SALINE DISTRICT LIBRARY
3 4604 91016 8342

W9-BUH-081

for Love & Liberty

THE UNTOLD CIVIL WAR STORY OF MAJOR SULLIVAN BALLOU & HIS FAMOUS LOVE LETTER

ROBIN YOUNG

THUNDER'S MOUTH PRESS
NEW YORK

To those loved ones who have gone on ahead . . .

FOR LOVE AND LIBERTY

THE UNTOLD CIVIL WAR STORY OF MAJOR SULLIVAN BALLOU & HIS FAMOUS LOVE LETTER

Published by
Thunder's Mouth Press
An Imprint of Avalon Publishing Group Inc.
245 West 17th Street, 11th Floor
New York, NY 10011

First printing January 2006

Library of Congress Cataloging-in-Publication Data is available.

ISBN: 1-56025-724-5
ISBN 13: 978-1-56025-724-0

9 8 7 6 5 4 3 2 1

Book design by Jamie McNeely
Printed in the United States of America
Distributed by Publishers Group West

Contents

ACKNOWLEDGMENTS v

PREFACE Conventions Used in the Book xi

INTRODUCTION "Go Tell My Wife Not to Grieve" xxi

CHAPTER ONE "Where the River Runs Like Silver" 1

CHAPTER TWO "Whose Sons Are Foremost in Duty" 21

CHAPTER THREE "Whose Daughters Are Peerless and Bright" . . . 41

CHAPTER FOUR "Joy Was in His Mild Blue Eyes" 59

CHAPTER FIVE "Our Lovings Prospered Well" 83

CHAPTER SIX "We Live in Hard and Stirring Times" 105

CHAPTER SEVEN "Our Cause Is Just and Holy" 135

CHAPTER EIGHT "The President Called on the Land for an Army" 177

CHAPTER NINE "I'm Off to the War with the Good Men and True, and Hadn't You Better Come Along, Too?" 209

CHAPTER TEN "Then to the South We Bore Away" 229

CHAPTER ELEVEN "From Hill to Hill, from Creek to Creek, Potomac Calls to Chesapeake" 271

CHAPTER TWELVE "In the Watch Fires of a Hundred Circling Camps" 297

CHAPTER THIRTEEN "Rally Round the Flag Boys" 335

CHAPTER FOURTEEN "The Most Glorious Scene" 379

CHAPTER FIFTEEN "How Many Miles to the Junction?" 423

CHAPTER SIXTEEN "A Cannonball Don't Pay No Mind" 461

Chapter Seventeen "The Murdering Cannons Roar" 509
Chapter Eighteen "Yankee Doodle Wheeled About and Scampered Off at Full Run, and Such a Race Was Never Seen as that He Made at Bull Run" 553
Chapter Nineteen "Weeping Sad and Lonely" 585
Chapter Twenty "Life's Tide Is Ebbing Out So Fast" 609
Chapter Twenty-One "And Our Hopes in Ruin Lie" 633
Chapter Twenty-Two "Though We Live in Winter Quarters Now, We're but Waiting for the Hour" 655
Chapter Twenty-Three "With Tender Care" 675
Chapter Twenty-Four "Wreaths of Glory" 701
Chapter Twenty-Five "The Eagle of Freedom Shrieks" 723
Chapter Twenty-Six "We Shall Win the Day" 741

Notes 783
Bibliography 819
Index 823

Acknowledgments

I would like to express my thanks to some very special people whose talented collaboration brought this project to fruition. To Lynne Rabinoff, the best agent a writer could have, whose belief in this project and author, ability to nudge when necessary, patience to tactfully teach a first time writer the facts of life of the publishing industry, and ability to make time and be there for all her clients simultaneously, establish her as extraordinary.

To my publisher, John Oakes, whose vision and faith in this project is appreciated more than he knows. To my three editors: Katherine Belden who provided early encouragement and guidance; Iris Bass, whose fine sense of history and amazing memory honed the story; and Jofie Ferrari-Adler, who worked tirelessly on weekends to pull together a complex manuscript and graphics and ready the whole for publication. To Ken Burns who provided the original introduction to Sullivan Ballou and his powerful letter.

My deepest gratitude goes to my friends and family who encouraged me, believed in my project, read parts of it, provided role models and inspiration, and traveled with me navigating strange roads while I researched it, namely, Vicki Scidmore, Jack Bornoff, Nancy and Shelly Zinberg, Pauline Rogers, and Sal D'Agostino. Special thanks to my mother, who aided and abetted my research trips while her health permitted, was the book's biggest fan, and whose tolerance of the long hours it took to write it is sincerely appreciated.

Researching this book has required me to crisscross the country, virtually and in person, and my special thanks go out to an unbelievable group of men and women who have often gone out of their way to assist me for no other reason than the shared belief that

Sullivan and Sarah's story deserved to be told. Time constraints often required me to rush archivists to call up vast stacks of manuscripts, photocopy everything relevant, and take it home to digest—sometimes on my way to the airport to catch a flight.

In Rhode Island, in Providence, the staff of the Rhode Island Historical Society, especially Jennifer Betts, Alison Cywin, Karen Eberhart, Robyn Flynn, and Rick Statler; Ray Bacon and colleagues at the Museum of Work and Culture in Woonsocket. The staffs of Grace Church Cathedral and Swan Point Cemetery, Sadie Barron, president; and John Myers at the Municipal Archives at City Hall. At the State Archives, Gwen Stearn and the amazing Ken Carlson. The staff of the State Library in the Rhode Island State House, and the Office of the Secretary of State. The incredible team of reference librarians at the Providence Public Library who never let me down. At Brown University: the Alumni Office; the John Hay Library: Manuscripts and Archives, Gayle Lynch and Ray Butti; the Anne Rice Brown Military Collection, Peter Harrington; at Providence College, Professor Mario Di Nunzio.

At the Providence Marriott Hotel, where Chevelle Mollock, Robert Greenwood, Dan Patterson, and their staff expressed their early faith in my project and passion for local history by assisting my research trips with a special rate for authors writing a book based in their hometown, feeding me, and configuring my room to hold the stacks of photocopies I hauled in daily.

Edna Kent, Glocester historian; and in Pawtucket, Betty Johnson, town historian; Jocelin and all the ladies from Daughters of the American Revolution. The staff at the City Clerk's Office, land records, and the cemetery maintenance crew in Public Works. Archivist Stephen Grimes at the Court Archives in Pawtucket and the reference staffs at the Warwick, Pawtucket, and Central Falls public libraries, including Tom Shanahan, and at Woonsocket-Harris Public Library, Bryan Strniste and Barbara Bussart. The staff of the City Clerk Offices of Central Falls, Valley Falls, Providence, and Cranston, especially Marlene. Jared Hartley, and the staff at the South County Museum in Narragansett. At the University of Rhode Island in Kingston, Sarina Wyatt. The RIGenWeb site, an amazing repository of transcribed documents about the state, and the chat list, a wonderfully helpful group of folks.

In Massachusetts, the staff of the American Antiquarian Society; the reference staff at the Worcester Public Library; Althea Church, and the incredible Brian Smith, author, researcher, and re-enactor. Jim Douglas at Conant Library, Nichols College; Peter Nelson at Amherst College; and the librarians at the Boston Public Library. In Connecticut, Tom Kemp, Godfrey Library; and the Reverend Susan Horgan, Petersham Orthodox Presbyterian Church.

In New York, the Association of Graduates of the United States Military Academy at West Point; Jeremy Dibbell and Teresa Finney at Union College; the amazing Steve Shumway of the Shumway Family Organization; and the librarians at the Poughkeepsie, Geneva, Cherry Valley, and Ballston Spa public libraries, especially Virginia Humphreys. In New York City, the Graphics Division of the public library, the Genealogical and Biographical Society; the Historical Society; the Museum of the City of New York; Jennifer Restak, Sharon Miller, Auburn Theological Seminary; and the staff of the East Side Marriott who provided special support during a family medical emergency during a research trip.

In New Jersey, reference services at the Newark and East Orange public libraries.

In Pennsylvania, at Carlisle Barracks, the staff of the United States Military History Institute especially Randy Hartenburg and Cliff Hyatt; the Free Library of Philadelphia.

In the South, the Historical Society of Washington, D.C.; the staff of the National Arboretum; the Architect of the Capitol; the National Park Service; the National Museum of Health and Medicine; the Armed Forces Institute of Pathology; and NARA researcher Beth Adams.

In Virginia, the staff of the National Park Service at Richmond, and Manassas National Battlefield Park, especially historian Jim Burgess. The pastor and congregation of Sudley Methodist Church, and the board of directors of the Women in the Civil War Conference. The Prince William County Public Library, Manassas Branch, and RELIC. The reference staff at the Virginia Historical Society in Richmond.

The Alabama Department of Archives and History, and Park Historian Rick Hatcher Fort Sumter National Battlefield Park in Charleston.

In the Midwest, the Chicago Historical Society Archives and the reference staff at the Evanston, Illinois, Appleton, Wisconsin, and Denver, Colorado, public libraries; the brainstorming of Keith Knoke; the team at the Church of the Latter Day Saints Genealogical Library in Salt Lake City.

In California, the staff of the Huntington Library in San Marino, and the staff in the History Department in the Los Angeles Central Library. Likewise to reference staff members at the La Habra, Sierra Madre, and San Jose public libraries, and the West Los Angeles and Whittier Church of the Latter Day Saints genealogical libraries. Thanks to my many friends in the re-enactment community; the American Civil War Society; and Ed Mann. Also the staff at Oak Hill Memorial Park, San Jose, and Church of Our Savior Cemetery, San Gabriel.

On the medical side, special thanks to Dr. Sheldon Zinberg for reviewing the medical passages; Dr. Richard Jantz at the University of Tennessee "Bone Yard"; and Dr. Douglas Owsley, forensic anthropologist and curator of the Museum of Natural History at the Smithsonian Institution for forensic details.

So as through a glass and darkly
The age long strife I see

—General George S. Patton, Jr.
Grandson of Confederate veterans

PREFACE

Conventions Used in the Book

It seems fitting at this point to offer the reader some explanations about the conventions used in the book, given the many period sources incorporated into the text. Each of the excerpts from diaries, letters, speeches, and reports was left in its own unique style. In most instances, these people were literate, articulate, and wrote effectively. However, spelling conventions from British English persisted, as did regional differences; for example, whether the village near Centreville was Sudley or Sedley. Also, some words were spelled differently then than now. The grammatical preferences and idiosyncrasies of these "contributors" are preserved intact, and the author trusts the reader can cope with, and perhaps enjoy, such inconsistencies.

For the convenience of the reader, definitions of unfamiliar words and other supporting information are provided in footnotes at the bottom of the page. Endnotes are citations of sources only. Dollar amounts from each historical period have been cross-referenced, within brackets, to year 2000 levels by the use of financial tables, so the reader may better understand their relative value.

It was necessary to decide which terminology to use for the first major battle of the Civil War—Bull Run or Manassas. The name "Bull Run" came into use later, and was used only by the North. Sullivan Ballou called it "Manassas," based on the nearby railway junction that was the strategic goal, as did contemporary letters, newspapers, and official documents; to maintain consistency, so has the author. Not until the second battle occurred in August 1862, did Sullivan's battle become "First" Manassas. Other battles gained double names as the war went on, the two sides no better able to agree on toponyms than on constitutional issues.

Finally, although each side certainly developed pejorative phraseology for its opponents, it has not been necessary to employ much of that in the narrative. The terms "Johnny Reb," "Billy Yank," "Secesh," "secession," and "secessionists," were common euphemisms during that time. So were other, more incomprehensible terms like "mudsill," and "black republicans"; and, of course, such generic pejoratives as "invader" and "barbarian," often employed in press reports. To maintain the authenticity of quoted material, the author has not altered whatever has been obtained from original sources to make it politically correct for the modern reader. Her sole concession has been to capitalize "Negro" and "Irish," then uncapitalized in common usage.

This is the most complete recounting of the opening hours of the Battle of First Manassas/Bull Run ever compiled. Hopefully, it is also the most accurate, but history remains open to constant revision as new personal accounts providing additional details are discovered in attics and archives. Indeed, based on just such reports, published for the first time, this book proposes some revisions in troop movements for the opening sequences of the battle.

All of the military information is presented in such a way that readers of many backgrounds and interests can follow the story without being military experts. In describing the overall development and progress of the battle, a special focus has been placed on the contributions of the two Rhode Island regiments, and their immediate opponents. To create this portrait, a number of eyewitness accounts from soldiers in many units were consulted, and their reports both compared and compiled. Often, one writer noted a detail that was unimportant to another. In the heat of battle, a soldier's position on the battlefield may have dictated which event he witnessed, and which he did not. For example, diarist Elisha Hunt Rhodes, a source used by many historians, missed several key sequences of the battle because he left the field to convey a wounded officer to the hospital.

All reports of the First Manassas battle were compiled into a table, and cross-checked for sequences of events, such as time and location of the enemy. Even accounts replete with exact times of battlefield deployment seemed to have been written by officers who had not synchronized their pocket watches! The exact sequence of several events is unclear but it has proved possible, by cross-referencing multiple sources, to postulate with reasonable accuracy the location and times of the key actions in which Sullivan Ballou participated. The same techniques had to be used when sources of personal data conflicted. The historian can but try to correlate as many points as possible in family history, make the most reasonable decision, and move on.

In dealing with the Civil War, people still tend to take sides. Regardless of victories in individual battles, the average fighting man on either side displayed equal bravery, forbearance, perseverance, and devotion to cause; almost all sacrificed personal business and economic interests to fight for the preservation of what they perceived to be their nation. Many suffered disease, slept outside in the rain and snow, felt homesick, and experienced hunger. It is therefore possible to honor the individual bravery and sacrifice of the combatants without necessarily endorsing their political cause.

In recounting the personal history of Sullivan and Sarah Ballou, this book details some particularly horrible and ghoulish behavior documented to a small group of soldiers. While such behavior can never be condoned or shrugged off as, "Oh well, it was war," it brings into the spotlight the difficulty of deciding what constitutes proper conduct when moral compasses are undermined by ambiguity. The experience of the Ballous reminds us that even war requires rules of conduct. At the same time, it would be wrong to generalize these misdeeds as characteristic of all soldiers, or all Southern fighting men. Both sides had their idiosyncrasies, their cowards, drunkards, and rotters, as well as their heroes.

The difficulties in military communication in 1861 seem almost incomprehensible to us in an era of cell phones, news footage from remote corners of the world, and spy satellites. And yet, to fully understand the realities of Sullivan Ballou's life and death, it is necessary to comprehend how things worked in those early days of the Civil War, before the great military machine was well oiled and organized, and what a huge impact the lack of even the most basic communications network had on this battle.

An expanded church facility serves twenty-first-century worshippers at Sudley Methodist Church in Prince William County, Virginia. *Author's photo.*

Built in 1835 in downtown Providence, America's first indoor shopping mall remains open for business in Rhode Island. *Author's photo.*

The era was not without technology. With the railroad, it was possible to travel back and forth between Richmond and Washington, D.C., the capitals of both nations, within a few hours. However, the middle chapters of the book, which focus on Sullivan Ballou's military career, concern events that took place in an area only eighty miles wide. In modern-day terms, the Northern and Southern armies moved around Ronald Reagan National Airport, Crystal City, the Pentagon Mall, the sea of parking lots surrounding the mighty Pentagon itself, CIA headquarters at Langley, and Occoquan Creek, which runs behind the MacDonald's where the marines from Quantico take their kids for Saturday morning breakfast. It moves through Arlington National Cemetery, the Alexandria Historic District, Gallaudet University, the National Arboretum, Kalorama, the Smithsonian Museum, and the Mall. In Rhode Island, Providence Place Mall, the ice skating rink, the Amtrak Depot, and the setting for River Fire are all locales where Sullivan Ballou walked and worked. All of these places are referred to by the names of the nineteenth century, and footnoted where additional orientation is necessary.

Civil War buffs are passionate about regimental identifications and providing them is conventional. From time to time, the book also provides sidebars containing more detailed information about a topic.

The chapter titles are excerpted lines from songs or poetry of the period. The abundant repertoire of music sung during the war years revealed the sentimentality, patriotism, martial spirit, and bravado, as well as the humor of the soldier and the folks back home. Common themes were missing loved ones, beating the enemy, overcoming the hardships of military campaign life, and dying bravely. The songs also reflect the viewpoints of different racial and ethnic groups caught up in the conflict.

Finally, Civil War battlefield medical practices were not delicate, but this book contains nothing worse than what may be viewed by the public in television shows on forensic investigations.

The majority of the illustrations used are from the period. The photography of the era concentrated on portraits; outdoor photography was in its infancy and because there were no action shots, important events were drawn for the newspapers, which were in any event unable to print photographs. The only Ballou to have a photographic image survive is Sullivan. Wherever modern or figurative illustrations are used to illustrate a point, they are so noted, and, of course, all photographs taken by the author are from the present day.

Sullivan's world view developed in, and was shaped by, his native state. The many fascinating details of the development of religious tolerance, democracy, and patriotism in the Ocean State could not be explored in depth due to the panoramic nature of his biography, but are well worth individual exploration, starting with the founding of the colony by Roger Williams.

Until 1863, Virginia and West Virginia were a single state. *Courtesy of the Department of the Interior, U.S. Geological Survey.*

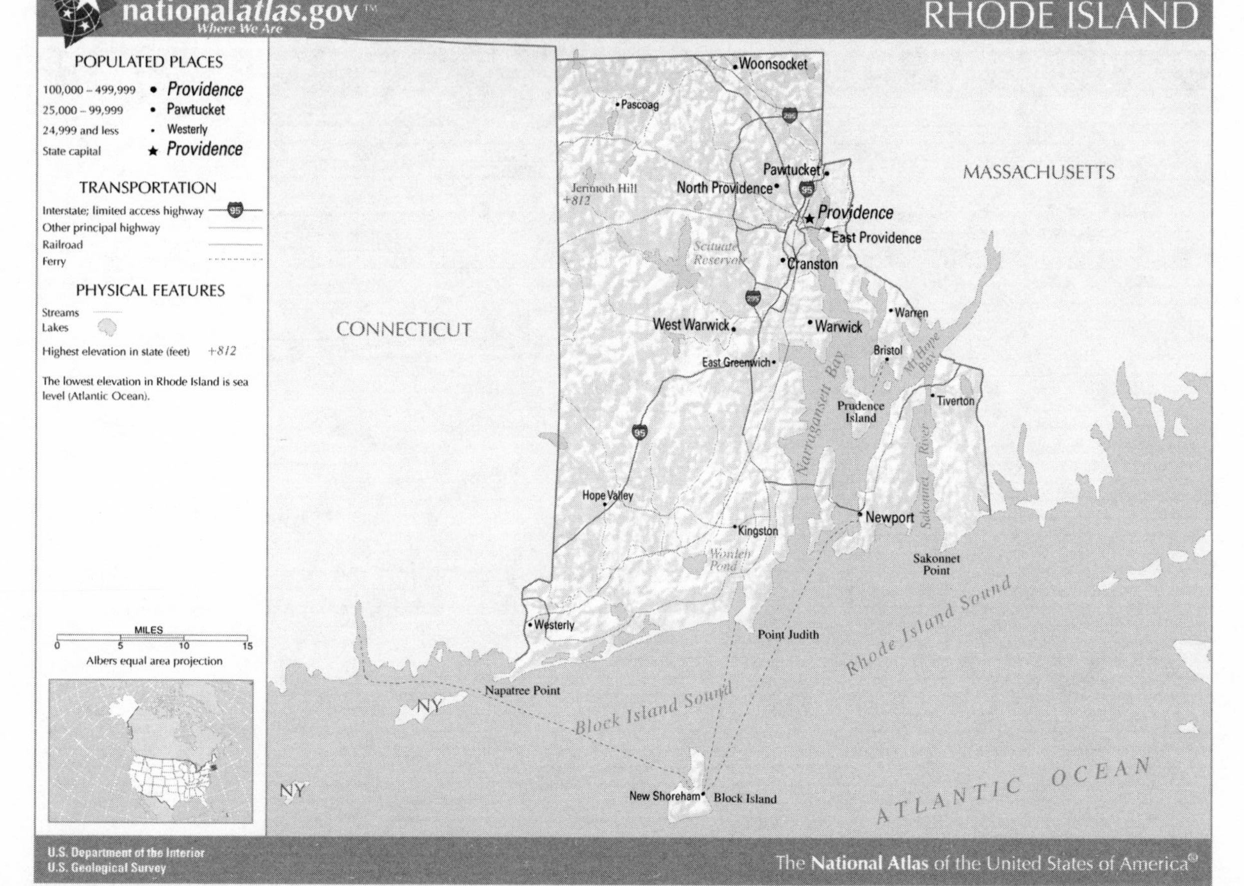

Rhode Island. *Courtesy of the Department of the Interior, U.S. Geological Survey.*

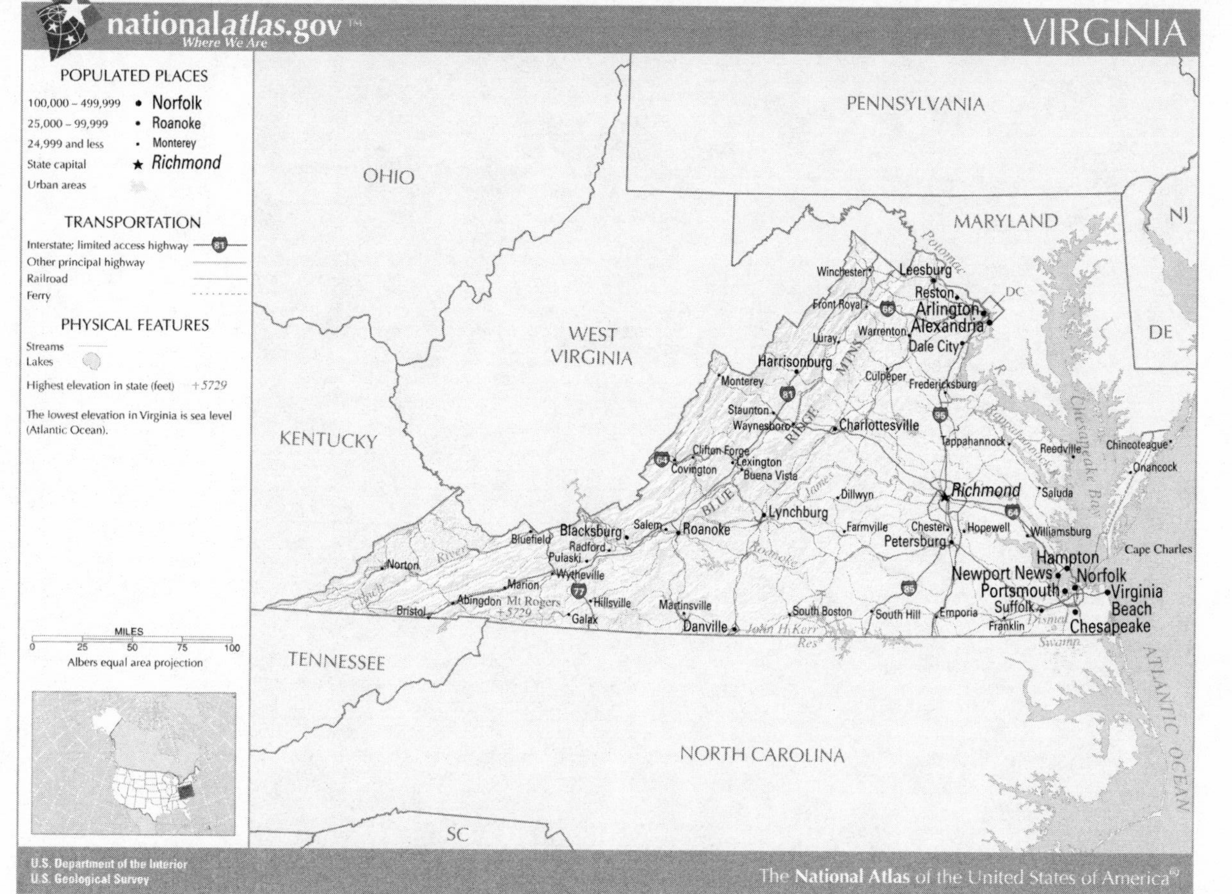

Virginia. *Courtesy of the Department of the Interior, U.S. Geological Survey.*

INTRODUCTION

"Go Tell My Wife Not to Grieve"*

The Letter

July 14, 1861

It was the hour when dusk slides into twilight. This warm July night might have passed like any other for Major Sullivan Ballou, except that he was camped in a glen of oak trees on the outskirts of Washington, D.C., five hundred miles away from home and his beloved wife and children. Here, the Army of the Potomac was slowly coiling like a massive snake, ready to strike a death blow at the rebellion against the United States. After days of rumors, indications were strong that the Rhode Island regiments might immediately move into Virginia to engage the Secessionists and stamp out their treasonous challenge to the young democracy. Sullivan had felt compelled to join the army and help save the country he loved so much.

Only four weeks a major in the Union Army, Sullivan's days

* From the Civil War era song "Brother Green."

were filled with the minutia of army life; the pace slowed down only in the evenings, when a glance at the sky revealed the tail of the Great Comet of 1861 grown fainter overhead. At the evening meal, the officers were quoting Shakespeare to each other as they passed the peas, "When beggars die, there are not comets seen; The heavens themselves blaze forth the death of princes."[1] Someone expressed the hope it would be *Southern* princes, and they had all laughed. Of course it must be so, another insisted, for in another play Shakespeare had said:

> Comets importing change of times and states,
> Brandish your crystal tresses in the sky,
> And with them scourge the bad revolting stars.[2]

To the Northern officers, who considered the South to be in revolt, the portents were clear. They would drive the Rebels from the battlefield in the next few days—if the Secesh did not run away first.

After returning to his own tent, Sullivan probably reread his wife Sarah's most recent letter one last time before packing it away in his trunk with all the other items he would not take on the march to Virginia. These letters were their lifeline and he waited for them eagerly; she was the only person who wrote to him. His friends, relatives, and law partner had not yet replied to the letters he had sent over the last month.

Over the years of their courtship and marriage, whenever he and Sarah were apart, if his law practice took him away from his hometown, or she went to visit her family, they had kept in touch by letters delivered overnight throughout New England by an excellent federal postal service.

Those letters were chatty and affectionate, replete with little personal details, sometimes nagging, often full of romantic longing and hand-wringing about the lack of money that sometimes kept them from traveling together. Underlying all the banter was a concern about each other's health and well-being, for this was an age when sudden illnesses could kill a child overnight, or carry off a hearty adult in a few days.

The Union Army understood the impact on morale of mail from home and, in this one aspect at least, was well organized. The postal service in the nation's capital sped letters efficiently to and from the soldiers in the scores of camps ringing Washington, D.C.

To Sarah, Sullivan's wartime letters boasted he could close his eyes and transport himself back into the house, drifting through the rooms, noting the placement of items on his desk, the mantel clock ticking confidently, the children's nursery, the brooch Sarah wore at her neck, the wisps of hair that escaped her coiffure and framed her face. Earlier this same day he had written her a chatty letter that said:

> I was never separated from my children before. I never knew the longing of a father for his children before. And you can scarcely imagine how my blood dances—my nerves thrill and my brain almost whirls, when with eyes wide open the world all becomes blank to me, and I see my little boys going through their childish pranks, and hear their singing voices, and even stretch my arms to catch them, and awake to touch the white walls of my tent.[3]

Orphaned himself at an early age, his younger years filled with poverty and hardship, Sullivan Ballou treasured his little family and their happiness together more than did the average man; he lavished powerful feelings of love and protection on them. Never would he have them go in search of attention, of crumbs of support from relatives, as he had done.

Some of his relatives considered him an unlikely candidate for a soldier, precisely because he was now so settled at home. Financial security finally seemed within reach as he concentrated on his law practice. His future in state politics also remained bright; and with his party in the White House, he hoped to be elected to a position at the state level, come the next election. He had campaigned tirelessly for Abe Lincoln and once this short war was over . . . well, there would be new opportunities for an honest, hardworking man with political talents and the right connections. Perhaps there would even be a seat in Congress, in the Capitol whose half-finished dome he could see from Camp Clark.

In the meantime, all around him, distantly, were the muffled sounds of a thousand men—the clanking of a tin cup, a cough, a harmonica, a raised voice, snoring. His lantern barely illuminated his own few square feet of ground, and the quarter moon gave so little light that, if he looked out into the darkness, all he saw was the fading embers of campfires, and fireflies floating up from the meadows.

The setting seemed ancient, primal, and he thought of others in his family who had known such a scene, ancestors who braved the unknown to settle Providence Plantations, and those who had followed Washington and Lafayette through an earlier war.

Thoughts came unbidden into his mind, a hoary hunch, and he decided to write a letter to his wife straightaway. Sullivan uncapped the inkwell, fixed a pen nib onto a wooden handle, smoothed out a sheet of paper, and wrote:

July 14, 1861
Camp Clark, Washington

My dear Sarah,
The indications are very strong that we shall move in a few days—perhaps tomorrow. Lest I should not be able to write again, I feel impelled to write a few lines which will fall under your eye when I shall be no more. Our movement may be one of a few days duration and full of pleasure—and it may be one of severe conflict and death to me. Not my will but thine O God be done. If it is necessary that I should fall on the battle-

field for my country, I am ready. I have no misgivings about, or lack of confidence in the cause in which I am engaged, and my courage does not halt or falter. I know how strongly American Civilization now leans on the triumph of the Government and how great a debt we owe to those who went before us through the blood and sufferings of the Revolution. And I am willing—perfectly willing—to lay down all my joys in this life, to help maintain this Government and to pay that debt. But, my dear wife, when I know that with my own joys I lay down nearly all of yours, and replace them in this life with cares and sorrows—when, after having eaten for long years the bitter fruits of orphanage myself, I must offer it as their only sustenance to my dear little children—is it weak or dishonorable, while the banner of my purpose floats calmly and proudly in the breeze, that my unbounded love for you, my darling wife and children, should struggle in fierce, though useless, contest with my love of country?

I cannot describe to you my feelings on this calm summer night, when two thousand men are sleeping around me, many of them enjoying the last, perhaps, before that of death—and I, suspicious that Death is creeping behind me with his fatal dart, am communing with God, my country and thee.

I have sought most closely and diligently, and often in my breast, for a wrong motive in thus hazarding the happiness of those I loved and I could not find one. A pure love of country and of the principles I have often advocated before the people and "the name of honor that I love more than I fear Death" have called upon me and I have obeyed.

Sarah, my love for you is deathless, it seems to bind me with mighty cables that nothing but Omnipotence could break. And yet my love of Country comes over me like a strong wind and bears me irresistibly on with all those chains, to the battlefield.

The memories of all the blissful moments I have enjoyed with you come creeping over me, and I feel most grateful to God and you that I've enjoyed them for so long. And how hard it is for me to give them up and burn to ashes the hopes of the future years, when, God willing, we might still have lived and loved together and see our boys grown up to honorable manhood around us. I have, I know, but few and small claims upon Divine Providence, but something whispers to me—perhaps it is the wafted prayer of my little Edgar, that I shall return to my loved ones unharmed. If I do not, my dear Sarah, never forget how much I love you, and as my last breath escapes me on the battlefield, it will whisper your name. Forgive my many faults, and the many pains I have caused you. How thoughtless, how foolish I have often times been! How gladly I would wash out with my tears every little spot upon your happiness and struggle with all the misfortunes of this world to shield you, and your children from harm. But I cannot. I must watch you from the Spirit-land and hover near you, while you buffit the storm, with your precious little freight, and wait with sad patience, till we meet to part no more.

But O Sarah! if the dead can come back to this earth and flit unseen around those they loved, I shall always be near you—in the garish days and the darkest nights . . . amidst your happiest scenes and gloomiest hours—always, always, and if there be a soft breeze upon your cheek, it shall be my breath, or if the cool air fans your throbbing temple, it shall be my spirit passing by. Sarah, do not mourn me dead—think I am gone and wait for thee—for we shall meet again.

As for my little boys, they will grow as I have done, and never know a father's love and care. Little Willie is too young to remember me long, and my blue eyed Edgar will keep my frolics with him among the dimmest memories of his childhood.

> Sarah, I have unlimited confidence in your maternal care and your development of their characters, and feel that God will bless you in your holy work. Tell my two mothers, his and hers, I call God's blessing upon them. O Sarah, I wait for you there! Come to me and lead thither my children.
>
> Sullivan[4]

He blotted the letter carefully, then folded it and put it into an envelope. He wrote on the envelope Sarah's name but no address and sealed it, then opened the trunk lid and placed the letter inside. Tomorrow morning before he marched off to Virginia, he would lock the trunk. A small detachment of men were remaining behind to care for the sick and guard the possessions left behind. If he died as he believed he would, the trunk and its contents would be delivered to her shortly afterward by a representative of the regiment. The letter would be a message to Sarah from beyond the grave, at the very time she was feeling most vulnerable and bereft. If he returned alive from battle, she would be spared the fright of reading it.

The letter first came to public attention briefly in the late 1860s, when the first biographies of Rhode Island war heroes were published, containing personal details that only family members could have shared. Because there were no photocopying machines or scanners then, the authors made hand copies of Sullivan's original letter to use in their publications. Sarah Ballou apparently next shared it with the now-defunct Sullivan Ballou Chapter of the Grand Army of the Republic in Valley Falls, and it was published locally. This may have occurred in connection with the placement of the memorial obelisk at his grave, which contained a line from the letter, "I wait for you there, come to me and lead thither my children."

Handwritten copies of the original letter reposed in various archives around the country, unknown but to a few scholars using the amazing collections of surviving letters written between soldiers and their families during the Civil War. One family in Massachusetts found a copy in their attic while this book was being written and, for a few breathtaking days, while a photocopy was in the mail, everyone held their breath to see if it was in Sullivan's handwriting. It was another period copy, in someone else's hand, but a great find nonetheless.

In the fall of 1990, Public Television opened its broadcasting season with a monumental nine-part documentary, *The Civil War*, by the brilliant filmmaker Ken Burns, which took Americans on a panoramic journey through the places and events of the war. This retelling of this most pivotal of American historical events so captivated average Americans that it was discussed at workplace water coolers, tire shops, hardware stores, and delicatessens all over the nation. Coworkers went into huddles each day to review the previous night's episode.

Viewers learned the politics and the military strategy and the hardcore statistics and facts, but what touched most people was how a generation of people long dead came alive again. Americans were glued to their television sets for nine hours, total, as Burns wove his spell, transporting them back through time by means of the photos, diaries, and letters of people who lived and loved during the five long years that the battle for liberty and freedom was being fought.

We heard these people through their own words, speaking through their own writings. We listened to the anxieties of rural wives, lonely and overworked in their efforts to keep farms going while their men were away, the lamentations of the slave waiting for freedom, and the bravado of the early days when all the soldiers, North and South, thought the other side would be easily defeated. We recognized the beginning of the women's movement as the ladies organized nursing corps and relief organizations. We heard the resignation of men ill fed, ill clad, and just plain ill as they saw the war through to its inevitable conclusion, and the pathos of dying men writing home one last time.

Americans marveled at the bravery of the these men—many not "career" soldiers but volunteers—who moved in steady long lines toward danger, destruction, and death—because it was their duty. We wondered how they did it, and we came to learn the toll it took on their loved ones back home. Respect developed for the courage and personal fortitude of the men who fought on both sides, regardless of the politics that drove them to the battlefield.

From all the letters, journals, and diaries, one stood out above the rest for its emotional impact, and became an icon that personified all the love and loss: Major Sullivan's farewell letter to his wife, Sarah. In episode 1, narrator David McCullough introduced Paul Roebling, who read Sullivan's letter to his wife as the haunting melody of "Ashokan Farewell" played in the background.

This tender, emotive letter summarized the yearning, hope, sense of duty, resignation, and patriotism felt by all the families separated by war, North or South. His eloquent affirmation that war and horror could not interrupt love, that this noblest of emotions was timeless, touched the hearts of Americans. Men were not ashamed to admit it made them cry. It was a message for all ages of American history.

After the letter was read on the show, switchboards at PBS stations all across America were jammed as viewers phoned in asking for more information on the Ballous. In this age just before the popularity of the Internet, people called and wrote in, wanting to know details about the Ballou family. So great had the identification been with his dear Sarah that people wanted to know if she was carrying his child when he went off to war, how she managed afterward, and whether the two little sons he mentioned lived "to honorable manhood?" At the time, there were few answers, for they still lay buried in a dozen archives across the nation.

The first three-day holiday weekend after the series ended, Columbus Day, visitors flooded into the national battlefield parks, eager to see for themselves the ground that men of both sides had hallowed with their life's blood. I was at Gettysburg National Park in Pennsylvania, which like all other parks that weekend, greeted the greater-than-normal number of its visitors under strange circumstances.

President George H. W. Bush, unable to come to an agreement with Congress on a federal budget, had shut down the federal government that weekend. No employees were allowed to work, under penalty of discipline, and this meant the employees of the National Park Service as well. At every national park the visitor centers were closed, there were no restrooms available for the relief of thousands of guests, and park rangers were forbidden to work, in or out of uniform, to protect the sites from souvenir hunters.

At Gettysburg, the local McDonald's restaurant adjacent to the battlefield heroically withstood repeated charges on its facilities, and the licensed battlefield guides, a private operation, worked from a card table in the parking lot of the closed visitor center. The wife of the park superintendent stood lookout over the park from its highest point, with the statue of General Warren as her companion, up on Little Round Top. Other unknown guardians in blue jeans prowled the lanes of the park, admonishing people not to dig for bullets on federal land, or climb on the cannons.

The frenzied tourism peaked, but still Sullivan Ballou remained popular; and when Burns's companion book to his Civil War television series was published, it included this letter. When the CD of music came out, it concluded with the reading of his letter, backed by Jay Ungar's poignant melody, a modern tune that sounded so much like one of the poignant ballads of the 1860s. Sullivan Ballou was written up in *People* magazine, a circumstance that would have likely amused him and appalled Sarah's sense of privacy. Less amusing were the conspiracy theories that began to circulate, suggesting the letter was phony, that no one could have so perfectly expressed those noble sentiments: perhaps, people suggested, it had been embellished by others after the war, to a purpose never specified, or perhaps Sarah had written it to herself, to gain publicity. There is however, convincing evidence presented in the book that Sullivan Ballou was the sole author.

For the next twenty years, the letter was read over the airwaves, even on Valentine's Day in Canada, and newspaper articles kept Sullivan's name before the public. The letter became part of classroom curricula on the Civil War in America, Britain, France, and Germany. It was excerpted in wedding vows, and also used in grief counseling centers, to help survivors cope with the loss of a beloved spouse. And it was picked up and used in many more Civil War books, but all without more information on its mysterious author.

Remembrance of the letter survived in the back channels of American consciousness so much so that it burst forth again in the great American paroxysm of grief and horror that accompanied the undeclared war on September 11, 2001. There were so many emotional similarities to the dynamics of the Civil War in this tragedy: the destruction, the inspiring bravery of men who walked into danger, to do their duty when others were fleeing it, the coming together in the face of horror, the patriotism, the determination not be cowed, and the number of families that suffered the loss of loved ones.

As Americans expressed their heartache, and mourned for loved ones who died in the World Trade Center towers, the Pentagon, and onboard the four airplanes hijacked by terrorists, Sullivan Ballou's letter found new purpose. It was read at memorial services and posted on Web sites dedicated to the victims. One hundred forty years after he wrote them, Sullivan's words were still consoling people with its message that the misery of grief is not the stopping place, that life and love continue on the other side.

Yet the letter had other messages, too, related to the other core values at the heart of America, which explain why Sullivan did not "hesitate to cast in my life if it is called for." He fought to support "American Civilization," which in 1860 did not mean avoidance of jury duty, free music downloads, voter apathy, SUVs, cell phones, frozen pizza, pat-down searches before boarding aircraft, and MacDonald's abroad. Sullivan's generation still felt a strong connection to, and appreciation of, the freedoms and values for which their grandparents had risked all by fighting the Revolution.

Sullivan's sacrifice cannot be understood without knowing something of his New England upbringing and the benefits of American life treasured there in the 1850s, which included free public schools, freedom of opportunity for upward movement for all who worked hard, and tolerance of diversity in religion and politics. Good roads, bridges in the right places, and tall steeples were achieved by people coming together and giving of their time in the endless committee meetings that made New England work as democracy at its most fundamental level.

When he says, "I know . . . how great a debt we owe to those who went before us through the blood and sufferings of the Revolution," he did know it intimately and personally because he heard the stories of their adventures and service directly from his grandparents and uncles, at Thanksgiving reunions and family events. Sullivan was closely related to individuals prominent in the American fight for independence, and was even named for one.

In his time, there were well-developed family legends of how the Shumway ancestors of Sarah, and the Ballous and Bowens of Sullivan's forebearers, came to America in search of liberty, religious freedom, prosperity, and education, and struggled to make a foreign land their own. This patrimony was an important part of what the soldiers fought for on both sides of the Civil War and is clearly stated: "I am willing—perfectly willing—to lay down all my joys in this life, to help maintain this Government and to pay that debt."

I found the answers to the questions people asked about Sullivan Ballou preserved in various archives around the United States. It took me three years of research to harvest them. Many of the precious records have survived thus far because of the American penchant for record keeping, but they are in danger, for the digital age has bypassed them. Had another twenty-five years passed before the harvesting of this data, parts of it would have crumbled into dust. Indeed, on occasion, the glass of the copy machine had to be swept clear of bits of paper records that crumbled off books and documents, history eroding in front of me. The state and municipal historical societies and archives remain on the lowest end of the food chain for money and resources to digitize their priceless records; unable even to afford modern copy machines that scan documents; lacking the staff to perform the digitization; ignored by federal, state, and local budgets. Our very history is at risk of "becoming history."

Through the use of these extraordinarily detailed records, Sullivan and Sarah, known only as shadow figures for a decade and a half, finally come alive—in this book. We recognize them through those characteristics they have in common with us today: love, bravery, humor, and persistence, as we come to appreciate the glimpse they give us into the otherness of their time and place.

The Honorable Sullivan Ballou, Esq. *Courtesy of Daughters of the American Revolution, Pawtucket, Rhode Island.*

CHAPTER ONE

"Where the River Runs Like Silver"*

The Beginnings of Sullivan Ballou and Sarah Hart Shumway 1800–1839

Sullivan Ballou and Sarah Hart Shumway grew up thirty miles apart, at almost opposite ends of the Blackstone River, he in the Cumberland District of northern Rhode Island, she in the city of Worcester in southern Massachusetts. The Blackstone had stretches of white water where it dropped an average ten feet per mile earning it the nickname of "the hardest working river in America," because its banks were lined with textile mills powered by water wheels. At the heartland of the American Industrial Revolution in the early decades of the 1800s, its rhythms shaped the lives of both children.

The stretch of land in between the two industrial centers was quite pastoral, providing food for many sheep and horses, and immense numbers of oxen, and the dynamics of the life of the

* From the Civil War song "Wait for the Wagon."

countryside also played a part in the childhoods of Sarah and Sullivan. One of the many common threads of experience they shared was the glory of a New England autumn when the surrounding forests ripened from gold to fuchsia to scarlet, until the leaves drifted down into giant brown carpets covering the ground.

Sullivan was the second child of Emeline Frances Bowen and Hiram Ballou, whose marriage merged two eminent Rhode Island families.

Emeline Bowen was the youngest child of Joseph Bowen of Glocester, one of Rhode Island's most renowned Revolutionary War–era doctors and adventurers. During that war, the aspiring surgeon was a young doctor treating patients at the general military hospital in Providence. This meaningful contribution to the war effort was not sufficiently exciting to a patriot who dreamed of striking a dramatic blow for American liberty, so Joseph found a way to combine medicine and swashbuckling adventure toward the cause. He signed on as surgeon for the sixty-five-member crew of the newly built Rhode Island privateer *Chance*, under Captain Daniel Aborn.

Privateers were commercial ships sailing under letters of marque from the Continental Congress or the various states. Outfitted with guns, operated by small crews, they sailed out of the many small ports along the eastern seaboard to harry, interrupt, and destroy British military and commercial shipping in the Atlantic, the Mediterranean, the North Sea, the Irish Sea, and the English Channel. Two thousand such ships, crewed by 58,400 men and carrying almost 15,000 guns, went to sea between 1776 and 1783, to even the odds in the sea war between the huge British Navy and the struggling American naval forces.[1] The *Chance* eluded the Narragansett Bay blockade in May 1782 and slipped into open waters.[2] Unfortunately, within a few days, the British ship HMS *Belisarius* captured her after a brief fight.* Joseph Bowen and his fellow

* HMS *Belisarius* was herself captured by Napoleon's navy in 1804.

crewmen suddenly found themselves prisoners of war on their way to His Majesty's death ships in New York Harbor.

The British had run out of prison facilities and assigned such prisoners to a flotilla of rotting, demasted hulks stuck in the mud in Brooklyn Bay. About eleven thousand men and women, two-thirds military, one-third civilian, perished in misery and desolation in Wallabout Bay, with the knowledge and acquiescence of British commanders General Howe and Clinton.[3] The death rate aboard the prison ships approached 75 percent.* Prisoners died from starvation, humiliation, misery, disease, heat and cold, and never received proper burial. Joseph was sent to the most notorious of these prison ships, the *Jersey*. Built for a crew of four hundred, the 144-foot-long *Jersey* already held eleven hundred prisoners when he arrived. The *Chance*'s master's mate, Thomas Dring kept a diary about his crew, but prisoner Reverend T. Andre noted,

> All the most deadly diseases were pressed into the service of the king of terrors, but his prime ministers were dysentery, small pox, and yellow fever.[4]

Joseph would have been a hero if all he did was provide medical treatment to the wretches on board, but he and the other Rhode Islanders dared to petition the British commander, Sir Henry Clinton, for permission to personally report conditions to General George Washington. To the astonishment of most on board, their request was approved, and young Bowen elected as one of the delegation.[5] Joseph's uncle was Jabez Bowen, deputy governor of Rhode Island, a close political ally and friend of Washington.**

* A rate not approached until the Nazi death camps of the 1930s. Even Andersonville Prison had "only" a 33 percent death rate.

** The family reused the name Jabez frequently, this one graduated Yale as a lawyer and was a prominent patriot businessman and politician married to Sarah Brown.

Washington had known of, and previously tried unsuccessfully to alleviate, prison conditions but the Rhode Island petition had produced a diplomatic breakthrough. Immediate improvements were made in the quality of the food, treatment of the sick, ventilation, availability of water, and cleanliness. The *New Jersey Gazette* reported on July 24, 1782, that "Sir Guy Carleton has inspected all the prison ships in New York and expressed his intention of having them better provided for."[6]

In an age before agreements on the treatment of prisoners of war, Joseph's part in negotiating more humane treatment improved the odds of survival for thousands of prisoners incarcerated for the remaining years of the war, and saved thousands of lives. Among his fellow internees and future patients, once he was exchanged and back home, were French soldiers and sailors, allies of the young democracy. It is obvious that Joseph admired the French: Emeline had an older brother and sister named for a French king and queen, Clovis and Marie-Antoinette, respectively. Although none followed him into medicine, all his children were educated, of upper-middle-class status, and knew more about nursing and healing than the average person of the era.

It is a mystery how Emeline even met Hiram Ballou, a man living on the far side of the state. The Ballou family was one of the oldest in Rhode Island, originally named Providence Plantations by its founder, Roger Williams.* The family's founder, a Norman from France named Mathurin Ballou, was among the second group of settlers, who, in 1645, "thankfully" accepted "a free grant of twenty-five acres of land," which included a town lot in the heart of Providence, a farm, and common rights in the meadows."**

* The term refers to the idea of the new settlements being "planted" in the New World.

** See Appendix One for a discussion of Maturin Ballou's route to the New World.

Mathurin married a twenty-year-old woman named Hannah Pike, who was the daughter of his neighbor and likely fellow shipmate, Robert Pike. Mathurin soon bought more land, first in town, then elsewhere in the colony.[7]

As Maturin Ballou's widow Hannah neared her eighties, the Ballou family had outgrown and sold its homestead plots in Providence. They bought additional land adjacent to an inheritance in the northeast, near the border with Massachusetts, an area later named for the English duke of Cumberland. Within a generation, so many Ballou progeny lived in the Cumberland that the area became known as the Ballou Neighborhood and is still marked as such on present-day maps.[8] Generations of Ballous attended town meetings and worshiped at the neighborhood meetinghouse, with its shallow seats and wooden rail at shoulder height across the back of the pew to ensure no one slouched while hearing the word of God.[9]

In the earliest days of the far-flung settlements, young men and women found it most practical to marry their neighbors. The choice of spouses had improved over the intervening two hundred years, but courting someone twenty miles away still posed logistical problems, despite the stagecoach that now traveled east–west across the state. One notable event occurred in the time frame of their probable courtship period, suggesting when they might have been introduced.

In 1824, Rhode Island was privileged to welcome the greatly respected war hero, Marie-Joseph-Paul-Yves-Roch-Gilbert du Motier, the Marquis de Lafayette, who had returned to America to see for himself the progress of the country whose freedom he helped establish. One of the few big-name generals still alive, Lafayette was now sixty-seven, still of military bearing and tall, with a full head of hair curled in the most current fashion. Americans had not yet forgotten they would not have been a nation without French military help, and the entire nation vied to honor him during this era of good feelings between America and France.

Providence has always been known for delightful and ingenious civic celebrations, and they had a showstopper planned for that part of the program when the marquis's coach pulled up to the long walkway in front of the statehouse building:

> The poplar avenue, leading to the building was lined on each side with nearly two hundred misses arrayed in white . . . holding in their hands bunches of flowers which . . . they strewed in his path.[10]

It was entirely plausible that eighteen-year-old Emeline was among them, looking like a classical goddess of liberty.

Lafayette was reportedly touched by this tableau. His open carriage, drawn by four gray horses, flanked on both sides by an honor guard, had been accompanied along the city's main processional route, Westminster Street, by a huge entourage consisting of the officers and students of Brown University, companies of military, retired military officers, a band, and groups of citizens, all on foot. The town council, officers of the government, and army and naval officers rode in carriages, and there were mounted units as well. At every stop on his tour, great pains had been taken to assemble and present to Lafayette all the old veterans whose health allowed them to attend, so inside the statehouse were even more dignitaries. The *Providence Gazette* reported, when he recognized, embraced, and kissed Stephen Olney, an officer who had served with him in many campaigns, "in a most earnest and affectionate manner . . . A thrill went through the whole assembly and scarcely a dry eye was to be found among the spectators."[11]

From Abner to Ziba, who was Hiram Ballou's father, all the Ballou men in the Cumberland had fought in the militia, most of them under the joint command of generals Lafayette, Nathanael Greene, and John Sullivan at the Battle of Rhode Island in 1778. Doubtlessly, many of them came to shake Lafayette's hand and brought their families to get a glimpse of him. After dinner and speeches, Lafayette traveled on to Massachusetts, along a route where the houses and gardens had been illuminated in his honor.[12] The families who had traveled into town to see him remained, continued the festivities, dined, and socialized.

Twenty-two years old, Hiram was one of a new breed of businessman, a merchant tailor. He had just completed a long, informal apprenticeship with his elder brother Johnathan, learning to craft the elegant new fabrics like cassimeres and merinos into the finely tailored fashionable garments now popular. One relative noted that Johnathan Ballou, the second son of Ziba, one of the first to enter this trade was a

> rarity in his line at first, among us country folks of his native town, who had always before been mostly accustomed to home-made garments of female construction. But the new styles and more polished workmanship soon took the lead and became indispensable.[13]

Clothing trends had simplified over the past couple decades. Gone were the George and Martha Washington–style brocaded and lace-lavished suits and gowns. Corseted bodices and huge petticoat structures had been replaced by more "democratic" fashions that hearkened back to classical Greece, a result of the fad for the ideals of classical Greece.

Up to this time in America, women had sewn most of the family clothing, at home, by hand. Only the wealthy had commissioned their gowns and suits. However, by the 1820s, achieving the lines of these new fashions required expert skill. Men's suits and great coats, for example, now had large, triangular lapels, which required skillful internal construction and trimming if they were to lay flat. The customer now visited the shop of the merchant tailor, who presented rolls of fabric for his inspection, and together they agreed on the style, price, and delivery date. Such clothing was also known as custom made or "bespoke," and the merchant tailor who made it also sold a few items on the side to complete an outfit, such as the cravat, or stock: seven yards of silk wound around the neck and tied in front. Gentlemen vied with each other to copy the latest knots to achieve a high-fashion look.

In the 1820s, the combined inhabitants of Woonsocket and the Cumberland numbered about ten thousand. Clearly there was room for multiple merchant tailors, and so Hiram and Johnathan could own separate shops in the same region.

However he and Emeline met, Hiram's business prospects demonstrated he could support a wife and family. There is no definite record of the date of the wedding ceremony, which occurred around April 1825. The lack of a marriage record for Emeline and Hiram is puzzling. Dates of births, marriages, and deaths are considered vital records; and Rhode Island's collections are in generally excellent shape. Had the couple married in Emeline's home parish and town, the normal procedure, the marriage would have been recorded in the parish ledger book. Also, Dr. Joseph Bowen served as town clerk of Glocester, so even if the church records of Emeline's marriage somehow went missing, it was implausible that he failed to note his daughter's marriage in his own annual list of record-worthy for the town.

In the absence of a marriage record from their own western Rhode Island—or anywhere else in the state—it is possible the couple eloped and were married in nearby Massachusetts or Connecticut. Emeline's mother had died in December 1824, so the need to elope would have inferred some disapproval of the part of her father, who may have found a health-related reason to object to Hiram as a son-in-law. Like many of the farm children who had lived through the starvation years of 1815 to 1817, Hiram was not especially robust, and the practiced eye of the physician may have seen the signs of early death in him and his siblings. If so, Joseph was correct. No father wanted to see his daughter left a young widow.

Mr. and Mrs. Hiram Ballou settled in the Cumberland, where their first baby was born on Friday, February 28, 1826: a healthy daughter whom they named Hannah Frances, after Emeline's mother.[14] Records kept within the Ballou family refer to the parents' marriage as having taken place in the summer of 1826, but these most likely concern the proof of marriage certificate that a couple had to file with the town authorities to show they were legally married out of the jurisdiction in which they had come to live. These were small certificates sent from the justice of the peace or minister who performed the ceremony, and commonly took six to twenty-four months to arrive and be recorded.

Their second child was born March 28, 1827. This boy received a single name, Sullivan. Family naming patterns still followed tradition at this point in time, and this blue-eyed boy ought to have been called Ziba, after Hiram's father.* Perhaps at the urging of the patriarch himself, most of his children broke with tradition and did not reuse his name for his male grandchildren. Emeline's own father had also been quite inventive when issuing names of French royalty to his brood, so perhaps such creativity was countenanced in the younger generation.**

At this point in time in Rhode Island, Sullivan was an Irish surname, an improbable source for the firstborn son of parents of non-Irish heritage. It was highly unlikely that the only other person with that first name, Sullivan Dorr, the scion of a wealthy merchant

* This name Ziba was not often seen, even in New England where biblical names remained fashionable for multiple generations. Perhaps his father, Noah, had opened the book at random to select this minor character from 2 Samuel 9:10; Ziba was a servant of Saul.

** The old biblical- and virtue-based names were dying out, and Hiram and Emeline were to give their third baby a popular girls' name of the 1830s, Janette, also a name not belonging to any forebear.

family, moved in the same circles as the merchant tailor of Cumberland Hill; Dorr was certainly not the godfather. However, Dorr, born after the Revolutionary War, was undoubtedly named for General John Sullivan, the hero of the Battle of Rhode Island, and a man with impressive credentials throughout New England. Given that all the many Ballou men in the Cumberland Rangers militia had fought under General Sullivan, he was definitely among the family's circle of contacts; if Hiram and Emeline desired a distinctive, elevated name, "Sullivan" made sense in that context.

During the early years of his life Sullivan encountered a large number of cousins and other relations living in the area, soaking up the Ballou Family's traditions and folklore.

Sometime in the 1830s, Emeline noted her husband was coughing more than usual. A doctor later confirmed her worst fears. Hiram had tuberculosis, known at the time as consumption for its devouring effect on its victims, or pthysis. There was much of it around, given there had been an epidemic only fifteen years before.

Not until the next century did scientists discover that tuberculosis was spread by aspirating dried and pulverized sputum in the air, or contact with pus from lesions. Because such particles are light and small, they are easily inhaled deep into the lungs of anyone who breathes the same air.[15] Yet, not everybody exposed to it catches the disease. In fact, as the human body naturally attacks intruders in the lungs, 95 percent of those who inhale the germs remain healthy. Even the remaining 5 percent may not become fatally ill, one of the great mysteries of science. Heredity, nutrition, general health, and age of exposure all matter. The most susceptible ages groups are infants, adolescents, and the elderly. In the 1830s, once the disease set in, 50 percent of the victims died within five years of onset; 20 percent remained chronically ill, and the rest recovered.[16]

A young father who needed to work to support his family,

Hiram was unable to take the recommended cure, an ocean voyage. Sullivan was five years old when his father worsened, and the household dynamics changed. Eight-year-old Hannah Frances was kept home from school to help as necessary. Sullivan's relationship with his father was by necessity confined to sedentary activities. There were no long rambles in the hills, coaching in ball playing, or trips to other towns.

When able, Hiram worked, completed orders, and had them delivered to customers. But certainly he was not out and about touting his services to prosper and grow his business. Evidence that the family's financial position slipped can be found in records that reveal the tailor began borrowing large amounts of money in 1832. Without prior records to evaluate the cash flow of his business, it is not possible to know precisely how much of the loaned money was diverted to supporting his family. His loans, eleven in all, often taken for periods of two to six months, totaled $1,900 [now $35,000] and he had another $1,200 [$20,500] in undated debts, some of which may have been normal accounts payable to suppliers of fabric. The short-term nature of the notes suggests his belief that he could pay the money back when he recovered. One payment of $400 [$6,000], possibly an inheritance, recorded against a loan of $600 [10,000], demonstrates faithful efforts to repay debts.[17] In August 1832, Emeline's father, Dr. Joseph Bowen, passed away in Glocester at age seventy-seven, after what seemed to be a short illness. An extremely religious man, his will committed "my soul to God that gave it and my body to Christian burial at the discretion of my executor," his son, Clovis Hildovus Bowen.[18] Emeline received a small inheritance equal to her sisters', indicating there was apparently no estrangement from her father as regarded her marriage.

In the Cumberland, Emeline could do no more for her husband than nurse him in the basic traditional female role, diligently administering home remedies, and keeping the patient warm, comforted, fed, and hydrated. If the body could effect a recovery on its own, such support activities made all the difference. As his condition worsened, and round-the-clock presence was required as a death watch, New Englanders had developed their own way of supporting each other. Neighbors, boarders, and friends took a shift at the bedside, especially during the night. They stoked the fire, kept a candle lit and provided a caring presence. There is no way to know if in its end, the disease took him slowly or quickly, but on Sunday, June 30, 1833, Hiram died at home, surrounded by those who loved him, and from whom he despaired to part.

This was the most pivotal event in the first half of Sullivan's life, and while its long-term effects took years to be felt, there were some immediate differences. His mother and house were given over at once to mourning. Harriet Beecher Stowe, in *Oldtown Folks*, noted,

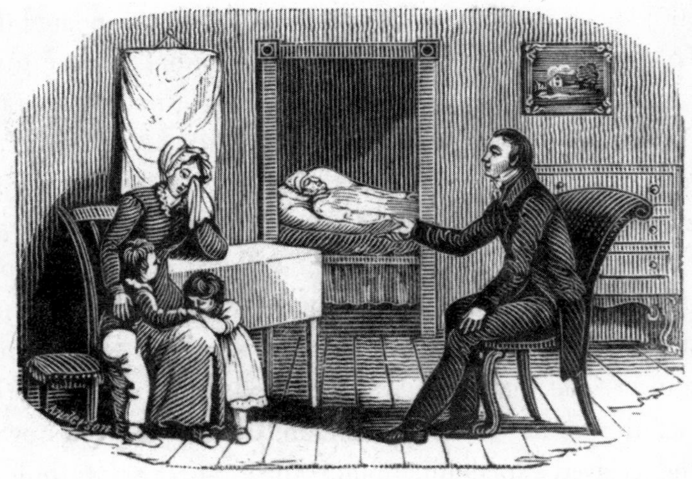

"The Sorrowing Family." In this woodcut (circa 1825), a family grieves over the loss of the husband and father while awaiting the arrival of the casket as the minister offers comforting words. Note the covered mirror, one of the ways the house was altered by death. *Courtesy Alexander Anderson Scrapbook, Volume X, Print Collection, Miriam and Ira D. Wallach Division of Art, Prints and Photographs, the New York Public Library, Astor, Lenox and Tilden Foundations.*

Hiram was buried in the Ballou family cemetery adjacent to the Elder Ballou Meeting House, located in the so-called "Ballou Neighborhood" of Cumberland. The structure served as town hall, militia headquarters, and church. *Courtesy of the Woonsocket Harris Public Library Historical Collection.*

> It was a doctrine of those . . . times that a house invaded by death should be made as forlorn as hands could make it. It should be rendered as cold and still, as unnatural, as dead and corpse-like as possible, by closing shutters.[19]

People dimmed their lights, covering mirrors with white sheets, removing flowers and "hiding out of sight any pleasant little familiar object which would have been thought out of place in a sepulchre."[20] Because the death rate was high, children of this era were more intimately acquainted with death than those of later centuries, but even so, to a six-year-old, the death of a parent would have been devastating. Compounding the family's grief, very shortly after, another trip was made down the long dirt road to the Ballou Cemetery to inter Sullivan's baby sister Janette, who died the same month as her father.[21] It had been a miserable year for Emeline—losing her father, her husband, and her youngest child—but the young mother still had to make do, financially and emotionally. Sullivan never forgot how hard these times were. In June and July 1861, more than three decades later, he recalled "having eaten for long years the bitter fruits of orphanage" and "felt too keenly the sufferings and pangs of orphanhood and . . . seen too many trials of the widowed mother."[22] These experiences shaped his aspirations as well as his definition of the roles of husband, father, and breadwinner.

Six days before Hiram's death, an attorney, possibly Christopher Robinson, had visited Hiram to prepare the will of the young father, "weak in body" and "considering the uncertainty of life." A woeful document, it records the pathetic last efforts of a man desperate to piece together some resources to succor the young family he was leaving behind. He left everything to "my beloved wife Emeline to take care of my children and bring them up out of my estate, should there be anything left after paying my just debts." He directed,

> As there will be some real estate which will fall to me or my heirs after the decease of my mother, [it is] my will that same estate should be sold by my executor . . . immediately at a public or private sale and the profits arising therefrom—minus the costs of the sale—to be paid over to my said wife for her to take charge of in the manner before mentioned, and should there remain any estate in the hands of my said wife, after my three children, viz Hannah Frances Ballou, Sullivan Ballou and Janette Ballou shall arrive to the age of twenty-one years, then the same shall be for the benefit of her, my said wife and at her disposal forever.

He directed that she receive "all the rents and profits on all buildings, lands and tenements I own in my possession"—after making any needed repairs; also that his brother, Henry, yet another tailor, should, "if he think it to his interest," "occupy the store and tailor shop wherein I now occupy."[23] Emeline notified the probate court that she accepted the terms of the will and relinquished her dower rights to her one-third of her husband's estate.[24] (In those times, a widow owned outright only her personal clothing, jewelry, and effects, and any items she had brought into the marriage by prenuptial agreement.)

The probate dragged on for two years, while Hiram's executors settled all his business affairs, paid his loans, and collected small amounts, ranging from $1 to $27 owed from some three hundred customers. Folks often bought on credit, intending to pay their bills when they had cash, but it appeared Hiram had not been well enough to follow up on obtaining payments from his clientele. Two years of rent on the shop and the tenement netted $240, which was put into the pot to pay off the debts.

A piece of scratch paper with tallies was uncharacteristically filed along with the will, showing the executors unsuccessfully trying to come up with enough cash to pay off the debt and end the probate. It showed Henry, George, and Hosea Ballou, and some others, finally chipped in about $1,000 to enable that to happen.[25] As inflation increased prices by 10 percent over the next four years, it appears they kept on paying. A family friend, Horatio Rogers, recalled, "a kind uncle . . . contributed much towards the support of the little orphans."* During this same time, Henry and Johnathan Ballou also absorbed the care of other widows and children of relatives who had unnaturally short life spans. Emeline, Sullivan, and Hannah Frances were never short of Ballou attention and friendship, just of cash. The Ballous closed ranks, supported one another however they could, and endured. Emeline coped, because she had to.

There were few options for a woman to earn money in the Cumberland in 1833. "School teaching, the boarding house, or work at

* In this era, fatherless children were called orphans even if their mother was still alive.

the mills" were the only choices for wage earning in New England, and none paid well.[26] Although women were restricted from many roles and occupations, Victorian society hallowed the role of a mother, who was believed to be the most important influence in her children's development. Mothers were venerated as the conduit of civilization, gentility, love of God, and education to their children.

It fell to the mother to instruct them in another important part of their religious world view, which in a society with many deaths, included the perception of death and the afterlife. Mrs. Child, author of *The Mother's Book*, reflected the Victorian belief that this life and the next were separated only by a thin veil when she said, "We ought not to draw such a line of separation between those who are living in this world, and those who are alive in another."[27] Sullivan was brought up to believe that his father was looking out for them from the afterlife, and he retained this viewpoint even after he forgot his father's face.

"Getting Dressed." In this woodcut (circa 1845), a mother helps her son get ready for church. In this era, most Americans washed hands, arms, and face daily using a pitcher of water and bowl, as in this summertime scene. In the winter, the family washed by the kitchen fire, also the site of the weekly bath. *Courtesy Alexander Anderson Scrapbook, Volume VIII, Print Collection, Miriam and Ira D. Wallach Division of Art, Prints and Photographs, the New York Public Library, Astor, Lenox and Tilden Foundations.*

Horatio Rogers wrote of her,

> Though Mrs. Ballou was not possessed of material wealth, she was blessed with maternal qualities, more valuable than silver and gold. She taught her children in their early years, that there was no royal road to success, and that if they hoped to achieve it, they must exert themselves to deserve it. She implanted in their breasts a spirit of self reliance and a determination to win the reward, which industry always attains. She impressed on their youthful minds the truth that honor and integrity were virtues without which, no success, however rapid or brilliant, could be enduring or even worth obtaining.[28]

Had Emeline chosen to remarry, her financial problems might have eased, and a prosperous stepfather might have had the means to provide an education that fitted Sullivan for a professional life. However, she was one of many widows who never remarried, and the family's financial problems never abated, requiring them to practice many economies. As Rogers remarked of their impact upon Sullivan,

> The slender means of his widowed mother could secure for him no other opportunities for mental improvement, than were afforded by the public schools of his native village.[29]

Sullivan obtained his knowledge of reading, writing, and arithmetic at the local one-room grammar school, as did the sons of even the richest men. It was an excellent grounding in the basics. In arithmetic, he learned to reckon in both American and English currency. He was taught, as well, the measurements for cloth, paper, foodstuffs, beer and wine, land, and linear distance; likewise the various weight systems: apothecary, troy, avoirdupois. By the time he left grammar school, Sullivan had also mastered all

Continental Army General John Sullivan, for whom Sullivan Ballou was named. *From* Thomas C. Amory's The Military Services and Public Life of Major-General John Sullivan (1869).

practicable mathematic methods enabling him to compute interest rates, perform ledger accounting, billing, profit, and commission calculations.[30] Remarkable as such an education may seem today, schoolmasters of that time anticipated that many of their students would need to go into some kind of business immediately upon leaving elementary school in their early teens or even younger. He would have been given a thorough course of study in reading and writing, again with immediate application in mind.

Sullivan's greatest passion, however, was that aspect of his education startlingly different from what is taught in the present day—rhetoric and oratory. In the 1800s,

> because oratory was considered an important part of Nineteenth Century American life, even very young children were expected to read, memorize, and deliver speeches . . . and to study speeches as a way of learning how to read, write, and speak . . . anthologies . . . were used to instill patriotic beliefs and American values in their readers.

It was believed a poor man could rise to prominence and prosperity through oratory, and schoolchildren of either sex were expected to be able to speak about local issues like libraries and schools, and perhaps discuss national issues as well.[31] Students might practice and give their speeches in front of their peers, parents, and siblings, but *The Mother's Book* advised against "parading" them before guests.[32]

Sullivan remained at the public schools in Smithfield to complete a full grammar school education, but the school district then lacked a high school. If he were to continue his education, it had to be in a private school, one that would cost more than Emeline could afford. It now mattered very much that he belonged to the poorest branch of the Ballou family.

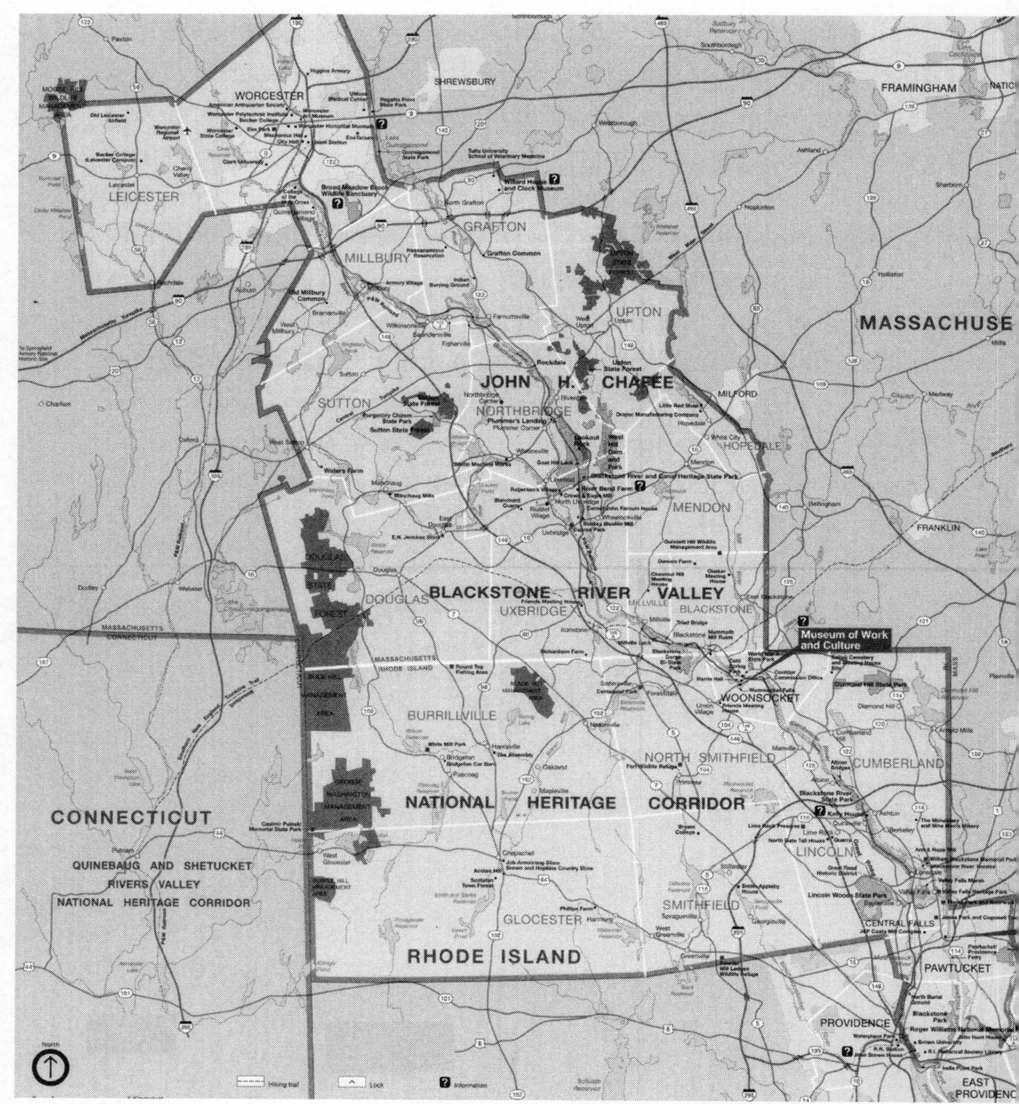

The Blackstone River ran between Sarah's hometown of Worcester, Massachusetts, and Sullivan's in Cumberland, Rhode Island. This area was the cradle of the American industrial revolution. *Courtesy of the National Park Service.*

CHAPTER TWO

"Whose Sons Are Foremost in Duty"*

The Education of Sullivan

1840–1845

Young Sullivan actually faced quite a dilemma. Lacking an inheritance of any kind, he had to set himself up from scratch in some occupation that would support him sufficiently to take care of his mother and, eventually, the family he hoped to have. One role model was his cousin Olney Ballou, "a prominent public man" and elected official, who in 1836 was a presidential elector in the election that brought Martin Van Buren to the White House. Another was the Honorable Jabez Bowen, esquire and graduate of Yale, who rose from a position on the town council to become chief justice; he served on the state's Council of War, was deputy governor, and counted generals George Washington and Lafayette among his friends. Bowen also owned land and was a partner in various maritime ventures, whose ships voyaged around

* From the Civil War song "Freedom's New Banner."

The Honorable Jabez Bowen, painted by John Singleton Copley before 1774. *Courtesy of Henry Dewey.*

the world;[1] despite the risk to his business ventures, he sided wholeheartedly with the patriots and independence—indeed, the Declaration of Independence was read out to the people of Rhode Island from his house in Providence.[2]

Sullivan faced formidable obstacles. While his family heritage was rich in honor, his economic heritage was poverty. Just before his birth, the Ballou family of Rhode Island split into three branches—poor, middle class, and rich—based on their ability to react to events and trends in post–Revolutionary War New England. Relationships between the branches remained cordial, and the family did have a history of helping each other. In 1829, when George Colburn Ballou's mill burned down, Hiram donated $25 to a fund to rebuild it, a large amount by his standards. Six years later, George and his brother Dexter contributed significantly higher amounts to pay Hiram's debts in probate. However, by Sullivan's time, such philanthropy toward poor relations had worn thin. The help received by any of them was never enough to lift widows and their children out of poverty, only enough to take the edge off it. In the whole family, in Sullivan's generation, only two of the orphan boys were sponsored for higher education and, when it happened, it was only for a year at a time: none of them had the security of a full commitment to pay for a complete education.

Sullivan's strategy came down to perseverance. He did what he could to help himself along; for one thing, he read, and developed a true love for reading, a reverence for books. Overall, he was an earnest, religious, hardworking boy who tried hard to please, and never lost his sense of humor. Plus, his mother was a Bowen, and Bowens had produced professional men all the way back to the founding of the colonies. She may have been his most powerful ally, and insisted that her son should not be deprived owing to an accident of fortune. The family had a history of bouncing back from disaster.

Molly and Ziba Ballou, Sullivan's grandparents, were the last of the huge Ballou farm families. Molly Mason, who married Ziba when she was only seventeen, bore him thirteen children in twenty-seven years; Hiram, her eighth child, was born just before the end of 1802.

"Resolute and industrious," Ziba and Molly had cheerful dispositions that seemingly could overcome any obstacle. The family relished telling Ziba stories, such as when he had set off in convoy with other farmers for Providence, all driving heavily laden wagons. They had only gone three miles when an axle broke on Ziba's wagon. He unhitched a horse, rode back home, made a new axle out of a piece of timber, and rode back to the wagon with the axle over his shoulder. He repaired the wheel, rehitched the horse into the team, and arrived in Providence no later than the others![3]

And yet, for all their spunk and hard work, Ziba and Molly almost lost their whole family when crops failed during the "Year without a Summer." Sullivan's father, aunts, uncles, and grandparents found themselves at the mercy of an environmental catastrophe. In April 1815, a volcano named Mount Tambora, located in Indonesia, blew up in a supercolossal explosion, sending four thousand feet of its mountaintop into the stratosphere in three columns estimated to have been twenty-eight miles high.* Ten thousand people lost their lives to the explosion itself or the pyroclastic flow; uncounted thousands more were killed by the tsunamis spawned by the force of the quaking ground.[4] The volcano wrecked the prosperity of New England, half a world away, when the amount of ash carried into the planet's atmosphere lowered the climate by an estimated three degrees, sufficient to cut the growing season from 160 days to 70.[5] In the northern hemisphere, the subsequent death toll from starvation was approximately 100,000 people.[6]

Other atmospheric changes occurred that year: In the third week of September 1815, a hurricane "far beyond any in the memory of any man living," blew into Providence. Water in the bay rose an estimated twelve to fourteen feet, and the high winds caused a tidal surge of almost eight feet to sweep through the city, which was evacuated. Buildings and farm crops were devastated as far inland as Worcester.[7]

In 1816, spring and summer never arrived. Snow, hail, and frosts continued through August. It was so cold that birds flew into barns and houses to survive; those that remained outdoors died, literally frozen stiff. Lambs and sheep perished in the fields, and the farmers were unable to raise crops.[8] Unable to graze, without hay or fodder, farm animals were slaughtered early in the season. Once their meat was consumed, there was nothing to eat. Panic, hunger, and poverty gripped New England. Hiram Ballou and his twelve siblings were utterly dependent for their sustenance on what their family farm produced. The fact that only one of the thirteen children lived a normal lifespan suggests their hardiness and health were undermined by that prolonged period of poor nutrition.

When it became clear that no farmland was coming their way, Hiram and his brothers needed to learn new skills. Many Ballou families began operating small manufacturing works that utilized

* A supercolossal category volcano equals 7 on the Volcano Explosive Index (VEI). For comparison, Mount St. Helen's in 1981 was a paroxysmal 5.

Author's photo at Old Sturbridge Village.

From author's collection.

Courtesy of the Woonsocket Harris Public Library Historical Collection.

Author's photo at Old Sturbridge Village.

Author's photo at Williamsburg.

The career paths open to a poor boy with no education around 1840 were limited. Sullivan could work at a mill, like his uncle George C. Ballou's on the left; farm; or open a modest manufacturing facility. But Sullivan aspired to a professional career, such as an orator (top right), and at a very young age opted to put in the hard work necessary to achieve his goal.

natural products obtainable locally to make shoes, saddles, harnesses, brooms, stone scythes, wagons, furniture, and cider. These employed few outside the immediate family.

At twelve, Sullivan knew no trade.

His father had tried to ride the wave of mill prosperity in a much more modest way, keeping his distance from the drudgery and danger of the mill itself. Having no real capital to invest, Hiram, like his brothers, became the merchant tailors, a much humbler line of work compared to the industrialists. While they were assured of steady supply of fabric from the family mills, and commissioned to sew the clothing worn by their wealthier cousins, they reaped little other benefits beyond a comfortable living. Wholly dependent on their own labor, if anything prevented them from working they were but one step away from insolvency and poverty. Sullivan did not desire to follow in his father's footsteps, and indeed he could not have done so in practicable terms: Hiram's business had died with him; there was no company Sullivan could take over to earn his own livelihood.

By 1840, when Sullivan had absorbed all the learning the Cumberland grammar school had to offer, the American industrial age had begun locally, financed by a group of farmers from the Ballou Neighborhood, who had the gumption to invest their cash in cutting-edge machinery and the manufacturing process.

Rhode Island had developed a market niche over the past hundred years of manufacturing raw materials into products, so it was natural for world-class entrepreneurs like the Brown family, of Providence, to pursue this opportunity for profit. They backed a prototype mill facility at Pawtucket, with seventy-eight thread spindles, which proved its ability to process large amounts of raw cotton. It was a greater leap of faith for the partnership of Ballou farmers—Ariel, Abner, and Nathan Ballou and four others—who "knew much more about manual agriculture than of running Cotton Mills," to open one.[9] Then again, in these early years, everyone running a mill was an amateur and it was a good time to break into the business. The Ballous appraised the area near tiny Union Village, by the waterfalls the Indians called Niswosakit. Here, in what had been an Indian campsite dating back 7,600 years, the Blackstone River fell thirty-one feet in a short distance, and others nearby had drops of sixty and fifty-two feet respectively.[10] The first cotton mill opened in Woonsocket in 1810, with two thousand spindles.

The original Ballou mill partnership sold out and returned to the line of business they knew best but, in 1817, another branch of the family moved their operations to Woonsocket in the ground floor of a thirty-by-seventy-foot building. Sullivan's uncle, Oliver Ballou, ran this in partnership with his three sons, Dexter, George Colburn, and Hosea. They had "mill fever," became capitalists, and rode the great wave of textile prosperity to eventual riches. In doing so, they backed a good trend: within twenty years, similar mills were being built on all the white-water courses of northern Rhode Island, crowding out the earlier occupants, the grist and sawmills, as well as the salmon, shad, and herring.[11]

Nature packages cotton in a tight wad, the fibers twisted every which way, inset with seeds. The task of "picking out" a single pound, for which Cumberland families formerly labored a full day and earned three cents a pound, was now accomplished by the cotton gin.[12] This device had been invented by a young Massachusetts man, Eli Whitney—a Yale graduate with a mechanical bent, who epitomized the "Yankee tinkerer" that loved experimentation, innovation, and had an insatiable longing for more and better tools—with the collaboration of Caroline, the widow of Revolutionary War general Nathanael Greene.[13]

Cotton immediately became a more viable commercial product, and its cultivation swiftly expanded throughout the South. So did slavery, then almost a dying institution. Cotton exports jumped from 140,000 pounds in 1794 to 18 million pounds in 1800.[14] A powerful bond of self-interest formed between the cotton-growing and cotton-spinning regions of the nation.

Mill operations streamlined in one building all the steps of the production process, and brought the workers to the machinery. Demand was such that Sullivan could have a job at a mill, any time he wanted one. The mills relied on a steady stream of children to feed the raw cotton into the carding machine, whose distance between rollers required workers with small hands.

This, in of itself, was dangerous work. Moreover, conditions inside the mills were unhealthy. The noise of the gears and machinery was constant.* To keep the thread flowing smoothly, the atmosphere was damp, and lint filled the air. Poor air circulation helped spread colds, influenza, and then-incurable diseases, such as tuberculosis. Injuries were rampant because the machinery never stopped. Most mills kept a surgeon on retainer to sew up wounds or amputate body parts too mangled to heal; workers injured too badly to return to work were not pensioned, just released.

Some worked at the mills for a while, accumulated savings, and left; more remained trapped in a work cycle of eight-to-ten-hour shifts that left little opportunity for schooling. A young man like Sullivan's cousin David, who would one day inherit the mill complex, might benefit from personal knowledge of the production line, but for Sullivan it was a total dead end. He escaped it only through the determination of his mother. No matter how broke or desperate Emeline felt while trying to make ends meet, she steadfastly rejected this source of income for herself, her daughter, and her son.

It finally became clear that the only resources Sullivan had were his intelligence, ambition, and persistence. To make the most of those, he needed to acquire those skills taught only in the higher

* The sounds of an operating mill can be heard at www.oregonlink.com/mission_mill.

educational institutions. Horatio Rogers noted how the youngster developed self-reliance: "Sullivan, . . . the youngest, early felt the necessity of depending upon himself for support and advancement." From the age of thirteen to twenty-five Sullivan would work many jobs, to earn the money to pay for his higher education.

But in about 1840, when he left Cumberland's grammar school, his mother wanted Sullivan to work full time, at least for a while. A strategy was needed to evade the mills without insulting their owners. Six years after her husband's death, Emeline sought a guardian for her son from among her own Bowen kin, and in November 1839, the Probate Court appointed her brother, Clovis Hildovus Bowen, then thirty-two years old, Sullivan's guardian, "hereby authorized to and empowered by said Court to exercise said office of Guardian and vested with all the power and authority of said office belonging."[15]

Sullivan's destiny was now linked to his uncle, a man of a very different temperament, outlook, and philosophy than his nephew. Clovis seems to have done his duty by the boy, but kept the purse strings tightly drawn against anything that smacked of indulgence. His only listed occupation was town clerk, a post he took over from his father, which probably paid a comfortable living, but he was an unlikely source of much additional funding. Living across the state, he was also an unlikely source of day-to-day contact or guidance, for all that he was Emeline's brother. However, Clovis used family contacts to get Sullivan a job so far away from the mills that it was several hundred miles away from home.

And so, between the ages of twelve and fifteen, Sullivan spent eighteen months as a clerk in a dry goods store in Rochester, New York, perhaps the one owned by Ira Bowen.[16] Dry goods stores of the time sold a profusion of the very textiles made in the mills of New England, as well as imported luxury fabrics, for personal and household use. Part of Sullivan's job was to measure and cut the yardage to the customer's specifications. His other duties included stocking merchandise, helping customers, adding up the bills and taking payments, sweeping up at night, and perhaps making deliveries. He did not like working as a clerk. Rogers related,

> This was a sore disappointment to the boy, and his letters home were filled with urgent entreaties that he might be allowed to obtain an education.

Sullivan's sojourn in Rochester had unexpected consequences, for the boom town was a microcosm of America's social, political, and religious precepts, as well as a perfect case study of the dynamics of westward expansion. A great many "isms" were spawned in Rochester: feminism, nativism,* abolitionism, millennialism, and religious revivalism. Many of the Rochester-born "isms" simmered in various underground movements and several short-lived nativist political parties for the next thirty years. When honed of extremism, they emerged as the philosophy and planks of a dynamic, new national political movement, the Republican Party, which Sullivan Ballou later supported as an early member. On his own, so to speak, without close family around him, Sullivan was to learn many lessons of life and politics there.

Settled by landless Yankees from New England, the town had gone from a junction of pathways in 1812 to a population of twenty thousand by 1840. Thanks to the Erie Canal (1821) and the later arrival of railroad transportation, it was "the marketing and manufacturing center for a broad and prosperous agricultural hinterland."[17] Surrounded by the vast farmlands opened up by General John Sullivan, Rochester capitalized on the water power of the two-hundred-foot drop of the Genesee River within its boundaries to become a milling and shipping center for grain: production

* An "Americans first" political philosophy spawned by the influx of immigrants, particularly the Catholic Irish.

jumped 2,000 percent in nearly twenty years. The city shared the same economic and political aspirations as the new states of the Midwest, aspirations that shaped the great American debate over slavery, public investment in transportation, and the continental railroad, all of which eventually led to the Civil War.

In an 1820s farmhouse nearby, Sarah Shumway Ballou's distant cousin, Joseph Smith, provided his own well-organized and compelling answers to the key religious questions debated in the Rochester area, including temperance, baptism, penance, redemption, and social obligations within the Christian community.[18] Absorbing local Native American mythology about superior earlier civilizations, the Mormon religion sojourned in Rochester before moving west to escape eventual persecution.[19]

Its proximity to Canada was to make Rochester a key station on the Underground Railroad, and its abolitionist-leaning Yankees efficiently helped many escaped slaves slip across the border to freedom. In Sullivan Ballou's native Rhode Island, slavery was more discreet, and had mostly operated in the lower half of the state he had had little opportunity to visit. Although Rhode Island businesses had transported 6 percent of all transatlantic slave traffic, mostly to the deep South or Caribbean, the small family farms in the Ballou neighborhood owned no slaves. Thus, Sullivan learned more about its tragic human consequences in Rochester than he ever did at home, and his stay there began to shape the antislavery beliefs he later professed during his political career.

In his early teens, however, Rochester proved a poor move for Sullivan. Sometime around 1843, he quit his job as a clerk and returned home. "At length, after dragging out a year and a half in this uncongenial occupation, his request was granted."[20] He came back amidst a time of upheaval and rebellion that had started in 1842, events whose outcome would grant Sullivan the right to vote and hold elected office when he reached age twenty-one in less than five years' time.

At that time, the right to vote was not consistently granted among all the United States. When Charles II had granted Rhode Island its charter in 1663, no one imagined the colonies would become independent and not have recourse to the king to update their charter. It therefore contained no provision for modification as the population grew and new towns were founded. By the 1840s, most states had overturned their colonial charters and replaced them with new constitutions, but Rhode Island had not.

Rhode Islanders thus lived via an antiquated system: Women and Blacks could not vote. A man owning real estate, and his eldest son, were eligible to vote; however his younger sons, and anyone who rented premises, could not. Under this system, Sullivan Ballou was part of the 60 percent of the state's white male population who had no right to vote.[21] As farmers became mill workers, and sold their land to rent cottages in the towns, they too lost that right. Ironically, all able-bodied men age eighteen to forty-five had to bear arms, but the majority were unable to vote on the matters that sent them to war.

In 1811 and again in 1824, proposals to redraft the state constitution were voted down by the rich landowners who dominated the legislature. The best minds in the state collaborated on how to fix the problem. One leader was Thomas Dorr, a Harvard-trained lawyer, son of Sullivan Dorr, the wealthy merchant of Providence. Christopher Robinson, the prominent Woonsocket attorney who had written Hiram's will, "prepared a few short essays on the subject of suffrage," and pamphlets were published and distributed.[22] All such efforts were ignored, "kicked under the table."[23]

By 1841, the reformers, including Sullivan's cousin Olney Ballou, decided to go around the legislature, straight to the people themselves, to convene a constitutional convention.[24] In Providence, in July, "the Suffrage Party held a mass meeting and roasted an ox on Smith's Hill . . . which did something to tone up public opinion in their favor." There was a procession through town that included some of the militia units, such as the Woonsocket Light Infantry.[25] The public demonstrations had the desired effect: the legislature belatedly wrote a new constitution, and, by the spring of 1843, Rhode Island found itself in the awkward situation of having two men with claims to the governorship under their respective old and new constitutions.

Thomas Dorr, the governor now locked out of the statehouse, gathered an estimated 250 men and a few cannon to his cause and holed up in the west of the state, near Chepachet, a suburb of Glocester. Exaggerated rumors flew around the state, of a force of three thousand men ready to storm all citadels of government and industry. Arsenals and factories alike were barricaded for protection. A militia force of three thousand men was then assembled to go west to do battle against Dorr and his inflammatory supporters; the bloodless Dorr Rebellion ended when he fled to Connecticut. A third constitution, passed overwhelmingly, took effect in May 1843, and governed the state for another eighty-five years. The state senate was reapportioned so that each town or city had only a single representative, which ensured rural dominance over the cities. It gave the vote to all native-born men over twenty-one years of age, regardless of race.* Blacks now had the vote in Rhode Island, and so would Sullivan Ballou once he came of age; women still did not.

One consequence of the Dorr Rebellion was the disbanding of the Woonsocket Light Infantry, whose members had paraded in support of Dorr. A new militia unit for the town was chartered by the legislature, the Woonsocket Guards. Two Ballous were among its earliest members: Henry Greene and Sullivan, uncle and nephew, carrying on a sacred tradition. Sullivan, then about fourteen years old, had not yet grown to his eventual height, and was

* Immigrants had to meet a lengthy residency requirement and a land-owning test equal to property worth $134 [now $2,400] to vote.

fondly remembered as being scarcely tall enough to carry the four-foot-long musket. For the first few years, he acted as "marker . . . orderly and Lieutenant."[26]

From the earliest days of settlement each region of each colony maintained for protection groups of volunteer, part-time, soldier-policemen known as the local militia. If the colony came under threat, these able-bodied men provided the first line of defense, sparing first Britain, then the state and federal governments of America, the expense of maintaining a professional army with little to do in between times of war but to get into mischief. The militiamen were able to fight and exercise some discipline, but were never trained as soldiers. The militia companies did sturdy service over a two-hundred-year period, dealing with threats from the Indians, Dutch, French, English, and occasional groups of rebellious colonists. They fought in the Revolutionary War, and the War of 1812. In the 1840s, they remained the second line of defense, behind a small professional army whose main activity during that decade was fighting with Mexico over ownership of the Texas border. They were to provide the initial troops for both sides in the Civil War twenty years later.

Civic-minded, sociable men joined up, and officers were elected each year on "muster day." In colonial times, these annual training days were held adjacent to taverns, where food and drink were available, and it was the custom for the newly elected officers to stand a few rounds for their men. As one man noted, "liquor was furnished in such overflowing abundance that some who attended training took many more steps returning home than they had in coming."[27]

For five to six generations, men of the Ballou, Shumway, and Bowen families maintained a tradition of service in these local militia units, often two generations at a time, the name of the grandfather being replaced by his grandson in the same unit. In the muster lists for 1756, for example, Second Lieutenant Benjamin

Bowen appeared with the Providence Troop of Horse, and Ariel Ballou as an ensign with the Second Company of the Cumberland Rangers. Such a contribution was considered by them to be a natural extension of their efforts to secure their homes and their liberties, just one more step in building America. The names of the units had gradually changed, but when Sullivan joined the Woonsocket Guards, he was the youngest member ever in a long line of his family to join the militia.

In colonial days, the local units were the Smithfield and Cumberland Rangers. In the muster rolls of "the Officers to command the several Train Band, or companies of Militia in the Colony, for Cumberland Second Company," were Levi Tower, Captain, and Levi Ballou, ensign. In the Revolutionary War, as in the Civil War, Tower and Ballou were fighting side by side.[28]

Still very much a boy, Sullivan spent his leisure time during fair weather with other teenagers, in games of townball, a nineteenth-century bat-and-ball game that had been played for generations in the towns of New England. Evolved from the game of "rounders" played in the sixteenth century, it was the immediate predecessor of baseball: The pitcher threw to the "striker," who was out after three strikes. If the catcher or another player caught his fly ball, he was out. Tagging had not yet developed, so the game was more lethal. A striker was also out if any of the players could hit him with the leather ball while he was running the four bases (then indicated by flat stones or wood stakes). The game was called townball because each town had its own variations on the rules. In some towns, like Dedham, Massachusetts, the game was won only when one team had scored one hundred runs.[29]

Sullivan was also expected to help out at home with various chores. One that was neverending was keeping wood handy for Emeline's use in cooking and for heating water and the house. One of Sullivan's duties was to fetch the chopped wood from the yard as needed, as storing it indoors was too risky a fire hazard.

During this period at home, Sullivan endeavored to borrow and read works by classical Roman and Greek authors whenever possible, to prepare on his own prior to enrollment in the 1840s equivalent of high school. To enter an academy or college, an entrance examination had to be passed, demonstrating basic skills in grammar, arithmetic, some Latin, and often one classical sage was particularly favored for study by an institution. Before even taking his entrance examination, a student was required to be at least fourteen years of age, and to be able to present testimonials giving "satisfactory evidence that he sustains a fair moral character."[30]

Much of the education of this era was based on the classics, in the belief that the wisdom of the great men of Ancient Greece and Rome had value and immediacy even nineteen hundred years later, and that their lives provided moral examples to the modern world.[31] The point of reading the histories of Ancient Greece and Rome, by both ancient and more contemporary writers, was to develop critical thinking skills, and the ability to analyze and draw conclusions from diverse accounts of events. Students needed to learn to present facts in a logical sequence, and facts about ancient times were believed as good as any, and perhaps less controversial than contemporary United States politics, especially when a class included boys from the South. Of course, the ancient writers also formed a large part of the body of study materials for rhetoric; notably Cicero, a Roman orator who was widely imitated.[32]

In rhetoric, clearness and directness were important, be the discussion the evils of slavery, or the benefits of the new heating fuel, coal. Those who were unable to achieve such convincing oration might practice elocution, the lesser art of clear and expressive speech, again in overt emulation of classical orators. As *American Eloquence* stated in 1854,

> a nation's eloquence is . . . a nation's power and glory. . . . The power and splendor of Rome . . . lay in her Senate and her

> Forum, more even than in the . . . prowess of her . . . legions. It was those living, undying voices, which thundered in her Capitol that made Rome great.[33]

In the early 1800s, producing such thundering voices was the real goal of the higher educational system that Sullivan sought to access. The system was focused on graduating men with communication skills able to influence others to action in business, politics, law, or saving their souls. Only those who spent years studying excellent speeches, giving their own and having them critiqued by their professors, might prove successful at what Walt Whitman called "the rarest and most profound of humanity's arts," oration.[34]

During the 1840s, tuition, room, and board at American academies and colleges cost between $21 and $100 [$386–2,150 present day] per third-year term, with fuel and washing extra. Many farmers struggled to educate at least one son per household.

In 1844, things began turning around for Sullivan, who left home for a destination much more to his liking than Rochester had been—a fine educational institution, Nichols Academy, in Dudley, Massachusetts. A progressive school that counted among its backers mill baron Samuel Slater, it had equal numbers of male and female students, about one hundred in all, and boasted a fine library.[35]

According to Horatio Rogers, Sullivan studied there for six months in 1844 "by the assistance of relatives."[36] There were three terms of three months each; the cost for tuition, room, and board was $21 [now $386] per term.[37] The students were expected to study algebra, grammar, geography, history of the United States and the world, and languages, especially Latin and Greek. Optional scientific courses in surveying, military tactics, or architecture were sometimes available to those intending such careers, depending on the institution. Sullivan apparently attended for two terms and had the opportunity to begin to learn public speaking, using Newman's and Whateley's *Rhetoric* among his texts.[38]

His classmates were all destined for careers in white-collar professions, the first time Sullivan moved in such a circle with so many other purposeful students. Certainly it was the first time he made the acquaintance of such a large number of young ladies his own age also bent on furthering their education.

Perhaps he absorbed all that Nichols had to offer, or perhaps the money ran out, because by 1845, Sullivan had come back to Rhode Island, "where for a year he studied the classics under Reverend Mr. Taft."[39] George Taft had come to St. Paul's in 1820, just after a bell made in Paul Revere's foundry was hung in the belfry.[40] For many years, he was also the principal of the Academy, a Pawtucket school begun in 1824, "the chief institution of learning in the village."[41] Taft was also the esteemed, high-energy pastor of St. Paul's Episcopal Church in Pawtucket, where Sullivan's family now lived. From this time, Sullivan appears to have been associated with the Episcopal Church. Interestingly, Sullivan was never found on the membership lists of any of the Baptist, Congregational, or Universal churches that were the mainstays of the Ballou family.

Taft tutored young Sullivan, loaning him books, putting questions to him, grading his essays, and coaching his declamations. The boy was able to live at home, saving money on room and board, the costliest part of an academy education. Whether Sullivan paid fees for this tutoring, or bartered his way by teaching the younger children, or helping at the Academy, is unknown. Rogers states Sullivan taught school at some point in his life, and it might have been here.

While studying with Reverend Taft, Sullivan may have assisted the pastor with charitable relief efforts Americans extended to Ireland during the potato famine. When details of the potato famine became known in January 1847, the local press leapt into action, the *Pawtucket Gazette* announcing, "Starvation of the most dire description stalked . . . the length and breadth of the land." Pawtucket was divided into districts, the clergy in each asked to solicit donations at Sunday services. The town bought 125 barrels of meal, which were shipped to Cork in May by the New York Irish Relief Committee.[42]

By working hard with Reverend Taft to master the ancient authors and their works, as well as participate in contemporary community activism, Sullivan was ready to move on to the next phase of acquiring those skills that opened, "in this country more than in any other, avenues to the very highest points of distinction, wealth and honor."[43]

CHAPTER THREE

"Whose Daughters Are Peerless and Bright"*

Sarah's Cosmopolitan Upbringing

1835–1849

One man had easily completed the sort of education for which Sullivan longed—his future father-in-law. The third son and fourth child of another prolific couple, Alfred Shumway and Elizabeth Steward, had also been christened with a name of honor: Christopher Columbus Shumway. The name enjoyed a brief popularity for babies born in Massachusetts around 1800.

Shumway was born in 1805, in his paternal hometown of Belchertown. According to contemporary records he was known alternatively by his namesake's full name, or by either portion; and he left behind no indication whether he appreciated the honor. Young Columbus must have demonstrated particular drive and talent, for he alone of all his seven brothers was singled out for higher education. He had no need of intermediate academies.

* From the Civil War song "Freedom's New Banner."

In 1826, at age twenty-one, Columbus Shumway entered the newly founded Amherst College, just five miles from his house. He attended for three years, then transferred to Union College, from which he graduated in 1830. That same year, Union was rated one of the Big Four, along with Harvard, Yale, and Princeton.[1] Immediately thereafter, he was counted in the 1830 census as living alone in Vermont, perhaps visiting one of the many Shumway families in that state, or perhaps interning at a parish. Then, for the next three years, Columbus attended the Presbyterian school, Auburn Theological Seminary, in central New York state, completing two degrees, one of them master of divinity.[2] Noted for theology that was "a little swerved" from the straight line of Calvinist doctrine, Auburn was by 1832 dispatching its graduates to be missionaries in Hawaii and Asia, and accepting students from China, Korea, and Japan.[3]

By the time Columbus Shumway came to the college, religion had mellowed out and moved away from its former zealotry in Massachusetts. The aspiring pastor expected to be an influential leader in any parish into which he settled, but not its sole source of law, justice, and social order as in the 1600s.

In sixteenth- and seventeenth-century Europe, and the American colonies, it was believed that a society's stability was guaranteed by having a single religion, and "religion was regarded by all governments as a part of the machinery of state."[4] A letter of that era describing the manner in which "malicious heretics were put to death" reads like a cookbook by Hieronymous Bosch. They were "scorched . . . hung . . . dismembered . . . boiled . . . broiled . . . stewed . . . grilled and barbequed. . . ."[5] Mercy was a name for daughters, not a quality practiced with dissidents.

Roger Williams, having seen the havoc that official religion created in society—his older brother, Sydrach, had been imprisoned during the Spanish Inquisition—was determined to create a settlement that welcomed all creeds and beliefs and treated everyone with respect, allowing them to speak freely without fear of reprisal.

He was the first American proponent of extending liberty to religious practice and the first colonial leader to advocate and practice the separation of church and state. It was his model of governance that set the colonial standard for liberty and justice that, when written into the Declaration of Independence and the Constitution, became the basis of America.

Once his exceptional, eclectic, and somewhat liberal education was completed, Columbus embarked on a career as a Congregational minister, never thinking to question the civil government that, comprised of councils and committees, really ran each town. Of his appearance, nothing is known except that most photographs of the next generation of Shumway men preserve images of their having very full heads of hair, and square faces. Now in his late twenties, and whatever his looks, Columbus had the prospects to support a wife and family. Whether his posting took him to a small mountain village or a booming town, his wife would be an important part of his ministry: interacting with parishioners, helping the sick and needy, taking messages for him, assisting with any number of small tasks. As an educated man he valued an educated woman able to hold up her end of conversation; at a minimum, he required a sufficiently pious spouse to create the appropriate household environment and lead her children, by word and example, to God.

Daughters of other ministers were perfect candidates. They understood the role, were devout and educated, and shared a common set of values. Because ministers were frequently in each other's company at meetings and events, there was always a way to arrange to meet suitable young ladies—as opposed to the high-spending, flighty, fashionable damsels who flirted in the churchyard each Sunday after services.

It was also no accident the daughters of ministers frequently preferred to wed ministers, to stay in the "family business." On her part, a woman desired a husband not given over to drink, one who treated her decently, a man who had been educated about self-control and the value of good deeds, and someone with some dependable means of earning a living, a profession that was not about to go under or out of fashion in a rapidly changing world.

In the end, Columbus chose Catherine Francis Fowler for his bride, a woman whose early families had founded the Connecticut colony and contributed amazing longevity to the gene pool. Many of her family lived into their eighties and nineties in the two hundred years since they had been in America. Her father, John Hart Fowler, trained as a lawyer at Yale, switched careers, was ordained, and became pastor of the Congregational Church in Exeter Society, a small parish of Lebanon, Connecticut. They lived there for eight years, until he was dismissed in 1821.[6] The minister who succeeded him there, Daniel Waldo, later resigned because the parish was unable to support him, a possible clue to why the Fowlers left.[7] From there the family moved on to Montgomery parish in Hampden County, Massachusetts, where Catherine grew up—a very small, mountainous town of three hundred souls.

Catherine was certainly educated—evidences of her signature in later years reveal a fine handwriting—but little specific is known about her. She seemed to have been a competent businesswoman in her own right, efficient, practical, and organized. Nothing exists in the family history to explain why she married so late—at age twenty-seven.

On September 2, 1833, Catherine and Columbus were married in what was then her home parish in Westbrook, Connecticut, by long-tenured pastor Sylvester Selden. At the time, Columbus was preaching in Sidney Plains, New York, a small town some fifty-six miles from Cherry Valley, in that part of the country pacified by General Sullivan's expedition against the Iroquois Confederacy.[8]

After their marriage, Columbus was ordained by the Black River Association in Smithville, New York, on February 4, 1834.[9] He then accepted a call to a church in Litchfield County, on the western side of the state of Connecticut. From 1834–5 he was pastor of the beautiful stone church in the village of Washington, the first town established in Connecticut after the Revolutionary War, named for the general who had stopped there twice. Situated in a very scenic part of the western Connecticut highlands, it had panoramic views, its hillsides banked with blooming laurels in June, and a vein of quartz near the river yielding semiprecious and other pretty colored stones.[10] In this pleasant place, Catherine gave birth to her first child on February 26, 1835.* In an unusual gesture, the parents reached back more generations than normal to name their daughter for her paternal great-grandmother, Sarah Hart, wealthy, well educated, and the most prominent woman in their family.**

According to customs still practiced in 1835, mother and baby lived a quiet and sequestered life the first few weeks, resting and being cherished. Most likely Catherine's mother, Phebe Lay Fowler, from the family that settled Saybrook, was there to assist her daughter with the birth and the transition, as was the custom. The new infant was not taken out of the house, nor were visitors initially welcome, probably sensible precautions given the prevalence of communicable childhood diseases in that era.

Once Catherine and Sarah were doing well and the household routine established to ensure their well-being, the family held a reception at which friends and additional family greeted the new arrival and toasted the happy but sleep-deprived parents. Sarah would have continued to enjoy a somewhat sheltered existence

* The month and date have never been in doubt, but the year of Sarah's birth has been stated in various documents to be anywhere from 1832 to 1838. The 1835 date, used on her marriage certificate, one of the few documents she and her mother cosigned, is also a good fit with her parents' marriage and her brother's birth two years later. It also coincides with some records that state her birthplace as New Preston, parts of which were absorbed by the new town of Washington.

** Daughter and heiress of Rev. John Hart, first graduate of Yale, the twice-widowed Sarah Hart Hill Adams enjoyed a long third marriage to the Rev. Amos Fowler.

within a quiet household. "In teaching a child to talk, low, mild tones should be used."[11]

There may have been an occasion when the reverend did not use gentle words, for after only one year, with no explanation in the records, the Shumways left this parish. According to writer Carolyn Lawes,

> Only God could save a soul, but a minister played a pivotal role. It was his responsibility to promote an awareness of sin in the unconverted, to guide the penitent through conversion, and to keep the converted on the path of righteousness through example and constant exhortation. A minister who did not inspire his congregation was the wrong minister for it, regardless of his doctrinal fitness.[12]

They went next to Townsend, Massachusetts, originally named for Viscount Charles Townsend. Its population of 1,500 supported four fine churches whose architecture reflected "credit upon the taste and good judgment of the men who designed the same and furnished the money."[13] Farming and coopering were the main occupations. Other members of the Shumway clan and their in-laws also lived here; and life in this town, set on a plain nestled among hills, seemed the best New England had to offer. Underneath, however, it simmered with religious turmoil.[14]

Revivalism was at the heart of the conflict: Townsend churches had a revolving-door policy—they had employed and dismissed five or six ministers in one six-year period, including a man who had served for thirty years. In the late 1820s the Orthodox Congregational Church of Christ split from the First Congregational meetinghouse and built their own fine brick meetinghouse, dedicated in 1830. Reverend Shumway became their second pastor on January 6, 1836. Between January 21 and October 27, "C. Shumway Minister of the Gospel in Townsend" married five local couples.[15] Although 1837 started out well enough for the couple, Catherine expecting her second baby, the spring brought startling news: The congregation was dismissing their pastor. The town history noted,

> In every particular, he was a respectable preacher. Mr. Shumway must have been placed in a delicate position, and experienced all the difficulties of being the successor of a first class man. Undoubtedly too much was expected from him. The notice of his dismission, tendered to him March 28, 1837, was a surprise to him, from the fact that up to that moment, everything on the surface indicated both unanimity and satisfaction.[16]

Traditional employment practices for ministers had lately changed in New England, following the powerful religious revival movement known as the Second Great Awakening. The Congregational churches enjoyed a great surge in membership and revenue, but their congregations were often divided between conservative and liberal groups. Christopher Shumway was just another victim of a typical tug of war between factions over control of the pulpit, and even the use of the church buildings themselves.[17]

In those days, "ministers were increasingly judged by the numbers of converts won and sustained," and if deemed "insufficiently orthodox," were soon exchanged for one who was more so.[18] Columbus was again out of a job, with a budding family to support.

However dismayed they were as the buggy took them out of town, the Shumways landed on their feet. References to the birth of their son, John Fowler Shumway, born in August 1837, read "Worcester," which could either mean the county or that the family sojourned in the actual Massachusetts town. On October 4, 1837, Reverend Shumway took over the pulpit at the Orthodox

A period etching of a fashionably dressed daughter from an upper-class family, circa 1840. *From author's collection.*

Congregational Church in Petersham, in Worcester County, and managed to stay four years, through the 1840 census taken that summer.[19] The parish recorded that a new minister started in April 1841, indicating the Shumways had left, again most probably back to the town of Worcester, the county seat. Petersham was Columbus's last parish, despite family legends to the contrary. Odd as it might seem given his distinctive name, there is a five-year gap in documentation of Columbus Shumway's career. There are, however, some clues.

In 1845, the family was irrefutably in Worcester, a town of 11,500 people, living comfortably. Situated at the crossroads of several stage and railroad lines connecting the town to Boston, Worcester was a

> smallish but growing urban center. . . . Large and diverse enough to accept change, but small and cohesive enough to remember community.[20]

The lack of water power in town meant no mill industry; instead, the city developed artisan shops and small manufactories as the base of its economy.[21] It was the terminus of both the railroad and the Blackstone Canal, by which crops, goods, and passengers moved from this landlocked part of Massachusetts through Woonsocket and the Cumberland, and on to the port of Providence.

In those intervening four years, 1841–5, a man of Reverend Shumway's superb education would have had many options available to earn a living. He might have tutored young men preparing for college, as Reverend Taft had done for Sullivan Ballou, or an academy might have employed him as an instructor, or he might have ridden the circuit. So many parishes were in need of someone to preach their Sunday services that a kind of domestic missionary program developed, which sent members of the large pool of well-qualified and trained ministers around as visiting preachers. While lacking the same social prestige, perquisites, and wages of their settled colleagues—no choice house on the village common with the cords of wood delivered to their yard each winter—they had the advantage of being paid in cash. If they were able to retain enough client parishes, they might prosper. Reverend Shumway owned a horse and buggy, and multiple suitcases, all of which suggest he was traveling regularly. He even had one of the then-popular buffalo robes to use as a lap rug in cold weather. His clothing was also that of a traveler, and included two dress coats and an overcoat, two pairs of boots, a woolen vest, and three hats and a fur cap, the latter quite useful in a buggy on a frosty day.

By 1845, the Shumways were known in Massachusetts as a widespread, hardy, and industrious clan of families who had settled by the 1570s. The timing of the arrival of Pierre or Peter Shumway, as he became known, followed a wave of persecution that occurred in France, as religious change swept the European continent.*

* "Shumway" is an anglicized version of the original, unknown name. Refugees often cloaked their identities to protect family members who remained behind.

Most of the Shumways lived in rural or semirural areas. Columbus broke with tradition by being the first to settle in a major city. Catherine and their two children remained in Worcester while he made his rounds. The Shumways rented a large house of two to three stories, with a parlor, kitchen, pantry, wash house, library or study, and five bedrooms—far too many for a family of four. Sarah was growing up in a sophisticated, comfortable house.

Many signs of middle-class life are revealed in the inventory taken in 1846. Those bedrooms were all furnished with bedsteads, linens, washstands, dressing or toilette tables, pitchers, and looking glasses. A trunk provided extra storage in each room. Twenty-eight chairs were tallied, including a child's chair and a rocking chair, plus abundant crockery and glassware. The stairs were carpeted.

There were three stoves—one for cooking, the others for warming—all using anthracite coal. The new stoves had dampers that allowed regulation of cooking temperatures; they even achieved various temperatures at one time. Meal preparation and menus alike became more complex now that Catherine was no longer cooking over a hearth with a single fire.

Many rooms in the home were lit by oil lamps. The library or study had a regular and a secretary desk. Both held books, as did a cupboard, for the Reverend Shumway owned a considerable personal library of at least one hundred books. Only a few are identified by name: *Josephus*, Stuart's *Commentary*, four dictionaries, an encyclopedia, Hopkins's *Divinity*, *Family Physician*, books of sermons, four volumes of church history, and, of course, Bibles.

In cities like Worcester, many homes had an alley in back of the house, used by tradesmen for deliveries. Even in the city, the Shumways' house lot would have been sufficient for a vegetable and herb garden, chickens, and their own cow. They may have even kept a pig, fed off scraps. The privy was at the farthest rear corner of the yard and, if there was a commode in the house, it was built to resemble a three-drawer chest.[22]

However, most homes at this level of modern outfitting now had a water pump in the kitchen, but rainwater was often stored in a cistern, to use for bathing. On Saturday nights, a portable bathtub was still set up as needed in front of the kitchen fireplace. Drinking water may have been purchased from vendors, who brought it from springs.

There were ways to put a home to work to earn money, and the Shumways may have done this. Most educational academies or schools had insufficient dormitory space to house all their students, and most lodged some students as boarding at the homes of ministers or former military officers in town. The biography of another Congregational minister of the time relates, "In order to earn extra money, Rev. Huntington opened his house as a boarding school."[23] Reverend Shumway is not listed in the city directory as operating a school at his home, but there is a high probability that Mrs. Shumway was using the extra bedrooms as a boardinghouse, to supplement the family income.

In 1845, just as the Ballou family began experiencing a respite from want, fortunes turned the other way for the Shumways. Columbus had been in vigorous health, vigorous enough to again impregnate Catherine that fall, a fact of which they had just become aware. The great Massachusetts holiday of Thanksgiving was almost upon them, and Catherine had already started the earliest of her food preparations—things that could be done in advance, like soaking raisins and currants, and preparing mincemeat.

Rather suddenly, Columbus complained of a bellyache, an ailment from which he ought to have recovered in a day or two. However, in his case, it progressed to acute pain and a high fever. A doctor was summoned and proved competent enough to recognize appendicitis. This was a devastating diagnosis because at that time surgery was not yet performed within the body cavity. There was no treatment and no cure.

If the doctor was correct, Catherine was to become a widow within hours, as soon as the infected organ burst and spewed its poisonous humors into the stomach and bloodstream. Columbus suffered miserably, his agonies assuaged with nothing stronger than laudanum.[24] Sarah and John were brought in to see their papa before he breathed his last, and then hustled out again to be cared for by relatives and friends while their mother kept the bedside vigil. He died so quickly on November 21, 1845, that there was no time to make a will.[25]

Sarah was going on eight when her father died, the same age as Hannah Frances Ballou had been. Her brother John was about Sullivan's age when he had lost his father. These children experienced the same bewilderment, fear, and sadness that the Ballou children had known thirteen years earlier in Cumberland. Catherine may have been even more shocked than Emeline, because she had had almost no time to prepare psychologically for her husband's death. Now, she, too, was forced into the black clothes and role of a widow. But while this family also shared the same grief as had the Ballous, they were better off financially at this tragic time. Catherine was going to have to work harder than ever before, but she did not need to rely on the charity of others to feed and clothe her little ones. The wolf never howled at her door as it had at the Ballous', or, literally, at her great-grandfather David's rock shelter in Sturbridge.

Within a month or two of Columbus's death, a prompt and efficient probate process had been concluded. The aforementioned inventory required of his possessions provided a glimpse into the family's lifestyle in Worcester. By early 1846, the probate court had awarded all the personal property—there was no real estate—to Catherine, "to retain as necessary for the use of herself and the family under her care," having taken due notice that the "deceased left two children dependent upon your petitioner for support." The probate records only alluded to the fact that all debts were settled; there is no way to know what amount of cash was left in the bank account, but it was a good sign the family was living on a cash basis, without high debt.[26] Catherine was fortunate:

> Until the passage of the married women's property act in 1855, a Massachusetts woman's property was liable to seizure by creditors to pay her husband's debts.[27]

Pregnant with her third child, Catherine continued her business as boardinghouse keeper, which was a good profession for women for its time and place. Worcester's population would double between 1840 and 1850, and the turnover rate of residency was twice what it had been in 1800. As many as 100,000 people would move in and out of Worcester in the 1850s.[28] Using college board rates as a benchmark, the widow Shumway would have been receiving less than $75 [now about $2,100] per year per boarder. Unless she doubled them up in a room, her revenue flow from four bedrooms would have been around $300 [$8,400] per year. By the time she paid the rent and other expenses, her income would have been so small that she would have been drawing on the proceeds of the sale of the horse, buggy, some of her husband's books, and perhaps a bank account. No wonder "widowhood was virtually synonymous with impoverishment."[29] "The suddenness and propinquity of death and economic failure . . . are unimaginable in America today."[30]

George Columbus was born June 8, 1846, and, at eight years of age, Sarah was considered more than old enough to help care for him, like many a girl of her times with younger siblings. Having someone new to love may have helped her move on from grief, as much as she and Catherine surely regretted that Columbus never saw his second son. Sarah's assistance would have enabled Catherine to concentrate her attention on running her boardinghouse.

These early New England boardinghouses had interesting social dynamics and often operated like an extended family. Catherine was nobody's servant, for all that she provided services. Male boarders helped out by chopping wood and bringing it to the fireplace. If John or Sarah were stumped with their homework, someone there might help. If a boarder became ill, others went for the doctor and helped tend them, and they, too, probably took care of little George. Everyone ate together, the menus planned and prepared under Catherine's direction. This was helpful, because the family could "eat off" the boarders, enjoying higher-quality meals and beverages. This dynamic was widespread; as the celebrated writer Lydia Child noted,

> French coffee is so celebrated, that it may be worth while to tell how it is made; though no prudent housekeeper will make it, unless she has boarders, who are willing to pay for expensive cooking.

Likely a servant or two was employed, and a woman came in to help with the washing each Monday. Probably these were day servants, because if they had lived on the premises, it meant less rooms to rent. By 1845, victims of the Irish potato famine were flooding into New England, and Irish women were hiring out as servants and washerwomen for very low wages.

Managing a boardinghouse was considerably more complex than running a household for a small family. Sarah's education in domestic management, not just cooking and child care, was jump-started by her participation in this larger enterprise at an early age. Like Sullivan Ballou, Sarah seems to have developed self-reliance at an early age, just as she learned the tricks of managing on a reduced income. She was in all likelihood a very busy child, because she was handling two educations at once.

The conversations Sarah heard as the boarders dined would have been lively and stimulating, for Worcester had the economic means to sustain a rich cultural and intellectual life. It had built halls and lyceums, and its churches hosted speakers from across the nation. It was "a seething center of all the reforms":[31]

> Campaigns against drunkenness, capital punishment, and slavery, . . . women's rights, dress reform, a ten-hour work day

> in the mills, existed alongside . . . new religions and utopian communities.[32]

Only forty miles by fast train from Boston, Worcester "was a regular stop on the abolitionist lecture circuit" attracting "a who's who of abolitionism"—Frederick Douglass, Lucretia Mott, William Lloyd Garrison, Lucy Stone, and Senator Charles Sumner.[33]

Worcester encouraged the education of its girls, and its thirteen district schools and various private schools provided many opportunities for the area's entire spectrum of students. The city had Latin, French, Apprentices', and African schools; and equal numbers of infant, primary, and two separate high schools each for girls and boys.[34]

The separation of girls and boys was seen as protective and necessary. Wrote Mrs. Child,

> Amusements and employments which led to exercise in the open air have greatly the advantage of all others. In this respect, I would make no difference between the management of boys and girls. Gardening, sliding, skating, and snowballing, are all as good for girls as for boys. Are not health and cheerful spirits as necessary for one as the other? When I say that skating and sliding are proper amusements for girls, I do not, of course, mean that they should mix in a public crowd. Such sports, when girls unite in them, should be confined to the inmates of the house, and away from all possibility of contact with the rude and vicious.[35]

The same arithmetic texts and readers were used for both sexes, and Sarah's basic elementary school education paralleled Sullivan's, the books having changed little in basic content in a decade. Still, society was concerned about a girl getting too much education, as Mrs. Child fretted:

> If a girl feels interested in nothing but books, she will in all probability be useless, or nearly so, in all the relations dearest to a good woman's heart; if, on the other hand, she gives all her attention to household matters, she will become a mere drudge, and will lose many valuable sources of enjoyment and usefulness.[36]

Sarah's other education came from her mother and the boarding-house environment. Even within a household that did not take boarders, a woman of this period was required to be a well-organized multitasker. If she did not soak the beans the night before, she could not cook the household's baked beans the next day; if she did not keep her yeast going, by replicating it once a week, she could not make bread, or had the humiliation of begging some off a neighbor. Mothers were encouraged to train all children, but especially their daughters, in the skills of economy and alertness:

> All the faculties of a child's mind should be cultivated, and they should early acquire a power of varying their attention, so as to be able to bestow it easily upon any subject whatsoever.[37]

Mothers were also encouraged to be strict:

> No single instance of carelessness should be overlooked. If a little girl cannot find her gloves, or her bonnet, when you are about to take a walk, oblige her to stay at home. Let no tears and entreaties induce you to excuse it.[38]

Because "making a home respectable and homelike was a woman's job," as was "keeping the family neat, clean and presentable . . . a practical necessity imbued with social meaning," Sarah's mother would have taught her to sew, as well. Girls began sewing about the time they went to school, starting with simple stitches in samplers, progressing to doll clothes—important practice because "women of all economic and social classes were expected to manufacture garments and to mend the inevitable rents and tears." Sewing also taught girls persistence, hard work, discipline, attentiveness, and how to take pride in their accomplishments.

> Learning to sew was an integral part of the training for womanhood, and entailed painstaking hours of practice under the guidance of a mother, a relative or a teacher.[39]

For the first few years after Columbus's death, Catherine incurred minimal expenses for the clothing of her children. At that time, children's clothing was very cleverly engineered to accommodate their growth. It was loose fitting, so when newest it might be baggy, and fit tightly only when almost outgrown. Girls wore a short chemise slip, the top of which served as a blouse; over this was placed a loose-fitting jumper that came down to their knees. From knees to ankles a pair of pantalettes would have been visible. All of these garments were originally made with extra fabric in the seams and ample hems. The pantalettes normally had tucks for expansion. All of these garments could be easily altered by reseaming, rehemming, and plucking out the tucks, as the daughter grew. Sarah probably helped let out and lengthen her own clothing, even if she did not sew the original garments. Little boys' shirts and trousers were similarly constructed, and George wore skirts, as did all infants and toddlers of that era, until toilet trained, for it made it easier to change diapers. Sarah's younger brother never reached the age of toilet training, however. He died in 1847, only a little over a year old, of seizures, probably an effect of a very high fever from a contagious disease.

Catherine Shumway supported her family in this way for another four years, until Sarah became a teenager. Catherine probably made the time to belong to one or more sewing circles during her life in Worcester where, during the 1840s and '50s, they became an important force in the development of women's intellects, self-confidence, and fund-raising organizational and political management skills. "Barred by their sex from holding formal positions of leadership and power," women in Worchester asserted themselves through the church and through women's groups.[40] The sewing circles made garments for divinity students at Amherst, foreign missionaries, and fugitive slaves transiting the town on the Underground Railroad. They produced items to be sold at bazaars to raise money for "temperance, foreign missions and relief for the poor."[41] The first Worcester County Anti-Slavery Bazaar was held April 26 to 27, 1848. The *Worcester Spy* carried a notice appealing to "all the friends of Liberty" to contribute, and the event raised an impressive $900.[42] "The move from sewing to benefit one's family to sewing to benefit society was a change many women eagerly embraced," in their long hours of sewing.[43] The movement also "grew out of an explosion of interest among middle-class women in reading and writing."[44] Mrs. Child, who after writing advice books, had gone on to become one of New England's most prominent female abolitionistist authors and speakers, offered her opinion on women and reading:

> While I condemn the excessive love of books, I must insist that the power of finding enjoyment in reading is above all price, particularly to a woman. A full mind is a great safeguard to virtue and happiness in every situation of life.[45]

The advantages to be had from both domestic and household education surely made their mark on Sarah. By the time Catherine Shumway moved her family from Worcester to places unknown, around 1849–50, the sum total of Sarah's experiences during her developmentally critical years had laid the foundations for a remarkable woman.

CHAPTER FOUR

"Joy Was in His Mild Blue Eyes"*

Courtship and Marriage

1850–1855

Part of the mystery of where Catherine Shumway and her children lived for the next four years involved her two brothers, the elder of whom was dismissed from his Presbyterian parish in 1838 for "gross immorality with a female parishioner."[1] John Walcott Fowler had been educated for the ministry, schools unknown, and practiced in New York State. He served at Binghamton and later moved to Utica, which was where he got into trouble. No records may be found indicating he was ever married, even to the lady in question in Utica. This was a career-ending dismissal, so Reverend Fowler followed the example of his father—in reverse—and switched to law, perhaps reasoning that few would complain if a lawyer was found out to be a scoundrel.

Working in his favor in either career was his ability to hold an

* From the Civil War song "The Vacant Chair."

audience spellbound. This very good orator loaned his talents to the political circuits in the 1840s, and made many important friends and connections as he stumped on behalf of various candidates. He decided to open a college of law in the Saratoga region of New York State, and purchased the former Sans Souci Hotel in the genteel spa town of Ballston Spa, where the upper crust came to take the waters in the mineral springs.

The State and National Law School had a stellar board of directors that included a batch of New York judges and a who's who of the United States Senate: Sam Houston of Texas, Henry Clay of Kentucky, Thomas Hart Benton of Missouri, and three other senators. In August 1850, when the school held its examinations—in public, as was traditional—former president of the United States John Tyler was present, and an overflow crowd was turned away. The guest speaker from Philadelphia "held the audience in almost breathless silence for nearly two hours."[2]

After three years in Ballston, in December 1852, the State and National Law School moved to nearby Poughkeepsie, a larger town with four female and three male academies.

Fowler was the first lecturer at the Poughkeepsie Lyceum of Literature, Science and Art course in 1852 to 1853 and spoke for two hours, "but who on Friday evening noted time," says the *Press* report of the lecture. "The man revels in the richness of fancy. There is no effort, the thoughts flow upon him eager for the drapery of his eloquence."[3]

The school struggled at times, but it remained open through 1860, until the young men who would have been its students joined the army instead.[4] Though Fowler was "undoubtedly a man of much ability" some people remembered him as a very pompous personage who "wore a much-padded coat."[5]

Transgressions aside, he was a reliable relation to Catherine Shumway, whom a single shred of evidence places in Poughkeepsie around this period of time: an 1856 letter from the Reverend

Henry Ludlow, pastor of the First Presbyterian Church of that town, addressed to Mrs. Sullivan Ballou. Expressing his regrets that he was unable to visit her in Rhode Island, he wrote in a fond tone as befitted a home-town pastor who had known a lovely young lady, married her to a wonderful young man, and was enthusiastic about her happiness.[6]

It may be surmised that Catherine either brought her whole family to Poughkeepsie, or somehow Uncle John traded a favor and got Sarah enrolled in one of the schools. Experienced as she was at operating lodging facilities, Catherine may have seized an opportunity to operate one of the academy dormitories or a private boardinghouse. In the former position, she might have escaped being listed in the city directories of the era. If she worked at an academy, her daughter might have had the benefit of its education. No housing records for Fowler indicate that he ever shared lodgings in Poughkeepsie with his sister.

Catherine's other brother, Johnathan Amos, had the family talent for music, and started out in life as a music teacher. By 1840, he was employed as such at the Cherry Valley Female Academy. By 1854, possibly sooner, he was its coprincipal, signing its diplomas in the same left-handed script that his niece, Sarah, used.[7] With 132 mostly local pupils, though some were from as far away as Louisiana, Georgia, Ohio, and Wisconsin, the academy's offerings parallels those of Nichols and Phillips, using many of the same textbooks.

In the 1850s, the closest thing to national magazines were *Harper's Weekly* and *Ballou's Illustrated*, both large-format newspapers, which ran extensive feature stories and illustrations, and carried advertising on a national basis. Academies wishing to attract students and staff advertised in these papers, advising interested parties to send for their printed catalogs. Anyone reading the September 26, 1857 edition of *Harper's* would have seen an ad for the Cherry Valley Female Academy, featuring the name of J. A. Fowler.

There was both an academic (classical) and an English course. French, Spanish, Italian, and German lessons were available, and the young ladies could learn Latin and Greek. The music department offered piano, organ, harp, guitar, and vocal lessons, and an art curriculum was available. Rhetoric, composition, and letter writing were practiced in regular exercises, and the three days of examinations, at which the students made oral presentations, were open to the public as at all institutions.[8] Students took regular daily outdoor exercise, and, when weather was bad, could use the "clean, comfortable plank walks" in the village.

The Fowler siblings had a tradition of holding a family reunion in Cherry Valley each summer; the exact year they started doing this is unknown. One possibility why Catherine Shumway and her children were not listed anywhere in the 1850 Federal Census, normally the most reliable guide to locating a family, is that they were traveling to or from Cherry Valley while the census was being taken. All school personnel and students are well accounted for, in the school records for Cherry Valley; clearly, Sarah neither attended that institution nor did her mother work for it. Sarah was in her early teens now, the only time in her life she could receive education beyond the level of grammar school.

Even assuming money was no issue, the upbringing and education of a daughter was subject to the dichotomies of the era. The only career to which Sarah could aspire in the 1850s was wife and mother. Because of this, she understood that "a woman's class standing" varied over time, sometimes significantly,

> keyed as it was to the luck and skill of her father or husband; rarely was an antebellum woman able to determine her class position through her own efforts.[9]

A woman of the nineteenth century was placed in a unique, circular jeopardy: unable to vote, she had no influence over the laws that controlled her property, her children, or her workday. Without this, she had no protection once the man upon whom she had depended for it, had died or left her. Reverend Theodore Parker noted a woman "can hold no office—cannot be on a committee of a primary school, overseer of the poor or guardian to a public lamp post."[10] Society believed the reason "women should not participate in politics" is because "their genteel sensibilities would reel at the uncouth behavior of male voters and politicians."[11]

Yet, if a woman was forced into the labor force, her choices were no better than were Emeline Bowen's twenty years earlier. A select few could go "into literature," the rest into domestic service, mechanical labor in the factories, or "trade in a small way." For example, it was appropriate for a woman to preside at her own dressmaking or millinery shop, and as the decade edged onward, her own photo studio. Few retail shops "venture[d] to brave public opinion [to] employ a woman at the counter."[12]

Although by 1850 90 percent of the teachers in Worcester were women, the salary of those very women who had educated Sarah Shumway was only 20 percent that of their male colleagues.

Abby Foster, a woman who divided her time between her family's farm in the Cumberland and their house in Worcester, pleaded with mothers to "educate your daughters, not to make them better wives and mothers," but to give them a skill "instrumental in gaining a livelihood," wrote Mrs. Child, lest they become "that most pitiable of all human beings, a helpless dependent upon the bounties of others." Helplessness and dependency, two of the central tenets of the alleged "cult of true womanhood"—were neither attractive nor desirable in the face of economic need.[13]

Mrs. Child also suggested that parents educate their daughters with any skills they could afford to teach them, such as the piano, not so they could show off to beaux, but because it gave the girls some occupation to fall back upon if ever they should need one.[14]

> I would indulge girls in learning anything that did not interfere with their duties, provided I could afford it as well as not; such as all kinds of ornamental work, boxes, baskets, purses etc. Every new acquirement, however trifling, is an additional resource against poverty and depression of spirits.[15]

Interestingly, Sarah Shumway was a very proficient piano player, although the instrument was not listed in the household inventory at the time of her father's death. It may have been a later purchase, or was her mother's property, which was not part of Columbus's inventory. To be so good at it, Sarah had to have started lessons at a young age, perhaps while in Poughkeepsie.

One of Sullivan's biggest breaks had occurred when his uncle, George, the wealthy mill owner, decided to send his son, David, to Phillips Academy, a top rated school, in Andover, Massachusetts,* and to pay his nephew's room, board, and tuition to attend as well. David was two years older than Sullivan; handsome and congenial, George expected him to take over the growing Ballou business empire.

Sullivan enrolled in August 1847, as a second-year student in the Classical course, which included beginning Greek grammar, Latin translations, geography, and arithmetic. The student-teacher ratio was generous:

> Each teacher devotes his whole time to two classes, giving twice the usual amount of time to each recitation. This has been found of very great service to the student . . . it is believed that few institutions present equal advantages to young men wishing to prepare for college.

* Another, unrelated Phillips Academy was located in Exeter, New Hampshire. Just twelve years later, Robert Todd Lincoln failed his entrance exams to Harvard, and was sent off to Phillips Exeter to get up to speed.

Sullivan's uncle, George Ballou, moved his family into this Greek revival mansion in Woonsocket in the early 1850s. The opulence of the house shows the financial gulf between the rich and poor Ballou families. *Courtesy of the Woonsocket Harris Public Library Historical Collection.*

A classroom photo from that period showed a large paneled and plastered room with niches containing busts of the great philosophers. The students sat on long benches with slatted backs, arranged in rows as if they were church pews. It was a blend of "Puritanism and Hellenism."[16]

Joining Sullivan in his course work as well as his dorm room—room 3 in building four of Academy Hall—were Charles Parkhurst, also from a well-to-do Providence family, and one Marcus Ames from Vermont. David Ballou was enrolled in the less demanding and more practical English course. Designed for future teachers, surveyors, and scientists, it was designed to be the equivalent of an English education. The dormitory rooms allocated to boys in that course were humbler, but David was permitted to room with Sullivan, Parkhurst, and Ames, perhaps as a result of his wealth, or signaling that Sullivan was charged with providing a good example and peer supervision.[17] Described as "commodious," the rooms for the classical students were "furnished with a bedstead, under-bed and table. A bed and bedding are usually brought from home."

Andover was also home to Abbot Female Academy, the type of school to which the young ladies were sent to gain above average educational skills to better prepare them to be wives of lawyers, politicians, and wealthy men, the same wish Mrs. Shumway had for her own daughter. The wives of such men were expected to be gracious hostesses, manage large households in their husbands' absence, and participate in intelligent conversation. Whether or not there were cotillions, or the young men took the young ladies skating on Haggett's Pond when it froze, these young ladies were also part of Sullivan's education. A young man striving to cultivate his talents and become exceptional, he knew perhaps for the first time that exceptional young ladies existed as potential soul mates.

Without Uncle George paying the $65 [now $1,200] costs, Sullivan might have been admitted as a "charity scholar," living in one of "the austere dormitories on Phillips Street" and supplementing his funds by "by digging rocks for Mr. Farely on the school farm at eight cents an hour."[18] As one graduate noted,

> Phillips Academy has ever been the poor boy's friend. . . . it encouraged climbing, it did not boost. It helped indirectly by stimulating the poor fellow to help himself. It stretched the sinews of exertion without cutting them. It cherished self-reliance and self-respect.[19]

The young men had all gone home for the July holidays, and were registered to go back to Phillips in the fall, when apparently they decided on a sudden change of course. In 1848, between September 2 and 7, Sullivan and Charles presented themselves at Brown University about seven o'clock in the morning to take the entrance examinations. To pass, they had to translate English into Latin and Greek, construe and parse any assigned portion of Caesar's *Commentaries*, Virgil, or Cicero's select orations, and prove a knowledge of quadratic equations in algebra. The professors worked fast to grade and provide the results. Both lads passed, and neither returned to Phillips. Both were admitted as freshmen at Brown University for the fall term beginning September 8, 1848—immediately. David Ballou were also admitted, again to the English course, presumably after a different entrance exam, and shared room 13 with Parkhurst at Hope College. Among the students were the Brownell brothers from Providence—William and Charles, sons of the physician, Richmond Brownell—with whom Sullivan was to become very close. Clovis Bowen was listed in college records as Sullivan's legal guardian.

Sullivan was a college man at long last, at the age of twenty. His unfailing persistence, and the piecemeal assistance of relatives now had him hiking up steep College Hill each morning, literally climbing the summit of his ambitions. Horatio Rogers supplied some details:

> Sullivan strove to make his obligations to the hand of kindness as light as possible. In his vacations he taught school, and, being an excellent flute player, he gave lessons on that instrument. As he could but ill afford college expenses, he boarded at home, every morning walking from his mother's house in Pawtucket to the University, a distance of four miles.[20]

The college catalog noted Sullivan living at Mr. Reynold's, but this was evidently temporary, unless it was a diversionary tactic using the name of his mother's landlord. College expenses were $63 per annum, [$1,633], and board another $68.25 [$1,774]. The first he had to pay, the second he did not. To save $1.29 in expenses each week, about a quarter a day, Sullivan walked eight miles per day to and from Brown, carrying his books. It took sixty to ninety minutes to get home, and then he would set out his books on the table and begin to write his compositions, surrounded by his family. Brown had an excellent library of 21,000 volumes in Manning Hall, and their records show that on October 19, Sullivan checked out the two-volume set of Keightley's *England*, and on October 24, Bancroft's *History of the U.S.*; both were returned with no fines assessed.[21]

The freshmen spent their first year perfecting their Greek, Latin, and geometry. Additional lectures on literature, animal physiology, American history, rhetoric, and the Christian religion were delivered, along with scientific topics.

The college gave prizes for Greek translations among other topics, and that first year Charles Parkhurst won $15; Sullivan none. That year, the college seniors were competing for prize money with dissertations on such topics as "Is there a right of revolution?" and "Can the institution of domestic slavery be defended on the principles of Political Economy?"

In his sophomore year, Sullivan learned French, and did more Greek and Latin, studying Herodotus, Thucydides, Horace, Euripides, and Sophocles, and in May again checking out Bancroft and a page-turner named *Dwight's History of the Hartford Convention*. For him, the best of all possible topics was rhetoric, and Rogers noted,

> At this time, like most boys, who have a decided bent in one direction, he did not excel in general scholarship. In declamation, however, of which he was very fond, he was distinguished among his fellows, and in it he was facile princeps.[22]

College-level rhetoric was the pinnacle of accomplishment, rising up to lofty heights from those little speeches the children of Cumberland had started giving in their one-room schoolhouses. By the time they got to the academies and colleges, students gave fully developed speeches up to three times a week.[23] Oratorical styles were dissected, and the students learned effective ways to compose the components of a speech.

In that time, the art of oration, in which a speaker used specific techniques to educate, inform, amuse, and move his audience to action, was cherished in America, and good speakers were revered. A single speech might be two to three hours long, but as Quaker Hannah Inman revealed in her Worcester diary, average people thought nothing of going to several in a day. Walt Whitman recalled he "haunted the courts to witness notable trials" and heard "Webster, Clay, Edward Everett, Phillips, and such célebrés," but preferred "the life-eloquence of men like John P. Hale, Cassius Clay," and an old preacher named Father Taylor who had "personal electricity" as he preached in a "little old sea church in Boston, those summer Sundays just before the Secession War broke out."[24] *American Eloquence* remarked,

> The people love to hear them, and love to read their printed speeches whenever they can get access to them. Hence, our public journals, which contain the speeches of our ablest orators, are sought with much eagerness and read with avidity.[25]

This article from *American Eloquence*, in 1854, went on to affirm,

> What a beneficent, blessed influence is that of a fearless, manly . . . eloquence, when employed on the side of truth and righteousness.[26]

Through oration, success was

> fully open to all our citizens alike, who have the requisite talents and enterprise to enter the lists of competition for possessing them . . . The man of humblest origin, and obscurest

condition, and narrowest circumstances, has the full privilege of putting in his claim, side by side with his competitors.[27]

All the colleges and academies stressed that their educators had perfected ways to groom

> young men who are on their way to those stations of power and trust, which will . . . give to them the opportunity of wielding . . . influence . . . in the widest and most effective manner . . . for . . . the high responsibility which . . . will soon be resting upon them.[28]

Rogers told how Sullivan Ballou availed himself of every opportunity to hear good oration:

> The court house, the legislative hall, and the lyceum, were to him places of frequent resort. No opportunity was allowed to pass unimproved, that he could in any manner conduce to the cultivation of his favorite study. His lectures and orations written while he was in college and a little later, testify that his style at that time was easy but forcible; and, as his delivery was graceful and earnest, his numerous audiences listened to him with pleasure.

Emeline's family attended Clovis's wedding to his second wife on August 1, 1849. Uncle Clovis had waited seven years to marry again. His bride, Nancy Steere, a descendent of the Wickendens, who founded the colony with Roger Williams, was nineteen years old, less than half Clovis's age. Just five years older than Sullivan, his aunt Nancy seems to have formed a good relationship with him and furthered his cause with his guardian, interceding on certain occasions.[29] Also that year, Sullivan's uncle Dexter, a man with huge business interests in banking and textile mills in Woonsocket, died, sending ripples through the network of Ballou finances.[30]

As the 1849 to 1850 school year neared its close, Sullivan was forced to concede that he could not return that fall; he would be compelled to leave Brown without graduating. Rogers revealed, "at the close of his second collegiate year, an uncle, who had rendered him pecuniary assistance," met "with business reverses" and withdrew his assistance. Although it is unclear which uncle this was, Sullivan, who was now so close to attaining his goal of becoming a lawyer, had to take matters into his own hands.

Sullivan learned that a teacher of elocution and rhetoric was needed at a reputable institution then located in Ballston Spa. Of interest to him was that the school offered its students both "a thorough systematic knowledge of law" and "every other intellectual acquirement essential to a public speaker," and promised a "full corps of able Professors . . . present in every exercise to explain, correct, enlarge, criticize and apply appropriate rules." Sullivan brokered an innovative deal in which he would be simultaneously a teacher of rhetoric and elocution, and a student of law, the salary from the one covering the expense of the other.

The National Law School used very advanced teaching methods for its time. There, students were assembled into mock courtroom scenarios, playing all the roles of witnesses, bailiffs, jury, and attorneys. The professors were the judges, and the teams of attorneys were given a set of facts to work from in building their case.

Course work included pleadings, evidence, criminal law, domestic relations, codes of procedure, the American constitution, duties of executors, patents, partnerships, even treaty law. Here at last was solid, practical education. Above and beyond this foundation, the school brochure promised that after two years, students would have

> acquired as much ease, elegance, and perfection in the utterance and style of their sentences in off-hand speech as we are accustomed to expect in the most finished written address.[31]

Sullivan was soon to have ample reason to be grateful he had ease and perfection in his ordinary conversation because, as of 1852, both he and Sarah were in the same neighborhood, at the same time, destined to meet through the good offices of J. W. Fowler.

Availing himself of every honorable means to replenish his scanty purse, Sullivan copied for the professors, in addition to his other labors. Letters written by him at this time show how straitened were his circumstances, and how rigidly he was compelled to economize. The following extract refers to the failure of a plan to visit the famous Revolutionary War battlefield of Saratoga, which was only fourteen miles distant; a visit which he had long promised himself. Sullivan wrote:

> The fact was that on Saturday I received a letter from Thomas, and the bad state of the finances at home on all sides, was quite a disappointment to me. I immediately examined my weak and sickly purse, and its long, lank, wasted condition spoke too plainly of the emetics I have given it. Therefore, begrudging the little expenses of the excursion, I thought it the part of duty to stay at home."

In a letter believed to have been written to his aunt, Nancy Bowen, with his uncle's name later omitted when it was published, he said:

> Have been waiting a long time, and patiently too, for money from ———, but it does not come, and I can now wait no longer. . . . Tell ——— I am 'broke'—'dead broke'—'hawk-struck,' and must have that money. . . .
>
> You ask if I am coming home this vacation. It depends as you see, upon what I can do with ———, as he is my staff after this term. Should I be able to raise thirty dollars out of

him, as I hope, why I shall stay and trust to Providence for eighteen or twenty dollars which I shall need next December. When I feel as I do to-day, I want to get home as soon as possible, and do something to earn my bread and butter. I cannot look forward with any degree of patience to next spring even, beyond which time my ambition does not impel me to stay. I know of no means, however, of staying beyond next Christmas, unless the Goddess of Fortune should appear in the sudden emergency, and boost me along, as she always has done. But lest she, who is so fickle with others, may fail me at last, I shall expect to come home 'for good' next Christmas.

Am getting along as well as could be expected with my studies. Sometimes I miss an exercise; but it cannot be helped. It is utterly impossible to accomplish all I have to do, and if I carry it half through, I shall do more than the rest. The first six weeks I stood it nobly. That good constitution, which necessity forced upon me amidst the dust, mud and rain of the Pawtucket Turnpike, has been worth a fortune to me within the present term. It is by no means overtaxed, but in this hot weather one feels a want of energy, a lassitude in driving business.[32]

While Sullivan was regretting his lack of resources, Sarah—and her mother—were deciding how she should best present herself to beaux. Once a girl's education itself had been obtained, the difficulty was what to do with it while the young woman was courting. In order to be married at twenty, the typical age, a girl began mingling with the opposite sex around age fifteen or sixteen. This allowed a couple of years to get the drill down, another eighteen months to sort through the offerings and opportunities, and a final six months to settle on one gentleman and get engaged. During this period, a young lady was advised to camouflage the extent of her education lest she scare off a potential husband. Emily Thornwell, writing in a book entitled *The Ladies' Guide to Perfect Gentility in Manners, Dress, and Conversation, in the Family, in Company, at the Piano Forte, the Table, in the Street, and in Gentlemen's Society* advised,

> Whether your pretensions to learning are well founded or not, the simple fact that you aim to appear learned, that you deal much in allusion to the classics, or the various departments of science, with an evident intention to display your familiarity with them, will be more intolerable than absolute ignorance.[33]

A letter written to a newspaper about this time noted, "Spinsters were women of superior minds and most men dread sensible women."[34]

No aspect of life received as much attention and advice as the selection of an equitable mate. Much of the advice was meant to be practicable. For example, a daughter should "Never consider seriously the attentions of one beneath her social class"; and a father could only approve a future husband who would give her "comfortable and respectable support."[35]

Each sex was advised against the dangers of coquettes or coxcombs, as well as of being too dull. Reverend Parker, one of the best-known preachers in New England, as part of a sermon arguing for the admission of women to spheres of influence outside the home, provided an interesting alliterative analysis of those who might not have such interests, such as the

> Domestic Drudges, who are wholly taken up in the material duties of their housekeeping, husband-keeping, child-keeping. In New England, a class of women getting smaller every year.

Although some considered the home to be the proper place for women, Parker validated the choices of some women, like Worcesterite Dorothea Dix, a "Non Domestic type," who deployed all their energies in social reform.[36]

Any courtship was managed under the strict protocols of the time. Girls were protected in multiple ways. Their sexuality was an undercurrent, not flaunted through exposure of flesh. In fact, throughout this time, a woman of courting age was covered from head to toe most of the time.

Women of this time wore full-skirted gowns down to their toes. Except for formal wear, these had long, full sleeves that fastened at the wrist. Rows of flounces were often added to both sleeves and skirt for a frilly, feminine look. Layers of petticoats or a crinoline hoop (the lighter option) held the skirts out in a big circle. A very tiny waist was ultra fashionable, achieved by means of a boned corset that also lifted and rounded the breasts.

All girls of marriageable age, whatever their shape or figure, desired to look dainty and feminine, and many gave in to the temptation to lace very tightly, which, if overdone, produced "an extreme heaving of the bosom, resembling the panting of a dying bird."[37]

It was assumed "women were more pious than men," and they were supposed to be superior to base desires and physical satisfaction; nonetheless young women were left alone in the company of young men only under controlled circumstances.[38]

> It was within the bounds of propriety for a young man to take his sweetheart for a ride or accompany her on a walk. They might be seen together at church or at the races.

Normally, her family took her to a ball or cotillion, where she might dance with the young man of her choice, or take supper with him, but was not under his control.[39]

In school settings, the sexes could mix: they might go to each other's recitals or declamations, and linger to chat a bit afterward—

anything in public was considered safe enough. Young ladies might, on their recreation day, go to see the young men play town-ball, and giggle for their team.

Group outings like corn husking, maple sugaring, or ice skating were decorous ways to put a group of young people together under the eyes of chaperones so they might get acquainted. Under such circumstances, a girl was advised:

> You may with propriety accept such delicate attentions as polished and refined men are desirous of paying, but never solicit them, or appear to be expecting them.[40]

As the relationship progressed, they had to take care to

> not be tempted . . . to address . . . your gentlemen of your acquaintance, who are unconnected with you, by their Christian names. It opens the way to unpleasant familiarities on their part, more effectually than you can well imagine.[41]

All these rules reflected a society that was only several generations into letting young folks choose their own spouses, and parents concerned for the happiness of their offspring. Especially in New England, there was a growing acceptance of respect of the strengths each brought to their still different roles in marriage, a philosophy that "woman shall not be subordinated to man, but the two coordinated together."[42] Sullivan Ballou and Sarah Shumway, both strong, capable people, must have been looking for these qualities, among others, in their ideal spouse. Neither was looking to get married immediately. Sullivan by now knew the caliber of woman he wanted as his wife; likewise Sarah knew her mission by age seventeen was to start making the acquaintance of men of the proper caliber from whom she could select a husband. The environment of her uncle John's law school was a perfect hunting ground.

It is not known precisely how Sullivan and Sarah met. But happily, for some twelve to eighteen months, they were able to casually spend enough time together to realize that the other had the desired qualities each was seeking, to recognize that they had met their respective soul mate, and to fall deeply in love. By the time Sullivan completed his studies and left to return home, their relationship had become serious, and they agreed, with the permission of her mother, to correspond frequently while apart. It was necessary for them to wait until he was established as a lawyer before they could marry.

Sullivan passed the bar in 1853 and was admitted to practice in the state of Rhode Island. He set up his first law practice in Pascoag, a small village near Glocester, having a post office,* eight woolen mills with five hundred employees, six stores, six shingle mills, one bank, seven saw mills, and five grist mills. The conceivable only reason he might have chosen it was because of an arrangement made there for him by his guardian who lived nearby, or because of some Ballou mill connection. Neither the work nor the environment suited him, and he soon left for Woonsocket, where his close cousin Latimer W. Ballou lived, as did his uncle, Henry Ballou.

By 1853, Woonsocket had grown into a flourishing post office town sprawled on both sides of the Blackstone River. Sixteen miles by railroad from Providence, it was connected by telegraph to the latter as well as Pawtucket. Home to 6,500 people in its principal village and satellite mill towns, such as Hamlet and Bernon, it had seven churches, a high school, a newspaper office, and six banks. The town also had eighty stores, three hotels, and six livery stables with a total of sixty horses. Woonsocket now concentrated on the

* A post office was a mark of distinction in antebellum America; it showed a town had achieved a level of cohesion, stability, and growth. Any post office town was surrounded by a dozen villages to which it provided mail service. Home delivery had not yet commenced, and residents called at the post office in person to collect their mail or arranged for a go-between to bring it.

production of fabric rather than thread. The very mills that Sullivan had evaded as a child and young man, were at the center of $2.3 million [now $64.4 million] in commerce annually. That was the equivalent of $100,000 in production for every resident, an astonishing figure. Its nineteen cotton mills with 73,304 spindles and 1,641 looms produced more than a quarter million yards of cotton cloth per week, and 33,000 yards of woolen fabric. The goods shipped from its factories totaled 20,000 tons annually, and the factories annually required 6,185 bales of cotton and 600,000 bales of wool. Supporting this industrial base were eight machine shops, two iron foundries, and miscellaneous spool thread factories, including one for silk thread. Other industries included extensive quarry operations, including two marble yards, four stove manufacturers, and three scythe stone production plants.[43]

Here indeed was work for a lawyer, in the tangle of contracts and incorporations, business deals, and personal legal business. The work was challenging, and the location invigorating. It was even close enough to the Ballou Neighborhood that his extensive clan of relatives could employ him. Sullivan's circle of friends increased, and he was marked now as a man on his way up, no longer a talent neglected and oppressed by poverty. Here, Sullivan found a mentor: the man who wrote Hiram Ballou's will, attorney Christopher Robinson, asked his young colleague to assist him with various cases. Sullivan not only learned some tricks of the trade from him, but was introduced around and made connections.

When Edward Harris, the great industrialist and benefactor of Woonsocket, offered a matching grant, challenging other manufacturers to raise a total of $3,300 [$82,500] to build a library in town, Sullivan stepped forward to offer his assistance in procuring the 2,600 books. The catalog states,

> Sullivan Ballou, Esq. our Librarian, has been more active than any other from the beginning of our movement. If "time is

money," his subscription is a very large one. To him, with Mr. Barnard, [commissioner of public schools for Connecticut] belongs almost the entire credit of selecting the books; and the efficient arrangement of the whole for the accommodation of the members belongs to him alone.

Along with his cousins Latimer and Hosea, Sullivan served on the board of directors, and also as secretary; Edward Harris was chairman. Sullivan was specifically empowered by the General Assembly, when it chartered the library, to publish notice and convene the first meeting. General membership cost $5 per year and had the right of survivorship to a widow and minor children, but the board might grant free use to "poor but deserving persons." Sullivan kept all the membership records. He was moving in very important circles now, among rich and powerful men, and certainly on his way to establishing himself as a public-spirited citizen, a public man.

The volumes in the library were eclectic, including an atlas and encyclopedias, and books on every religion except Judaism. The library's catalog, also put together by Sullivan, was fifty-six pages long, single spaced. There were numerous books by female authors, and sixty-five books for juveniles. The two biographies of General Winfield Scott, the hero of the war with Mexico, were to be found on shelf ten, and the fiery, passionate speeches of Thomas Frances Meagher on the *Independence of Ireland* on shelf five.[44] Ironically, both men were later to play important roles in the military career of Major Sullivan Ballou.

After the years of striving to become a professional man, Sullivan wasted no time in establishing himself. During this time, he also served as town moderator for Valley Falls, attending their council meetings as an organizer and referee, and was hired as the clerk to the House of Representative of the General Assembly in 1854, along with Charles Brownell, his old college classmate. That position required him to attend the twice-yearly sessions of the state legislature and keep the business records of the House. He sat in chamber while the house was in session, taking notes, recording votes, and hand-carrying items to and from the Senate as the flow of legislation required; entered the election results into the state record; kept the legislative calendar; and handled the flow of documents to and from committees, making sure no items were forgotten. He was responsible for the accurate printing and distribution of all laws and appointments, and payment to the printer and other vendors.[45] Sullivan either wrote out the motions and resolutions longhand in the big ledger book, or, if they were written by a petitioner, he pasted them into the book, with annotations. Numerous pages in his handwriting in these extant public records document his handwriting.

The job was important, and required someone well organized and not easily flustered, a man who could handle pressure. It was the kind of work Sullivan proved himself expert at performing—the organization of complex, multifaceted public tasks. Its most important aspect was the fact that it brought him into contact with all the important people in the state, who were either in the government, or had business before it. It would lead to bigger things. The salary was not great, just as that of the Carrington librarian was not great, but everything that helped him establish his financial base brought him closer to marrying Sarah Shumway.

This is the period of time he later spoke of, when he and Sarah, living so many miles apart, shared their thoughts, feelings, and dreams by letter. They did not have the luxury of courtship in person; the costly, time-consuming journey between them, not conveniently joined by rail, limited the times he could visit her. If she ever saw the town or met his family before the wedding, it would have required him to travel to Poughkeepsie, bring her and her mother (as chaperone) to Rhode Island, and take them home again. Probably his family took her solely on faith. But having established himself in his occupation in a suitable location, he now

Influential on both sides of the Atlantic, *Godey's Lady's Book* printed fashions for hometown dress makers to adapt. This image dates from about the time Sarah Ballou was a bride. *From* Godey's Lady's Book, *author's collection.*

convinced Sarah's family of his ability to provide for her. In the absence of both fathers, from whom it was traditional to request permission to marry, the couple likely sought the approval of both mothers, and perhaps Uncle John W. Fowler. Then their engagement was short, only a few months.

Wednesday, October 15, 1855, arrived at last. Weddings by custom, and in some places law, took place before three o'clock. Married by Reverend Henry Ludlow, in a simple ceremony at the newly built First Presbyterian Church, Sullivan and Sarah exchanged vows in the presence of family and friends. The legal witnesses were Sarah's mother and uncle.

With Uncle John standing in loco parentis for his niece, it was probable the reception was held at the National Law School rather than at his lodgings. The wedding party walked there from the church.

At the very least, tea and punch were passed around as beverages. If it was not a temperance ceremony, then brandy, cordial, and toddies were served. Every reception had a wedding cake, usually a very rich fruit cake, made with currants, raisins and citrons, cinnamon and cloves, and covered with a thick white icing stiffened by a great many egg whites and decorated with glided almonds, artificial flowers, and real vines.

It is unclear how many of the Ballou clan were able to make the journey from Pawtucket, but certainly Sullivan's former colleagues on the faculty were on hand. If unable to afford "a nuptial journey," the Ballous then went home to Woonsocket to settle into their home. There, Sullivan introduced his bride to more family and friends at a second reception given in Rhode Island.

CHAPTER FIVE

"Our Lovings Prospered Well"*

Building a Family and Career

1855–1857

Sullivan and Sarah Ballou began creating a life designed to avoid the miseries of their childhoods. They built a marriage based on open communication, mutual respect, passion, the gregariousness of her family and the closeness of his, public service, and their common New England religion, background, and upbringing. The extremely sentimental Victorians of their acquaintance would have found special significance in two orphans from incomplete families now making one whole family of their own.

Sarah now moved full time into the circle of Sullivan's love and protection. After a courtship spent living far apart, requiring them to express their thoughts and feelings only in letters, the constant presence of each other was a great joy to a couple so much in love. Sullivan was to remind Sarah of those days of separation in one of his letters from the battlefield:

* From the Civil War song "Lorena."

> There have been many times since we were first acquainted where I have been separated from you, and longed to see & be with you with all the deepest fervor of my heart.[1]

Sullivan did more than move Sarah into his house; he also moved her into the close circle of his approving friends and family, near the area where he grew up, the Ballou Neighborhood. Half the size of Worcester, more intense than Poughkeepsie, the region and its people captured Sarah's heart. She chose to make it her home for the next four decades, even when she could have lived anywhere. It proved an auspicious move for Sarah, for "within very convenient distance all the pleasures of refined and intelligent society may be easily enjoyed."[2]

From Woonsocket, the newlyweds could go by horsecar to Providence, where there were greater social, cultural, and retail opportunities. The 42,000 residents of Providence supported libraries, theaters, and concert halls; the Athenaeum on Benefit Street, another Greek

Woonsocket Falls was surrounded by little mill villages like Bernon and Globe that eventually formed the city of Woonsocket. When the Ballous lived here, it was a high-energy regional market town. *Courtesy of the Rhode Island Historical Society, artist unknown.*

A view of Providence from one of its seven hills. *From author's collection.*

temple–style edifice, had been collecting books since 1753. (It even owned an original copy of the spectacular, multivolume set, "Descriptions of Egypt," published by the French scientists who had accompanied Napoleon's expedition. The librarian, John Russell Bartlett, a contemporary of Sullivan's at Brown, had a local craftsman build an Egyptian temple–style display table to hold the massive folios.[3]) The locals knew they lived in a city of culture, with a proud heritage already dating back two hundred years.

Settled comfortably in this agreeable locale, Sullivan and Sarah concentrated on each other and the hundred little compromises that made for a happy marriage. One such compromise must have been the allocation of storage space for clothing in their bedroom. Having lived in male dormitories or bachelor quarters for much of the last dozen years, Sullivan likely had no real idea how much clothing a woman actually wore until Sarah's trousseau arrived. An avalanche of feminine garments arrived in his house along with his bride.

Each morning, sufficiently well-to-do to have separate nighttime and daytime underclothes, Sarah first donned a full-length chemise, a garment designed to protect her outerwear from perspiration. Underclothing was washed each Monday in a daylong ordeal of soaking, boiling, soaping, rinsing, drying, starching, and ironing. The elaborately trimmed outergarments, usually decorated with trim and buttons that withstood washing poorly, were not.

A lady donned the rest of her underclothes in a specific order. Next came the corset, which she might well lace up herself if she strung the laces a certain way, then her knee-length drawers, or pantalettes, which could open at the back to facilitate bodily functions. Next she put on the hoop, which tied at the waist and enough petticoats to achieve the desired fullness. Only then was the dress pulled on over the head, tugged into place, a collar affixed and held closed with a brooch.

The Lady's Guide to Perfect Gentility admonished,

> It is not in good taste for a lady to appear at the table in the morning without being laced at all; it gives an air of untidiness to the whole appearance.[4]

A rich treasure trove of fashion images is available in the form of thousands of photographs from the era, several of which are of unidentified Ballou women. Photography was becoming both popular and affordable at this time, and many people had their photographs taken for cartes de visite, photographic calling cards. Distributed to family and friends, these small images on cardboard backings provide a thorough documentation of the fashions of the period. Regrettably, no photographs of Sarah in this time period appear to have survived, although she did sit for a photographic portrait prior to 1862, at Emerson Goddard's Photographic Studio at 21 Main Street in Woonsocket. At least one large copy of this portrait was sent to her family in New York.[5] Goddard had trained in Boston and operated the studio in Woonsocket for many years; he, too, was married to a Worcester girl.[6]

The Victorians adored adjournment, and female clothing and hats were covered with as much lace, braid, ruffles, fringe, artificial

Photography in this era focused on portraiture like these *cartes de visite*—visiting cards—of upper-middle-class Providence women, contemporaries of Sarah Ballou. The Ballous patronized Goddard's. *From author's collection.*

flowers, and ribbons, as the wearer's social status and budget allowed.

Fashion might make her look like a china doll, but Sarah was a strong and capable woman. It was just one of the many contradictions of the Victorian age that women worked arduously to accomplish all that was theirs to do for their families, but were put on a pedestal and thought of as fragile, a perception reinforced by all their ruffles and bows.

Because none of her letters have survived, Sarah is revealed only through the mirror of Sullivan's comments about her. He was an emotional, extroverted person who did not hesitate to tell his wife he loved her. There is no doubt that Sarah returned his affection, but she was never as open in demonstrating it before others, or writing or speaking about her feelings and personal issues. As their relationship developed, Sullivan was always urging her in his letters to express herself more and, when she obliged him, he was full of praise for her. He wrote, "I beg of you do not let me suffer and complain as I have in years gone by, about your letters,"[7] and,

> You know I need to be in some fault with your letters—because they were so short and told me too little of your everyday thoughts & feelings—But I find a happy change in your style now; and I know when the mail comes I shall find a missive full of tenderness and affection.[8]

Sarah did not seem to be afraid of her own sexuality or of expressing it, though she did not wish to display it for eyes other than Sullivan's. In private, their affection seemed unbounded and, in Sullivan's own words, their enjoyment of physical love was unrestrained, by Victorian standards. He wrote, "Few men can boast a wife's love as I can; and it is a pride I can feed upon in secret and never be sated,"[9] and,

> I have so long clasped you in my arms and told it to you with my own lips and seen your warm return of it in your own eyes and felt your responsive heart on my own bosom.[10]

Although eight years her senior, Sullivan did not treat Sarah as a child. This was not a marriage in which the wife need "give up her heart, feelings, fancies and opinions to her husband," as some advised. Nor did Sarah need to "watch well the first moments when your will conflicts with his to whom God and Society have given the control."[11] In addition, Sullivan never used simplistic language or diminishing names in his letters to her, such as "little pet," "your little head," or "my little woman," as some of his contemporaries did.[12] Instead, he included classical references in a way that indicated she was familiar with and understood them.[13]

Queen Victoria and Prince Albert were considered the ideal Victorian family, and were imitated on both sides of the Atlantic; her pose shows the wifely deference expected even from a queen. *Photo by Mayall, author's collection.*

They had lively intellects and shared a keen interest in the news and current affairs. The couple read the Providence papers, which could be bought for a penny or two, and if they wanted a New York paper, like the *Times* or Horace Greeley's *Tribune*, these could be obtained the next day from one of the booksellers in town. So long as Sullivan still served on the board of the private Carrington Library and kept up his role as librarian and book purchasing agent, they had access to newly arrived books.

In 1855, Sullivan was continuing to develop himself in the mold of a public-spirited American patriot. He felt the same calling to public-service that many of the Ballou men in previous generations had felt and answered. While the focus of Sullivan's career was his law practice, he made the time to be active in a variety of civic functions. Following his marriage, he continued his important job as clerk to the General Assembly, which met twice a year for several weeks at each session. He continued to serve with the Woonsocket Guards and on the library board. All of these were ancillary to his law career, in which his "uprightness, urbanity of manner, industry, and enthusiastic love for his profession, at once secured him a lucrative practice." His friend, Horatio Rogers, commented that "his reputation as a good lawyer was wholly merited," and that Sullivan "had the temperament of an orator, and . . . demonstrated there is room for eloquence in transacting the business of the world."[14]

In the evenings, Sullivan probably came home and told Sarah all about his cases, the issues he must advocate, and the personalities involved. In all these things, Sarah was likely both his sounding board and his champion.

In the 1850s, the key issues in America were slavery, improvements in transportation, economic development, and territorial expansion. All these issues fed into each other in a continuous circle, and people's viewpoints on these tended to be regional. The North saw them differently than did the South. Many politicians tried to tiptoe around the controversies, and the presidential candidates elected during that decade were compromise men whose main job was to hold the country together just a little bit longer.

But every year or so, some key event or crisis exacerbated the national debate, fraying trust, and national cohesion just a little more each time. The two-party system that had governed America for the last twenty years began to fall apart. Party affiliation was very fluid in the later 1850s as new parties evolved. The first to totter and collapse were the Whigs, although the name hung around, as in "Cotton Whigs," Northern manufacturers whose dependence on cotton made them pro-South. "The Democracy," as the Democratic Party was then called, had "doughfaces," meaning they were Northerners with Southern sympathies. Often short-lived and focused around a few issues, the new parties had interesting names, like the Free Soil Party (Slave-free Kansas), the Know-Nothings (Temperance and immigrant voting restrictions), and the Constitutional Union Party. The Republican Party began to gather to itself the entire spectrum of antislavery people, from the fiercest abolitionists to moderates.

Married into a family that cared passionately about politics, Sarah was exposed to enough discussions that she likely formed and articulated her own viewpoints to family and friends. Of course, women had no sanctioned public political presence or life at that time, and were unable to vote. Still, women could attend political gatherings and government meetings, so some days Sarah might have donned her most fashionable promenade gown and accompanied her husband when he had to conduct a case in court. There she could sit in the audience with others who enjoyed lively debates and dropped into the courtroom whenever one was occurring—just as Sullivan had done as a teenager.[15]

Sullivan was continuing on a course already established, but Sarah's was new. At this point in her life, her main jobs were to adjust to her married relationship, and to take over the management of their domestic life and excel at it. She was self-reliant and able to make many of the household decisions by herself, though she consulted him on various items. He supported and complemented her self-reliance.[16] It benefited them both, for she was still a very young woman, living away from her family in a new locale, and his work sometimes took him out of town for a fortnight at a time.

Sullivan and Sarah lived their entire adult lives in rented housing, moving frequently in response to the demands of work and schooling. They never expressed regret at not owning property; and the cost, comfort, and suitability of their dwelling place figured more importantly in their happiness than did ownership. They lived in small towns bordered by rural areas, in houses set on large enough lots that they remained in close touch with the rhythms of the rural life that their parents and grandparents had lived. They planted and harvested gardens and kept livestock, without being tethered to the brutal calendar of full-time farmwork and crops. Sarah Ballou moved at least a dozen times throughout her life. Home was a spirit she carried with her and created for her family in whatever dwelling she occupied, as women have done for centuries.

Despite her youth, Sarah Ballou shouldered huge responsibilities for the well-being and comfort of her husband and, later on, her babies. Many of these were unique to the state of housekeeping at the midpoint of the nineteenth century. By 1855, some prepared food could be purchased, but it could be unreliable in quality or expensive, so it was Sarah's job to produce and process much of the household's food in addition to cooking and serving it. She was the family baker, making all their bread, muffins, pies, and cakes. The young wife knew that hams kept best wrapped in paper and packed in boxes of ashes; that smoked herring could be kept in the cellar; and that if a family could stand having dried codfish hanging in the house, it must be moved from garret to cellar when the weather warmed up. Women of her class were also the family nurses, laundresses, and seamstresses.

Sarah had been well trained in the many aspects of household management by her mother, and surely set up their home from scratch. Ballou probably had not kept his own home. Most young, unmarried lawyers boarded with families.

In January 1856, Sarah began to suspect she was pregnant. In any event, the honeymoon phase could not go on forever, because Sullivan's presence was required at the legislative session in Providence, when the General Assembly reconvened in its second session of the legislative year. One issue that session was a proposal to restrict immigrant voting by requiring twenty-one years of residence. Sponsored by the Know-Nothing Party, it died in conference committee.

Temperance remained a strong issue as long as immigrants clung to the camaraderie of their working-class taverns, but antislavery was moving up in the charts. The Republicans usurped all the key issues, including "honest and vigorous enforcement of laws prohibiting the liquor traffic," in their 1856 platform. Anti-Catholicism soon gave way before the greater evil and unifying issue of slavery. The victory in the spring 1856 Rhode Island state elections of a multiparty, "fusion" slate, dominated by Know-Nothing candidates was their last hurrah.

All throughout 1856, newspaper headlines would keep people's attention riveted to the issue that would soon be the major political issue in America—slavery. At first, with so much of the news happening far away, the debate on slavery must have seemed like background chatter to the Ballou family but, as time passed, it would come to mean life or death to them.

At the midpoint of the nineteenth century in America, interest in politics took the place of all other forms of news-related entertainment. It was a passion. People did not follow major sporting events or celebrities, as there were few of either. Crime news was always welcome, but rarely sensational. Politicians were the celebrities, and great debates, whether witnessed locally in the courthouse, or followed in the newspapers, like the Lincoln-Douglas debates, were closely followed and discussed.

Reports from two Yankee merchants who had actually lived or traveled extensively in the South, as most readers had not, had a significant impact on Northern newspaper audiences. George Opdyke, who would later become the mayor of New York City, wrote in *Treatise on Political Economy*, 1851,

> . . . with the exception of property in slaves, the south is possessed of but a thin drapery of productive capital,—so thin that with the aid of an abundant and fertile soil and the cheap labor of slaves, the net profits are so meager that the proprietary class, although it shares the whole of these profits, is compelled to forgo many of the comforts of life and most of its luxuries. . . . It may be remarked that the people of that section have but few railroads and canals, and scarcely a turnpike-road or other highway that can be called passable. The steamboats which navigate their noble rivers, and the ships that visit their sea-ports, are mostly owned either in the free States or abroad.[17]

Frederick Law Olmsted traveled "from the banks of the Mississippi to the banks of the James," and found very few instances of people informed about or engaged in national issues, or widely read.

> I could find no reading-room; no recent newspapers except the Natchez Free Trader, which has nothing but cotton and river news and steamboat puffs; no magazines but aged Harpers; and no recent publications of any sort are for sale or to be seen at the booksellers.[18]

Recounting his journey to Natchez, Mississippi, in *The Cotton Kingdom*, New York 1853, Olmsted compared it to one of the same population in Illinois, and noted the Southern town had 10 percent of the library books, 25 percent of the church seats, and 33 percent of the children enrolled in school compared to its Northern counterpart.[19]

Published in such papers as the *New York Times*, these analyses were widely read and discussed throughout the Northeast. Coupled with the more salacious allegations of the abolitionists, about beatings, and of masters breeding with slave women to increase their property while the legal wife and mother of the plantation heirs pretended not to notice, such reports fueled public opinion against the merits of the Southern way of life.

The South found this viewpoint insufferably Yankee-centric, and countered with its own assertion of Southern manifest destiny. Senator James Hammond from South Carolina articulated it all in a single speech, in which he discounted "trashy census books, full of falsehoods," and boasted the South is

> as large as Great Britain, France, Austria, Prussia and Spain. Is that not a territory enough to make an empire that shall rule the world? . . . We own . . . the most of . . . the great valley of the Mississippi . . . as great as ever the Nile knew in earlier ages,

. . . slave labor will go over every foot of it. . . . the greatest strength of the South arises from the harmony of her political and social institutions . . . In all social systems there must be a class to do the menial duties, to perform the drudgery of life . . . a class requiring but a low order of intellect and but little skill. Its requisites are vigor, docility, fidelity. It constitutes the very mud-sill* of society and of political government. . . . Fortunately for the South, she found a race . . . inferior to her own, but eminently qualified in temper, in vigor, in docility, in capacity to stand the climate, to answer all her purposes. We use them for our purpose, and call them slaves. . . .

Your whole hireling class of manual laborers and "operatives," as you call them, are essentially slaves.[20]

At this point, neither the great national debate nor specific events in the South directly impacted the Ballous' daily lives. The factories of Woonsocket still hummed as Southern cotton imported on Northern ships and railroads was spun into thread and cloth. These factories were so busy they needed foreign labor to meet their production demands, and with new incorporations and land deals, there was plenty of work for an attorney with a good reputation. Whatever the national debate, America in 1855 was "buoyant with hope and expectation."[21] Sullivan and Sarah's future—his career and their prosperity—looked auspicious. Underlying this, however, was Senator Hammond's threat:

What would happen if no cotton was furnished for three years? . . . No, you dare not make war on cotton. . . . Cotton is king. . . . The South . . . is satisfied, harmonious, and prosperous, but demands to be let alone.[22]

* As in door sill.

Sullivan and Sarah had a wide range of friends and relatives with whom they could socialize, and it likely took the new bride some months to visit or be visited by all the Ballou cousins. Although Sarah was not an uncommon name, all the men with whom Sullivan was closest had wives named Sarah, and it took the newest Sarah a while to sort them all out. They were especially close to Uncle Henry and Aunt Sarah (Fales), who had been Sullivan's benefactor after his father died. Closer to his own age was Sullivan's dear friend, his cousin Latimer Whipple Ballou, whom Sullivan considered "the truest friend I ever had."[23] Latimer, who was likewise married to a Sarah (Hunnecutt), was the son of the distinguished attorney, Levi Ballou, whose fifty-year-long career in public service had seen him repeatedly appointed to every major local office in northern Rhode Island.

There were friends outside the family circle, too. Sullivan's law partner, Charles Parkhurst, was a close friend, and their acquaintance with the Brownell family was turning into friendship. The eminent lawyer, Christopher Robinson, who had taken Sullivan under his wing by having him help on major law cases, along with his wife, mercifully named Louisa, may have helped ease the new bride into the local social scene.[24] Through these friendships, the newly married Ballous moved among the social, business, and political movers and shakers of Providence County, attending dinners, dances, plays, weddings, and holiday events.

The newlyweds visited Sullivan's family in Pawtucket, a town of four thousand divided across the banks of the Blackstone River, its eastern half in the state of Massachusetts, its western in Rhode Island. The town still had five working mills, including the region's first, Slater Mill.* Served by the railroad and a stage coach, the town even had its own temperance publication *The Battle Axe*.[25]

* A prominent Rhode Island tourist attraction, the mill complex re-creates life in industrial New England. For more information visit Pawtucketri.com.

Emeline shared a home with her daughter, who had married Peter Bogle, a Gorham Silversmith, on the corner of Church and Garden streets, in a lively household that included William (nearly eight), little Sullivan (two), and baby Jeanette (not yet a year old).

As her girth increased with the new life within, Sarah altered her wardrobe by letting out the seams of her underwear and hiking her hoop petticoat up a notch to camouflage her delicate state. This often worked nicely for the first six months or so. After that, she wore looser, unfitted clothing, such as a sacque, a top that hung in an A line from the bosom to the hips, where it joined the broadness of the skirt. It prevented the rounded belly from being seen during an era when the highly embarrassing state of being pregnant needed to be camouflaged.

At the same time when Sarah's baby began kicking so vigorously in her womb that both parents would have felt his little blows, there were blows of a far different kind rocking the nation. Pro- and antislavery partisans were shooting at each other in the cornfields and burning each other's homesteads in "Bleeding Kansas." Each sought to drive the other side out of the territory before the vote on the referendum on whether Kansas should allow slavery. Lawrence, Kansas, and nearby towns along Pottawatomie Creek had been settled by farmers financed by Providence and Worcester mill barons. Lawrence was raided by proslavery militia determined to stamp out illegal government. A few days later, antislavery vigilantes led by John Brown went from homestead to homestead, murdering adult males in an action known as the Pottawatomie Massacre. Further mayhem was to follow, and the telegraph kept the nation up-to-date.

On May 22, 1856, the bloodshed from Kansas spread to the floor of the United States Senate Chamber itself, where the junior senator from Massachusetts, Charles Sumner, was assaulted by Congressman Preston Brooks, the nephew of Senator Andrew Butler whom Sumner had castigated in a speech three days earlier.

Sumner, a fierce antislavery advocate and master of invective, had given a long incendiary speech against slavery in Kansas in which he called Senator Butler "one of the maddest zealots" of "tyrannical sectionalism," a self-proclaimed "chivalrous knight" who "has chosen a mistress to whom he has made his vows, . . . the harlot, Slavery."[26]

With Butler out of the capital, his nephew decided to act in his behalf in accordance with the Southern code of punishment, which called for using a cane or horsewhip on "an insulting inferior."[27] Perhaps thinking that carrying a horsewhip into the Capitol building might be indiscreet, Brooks instead brought one of his walking sticks made out of an early, hardened rubber product known as gutta percha.

Confiding his plans to Southern colleagues in Congress, Brooks lurked around the Capitol building some three days before he was able to catch Sumner alone at his desk in the Senate Chamber concentrating on paperwork. After striking the first blow, Brooks apparently lost his self-control and repeatedly thrashed Sumner about the head with his metal-headed cane, administering some thirty blows in all. Sumner's face was split open down to the bone, and several cuts were two to three inches long.

Trying to get away from Brooks, Sumner overturned his desk and staggered around the chamber, dazed, and ineffectively trying to protect himself, his wounds bleeding profusely as only scalp wounds can. Brooks continued striking until his cane broke into pieces and he was pulled off by New York Congressmen Ambrose Murray and Edwin Morgan, who came rushing in after hearing the altercation. They caught Sumner just as he collapsed, and lowered him gently to the floor.

More honorable members ran into the chamber, Senator Crittenden of Kentucky telling Brooks not to kill Sumner, while Congressman Keitt of South Carolina yelled and brandished his own cane, ready to strike anyone who was breaking up the fight. Senator

Toombs of Georgia shouted at Keitt not to hit Crittenden, while Brooks struggled to break free and continue beating up Sumner until he was hauled off to the washroom by friends to wash the blood off.

Sumner remained "senseless as a corpse," for several minutes. Blood had soaked through his frock coat, saturating his shirt. A doctor was summoned and stitched up the wounds without disinfecting them or the sutures. Sumner was taken home to recover, and Brooks, who had not been detained, was found, arrested on assault charges, allowed to post bond, and released.[28] Washington was on edge. "Everybody here feels as if we are on a volcano," wrote Congressman Keitt.[29]

The assault united the North and South—against each other. Both men became heroes for their respective causes and received fan mail, as the newspapers again weighed in with their own commentaries, predictable by state. In New York, the *Albany Evening Journal* noted, "For the first time has the extreme discipline of the Plantation been introduced into the Senate of the United States."[30] The *Richmond Enquirer*, always good for a pithy quote, opined that "Abolitionists could only be governed by a penitentiary system. They are as unfit for liberty as maniacs, criminals or wild beasts."[31]

Providence held a protest rally, as did New York, Boston, Philadelphia, and dozens of cities throughout the North. While many in the North felt Brooks should be punished, Southern congressmen blocked a censure motion recommended to the House by its own select committee on the assault.

Five days after the assault, the Rhode Island General Assembly convened its May session in Newport. With the Sumner affair foremost in every member's mind, the lawyers discussed the legal tradition of absolute immunity of speech on the floor of the Congress. In clear contrast to the dysfunctional national legislature, Sullivan Ballou and the members went about the nuts-and-bolts work of functional democracy. On Tuesday, May 27, they met all day, counted and verified the votes, affirmed the election certificates, and once again elected Sullivan Ballou Clerk of the House.

On Wednesday, May 28, starting at 10 A.M., the agenda was a fairly easy one, but it was very labor intensive for Sullivan inasmuch as a stack of reports and petitions were read and referred out to committees for further action. That same day in Washington, D. C., Sumner's wounds were turning septic and he was in danger of succumbing to blood poisoning. The doctor was summoned, opened the wound, applied a poultice to draw out the infection and gave his patient opiates to relieve the pain. The nation's newest media celebrity remained weak and debilitated, moved between the homes of friends as updates were issued on his condition.

In Newport, on Friday, May 30, the House announced appointments to the various offices that represented democratic government in each village and town, the justices of the peace, judges, and notaries public. Sullivan Ballou was appointed one of seventy-five notaries for the state who witnessed deeds for sales of property as well as last wills and testaments. Notaries received modest fees for these services. For Sullivan, it also put him in touch with potential clients for his law firm. The legislature then adjourned until June 28 and everyone went home for a month with the prophecy from Sumner's speech fresh in their minds:

> Even now while I speak, portents hang on all the arches of the horizon threatening to darken the broad land, which already yawns with the mutterings of civil war . . . fratricidal, patricidal war . . . beyond the wickedness of any war in human annals . . . wickedness which the imagination toils in vain to grasp. . . .[32]

The author of these words remained a semi-invalid, dragged his feet, perhaps indicative of spinal or lower back nerve damage.[33]

Unsure if he was fit enough to serve, his Massachusetts constituents wondered whether to reelect him, but did. The Southern press jeered that he was malingering. To complicate matters, his mail contained death threats, and the Southern newspapers published a steady stream of menacing warnings and letters from braggarts offering to go and finish what Brooks started.[33] (Not until 1861, when Northern troops garrisoned Washington, D.C., and the Southern Congressional delegation left town, did he once again feel completely safe in the Senate.)

Events in Washington receded in importance for Sullivan Ballou as he returned home to complete the preparations for the baby and attend the arrival of his mother-in-law, Catherine. With his wife in good hands, Sullivan again dashed South for the balance of the session, which he was powerless to speed up.

Underlying the cheerful bustle of preparation for a home birth was a certain tension, caused by the knowledge that childbirth in 1856 was painful and medically hazardous. There were no analgesics to ease the pain of labor or delivery. Difficult births did not end in Caesarian section operations with a drowsy mother and calm baby—they ended with one or both dead from complications. Without medicines to help the new mother fight off the bacteria from unsterilized linens, hands, or forceps, "childbed fever" could become systemic and kill her within a week. Even without infection, a woman with undiagnosed or untreated health problems was at special risk during delivery. There were also risks for the newborn, and statistically, more of them died than did their mothers. Despite this, more mothers and babies survived than did not.

In the middle of the nineteenth century, a woman who lived near family and friends normally gave birth at home, attended by her own mother, if possible, and by other female relatives and friends who had previously given birth. While a midwife or nurse might be employed, a physician rarely was. This gathering of female resources at the mother's home provided experience, reassurance, sociability, and many helping hands to tend and feed other children and nervous husbands. Only women with no support group to assist their delivery, such as immigrant mill laborers living far from family, went to a hospital for childbirth.

As was the custom, Sullivan would have been kept as far away as possible during Sarah's hard labor. Another man would have been assigned to keep him company, perhaps his brother-in-law, Peter, an experienced father of four. They did not have long to wait, for after a reasonable length of time, Sarah gave birth to a son.

The date was August 21, ten months after her marriage. Sarah came through the delivery safely, with no complications or impediments to future childbirth. When Sullivan was admitted to the "borning room," after mother and babe had been made comfortable, he would have found his wife lying in bed with the little boy swaddled in her arms, all messes cleared away. Sullivan was amazed that his son had his own blue eyes.

Sarah and Sullivan's son was named Edgar, *the* fashionable name at the moment, perhaps because of the popularity of the famous New England author, Edgar Allen Poe. Poe was a regular on the lecture circuit throughout New England and had quite a following. The Shumway and Fowler clans both had little Edgars born in the 1850s. By rights of the naming conventions still in use in New England families at that time, Edgar's middle name should have been Bowen, to honor his papa's mother. High honors were paid to Sarah's mother to have the first son given her maiden name of Fowler, and it confirmed the high esteem in which she was held.

In November of that year, the Republicans had made a decent showing in their first national election but, despite Rhode Island voting that ticket, there was no guarantee the party would even be around in four more years. It seemed the great national tightrope walk was to continue for another four years, and it is likely that this is when Sullivan began to consider elected office as his next step. Half a continent away, another attorney who aspired to politics,

Abraham Lincoln, whom Sullivan had yet to meet, expressed similar thoughts:

> I think I am a Whig, but others say there are no Whigs and that I am an Abolitionist . . . I am not a Know Nothing. That is certain. How could I be? How can anyone who abhors the oppression of Negroes be in favor of degrading classes of white people? Our progress in degeneracy appears to me to be pretty rapid.[35]

Meanwhile, the Democrats, secure in their hold on the White House and the nation for another four years, prepared to inaugurate James Buchanan as the fifteenth president of the United States.

CHAPTER SIX

"We Live in Hard and Stirring Times"*

Americans Debate the Sharing of Wealth and Prosperity

1857–1858

That March of 1857, it was not politics as usual, and little went as planned for the Democrats. Death stalked the inauguration of the fifteenth president. Silent and unseen, the peril came from an unexpected quarter and attacked the first family in their lodgings.

The Buchanans and some of the Inaugural Committee had checked into the huge National Hotel on Sixth Street in advance of the family's move into the White House. One of Washington's major hotels, the National was a great favorite with Southerners. Its sidewalks were normally ringed with slaves awaiting their masters inside.

The inaugural festivities included a parade, a festive ball, and a reception for more than a thousand guests, scheduled around the

* From the Civil War song "What's the Matter?"

formal swearing-in ceremony and delivery of the Inaugural Address. For those participants who had checked into the National in advance of March 4, this gaiety was, unfortunately, overshadowed by illness. The president-elect and dozens of others became ill with dysentery from contaminated food. Since everyone afflicted had stayed or dined at the hotel, it became known as the "National Hotel disease," and business plummeted at the establishment.[1]

Given the climate of hostility and suspicion that characterized politics of that era, there were immediate suggestions that poison was to blame. Newspapers all over the country weighed in with their favorite conspiracy theories, each region airing its views on the identity of the culprits. Some factions blamed the Jesuits; others accused the Republicans of attempting to do away with the entire Democratic leadership in one fell swoop. Journalists speculated on which poison had been used, and published graphic accounts of the victims' symptoms. Sectionalism was becoming such a habit, the reactions so automatic, that taking sides on every news story became inevitable.

In all likelihood, the hotel's kitchen had become contaminated in a manner unique to the times: In cold weather, portions of Washington's notorious sewer system froze, creating blockages that caused raw sewage to back up and overflow at its source. While an affected kitchen was cleaned up, it was not disinfected, as there was still little understanding of the connection between germs and disease. Also, in cold weather, omnipresent rats liked to crawl into warmer places, where they sometimes became stuck and died. A dead rat in the hotel's water supply was also suspected as a cause.

President-elect Buchanan himself became ill, and remained under the care of his personal physician for two weeks. His malaise and some immediate political blunders by Buchanan combined to get his administration off to rather a bad start.

Refusing to heed seasoned political advisors, Buchanan used his

James Buchanan, president of the United States, 1857–1861. *From* Harper's Weekly.

inaugural address to state his position that slavery could not be prohibited in a federal territory. Firmly placing himself on one side of that enormous controversy undercut his opportunities to act as national mediator and leader. By announcing he would not seek reelection, Buchanan became an instantaneous lame-duck president, with diminished power to hold the Union together.

When, to placate the Southern wing of his party, Buchanan passed over some of his powerful Northern political supporters and allies who had expected to receive cabinet appointments, appointing instead a majority of slaveholders, he essentially surrounded himself with a majority of men who had no stake in the Union. As the disagreement between the North and South over slavery became more and more polarized, each side blocked the ambitions of the other, causing paralysis within the administration.

The Supreme Court was at this time finalizing a major decision on slavery, the Dred Scott case. Denied the opportunity to buy his liberty, and that of his wife and two teenage daughters, the slave, Dred Scott, had begun the case many years before by suing the widow Sanford for their freedom. For thirty years, slaves had successfully brought suit in Missouri courts—some 278 cases—complaining of unusually cruel treatment or punishment by their masters.

In 1857, the Supreme Court justices were evenly divided between Northern and Southern states. Chief Justice Roger Taney was a frail seventy-seven-year-old Marylander, who had owned and emancipated his slaves but was philosophically proslavery. It was also a geriatric court, with a generation gap that caused additional friction between its members.

Buchanan was apparently worried what public reaction would be if the Court appeared to rule along regional lines. To mitigate the appearance of bias, he attempted to convince his fellow Pennsylvanian, Justice Robert Grier, to vote in favor of slavery, and Grier indeed did so, though whether this was a result of Buchanan's interference is unclear. Although Buchanan's actions might not have changed the final outcome of the verdict, as president he was in ethical, if not technical, violation of the separation-of-powers doctrine between the executive and judicial branches of government, set forth in the Constitution.

On March 6, the same week when the Rhode Island General Assembly reconvened in Providence, the Supreme Court announced its constitutionally skewed decision on the case, 7–2 against Dred Scott; only Benjamin Curtis from Massachusetts and John McLean from Ohio voted against the decision.

Providence buzzed with disapproval, as did every other Northern city. Only in the working men's taverns frequented by Irish laborers, who competed with free Blacks for the same jobs, and in the grand houses of the Lords of the Loom, was there approval.

With the Dred Scott decision, Northerners realized that the Southern political agenda had totally dominated the outcome of national events for decades and would continue to do so long as the Southerners held power. Northeasterners needed more powerful political representation than the Know-Nothing Party was providing, and, as they searched for alternatives, they discovered the new, energetic, and viable Republican Party, which attracted new members by focusing on the key issues of the times: those which held back the prosperity of the majority.

Sullivan Ballou's own personal experiences convinced him the Republican Party platform was the right choice, as was obvious from a speech he later gave. He was born in and understood the industrial North, knew the value of economic growth, and he had watched Woonsocket and Providence expand and prosper. He knew the stories of mill owners who had rebuilt from scratch, bigger and better, after fire destroyed their mills. Among his clients were businessmen who sold goods to mill workers and owners alike. Inevitably, he recognized the improvements in domestic life at that time as compared to that of his childhood—brought about by the introduction of the cotton gin, kitchen stoves, iceboxes, and sewing machines.

Sullivan worked daily with investors and was aspiring to become one himself.[2] He understood the value of moving goods and raw materials to and from markets. The Pacific Railroad and navigational improvements in the Great Lakes would benefit New England—and its investors—just as previous advancements had done. But the deadlock over slave vs. free states held the national economy hostage, and had delayed the construction of the much-needed transcontinental railroad by twenty years, causing its investors to default on their notes and triggering the Panic of 1857, which ruined businesses throughout the North.

The fair and appropriate allocation of the national wealth was another issue dividing North and South. The merchants, bankers, mill owners, and farmers with whom Sullivan Ballou worked each day complained about many examples of unfairness: While the Southerners were disgusted that the North had received more lighthouses, a low-end expenditure, Northerners bewailed the lack of expenditures on navigation and ports in the Great Lakes. In the higher latitudes, multiple ports were required to avoid seasonal disruptions in shipping routes caused by flooding or freezing. Northerners paid more for grain shipped to their densely populated cities in a triangular route through New Orleans, than they would if it came straight from Ohio or Rochester. Northerners recalled the many years their tax dollars had gone to improve navigation along the Mississippi River, and wondered when the Southern legislative caucus would ever approve money for their needs.

Yankee manufacturers also wanted protective tariffs on manufactured goods to keep out cheaper European goods, and keep Americans employed. Southern legislators opposed all tariffs except the one that threatened Southern-grown sugar, because the South imported many of its manufactured goods from Europe and benefited from cheaper goods.

The Republicans heeded these Northern voices, eager to turn business owners and workers into Republican voters.

It must be said that, in the 1850s, Northern beliefs in free labor and freedom for slaves were not the same as supporting fraternization or social equality. Sullivan considered the Irish and Blacks to be his social inferiors, even while convinced it was right to open up to them the opportunities for betterment offered by free labor.[3]

In 1857, the candidate for U.S. Senate in Illinois, Abraham Lincoln, prophesied eloquently,

> "A house divided against itself cannot stand." I believe this government cannot endure permanently half slave and half free. I do not expect the Union to be dissolved—I do not expect the house to fall—but I do expect it will cease to be divided. It will become all one thing or all the other.[4]

This transformation played out subtly in Rhode Island that year.

In the State House, it seemed like business as usual, except that behind the scenes, at meetings and dinners, the members were changing their political allegiance, as men of power, wealth, and influence came together to share ideas and discuss ways of ending the national stalemate. Present at these informal caucuses, Sullivan Ballou participated in these discussions and expressed himself with his customary eloquence—as he could not while taking notes in the House. Men of importance listened, were impressed, and decided to back him politically. Possibly they had already sounded him out concerning a candidacy for elected office.

When Sullivan returned to Woonsocket, to the routine of his law practice, he seemed not to have experienced the awkwardness that some new fathers felt. He was an interactive father, playing with his infant son and participating in some of his care, like putting the baby to bed, taking care to "lay him on a pillow and whistle him to sleep."[5] Sullivan's hopes for the future were centered in his family, and he saw the Republican Party as offering him a way to realize them.[6]

Sullivan spoiled Sarah as much as their budget would allow, including some luxuries. Musical talent ran in Sarah's family; witness her brother Johnathan. Sullivan owned and played an ivory-topped flute and, by his own admission, he also whistled quite merrily. 1857 was most likely the year that he presented Sarah with a piano. An extravagance given his present income, he had to pay for it on credit for at least a year.[7] It probably cost him at least $350 [now $9,000] plus delivery.[8]

Rhode Island elected its state legislators on the first Wednesday in April, for an inauguration the last Tuesday in May.[9]

By the time the state elections rolled around, no party was dominant in Rhode Island politics, so another "fusion ticket" was run for the state-level offices. The only noticeable change was that, this time, Republican candidates now predominated. The fledgling party was getting its feet under itself, and, fueled by temperance and antislavery, began to assimilate the voters of the various single-issue parties, the fusion parties, and the Know-Nothings. The canny politicians among the Know-Nothings had sniffed the wind, seen where the voters were going, and hurried to change parties—"the better to get out in front and lead."

The Ballous had highly personal reasons to await the outcome of this particular election, for Sullivan himself was on the ballot for a House seat. He had been nominated to represent Smithfield in the General Assembly. The average age of legislators was then forty-five years, and their average personal wealth was $11,833. [$308,000][10] Sullivan Ballou, at age thirty, with less than $1,000 [$26,000] in assets, was atypical; his nomination was a singular honor.[11] Not only was it a recognition of his hard work, and an encouragement for his talents, but an indication that he was being groomed for even higher things. He had won the patronage of the Rhode Island civic fathers, who were helping to open doors for him. With further hard work, even higher levels of success were now possible.

The statehouse in Newport where, in May 1857, Sullivan was elected as Speaker of the House of Representatives. *Courtesy of the Rhode Island Historical Society.*

Duly elected in April, Sullivan undertook his traditional journey to Newport for the May session, this time to be seated as a legislator and to start drawing the dollar-a-day pay, plus eight-cents-per-mile transportation reimbursement. Charles Van Zandt stepped up to the job of first clerk and a new fellow was hired as recording clerk. Alas, he could not fill the shoes of Sullivan Ballou and quit after only two days. He stayed only long enough to assist in the first task—certifying the election results.[12]

Remarkably, the same day Sullivan was sworn into office, the members immediately and unanimously chose him to serve as Speaker of the Rhode Island House of Representatives. Now, his place was at the architectural focal point of the entire chamber, beside the American flag, backed by a large, twenty-four paned window. Just in front of him was his former desk as clerk. Three elegent tiers of curved benches for the legislators, carved and turned from dark cherry wood, circled the room facing the speaker's desk. Serving as Speaker made Sullivan the second most important elected official in Rhode Island. The governor was technically first in importance, but under the 1842 State Constitution, the governorship was a weak position, serving as the commander-in-chief of the militia and able to grant temporary reprieves to prisoners. With the governor more of a figurehead, without even the power of appointments, the real power lay with the legislature.

It was the legislature, for example, which annually appointed the officers of the militia regiments, judges, justices of the peace, notaries public, and a host of other administrative and judicial offices. The General Assembly had all existing powers, except those denied to it by the Constitutions of the United States or Rhode Island. The "power of the purse strings" allowed it to raise money to fund the central government by apportioning levies to the towns. The towns in turn added these to the local real estate tax.[13]

The Speaker had both public and behind-the-scenes power, and so the rich and powerful elite of the state cultivated whoever held that position. It must have been an interesting turn of events for the young man who had to beg for money to attend college.

The offstage part of Sullivan's new job was that of political power broker, and involved negotiating with the governor, taking the initiative with other powerful members who were leaders in crafting major legislation, and controlling the flow of legislation during each annual session. He could bring petitions to the floor quickly, or let them languish. Through influence and example, he was also the leader of the Republican Party in the House.

Sullivan now began to play a central role in the administration of the General Assembly, meeting with the clerks to make sure the body functioned as efficiently as possible. The elected officials of New England valued proper behavior in their peers.[14] It was up to the Speaker to enforce it, for he was the guardian of the honor and prestige of that institution.

Thirty-year-old Sullivan was up to the task, presiding over the seventy-two-member House with flair and fairness. His "strict impartiality, unfailing courtesy, and eminent fitness for the position, won for him a merited popularity."[15] In his public role, he acted as a kind of referee, maintaining order, making parliamentary rulings, and overseeing the general conduct of business.

At the start of each day's business, Sullivan took his special seat in the middle of the chamber, and raised his voice to call the House to order. All members rising from their seats and wishing to speak, first turned to him, and making a little bow or nod of the head, addressed him, and asked for permission to speak. Ballou assigned the order of speakers, the time allotted each, and how many times a member might speak on the same issue. He had to make sure all sides were heard on any issue, and had to refrain from showing obvious favoritism at any time. The Speaker had the authority to compel absent members to attend either the morning or afternoon sessions each day, and to fine them twenty-five cents for unexcused absences.[16]

His efforts to preserve decorum and order among the members was perhaps most sorely tested on an unlikely issue. While America's eyes were on "Bleeding Kansas," Rhode Island's were often on the State Normal School: its first school for training teachers. Every city wanted to be its site, just as they had wanted Brown University a hundred years earlier. It was that session's issue from hell, the agenda item that would not die. In his role as arbiter of all points of parliamentary order and proceedings, Sullivan ruled on it—every single time it came up. The first time around, Providence and Woonsocket both wanted the school but finally, after several votes, Bristol won. However, the Senate could not concur, and wanted to refer it to a committee, so it came back to the House, was discussed, another motion was put forward, and it failed to be carried, by 27 to 37 votes. On yet another occasion, a motion was put forward for Woonsocket. That failed 13 to 47. Perhaps the wiser head of the Speaker then prevailed, and the item was postponed indefinitely. Just before the session adjourned, a motion again passed to locate the school in Bristol, but only for a period of four years, after which its location would be reconsidered.

For the rest of the session that spring, the members of the House approved measures that furthered economic development, infrastructure, and transportation improvement—the same kinds of actions needed at the national level, which floundered over the schism in consensus caused by the slavery issue there. For example, the members approved the incorporation of the Hope Iron Foundry, and the macadamizing of the streets around the courthouse in Providence. The town of Warren received approval to establish fire districts for the protection of life and property.[17] Salaries were set for the members—a mere $6000 [$156,000] covered the cost of the whole House—with another $2500 [$65,000] appropriated for both clerks and their stationery budget.[18] As Speaker, Sullivan was able to speak "as other members" did on general issues, but found his ability to debate hampered by his supervisory position.[19] The session adjourned until the first Monday in January 1858, and all the members went home, their ears still ringing with counterproposals for the normal school.[20]

This summer, with their finances in tolerable shape, Sullivan was able to take Sarah on a summer holiday to see her family in idyllic Cherry Valley in New York, for little Edgar to meet Sarah's uncle Jonathan and aunt Eliza. Her relatives would have seen a woman who was happy, self-confident, and blooming in her marriage, and were surely pleased with her husband's care of her and his growing prospects.

While the Ballous and their Fowler kin enjoyed mountaintop vistas and clean air, national politics continued to absorb every one's attention. 1857 represented the high water mark of the proslavery South's national political power. The president, the Supreme Court, and the proslavery Democratic majorities in both houses of the Congress exercised little restraint and consistently acted beyond the pale of the national political conscience. It seemed as if no idea was too extreme for the ruling majority, and the Northern rank-and-file Democrats became alienated.[21]

Proposals were floated to reopen the African slave trade; another to extend the Mason-Dixon Line clear across the continent to the Pacific Ocean. The Mason-Dixon line, named for its surveyors, established the border between Maryland and Pennsylvania, and formed the boundary between free and slave states. Had the proposed extension been implemented, it would have divided California into two states around Fresno, and admitted Kansas, New Mexico, Arizona, and Hawaii as slave states.

Another scheme, proposed by the Knights of the Golden Circle, a Southern group that claimed to have 100,000 members, was to negotiate the annexation of Mexico, creating twenty-five more slave states, to form an empire arcing from the tip of Florida to the Yucatan.[22] Buchanan advocated the annexation of the island of Cuba, with its plantations and slaves.

Disagreements about slavery permeated many aspects of daily life. The schism over slavery split the Presbyterian, Methodist, and Baptist churches into Northern and Southern branches. Southern students walked out of the Philadelphia Medical School. Southerners decried the use of Northern textbooks in Southern schools, because they taught "alien" cultural values.[23] At Phillips Exeter, Southern students withdrew when a Black student was admitted.[24]

The Panic of 1857 struck later that year. Grain had led a decade-long boom of prosperity that showed every sign of becoming a recession in 1857 now that a Europe at peace once again bought Russian grain and abruptly stopped purchasing it from America. The price of grain dropped 75 percent, Providence ship captains had no cargoes, and the stock market declined 50 percent.[25] On the day the Ohio Life Insurance and Trust Company announced it was the victim of a massive embezzlement and shut a branch office, the stock market dropped another 10 percent.[26]

The Ohio owed money to many banks, whose liquidity was now jeopardized. Americans holding paper money were jittery, because banks held only small gold reserves to back up the paper currency in general circulation and there was no way they could pay off all depositors at once. A major shipment of gold equal to 20 percent of the total amount on hand was expected from the California gold fields and might have averted the crisis. As luck would have it, after battling a hurricane for four days, the SS *Central America* went to the bottom of the ocean on September 11, 1857, taking with her 450 men and 30,000 pounds of gold, after getting the women and children off in lifeboats.* The news reports of the loss caused a

* Standard nineteenth-century marine procedures required a few lifeboats to make multiple trips evacuating passengers to rescue vessels. This is why the *Titanic* did not have lifeboats for all her passengers. The procedure was only moderately successful because panicked crews commandeered lifeboats, rescue vessels were scarce, or sea conditions did not permit multiple trips.

general run on the banks and created a panic that was illustrated in contemporary cartoons as a runaway horse.[27] There were no federal bank regulations to deal with such a crisis, and the Panic of 1857 caused major economic disruption.

In Pawtucket, all the shops and stores closed except for a single grocery store on each side of the river.[28] Mill workers used to buying on credit went hungry until payday. Sullivan's income dropped, like that of men all over the Midwest and East. Only the self-sufficient plantation economies came through relatively unscathed, though census records in northern Virginia reveal that cash-poor planters increasingly leased or sold off parcels of their patrimony to free Blacks; and Northern or Border State farmers, to raise cash for luxury and manufactured goods.

The South was aware of the hard times in the North, and felt that the Panic of 1857 proved the validity of the Southern economic model. Their slaves were not starving, unlike the mudsills who worked in the Northern mills and factories. For three more years, the South was to take full advantage of the economic discomforts the nation experienced in 1857, demanding better terms in every way and threatening to leave the Union if they did not get them.[29] "Or else!" was the first version of the rebel yell, the phrase thrown defiantly into the faces of political adversaries on every issue; it was "yield or we secede," an attitude that brought American politics to a standstill.

By the time the nation's calendars read 1858, the trend toward "substituting stereotypes for realities" also continued its dangerous, downward spiral. Northerners and Southerners "continued to lose sight of how much alike they were and how many values they shared."[30] In the last two years of the 1850s, the nation became stuck on the slavery issue.

> [This] had an effect of changing men's attitudes towards the disagreements which are always certain to arise in politics:

ordinary, resolvable disputes were converted into questions of principal, involving rigid, nonnegotiable dogma. It transformed political action from a process of accommodation to a mode of combat." Americans may have deplored it, but no one seemed able to stop it.[31]

All the piecemeal attempts to resolve the problem, by the Cotton Whigs, and a host of others, failed.

With the exception of a few who stood out for their adamant views, most American politicians strove to avoid disunion by treading cautiously through the quagmire, but it seemed that the quicksand only spread. The situation was almost impossible, and the blame was not the president's alone. Buchanan could not prevent the growth of the crisis, but many of his actions inflamed it. Accusations of chicanery, and of secret political deals on the upcoming referendum in Kansas, further hurt his presidency. An exceptional president and Congress were needed, and in 1858, America had neither.

In the winter session of the Rhode Island House of Representatives in Providence, Sullivan Ballou had a chance to cast a vote on

The statehouse in Providence, site of the January and special legislative sessions, where Sullivan worked as clerk, speaker, and representative. *Author's photo.*

the future of Kansas, as well as on more prosaic, local matters. The General Assembly established $20 fines for cockfighting and animal baiting offenses, and adopted measures regulating rabbit hunting, "tippling houses," banks, the railroad, privy vaults, and cesspools. On February 4, 1858, the House debated and took a stand on the conditions of the admission of Kansas to the Union. The purpose of their vote was to advise Rhode Island's Congressional delegation in Washington, D.C., how to vote. At issue was the product of a proslavery constitutional convention held in Kansas in 1857. If the Congress and president approved this "self-governing" plan, it would be submitted to the voters of Kansas. However, there was a catch.

The vote on the so-called "Lecompton" State Constitution was confusing, something of a "vote no on yes." The main constitution was approved whether the votes were yes or no. The only item of choice that would come before the voters was a clause regarding *additional* slavery. If the "yes on slavery" clause was approved, Kansas would immediately be admitted as a slave state and there would be no limit on how many slaves could be imported. If the "no on slavery" clause was approved, admission to the Union would be delayed, and Kansas would still have slavery, because the language "grand fathered in" all the slaves then living in the territory.[32]

Voters read this twice, scratched their heads, and knew they had been had by the politicians. Of course, such obvious manipulation generated a firestorm of criticism around the nation. President Buchanan backed the maneuver. In Providence, the House voted 57–2 against the admission of Kansas by this flawed constitution, and Sullivan surely voted with the majority.[33*]

If the State Constitution had been submitted in a format that permitted a free and honest vote, with no proposals to fiddle

* At this time, only vote tallies were reported; no records were kept how each representative voted on issues.

with the boundaries of Kansas, events would have taken their course, and the crisis might have defused. The Northern Democrats would not have defected and joined the Republicans in a coalition that eventually won the White House. If compromise could have been achieved, the nation would not have careened toward civil war in 1861.

In late April, tragedy struck closer to home, in Pawtucket, when young William Bogle, Sullivan's nephew, in an accident received a blow to the head that killed him.[34] He died on April 22, 1858, at only eleven years old, "a child of rare beauty and promise."[35] Frances and Peter had now lost their two eldest sons. Only little Jeanette and Sullivan Bogle remained. As close relations, Sullivan and Sarah would have observed mourning for the dead child.

More happily that April, Sullivan was reelected to the House of Representatives. "So acceptably did he fill the chair, that when his constituents, in the succeeding year, returned him again to the house, he was again proposed for the Speakership."[36] The thirty-one-year-old had evidently presided with flair and calm authority. However, when he took his seat in May 1858, "he declined a re-nomination to the Speakership, as the duties of the chair interfered with his freedom for debate."[37]

In the May session, the House dealt with repairs to the State House building, the streets of Woonsocket, publication of the colony's colonial records, and regulated grain sales. They agreed to give two days' pay to the clerk who had resigned after only two days. Meanwhile, Buchanan and the Congress, voting along sectional lines, approved the submission of the Lecompton constitution to the voters of Kansas.

In the summer of 1858, Sullivan arranged for Sarah and Edgar to once again have a long visit with her family in New York State. Cherry Valley's high elevation made it a cool and refreshing place to pass the summer. America's first best-selling author, James Fenimore Cooper, praised "that verdant and undulating surface of forest, which spread itself unbroken, unless by stream or lake, over such a vast region of country."[38*]

In this quiet hamlet, in the workshops of Samuel Morse and his colleagues, the first working telegraph machine and telegraph office were invented, using a binary code. The telegraph system that was to play a vital role in the lives of Sullivan and Sarah Ballou provided the Victorians with the same sea change in communications as the Internet did for people of later centuries.[39]

Johnathan Fowler, and his wife, Eliza Little, lived in Otsego County; Sarah's younger brother, John, came with her mother, Catherine, and there were other Fowlers living in nearby villages who came calling; and even J. W. slipped away during the Law School recess.

As much as he had enjoyed himself there the previous year, Sullivan would have again been feeling the pinch of finances: thanks to the 1857 recession, he could not in 1858 sustain any dip in his income that would result from a prolonged absence from his law practice, and he hesitated even to spend the cost of his train fare.[40] Besides, the Court of Common Pleas, the Civil Court, held its summer session starting the first Monday in June, the U.S. Circuit Court met on June 15, and the U.S. District Court began the first Tuesday in August. Summer was a busy time for lawyers in New England, because their clients were catching up on lawsuits deferred when every one was snowbound.[41]

That summer, Sullivan was representing a client accused of perjury in an important criminal case that had political repercussions in Cumberland. He remained at home, uncomplaining, and corresponded with Sarah while she was gone. One letter survived, a letter that any woman would have felt proud to receive.

[*] A film version of this book *The Last of the Mohicans*, released in 1992, lyrically portrays both the vast American landscape and the life and travails of the people of the mid 1700s.

It is a touching love letter in which Sullivan told her explicitly, and in many fond little ways, how much he adored her. He marveled that a man so long married should love his wife so much. That summer, Sarah was in the first half of her pregnancy with their second child; he is worried about her well-being but, Victorian to the core, neither of them overtly discussed the pregnancy. Reading between the lines, it seemed she was experiencing morning sickness.

My Dear Sarah

After I wrote you on Sunday, now I counted the long long hours till Tuesday night, when I knew I should receive your letter! I was very much occupied Tuesday taking depositions with Robinson in Providence but I lotted on coming home and reading your letter all the evening. I followed the mail to the Post office and watched the Box till the last moment, and saw nothing there. I asked the boy if the down mail was open? "Yes." I could have clutched him by the throat and told him he lied. I looked in Henry's box to see if there was not some mistake and finally turned my sad steps away, realizing a heart sickness that I never felt before. Never, when a lover, "sighing like a furnace" did all my disappointments together amount to one half the sadness of this. No matter about the night I passed. In the morning I thought your letter must come up from Providence. I was to go down that day to try a case for Perjury; and so I hired Peter to carry the mail and boy to the office—the latter to hunt the bag for something for me, and Peter to bring it before the down Train. And lo! Peter appeared just in time with your welcome thrice welcome letter. I cannot tell you how it cheered my heart to learn of your safe arrival and good health and all about you. I read it over till I was ashamed to be seen pouring over it any longer; and then went into the baggage car and read it over and over again till I got to Providence. I repented of my threat to send it back if it was upon note paper, I could not spare it; and at that time I would have put up with a single word.

I reproached myself much, for loving you so—making an idol of you—making more than a goddess of you. I thought how foolish, a man of my age—who had been married three years—should still be really in love with his wife (should a husband ever be otherwise!) should be disconsolate without her, and stake his happiness or misery on the receipt of her letter! I don't care for the folly, nor the blind idolatry! I'll plunge headlong into them both. There is something in the fanaticism of such heart devotion (if you call it such) that fills my whole soul and feeds its warm fires. I have centered all my earthly ambition and joys in you my own dear wife, and cannot move one of them out of the circle of your own heart. How boyish seem the affections of former years compared with the love that now stimulates every heart throb! And how it gilds and ennobles every struggle of life to be inspired by love for one so loved as you. I know you will not laugh to think of my writing you a bona fide love letter; besides always helping my feelings to write you anything else I am peculiarly situated now. I have no creature or thing to pet or fondle or love in this house but my pen; and I should be cruel to myself if I did not let it write some of my wayward but affectionate thoughts.

Your letter fairly inspired me. I went to the trial of that case with a heart full of enthusiasm as well as consciousness of my client's innocence and I think I made the best argument—the clearest analysis of testimony in my life with one exception. The case was a mere preliminary examination and occupied a day and a half. My client was discharged. Why I speak of it is, that the case sprung from political animosities and enlisted wide spread feeling, in the lower district of Cumberland where I was glad to make some political friends. They were well satisfied with my efforts and complemented me highly. And I think it will have an important bearing on my political prospects next spring. Several other things of minor importance in themselves have transpired that give me great encouragement and if I am fortunate next winter in the legislature I am quite certain of becoming an M.C.*

I have been quite busy this week and by the aid of your letter in my darkest moments have dragged out my life more comfortably than last, and soon I shall hear from you again. You must not be homesick—adopt the Epicurean philosophy and enjoy yourself while you can, and when sated with pleasure come home to me, and make my heart glad once more with your constant presence. I hardly know how to write you about coming on there. Have not heard from the west** yet and unless I do, I can not feel that I ought to indulge in the expense. I know you will feel much disappointed and I almost wish I had waited till my next letter before writing about it, to see "if something wouldn't turn up." I would not care to come, but to make your visit more pleasant; and if I have to give it up you must try to enjoy yourself more some other way. My last note on the Piano comes due soon—the first payment on my life Insurance also comes due this month. I find it very difficult too, to raise any money from collections, and all things considered I better give up my jaunt this season. I will how[ever] come to Albany after you; unless you should happen to know of some one coming right through from Cherry Valley to Boston who would take charge of you. But you may not take this as final. Wait till my next and then I will write you conclusively about the matter. Of course I need not charge you to keep my

* Member of Congress

** Uncle Clovis? Perhaps Sullivan had loans to repay to him.

prudential reasons to yourself. You may tell Jonathan I fear my business which at present controls me almost entirely, will prevent me visiting him and that I hope some day to make up for my absence this time.

Mattie came home last Tuesday and says she is very lonesome without you. I have not been home enough to know if Charlie is as devoted as ever. Lucy Whipple (that was) went home yesterday. I did not go up to see her in fact I have not been even to Mrs. Talbot's nor Mattie's. When at home I go from the office to the house and hope and wish and wish and hope I could sleep till you come back (pardon the grammar of that last sentence.) I long to hear from Edgar again and still more to see him, I wish you would write me more particularly about him and his health and your own too. You are too general altogether in what you write. You can write me on a little slip of paper about yourself and I can destroy it on reading it. Have you taken Dr. Okie's medicine and has it benefited you?* How is your general health &c? I write this on Saturday for I shall go down to Pawtucket and spend the Sunday with Mother. Next week I shall take the jugs and things down there & make some wine and jelly. The House is in excellent order and the garden growing finely and the whole week has been rainy and cool. Give my love to your Mother and all the rest and believe me

as ever
Your Sullivan[42]

* Mattie is possibly Mathilda Ballou who lived in Woonsocket; Charlie is almost certainly Charles Brownell, whom Sullivan called Charlie; Lucy Whipple may be either the daughter of Sullivan's cousin Lucy Ballou, or an Otsego girl of Sarah's age. Dr. Okie was a prominent homeopathic practitioner in Providence who dispensed a variety of potions and tonics.

Sarah's idyll in the countryside was interrupted by more bad news from home, however. Her niece, Jeanette, died on July 27, on her third birthday. The family had yet to abandon their mourning clothes for William and remained in black. For Sullivan, Emeline, and Frances, it must have been an unhappy reminder of 1833, when two deaths had occurred so close together. Little Sullivan was now an only child, and his parents and the rest of the family probably lavished care on him, as they overprotected him. Uncle Henry and Aunt Sarah had also lost six-year-old Emma Louisa on March 1 of that year, underscoring how vulnerable little children were in the 1800s.

Peter and Frances seemed to have clung to each other for comfort in their grief, for by Christmastime, the family knew Frances was expecting a new baby the following summer. Peter returned to his work at Gorham, where everyone worked ten-hour shifts, and life went on.

While the death of a child was a family tragedy, the death of a father and breadwinner was catastrophic. Sullivan and Sarah knew this only too well—both had experienced their family's sudden slide into poverty. Determined to prevent this from happening in their lives, they now decided to take out a life insurance policy on Sullivan. Such policies had been available from insurers since 1825, and by 1855, a hundred million dollars of policies were in force, some from mutual insurance companies located in New England and New York that paid annual dividends.[43]

The maximum benefit for a forty-year-old man was $10,000, for which the premium was $300. The proceeds from insurance policies could be used to pay off creditors, support the family, and were inheritable by the children, should the wife herself die. However, the policies were normally voided by military service. In his writings, Sullivan refers to making installment payments on his insurance policy, but does not give any specifics.[44]

* * *

On August 4, 1858, the people of Kansas voted down the Lecompton Constitution by a vote of 11,200 to 1,788. Statehood went back to the drawing board. On August 18, the completion of the laying of the telegraph cable across the Atlantic Ocean was celebrated in Poughkeepsie, New York, the town where the Ballous were married. The Cherry Valley inventor, Samuel Morse, was honored by a long poem about the glorious future of technology. The whole nation envisioned a sea change in communications efficiency, with telegrams plying back and forth among England, continental Europe, and America. Queen Victoria telegraphed President Buchanan.

By September 1, however, the cable had failed. The high-voltage frequency chosen for transmission rendered the wire so hot that its conducting core burned through its insulation and exposed the cable to seawater. The entire project was a washout. After an investigation, however, planners immediately began organizing the next attempt.[45] It was amazing how fast nineteenth-century businessmen could move when slavery issues did not interfere.

In 1858, the businessmen and town fathers of Pawtucket had decided to replace the bridge joining the Rhode Island and Massachusetts sides of town with a new stone structure. After a temporary pedestrian structure was put up, the old bridge was torn down and the new one inaugurated that same year. Many local dignitaries were invited to make remarks, but Sullivan Ballou's were wonderful. Not only was his short speech appropriate for the occasion, but by connecting the opening of this single bridge with the nation's push for greater development and prosperity, he imbued the event with symbolism. It is not hard to see the key issues of the Republican platform behind his statements, and yet it was not a partisan speech. It is also the only speech of his to have survived, probably because he handed his text to the local newspaper reporter.

Mr. President—It has always been a source of pride to me to hear the American people rejoicing over those great improvements that tend to uplift the race and develop its moral, intellectual and physical power; and I am no less proud to be here today to rejoice with you over the completion of this work of internal improvement; that adds more than its cost to the wealth of the community in which it is located—exhibits its beauty to all who will behold it—and pledges safety to all who would pass over it.

It is one of those works that help make up the wealth of the country, and I would we had more of them; that every stream in the land had these granite spans from shore to shore; that all our sister States, Massachusetts and Rhode Island now are, bound together with those links of rock—that time can never crumble nor the wildest contention shake.

Our national prosperity and wealth would be unparalled and boundless if all our labor was turned to the production of the durable and useful, instead of that vast amount of useless and perishable production that modern life is made to require. Gaunt poverty would be banished, and industry, stern and honesty, would deck the whole land with such proud trophies of its perseverance and skill.

Every such work as this, whether it assume more than a local importance or not, is not only in itself worthy of commemoration, but the very ceremony of commemoration tends to increase the stability of our national character and our love for the durable and useful.

But I derive additional pleasure from this celebration because this is the work of the State. It is true, the individual enterprise and public spirit of these citizens of Massachusetts and Rhode Island put the keystones in those arches, but their strong foundations are the work of the State. And I hail it as exhibiting a regard for the material interest and prosperity of

> the people, and a disposition to secure uninterrupted forever the intercourse with our old mother State, Massachusetts.
>
> It was truly put in the most appropriate place, without regard to necessity—at the head of the tide water that washes the shores of both States, and where the distilling dews and descending rain from Massachusetts and Rhode Island hills—flowing down past the grave of Blackstone—turning a thousand wheels and exhausting all their power for the benefit of man, dash down at the last beneath it to the embrace of the sea, ever moistening its arches with the spray of the glad meeting.
>
> Mr. President—May the citizens of both States that pass over it, like shuttles, carry the threads of a common interest and weave the texture of an unbroken friendship.

The band then struck up the "Grand Troop Waltz," after which Sullivan's former teacher, the Reverend Mr. Taft, stepped forward and made an "exceedingly interesting speech." He was most pleased with his former pupil.[46]

In contrast, for many in Rhode Island, the center of U.S. textile manufacturing, slavery remained an especially complex issue. Not only did it seem like economic folly to interfere with anything that kept the cotton flowing into Northern mills, but family relationships further complicated the dynamics: To guarantee the flow of raw cotton to their factories, the Northern mill owners had cultivated political, social, and often, family ties in the South. The business dealings were often family to family: the mills owned by a Northern family bought their cotton from plantations owned by extended families in the South.

Since the 1840s, these families had visited back and forth, sharing hospitality—going South for the winter or North for the summer. Newport, Rhode Island, and the spas at Saratoga and Ballston in New York, were popular destinations for Southerners.

Every school Sullivan Ballou attended had Southern students, as did the Cherry Valley Female Academy of Sarah's family. The adult sons of the Lords of the Loom and the Lords of the Lash were sent on fact-finding journeys to each other's families, to learn various aspects of the business. Intermarriage among the families had occurred over several generations. This layer of personal relationships complicated the political situation and made the mill owners reluctant to embrace Republicanism and its call for abolition.

Indeed, for many Northerners, it was enough that they had outlawed slavery in the Northern states. Additional degrees of virtue were achieved by opposing its expansion in the new federal territories. Few proposed its abolition in the South, where it was seen as practically impossible to eradicate. If eradicated, one very real concern was what to do with the freed slaves. The wife of Senator James Chesnut, Jr., of South Carolina, diarist Mary Boykin Chesnut, had some acerbic comments on freedom for Blacks:

> It is a crowning misdemeanor for us to hold still in slavery those Africans whom they [Northerners] brought here from Africa, or sold to us when they found it did not pay to own them themselves. Gradually, they slid or sold them off down here; or freed them prospectively, giving themselves years in which to get rid of them in a remunerative way. We want to spread them over other lands, too—West and South, or Northwest, where the climate would free them or kill them, or improve them out of the world, as our friends up North do the Indians. The best way to take Negros to your heart is to get as far away from them as possible. . . . People can't love things dirty, ugly and repulsive, simply because they ought to do so, but they can be good to them at a distance; that's easy.[47]

Faced with this conundrum of freed slaves, most Northerners were content to fight slavery in small steps, like opposing the Fugitive

Slave Law and the spread of slavery; the bigger picture would have to wait for events to take their course. While falling short of full integration, and seeming in hindsight to be half measures regarding the freedom of Blacks, the policy may have been all those times could have borne. No one in that period of history, North or South, Black or white, advocated intermarriage, integrated schools, or social contact between the two races. Dred Scott did not want to be invited to a clambake; he wanted freedom for his girls who were born in a free territory. He was no longer fighting for himself; more than sixty years old, he likely knew his tuberculosis was terminal and his life would soon end.[48]

As a radical Republican, Sullivan Ballou's views on slavery were clear. He opposed it and approved proactive means to end it. His personal role at the end of the decade seems to have focused on speaking out against it.

A few Rhode Islanders were activists on a more physical scale—some of the more daring abolitionists literally freeing slaves—once the latter arrived in New England, that is. Slaves who escaped from their masters down South had to go all the way to Canada, or risk being tracked and captured by bounty hunters and returned south under the provisions of the Fugitive Slave Law. Escaped slaves traveled north at night, navigating by the North Star and the constellation of the Big Dipper, the "Drinking Gourd" celebrated in slave songs. A network of helpers fed and sheltered them, in barns, outbuildings, or secret rooms in their own homes. This system was known as the Underground Railroad, and many of its partisans were Quakers, known opponents of slavery. In Rhode Island, the Underground Railroad reputedly ran through Woonsocket and the Blackstone Valley, right through the Ballou Neighborhood that had an old Quaker meetinghouse.

Escaped slaves making their way through Massachusetts and Rhode Island had the help of a network of sympathetic persons and safe houses. In the middle of the night, closed carriages shuttled fugitives between the safe houses run in the homes of two sisters, going from the Fall River home of Lucy Buffum Lovell to the house of Elizabeth Buffum Chace at Broad and Hunt streets in Valley Falls. Mrs. Chace gave the fugitives an envelope addressed to her, which they were to mail from Toronto to confirm their safe arrival.[49] Elsewhere in Cumberland, farms and an old home on the Mendon Road performed the same function. In Providence, the A.M.E. Bethel Church, at its original site, and the home of wealthy slave trader turned abolitionist, Moses Brown, were also safe houses. The transportation infrastructure of Rhode Island may also have been used to move fugitive slaves. The towpaths of the Blackstone Canal made excellent pathways if used at night, or in between the known movements of canal boats.

Sarah Ballou may not have realized that just a few paces from where she did her shopping and errands, fugitives were scurrying to freedom at night. Also, free Blacks working on the Providence–Worcester railroad were said to smuggle escapees on and off trains. It is unlikely that Sullivan ever knew whether an escaped slave was riding on his train, though he might have bumped into one indistinguishable from a railway worker.

The Black dock-worker community at Fox Point Harbor was then thought to operate another transmigration stop.[50] Providence and Woonsocket had African-American neighborhoods—Snow Town, Hard Scrabble, and Cato Hill—where free Blacks lived, and these provided a sympathetic refuge where fugitive slaves could blend in while they rested or recovered from their arduous journey. The technically illegal activities of the Underground Railway worked best when invisible. These traffickings were perhaps the only invisible part of the slavery crisis, which continued to wrack Rhode Island and America.

· CHAPTER SEVEN ·

"Our Cause Is Just and Holy"*

The Nation Accelerates Toward Disunion

1859–1860

Sullivan and Sarah welcomed the New Year of 1859, and their second son, all at once. William Bowen was another healthy, blue-eyed, Ballou baby. His middle name was of course, Sullivan's mother's maiden name; his first, probably chosen to commemorate their nephew, William Bogle, who died in 1858. Victorians often reused the names of dead children, because they "wanted one in the family [with the same name] as a substitute for . . . one . . . lost."[1] It was not an unusual experience for a Victorian child to accompany his parents to the cemetery, to place flowers at the grave of a predeceased sibling with the same name as his.

This second child was born in their new house. Sometime after Edgar was born, the Ballous moved to Bernon Village, about a mile away from their former house, but still in Woonsocket. Bernon was

* From the Civil War song "The Southern Wagon," a version of "Wait for the Wagon."

prettier, part of the mill complex that was designed with greenery and open space around the housing areas. The neighborhood was built on flatter ground, making it much easier for Sarah to manage outside errands. Likely Sarah's mother once again attended the birth and stayed on to lend a hand, because Sullivan had to immediately turn his attention to the January session of the General Assembly, where, as a member, "his attention to business, and his effective oratory, made him a leading legislator of the State."[2]

In January, the rotation policy called for the meeting to be held in the historic Providence State House building, which had hosted presidents Washington and Jefferson, and the celebrations for the Marquis de Lafayette. Here, Sullivan's cousin Jabez Bowen had attended meetings of the Council of War during the Revolution. It sat on a slope, with its main entrance on Benefit Street and its southern facade facing a long promenade lined with trees. The House used a newly renovated chamber on the first floor, illuminated by natural light through large windowpanes.[3]

This was the session at which Sullivan hoped to lock in support for a congressional seat. Instead, at its January 1859 session, the House appointed him to serve on a special committee to investigate what rights the State and various individuals had by title or easement in the lands that bordered the Woonasquatucket River, which formed the border between the cities of Providence and North Providence. Now that the railroad had come through the area, the derelict reed beds were prime development land, and ownership needed to be clarified. The committee was also charged with providing a plan for the straightening of the channel of the river.[4] At stake was a bill pending before the legislature that might affect the land rights of some of Rhode Island's oldest, most prestigious, and wealthiest families.

At its initial meeting on April 2 in Providence, the first act of the committee was to elect Sullivan its chairman.[5] The assignment was high-profile, one that put Sullivan's legal talents fully in the spotlight before the most important families and government officials in the state. If he could successfully navigate the political quicksand and legal complexities of this case, he would prove himself worthy of higher office. It was in many ways a dress rehearsal for more important things to come, and he certainly applied himself with vigor, and yet, there was disappointment, for this was not the next step he had been anticipating. Wrote John Russell Bartlett,

> During his short service in the House of Representatives, he was a prominent member, being possessed of unusual powers of debate and eloquence as an advocate, and his gifts were never used except for the cause of justice and right. In whatever position he was placed, he was always distinguished.[6]

While no records exist in the personal papers of the Ballous or the state legislature, it was evident that much happened behind the scenes.

The Republican nomination for the vacant congressional seat of retiring congressman Nathaniel Durfee, the one to which Ballou aspired, proved troublesome in all respects. The party could not agree on a candidate. It was split, likely along radical-conservative lines, between attorneys Thomas Davis and Christopher Robinson, so both went on the ballot. In the April 7 election, neither Republican nor the single Democrat won a clear majority. In a runoff election held on June 22, Christopher Robinson won the seat by 730 votes. And so it did turn out that the "politically significant" law case in Cumberland paid off—but for the senior counsel, not the junior one, Sullivan Ballou. Rhode Island's other congressional seat was held by a south state Republican in his second term and was not up for grabs.

Perhaps Sullivan had aimed too high, too young, because Rhode Island tended to send to Washington men who had much more experience than he did in 1860. Men with a decade in the General Assembly, a former attorney general, two former governors, these were the credentials of the current congressional delegation. Just as the legislature divided its meetings between the two main population centers of Providence and Newport, so the state tended to alternate between northern and southern counties in choosing whom to elect for various offices. It was a delicate balancing act.

Newport, a southern Rhode Island seaport, had become depopulated after the Revolutionary War after the British expelled the Jews and burnt a goodly section of the thriving coastal town, including the residence of one of the signers of the Declaration of Independence. Newport never recovered its prominence, lost much of its impetus to growth, and closely guarded its prerogatives to a fair share of state government.

Providence, on the other hand, was attracting all the growth, and its satellite cities in the northern half of the state were also expanding. The 1842 Constitution went to some pains to prevent Providence from dominating the state. The State Constitution guaranteed each town at least one representative—and one state senator—but stated that no town could have more than one-sixth of the state's representatives. This meant that the large population of Providence, competing with Warwick, Bristol, Tiverton, Kingston, Woonsocket, Newport, and a host of others, was always underrepresented. It also meant that only so many aspiring politicians could live in the state capital, because the competition for office was too intense for most of them to get elected.

This time around, Woonsocket, ably represented by the distinguished Robinson, got the nod for the congressional seat. When and if Robinson was through with it, the seat would rotate to another town, so there was little point in Sullivan expecting to get the nomination in a few years . . . assuming he remained in Woonsocket. All things considered, it would have been awkward for the young man to openly begrudge the success of his older, more experienced friend and benefactor.

Still ambitious, Sullivan evidently calculated that he needed to take steps to reposition himself—geographically and careerwise—because, in 1859, he started making some major changes in his life. For the last four years—the length of their marriage—Sarah had been the person experiencing the biggest life changes and needing to make the biggest adjustments. Starting in 1859, it was now Sullivan's turn. Rogers said,

> At the close of his second year of legislative office, he persistently declined re-election, having determined to apply himself with undivided attention to the engrossing cares of his profession.[7]

Members of the General Assembly were prohibited by conflict of interest rules adopted in 1842 from representing clients on business before the legislature. Sullivan might have determined there was more money to be made in private practice, utilizing his extensive contacts, than there was from the $50-odd a year he made as a legislator.

Sullivan's eye was on large cases for governments or corporations. The State paid $1,100 to the law firm that litigated the border dispute with Massachusetts. Abraham Lincoln earned a $5,000 fee in a railroad case. An attorney handling a libel suit brought by New York Buchanan supporters against the Republican Party earned a $2,000 fee.[8] Sullivan could practice law, build up his personal financial position, and try for higher office later; remaining in the legislature was not absolutely necessary for a career in politics.

During the first half of 1859, Sullivan established a new partnership with attorney Charles F. Brownell, and moved his practice to the city of Providence. Brownell was a bachelor, a few years younger than Ballou, and the son of a prominent physician. He and Sullivan had been clerks of the House together in 1855, before Brownell moved over to the Senate as clerk. Their offices were on

Weybosset Street, downtown, near the Salt Cove. It is likely these two partners occupied a typical young lawyer's office, practicably furnished, not as fancy as some in town, and located on a lower floor of their building. Only the town's most venerable attorney, Richard Green, dared take an office on an upper floor that required his clients to climb two flights of stairs.

Providence was the economic, social, and governmental capital of the state, and Sullivan could score more major cases there than in Woonsocket. As one contemporary put it, after "a few years, [Woonsocket] also became too cramped for him, and he opened an office in the city of Providence."[9] For his new assignment Sullivan published notices in the local newspapers, held public hearings in the Senate Chambers, and started research on an extremely complex maze of riparian land rights, tracking the land ownership back some 230 years and obtaining the earliest land records of the colony, including some from "the Indian bag," which contained the contracts the first settlers had made with the Narragansett.

In addition to this assignment, two events stood out above the routine in the usual fall bustle to get ready for winter in New England. The happy one was the Ballous' fourth wedding anniversary as a loving and devoted couple. They prided themselves on their modern relationship; he talked to her openly and equally, as many an older man would not. Her opinions were always heard, and he provided no interference in the things that were hers to manage. She had help and support when she needed it, but her independence was always encouraged. Their relationship had a good balance and they were proud of all they had built and accomplished in so short a time.

Following right on the heels of their anniversary was the latest, bizarre episode of bloodshed in the struggle against slavery. The John Brown raid at Harper's Ferry occurred on October 16, 1859, and dominated the newspaper headlines and church sermons for months.

The setting of the raid was the sturdy little hamlet of Harper's Ferry, nestled against the scenic golden hillsides of one of America's most beautiful river gorges, where the Potomac and Shenandoah rivers crashed together. Thomas Jefferson called this site "one of the most stupendous of nature . . . worth a voyage across the Atlantic."[10]

Railroad bridges spanned both rivers, making Harper's Ferry a key railroad junction. It held major stockpiles of weapons in a rifle factory, as well as in a federal arsenal established at this strategic spot by George Washington himself. Under cover of darkness, abolitionist John Brown of Pottawatomie Massacre fame, described as:

> a stone eroded to a cutting edge
> By obstinacy, failure and cold prayers
> And with a certain minor prophet air
> That fooled the world to thinking him half great[11]

raided the town to seize the weapons to arm a slave uprising he hoped to trigger. Twenty-one men, three of whom were his sons, rode with him. After taking sixty local persons hostage, including the great-grandnephew of George Washington, Colonel Lewis Washington, they seized the arsenal, rifle works, and railway facilities. They halted a Baltimore and Ohio Railroad train on the bridge, killing a guard and a porter before letting the train continue.[12]

After daybreak, local residents and militia pinned down the raiders in the railway's gatehouse in a dead-end area of the town. Brown and his followers waited, expecting to be joined by thousands of rebellious slaves whom they unrealistically expected to flock to their cause in this well-guarded canyon. Brown planned to lead this "army of emancipation" to free the slaves of Virginia, followed by those in the rest of the South.

The slaves never came, but the U.S. Marines did. Colonel Robert E. Lee brought them in by railroad, then a unique way to move troops. Lee sent Lieutenant J. E. B. Stuart to offer Brown terms of surrender. When no terms could be reached, Stuart's men assaulted the position, on Lee's signal. In the ensuring firefight, twenty-three men mingled their blood with the red autumn leaves, fifteen killed and eight wounded. The dead included two of Brown's sons, the mayor of Harper's Ferry, and a marine. Five of Brown's men were never captured and escaped to Canada.

John Brown and his surviving followers were jailed in nearby Charlestown, whose residents trembled in fear of a retaliatory attack. The Ballous followed the developing story via reports telegraphed to key newspapers. The major newspapers of the North and South squared off to comment and hurl invective at each other until autumn turned to winter.

The Concord *New Hampshire Patriot* condemned the loss of life "wantonly taken away by lawless violence." In Milledgeville, Georgia, the *Federal Union* alleged that "this was a regularly concocted, and premeditated attempt of Abolition Fanatics to overthrow the Government, and emancipate the slaves." In Ohio, the *Cincinnati Enquirer* was droller: "the negros of Virginia are not insurrectionally inclined."[13]

New England was sharply divided over the Harper's Ferry Raid. Some of the most radical abolitionists sided with Brown, raised money for his defense, and offered to look after his family. In Rhode Island, the Republican *Providence Journal* labeled the raid a "foolish, riotous, and bloody work. All lovers of good order and decency and peace will unite in uttering their abhorrence of this mad and criminal attempt."[14] The *Journal* insisted that the South must give Brown a fair trial, and the *Woonsocket Patriot* urged "Of their guilt . . . there can be no doubt . . . but they are entitled to sufficient time to prepare for trial."[15]

Brown's trial began just eleven days after the raid, and finished four days later. He was convicted of treason against the State of Virginia,* a capital crime, and two lesser charges.

* The last time the crime of treason against a *state* was prosecuted was Thomas Dorr's 1842 Rhode Island Rebellion.

The *Woonsocket Patriot* published its opinion on John Brown's imminent demise: "he should no more be hung than . . . James Buchanan."[16] But hung he was on December 2, 1859, as Major Thomas J. Jackson, commanding the cadets of the Virginia Military Institute, deployed to Charlestown as a security force, prayed for his repentance and salvation.[17]

Throughout New England, church bells tolled and rallies were held in sympathy. In Rhode Island, the church bells remained silent, and a single, tame meeting was held, attended by a mixed crowd of free Blacks, Brown supporters and detractors. Shock waves of indignation and accusation continued to roll across America. The eminent Black spokesman, Frederick Douglass, deemed it prudent to flee to Canada, because his correspondence with Brown caused some to perceive him as an accomplice.

Sullivan Ballou's thoughts on the John Brown raid were not recorded. Despite having the antislavery beliefs of a radical Republican, he was probably too much a legalist to approve.[18] His work on the Report of the Woonasquatucket River Committee demonstrates his reverence for the law, and for courses of action that have a legal basis. Most likely he sided with the majority of Rhode Islanders who believed Brown was a criminal.

However noble the goal, or righteous the cause, the sad fact was that John Brown's act of terrorism blew away any remaining chance at reconciliation between North and South. It sounded the death knell of compromise and the various fusion party efforts at the national level; the existing parties became even more rigid.

The thirty-sixth Congress of the United States convened for its first session on December 5, 1859, new congressman Christopher Robinson in attendance, just three days after John Brown's execution. The Democrats controlled the Senate, but no one knew who controlled the House, because neither party held a clear, loyal majority. The fight over the Speakership went on, with the House in disarray and unable to conduct business for two months, until

February 1, 1860.[19] The Southern Democrats paralyzed the House in retaliation for Republican funding of 100,000 copies of the 420-page antislavery tome *The Impending Crisis*, written by a white abolitionist Carolinian.[20]

The former Speaker of the Rhode Island House did not have much spare time to monitor this particular political white-water raft ride. Despite leaving the legislature, Sullivan continued with the heavy workload of the special committee. It seems impossible that he was not paid a fee for this work, but no such payment is recorded directly to him by the legislature. Unless it went through another firm, it must have been pro bono. He held public hearings on January 5, 11, and 18, 1860, then it was time to write the report.

Reading his words on paper is the closest approximation of watching him in court, laying out his arguments, explaining the proper conclusions to be drawn, and asking for a specific action. In this case, his jury was the seventy-one members of the House. The forty-four-page printed report is a showpiece of elegant phraseology, impeccable grammar, intelligent organization, and careful legal reasoning. He wrote,

> The filling up of the Cove, for railroad purposes, so greatly benefiting and improving the city of Providence, has brought these salt marshes in the Woonasquatucket valley into close proximity with the centre of the city, added much to their value and importance . . .[21]

After a lengthy review of the legal principles at stake, Sullivan wrote the government's rights included "power over all sea shores and tide water" to be held "in trust for the public."[22] Without such protections, all beachfront land would have been in private hands with no public access.

He spent several pages laying out the precedents established by the governing bodies of all levels of Rhode Island government and described a clear pattern where these agencies believed and acted as if they had jurisdiction, so that the issue was "definitely and unalterably settled." He also reviewed U.S. Supreme Court decisions on tidewaters.[23]

Sullivan left no stone unturned and no argument unanswered. It was a most thorough analysis, written in plain language so the one hundred members of the state legislature—most of whom were not attorneys—could understand it. If the vote went against the landowners, Sullivan knew the matter could tie up the courts for years, and so he urged the matter be referred directly to the Supreme Court to prevent all the intervening litigation. He turned in his report and waited.

In February 1860, Providence buzzed with the news that the famous orator, Abraham Lincoln, was coming to New England. The 1858 Lincoln-Douglas debates had brought Lincoln a measure of national fame, and he was considered the foremost spokesman for Republicanism. The official reason for his journey was to check on his seventeen-year-old son, Robert Lincoln, now attending Phillips Academy at Exeter, to prepare for college.

Lincoln's last visit to the Northeast had been twelve years ago. Now, the region was a stronghold of the Republican Party, and Lincoln, as an aspiring presidential candidate, thought he might test the depth of these waters along the route of his journey on a trip underwritten by a contract to speak at a church in Brooklyn for a $200 honorarium and travel expenses.[24]

Eager for a hot bath and change of clothes after three days spent in smoky and uncomfortable railroad cars, a rumpled Lincoln checked into the elegant Astor House Hotel in New York City. There he was handed a stack of invitations from Republican leaders clamoring to have the powerful speaker appear in their hometown.[25] He also learned that the venue of his New York speech had been moved from Brooklyn to the larger and more prestigious Cooper Union Hall in Manhattan.[26]

The next day, Lincoln had a few hours of rest before embarking on a grueling schedule. He reviewed the speech he was to give that evening and declined most of the invitations. He agreed to speak the following day in Providence, Rhode Island. Providence attorney John Eddy, a man as tall as Lincoln and twice as wide, and another former clerk of the House, hoped the Rail-splitter could persuade the Cotton Whigs of Providence, the powerful textile manufacturers, to support and fund the Republican Party in Rhode Island.[27]

The Cooper Union speech is the only fully transcribed version from that speaking tour, because Lincoln gave copies of his speech to the New York press who, by publishing it, preserved it for history. Except for some extemporaneous remarks topical to each locality, it was basically the same speech he was to give throughout New England during February and March 1860. The enthusiasm of his audience at Cooper Union and the simple elegance of the speech gained Lincoln rave reviews from the press, which resulted in even more invitations to speak throughout the Northeast. He accepted as many as he could fit in, while still leaving some private time with his son, Robert.[28]

To keep his appointment in Providence, Lincoln boarded an 8 A.M. northbound train and journeyed for eight hours, changing trains and ferries. His host met him and took him home for dinner, where legend held that Lincoln gave red gumdrops to little Alfred Eddy.[29]

After dinner, they set off for Railroad Hall, a huge assembly hall on the second floor of the downtown railroad depot. There, an overflow crowd heard Lincoln's speech, while those who could not gain entry gathered by the railroad tracks outside. Three-term governor William Hoppin, a moderate Republican, called the room to order, and Thomas A. Jenckes introduced the speaker. The local press reported on the size of the crowd, Lincoln's good humor and pleasant satire, saying he seemed a man of "thorough honesty and of sincere and earnest belief in all that he says."[30]

It is likely Woonsocket's leading Republicans were present and persuasive because, that very evening, Lincoln agreed to speak in Woonsocket on his way back to New York later that month.[31] Latimer and Sullivan Ballou may have played a role in this invitation. Having secured Lincoln's promise to speak, a Woonsocket organizing committee was surely formed, for that was the Rhode Island way of things.

The morning of the event, March 8, the wives and adult daughters of the male committee members decorated the hall with patriotic bunting, flags, and whatever greenery could be cut from the snow-covered lanes and gardens. Sarah Ballou was probably a participant. Meanwhile, the Republicans of Woonsocket had organized one of the most unique and touching welcomes Lincoln had experienced on his tour:

Not wanting their guest to make the forty-five-minute commute by railroad from Providence to Woonsocket alone, some five hundred Republicans paid fifty cents apiece to take the train down to Providence to join Lincoln on the journey. The American Brass Band accompanied them.[32] Although older, higher-status members more likely waited in Woonsocket to receive Mr. Lincoln, Sullivan may have been part of Lincoln's escort on this half-hour journey. When this party train pulled into Woonsocket, the throng bore

The Woonsocket railway station. *Courtesy of the Rhode Island Historical Society, artist unknown.*

Lincoln along on their tide of goodwill to Harris Hall. There, a packed house awaited him.

The crowd saw before them a craggy-faced, lean man, a man who, when he rose to speak, moved ungracefully in his tallness, yet was at ease on the platform. Although his clothes were rumpled from travel, and ill fitting, he nevertheless exuded a quiet confidence.

From his place on the platform, the speaker saw a sea of Yankees, the ladies practically elegant rather than ostentatious, the men well tailored in somber winter coats, their top hats perched on their knees.

Latimer introduced Lincoln, who delivered "one of his most powerful addresses," speaking so forcefully for two hours that his tie went awry.[33] His topic was slavery, specifically the national debate over the Kansas-Nebraska territories. Devoid of his usual prairie witticisms but full of style and humor, his words led his listeners step by step through the wording of the Constitution on property rights and an interpretation of the intentions of the men who wrote it, and the crowd roared its approval.

Taken at the New York Brady studio ten days before he spoke in Woonsocket, this is the beardless face of Abraham Lincoln that Sullivan and Sarah first knew. *Photo by Matthew Brady from the Library of Congress Prints and Photographs Division.*

Lincoln noted that the words "slave" and "slavery" are nowhere to be found in the Constitution, and that "an inspection of the Constitution will show that the right of property in a slave is not distinctly and expressly confirmed." Indeed, the Constitution speaks only of debts to be paid off in labor, as in apprenticeships or indentured servants [a seven-year labor contract].[34]

Lincoln then changed the tempo of his speech, beginning a dialogue with absent Southern opponents—"if they would listen,—as I suppose they will not"—using humor to keep his audience with him. He wondered why people who "in the general qualities of reason and justice . . . are not inferior to other people," persist in calling Republicans "reptiles, or, at the best, as no better than outlaws. . . ." He avowed that no speaker has the

> right to mislead others, who have less access to history, and less leisure to study it, into the false belief that "our fathers who framed the government under which we live" were of the same opinion—thus substituting falsehood and deception for truthful evidence and fair argument. . . .[35]

He had started the speech with one of his usual, moderate statements about the reality of slavery in the South:

> Wrong as we think slavery is, we can yet afford to let it alone where it is, because that much is due to the necessity arising from its actual presence . . . but can we . . . allow it to spread into the national Territories, and to overrun us here in these free States?[36]

And he continued the theme by saying,

> Republican doctrines and declarations are accompanied with a continual protest against any interference whatever with

> your slaves, or with you about your slaves. Surely this does not encourage them to revolt. . . . Occasional poisonings from the kitchen and open or stealthy assassinations in the field, and local revolts extending to a score or so, will continue to occur as the natural results of slavery; but no general insurrection of slaves, as I think, can happen in this country for a long time. Whoever much fears, or much hopes, for such an event, will be alike disappointed. . . .[37]

Chuckles from the audience and applause interrupted him, but he talked on, still addressing the South, but smoothly turning the event into a Republican campaign rally:

> There is a judgment and a feeling against slavery in this nation which cast at least a million and a half of votes. . . . You will not abide the election of a Republican president! In that supposed event, you say, you will destroy the Union: and then, you say, the great crime of having destroyed it will be upon us! . . .
>
> Your purpose, then plainly stated, is that you will destroy the government, unless you be allowed to construe and force the Constitution as you please, on all points in dispute between you and us. You will rule or ruin in all events. . . .

He stated that the only way to satisfy the South was to stop calling slavery wrong, to which effect Senator Douglas had introduced a new sedition law, a "wrong law," to make it illegal to say "in politics, in presses, in pulpits, or in private," that slavery is wrong.[38] He urged Southern politicians to return to the Constitution, "let all the guaranties those fathers gave it be not grudgingly, but fully and fairly, maintained." His final words to the audience in Woonsocket were not only a personal pledge but a statement of what later became the core values of his presidential administration:

> Neither let us be slandered from our duty by false accusations against us, nor frightened from it by menaces of destruction to the government, nor of dungeons to ourselves. Let us have faith that right makes might, and in that faith let us to the end dare to do our duty as we understand it.[39]

Lincoln had treated his listeners as intelligent people, and this was flattering to them. It was the kind of speech a lawyer might make to a jury, and the Rhode Islanders loved it, just as New Yorkers had. His listeners had to have gone away pleased with their newfound ability to understand the ins and outs of this complicated issue. The speech followed the precepts of good rhetoric as Sullivan knew them.

Sullivan could have come away with much more than the average listener. Renowned locally as an excellent speaker, sharing Lincoln's height and slim build, he would have eagerly observed this nationally renowned orator, some twenty years his senior, curious to see how he gestured and moved. Hopefully, he opted not to copy Lincoln's habit of bending his knees just before he made a key point, only to straighten them and rise back up to his full height to emphasize the statement he was making.

After the speech, Lincoln was the guest of the Harris family at dinner and overnight. Whether the guest list included the committee members was not noted, though the Harris family recalled the tall westerner leading his very diminutive hostess, Mrs. Harris, into dinner, and telling her, with tongue in cheek, that the only possible solution to the slavery crisis was to send all the slaves back to Africa.[40]

The next morning, Lincoln headed off to make his last two speeches in New England before going home to Illinois to confer with his campaign managers; the presidential nominating conventions were only three months away. The *New York Tribune* said of his swing through New England, "Mr. Lincoln has done a good work and made many warm friends."[41] Lincoln's impact on Rhode Island had been profound. For the Ballous, it was life altering.

At this point, Sullivan made another career move. Perhaps tired of spending one and a half hours on the trains each day, along with the cost of the railroad fares, he moved his home closer to his law practice in Providence. Possibly, too, as Edgar approached school age, the Ballous were troubled that Bernon Village did not have its own schoolhouse, but held classes in a building rented for that purpose from the Woonsocket Company.[42] Sullivan opted not to move into Providence itself, where any good locale was going to be too expensive, and where the competition for its fixed number of seats in the government too intense.

Instead, he moved to Cranston, a suburb four miles south of Providence and fifteen miles south of Woonsocket. For a man who had lived all his life in northern Rhode Island, and whose wife was comfortably settled into a social environment there, this was a huge upheaval. It took them away from friends and family, but did place them in an affluent, up-and-coming suburb of the newly wealthy.

The town was allowed two representatives and a senator.[43] The city of Cranston had a population just under five thousand, slightly bigger than Pawtucket, and although it had the inevitable mills, it was mostly farmland and nurseries; in the nineteenth century, it was home to many ice works. It was crisscrossed with ponds, rivers, brooks, and streams, flowing eastward into Narragansett Bay. The neighborhood that the Ballous chose was served by two railroads and an omnibus company providing commuter service to Providence.[44]

By July 10, when the Federal Census was taken, the Ballous were settled in that part of Cranston known as Elmwood,* which bordered South Providence, starting just below the triangle of the new Grace Church cemetery. They lived at the corner of Peace and Elmwood

* In 1868, Elmwood was annexed to Providence and remains within its municipal boundaries in the present day.

streets, a tree-lined north–south thoroughfare in a neighborhood of attractive, mostly two-story, wood frame houses.

Sullivan and Sarah's new house was two stories, with a lot large enough to keep their own cow. Living with them that year was thirteen-year-old Catherine Curry, daughter of an old Providence family, and an Irish maid of all work, thirty-five-year-old Mary Block.

Their neighbors included cotton and rubber manufacturers; there were also small family units of less-glorified occupations: a jeweler, a coachman, laborers, a boot maker, and a laundress. These were Black, mulatto, and Irish, many of them owning their own homes. Within Elmwood, there were wealthy districts, a haven for the rich folks who wished to escape the growing commercialization of downtown Providence; the town also had areas where the lower middle class could afford to buy property, and became one of the first neighborhoods where the Irish built their own houses. The low cost of housing might have been another reason that made Elmwood attractive to Ballou.[45] The tax rate was moderate, only thirty cents to the dollar.

In the decade before they moved there, many tracts of land in Cranston had been subdivided by Providence business investors, intent on developing Elmwood as an attractive, middle-class neighborhood, with wide streets lined with stately elm trees. These investors, however, did not get rich. One prominent builder in the 1850s was Joseph Cooke, another was S. V. Potter, who built a tract of brick houses intended for sale or rent. Cooke's tract took some ten years to build sixty houses, and Potter's was a business failure, both perhaps hurt by the recession of 1857. Potter died, and the land was put up for sale. Charles H. Tompkins, cashier of the Mercantile Bank, and captain of the Marine Artillery, cosigned a one-year mortgage contract for $10,000 with his wife, Jane, to purchase four square blocks of land and buildings along Elmwood Street, between Peace and Plenty streets, in Cranston. Tompkins held the rights to rent out any premises on the land, and promised to make semiannual interest payments in advance.[46] The Ballous were apparently tenants of the Tompkins, whom Sullivan may have known through business dealings. The Tompkins lived nearby, with their year-old daughter.[47]

In the flurry of moving, Sullivan seemed not to have completed his voter registration paperwork because, not until their meeting of April 2, 1861, did the town council of Cranston add him to the voting rolls by Certificate of Real Estate; it was done as a correction prior to that year's April election.[48]

Sullivan had relocated, but nothing had been resolved in the key conflicts paralyzing America. Buchanan still harangued Congress about the need to build a transcontinental railroad, but the railroad was stalled. The only way for Americans to get to their Pacific Coast was by wagon train across the North American continent; by a long and dangerous ocean voyage around the tip of South America; or by ship to Panama, by donkey trains across the fever-ridden isthmus, and onto another ship to cross the remaining ocean. Americans taking the latter route were still being attacked. President Buchanan was ready to declare war on Columbia for not controlling the banditos in the steamy jungles of its distant Central American provinces.

In this atmosphere, the Rhode Island state elections of April 1860 took place amid a great clash of ideologies. So many of the Cotton Whigs were still hurting economically from the Panic of 1857 that they remained reluctant to do anything to antagonize the South, the source of their raw cotton and the buyers of their cloth. Their main issue was holding onto their wealth. In Rhode Island, as in Massachusetts, it was said that they were allied with the slave-owning cotton producers.

For the past two years, the textile barons had tried unsuccessfully to form several versions of some new party but were unsuccessful. The Republicans ran a radical/abolitionist ticket for the state offices in Rhode Island, headed by Seth Padelford. Padelford had ties to prominent abolitionists Lawrence, Hale, and other backers of the Emigrant Aid Society who had armed settlers in Bleeding Kansas.[49] The supporters of those Republicans who lost the party nomination to Padelford joined with Democrats and the textile barons to nominate a fusion candidate on a "Conservative" ticket that opposed war. The campaign evidently captured public interest, because double the number of voters turned out over the previous year's election. The results were:[50]

Governor	William Sprague (Providence)	12,278
	Democrat/Conservative	
	Seth Padelford, (Providence)	10,740
	Republican/Radical	
Lt. Governor	J. Russell Bullock (Bristol)	12,240
	Stephen N. Mason (Smithfield)	11,050
Attorney General	Walter S. Burgess (Cranston)	12,064
	Thomas A. King (North Providence)	11,139
Secretary of State	John R. Barlett (Providence)	23,341
	unopposed for 5th term	
Treasurer	Samuel A. Parker (Newport)	23,346
	unopposed for 6th term	
	Both previously elected as Know-Nothings	

The textile interests of Providence gave Sprague fully half his margin of victory, voting Conservative 3,578 to 2,761. He was a bachelor, twenty-nine years old and heir to a Cranston textile fortune. He served with the Providence Marine Corps of Artillery, one of the state's militia units. Southern interests were so overjoyed at this rebuke to abolitionism, so happy at results so sympathetic to their cause, that Savannah, Georgia, fired a hundred-gun salute in honor of Sprague's victory—an action that would seem incomprehensible only a year later.[51]

That same spring, the same drama played out on the national

stage. The breakdown of America herself was foreshadowed by the breakdown of her political parties. While this process had been ongoing for some ten years, the spring of 1860 brought the same kind of disaster to the major political parties as the John Brown raid brought to general public opinion. This political chasm would never be closed, and forevermore made America a different place. Come April 1860, no candidate for president could run a campaign that was truly national—because there was no political party that still operated nationwide.[52]

The location of the quadrennial presidential nominating conventions of American political parties was always important, but that year, the choice of cities played an unusually critical role for all the parties. It was customary for the Democrats to choose their candidate first. Alas for the Union, in April 1860, the Democrats convened their convention in beautiful Charleston, the most militant of Southern cities, and the one most vocal in defense of continued slavery—a city unforgiving of compromise.

After ten days, and more than fifty-seven ballots, the Democrats failed to select a candidate. Although the forty-seven-year-old orator from Illinois, Stephen Douglas, "The Little Giant," was the front-runner, he could not muster sufficient votes to win the nomination. At this point, the delegations of some states, approximately one-sixth of the total delegates, "seceded" from the convention.[53]

It was deemed prudent to adjourn the convention for six weeks to allow for further campaigning and the subsidence of tempers that had flared out of control. The Democrats reconvened in Baltimore on June 18, with competing Southern delegations clamoring for credentials. For another six days, the convention struggled to select a candidate. The first ballot of this convention was inconclusive because the Southerners withheld their votes altogether, denying Douglas the nomination.

His people gave up on trying to reason with the Southern delegates and introduced a simple resolution declaring Douglas "unanimously elected" as the candidate. This passed by simple majority—the Northern votes.[54] The "Great Orator" was now the Democratic nominee. Or was he?

The Southern Democrats walked out, rented another hall in Baltimore, and the next day nominated their own candidate, the currently serving vice president, John Breckenridge, from Kentucky.[55] President Buchanan promptly endorsed Breckenridge.

In the interim, the Republican convention had been held in Chicago in May. This was the westernmost venue to date for any U.S. political convention, and reflected the growing significance of the electoral votes of Illinois and the other midcontinent states. The level of energy released at this convention was unlike anything seen before; it was the crusading zeal of a political movement that knew its time had come at last.

The 1860 Republican Convention was the most exciting political event ever seen in America up to that point. The delegates assembled from all over the nation, meeting in "the Wigwam," a brand-new hall specially built for the convention. All white males, they nonetheless reflected the diversity of the states, occupations, and economic strata of the nation. Swarms of people traveled into Chicago, filling all the hotels and boardinghouses. The ten-thousand-seat Wigwam was always packed to the rafters, and crowds of twice that number assembled outside the building. Liquor flowed freely—this was not a temperance convention, despite earlier flirtations with that plank. Cases of champagne were shipped to the convention, along with carloads of political supporters.[56] The Lincoln team had planned an effective floor strategy: They printed extra admission tickets to the Wigwam, and made sure these were put in the hands of Lincoln supporters, men specially chosen for their ability to yell loudly and cheer for their candidate at the critical moments. They were successful in packing the hall with the enthusiastic claque.[57]

Abraham Lincoln and his team of handlers from Illinois developed and waged a brilliantly effective campaign strategy. The Republicans, after all, would not be on the ballot in all states; they would not be on the ballot in the South at all. They could only win the presidency of the nation if they could nominate a candidate who could capture the heavily populated Northern manufacturing states, the key Midwest states, and at least some of the border states. His advisors used four successful approaches to make sure the delegates knew Lincoln was that man: Lincoln took care not to be the front-runner, on whom all other candidates would focus their attacks. His team positioned him as a moderate and centrist candidate. If the abolitionist Eastern politicians seemed too rabidly antislavery, he presented a choice—a man of reason who had shown in his Cooper Union address that he could assess the pros and cons of any issue. Also, Lincoln carefully avoided becoming a warmonger; any look at his record of debates from the past four years showed he never proposed abolishing slavery in the South itself. He was presented as the ideal second-choice candidate, once it became apparent that the front-runners were too radical to accumulate sufficient electoral votes for victory. Born in Kentucky, and a favorite son of Illinois, he was also likely to carry nearby Indiana. Finally, momentum would work in their favor; "they were in position to show startling gains as the first choice candidacies evaporated."[58]

Lincoln was selected on the third ballot of the Republican convention, and the vice presidential nod went to Maine Senator Hannibal Hamlin, a former Democrat, selected for his "sterling integrity and nice sense of honor."[59]

Next on the agenda was the platform, which denounced secession, efforts to reopen the African slave trade, the extension of slavery into the territories, and John Brown's raid as "among the greatest of crimes." It supported tariffs, the transcontinental railroad, the right of new citizens to vote, and the Homestead Act, twice blocked by the Buchanan administration.[60]

The delegates were in high spirits. With the passage of the tariff plank in the platform the Pennsylvania delegation went into "spasms of joy . . . the whole delegation rising and swinging hats and canes."[61]

In May, the Constitutional Union Party nominated the fourth man running for president that year, John Bell of Tennessee, a former Speaker of the U.S. House of Representatives. Backed by border staters and some former Southern Democrats, he ran on a generic platform of support for the Union and the Constitution—whatever that meant. One wag noted,

> Everybody is eminently respectable, intensely virtuous, devotedly patriotic, and fully resolved to save the country. They propose to accomplish that political salvation so devoutly to be wished by ignoring all the rugged issues of the day.[62]

All four candidates began campaigning only in regions where they were strong—and on the ballot. One of the queer details of the 1860 "national" presidential election was that not all candidates' names were on the ballots in every state. Out of thirty-three states, Lincoln's name did not appear on the ballots of ten Southern states. Douglas was not on the ballot in Rhode Island, New York, or New Jersey. Bell did not appear on the previous three nor Minnesota and Michigan.[63] This further complicated each party's strategy, because of the need to amass enough of the national electoral vote total to win. For example, the ten less populous Southern states had an aggregate of only seventy-three electoral votes, just 24 percent of the national total—far short of the tally needed to elect a president. Without slaves, who counted as three-fifths of a white man in apportioning electoral votes, there would have been still fewer Southern electoral votes—another reason not to free slaves, according to statements of the time. Just three large Northern states, New York, Pennsylvania, and Illinois, counterbalanced the entire South.

A political cartoon showing the four presidential candidates in the 1860 election and the sectional schisms in America. *From* Harper's Weekly. *Library of Congress Prints and Photographs Division.*

Most of the candidates did not even attempt to campaign in all states. The absence of mass media, the rigors of campaign travel by train and buggy, the lack of voice amplification systems in large halls—all worked against candidates. The long distances between major cities—California was twenty days by stagecoach from St. Louis—meant the candidates stayed home and relied on others to get their message out.[64] Only Stephen Douglas broke with tradition and personally campaigned around the country, emphasizing the danger of disunion, and for this breach with tradition he was roundly criticized, as by the *Carolina Spartan*:

> We have fallen on evil times when the high office of President can be sought by arts of electioneering. Alas for our country . . . Shame! Shame![65]

Douglas wore himself out to the degree that his health broke down. In contrast, Abraham Lincoln opened an office in Springfield, Illinois, received callers, and wrote to a friend, "by the lessons of the past, and the united voice of all discreet friends, I am neither [to] write nor speak a word for the public."[66]

With the presidential candidate traditionally going undercover to avoid making a career-ending mistake, politicians relied on their own campaign "newspapers," which both raised funds and publicized their platform, on friendly general-circulation newspapers, and on a phalanx of speakers to relay their messages to the voters.

Many speakers relied on the "Wide Awakes," members of political clubs, who paraded through towns carrying torches, calling upon the citizens to "wake up" to the dangers facing the nation and elect a wary candidate who could solve them. They were showy, nouveau, and people turned out in droves to watch and listen.

All over Rhode Island, campaign clambakes, logistically suited to feeding the masses, were held at the seashore. Voters were served a huge feast of clams, fish, lobster, potatoes, and corn on the cob steamed in a pit lined with seaweed and rocks, with fried seafood, more vegetables, and watermelon for the last course.[67]

Some of the "wide awake" torches carried in after dark political parades for the Lincoln campaign. *Author's photo at Mystic Seaport.*

Encouraged by depictions like this one, the temperance movement swept over the North and was merged into the Republican Party reform platform. It never made similar inroads in the South. *Courtesy Alexander Anderson Scrapbook, Volume X, Print Collection, Miriam and Ira D. Wallach Division of Art, Prints and Photographs, the New York Public Library, Astor, Lenox and Tilden Foundations.*

Sullivan Ballou and the other Republicans of Rhode Island worked hard for Lincoln. Latimer Ballou was Lincoln's Rhode Island campaign chairman, and it was inconceivable that he did not use his cousin's talents to the utmost. Horatio Rogers, by then a fellow attorney, said of Sullivan Ballou,

> A radical republican in politics, he could not keep aloof from the exciting canvas of 1860, and he exerted himself to the utmost for the elevation of Abraham Lincoln to the presidency.[68]

The state only had four electoral votes but, if they went to Lincoln, they might offset those of California, a state whose voters were evenly split over slavery. Or, they might cancel out the four votes of proslavery Texas or Arkansas.[69]

As a local orator popular for his inspiring, patriotic style, Sullivan was in demand and undoubtedly spoke at many campaign-related events. After all, how often had a presidential candidate ever come to Woonsocket to solicit the votes of the people of the Ballou Neighborhood and the Cumberland? If he needed details of Lincoln's life, he could look them up in a long biographical guide that Lincoln had written for his campaign speakers to use.[70]

Political campaigns were often rough and tumble, filled with vitriolic cartoons and sarcastic jibes. The tall and gawky candidate's weak spot was his appearance, and his picture was rarely used, even in his own campaign materials. Pictures of vice presidential candidate Hannibal Hamlin, who had a patrician Roman nose and straight hair, could not be shown in the South, lest they contradict allegations printed in papers like the *Montgomery Mail*, which told its readers, "Hamlin, who is on the ticket with Lincoln, is a free negro and boasts of his African blood."[71] Southern newspapers voiced a fear of being ruled by Negroes. The *Memphis Enquirer* lamented,

> Think of it—a *nigger* in principle, elected President, and a mulatto, for Hamlin is said to be one, sitting as Vice President and presiding in the Senate. What Southern man could submit to sit under the shadow of such a creature? It would be disgraceful in the extreme.[72]

All of this was an example of the sort of thing Sullivan had to contend with while extolling the virtues of the Lincoln ticket.

This campaign effort—negative and positive—was directed only at those states where the Republican ticket was on the ballot. Because Lincoln was not on the ballot there, Southern papers carried little real coverage of his background, statements, or platform, just hyperbole that inflamed readers' fears. The *Atlanta Daily*

Intelligencer explained, "Mr. Lincoln having no party in our State, we have not thought it proper to spend much of our ammunition upon him."[73]

What little coverage found its way into print supplanted hard facts with melodrama. Incorrect assumptions were widespread—such as the Republican platform condoned racial equality, enfranchisement, and miscegenation. The *Athens* (Georgia) *Southern Banner* gave voice to the prevailing apprehension about the policies of a Republican administration that might

> build up an abolition party in the Southern States, who would distribute arms and strychnine among the slaves with which to murder their masters.[74]

Southern fear of the Republican ticket skyrocketed when Republican candidates swept to victory in the Northern state-level elections during October. For the first time, the South realized it might lose control of the White House. Anxious at the eleventh hour to know more about Abraham Lincoln, they turned for information to the most jingoistic and radical Northern newspapers, like Horace Greeley's abolitionist *New York Tribune*. It was ironic that as hard as Lincoln worked to choose his words to allay Southern fears, moved to the center, and proclaimed a policy to *not* terminate slavery in the Southern states, the very people for whom his moderate messages were intended never heard them. Below the Mason-Dixon Line, they knew only a caricature.

While women themselves did not yet vote, their behind-the-scenes influence might sway a few votes. Ladies went to public assemblies and dinners, but not to association or society meetings and dinners.[75] Sarah might have played a role in talking up Lincoln at ladies' teas, or organizing bake sales or dinners in support of the Lincoln-Hamlin ticket. This may have been the busiest social year since her marriage.

After weeks of bombast, the nation voted on Tuesday, November 6, 1860. Thanks to the new telegraph system, the country no longer needed to wait days or weeks to learn the election results. As soon as the states tabulated their votes, a courier raced the totals to the telegraph office so the figures could be sent to Washington and the big newspapers. Lincoln was one of the first to learn of his victory. On this election night, he began a pattern of behavior that he would follow throughout his years in the White House: sitting for hours at the telegraph office, waiting for critical news to come in. On November 6, it was the election returns; during the war it would be casualty figures and outcomes of major battles.

That same night, enough of the vote had come in to give Lincoln an unbeatable majority of electoral votes, and he knew he had won. He went home and called out to his wife, "Mary, we've been elected!"[76] The news flashed around most of the nation the next day, although it took three weeks to get to distant Oregon and California. In Rhode Island, the Ballou cousins rejoiced and celebrated late. The *Harrisburg Telegraph* November 7, 1860, printed a stirring report of the partisan jubilation:

THE UNION SAVED!
Lincoln Elected President!
Freedom and Free Labor Gloriously Triumphant!
Pennsylvania Gives "Old Abe" Sixty Thousand Majority—
An Avalanche of Republican Victories
Treason Crushed Out—The Fusionists Confused

We have received returns enough to indicate the Republicans have achieved one of the greatest victories ever gained, by any party, in this country . . . our sanctum and the street in front of the TELEGRAPH office are crowded with jubilant Republicans who make the welkin ring with cheers, as the reports roll in over the magnetic wires from every direction, bringing

> the glorious intelligence that State after State has gone for LINCOLN . . . The Wide Awakes are parading the streets, in uniform, with much and brightly burning torches, cheering enthusiastically as they pass through the city on their triumphal march.[77]

Abraham Lincoln won the presidency with only 39 percent of the popular vote. With four candidates running, the odds were stacked against anyone getting a clear majority. The placement of Lincoln's 39 percent, however, bore out the wisdom of his campaign managers—his popular vote totals were concentrated in the key states that had the most electoral votes. Lincoln carried all the free states except New Jersey, which split its votes, giving him half. By the time the most distant states reported in, Lincoln won with 180 electoral votes, 27 more than needed for victory. He won California by a mere thousand popular votes, but won the North with 55 percent of its votes. His greatest strength had been in rural New England and the Northeast. (Large cities, home to major populations of immigrants, voted Democratic. Lincoln lost seven of the eleven cities in the Northeast with populations of fifty thousand or more.[78])

Stephen Douglas, the Northern Democrat, ran second in the North and border states, collecting just half the popular vote Lincoln got. In electoral votes, Douglas won only Missouri and the other half of New Jersey. John Breckinridge, the Southern Democrat, won Delaware, Maryland, and the eleven Southern states. John Bell, the candidate of the Constitutional Union Party, won Virginia, Kentucky, and Tennessee.

The results proved to the South that her policy on admitting more federal territories to the Union as slavery states had been right. Without these additional states, the North could continue to outvote the South, as it had done in this election. It was not that the Southern states feared Lincoln the man, for they never knew him; Lincoln's attempts to mollify the South had little to no impact on that region. The real issue was that the South would not be mollified, would not be reassured, and would not engage in dialogue. It had made up its mind to secede if *any* Republican won.

Lincoln's victory was the South's second worst nightmare come true—the first being a widespread slave insurrection. As Southerners grappled with their fears, a few newspapers suggested giving him a chance, especially since the new Congress and Supreme Court were Democratic and proslavery. Other papers took their cue from the inevitable, over the top, "go get 'em Abe" hoopla that came out of his hometown newspaper and other radical papers; they vowed they would not live with the unfavorable election results. One Alabama paper intoned, "Lincoln never can be President of the Southern States."[79] Suggested another, "Would it not be better to [secede] immediately . . . while Buchanan and his Cabinet who are friendly to the South have the reins in their hands, than to wait till Lincoln and his Wide-Awakes get possession of the purse and the sword?"

In the frenzy that surrounded the Republican victory, the South searched for a way out. South Carolina was the first state to announce its intention to secede. At the time, the reaction in the North was blasé. In Springfield, the *Illinois Republican* said, "If South Carolina wants to go out of the Union, let her go and say no more about it."[80] So often had the Southern states cried the wolf of secession that few took them seriously, even when more states threatened to leave.

Senator Charles Sumner was happy to be rid of them; he was of the opinion that if up to five Southern states stayed away from Congress for a few months, their majority voting block in Congress would be broken and the nation might get some business done before they came back.[81] One Kentucky newspaper proclaimed,

> Their absence would be an incalculable and invaluable relief to the balance of the people of these United States. We should

> escape large quantities of quadrennial gas and noise and confusion . . . Every four years these Southern Quixote's swell up with bad whiskey and worse logic, and tell the balance of the people if they don't do so and so, . . . that they will secede. Let them secede and be—blessed. We are tired of their gasconade, their terrific threats . . . their bombast is absolutely sickening.[82]

In pro-Union Charlestown, Virginia, later West Virginia, the *Free Press* labeled the secessionists "pestiferous grumblers."[83]

The South fired back with all the fury of a spurned lover. The *New Orleans Daily Delta* opined,

> Why, then, should we desire to consort any longer with a people so antagonistic to us in feeling, principles and interest? Why, with one effort, not heave off this incubus, which is oppressing our energies, strangling our commerce and dwarfing the natural growth of our natural proportions?[84]

Slaveholders had held the presidency for fifty of the seventy-two years from 1789 through 1861. In all that time, no major party had ever expressed clear opposition to slavery until 1856. But in 1860, the party that won the election was explicitly committed to the position that the normal condition of all the territory of the United States was that of freedom."[85] During the three months before the Republicans took power, in ways both subtle and obvious the nation accelerated toward disunion.

Two weeks after the election, in the third week of November, a routine change of command took place at a fort in South Carolina. The arrival of a single army officer at his new command normally had little significance; in this case it was a minor transformation, destined to play a major role in national events. Major Robert Anderson, a former instructor in artillery tactics at West Point Military Academy, was assigned to command the garrison at Fort

Moultrie in Charleston, South Carolina. The fifty-five-year-old Kentuckian came from a distinguished military family: eight of his forebearers had served in the Revolutionary War. Fort Moultrie was an ironic and poignant assignment for Anderson, whose father had been captured by the British and imprisoned at Moultrie for nine long months. A career man himself, Anderson junior had inducted a young Abraham Lincoln into the militia during the Black Hawk War in 1834.[86]

En route to his new command, Anderson visited his mentor, General Winfield Scott, in New York City. The nation's military commander lived there instead of Washington, D.C., because President Buchanan neither sought his advice nor listened to his opinions on military issues. General Scott knew the layout of Charleston's defenses and that only five hundred men were deployed close enough to answer a summons for help. Scott encouraged his protégé to be alert for surprise attacks. Ever meticulous, Anderson next called on a military engineer who had spent five years working in the chain of forts in Charleston Harbor. From him, he learned the key defensive points of the complex.

Major Anderson left his ailing Georgia-born wife, Eliza Clinch Anderson, behind and went to Washington to receive his orders. The daughter of a general, she understood duty and the role of a military wife. Arriving at Fort Moultrie during Thanksgiving Week, Anderson sized up his command and found all he had to work with were two companies from the First Artillery and nine band members. Captain Abner Doubleday, an avid townball player and fan, and an outspoken Republican, commanded one company. The other officers were a brevet [honorary] captain and two lieutenants. The major's inspections of the fortifications revealed the situation to be more dismal than his briefings had warned; he telegraphed the capital with a request for reinforcements.

In 1860, Thanksgiving Day in New England dawned with the usual chill in the air; it was the last major holiday the Ballou family celebrated before the war. As in years past, families went to noon church services, where it was traditional for the minister to deliver a sermon on politics and the role of Christians in a democracy. In 1860, their duty toward the evil of slavery was preached throughout New England, albeit in varying shades of fervor.[87]

Long before it became a nationwide tradition, locals kept covenant with the memory of "pious forefathers," recognized the "civil and religious blessings" enjoyed by all, and celebrated the strength of the New England family. Even then a holiday of reunion, all families had their own traditions for expressing their pride in their "abundance and prosperity," with members traveling inconvenient distances by oxcart, sleigh, or carriage to celebrate together.[88]

In Washington, the Buchanans celebrated their last Thanksgiving in the White House, in and of itself reason for the president

Even in the 1850s family members traveled great distances to be together for New England Thanksgiving celebrations. If there weren't enough chairs, children stood behind their parents and ate standing up. *Alexander Anderson Scrapbook, Volume IV, Print Collection, Miriam and Ira D. Wallach Division of Art, Prints and Photographs, the New York Public Library, Astor, Lenox and Tilden Foundations.*

to be thankful. The president then turned his attention to his twenty-three-page State of the Union address. On December 3, 1860, he stood before the assembled Congress and noted that Northern agitation had so excited the slaves to insurrection that "a sense of security no longer exists around the family altar." He scolded the Northerners that they "have no more right to interfere than with similar institutions in Russia or in Brazil." The outgoing president urged the Southern states to "wait for some overt and dangerous act on the part of the President elect" before dissolving the Union, and urged the nation not to rush into war.[89]

He noted that the sum of $61 million [now $1.2 billion] had been allocated for the expenses of the federal government in 1861 and was expected to be sufficient. He chided the Thirty-sixth Congress for adjourning the previous March without appropriating any money for the Post Office, and noted that after no mail had gone out west for four months, Cornelius Vanderbilt had volunteered to carry the mail to California and the Pacific Coast on his own ships, out of goodwill and the hopes of eventual reimbursement from the government.[90]

The speech did not provide any position or course of action around which reasonable men could rally, so unreasonable men took action. Old allies stopped talking to Buchanan, his Cabinet members started resigning, and the president's fragile people skills evaporated as he snapped at everyone, driving away even old friends. Everyone in Congress vilified the president for one reason or another. Buchanan became so isolated that he actually telegraphed General Winfield Scott to come down to the capital.

"A sense of impending calamity hung in the air," Senator Grimes of Iowa noted, "secession of one or more States is inevitable." Senator Benjamin of Louisiana felt, "A revolution . . . of the most intense character" was imminent, and "I see not how bloodshed is to be avoided." Congressman McClernand of Illinois lamented, "A fanaticism, an infatuation has seized the minds of many."

South Carolina was fast tracking an ordinance of secession and threatening to seize the forts in Charleston Harbor. Buchanan's earlier interest in reinforcing Major Anderson's command now stalled under the barrage of opinions for and against it. In the second week of December, Eliza Anderson became so frantic about the danger her husband was in, that she took the train from New York and came to the White House to implore Buchanan to send troops. Although moved by her pleas, the president did not act, continuing to search in vain for a way out of the predicament. He feared triggering hostilities, and did not believe he could order the use of force to preserve federal custody of the forts. Open charges of "traitor" and "imbecile" were publicly hurled, and there was open talk of impeachment. General Scott had begun clandestinely briefing the president-elect, Abraham Lincoln, about the military situation.

Inflamed by a series of barn fires, known as the Texas Troubles, the Southerners feared their slaves were inflamed by Republican propaganda and would slay their masters in their sleep, as had happened to the brother of Senator Keitt at his Florida plantation. The South began to be seized by rumors of impending slave uprisings, supposedly timed to coincide with Christmas. On December 11, a newspaper in the state capital of Alabama, the *Montgomery Mail,* disclosed, "We are now whipping our negroes [to force confessions]. We hear some startling facts."[91] A North Carolina paper instructed,

> Let the slaves know that the first attempt at revolt will be met with speedy vengeance. And that every offender will be swung to the first tree. Le them know that the white men of the South have determined, whether the Union be dissolved or not, that they shall be obedient, submissive and quiet, and that they shall continue to serve their owners in the future as in the past.[92]

On December 20, South Carolina seceded from the United States. Secession in Charleston was celebrated as the first Independence Day had been, eighty-four years earlier: Marching bands played martial music, bonfires were lit in the streets, the Liberty Pole was lit, and cannons boomed. Rifle salutes were fired and the populace pinned blue cockades to their lapels as they surged through the streets. The Palmetto state flag was everywhere.

Still, Carolina was only one state, and had long been the most boisterous in crying for secession. The nation remained uncertain about what the trend would be, so celebrations were held as normal around the country for the Christmas holiday.

The Ballous celebrated Christmas with joy, still hopeful about success and prosperity. A beef or pork roast was the usual centerpiece of a festive dinner and everyone exchanged presents. American families now placed Christmas trees in their parlors, decorated with candles, gilt nuts, and edible confections. Their own future looked promising—the Republicans were rewarding Sullivan's efforts in Lincoln's campaign by offering him a chance at statewide office in the upcoming spring elections. One short month after Lincoln's inauguration, Sullivan would be on the ballot for attorney general of Rhode Island, hoping for a ride on Lincoln's coattails.

In Washington, D.C., the president's last holiday in the White House was not as happy as the Ballous'. On Christmas Day, the *Washington Constitution* blasted the president for his viewpoint that secession was illegal, while a blizzard howled outside. Members of Buchanan's Cabinet continued to resign, and a public scandal was brewing regarding a million dollars in Indian bonds "borrowed" by a relative of the Secretary of War.

Snow and ice were not the only things swirling around Washington. Secretary of War Floyd and Texas Senator Wigfall discussed participating in a plot underway by unknown perpetrators, a plot to kidnap the indecisive Buchanan and replace him with the current vice president, John Breckenridge, younger, more vigorous, and a Southerner. Floyd opted out and the plot was never successful. In Richmond, the capital of Virginia, the *Enquirer* printed Christmas tidings of comfort and joy:

> The hope of settlement . . . has been abandoned in Washington . . . no compromise that would protect Southern rights and Southern honor will be permitted by Mr. Lincoln and his party.

How this was determined "in Washington," before Lincoln ever set foot in the town, is not noted. The *Enquirer* then went on to suggest that Lincoln should never be allowed to set foot in Washington at all, a course of action that was both seditious and ominous:

> If Virginia and Maryland do not adopt measures to prevent Mr. Lincoln's inauguration at Washington, their discretion will be as much a subject of ridicule as their submission will be one of contempt.[93]

The church bells of Charleston pealed for Christmas Day over a changed city. The residents were giddy with a spirit that owed more to secession than to Christmas itself. The holiday notwithstanding, the Secession Commission met to work out details of seizing additional federal property, like the Post Office and Customs House. One burning question remained: What to do with the ring of federal forts at the Battery?

The federal defensive infrastructure in Charleston Harbor consisted of four forts, all designed to repel invaders from the sea. Three of these, Moultrie, Pinckney, and Johnston, were more or less connected to spits of land; the fourth, Sumter, was located on island that had been built from landfill in the middle of the harbor. Its only occupants during the holiday were the construction crews upgrading it; however, its armaments had already been installed and its magazines stocked with cannonballs and powder. A formidable fortress with walls sixty feet high and eight to twelve feet thick, it could only be seized with great bloodshed.

Major Anderson's federal military force of some sixty men and a few family members lived at Fort Moultrie, a crumbling edifice with cracked walls. Wave action had deposited enough sand on the beach adjacent to Fort Moultrie that high dunes had formed along two sides of the fort's walls—so tall that riflemen standing atop them could fire down into the fort.

That Christmas in Charleston, St. Nick and his reindeers were not the only ones sneaking around in the night. As rumors abounded that South Carolina was about to seize the forts, Major Anderson understood only too well that Sumter's guns could be trained on Fort Moultrie, which could never hold out against an attack.

Although telegrams flew between Washington and the arsenal in downtown Charleston, all of Major Anderson's reports and requests for reinforcements had been ignored; no orders came for him. He had to rely on the last set, the ones he had received personally from the secretary of war, one long month ago. Floyd had instructed him not to initiate war, to avoid bloodshed, to defend the forts if attacked, and to consolidate his men as the situation dictated. Major Anderson made up his mind to merge his forces within the stronger fort, Sumter, and planned to withdraw there unobserved on Christmas Day, when Charlestonians would be busy celebrating.

To this end, he chartered boats for the ostensible purpose of sending the women and children ashore. It rained all day December 25, so the major held off until the next day. Without revealing his true intentions, Major Anderson loaded four months of provisions and all the women and children onto some of the boats, and sent them off across the harbor on a tack toward Fort Johnston, with orders not to land. At sunset, giving his subalterns only twenty minutes notice, he ordered an evacuation to Sumter. At 6:00 P.M., Captain Doubleday's company marched to a rowboat, where he ordered his men to remove their military insignias. As the soldiers rowed their boat to Sumter, past the harbor patrol boats, they looked like workmen returning to work, and were not challenged. Doubleday then secured the fort, and sent the boat back to bring over the remaining troops.

Stealthily, under cover of darkness, the rest of the military forces and weapons were brought to Sumter. Only then were the women and children allowed to land. Next, any secession sympathizers among the construction workers were sent ashore, because only workmen loyal to the Union could be allowed to remain. By 8:00 P.M., Major Robert Anderson completed the transfer of his entire garrison, without being observed, and everyone was settling into their new quarters.

So successful was the undercover operation that, the next morning, they still had the opportunity to send boats back to retrieve all their hospital supplies, additional food, fuel, and personal effects. The housekeeper for the officer's mess was also brought over, with a ready-cooked meal. The cannons, which could not be moved, were set afire and burned, to prevent their use against Fort Sumter.

When the South Carolinians discovered the move, after seeing the smoke from the cannons, they insisted that Major Anderson and the garrison return to Fort Moultrie. He declined. He had bought time for the politicians at the cost of cutting himself off from all communication with the outside world. Now, sitting in the middle of Charleston Harbor, he would definitely obtain no reinforcements, no more weapons, no additional provisions, and no word from Washington, D.C. At noon on December 27, the troops, families, and 150 workmen gathered on the parade ground inside Fort Sumter. The band climbed up into the ramparts and played the "Star-Spangled Banner" as the Stars and Stripes was run up the flagpole to fly over the harbor—visible to all who lived in the South's most rebellious city.[94]

CHAPTER EIGHT

"The President Called on the Land for an Army"*

The Chain Reaction Cannot Be Stopped; America Splits Apart

January to April 15, 1861

In January 1861, the breakup of the United States accelerated. The ensuing turbulence began to buffet the Ballou family. Focused on his joy over Lincoln's election, the countdown to the start of the Lincoln presidency, and his own hopes to be a nominee for statewide office in the spring balloting, Sullivan did not yet fully apprehend how massively the cascade effect of secession was menacing his family and millions of other Americans. Still, he and Sarah sympathized with those brave soldier boys, immured in Fort Sumter, surrounded by enemies, and devoured every article about them with avid interest, as did all Northern newspaper readers.

When Major Robert Anderson's men first took over Fort Sumter, it was an unfinished construction site, "filled with building materials, guns, carriages, shot, shell, derricks, timbers, blocks and

* From the Civil War song "Paddy and the Know-Nothings."

tackle, and coils of rope in great confusion." Major Robert Anderson and his officers had to sort through all this and develop a realistic plan to defend this tiny, symbolic outpost of Union authority.

> The possibility of a sudden dash by the enemy, under cover of darkness and guided by the discharged workmen then in Charleston, demanded instant attention. It was impossible to spread 65 [men] over ground intended for 650, so some of the embrasures had to be bricked up. Selecting those . . . essential to artillery defense, and mounting guns in them, Anderson closed the rest.

Despite the threat of attack, the garrison still had food, and morale was kept strong by competitions of running 128-pound cannon shells up several flights of stairs to reposition the ammunition supply.[1]

As the small band of soldiers prepared their fort to withstand a Southern onslaught, it was ironic that the garrison at Fort Sumter was actually in less danger than was Abraham Lincoln that winter. On January 2, 1861, the *Washington Star* reported that "it seems that Messrs. Lincoln and Hamlin have both received anonymous letters threatening violent opposition to their inauguration."[2]

As did other Northern politicians and businessmen, Sullivan believed that once Lincoln was inaugurated and implemented his firm but fair policies, the threat of secession would wane. However, many in the South were afraid to wait and see.[3] Fearing the loss of decades of party and regional influence in Washington, appalled that the nation had elected such a humble man rather than a gentleman to the exalted post of president, afraid of Republican radicalism, the South acted upon its desperation.

Eliminating the incoming president by kidnap or assassination was well publicized and openly discussed in the South; the prevention of Lincoln's inauguration became an ominously persistent theme in the Southern papers. For those who dreaded a Lincoln presidency, the first two months of 1861 were spent evaluating the logistics of how best to accomplish the crime. Aware of the plotting, New York Republican leader Senator William Seward noted,

> It seems to me that the inauguration is not the most dangerous point for us. Our adversaries have us more clearly at disadvantage, on the second Wednesday of February when the votes should be officially counted.[4]

Reported plots to prevent counting of the electoral ballots, by interfering with the meeting of the electoral college, seemed to have little real chance at success.[5] Obstructing the actions of the electoral college on Wednesday, February 13, meant assaulting the Capitol Building and the entire United States Congress—actions that could backfire with the public as well as with the Confederacy's potential European allies, Britain and France.

Seizing the entire city seemed more practical, at least to Governor Gist of South Carolina, who pledged, "I will have a regiment in or near Washington in the shortest possible time."[6] However, the timing was still wrong for the South to send troops into the national capital, so the plotting went to ground for a few weeks, although the *Washington Star* reported in its January 17 edition that a visitor returned from Maryland reported, "10,000 men have been secretly organized in Maryland and Virginia to prevent inauguration of Lincoln."[7]

James Buchanan and his secretary of war, John B. Floyd, of Virginia, did not allow the federal military to take steps to "harden" the federal forts and arsenals located in Southern states, to improve their defenses. Neither did they remove any weapons or munitions. Floyd was privy to inventory lists of armaments, and may have shared them with the states. South Carolina's seizure of forts

Moultrie, Pickney, and Johnston on January 2, followed by Georgia's seizure of Fort Pulaski on January 3, started the rush. Throughout the month of January, the Confederate states armed themselves by continuing to seize arsenals and forts, and appropriating "their fair share" of federally funded armaments.

Meanwhile, on January 9, Florida left the Union, and the next day, Alabama seceded. Also on the ninth, the merchant vessel *Star of the West*, under the direction of the U.S. Navy, tried unsuccessfully to resupply and reinforce Major Anderson's command at Fort Sumter with two hundred men; Charleston had been warned, and fired upon and drove off the ship before she could dock. On January 11, Mississippi was propelled into secession by her major slaveholders after poor voter turnout for that election.[8]

Public opinion in the North was confused. In New England, the prevailing sentiment was hope that the Union could still be saved by persuasion. Cotton Whig Amos A. Lawrence wrote to friends, "Nine out of ten of our people would laugh if told that blood must be shed" to preserve the Union.[9]

Lincoln had made moderation and flexibility the hallmarks of his campaign platform. He hoped to encourage the Southern politicians to keep their states in a Union governed by a centrist inclined to deal with them fairly once in office. He was a moderate reaching out to moderates—but every week there were fewer moderates still left in the South, which was

> united by a sense of terrible danger. . . . in a determination to defend slavery, to resist abolitionists and to force the Yankees to recognize not only their rights, but also their status as perfectly decent, respectable human beings.[10]

In Washington, and in the state capitals, a cadre of resolute, radical secessionists manipulated half-formed public opinion, and rushed the issue along to take advantage of the situation. Senator Howell

Cobb of Georgia noted, "It looks as if they were afraid that the blood of the people will cool down."[11] Southern members of Congress coordinated the supposedly independent actions of the Southern states, acting informally, but lethally, to organize secession.[12]

Back in the state capitals of the South, educated individuals who knew about these things, and who made up the ruling class of Southerners, including State Senator Egbert Jones of Alabama, were further united in their view that the Constitution had created states as sovereign entities, which only lent their authority to the federal government to act on their behalf. If the states became unhappy with how it was used, as they were now, they could take it back.[13]

On January 19, Georgia seceded, followed by Louisiana on the twenty-sixth. In Louisiana, secession had won by less than 1,800 votes out of 40,000 cast.[14] Six states had now left the Union and several others had popular referendums pending.

In the North, many were starting to question the wisdom of just waving good-bye to the Southern states and saying good riddance to political feuding. More voices began to say that the Union was worth preserving, and that if it took a fight, so be it. It now looked like Pharaoh might pursue the Israelites after all.

There was still hope that the awful alternative could be avoided if a figure with moral authority just stepped forward to dissuade, persuade, or compel. But who could apply such pressure when, as Henry Adams said, the very "Government had an air of social instability and incompleteness"?[15] America in 1861 lacked a national media apparatus to focus attention on the severity of the political crisis and hound its government into reacting, so the press could not help.

Certainly the lame-duck outgoing president, James Buchanan, could not apply such pressure. He was now held in such low esteem that during his pathetically ill-attended New Year's reception, normally the formal kick-off of Washington's winter social season, many in the receiving line refused to even shake the president's hand! The *Harrisburg Pennsylvania Telegraph*—from his own home state—labeled him "that miserable old man," and suggested, "he is open to the suspicion that he is ambitious to be the last President of the United States."[16] A diligent man who had worked hard in many government jobs his whole adult life, Buchanan must have found it bitter to not matter anymore. He lamented, "The office of President of the United States is not fit for a gentleman to hold!"[17]

Sadly, when Buchanan at last tried to ring the national fire alarm, everyone had stopped listening to him. By his many jabs at the North, he had forfeited his ability to engage meaningfully with them, and hence irretrievably lost his credibility as a national leader.

During the four-month period of time in between the election and inauguration, Cabinet secretaries and other executive staff traditionally abandoned the ship of state as they sought new jobs or returned to long-neglected farms and businesses. Unhappily for the Union, many of the "new jobs" that Buchanan's appointees accepted were with the Confederate government, then organizing in Montgomery, Alabama. Secession fever had so infected the administration that even lower-level political appointees, like government clerks, sported blue ribbons—secession cockades—on the lapels of their coats.[18]

The Supreme Court, never a proactive body, never designed to initiate action or policy, and well-composed of Southerners, was unlikely to ever rule against slavery.

The legislative branch, Congress, in which the slavery crisis had simmered for decades, could not resolve what the states individually would not. Tension, not compromise, reigned in both chambers in early 1861. Congress had been set up to debate ideas and develop policy by means of consensus. But, during this time, members displayed such hostility that the House ceased to function as a deliberative body, becoming only an arena for combative debate. Speeches reached an unprecedented level of acrimony. Most politicians found threats and warnings in their mail.[19]

Senator Grimes, of Iowa, wrote, "The members on both sides are mostly armed with deadly weapons, and it is said that the friends of each are armed in the galleries," and Senator Hammond, of South Carolina, said, "The only persons who do not have a revolver and knife are those who have two revolvers." During one bitter debate, a pistol fell from the pocket of a congressman from New York, and, thinking that he had drawn it intending to shoot, other members went into a near-panic.[20] Senator Benjamin Wade, of Ohio, carried a brace of large pistols into the chamber every day and ostentatiously thumped them down onto his desk, making sure everyone knew he was not one of those allegedly cowardly Northern legislators who would not fight. The widespread expectation of a shootout on the floor of Congress did not seem far-fetched.[21]

In this atmosphere, it was no wonder that the special committees set up by both houses to try and solve the secession crisis failed. Still, the legislators got some work done. Three new federal territories—Dakota, Colorado, and Nevada—were established without any friction over slavery. Following a legitimate referendum of her people, Kansas was finally admitted as a free state. When a thirty-four-gun salute to welcome the newest state was fired by a light artillery battery, it nearly caused a panic among nervous Washingtonians, who thought the secessionists were invading from Virginia![22]

On January 21, known as "Withdrawal Day" by the South, members of all congressional delegations from seceding states delivered emotional farewell speeches in the House and Senate. Benjamin Fitzpatrick, the senior senator from Alabama, proclaimed, "I acknowledge no loyalty to any other Power than that of my sovereign State."[23] Now that their states had left the Union, these senators and congressman were no longer able to participate in the governing process of the United States. Virginia Tunstall Clay, wife of the junior senator from Alabama, who witnessed the event from the galleries, wrote,

> There was everywhere a feeling of suspense, as if, visibly, the pillars of the temple were being withdrawn and the great Government structure was tottering; nor was there a patriot on either side who did not deplore and whiten before the evil that brooded so low over the nation.[24]

In early February the secession of Texas—for which the nation had gone to war just thirteen years earlier—brought the total of Confederate states to seven. The entire tier of Gulf Coast states had joined the Confederacy, as had the Atlantic Coast states as far north as South Carolina. Flushed with its success the Confederacy was becoming deliriously illogical. The *North Carolina Ledger* opined that, after subduing the Northern "incubus," the Confederacy should annex first Mexico and all of Central America, then "Cuba afterwards either by negotiation or conquest" to make the Caribbean a Confederate lake—or perhaps the new Mediterranean![25]

The North came up with its own share of loony ideas during the crisis. One man proposed four "union republics" balancing each other's power. The mayor of New York, Fernando Wood, proposed secession for his city to be an independent nation. Senator William Seward, went so far as to quietly suggest it might be useful to start a war with England, France, or Spain in order to unite the country.[26] The still-tenuous communication links with the nation's West Coast were reflected in yet another discussion of an independent Pacific Republic of California and Oregon.[27]

Only one other player in the national drama remained, and Abraham Lincoln was as yet offstage. Could he save the Union? If so, when? During a period when the nation was cascading out of control, the four months mandated between the election and inauguration of a president was especially disastrous timing. This interregnum was an anachronism, left over from an era before railroads and the telegraph, when the victor might not even learn of his election for as many as three weeks.

Lincoln was to have no official power until he assumed office on March 4, 1861. While he waited out the transition period in Springfield, Illinois, he was neither able to influence much of the course of national events, nor tell the incumbent president how to govern. At least it was now proper for him to begin receiving military and security briefings, and General Scott began providing them. However, Lincoln was not yet legally permitted to make executive decisions. He had not even yet personally met all of the men he was considering for his Cabinet, let alone appointed them.

In late February, his most pressing concern was to finalize his Cabinet. "Lincoln decided that a broadly representative cabinet was more essential than a doctrinally cohesive one," but the negotiations with the proposed Cabinet members and all their supporters or detractors were excruciating.[28] The Cabinet was not to be finalized until the day before his inauguration:

Montgomery Blair, Massachusetts Postmaster
William Seward, New York State
Salmon Chase, New Hampshire/Ohio Treasury
Simon Cameron, Pennsylvania Sec War
Gideon Welles, Connecticut Navy
Caleb Smith, Indiana Interior
Edward Bates, Missouri AG

Lincoln had been absent from Washington, D.C., for a decade; he was fundamentally an outsider with no network of personal familiarity. He could not take over any existing Republican network or base of operations, because his party had never before held national office.[29]

However, two appointments were easily made—the president-elect decided that two talented young lawyers he knew from Springfield, John Nicolay and John Hay, were to travel to Washington with him to become his private secretaries. A graduate of

Brown University class of 1858, John Hay was the son of a Rhode Islander. Hay had studied law with his uncle, whose law office was next door to Lincoln's in Springfield.[30]

It was going to take some months to make all the other appointments for territorial governors, postmasters, customs inspectors, collectors of revenue and ambassadors; and since Rhode Islanders would surely receive some appointments, Sullivan might even have been in line for a federal post. Certainly Sullivan's destiny had become entwined with Lincoln's on that fateful day the previous year in Woonsocket, and would remain so whether the president gave him a job or not. His and Sarah's future happiness now rested on the same things that were impacting their new leader.

Despite the national turmoil as Inauguration Day approached Sullivan and Sarah were still living normal lives. Edgar was now four and a half, and his younger brother two. On the extended family front, favorites Uncle Henry and Aunt Sarah Fales Ballou left Woonsocket and moved to a large tract of land outside the port city of Bristol, the Fales's hometown. Sullivan and Sarah visited them often.

In Springfield, Illinois, Lincoln began to plan a far greater journey, of the nineteen hundred miles to Washington, D.C. It would be an endurance test, requiring thirty changes of trains on twenty railroads over twelve days, and a multitude of speaking engagements.[31]

Lincoln, a brilliant politician, calculated that he could accomplish something very special on this trip if he organized it as he had the one to New England just a year earlier. He knew that many of his oratorical appearances would be written up in the newspapers of the state in which they occurred, and often telegraphed across the nation. He shrewdly surmised that he could build support for his presidency and continue to get his message out in a low-key way if he avoided the pitfalls of announcing major policy shifts, controversial action steps, or political appointments. He could take the pulse of the nation while they took his measure.

On February 11, 1861, the two men who were to become the respective president of each half of the former United States left their hometowns to journey to their capital cities. Jefferson Davis left Mississippi. The Lincoln family also left on this same date for his March 4, 1861, inaugural.

By the time he arrived in Washington, Lincoln had interacted with 200,000-plus people during his journey. He had spoken to city councils and state legislatures in each capital. He had addressed huge groups of people, in halls and from hotel balconies. He had made remarks from his train as it stopped at dozens of small towns in each state, and had dined with societies and welcoming committees.[32] In this way, in an era before public opinion polls, Lincoln learned that the country remained behind the policies he had first articulated six months earlier and behind him as he took over the reins of government.

The ten square miles of the District of Columbia sat squarely in the midst of secessionist sentiment. If it were a clock face sitting on the map astride the Potomac River, it would share a border with the State of Maryland from ten o'clock to six o'clock, and with Virginia over the Potomac River, from six o'clock to ten o'clock. The district was wholly dependent on its two neighboring states, and while all three entities had worked cooperatively enough over the last seventy years, continued cooperation was no longer a given. In 1861, Virginia and Maryland had large populations of secessionists.

At that time, there were few public buildings in Washington, D.C. The Capitol Building was being remodeled and was shrouded in scaffolding, surmounted by a tall crane. The giant dome of the edifice, still unfinished, dominated the scenery: to the South, the incomplete dome represented a failed experiment in nationhood; to the North, a nation still building its young democracy—the noblest form of government on the globe—and still perfecting the boldest experiment in self-governance the world had ever known.

The Executive Mansion had a different silhouette then. Rebuilt after the British burned it in 1814, the main building with its elegant portico was, in 1861, surrounded by greenhouses, sheds, outbuildings, stables, herb and vegetable gardens, and modest fruit orchards. It looked little different from the plantation houses nearby in Virginia, just across the Potomac River.

On the north side of the mansion, an extension of Pennsylvania Avenue had replaced the northernmost edge of the President's Park, and omnibuses now plied "the Avenue" between the Capitol and Georgetown. The president had little privacy—many strollers on the Avenue reported glimpsing him as he left the White House, on foot, or on horseback, on business about the city.

The south lawn of the Executive Mansion meandered down toward the malarial swamps of the Potomac River. The river could be reached by crossing one of the iron bridges spanning an abandoned old canal filled with sewage and refuse. The area south of the canal was known as "the Island," and it ran on for some miles, comprising southwest Washington, D.C. On the Island were located the Smithsonian Institute, the partially finished gardens of the Mall, the Arsenal, the armory, and the penitentiary. The distinctive, castlelike cherry-red brick structure of the Smithsonian Institute, which housed a "fine library and an extensive gallery of paintings" rose prominently on their knoll.[33]

The same could not be said of the Washington Monument nearby, which was only one-third built—donations having run out—and its blocks lay in pieces around the truncated shaft. Mark Twain noted,

> It has the aspect of a factory chimney with the top broken off. The skeleton of a decaying scaffolding lingers about its summit, and tradition says that the spirit of Washington often comes down and sits on those rafters to enjoy this tribute of respect which the nation has reared. . . . The memorial Chimney stands in a quiet pastoral locality that is full of

> reposeful expression. With a glass you can see the cow-sheds about its base, and the contented sheep nibbling pebbles in the desert solitudes that surround it, and the tired pigs dozing in the holy calm of its protecting shadow.[34]

Despite the livestock, the city was a lively place, especially when its population of 61,000 swelled by several thousand whenever Congress was in session. Many long-term visitors, who came for what Henry Adams called "its primary business: politics," were accommodated in entire neighborhoods of boardinghouses.[35]

Early 1861 also saw an exodus: As the secession procession continued, Southern army and naval officers shook hands with Northern colleagues, resigned their commissions, and left for their home states to offer their services to the Confederacy. Many officers were recalled from distant posts to Washington, to the service of the Union, only to resign upon arrival. Nearly one-third of the army officers, and one-fourth of the naval officers, joined the Confederate military.[36]

The general in chief of the army, Winfield Scott, now returned to the capital after nine years of self-imposed exile, after having left the 1852 election as the Whig Party candidate for president of the United States. Scott came back after the 1860 election, at Buchanan's request; as the secession crisis deepened, he offered advice on the defense of the city and measures to be taken to redistribute arms, weapons, munitions, and ships situated in Southern forts to Northern arsenals—advice that Buchanan chose to disregard, fearful of further antagonizing the South. As a result, much of that materiel was lost to Northern use, as the South seized or burned such facilities that January.

A Virginian born and bred, Scott moved in Southern social and political circles, and showed a marked partiality for advancing Southern officers in the military. Only one of the six departments of the Regular Army in 1860 was commanded by a Northerner, and the sole Northerner serving on the General's personal staff was his military secretary, Lieutenant Colonel Erasmus D. Keyes, an appointment made after Virginian Robert E. Lee turned down the post.[37] Yet, his loyalty to the Union was beyond question.

Washingtonians sized up the nation's military leader and concluded he was, "the very figure to satisfy a peaceful people, fond of bragging of their bygone belligerence . . . the General was as magnificent as a monument . . . and nearly as useless."[38] It was noted, "the General is older than the Capital."[39] As senior military advisor to the president, this was the man Abraham Lincoln, the Cabinet, and Congress would have to rely on for all their military advice and strategy for the next eight months. There was no alternative.

Scott understood the immediate need to protect the Capitol, the Congress, the Peace Conference, the electoral college meeting, and both presidents through the inauguration. He appointed Colonel Charles Stone, who had served with him in the Mexican War, to develop a security plan and organize the local militia. They scrounged the eastern United States and the military academy for army units that could arrive in Washington in time, and found

Seventy-five-year-old general in chief of the United States Army, Winfield Scott suffered from gout, poor circulation, and swollen limbs. Weighing over three hundred pounds, Scott was barely ambulatory and could no longer ride a horse. *From author's collection.*

only eight companies—a mere eight hundred men. One of these was the Military Academy Battery, commanded by First Lieutenant Charles Griffin.

The threat level was so high that the congressional committee established to investigate plots to prevent Lincoln's inauguration found them sufficiently viable to appeal to the chief of police of the city of New York to send undercover detectives to infiltrate radical groups in Richmond, Alexandria, Baltimore, and Washington, D.C.[40] The committee members had only to frequent the same capital bars to hear whiskey-drinking government clerks boasting that the new president would never take the oath of office.[41]

So many reports came from so many places—Cincinnati, Pittsburgh, St. Louis, Chicago, New York, Philadelphia, Baltimore—and so many sources—detectives, General Scott, a railway president, a former governor, a cabinet minister, and worried citizens—that it was necessary to take seriously and investigate the high level of chatter.

One rumor was that two antifederal militia groups within Washington itself were assigned the mission of seizing of all the money stored in the Treasury Building, along with the official seals of the U.S. government.[42] To counter such homegrown guerrilla units, Colonel Stone had to use his creativity. He solicited the cooperation of already established neighborhood fire-fighting companies, such as the Northern Liberties Fire Insurance and the Liberty Hose companies, and they agreed to help defend the capital. Stone also applied to various cohesive trade associations working within the district: the carpenters, turners, masons, stonecutters, and painters agreed to form militia units on the spot.*

* Just a few months later, these militia units were given the honor of leading the federal advance into Virginia for the capture of Alexandria.

As he took steps to defend the nation, General Scott's mail grew "heavy with threats of assassination," and the students at the University of Virginia burned him in effigy. He was persuaded to move to a boardinghouse directly across the street from the War Department, so he could be better guarded.[43]

Meanwhile, Lincoln's campaign team from Illinois was equally determined that the Republican winner would be inaugurated, so they hired Alan Pinkerton's Chicago-based private detective firm, one of the first of its kind in the nation, to provide personal security to the president-elect.[44]

On February 21, while in Philadelphia, almost the last leg of his journey to Washington, Lincoln's security team received what they considered to be solid intelligence regarding attempts to kill him in Baltimore during his one-mile trip between train depots. Unable to determine definitively which of these plots were real, the Lincoln team could not afford to take any chances. As Lincoln later said, "I did not then, nor do I now believe I should have been assassinated; but I thought it wise to run no risk where no risk was necessary."[45]

Thomas Scott, president of the Pennsylvania Railroad, on whose trains Lincoln would travel for the first four hours out of Philadelphia, made arrangements for the president-elect to secretly board the night train to Baltimore, traveling incognito and accompanied only by Pinkerton and Ward Lamon, Lincoln's close personal friend, who was heavily armed.[46]

Scott put in charge one of his own most trustworthy engineers of Lincoln's train Edward R. Black, the husband of Sarah Ballou's first cousin, Celia Shumway. Black described the drama:

> I was told to make no stops, and when obliged to take water, to do so at the most secluded places I could; to keep a sharp lookout, and to arrive at 30th Street, West Philadelphia, by 10 o'clock sure. Feeling the great responsibility upon me, you may be sure I looked after things mighty sharp.

Lincoln thus safely passed through Baltimore around 4:00 A.M., many hours before he was expected, and while the conspirators were still asleep.[47] He arrived safely in Washington at 6:00 A.M., and was driven to Willard's Hotel by Illinois congressman Elihu Washburne. Edward Black reported that Lincoln's staff in Harrisburg, and railroad director Scott

> all passed a sleepless night, but as day was breaking, . . . Scott received an unsigned dispatch reading, 'Plums delivered nuts safely,' which had been previously arranged, and their anxiety was relieved.[48]

Mary Todd Lincoln, her children, servants, and the balance of the presidential staff took the originally scheduled train, and were met in Baltimore by a jeering crowd of ten thousand at 1:00 P.M. The security team was apparently correct in their assessment that the Lincoln women and children would not be harmed by the mob; Mrs. Lincoln entered Washington, D.C., without incident.

Amid Southern rumors that a slave uprising was timed for March 4, General Scott, was now able to step up his military briefings to Lincoln. On March 2, he counseled the incoming president that the logistics of the forts in Charleston Harbor made it "not practical" to defend Fort Sumter.[49]

Inauguration Monday dawned dark and gloomy, but brightened up in time for the ceremonies that were to be held outdoors, on the steps of the Capitol Building. The security on March 4 was extreme, some of it obvious, some not. The threat matrix for this day included attacking Lincoln on the journey from Willard's to the swearing-in, as well as blowing up the platform upon which he and the leadership of the nation would be gathered for the ceremonies. Seemingly somewhat after the fact, since it would still leave the hated Republicans in power, the final menace was a plot to kill him during the inaugural parade.[50]

As etiquette and courtesy demanded, President Buchanan called for his successor in the White House carriage at noon. Sitting side by side, under bright blue skies, they rode the one and a quarter miles up Pennsylvania Avenue from Willard's Hotel to Capitol Hill, waving to the gathered crowds. By prearrangement, their cavalry guard did not ride in precision formation; they pretended their horses were disorderly, to prevent a marksman from taking aim at the presidential carriage.[51]

Salient points on the line of march to the Capitol were defended. "The housetops along the avenue bristled with riflemen," watching the windows of the houses opposite, with orders to open fire if any shots were fired on the presidential carriage. Additional cavalry controlled the intersections along the route, using a kind of protective leapfrog movement to stay in advance of the presidential carriage.[52]

"The Capitol building was in possession of the army and a battery of flying artillery was stationed at the northern entrance to the plaza at Delaware Avenue and B Street, for the protection of the platform reared over the steps upon the east front."[53] Each window of the Capitol held two riflemen.[54]

To counter the plot to blow up the platform on the steps of the Capitol where the new president and vice president would take the oath of office, the premises had been immediately searched when the plot was discovered. Colonel Stone then stationed men under the stairs and put plainclothes policemen throughout the crowd. At daybreak on inauguration day, a full battalion lined up to cordon off the steps.[55]

Lincoln and Buchanan entered the Capitol together, via a boarded tunnel. They went first to the Senate Chamber for the swearing-in of the vice president, former Senator Hamlin, whose brief and modest words allowed the dignitaries to promptly move on to the main event outside.[56] There, on a canopied platform draped with the national colors, the order of events was the inaugural address, followed by the administration of the oath of office. Journalist William Croffut reported,

> Never before was such a multitude present at an inauguration as that which faced and surrounded the president-elect when he took the oath of office. . . . It was estimated that two thirds of the audience were secessionists, and their sympathies were indicated by the frequent interruptions, sometimes quite drowning out the voice of the speaker. . . . Some of the exclamations heard during the delivery of the address, uttered in so loud a tone as to be a serious annoyance were: "That won't do!" "Never! Never!" "Worse than I expected!" "Too late!" "We defy your threats!" . . . During the first two minutes it became obvious that Mr. Lincoln possessed a voice of great carrying power and that his words would be conveyed to the auditors who were most remote. He was tall and unperturbed and his tall form overtopped the distinguished assembly. . . . At the close of the exercises hisses and denunciations were renewed. . . .[57]

Lincoln supporters led loud cheers and applause, attempting to drown out the hecklers.

Lincoln's closing words rang out over the assembled multitude of thirty thousand:

> In your hands, my dissatisfied fellow-countrymen, and not in mine, is the momentous issue of civil war. The Government will not assail you. You can have no conflict without being yourselves the aggressors. . . . We are not enemies but friends. We must not be enemies. Though passion may have strained, it must not break our bonds of affection. The mystic chords of memory stretching from every battlefield and patriot grave, to every living heart and hearthstone over all this broad land,

> will yet swell the chorus of the Union, when again touched, as they surely will be, by the better angels of our nature.[58]

At the close of the address, eighty-three-year-old Chief Justice Roger Taney, "looking like a galvanized corpse," rose from his seat and stepped forward to administer the oath of office. Lincoln was the eighth president he had sworn in. Afterward, Lincoln kissed the Bible, and the customary gun salutes began reverberating all around the city.

The anti-Lincoln press heard and reported only the message they wanted to hear: "There is no mitigation of Lincoln's fanaticism in this Inaugural Address," declared the North Carolina *Wilmington Daily Herald.*[59]

An inaugural parade had been a tradition since George Washington, and Lincoln's proceeded without any assassination attempts. Following the ceremonies, the new first family dined in the White House and later danced at the gala inaugural ball at the marble-columned Post Office Building. The new president left Mrs. Lincoln dancing happily at the ball, and returned to the White House. Around 1:00 A.M. he performed his first official act as president when he read the latest dispatch from Major Anderson at Fort Sumter, who disclosed their supplies would run out before a relief expedition could reach them.[60]

The pressure was on, yet Lincoln was not free to devote much time to it during the first two weeks. On March 6, delegations from ten states, including one from Rhode Island, called on him.[61] The purpose of these visits was to congratulate the new president and make contacts to establish a proper working relationship between the states and the administration. The Rhode Island delegation likely did not stay in Washington very long, they had to get back home and campaign for the April election.

Sullivan was once again running for office, this time much more prominently than before. Horatio Rogers reported, "In the spring of 1861, the Republicans in grateful recognition of his services, nominated him for the office of Attorney General of the State."[62] As part of his campaign effort, Sullivan took every opportunity to advocate his beliefs on the state and fate of the Union, speaking to the people at frequent political rallies and at events on patriotic holidays, such as Washington's Birthday, and attending many political dinners.[63] He kept in touch by letter with those political friends from whom he was separated by distance, like George Manchester, and they talked him up in their own circles.[64]

There were four main political factions in Rhode Island in 1861, all centering on the major issue of American politics—slavery. These were:

- The super radicals, the abolitionists, who aligned themselves with the Republican Party, but were only a fringe element, not its majority. They supported civil disobedience, insurrection, and war to free the slaves. They were widely believed to have been behind John Brown's raid in 1859.
- The mainstream Northern or Lincoln Republicans, who held moderate viewpoints. They believed the young nation could neither move forward with its development nor be true to its democratic roots, so long as slavery undermined free labor and caused apolitical checkmate. Because they favored breaking the gridlock, with force as the last alternative, conservative campaign rhetoric put them in the same box with the super-radical abolitionists.
- The super conservatives, former Whigs, who usually allied with the Southern Democratic Party. They preferred to offer no opposition whatsoever to slavery or its expansion.
- The moderate conservatives, former Whigs, who usually allied with the Northern Democratic Party. They believed slavery was morally and philosophically wrong, but did not wish to incur the disruption that would inevitably follow attempts to curb it.

For the spring 1861 state election, the last two groups formed the "fusion party"; the second group made up the Republican, or radical ticket; and the abolitionists were not on the ballot at all as such. Sprague, the mill owner, was opposed this year by another wealthy cotton mill owner, James Young Smith. Smith was Connecticut born, from the same area as Sarah's grandparents, and owned mills in Woonsocket and Willimantic. He had served as mayor of Providence for two years, was the president of the State Mutual Fire Insurance Company and the City Savings Bank, and seemed a solid businessman.[65] Sullivan's opponent was Timothy S. Burgess, another attorney. The only easy votes were for the venerable academician, author, and longtime incumbent secretary of state John Bartlett, and treasurer Samuel Parker, both running unopposed.

The Republicans had high hopes of riding to victory on Lincoln's coattails to sweep the statehouse in Rhode Island. They needed to gain back some ground after losing Christopher Robinson's congressional seat to a fusion candidate the same day Lincoln had been elected. Newport, in the southern part of the state, had sent a new Republican to Congress in that election, and both senators were Republican, but Rhode Island voters seemed to prefer to split their ticket and keep the statehouse under the control of the fusion candidates. Given that incumbents almost always have an edge in reelection, and that the secession crisis kept all the big-name Republicans in distant Washington, far away from the Rhode Island campaign trail, it was a huge question whether the Republicans could wrest power at the statehouse in April.

If elected attorney general, Sullivan would have held a uniquely powerful office, because under the Rhode Island constitution, that office prosecuted all criminal cases—a task normally performed in other states by district attorneys. He would interface with the Court of Common Pleas, the lower court, as well as with the State Supreme Court and the U.S. District and Circuit Courts. As attorney general, he would have overseen the central legal agency of the state, and prosecuted all felony criminal cases, misdemeanor appeals, and misdemeanors in the district courts. (When the office was first instituted, back in 1650, the elected attorney general received no salary, but could charge the General Assembly for his services, including "ten shillings for every criminal executed to death," a payment plan that might have triggered an interesting rush to the gallows.)

As in all states, the office also provided legal advice to state officials and the legislature.[66] The attorney generalship was a statewide office within Sullivan's grasp; one in which he could perform brilliantly. After a term or two, he could aim for deputy governor and even governor, if he played his cards right. Many Rhode Island governors "moved up" to win election to the United States Senate. Sullivan was on the threshold of something great, at a time when the state was ripe for change. It seemed reasonable to hope that the old boy network of men who had made all decisions based on the cotton economy, would be hard pressed to hang on to power during the Lincoln administration, and that a new generation of leaders would be coming to power in Rhode Island, among them Sullivan Ballou.

Political wrangling was going on in the halls of power in Washington, D.C., as well. The power struggle in Lincoln's cabinet was in full throttle, with both Chase and Seward threatening to reject their appointments.[67] The first Cabinet meeting could not be held until all ruffled feathers were settled, and so it was not until March 9 that they met to discuss Fort Sumter. Two days later, the Cabinet recommended withdrawing and surrendering. Their stance was influenced by the hope of yet keeping the border states within the Union. Lincoln met with his Cabinet almost daily. On March 15, not content to defer to his Cabinet as Buchanan had done, the president presented a plan to resupply the fort on which he had been secretly working with postmaster Montgomery Blair. He asked the Cabinet to respond in writing. Their vote was 5–2 against resupply.[68]

President Lincoln, his cabinet, and General Scott. *Courtesy Library of Congress Prints and Photographs Division.*

On March 29, Lincoln finalized his plan; he was determined to resupply Fort Sumter with food and medicines, notifying the South in advance of the nature and terms of the cargo. He did not get the cooperation he expected from his military forces or Secretary Seward.

On Tuesday, April 2, when Rhode Island turned out to vote, the battlements of Fort Sumter, where Lincoln had drawn a line in the sand 950 miles to the south, loomed over the election. No polling was done to give feedback to candidates. After Sullivan voted in Cranston, he awaited the results with hope, having done his best. That same Tuesday, President Lincoln visited the Washington Navy Yard and various military barracks in D.C. to inspect their state of readiness for the hostilities he feared were close at hand.[69]

Sullivan did not win the attorney general's race. It turned out that the prevailing mood of the 22,355 Rhode Island voters was still conciliatory to the South, still reluctant to take a stand on expansion of slavery in new states and territories, for fear of driving the South out of the Union. They instead voted for jobs, for keeping the economic engines of the state turning, returning to office another "fusion" ticket of conservative incumbents headed by a Democrat, Governor William Sprague. This year, Sprague won by 54 percent, just a single point higher than in 1860.

To his credit, Sullivan actually did the best of anyone on his ticket, losing by the smallest margin of any statewide candidate, just 4 percent, but Secretary of State Bartlett noted that "even his popularity did not suffice to turn the tide in his instance."[70] Rogers commented,

> The whole ticket was defeated by what was called the conservative party, and Mr. Ballou remained in private life, anxiously watching the development of the conspiracy which then threatened our national life.[71]

Votes Cast for State Wide Offices In Rhode Island, election day April 2, 1861

Office / Candidate	Party	Ticket	Votes	%
Governor: 22,321				
William Sprague	Democrat	Conservative	12,005	54%
James Y. Smith	Republican	Radical	10,326	46%
		Majority	1,669	8%
Lt. Gov.: 22,421				
Samuel G. Arnold	Democrat	Conservative	11,966	53%
Simon Henry Green	Republican	Radical	10,455	47%
		Majority	1,511	6%
Secretary of State				
John R. Bartlett	unopposed for 6th term		22,355	100%
Attorney General: 21,557				
Timothy S. Burgess	Democrat	Conservative	11,157	52%
Sullivan Ballou	Republican	Radical	10,400	48%
		Majority	757	4%
Treasurer				
Samuel A. Parker	unopposed for 7th term		100%	

To a highly emotional man like Sullivan Ballou, such a blow would have taken some time to heal, in any year. Given the uncertainty of such inflammatory national events, Sullivan would have been fearing for his country's future as well as his own.

On April 3, the *New York Times* reacted to events in the North by printing the headline "WANTED—A POLICY!" The paper called for the North to display as much cohesion and initiative as the South.[72] Lincoln, of course, could not make public the behind-the-scenes maneuvers and negotiations he was pursuing, and his silence was construed as inaction. Had they been known, the Rhode Island vote might have gone differently.

On April 6, the president sent a messenger, a State Department clerk, to tell the new governor of South Carolina that he planned to reprovision the fort but would not reinforce the federal forces still holding out on the rocky island. On April 7, the South severed all communications between Sumter and Charleston, the fort's only link to the outside world, thereby cutting off all contact with President Lincoln. On April 8, all South Carolina forces were placed on alert status in the harbor.* Within Sumter, the Union forces prepared to defend themselves as best they could with materials on hand.

Just thirty-four days into his presidency, the first great crisis of Abraham Lincoln's administration had now come to a head. "The interest of the nation centered at a small fort in the harbor of Charleston," where the two halves of a great nation were staring at each other, waiting to see who will be the first to blink.[73] It would not be South Carolina.

On April 9, the Confederate government ordered General Pierre Gustave Toutant Beauregard, commanding the defenses of

* Exactly four years later, Confederate General Robert E. Lee surrendered his army at Appomattox Court House.

Fort Sumter, in the middle of Charleston Harbor. *From author's collection.*

Charleston, to acquire the fort.[74] Beauregard received the order on April 10 and conveyed it to Major Anderson on April 11. On April 12, Beauregard asked Anderson to finalize the hour of surrender; Anderson tried to stall until April 15, but the Confederates decided it would be imprudent to wait, fearing the North might send additional ships or reinforcements. They notified Anderson that an attack was imminent.

At 4:30 A.M. on April 13, the bombardment began, making red arcs in the dark sky. News reporters cabled out their dispatches and the story flashed around both nations. In Cranston, Sullivan and Sarah read the Providence papers and found their worst fears confirmed:

> *dateline April 13 3 pm*
> A terrible fight is at this moment going on between Fort Sumter and the fortifications by which it is surrounded. . . . The excitement in the community is indescribable. With the very first boom of the gun, thousands rushed from their beds

> to the harbor front, and all day every available place has been thronged by ladies and gentlemen, viewing the solemn spectacle through their glasses.

Sumter fired back methodically, but less frequently, than its opponents.

Major Anderson remained unable to get messages out during the fighting; in absence of any direct communiqués from Charleston, the White House got all its news through the press as late as April 13.[75] *New York Herald* reporters in Charleston telegraphed a series of breathless dispatches to their newspapers every few hours, chronicling the developments. These were printed verbatim, all at once, in the *Providence Journal:*

> *Fourth Dispatch*
> The bombardment of Fort Sumter continues. The floating battery and Stevens battery are operating freely, Fort Sumter returning their fire. It is reported that three war vessels are outside the bar.[76]

Choked by acrid smoke, exhausted, and outgunned, Major Anderson's little band was sorely pressed. He had hoped to surrender peacefully, once his rations had run out. Instead, he and his command were forced to fight for their lives as a nation breathlessly followed the news reports.

On Saturday, April 13, this headline opened the *Providence Journal* :

> WAR HAS BEGUN
> These words, so full of solemn meaning, must be spoken. The government of the Southern Confederacy have deliberately began war. By their express order the forts and batteries near Charleston opened fire on fort Sumter yesterday

> morning at 4 o'clock. . . . Major Anderson's whole course has been noble and patriotic in the highest degree, and he and his gallant little band will never be forgotten by his grateful countrymen.[77]

Throughout the nation—North, South, and in the White House itself—everyone waited for the final act of the drama. The bombardment ended at 2:00 P.M. on the fourteenth. Major Anderson reported,

> I accepted terms of evacuation offered by General Beauregard and marched out of the fort Sunday afternoon, the 14th instant, with colors flying and drums beating, bringing away company and private property and saluting my flag with fifty guns.[78]

On April 15, the populace of Richmond, Virginia, exulted at the news of the fall of Fort Sumter. John Mercer Patton, prominent attorney and captain of the Kanawha Rifles Militia Company, told a jubilant crowd of thousands gathered at the State Capitol "that we rejoice with high, exultant, heartfelt joy at the triumph of the Southern Confederacy over the accursed government at Washington in the capture of Fort Sumter."* Fireworks and illuminations lasted long into the night as the celebrations continued.[79]

That day, after conferring with his Cabinet 106 miles away in the federal capital, President Lincoln issued a proclamation asking the governors to activate and deploy their state militias in the service of the federal government. The thousands of men in the state militias were needed because, in 1861, the Regular Federal Army consisted of 16,317 men, only 1,108 of them officers.

* John Mercer and five of his brothers joined the Confederate Army, including Colonel George Smith Patton, the grandfather of General George S. "Old Blood and Guts" Patton, Jr., of World War II fame.

During Buchanan's term, the majority of the armed forces were strung out in lonely outposts across North America, like Fort Bragg, Fort Mojave, Fort Laramie, and Fort Leavenworth, stretching from the Oregon Territory down through the forts controlling the Great Plains Indians and Mormon raiders. Only one company of engineers and sixteen of artillery were even stationed east of the Mississippi River and none of these were near Washington, D.C., nor in any position to defend it. Some felt this was a deliberate action on the part of the secessionist Secretary of War John Floyd.[80]

The fastest way to get additional troops where they were needed in this crisis was to work through the states, which had armed and uniformed volunteer forces that they could loan to the federal government for ninety days.

The states moved quickly to supply the regiments requested by the president. Existing militia members were given the choice of volunteering to join federal service; vacancies were filled by new recruits.

"It was like the peal of a trumpet. The people of the North rushed to arms," wrote the pastor of Grace Church Cathedral in Providence.[81] Senator Sumner, who had been beaten in the Senate over slavery, wrote,

> I never believed the North would be practically divided when the conflict came; but I did not expect the ferocious unity and high-strung determination which are now witnessed.[82]

"Within a week, five Massachusetts regiments started South"—the Third, Fourth, Fifth, Sixth, and Eighth, who had been drilling for two months in anticipation of war. The state also sent artillery and a rifle battalion.[83] In New York, the Seventh and Seventy-First readied for action. Kentucky sent the Clay Battalion, a rough-hewn group of squirrel shooters whose loyalty to the Kentucky-born president was unquestioned. Vermont telegraphed, "Vermont will do her full duty."[84] It was just as well, because the governors of the border states—Maryland, Virginia, Kentucky, Delaware, and Missouri—sent indignant, often pithily worded refusals.

In Rhode Island, Governor William Sprague, whose constitutional role as commander of the militia gave him a meaningful role at last, reacted swiftly to Lincoln's proclamation. Ironically, the very man elected to keep the state out of an unwanted war now became the prime force behind organizing Rhode Island's zealous response. His state's artillery units were generally acknowledged to be among the nation's finest and had traveled extensively throughout New England, training by invitation those of other states. Rhode Island had more than ten militia companies, including the Woonsocket Guards, the unit Sullivan had served with since he was a teenager. In addition to activating a thousand-man infantry regiment from the existing militia units and volunteers, Sprague telegraphed the Lincoln administration to offer a unit of artillery that could be ready to take ship for the South in a week's time, along with the militia. This White House readily accepted the offer.

Along with the rest of the North, public opinion in Rhode Island was changed radically by the capture of Fort Sumter, but this occurred too late for Sullivan Ballou. Ten days earlier, the voters had put a peace coalition in place, rejecting those who were prescient in realizing stern measures and sacrifice would be needed to save the Union. All of a sudden, the Republicans were no longer radical—but neither did they hold power. Now, Sullivan and his running mates had the frustrating experience of watching from the sidelines while the peace-candidate victors ran "their" war. What a difference ten days had made to local politics. Sullivan was surely struck by the irony of these words in the *Journal*:

> From this day let there be no parties amongst us. Let us with one heart sustain our government against the rebellion which defies and insults us . . . Heaven protect the right![85]

Sarah's hometown paper *The Worchester Spy*, said much the same thing:

> At once partisan differences were forgotten, partisan antagonism melted away, the hearts of the people united in a mighty cheer for the old star spangled banner and in a mighty purpose to maintain our republican institutions against the conspirator that would destroy them.[86]

Sullivan faced a hard choice. The nation needed the utmost from men with courage and talent. Shut out of government, searching for a new way to make his mark, the young husband and father would now consider enlisting in the army.

CHAPTER NINE

"I'm Off to the War with the Good Men and True, and Hadn't You Better Come Along, Too?"*

The Response to Fort Sumter

Late April, 1861

Washington, D.C., was accustomed to receiving mail, newspapers, grain, meat, produce, and other food from Virginia. But on Wednesday, April 17, the State of Virginia passed its ordinance of secession by a vote of 83 to 55. Now, the only connection between the nation's capital and the outside world was through Maryland, a border state with secessionist sympathies, which had yet to decide if it would be staying in the Union.

In Providence, Rhode Island, Governor Sprague called the General Assembly into special session that day, citing the "extraordinary occasion." One action taken was approval of an urgent revision and modernization of all the state laws relating to its

* From the Civil War song "The Why and the Wherefore."

Governor William Sprague in civilian dress and military uniform as head of the state's militia. *From author's collection.*

militia, almost certainly prepared in great haste by Sullivan Ballou. Familiar with both the militia and government processes, with wording similar to other legal documents Sullivan prepared, he probably stayed up all night on the sixteenth to complete it. The revised laws authorized the governor

> to raise, by detailing from the chartered companies of this State, or by voluntary enlistment, or by draft, so many regiments, battalions, or companies of troops for service within or without this State, and to arm and equip the same . . .[1]

As commanding officer, the governor appointed the regimental officers—colonel, lieutenant colonel, major, chaplain, surgeon, and quartermaster. The colonel of any regiment was authorized to enlist his own aides, as well as a band, subject to gubernatorial approval. The companies, once raised, were to elect their own field officers—lieutenants and captains—plus a drummer and fifer.

Rhode Island troops were going to be paid the same pay scale as the regular army, a canny move to short-circuit griping; and all noncommissioned officers, privates, and band members received an additional monthly "bounty" of twelve dollars. To encourage "experienced" militia officers to volunteer, promotions earned while the regiment was in federal service would be permanent. Additional artillery officers were authorized, and a second surgeon's mate was funded for each regiment. Three local militia units were revivified, one under the new name of the Narragansett Guards.[2]

The state treasurer was authorized "to hire" the use of $500,000 at 6 percent interest, to equip and transport the troops Rhode Island would send to Washington. Ten banks in Providence, one in Fall River, and the firm of A. W. Sprague loaned the money.[3] After passing resolutions thanking the governor for "his prompt and efficient action," the legislature adjourned on April 18 until its regularly scheduled session on May 28.[4]

In Rhode Island, as throughout the North, men in the thousands began to flock to army recruiting stations.

The *New York Times* commented,

> Not for fifty years has such a spectacle been seen, as the glorious uprising of American loyalty which greeted the news that open war had been commenced upon the Constitution, Government of the United States. . . . millions of freemen rally with exulting hearts, around our country's standard.[5]

As one Northerner wrote, the Yankees'

> self respect, their intelligent and conservative love of order, government, and law, all their instinctive love of liberty and their sense of responsibility for the safety of the blessings of freedom and popular government were stirred to their very depth.[6]

As the men rallied to war, women raided the dry goods stores to buy red, white, and blue ribbon to stitch into cockades to wear on hats, jackets, or dresses. Sarah Ballou probably fashioned some for her family, to wear whenever they were out of the house. Soon, the savvy clothiers were selling ready-made ones. There were "banner raisings" in Providence, and soon the city was festooned with the national colors.

It was a week to remember in Rhode Island, where "two thousand five hundred men volunteered for the defence of the Government," and but only twelve hundred were needed.[7] One young man who made the cut, Private Albert Sholes, recalled, although Fort Sumter was

> fired on Friday at daybreak, it was not until Saturday that here the certain news was known. . . . Wherever men congregated, the question was prominent as to what would be the outcome. On the Sabbath, in every church, patriotic sermons were preached. That Sabbath was a day of anxious waiting for all our people, old and young, and on Monday morning, everybody was out early for the morning papers.

Sholes vividly detailed the high tension that prevailed throughout the entire Civil War in a populace dependent on the printed page as its sole form of news media. Not always able to wait for the news to reach them, people eagerly went to the news.

The First Regiment needed to fill seven companies of men sufficiently fit to see real action. There was no guarantee that the many volunteers were healthy enough to serve, so a formalized selection process was established. In his capacity as Judge Advocate General of the Militia, Sullivan spent a very busy week helping to organize the regiment, as new enlistee Albert Sholes noted,

> On Wednesday morning, the two hundred gathered again at the armory where inspecting officers John S. Slocum and Sullivan Ballou were to select the fifty to fill the company.

Captain Slocum mounted a table at the west end of the room and with the men clustered around him, he selected one after another to go to the room at the other end, where Dr. Rivers would examine them.

Sholes caught "Slocum's eye and he came down. He called Major Ballou to the table" to take his place selecting men. After trying to dissuade Sholes, and suggesting he return instead to school, Slocum gave in, threw his arm around the young man's shoulder, and personally took him in to Dr. Rivers. The doctor "turned me about, patted me on the back and chest, and said, 'All right, you'll do.' "[8] Sholes was made a private.

A full-strength regiment was twelve hundred men, divided into companies of one hundred apiece. Most Civil War companies, North and South, were formed from within a community. Their men lived near one another or worked together; many were related, some brothers. In the First Rhode Island, more than half the men were from Providence; Woonsocket, Pawtucket, Westerly, and Newport provided the other companies.[9]

The makeup of the regiment reflected the diverse urban workforce of the industrial north. As a rule, these occupations required literacy, and so the regiment was well educated by the standards of the time. There were men who worked in counting houses, shops, and mills. To be sure, 3 percent of the regiment were farm boys, but there were also fishermen and master mariners, an actor, an aeronaut, a dentist, a horse jockey, and a cigar maker. Thirteen percent of the First Regiment were jewelers.

Their names reflected their French, German, and Irish heritage, along with the familiar Anglo Saxon names of the founding families. British-born soldiers made up 4 percent, as did the Irish and Germans; 47 percent were Rhode Island–born and 14 percent from Massachusetts. There were a half dozen Ballous. The militiamen's average age was twenty-five; the oldest among them fifty-nine and the youngest only sixteen.[10] In forming the First Rhode Island Regiment,

> class, caste, sect, party, were all forgotten and rich and poor, native and foreigner, Protestant and Catholic, Radical and Conservative, Republican and Democrat, alike felt the mighty impulse . . . the names of several [were] identical to those of the officers of the early regiments of the Revolution . . . Thus, the spirit of the heroes of the Revolution lived again in their descendants . . . . Animated by the same deep love of country, the sons proved themselves worthy of their sires.[11]

There were other reasons to go, too. For some of the volunteers, the element of adventure figured as prominently as patriotism in their enlistment. A ninety-day tour of duty provided a chance to see the South and the national capital, "to see the elephant" as the contemporary phrase had it. The modest pay of the soldier subsidized what for many young men was a chance to experience some excitement, away from the drudgery of mucking out the stables or the monotony of tending machines in the mills. Wives, mothers, and sweethearts fretted about the risk, but for the men it was a chance to go camping and be a patriot all at once. Few seriously thought they would die—or even see much action—for it was commonly believed the Southerners would back off once the North had rallied its army. As one Regular Army officer wrote another who was leaving for service to the Confederacy,

> Your whole population is only about eight millions, while the north has twenty millions. Of your eight millions, three millions are slaves who may become an element of danger. You have no army, no navy, no treasury, and practically none of the manufactures and machineshops necessary for the support of armies, and for war on a large scale. You are but scattered agricultural communities, and you will be cut off from the

> rest of the world by blockade. Your cause must end in defeat, and the individual risks to you must be great.[12]

The most basic math revealed each Southern soldier would face four counterparts from the North. Bluster and patriotic fervor aside, the South's best chance lay in the North letting them leave the Union uncontested.

That April, Sullivan Ballou's love for his family collided with his love for his country. Sarah and the boys won. Despite knowing that four Ballou cousins, three Bowen cousins, and a passel of more distant relations, among them members of the Bliss, Bosworth, and Razee families, had already signed up, Sullivan did not enlist in the First Regiment. However great his anguish over his defeat at the polls, he did not seek the consolation of rushing into battle.

He and Sarah understood two things: He could do more for the war effort using his organizational skills through his position as judge advocate general than he could as a common soldier in the field. Also, Ballou was no close friend of Sprague, Burnside, or Slocum, the three genii behind the regiment so, practically speaking, he did not have the connections to get an officer's commission with the greater pay that would allow him to support his family. Having "felt too keenly the sufferings and pangs of orphanhood" in his own life, Sullivan knew his family would suffer if he left them unprovided for while he went off to serve on a mere private's pay of eleven dollars a month.[13] He had no other means to support them, no great savings, no property to sell off, just his earnings from his law practice, which would cease if he was gone.

Together, Sarah and her mother also urged her twenty-one-year-old younger brother, John, not to rush into anything they would all regret. The family already had plenty of kinfolk in the Third Massachusetts Rifles, the First Connecticut Volunteers, as well as in the First and Twentieth Ohio. Thankfully, Sarah's own sons were too young to go to war.

* * *

In response to the enlistment program in the North, Virginia's militia was mobilized to form an army massed just across the Potomac, ready to strike the national capital. Lincoln, his Cabinet, and the general in chief planned their next strategy. Alas, the elderly Scott's health was worsening, in correlation to the increase in his duties. The man under whose command the Rhode Island troops would be placed was bedridden, holding conferences from a chaise longue set up in the drawing room.

> "I am an old man," he said [to Lincoln]. "I have served my country faithfully I think, during a long life. I have been in two great wars and fought them through, and now another great war is on and I am nominally at the head of the army, but I don't know how many men are in the field, where they are, how they are armed and equipped or what they are capable of doing or what reasonably ought to be expected of them. Nobody comes to tell me and I am in ignorance about it, and can form no opinion respecting it."[14]

Nevertheless, Scott pushed himself and his small staff to complete the mountains of paperwork needed to mobilize an army. He and the president ordered several basic defensive actions to be taken. First, the Union forces burned their armory and depot at Harper's Ferry and evacuated the troops stationed there. Likewise, on Virginia's Atlantic coastline, at the key naval port of Newport News, a similar "scorched earth" plan was activated, destroying ships and docks. Unfortunately, in both places, the destruction was incomplete, and Southern troops, moving in on the heels of the Union forces, were able to salvage considerable materiel. On April 19, a small Virginian newspaper *The Republican Vindicator*, failed to publish because all its staff who were "members of the local militia companies had to march to Harper's Ferry immediately," to help capture its rifle-making machines.[15]

In Rhode Island, a de facto council of war had formed, and was completing the last arrangements for the First Regiment to ship out Saturday, April 20. Horses, fodder, artillery, men, rations, uniforms, ammunition—all had to be ready to go.

On Friday, April 19, there was still time for measured action. Lincoln issued a proclamation ordering a blockade of ports in the South, and the small Union Navy set sail to implement this order. Suddenly, the crisis exploded in all directions. Hostilities took place simultaneously on many fronts. That morning, Washington, D.C., learned that Harper's Ferry had fallen to the Virginia militia. In southern Virginia, the Norfolk Navy Yard was refusing to allow ships to sail out of the harbor, fearful they would reinforce the Union Navy. Regiments from New York, Pennsylvania, and Massachusetts were already traveling by train to the capital, retracing Lincoln's footsteps through a pandemonious Baltimore:

> At that hour, Baltimore was in the hands of a mob, which had sacked the gun shops and the liquor stores; the streets were barricaded and guarded by artillery and cavalry, and companies of secessionists were hurrying in from the neighborhood.[16]

In 1861, April 19 still remained something of a patriotic holy day in America, the anniversary of the Revolutionary War Battle of Lexington in Massachusetts, in which Minutemen had faced British Redcoats. This April 19, another group of Massachusetts men faced another battle, this time on the streets of hostile Baltimore. They were the men of the Sixth Massachusetts Regiment, whose hometowns were Lowell, Lawrence, Stoneham, and Boston. The men of Company G were from Worcester County—Shumway country.

Like Lincoln before them, the Sixth had to complete a transfer between railway stations. Where the route was narrowest, nearest the bay, the mob had taken anchors and chains off ships in port and barricaded the street. They attacked the cars using cudgels, throwing paving stones and yelling epithets like "Kill the white niggers."

Unable to remain in the cars once surrounded and halted, companies C, D, I, and L battled their way off the train. At first, they used only bayonets and rifle butts to push their way through the rabble, but the mob was armed and may have wrested guns away from the soldiers. Their commanding officer, gone ahead with the first companies that had managed to get through without incident, had given permission for his regiment to load their rifles with live ammunition for the passage through town.

The Sixth had no orders to fire their weapons, but, as the mob swarmed around them, pistol shots felled soldiers in the front of the line. The appearance of the mayor of Baltimore did not quell the rioters. Soldiers individually opened fire on the throng, and as many as twelve civilians lay dead in the streets of Baltimore. Had they fired by platoon, the death toll would have been huge.

The sound of gunfire brought the Baltimore police running from Camden Station, rather belatedly it would seem. They put themselves between the crowd and the rear guard of the soldiers, and loudly threatened to shoot anyone trying to breach their line. With the front ranks brandishing their loaded weapons, the Massachusetts militia were able to evacuate their four dead and thirty-one wounded, and reach Camden Street railway station.*

The mayor of Baltimore telegraphed President Lincoln with the horrifying news, which "rocked Washington to its foundations."[17] When the news reached the Northeast, there was alarm in Rhode Island, whose regiment was due to leave in just a few hours and travel the same route.

When the train carrying the Sixth Massachusetts huffed and puffed its way into the railway station for Washington, D.C., a

* Now the site of Camden Yards baseball park, home to the Baltimore Orioles.

friendly crowd was already waiting, among them women spontaneously come to nurse the wounded. Led forward by Clara Barton, they began to bandage wounds and staunch the flow of blood. The Barton girls had grown up in Shumway country and had come to the station to assist their old friends and neighbors. Washington did not have a hospital large enough to treat thirty-one wounded men—the closest military hospital was at Fort Leavenworth, Kansas! When the little E Street Infirmary could take no more wounded soldiers, Clara Barton and her sister, Sally Vassall, took these hometown folks back to Sally's house to nurse back to health.[18]

The president and his advisors immediately focused on the issue of moving troops safely through Maryland. It was hoped that Baltimore could be pacified but, temporarily, an alternate route was established, whereby troops disembarked at Annapolis, marched to the railway junction, and caught a train for the capital. The First Rhode Island was duly notified and diverted to this itinerary. Notice of this change, necessarily sent to all the states, ports, and railways, was hardly a secret. Rebel sympathizers promptly tore up twenty miles of track to foil the plan.

The good citizens of Baltimore petitioned the president and argued that no more troops should cross through their city. Others threatened that 75,000 fellow Marylanders would fight and repel any Northern troops transiting their state. Lincoln laconically replied that he reckoned that Maryland had sufficient ground to dig 75,000 graves.[19]

Maryland teetered between Unionism and Secessionism, and this weekend of April 20 to 21, the partisans of the latter held sway. Inflamed by the encounter with the Sixth Massachusetts, plans for retaliation for the civilian deaths were not long in coming. The wooden railroad bridges west and north of Baltimore were burned on April 20.

Washington awoke on Saturday to find itself without railway connections or communications to the loyal states, without any means of exchanging mail or newspapers from the North. Over the weekend, women and children were sent out of the district, while Southern sympathizers created an exodus over the bridges to Virginia. The hotels were empty, shops shuttered, and the streets deserted. Hoarding of food began in anticipation of a siege, but was short-lived when the government seized barrels of flour from the mills in Georgetown, and began storing them in the basements of federal buildings.

On Sunday night, April 21, the telegraph lines were cut; the president, Cabinet, general-in-chief, newspapers, and the entire remaining population of Washington were then completely cut off from the outside world. Lincoln had no way to know if, or how, the states were following through on their promises of sending soldiers.

The military situation in Washington, D.C., was critical. Those few Regular Army units in place, or recalled to the national capital to bolster its defense, lost soldiers as their Southern-born army and naval officers resigned their commissions and left for home. As the state militias of the Confederate states organized, the Regular Federal Army eroded. Desperate plans were made by the government to try and protect critical locations with the few loyal troops on hand.

The district entered a state of near hysteria, thanks to the boast of the Confederate secretary of war that the Stars and Bars would fly over Washington by May 1, and such reports as this one in the *Vicksburg Whig:*

> Major Ben McCullough has organized a force of five thousand men to seize the Federal Capital the instant the first blood is spilled.[20]

These bravura exhortations were Southern bluster, but terrified the residents of the capital. Lacking any natural defenses, it required for its protection a degree of manpower that was virtually nonexistent. Had Southern leaders been able to organize a concerted action and move on D.C. that weekend, they could have taken it.

General Scott's version of a bunker plan called for the president and Cabinet members to seek refuge in the sandbagged Treasury Building, which had new iron doors and a reliable supply of food and water. Colonel Irvin McDowell commanded the fortified Capitol Building: boards, stones, and casks of cement blocked the windows and casements. Heavy iron plates, destined for placement in the dome, instead formed breastworks on the porticos. Inside, statuary was boarded up for safekeeping. The militia, including the Clay Battalion, commanded by Kentucky orator Cassius M. Clay, guarded public buildings, and the two companies of Regular Army soldiers that had just returned from Texas stood watch over the bridges.[21]

Major David Hunter, who had become a personal friend of Lincoln while accompanying him from Illinois to Washington, D.C., was ordered by General Scott to take charge of the presidential mansion and coordinate security with John Hay. Hunter's guard detail "consisted of about one hundred gentlemen from all parts of the Union, who, on being apprised of the danger, cheerfully enrolled themselves for service."[22] The loyal Republican and senator-elect from Kentucky, Jim Lane, commanded these "Frontier Guards," a motley crew of treasury messengers, government clerks, and office seekers who had come to town in search of a political appointment and instead found themselves holding a musket and garrisoning the White House.[23]

Probably, during the day, they put on enough of a show outside on the grounds to let people know there were guards. At night, those men not on guard duty camped inside the White House, sleeping on the floor. The Lincoln women and children had not been sent out of town. Armed with pistols, David Hunter himself slept for six nights on the carpet of the East Room, defending the

Major David Hunter. *Courtesy of the Gil Barrett Collection.*

entrance to their quarters. (Lincoln was by now so fatalistic about the dangers surrounding his own life that, by April 18, when John Hay awakened him in the middle of the night to tell him of a new plot against his life, he just grinned and went back to sleep.)[24]

Arriving in New York harbor on April 21, the first batch of men of the First Regiment first learned they would have to proceed to Washington by a roundabout route to avoid the instability in Baltimore. Attending Sunday church services conducted on board their ship, the men could see the stars and stripes flying from all the buildings visible from the harbor, but they were not allowed shore leave in New York City before they boarded another boat to take them south.

That day, Lincoln and Hay went up on the roof of the White House to see if any Northern troops were yet entering the capital. They saw nothing through their telescope but the rebel flag flying over the rooftop of a building in Alexandria to the west.[25] Several more days tensely passed.

On one occasion during this waiting period, the president thought he heard cannon fire. No one else heard it, but Lincoln

This drawing conveys the sense of urgency surrounding the departure of the First Rhode Island Regiment and its battery. *From author's collection.*

went off alone to search for its source. He wandered the entire length of "the Island" by himself, until he came to the Arsenal. Its doors were flung wide open—there were no guards—its three officers and fifty-three ordnance men had fled.[26] The guns within could have been seized by anyone and put to any malevolent purpose. This did not bode well for the defense of Washington.

On Wednesday, April 24, the president received the wounded men of the Sixth Massachusetts at the White House, to thank them for their sacrifice. He seemed moody and despondent during most of the event, no more so than when he told them,

> I don't believe there is any North. The Seventh Regiment is a myth. Rhode Island is not known in our geography any longer. You are the only Northern realities.[27]

The blackout in communications had prevented the president from knowing that other troops were indeed on the way. As many

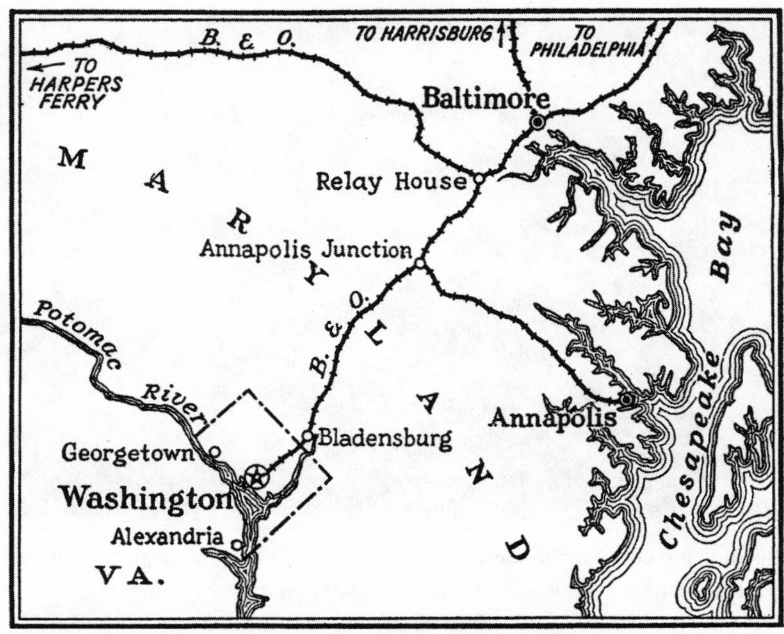

This map shows the railroad routes in Washington, D.C., in 1861. *Map by the Manhattan Drafting Company, originally published in* Reveille in Washington.

as five thousand more men were then pushing toward the national capital, if only they could get through. Their progress was hampered by efficient sabotage; along the route in Maryland, locomotives had been sent away or disabled, bridges and tracks burned or ripped up. But the Union troops were determined to protect their nation, and they had a trick or two up their sleeves as well.

The rail journey of the Eighth Massachusetts Regiment had been interrupted at Perryville, Maryland. Undaunted, they commandeered a ferryboat and sailed down the Susquehanna River to Annapolis and the hospitality of the Naval Academy, where they linked up with the Seventh New York. Their plans to ride the Elk Ridge–Annapolis rail line to the junction with the Baltimore and Ohio line to Washington were thwarted by destroyed bridges and lack of locomotives. As they prowled the deserted railroad station, they found a single, disabled locomotive left behind, and, as luck had it, among the soldiers were mechanics whose recent peacetime jobs had been building these locomotives in their home-town factory. They soon had it fixed, working, and coupled to a train, but the problem of the rails remained.

Thomas Scott, president of the Pennsylvania Railroad and a loyal Union man, had sent experienced crews to relay the tracks, and the men of the Seventh New York lent strong backs and willing hearts to the unaccustomed labor, helping to rebuild a bridge. Overseeing the work of Company H that day was Captain Henry C. Shumway, a fifty-three-year-old volunteer who had put aside his paint brushes and portraits to save democracy. The men continued their work by moonlight, so urgent was the need to complete the track to Annapolis Junction.

Scott had also brought along his personal telegraph operator, a talented young Scottish immigrant named Andrew Carnegie. Noting the telegraph lines alongside the railroad tracks had been damaged, Carnegie took the initiative to organize a crew of operators and linesmen, who helped the War Department reestablish telegraph connections with the capital. Carnegie personally drove the first troop train into the District on Wednesday, April 24, bringing with him the Eighth Massachusetts and the Seventh New York.[28]

The latter marched out of the railway station with perfect precision. Straight from their hard labor on the railroad, these elite young gentlemen from the drawing rooms of New York paraded first to the White House to salute the president, and then back to their assigned campsite at the Capitol Building. There, they set up bunks on the benches of the galleries, washed up in the congressional lavatories, and paraded back down the hill to dine in one of the hotels. The Eighth Massachusetts also bivouacked there.

The Rhode Islanders were just a day behind them, their three-day journey stretched to six by the circuitous route and a traffic jam at the docks of tiny Annapolis. After a nervous journey through Southern waters, where lighthouse beacons along the rocky coast had been extinguished by the Confederates, the steamer *Coatzacoalcus*, bearing the Rhode Islanders rendezvoused with the *Baltic*, carrying the Seventy-first New York Regiment, and escorted by the same ships that had been at Sumter, the convoy sailed north up the Chesapeake Bay, making for Annapolis on the western shore. The frigate *Constitution* was already docked at Annapolis, preparing to evacuate the Naval Academy staff and cadets to a location safe from Southern attack—Newport, Rhode Island.[29*]

After spending the night on the pine floors of empty buildings at the Naval Academy, at 5:00 A.M. on April 25, the half-strength First Rhode Island marched out of Annapolis, one hour after the full-strength Seventy-first New York. In seven hours, they covered an unremarkable eight miles, caught up with the New Yorkers marching in new shoes and carrying backpacks that were still too heavy with "all the comforts of home." As much burdened as aided by the "sundry broken down horses and mules," which pulled the "few rickety carts . . . procured at fabulous prices" in Annapolis, which creaked and groaned under the heavy military supplies, they made slow progress on the rutted dirt roads. The Rhode Islanders progressed another nine miles before they bivouacked for the night in the unsympathetic countryside of western Maryland. Whenever they asked the locals how far it was to the Annapolis [railway] Junction, the answer was always the same: "nine miles," a phrase that was to take on special meaning for them.

In the morning, they had only to march another four miles to the railway junction where thanks to the restored rail service, they boarded a train for Washington, D.C. A few hours later, at midday, Friday April 26, they arrived at the railway station near the Capitol, "were welcomed with every expression of delight," and

* Classes reconvened on May 13 at Fort Adams in Newport Harbor. The Naval Academy moved back to Annapolis on August 9, 1865.

were dispatched to quarters in the Patent Office.[30] There, they spread their bedrolls and red blankets and camped between Benjamin Franklin's printing press, George Washington's uniform, and "a menagerie of 'stuffed birds, beasts, fishes and insects.' "[31]

The second detachment under Pittman had left Providence on April 24; on the twenty-eighth, they sailed up the Potomac escorted by the omnipresent *Powhatan*, whose firepower discouraged the Confederates from shelling them though, just before the ships passed Alexandria, the men were ordered belowdecks as a precaution. They landed at the newly restaffed Washington Arsenal, just below the canal, where they spent the night. Compared to the cross-county adventures of their comrades, these men never even got their shoes dusty.

The next day, their comrades marched down to claim them, and the now-complete First Rhode Island Regiment paraded to the White House to be received by the president, the secretaries of war and state, and General Scott. It was noted that they marched especially smartly. As they passed by, Joe Green's band played "The Girl I Left Behind Me."[32] They next marched to the Patent Office to bivouac with the earlier arrivals.

The militias' very presence, combined with that of other regiments now arriving daily, was a deterrent to attack by organized Confederate forces or hostile mobs. Five regiments now in town meant that five thousand loyal troops were guarding the president, Congress, and the capital. Even the boldest of Confederate generals would have had serious second thoughts about attacking Washington now.

CHAPTER TEN

"Then to the South We Bore Away"*

Sullivan Ballou Joins the Army

May–June 1861

By the first of May, four thousand men at a time marched down the avenues of Washington, D.C., as the first regimental representatives of even the most distant states arrived to defend the Union. Most were first-time visitors to the capital. Each triumphant arrival was reported in the papers back home, the news avidly devoured. The men were safe after all, and having a wonderful time, and in their hometowns, their younger brothers and friends became eager to follow them. At first, the residents of Washington, too, were fascinated by the novelty of it all.

Northern public opinion followed the shift in strategic outcomes without blinking an eye. A sermon preached in Boston

* From the Civil War song "The Girl I Left Behind Me."

during the last week of April clearly affirmed the defense of the national capital was the prime objective:

> The struggle now is, not of opinion, but of civilization. . . . The war is not of aggression but of self defence; and Washington becomes the Thermopylae* of liberty and justice. Rather than surrender it, cover every foot of ground with a living man. Guard it with a million men, and empty our bank vaults to pay them[1]

President Lincoln, however, breathed only half a sigh of relief. Phase two of the war plan had begun in late April, as both sides started to organize and mobilize for the forthcoming conflict. Their numbers were sufficient if the sole intent was to garrison the capital, but it was not. Southern regiments were pouring into Richmond as the Confederacy built her own army and navy. The Union government could not cower in its fortified city forever; the threat had to be removed. It was now necessary for the North to build an army to meet the South in battle. For this, the Union needed not only more soldiers, but soldiers whose term of service allowed them to be extensively trained and used in offensive battles. So on May 3, the president called for yet more volunteers to form additional regiments; this time their term of enlistment was three years. The states needed to continue to mobilize their citizenry.

These militia units had to be made into an army, and only General Scott and Brigadier General Wool, two years older even than Scott but still able to mount a horse, had ever commanded anything as large as a brigade of several thousand men. At one point, Secretary of State William Seward asked Scott, "What shall we do for generals?"[2]

* Meaning a battle to the death; a classical reference to the climactic battle between the Spartans and Athenians in Ancient Greece, in which the Spartans perished trying to save their culture.

A successful army requires many different kinds of talents from its leaders—political, logistical, tactical planning, intelligence, and field command, to name a few. Only in the most exceptional cases are all these present in the same individual. At this early stage of the war, neither individual officers nor those in command in Washington knew where these talents were. They hoped experience would bring them forth, as it had in the Revolutionary War. When it came to "getting generals" from the Regular Army, it was a natural enough dynamic for Lincoln, Scott, and Stanton to turn to those they had come to know during the present crisis, those who had demonstrated leadership and loyalty, albeit in limited circumstances, men like Keyes, Hunter, and McDowell. North and South alike promoted new generals from among the West Point Military Academy graduates amid intense, behind-the-scenes wrangling. High-ranking military commanders, aided by politicians from their home states, struggled for preeminence among their peers, rapid promotions, and the "best" commands.

The states had the right to name the generals commanding their respective militias, and these appointments often went to politicians, like attorney Benjamin Butler of Boston, who commanded the Sixth and Eighth Massachusetts regiments, among others; State Senator Egbert Jones who got the Fourth Alabama; and Francis Bartow, who led the Seventh and Eighth Georgia.

For the Union, fifty-four-year-old Irish-born Robert Patterson was commissioned a major general and given command of the districts of Delaware, Pennsylvania, Maryland, and Washington, D.C.—a command that only lasted eight days before it was divided among himself and generals Butler and Mansfield.

In the last week of April, military security was still so elusive that the commissioner of public buildings requisitioned more guns, doubling the number of Colt revolvers at the White House from six to twelve.[3] The *Staunton* [Virginia] *Spectator* urged laying siege to Washington to force the capitulation of the president.[4] And young Johnston Hastings Skelly,* writing home to Gettysburg from the camp of the Second Pennsylvania, expressed the ongoing uncertainty about Maryland's loyalty: "I suppose we will leave here sometime this week for Washington. I don't know whether we go through Baltimore or not."[5] The governor of Maryland withdrew with the legislature to the more northerly city of Frederick, astride the key Baltimore and Ohio railway line to Harper's Ferry. On April 27, Corporal Sumner Henry Needham, Sr., one of the wounded soldiers from the Sixth Massachusetts Infantry, died of his wounds. The same age as Sullivan Ballou, Needham left behind a newborn son, Henry Junior.[6]

Also on April 27, Lincoln found it necessary to vacate constitutional guarantees on incarceration, search, and seizure in the specific geographic area along the railroad lines from Philadelphia to Washington, D.C. He suspended the habeas corpus right to a prompt hearing after arrest. It was a desperate move to keep the railroads moving by going after the guerrilla secessionists that were crippling them. The processes of justice in that area were militarized and placed under the authority of General Scott. Military courts were henceforth to try railroad terrorists. The Lincoln government was neither the first nor the last, while under duress, to resort to repressive measures that eroded civil liberties.

On Thursday, May 2, "there was a grand celebration at the Patent Office, where the president hoisted the big new flag contributed by the clerks of the Interior Department."[7] The entire First Rhode Island Regiment turned out, paraded, and sang "Our Flag Still Waves." They later marched to the Capitol grounds for their formal induction into federal services. There, the companies lined up forming a hollow square around the American and Revolutionary flags. With the sunset "lighting up the front of the

* Skelly was the fiancé of the only civilian casualty during the Battle of Gettysburg in 1863, Jenny Wade.

Capitol," eleven hundred voices "rose in one volume in the air" taking the oath of allegiance:

> I ______, do solemnly swear that I will bear true allegiance to the United States of America, and that I will serve honestly and faithfully, against all their enemies or opposers whatsoever, and observe and obey the orders of the President of the United States, and the orders of the officers appointed over me, according to the rules and regulations for the government of the armies of the United States.[8]

The ceremony completed, the men broke into columns and unfurled their red blankets to use as overcoats against the chill spring air. The dapper Governor Sprague, astride a white horse at the head of the column, led their march back to the Patent Office Building.[9] Later this same day, the Providence Marine Corps of Artillery, commanded by Colonel Charles H. Tompkins, Sullivan and Sarah's landlord in Cranston, arrived in Washington via the Potomac River.

On May 4, in the wee hours of the morning, a fire broke out in a tailor's shop adjacent to the fully occupied Willard's Hotel. The alarm was raised to summon the local firefighting volunteers, but they had unexpected reinforcements. The men of the Eleventh New York had been recruited from the volunteer firefighters of New York City by a close friend of the president, Elmer Ellsworth. Outfitted in the flamboyant Algerian-style uniforms known as "Zouaves," they had kept in shape by climbing the unfinished Capitol dome and swinging from lightning rods. They turned out en masse and, for five hours, from 3:00 to 8:00 A.M., the firemen of New York City, nicknamed "Lincoln's Pet Lambs," battled the fire and succeeded in extinguishing it. Washingtonians had never seen anything like the acrobatics of these men who formed a human ladder to pass along buckets of water. Willard's invited them in for breakfast to say thank-you and they were the talk—and the toast—of the town for days.[10]

As North and South began to mobilize, it was inevitable that both jockeyed for control of Alexandria. On May 5, the Confederate commander in Arlington pulled his troops out. Pitifully equipped with the Revolutionary War flintlocks of their grandfathers, without ammunition, each local man spending the night in his family home, this was no fighting force capable of repelling or delaying a Union advance.

The Union was likewise not in any position to advance west that first week of May; their highest priority was to stabilize Maryland, their chief route to the north. General Scott assigned General Benjamin Butler and his Massachusetts men to occupy an important railway junction in Maryland, to guarantee the passage of troops. Called "Relay" because it represented the distance that a team of oxen could drag a rail car between sets of tracks in years past, Relay House, or "the Relay," controlled the main line between Baltimore and the North.

On May 6, Jefferson Davis signed the South's bill of war, commenting, "We desire peace at any sacrifice save that of honor and independence."[11] That same date, Arkansas seceded, followed in a matter of days by North Carolina and Tennessee, swelling the ranks of the Confederacy to its final tally of eleven states.

On May 8, the First Rhode Island was assigned to a rural campsite north of the city boundary, among the plantations outside the capital, and dispatched a committee of men to negotiate specifics with the landowner, Mr. Keating, and to survey, design, and build the camp.

> A broad lawn became the parade ground, and the Keating House became a "comfortable hospital." . . . in two weeks' time, a miniature village for the accommodation of twelve hundred inhabitants was built, planned by Private Henry De Witt of Company C. Rough board huts with sleeping

arrangements for eighteen persons each, and with a porch in front for the dining hall, were our habitations. Our streets received the names of those familiar at home, and our village was named for the Governor of the State.[12]

Company D, under Second Lieutenant Henry Prescott, was the first to move in on May 14, and was followed by all the others, so that by May 18, the camp was fully populated. The bunks were filled with fresh straw for bedding, and the men personalized their huts with signs and decorations. The camp had officers' quarters; a regimental street for the commanding officer, chaplain, and surgeon; streets of huts, "roofed in felt," for each company; a commissary and a hospital; strategically located latrines; and a designated meadow for the horses. Their neighbors were the New Jersey Brigade, camped on Meridian Hill, near the Seventh New York. The First and Second Connecticut regiments were assigned a campsite on the grounds of Glenwood, W. W. Corcoran's "fine estate" two miles north of the city. Between their camp and the Rhode Islanders', not far from the Bladensburg Road, was Glenwood Cemetery.[13]

As the rather sleepy city began to fill up with regiments, the caliber of the street theater increased dramatically. Secession-minded residents taunted and insulted the Union soldiers, who were sorely tempted to brawl with or arrest them. A herd of cattle, bought to provide fresh beef for the soldiers, was put to pasture in the grounds of the Washington Monument only to fall into the canal. It took a day and a half to drive them back ashore.[14]

On May 10, relieved by the newly appointed major of the First Rhode Island, druggist Joseph Balch, Major John Slocum returned home to Providence to recruit the next regiment, the three-year men Lincoln had requested a week earlier: another twelve hundred men and officers to defend the Union and liberty. Luckily, they were already partially enlisted.

On the night of May 13, displaying considerable verve and total disregard for his chain of command, General Butler realized he could enter Baltimore by stealth, occupy it, and present the Union with a pacified railroad hub. He did so unobserved during the early hours of the morning. The residents of Baltimore awoke to find a regiment of Union troops in town, and a battery of artillery planted on top of Federal Hill from where it could fire on the harbor or any other sector of town. The Sixth Massachusetts now controlled Baltimore, and could ensure that no other regiment received the same bloody welcome they had.

By May 14, the *New York Herald* could report,

> The railroad through Baltimore is open, the route clear, and the bridges all secure and well guarded. . . . The capital is now completely encircled with encampments, controlling all the railroads. . . . strong efforts are being made even by members of the Cabinet, to induce [General Scott] to advance his forces into Virginia, but he is resolute in maintaining his present position until he is quite ready to move.[15]

Several important promotions were made within the Union Army command that Tuesday. Irvin McDowell and Joseph Mansfield were promoted to brigadier general. Both had held only staff positions since the Mexican War, and neither had experience in commanding large-scale operations on a battlefield. So the military trio upon whom Lincoln had to rely consisted of an aged war hero with command experience yet who was too frail to go to the field, and two untested staff officers. It was the best the rusty Regular Army could provide in 1861, and was the harvest of a peaceful nation. As described by his adjutant,

> Major Irvin McDowell was 43 years of age, of unexceptionable habits and great physical powers. His education, begun

> in France, was continued at the United States Military Academy, from which he was graduated in 1838. Always a close student, he was well-informed outside as well as inside his profession.
>
> Distinguished in the Mexican war, intensely Union in his sentiments, full of energy and patriotism, outspoken in his opinions, . . . he had at once secured the confidence of the president and the Secretary of War, under whose observation he was serving in Washington.[16]

Mansfield was fifty-eight, from Connecticut, and after graduation from West Point, second in his class, entered the Engineering Corps. Like Lee and Beauregard, he had been assigned to supervise southern coastal forts, and had participated in the Mexican War.[17]

On May 16, Ensign Levi Tower of the First Rhode Island was given top-secret orders to assemble a boat detail, consisting of twenty-five privates and one sergeant, whom the authorities had hoped had some sailing experience. While they remained ready to deploy at a moment's notice, they were still in Washington as of May 23, 1861. Their mission was to prepare a military ferry service across the Potomac River between Washington and Alexandria, so troops could be landed secretly to seize the town.[18]

On Monday, May 20, the Confederacy transferred its national capital to Richmond, Virginia, a rail hub located close enough to the Northern border to be an effective military command and control center; and Jefferson Davis prepared to depart the old capital in Montgomery, Alabama. When the voters of Virginia ratified secession on May 23, the Union Army created the Department of Virginia to control all military actions expected to take place within that state. Under cover of darkness on May 24, with no advance fanfare, and no bands playing, the Union Army advanced nine regiments in a three-pronged movement across the Potomac. Using the bridges and the ferry service, they quickly took control of Alexandria and its port, which surrendered without contest. The vanguard leading the march across Long Bridge were the Washington, D.C., home guard units formed just a month before, followed by regiments of New York volunteers. The Union now established a toehold on the river's western bank and secured the bridges across the Potomac against sabotage.

One act of Union bravado on the first day of occupation turned out tragically, however, giving the Union its first major hero of the war. Young, dashing Colonel Elmer Ellsworth, of the Eleventh New York, entered private property—a hotel flying the Confederate flag from a tall pole atop its roof, a flag that could be seen from the White House. Ellsworth ripped down the offending banner and returned down the staircase to exit. The homeowner emerged from an upper room and shot the trespasser dead on the spot—and was himself immediately killed by Ellsworth's backup.

Both were needless deaths. Because they occurred at a time when people's sensibilities were not yet bludgeoned by body counts, both sides were able to focus attention on the deaths and each man became a hero to his respective cause.

Ellsworth's funeral was held at the White House, where Lincoln cried openly over the loss of his young friend. Images of the Union champion loomed large in the press and served as the basis for an unofficial "Remember Ellsworth" campaign that boosted recruitment efforts.

Rhode Island needed no help raising regiments—in fact, they had more men than they could handle. No sooner had the First Regiment departed than the governor and commander of the militia had thought it prudent to create a second regiment—just in case—and had posted recruitment notices. So great was the response to the call in Rhode Island that a diplomatic balancing act was required to let every section of the state be represented in the Second Regiment. The governor had to issue a decree merging various Providence militia companies.[19] "The State was all astir, and every town wore the features of a military camp."[20] The newspapers breathlessly announced every piece of trivia associated with the mobilization, such as the arrival by "propeller" ship of "150 light artillery sabers" for the personal defense of the members of the Rhode Island Battery.[21] Women hurriedly sewed uniforms, flags, and havelocks.

Elisha Hunt Rhodes, a young store clerk in Providence, kept a diary that provides a reliable and lively record of this Second Rhode Island Regiment, from its earliest days. Like Sullivan Ballou, Rhodes's family situation had prevented his enlistment in the First Regiment though for the young clerk, it was a widowed mother whom he had to support. She at last relented, showing "a patriotic spirit that much inspired my young heart."[22] Throughout the state, similar scenes were being played out, as families struggled to decide what precedence love of country, patriotism, and a sense of adventure had over their personal and business responsibilities.

Sullivan discussed his options with his friends when he had the chance, as did his cousin in Ohio, James Garfield, whose friend wrote,

> We talked of our personal duty, and though both Garfield and myself had young families, we were agreed that our activity in the organization and support of the Republican party made the duty of supporting the Government by military service come peculiarly home to us.[23]

Many found themselves seduced by the ongoing need for soldiers. One such soldier confessed,

> As the war progressed, and our brave three months men met with misfortune, the President was authorized by Congress to call for 500,000 vols. for three years. Then I could hesitate no longer. . . . [My wife] . . . did not like to have me go but said very little.[24]

It was unlikely that Sarah Ballou said little about Sullivan's future. Indications are that the couple maintained a dialogue about the implications of his service, including their finances, their living arrangements, and his health and well-being in the field.

A second physical examination was set up for inductees, in the hopes of reducing the overenlistment; men known to be bullies were also turned away.[25] Colonel Slocum, and the man who was to be surgeon to this regiment, Dr. Francis L. Wheaton, presided over the selection. About-to-be Private Rhodes was appointed clerk and wrote down the names of the men the doctor passed. Wheaton did not want to sign Rhodes up, telling Colonel Slocum that the slightly built boy "will be in the hospital in a week and we shall have to send him home." The Colonel was not fazed and insisted the eager young man should be allowed in, even if they had to send him home later.

The contingent of young men accepted along with Rhodes were sent to Captain William Steere, who had already mustered a full complement of one hundred men for his company. Informed by the governor that room must be made for twenty-five volunteers from the three Providence Guard companies, he grudgingly accepted the newcomers, busted them in rank, and detained the whole company in the Armory where they "howled most of the night, much to the disgust of the Captain," but soon all settled in to soldiering.[26] By the first of June, the companies were formed and beginning training at the Cadet Armory near the State House in Providence.

Coming less than a month after the exertions to hasten the First Regiment to Washington, the state once again mobilized its business, financial, and political resources to organize, equip, and prepare "a thousand comforts for those who went to the front."[27] It was obvious to the government and business leaders in Providence, from the news from Washington, that this was no sixty-day crisis, and it was reasonable to put the state on a war footing. All of the ad hoc committees trying to organize regiments made for too chaotic and disruptive a process. On May 30, the General Assembly further organized the Rhode Island military forces, appointing three new statewide militia officers to join Sullivan, now reappointed to his fourth straight term as judge advocate general of the Rhode Island Militia.[28]

The officers were an adjutant general to keep the records of all enlistments, commissions, and discharges; a commissary general to provide food while the troops were in Rhode Island; and a quartermaster general to purchase, issue, and monitor all uniforms, weapons, supplies, and materiel. Rhode Island also supplied their own distinctive uniforms, rifles, cannons, and initial ammunition. After the troops were mustered into and deployed with the Union Army, their food and replenished ammunition was provided by the federal quartermaster. The mayor of Providence, Jabez Knight, doubled as militia paymaster general. A respected local physician, Francis L. Wheaton, became the surgeon general.[29]

With thousands of men under arms, Sullivan now had a more lively role to play the war, eventually providing real courts martial instead of the peacetime tiffs of feuding commanders. To oversee the legal integrity of the processes of justice, and guarantee that the standards of justice of their home state continued to protect them even when serving far from home, Sullivan managed all courts martial involving men of the rank of captain and below. He had the powers of arrest and subpoena, and prosecuted each case himself or assigned another counsel. A three-judge panel heard the cases, and a conviction required two votes; the verdict of the court was then sent to the governor for his review, approval, or alteration.[30]

It is unclear what this position paid, if anything, and while it lacked the excitement of combat service, Sullivan was still able to keep his civilian law practice. He and the two Charlies—Brownell and Parkhurst—were again reappointed as notaries public for Providence County.[31]

Regular Army men were engaged to drill the raw recruits but the Second Regiment still lacked field officers to oversee innumerable complex preparations: Tents, ammunition, boots, hats, haversacks, and canteens needed to be purchased for a thousand men, and flags sewn. Guns had to be transferred from the State Armory. Sturdy and suitable horses were needed, and many were purchased from Vermont or neighboring states, which required contacts with the horse dealers. There needed to be coordination with private benefactors who provided drill barracks and meals. The pastors of churches had to know when and where the regiment would worship. The press needed a liaison contact, so they could keep the populace informed of the troops' activities. A schedule had to be made for each ceremony, and all participating dignitaries notified in advance and accommodated.

Governor Sprague again stepped in and loaned one of his aides, Lieutenant Colonel Robbins, originally slated to command the Second, to assist Colonel Slocum. Now, appointments needed to be made from the top down. A small state, Rhode Island boasted few West Point graduates. Accordingly, Sprague sought men from everyday life with a commanding presence: brave, intelligent, and reliable men, who could be counted upon to be industrious in acquiring knowledge of their profession, and conscientious in the performance of their duties; driven men willing to lead others to victory following the precepts for the ideal officer in the military manual from which they were to learn their new craft.

> He should possess a high sense of honor, a great pride in his peculiar arm of service, and confidence in himself to perform the tasks assigned to him. . . . pursued persistently in spite of all obstacles; energy and perseverance will compensate for lack of genius and anticipate ill fortune. With these qualifications in his mind and at his command, no officer will fail to realize an enviable future.[32]

The Second Rhode Island Regiment in late May

Colonel John Slocum
Adjutant—vacant
Lieutenant Colonel—vacant
Major—vacant
Chaplain—vacant
Surgeon Francis L. Wheaton

Company A	
Captain Cyrus Dyer	Aponaug, Natick, and Phenix
Company B	
Captain John Wright	Scituate, Johnson, and Cranston
Company C	
Captain Nelson Viall	Providence
Company D	
Captain William Steere	Providence
Company E	
Captain Isaac Rodman	South Kingston
Company F	
Captain Levi Tower	Pawtucket, Valley Falls, Central Falls
Company G	
Captain Nathan Goff, Jr.	Bristol County
Company H	
Captain Charles W. Greene	East Greenwich & environs
Company I	
Captain S. James Smith	Smithfield, Woonsocket, and Greenville
Company K	
Captain Charles W. Turner	Newport County

In Providence, after the white-hot excitement of the departure of the First Regiment cooled, Sullivan, one of Rhode Island's earliest advocates of action, found himself still on the sidelines as he attended the General Assembly meeting in Newport. Military affairs dominated that session, during which a resolution was passed welcoming the U.S. Naval Academy to the State and offering to cede jurisdiction of the 150 acres of Victorian buildings it was occupying to the federal government.[33]

Before 5:00 A.M. on May 28, 1861, phase three of the Northern war plan began when Brigadier General McDowell moved across the Potomac to personally oversee the gradual assemblage of two divisions of troops around him in Arlington. The port of Alexandria, the turnpikes, the fields, and hillsides became a beehive of activity. It was prudent to establish headquarters on an elevated position that could literally oversee all Union positions on the western bank of the Potomac as well as the fortifications they would begin building as almost every acre of land was being converted to the use of the army. McDowell chose to use the grounds of Arlington House, the elegant, Greek-pillared mansion sitting on 1,100 acres overlooking the Potomac. It was General Robert E. Lee's home.

The house was built by the grandson of Martha Custis Washington by her first marriage; Robert E. Lee married Mary Custis, the daughter of George Washington's godson, in 1831, and for thirty years, the estate was their home base and the birthplace of their seven children. Lee wrote a cousin that at Arlington House "my affections and attachments are more strongly placed than at any other place in the world." He had left the estate on April 22, 1861, when he followed Virginia in her secession from the Union and went south to Richmond to accept command of Virginia's military forces. Mrs. Lee, an invalid who suffered from rheumatoid arthritis, left about a month later after being notified by General Scott that the Union Army required the use of her house. Indignant but resigned, she moved eleven miles away to the home of an uncle, taking with her some furniture, personal valuables, and priceless family heirlooms of George Washington, including his uniform, papers, and artifacts.[34]

McDowell's presence protected the Lee-Custis family mansion; he posted a guard at the door and slept in his tent on the lawn. McDowell served at the displeasure of his own commanding officer. General Mansfield had been Scott's preferred choice—Scott had persuaded Lincoln to let him backdate Mansfield's date of promotion so McDowell could not be considered the more senior general—but Mansfield was deemed essential to the defense of the capital itself and had to remain there. Outmaneuvered by politics, Scott had no choice but to appoint McDowell to command in Virginia, but went so far as to suggest he decline the appointment. McDowell related,

> I said I could not do that. . . . Just appointed a general officer, it was not for me to make a personal request not to take the command to which I had been ordered. . . . I refused to make any such application. . . . General Scott was exceedingly displeased that I should go over there. And he was piqued and irritated that I was sent over there . . . The general had opposed my somewhat rapid promotion. The general was cool for a great while. . . .[35]

It did not bode well for the future effectiveness of military operations that such strong, interpersonal rifts had already developed only six weeks into the war-planning process.

The Union hugged the riverbank, not daring to push farther inland to scout the foe until May 31. On that date, some of Company B of the Second Cavalry USA skirmished with an equal force of superior Confederate cavalry from a battalion commanded by Brigadier General Richard Ewell, at Fairfax Courthouse, a small town that the federal forces might have taken without resistance earlier in the week. On that Friday, they were twice repulsed and sent galloping back to their own lines before they could learn anything about the enemy's deployment or numbers.

As frequently happened when men retreat, they attribute it to having run into a much larger number of troops—heaven knows it could never mean they were outsoldiered—and the Second Cavalry were no different. This perception of superior numbers, which was later proved inaccurate, had the unfortunate effect of postponing any further reconnaissance missions into Prince William County for a critical two weeks. Wags referred to it as the "Charge of the Light Brigade," a tongue-in-cheek reference to a disastrous British cavalry movement in the Crimean War.

In Rhode Island, the military happenings were more positive, even festive. On June 5, the men of the Second Regiment were "mustered into the U.S. Service" and that evening were fitted out with their uniforms, "a blue flannel shirt worn with the flaps outside of the pants, grey pants, fatigue or forage cap and shoes."[36] Corporal Rhodes, having won back part of his lost promotion, immediately donned his new uniform and got permission to make the ten-mile round trip walk home to show it off to his mother and envious friends. It was his last visit home before the regiment shipped south.

That week, the men moved to the Dexter Training Ground, south of Federal Hill, and set up their tent city. The regiment had been provided with the excellent, cone-shaped Sibley tents, which housed ten men apiece. Here, the men learned the basics of outdoor camping and group discipline, in the camp where "everything is conducted according to the formal regulations of the army."[37]

Militia veterans knew army structure, but now hundreds of men had to learn the command hierarchy just to understand their role in the larger system. The informal, smallest unit was a mess, usually about half a dozen men who cooked and ate together and were often tent mates. The company was the basic official unit, purportedly one hundred men, but in practice often only sixty to eighty. If a company needed to divide in half, each half was a platoon, which was thirty to fifty men. The predominant rank was private, with as many as eight corporals and five sergeants, the latter known as first through fifth. Each company was commanded by a captain, often a man from the same county or town as the men, having

> one to three lieutenants to assist in the duties of running the company. These include being present at roll calls, pay call, preparing paperwork, inspecting the quarters, kitchen and latrines, and stable duty. The lieutenants make sure that all tasks are performed to the proper standard.[38]

At this level, no military experience was required, and the captains of the Second Rhode Island came from various nonmilitary backgrounds, and included a stone mason, a railroad ticket master, and a molding maker.

Sullivan knew at least half these men. Twenty-five-year-old bachelor Levi Tower, whose family lived down the street in Pawtucket from Sullivan's mother and the Bogles, was carrying on a tradition of service dating back to an eponymous forebear in the Revolutionary War. Coincidentally, Colonel Slocum was a Pawtucket man. With all his commuting around the state, Sullivan surely knew the ticket master, and he and Sarah knew James Smith and his wife, the apothecary from Woonsocket. Cyrus Dyer, commanding Company A and something of a John Mosby look-alike, wore a bushy beard that reached to his collarbone, and ostrich plumes pinned to his hat.

Ten companies made up a regiment, commanded by a colonel, and always designated as being from the single state that raised it, even though some of its soldiers may have joined from adjoining states. The rest of the field staff was the lieutenant colonel and a major. A small headquarters staff included a chaplain, at least two surgeons, hospital stewards, and an aide or two for the colonel. The Rhode Island regimental band members carried their instruments and played music while going into battle, and carried the wounded out on stretchers to the hospital after the battle.

Unofficially, behind the scenes, a variety of servants who had worked for the officers in peacetime, or who were hired locally to cook, fetch water, chop wood, do laundry and mend clothes, supported the regiment. Seen moving around the camp were two Black servants, Robert Holloway and Frederick Bub, in the employ of officers Ambrose Burnside and William Reynolds.

As many as four regiments combined to make a brigade, commanded by either a brigadier general or a colonel. The Confederates really only used brigades at First Manassas, despite Beauregard titularly controlling I Corps. They also used the term, "legion," meaning a subbrigade. Next was the division, composed of three to four brigades. The Union Army organized at this level for the battle of First Manassas. As time wore on, the men identified themselves with the commanding officer, and wrote home that they were in Burnside's Brigade or Hunter's Division or Hampton's Legion.

The use of army corps was not established until later in the Civil War, when a corps meant one or more divisions, or sometimes a division and remnants of regiments. Northern corps were identified by a Roman numeral, and a distinctive design, like a diamond, sewn onto caps and flags, to help the men distinguish their own when the size of the fighting force swelled. Multiple corps made an army, which normally had a geographic name related to the theater of war in which it fought, such as the Army of Tennessee, or the Army of Virginia. To support such a huge army, the secretary of war established a department, normally congruent with the state in which it was operating. When the voters of Virginia approved secession, the Union promptly created the Department of Virginia.

In early June, the Second Regiment paraded through Providence, going about its business, warming the patriotic hearts of the citizenry who

> enjoyed the unusual spectacle of a field camp, of reveilles, dress-parades, firing of artillery by sunrise and sunset, of tattoo and taps. The unusual sight attracted multitudes of men, women and children, day after day. While in camp, mounted battery drills wore away the hours of impatience.[39]

On June 7, the Second Rhode Island, now numbered into companies A through K, minus a "J" to avoid visual confusion, formed up as a regiment for the very first time and marched to the heart of town, to Exchange Place, to participate in the memorial services for a great patriot: the late Senator Stephen A. Douglas had worn out his health during his energetic presidential campaign and his efforts to save the Union, and had recently died.

This was a major event with military and political overtones, and both Governor Sprague and Sullivan Ballou were probably there. The two men did not move in the same financial or social circles. They had missed being in government together by a couple of years, and of course, had run on opposite tickets in the recent election; but somewhere along the line, the governor would have noted the many civic activities and organizing abilities of Ballou, who was two years his senior. Their coming together may have provided the moment for William Sprague to discuss with Sullivan the still-vacant post of major in the Second Regiment. Sprague

> had early learned that the wisest choice of material for officers, where all were unskilled in the art of war, was to select men of ability and education, who would be apt at learning from books, and who would make the most of experience as they obtained it.[40]

Surrounded by the reality of another set of friends and acquaintances going off to war, and the deluge of patriotic feeling that accompanied it, and surely embarrassed that his financial situation held him back, Sullivan would have listened attentively. That day, or shortly thereafter, Sprague offered him the post, and probably required a response within a day or two. Whoever accepted would need to set his personal affairs in order in great haste and begin to assist Colonel Slocum.

To move the men, gear, guns, and horses from the Dexter Training Ground to the capital required a journey of more than a dozen stops and three different kinds of transportation. A detailed schedule was necessary to avoid a traffic jam through downtown Providence, or at the docks. Food for the journey had to be arranged.

Coordinating the arrival day and time, and camp space in Washington with the War Department was ever more complicated, and necessitated frequent use of the telegraph. Once in D.C., the regiment would require such federally issued items as ambulances, wagons, supplies of forms, mail bags, and a chain of command.

A major would assist the colonel in all matters related to the care of the men—their pay, provisions, shelter, transportation, and armaments.

> In the field, whilst with his regiment, he has to see to the drill and equipment of the men in conjunction with the Adjutant. Being a field officer, he is mounted on all parades and in action.[41]

Moreover,

> When any commissioned officer shall die or be killed in the service of the United States, the major of the regiment . . . shall immediately secure all his effects or equipage, then in camp or quarters, and shall make an inventory thereof, and forthwith transmit the same to the office of the Department of War, to the end that his executors or administrators may receive the same.[42]

Becoming a major immediately cast Sullivan into a prominent position; though the lowest level of field officer, he still outranked the company officers. Major was a distinguished position: Major Anderson had commanded at Fort Sumter, Major Hunter had escorted president-elect Lincoln to Washington. It was easy to see it as another honor come to his career, another step that might well pay off in the future. Rogers related,

> The offer was entirely unexpected and unsolicited on the part of Ballou . . . In such a crisis, when office sought him, he did not feel that he could decline the appointment.[43]

Sarah was as much a patriot as he, supported the Union cause, and understood that the women of her family had sent their men off to war in the past. In June 1861, Sarah conformed to the behavior many other women were demonstrating, "those whose hearts have been too brave to be selfish, and too faithful to duty, even to listen to the voice of love itself." Women had an expected role to play, too, and the emphasis was heavy on sacrifice: "Brave Women! Let us honor their self-denying virtue."[44] There was no mention of her having raised objections.

By June 11, Sullivan accepted the appointment and it was announced. Unable to travel up to Woonsocket, he wrote his cousin Latimer the following revealing letter:

> Providence June 11 1861
> My very dear Friend
> Gov Sprague has tendered me the Commission of Major in the 2d Regiment of R.I. Detached Militia and I have accepted it. In the hasty and somewhat confused contemplation of my new position which I have been able to give it, my heart yearns for friendly converse with you. You have long been too kind to me—and I have too long resorted to you for

encouragement and advice not to think of you now when I realize the full value of all my friends and the pain & loss of parting from them. God bless you and reward you as the truest friend I ever had.

I have searched my conduct and motives to know if I have done wrong in thus changing and perhaps periling the course of my life, and I am not sensible of having wronged myself or my family; but the base thought of leaving my wife and little boys is full of intense pain. It was one thing to talk over the matter before I accepted the commission and a very different thing to feel that I am now under marching orders.

If I fall, I know it can never be in a better cause. I am too thoroughly convinced of the justice of this war—know too well the peril of our free institutions and the value to the world of our American civilization, even to hesitate to cast in my life if it is called for; but I have felt too keenly the sufferings and pangs of orphanhood and have seen too many trials of the widowed mother not to fear for my dear little boys and tremble for my wife. If necessary will you not sometime give them that kind and effective counsel you have often given me.

Do not think me weak or lacking in courage in thus expressing this only feeling that burdens my heart. I could not help doing it to you.

I shall doubtless see you before we leave as I must come to town and arrange a few little matters I have there. Can you not induce Smith to pay that draft before I go; He is not aware how much I need that money, or he would pay it promptly.

Yours affectionately,
S. Ballou[45]

Sullivan and Sarah started a crazed round of tasks to get him ready to leave with the regiment in a week. He had to be fitted for an officer's uniform, acquire a sword, and purchase various trappings, such as gloves, hat, sash, and probably, boots. No one else but Sullivan mentioned being vaccinated for smallpox, but at some point over the next ten days he was, a rather risky thing to do just before departure. He spent hours at camp at Dexter Training Ground, around town as needed for regimental business, and probably met with his mother and sister to say good-bye. Perhaps Sarah brought Edgar and Willie to see their papa and all the soldiers at their camp. One of the last things he did before leaving on Monday, June 17, was to dictate his will, in the presence of his close friend and later biographer, Horatio Rogers, Jr. The short document named Sarah as executrix of his estate.

In the 1800s, wills were usually made when individuals were experiencing their last illness, and were normally witnessed by mature men who were close friends of the deceasing. Rogers witnessed the will, and then for the other two signatures seemed to have pressed into service two young men who happened to be handy, the young Bolles brothers. Twenty-three-year-old Lucius, a graduate of Brown in 1859, was still a medical student, living with his widowed mother; and Nicholas was a bank clerk who worked downtown. Sullivan, "with tender earnestness," advised Rogers and the young Bolles boys not to hasten to join the army, "unless his services were imperatively demanded, as if the uniform of the soldier were the pall of death."* Rogers was struck by Sullivan's sixth sense:

> Those of us, who knew him well and watched his arrangements preparatory to his entrance upon military duties, could

* To a point, they followed his advice. Nicholas joined the Tenth Rhode Island as a first lieutenant in 1862, served on special duty, and mustered out four months later. Lucius enlisted as a surgeon with the Second in 1863, resigned when his brother died that fall, rejoined three months later, and survived the war.

> easily see that the terrible and unerring presentiment that he would never return, haunted him from the very acceptance of his commission.[46]

Perhaps Sarah and Sullivan were present at the evening dress parade ceremony on the twelfth, in which the ladies of Providence presented an "elegant stand of colors" to the regiment. Like other women all over the North and South, their needles had been flying in and out of wool and silk. Probably organized at the sewing-circle level, they had sewn two full-size, square-shaped flags. One was the Stars and Stripes, a "beautiful American ensign of [white] silk, with gold fringe and tassels, and having the name, "2d Regiment R. I. V.," inscribed in gold letters on the center red stripe. The red stripes were all appliquéd, as was the blue field with a circle of thirteen five-pointed stars bounded by two rows of more stars at top and bottom.

The other, regimental flag featured Rhode Island motifs, since the state had no official flag. "The regimental standard of blue, with gold fringe and tassels and bearing on its fold the arms of Rhode Island, was passed to Lieutenant Munroe of the artillery."[47] The design was embroidered in silver thread, a decorative scroll surrounding an anchor and the name, 2nd Regt. Rhode Island D. M. Cabling on the anchor and the motto were embroidered in gold thread on the blue silk.[48] It was one of the more stunning battle flags sent to war on either side. They also made a set of "proper" guidons, small triangular flags used to mark company boundaries on the march.

The mayor made the presentation, because ladies did not normally speak in public in those times:

> On behalf of the ladies of our city, I have the honor to present you with these regimental colors and the national banner, which they have prepared for your acceptance and use. In placing them in your charge, I desire to express the high degree

> of confidence these ladies entertain in your ability and courage at all times to guard, protect and defend them. . . . Take these colors and cherish them, and in the hour of battle remember, that the wishes and prayers of the fair donors are ascending to heaven for your welfare. Wave them in triumph and in defence of the right, and bring them back with you. . . .[49]

Embodying the pride and love of the home folk who were sent their men off to war, such flags might be ripped by bullets and shells during battle, but the men went to great lengths to prevent the capture of their colors. So powerful was the symbolism that most Medals of Honor awarded by the Union were for the capture of Rebel flags.[50] Custody of these flags was assigned to one company of the regiment, known as the color company, whose job it was to deploy them to guide the regiment in battle and to protect them. After the ceremony, the regiment drew lots to see which company was to have that distinction; Company C won.[51]

As they prepared for imminent departure, the new soldiers were feted. "All sorts of useful and ornamental articles were given to us by our friends. . . . supposed to be of use to me," noted Corporal Rhodes, who also received "a Smith and Wesson seven shooting revolver and a holster to carry it in."[52] Each man was given two havelocks, one for sun and one for rain. Named for Sir Harry Havelock, a British commander in India during the Sepoy Mutiny, they were a hat cover rigged with a cloth drape down to the shoulders to ward off sunburn, and were the ultimate fashion accessory for the first month of the war. Official Rhode Island agreed they could skip the annual banquet given at the end of the court term, and spent the money instead on one thousand rubber blankets for the men.

Ministers preached blessings on them:

> It is a brave thing for a man, even with arms in hand, to enter into a systematic warfare with his fellow man. It is a heroic

> thing when that warfare is waged for the sake of a principle, for the sake of justice, liberty, and right. The action approaches sublimity when a man, from a sense of overpowering duty, and with an earnest, serious, prayerful patriotism, leaves the comforts of home, and the endearments of the family circle, and cheerfully gives himself to his country' service, and lays his life as an offering on the altar of his country's freedom.[53]

On Wednesday, June 19, 1861, Corporal Rhodes wrote in his diary,

> Today we have orders to pack up and be ready to leave Rhode Island for Washington. This is new business for us and the work of taking down the tents is slowly performed.[54]

Major Sullivan Ballou embraced his wife one last time, tenderly kissed his little boys good-bye, and rode off to join his regiment. The departures were timed like clockwork, and provided a daylong spectacle. The battery left camp first, by 9:00 A.M. By midafternoon, the tents were down, the local newspaper noting that "the canvas cones, which had somewhat resembled a good sized village laid out with more than usual regularity, all disappeared."[55]

Word may have been relayed back to camp when the steamship, the *Kill Van Kull*, was loaded and ready to sail, about 4:00 P.M. About 4:40 P.M., in a sprinkle of rain, the Second marched into Exchange Place, accompanied by the governor, colonels Goddard and Gardner of his staff, Secretary of State Bartlett, Mayor Knight, and Judge Samuel Ames, and paused for a "short and spirited address" by Bishop Thomas Clark, "who also invoked the divine blessing."

Rhodes noted they marched eastward to Fox Point, "an isthmus of land jutting out 500 feet from [the] harbor [which] contains the wharves of New York steamers."[56]

> Toward night we slung our knapsacks and moved down High, Westminster, and South Main Streets to Fox Point where we went on board the side wheel steamer *State of Maine*. The streets were crowded with people and we were observed continually. My knapsack was heavy; in fact it was so heavy that I could hardly stagger under the load. . . . At the wharf an immense crowd had gathered and we went on board our steamer with mingled feelings of joy and sorrow.[57]

The officers all boarded the *Maine*, along with their guests, various businessmen, the mayor, Bishop Clark, John Bartlett, and the governor and his two aides Goddard and Gardner.[58]

A great many wives and sweethearts had come to wave the ship off. Ladies had a hard time keeping on their feet on the dock as their hoop skirts were pushed on from all sides; hems were stepped on and ripped by men pushing through the crowd. Bishop Clark spotted his own wife trying to follow the ship as it eased out of its berth.[59] Was Sarah Ballou there, too, or had her husband encouraged her to skip the mob scene in favor of a more private good-bye?

After leaving Providence, the "uncomfortably crowded," ship sailed south and into Newport Bay, where "we sent some companies to the steamer *Metropolis*, after which we got on very well."[60] Departing Newport, the new home of the United States Naval Academy, the guns of Fort Adams boomed out a salute. Wrote Rhodes,

> The Colonel made us go to bed early in so spreading my blanket upon the floor of the saloon I went to sleep. We were not allowed to make any noise and soon all was quiet.[61]

Well, maybe not.

> The soldiers sang occasionally and behaved in all respects with great propriety with one exception. He was a hard case and the Colonel had to lash him to the mast till he reached New York, where he was let loose on shore.[62]

To while away the hours of the journey through Block Island Sound and Long Island Sound, the officers got up a unique entertainment for themselves in their quarters on board. At the suggestion of Bishop Clark, they held a mock court-martial:

> Colonel Slocum had Captain Reynolds, of the Light Battery regularly indicted and tried. The whole thing was carried out with perfect conformity, and made a great deal of amusement.[63]

Undoubtedly Sullivan, as judge advocate general, was either the prosecuting or defending attorney and had a star role in the merriment. The ship sailed eastward toward New York harbor, through Long Island Sound, a safer route than the open ocean. Around dawn, they sailed by the city of New Rochelle, the most successful and long-lived of the French Huguenot colonies in the New World. The refugees fleeing the violence and persecution in their homeland had founded this thriving town situated on the coast, like its namesake. The ships sailed past the 452 guns of Fort Schuyler, guarding the East River entrance to New York Harbor, past Brooklyn and the site where the British prison ships had been moored and Sullivan's grandfather imprisoned, and into the harbor.[64]

Private Rhodes chronicled their arrival in New York City, where like the First Regiment they were destined not to get off their ship. Still, for many of the men who had never even been out of Rhode Island before, the glimpse of the thriving port, its commercial buildings lining the waterfront patriotically festooned in red, white, and blue bunting and flags, was impressive.

> Thursday, June 20th 1861—we arrived this morning in New York, and as I had only visited New York once before I enjoyed the sail up to the city. We touched at a wharf and after remaining a few minutes steamed down the harbor and landed at Elizabeth Port, New Jersey.[65]

Likely they received orders from an officer there directing them to rendezvous with their train directly on the New Jersey side of the Hudson River. Trains from the west did not yet run into New York City proper, and an additional transfer by ferryboat was very cumbersome. The steamer left New York Harbor, sailed through the tidal strait for which their battery's ship was named, the Kill Van Kull, into the southernmost edge of Newark Bay to Elizabeth Port. But what was the army without snafus?

> On approaching Elizabethport, we ran into the mud, and there it was said we must remain some hours until the tide had time to rise, but, before long, a huge ferryboat put off from the wharf and took us to our trains.[66]

There was another massive unloading and reloading onto the trains. "It required two hours to get our cars underway. We started with ninety-two cars in three separate trains."[67] The ratio was two-thirds baggage cars to one-third passenger cars, so the men were packed in fairly tightly as they started off for Harrisburg, Pennsylvania.[68]

> The sight was magnificent, and everywhere, as we moved along, the workmen stopped digging in the fields, children rushed to the doors, and the whole population turned out, keeping the air ringing with shouts and huzzas.[69]

As the trains moved through the New Jersey countryside,

> much sympathy was displayed by the people of New Brunswick, Trenton, Easton, and other places we traveled through. Loud cheering hailed us at every station; strawberries, pies etc., were freely handed in the cars.[70]

Rhode Island soldiers, like those of other states, complained about the tedium of the train rides.

> All day we dragged along or waited at stations for other trains. We moved so slow that at times the men got off and walked. We had to sleep on the train and being crowded the night was one of much discomfort, and when morning came showed a party of very weary men. We descended upon the contents of our haversacks for food and the supply was limited.[71]

Happily though, the women of Harrisburg had already organized the first of many eventual depot-based relief societies at the major railway transfer points, to feed soldiers so the men did not have to travel hungry. The men were brought hot coffee, bread, and pies when the train pulled into that depot. "After a short halt," the trains moved on, and the Rhode Islanders got to cross the mighty Susquehanna River in daylight. The little town of York was the last Northern outpost they saw.[72]

As the train chugged across the Mason-Dixon line and into Maryland, they found they had entered a different reality. Bishop Clark noted a touching dynamic,

> The reaction of the Negroes was peculiar; they rarely shouted, but just dropped their hoes and stood bareheaded, in silence, sometimes with their hands clasped and lifted a little as if in prayer, and sometimes with one arm raised almost straight in the air.[73]

The men had seen raggedness and poverty in Northern cities,

> but Maryland was raggedness of a new kind. The railway . . . rambled through unfenced fields and woods, or through village streets, among a haphazard variety of pigs, cows, and negro babies, and cabins so ramshackle it could not be determined if they were for man or beast.

Some felt "struck . . . in the face" by slavery. These Northern boys had heard many a sermon against slavery in church; now, seeing it with their own eyes for the first time, "it was a nightmare: a horror; a crime; the sum of all wickedness! . . . Slave States were dirty, unkempt, poverty stricken, ignorant, vicious!"[74]

Already on the road for almost forty-eight hours, the men had the tensest part of their journey yet ahead of them—a "terribly hot" Midsummer's Night march through Baltimore. The three trains came in one after another for over an hour, starting about 8:00 P.M.[75] The battery was the most vulnerable:

> Our battery was immediately loaded on flats, drawn by horses to the top of the hill, the horses unhitched then, and the cars rolled down the other side to Washington depot. Order was given not to accept of any refreshments from the citizens. Bricks seemed to be the favorite weapon of the day, mostly thrown inaccurately from a distance. The artillerymen got through without injury.[76]

Corporal Rhodes related how the infantrymen had made their own, secret preparations:

> Rumors had been heard along the route that an attack was to be made upon us while marching through Baltimore, and the excitement in the regiment ran high . . . Most of

> the men carried revolvers, although strict orders had been issued against the practice. In the search which was made by the officers for concealed weapons, I managed (as most of the boys did) to save mine from capture. It was dark when we disembarked at Baltimore and we found the streets crowded with people.[77]

Seven weeks after the incident with the Sixth Massachusetts, the good citizens of Baltimore were still turning out en masse at inconvenient hours to harass the trains carrying troops. It showed a persistence of sentiment, and as Chaplain Jameson noted, an "impertinence of manner."[78] Rhodes continued,

> Strict orders had been given us to answer no questions and hold no conversation with any one. Silently we slung our knapsacks, and taking places in line began the march. Cheers for Jeff. Davis were given by the crowd on the sidewalks, and some abuse was heaped upon us, but we kept on our march, ready to repel an attack. My knapsack contained a load sufficient for a dozen men, and with aching back I tramped on, not daring to stop for fear of the crowd. . . . But I learned a useful lesson: never to put more in a knapsack than I could comfortably carry.[79]

Sullivan Ballou then picked up the narrative, and revealed how the Rhode Islanders were determined not to be cowed that summer solstice by the Secessionist sympathizers in Baltimore:

> Our journey was very tedious and uninteresting till we arrived in Baltimore, where we "did the thing brown" our [illegible] servants and baggage men rode through on the baggage train singing the Red White and Blue Yankee Doodle and Star Spangled Banner with all their might. They however got two

brick bats that did no harm and were not noticed. The troops marched through in utter silence—but the Band played the above airs with good strong breath. Our muskets were unloaded; though the men had ten rounds in their cartridge boxes. And we were the first that had been through without muskets being loaded since the 19th of April. The officers however all had their revolvers loaded—I had a pair in my belt—and we all marched on foot. We rested occasionally, for the heat was very oppressive, and marched with a very apparent impudence and indifference. The head of the line was abundantly cheered, for all opposition was evidently cowed; but as the left of the line came along and passed by, the "seshers" ventured to let out some hearty groans. Those who did not know us, took us for "regulars" and would frequently compliment us with this & kindred expressions—"when d[amne]d regulars can show you how to march."[80]

Once settled into their new train in Camden Yards, the infantry men remained uneasy:

After taking the cars for Washington, we heard many rumors of intentions to run us off the track, which kept the men on the alert, and fears of an attack caused sleep to be out of the question.[81]

The bishop was more upbeat:

Our ride from Baltimore last night was very exciting. We got away about midnight. The moon made it almost like day, and, as we passed the sentinels, the splendid and vast encampments with their white tents and smoldering fires, it seemed like history and romance made real.[82]

But the rest of the trip was indeed uneventful and fairly rapid. On June 22, at 3:00 A.M., the Second Rhode Island arrived in Washington, D.C. The men unloaded horses, cannon, and themselves, and marched from the depot to the camp, moving easterly on the diagonal of New York Avenue. At least some of the officers and Bishop Clark made other arrangements:

> The arrival and reception here this morning in the gray of dawn, was still more impressive. We took a carriage and drove at once to the camp of the First Regiment.[83]

Corporal Rhodes took in a lot on that short march:

> Saturday Jun. 22nd 1861 Hurrah we are in Washington and what a city! Mud, pigs, geese, negroes, palaces, shanties everywhere. We marched out to a place called Gales Woods where we are to camp and stacked arms in Camp Sprague, home of the First Rhode Island Detached Militia.[84]

Of course, at this point in time, they had seen only the depot. At Camp Sprague, the

> unseasonable reveille of Saturday morning brought upon the parade ground a thousand unwashed, unkempt, sleepy, growling men, trying to make believe glad . . . but wishing that the train had delayed its coming until after sunrise.[85]

Even the band of the First Regiment turned out with their instruments, and perhaps the peppy music cheered the men of the First even as it must have done the residents of semirural New York Avenue who were treated to a predawn concert by the band of the Second.

> In a few moments we heard the distant sound of music approaching from the Capitol. The Second Regiment soon marched into the ground, and as they filed before the ranks, one shout after another rent the air while the music of our band mingled with that of the other.[86]

In a few moments the ceremony of reception ended and the men scattered over the field to find their old friends. Many in the two regiments knew each other, and the "fresh fish," the newcomers, could not wait to hear the "war" stories of the three-months men. These, in turn, were anxious to learn the latest news from home. "Breakfast was soon ready and a hungrier set you never saw. No rations had been served for twenty-four hours, and they were all ready for the onslaught."

The bishop joined Colonel Burnside and others in the colonel's tent, and enjoyed the novelty of the tin plates and mugs: "We had a rich time." Colonel Tompkins's battery hosted the newly arrived artillerymen to a breakfast of "roast beef, soft bread and coffee."[87] Major Ballou brought greetings, and possibly a letter, from Tompkin's wife, Elizabeth, in Cranston. The Second Regiment proceeded to pitch their tents in the "beautiful grove" to the east, adjoining the first camp. The streets of white tents looked impressive and created a different impression from the wooden huts of the first camp. "The location of the camp is magnificent. All the main points of interest are in full view."[88] Chaplain Woodbury was more specific:

> A site had been selected on the slope of a hill, about a mile to the north of the Capitol, and near the road leading to Bladensburg. The environs of Washington are eminently beautiful, and the position of our camp, in this respect, was unsurpassed. Arlington Heights, then free from fortifications; Georgetown Heights, and the elevated land upon the south

> and east of the city were in full view; the silvery Potomac gleamed in the distance, while immediately below and in front lay the city itself, with its unfinished public buildings and its clustered dwellings, to which distance lent an enchantment which they themselves did not possess. Upon the brow of the hill, our artillery was planted.[89]

All in all, it was a delightful place from which to anticipate war. The two regiments assembled together for church services on Sunday, July 23, during which Bishop Clark preached "an impressive sermon . . . In the afternoon, passes were given to the men to visit the city."[90] With the men gone, Sullivan found time to write to Sarah again before President Lincoln and other dignitaries came to the evening dress parade.

> Camp Sprague
> Sunday June 23d/61
>
> My dear Sarah,
>
> I wrote to you very hurriedly and confusedly yesterday soon after our arrival; and felt again as tho I wanted to write you a little more. We are encamped in Paradise. There certainly never was a more beautiful spot. It is an oak grove—the trees are tall and large and the ground free from shrubs. The space we occupy is about half the size of the camp at home and while the sun is pouring down its oppressive heat out side, we are as cool and comfortable as you could wish. While the first regiment is encamped close beside us in booths or sheds and rather cramped for room and oftentimes go outside on the ground to sleep, we are all cool and our white tents in the green wood look more inviting than anything else. Our baggage waggons stand close behind our row of tents—one just at the back door of my tent to which my good horse "Jennie" is tied night and day. My man sleeps in the baggage

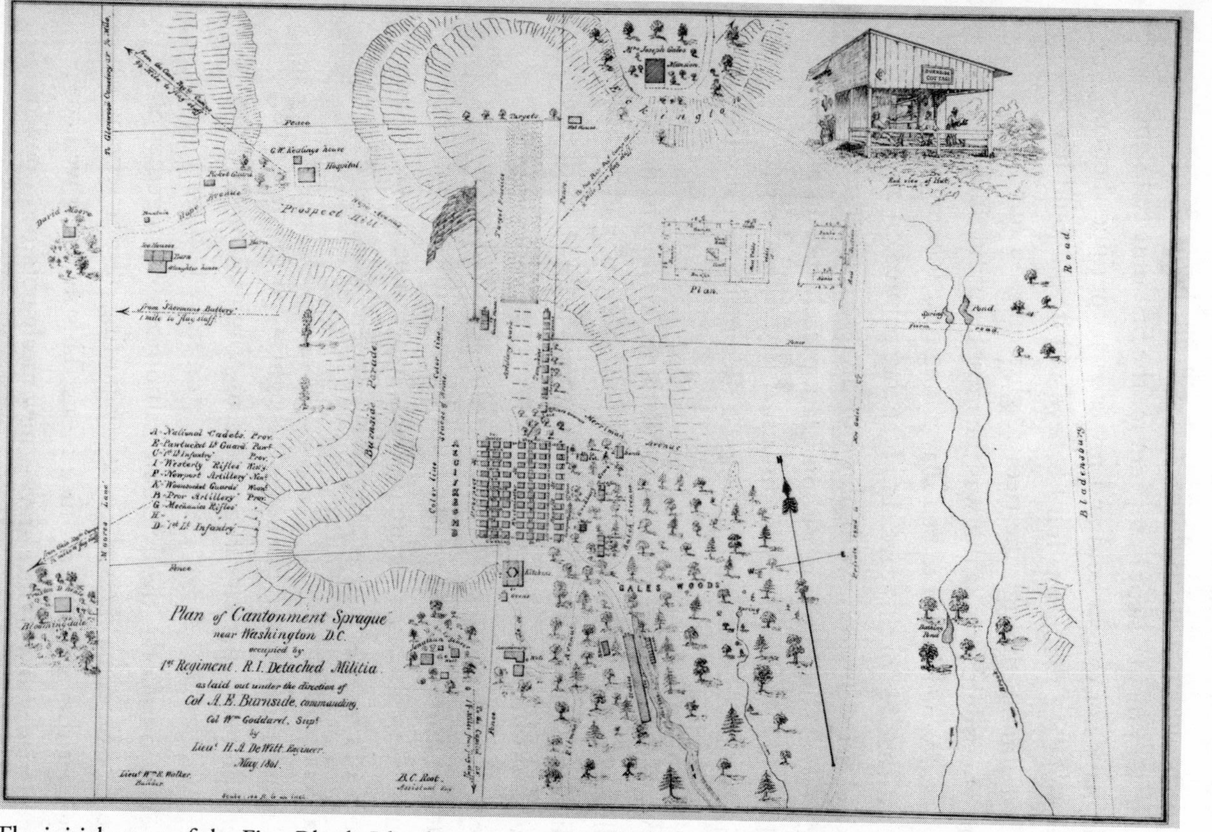

The initial camp of the First Rhode Island was surveyed and laid out on Eckington Plantation, owned by the widow of the publisher of the *National Intelligencer* newspaper, Joseph Gales. When the Second Regiment arrived, they camped directly adjacent in Gales Woods, and Sullivan described the trees in writing home to Sarah. *Drawing by H. A. DeWitt and B. C. Root. Courtesy of the Rhode Island Historical Society.*

waggon and I occupy my tent alone much to my delight—he is a kind good natured fellow and I like him much. He now begins to understand his duties and will fill them I have no doubt. Last night I slept in my tent for the first time & I slept well; have not caught cold and my catarrh continues better. Last night the moon was full I believe and if you could have seen it shining through the trees & glistening on our white tents you would have said it was the most beautiful sight you ever saw. When I went to bed I lay a long time looking up to see the shadows of the leaves and branches painted on my tent and at last went to sleep thinking of my loved wife and my little boys. This morning Bishop Clark preached to us about half an hour and spoke with his usual [style?] and elegance. The band and the choir of the 1st Regiment gave us the music.

We are about two miles from Washington: and from the hill where the 1st Regt' are encamped, the city and all its buildings can be seen. Tomorrow afternoon at 3 P.M. we are to march down to the White House to be reviewed by the President & Genl Scott. What is to be done with us I know not, but feel quite satisfied we shall not be moved from here for some weeks although we are probably liable to be moved at a moment's notice just as the 1st Regiment was moved to Harpers ferry and then came right back. This week I shall try to move round a little and see the sights—go to the city & perhaps get a permit to go over to Virginia to view the defenses.

As to our food—the field and staff officers sup together & use Col Slocums mess chest & try putting all our servants together they get us some nice meals. This morning we had some fried veal with nice gravy—new mealy potatoes—boiled eggs—coffee & excellent bread and butter etc etc. Tonight we shall have some fried cakes—poached eggs—& tea. You need not think of sending me any food because we fare poorly, for we live well—and so far as health is concerned—the mere living in camp will improve my constitution 50 percent. The first regiment are in splendid health—they are brown and stout as you can imagine. On their return from Harper's ferry they marched 32 miles in 17 hours & feel very proud of it. Our Regiment are all well—among the whole 1000 there is scarcely an ail. You need not think I have put a shining face on, to cheer you up. I really have not exaggerated our agreeable situation. At the same time do not harbor the thought that I fail to think of my loved ones at home—they are always in my heart and scarcely ever absent from my mind. I have just begun to realize that though I came here with 2000 men I am yet alone. I am far away from you Sarah and my beautiful boys—and it seems strange to me that I have never prized you as I ought—however much I may have loved you. I yearn to see you now so much, when I know I cannot, that all the love I have heretofore poured out for you seems insignificant. When I could go home every day & see you all, I did not think to weigh you in the scales with my affection; but now I think day by day what a trio I have, far away in my home.

When shall I hear from you: perhaps you are writing me today, I hope so—& that you will write me long letters full of all the little incidents of your daily life & that of the children. Be of good cheer & bear our present separation like the noble christian woman that you are. I already look forward to the time when I shall come home to you safe & well. I pray God I may find you & my dear children all well and rejoiced to see me. I wish you would go out & see my mother often and comfort her. I cannot write her many letters unless I lessen the number to you & that I do not wish to do. So you must see her and tell her all the news from me. You must not wait for letters from me, dear Sarah, but write me as often as you can find a few moments to spare for I shall look for your letters now, with as much impatience [as long ago?] when a lover's ardor fired me almost to a [?].

I ought to say that my vaccination has taken finely and provided no unpleasant feeling whatever.

There is a rumor tonight that the rebels will attack our lines on Arlington Heights tonight and that the First Regiment had marching orders—and there are so many rumors of the same kind that nobody takes very[seriously?] I doubt the rumor and rather believe that there will be no general battle for some time. It will be many [days?] to put our regiment into the field [since we came with?] bad arms. We shall probably be furnished with rifles & we must be drilled with them some time before the men can use them well.

Today I saw Sammy from Sherman's store and he looks the picture of health. Capt Tompkins also looks remarkably well.

Goodbye My dear Sarah
& believe me
Yours affectionately

Sullivan

The adjutant here is a fine flute players & has his flute with him & good music. When you learn of some one coming directly here send my ivory topped flute by him.[91]

Sullivan's life had now come full circle. As a radical Republican who advocated war to end slavery, he had helped elect Abraham Lincoln, a moderate who hoped to prevent war; events forced Lincoln to call for volunteers to defend the nation and the capital, creating the means by which Sullivan became a soldier. Now Sullivan was in that capital as a field officer whose fate was tied to a regiment bound for the battlefield.

CHAPTER ELEVEN

"From Hill to Hill, from Creek to Creek, Potomac Calls to Chesapeake"*

The Secessionists and Their Strongholds

June–July 1861

As the heat and humidity of a midatlantic summer escalated, both the United States and the Confederate states readied military forces on either side of the Potomac to go forth as the champions of their respective causes, and "every man was a hero in immediate prospect."[1] Throughout June and July of 1861, while these armies prepared to face each other at Harper's Ferry and near Alexandria, a powerful third force was already shaping the nature of the contest—the battleground itself, the topography of northeastern Virginia.

The Rhode Islanders were making their preparations at the most northeastern corner of the capital, less than a mile from the Maryland border. Before now, Sullivan Ballou had never visited Virginia, as neither had most of the Union command. Beyond the rabbit

* From the anthem of the state of Maryland "Maryland, My Maryland."

warren of their own fortifications along the riverbank, their commanders knew little about Virginia, few details beyond an outline of her topography and railroads. Their first cavalry reconnaissance had been disastrously unfruitful and they were leery about chancing another.

In 1861, Virginia was a giant square covering three degrees of latitude. Roughly speaking, her top and bottom boundaries were straight lines, shared with Pennsylvania and North Carolina. Her eastern boundary ran its fingers into the Chesapeake Bay and the Atlantic Ocean. Her western boundary was irregular, generally following the course of the Ohio River.* Her border with Maryland ran along the Potomac River, which first broke ground at 3,100 feet in the plateau of the Allegheny Mountains, a range that divides the northern Adirondacks from the southern Appalachians. This untamed wilderness more resembled New England than anywhere else in Virginia. After a 2,000-foot descent, the Potowmack, as it was spelled originally, spread out and was joined by other rivers, supporting ever-changing ecosystems as it descended. Nestled between the Blue Ridge and Shenandoah mountain ranges, sat a 20-mile-wide swath of superbly fertile farmland, the Great Valley of the Shenandoah River, known as the "breadbasket of the Confederacy." This rich country produced more foodstuffs than it could consume, and exported them predominantly to the eastern part of the state, along a network of independent railroads built for that purpose. Both nations immediately recognized that control of this valley was critical to the conduct of the war for either side. These western mountain ranges shaped what lay below and to the east, the ground over which Sullivan and the Union Armies were going to make their first advance. As the river flowed southeast,

* Not until 1863 did the pro-Union populace of West Virginia become a separate state, removing the northwest part of the square and leaving Virginia with the familiar triangular shape of present day.

forming the boundary between Virginia and Maryland, more tributaries, like Antietam Creek, joined it along its route.

Near Harper's Ferry, the Potomac met the Shenandoah, and both rivers cascaded through a spectacular gap in the Blue Ridge Mountains. Just as falling water had powered early industrial development in Rhode Island, here too it supported early industrial development and military arms manufacturing. A railroad now ran through the area, whose overall strategic importance near a border state made it the northern front of the Civil War that early summer of 1861. Confederate general Joseph E. Johnston and Union brigadier Robert Patterson maneuvered around each other for weeks without closing in battle.

White's Ferry, operated by Jubal Early, provided a means of crossing the Potomac at one of its quiet bends, above Ball's Bluff, but the river then erupted into a 10-mile course of whitewater. Starting at Great Falls, the river dropped 60 feet in less than a mile, and navigation was not possible again until the southerly side of Little Falls, where the herring and perch still spawned. Ocean-going ships called at Georgetown, the first major port on the Potomac, and terminus of the canal system, which did a thriving business shipping up and down the river.

Below Georgetown, the land was low lying and flat, suitable for the construction of good-size towns. Established in Colonial times and venerable in terms of American settlement in the wilderness, the large port town of Alexandria served as a market town for the region. Many great Virginia families, the Curtises, the Lees, the Randolphs, and the Washingtons, lived within a 20-mile radius, in great plantation houses like Mount Vernon and Arlington House, which dotted the heights and landings along the riverbank for miles southward.

Opposite, on the swampy, low-lying bottom land of the eastern bank, George Washington, an experienced surveyor, had selected a safe site for the national capital city. Far enough upstream to prevent easy attack by foreign fleets, D.C.'s main battles to date—with the exception of 1814—had been with its swamps.

Bridges were few and far between, due to the cost of construction, maintenance, and the raging fury of the Potomac in flood. Only three spanned the 270-mile-long Potomac, all near Washington, where Civil War military strategy was influenced by their placement if not their innovative nomenclature. The most northerly of the capital city bridges, Chain Bridge crossed the Potomac just below Little Falls. At first a wood-covered bridge built in 1797, whose twenty-five-cent toll George Washington used to complain about, a 1,350-foot-long chain and stone structure built in 1810 now gave the bridge its name—and upped the toll to a full dollar. It connected to the Virginia Turnpike, Leesburg, and Harper's Ferry.* The second, Aqueduct Bridge, was the towpath of one built to carry canal boats over the Potomac to the port of Alexandria. The third, and longest, a wooden structure named Long Bridge, crossed the river on pilings at the southernmost end of Washington, linking the capital with Virginia.

The Anacostia River joined and widened the Potomac as it flowed onward into the headlands of the mighty Chesapeake Bay, the mother of all wetland habitats. The easternmost part of Virginia, transected by mighty rivers like the James, the York, and the Rappahannock, extended three giant prongs of land into the vast waterway of the Chesapeake Bay. Smaller but still powerful rivers like the Chickahominy further interrupted the landscape. The tidal action of the bay influenced the river and its inlets all the way to Little Falls, so this part of coastal Virginia was called "the Tidewater," known for its oyster beds and waterfowl, plantations, and occasional, small, regional tobacco shipping ports like Dumfries.[2]

Sitting at the head of the third prong of land extending into the

* In today's terms, the toll went from approximately $12.75 to $47 for a two-wheeled vehicle.

Chesapeake, on a line drawn straight down from Washington, some 90 miles due south, was the major port and Confederate capital, Richmond. In the 1850s, two thousand ships called there annually for the wheat trade alone, and more than 300,000 barrels of flour were sent to the Port of San Francisco to feed the miners of the gold rush. Warehouses lined the low land along the river, with one whole section devoted to tobacco storage, while the comfortable homes of their owners graced the tops of the bluffs above.

Like other states, Virginia had gone on a railway-building binge in the two decades prior to the Civil War, and was criss-crossed by eleven independent railroads, four of which intersected in Richmond, making that town the state's major railway hub. In northeastern Virginia, the aggressive Scots merchants and civic leaders of Alexandria were in competition with Richmond for business, and financed the construction of turnpikes and railroads to direct business to their own deep water port. Part of this planning included the Manassas Gap Railroad, designed to bring riches from "the fertile valley of the Shenandoah, then teeming with livestock, and cereal substances," to Alexandria through the pass or gap in the Blue Ridge mountains. However, the Panic of 1857 had undermined its funding, so even though a roadbed had been cut out for it as far northeast as the Sudley Springs area, this railroad ran only as far as Manassas.[3]

Manassas got the railroad-related jobs, while the farmlands to the east remained isolated. Here, at the "Junction," all passengers and freight had to transfer over to the Orange and Alexandria railroad to reach the port on the Potomac. This key junction was close to the Potomac River, the Baltimore and Ohio Canal, and Washington, D.C., and whoever retained control of this junction and its railroads could move food, armaments, and general freight throughout the region.

The topography of Virginia made it unlikely for the federal government to attempt to strike the Tidewater region or try to move large armies north along the Potomac near Great Falls. The most logical first move was a direct one, to surge across the bridges to strike at the state's railroads.

One of Jefferson Davis's first tasks, after being sworn in as president of the Confederacy on George Washington's birthday, was to begin organizing the Confederate military. Edward Porter Alexander reported there was an understanding among Regular Army men from the South, that "with few exceptions, the creed was held that, as a matter of course, in case war should result from secession, each officer would go with his state."[4] It was a fine balancing act. If officers resigned at their distant posts, they had to pay their own passage home, and that of their families, if accompanied. Nearly all waited until recalled by Scott back to the East Coast, and then tendered their resignations from the Union forces. During Beauregard's stint as commanding officer of the West Point Military Academy, cut short by the secession crisis, he told a nervous Southern cadet at the academy, "Watch me; and I when I jump, you jump. What's the use of jumping too soon?"[5]

After Fort Sumter, the Confederacy was able to call upon the services of the South's share of West Point graduates, and by late spring, a host of them had assembled and began to organize forces, either under the banners of their states, or the Confederacy. Men who continued to flock to recruiting stations, even though the South had begun mobilizing six weeks earlier, firmly

> believed that every man's allegiance was due to his State only, and that it was only by virtue of the State's continuance in the Union that any allegiance was due to the general government at all; wherefore the withdrawal of a State from the Union would of itself absolve all the citizens of that State from whatever obligations they were under to maintain and respect the Federal constitution.[6]

Companies were raised around themselves at the county level, by local gentry, militia commanders, and Regular Army officers.

> Public opinion said that every man who did not embrace the very surest and earliest opportunity of getting himself mustered into actual service was a coward, and so, to withdraw from the militia and join a volunteer company, and make a formal tender of services to the State, became absolutely essential in the maintenance of one's reputation as a gentleman.[7]

The agrarian South would be fighting an industrialized North. Civilians did their part. In Virginia, C. R. Mason, esquire, "offered the Governor the use of two hundred slaves, three hundred mules and cars, and himself to serve during the war." The County Court made an appropriation of $3,000 to equip their company [the Augusta Rifles] even though no one expected the actual cost to exceed $500. Another patriotic gesture was made by

> the Reverend R. H. Phillips of the Virginia Female Institute [who] furnished the material, and the young ladies of the school manufactured three or four hundred jackets after the sailor fashion, for the use of the . . . Volunteers from the country.[8]

Each side surprised the other with the vehemence and rapidness of its mobilization. The citizens of Savannah, who had fired the hundred-gun salute when Rhode Island elected an antiwar governor in 1860, found to their astonishment that the Northern textile industry states were not "wholly choked with cotton dust," but could act with alacrity to send troops against them. Young Governor Sprague was no longer their hero.

In the earliest months of the war, Virginia had four specific functions to accomplish: When the Confederate capital moved to Richmond, Virginia became the headquarters state of the Confederacy, which had both political and military implications. As a member of the Confederate states, she was mobilizing her militia in response to President Davis's summons. As the most likely route of invasion, she had to prepare a military defense. The Virginia militia, already on hand, were to be the first responders, the primary line of defense. In this regard, Virginia was the counterpoint to Washington, D.C., mobilization central for all the troops of the nation. Leaders in the Old Dominion not only mustered, transported, trained, and equipped their own troops, but prepared training camps to receive those from all the other Confederate states. Their private homes and churches geared up to offer food and lodging to thousands of visitors and soldiers. They also began to prepare a medical infrastructure. One woman spent her entire private fortune, $22,000,* on a private hospital in Richmond.[9] Not only did Virginians procure a large portion of their new nation's armament by seizing munitions and guns from Harper's Ferry and Norfolk Naval Yard on behalf of the Confederacy, they prepared a battleground as well.

In the spring and summer of 1861, there were two centers of military assemblage in Virginia: Richmond, and Manassas Junction. While some freelancers, such as the precursors of the Texas Rangers, headed straight for the latter to offer their volunteer services, most out-of-state troops were sent first to Richmond. Given financial and transportation issues, it was often more practical to assemble regiments in Richmond, rather than in their home state, and the men appreciated the warm welcome they received once in the Old Dominion:

* Approximately $1 million, but the model does not factor in wartime inflation in the Southern capital.

> At every depot the platform was crowded with men, women & children & negroes to welcome the troops. Every lady, almost, had a bouquet for a soldier. I received several. . . . We passed several hundred on the road which have not yet reached here. While there are so many coming in, they send others out the Seat of War. Most of the troops are now being sent to Manassas Gap, some to Yorktown, and some to Harper's Ferry.[10]

Richmond had the good fortune to sit on the powerful James River, at a spot where the river dropped 100 feet in 7 miles—perfect for using water power for manufacturing. It was the most industrialized city in the South, with fifteen foundries. The Kanawha Canal, one of several lines that bypassed the river's rapids, brought pig iron into Richmond for use in the foundries and armory. A natural center of trade for the eastern shore, it was a city of culture, wealth, and opportunity. Richmond's population was fifty thousand, comparable with that of Washington, D.C. There were 38,000 whites; of the 12,000 Blacks, most were slaves. By late June 1861,

> nine out of every ten men you see is dressed in a military suit. This is a perfect military camp. Thousand of troops are encamped here. Many are quartered in the different churches . . .[11]

and others camped at the fairgrounds and the racetrack, all learning the basics of soldiering. Here, these regiments were mustered in, trained and began to receive such equipment and armaments as the South possessed in the summer of 1861.

In the South, as in the North, officers had difficulty impressing the need for discipline and uniformity upon the recruits. Whether cocky Yankee individualist, or hardy, independent Rebel farmer, none had much experience in following orders for orders' sake. In turning these free and independent volunteer spirits into soldiers, Southern officers faced different problems than did their Northern counterparts. For those that had them,

> Every man brought a servant or two with him, of course. How else were his accouterments to be kept clean, his horse to be groomed, and his meals cooked?[12]

A Texas officer wrote his mother a gentle reprimand after learning she had let his two younger brothers go off to war without sending any slaves with them:

> And I wish, Mother, if you could have spared any of them, that you had sent with them one of the boys [slaves] . . . to have waited on them and cooked for them . . . you cannot imagine how much assistance it would have been.
>
> For instance, the boys will have to go out on picket duty, march 6 or 8 miles, and when there, will have to stay out on picket for 24 hours before they are relieved. Now, it would be very pleasant to have someone to cook their meals and have them ready for them when they come in, to dry their clothes when wet, & perform all these little offices.
>
> I have seen soldiers on the march throw away all the blankets they had in the world just because they were tired, when, if they had had a servant along with them, he could have relieved them of much of their load.
>
> I do wish Mother, the boys had a servant with them, not only to wait on them when well, but to attend them if they get sick. There are a great many negroes with the soldiers, and they all seem pleased and enjoy life very much.[13]

Some of the Southern gentlemen also had novel ways of enforcing military regulations. When a detail was formed for the purpose of cleaning the campground, the men regarded themselves as responsible for the proper performance of the task by their servants, and uncomplainingly took upon themselves the duty of sitting on the fence and superintending the work.[14]

In the early days of the war, there was also a clear hierarchy among white Southerners:

> The two or three men of the overseer class who were to be found in nearly every company turned some nimble quarters by standing other men's turns of guard duty at twenty-five cents an hour.[15]

Confederate men were no more fond of repetitive drill practice than were the Yankees. In June, Colonel Egbert Jones, a former state legislator like Sullivan Ballou, and one of the political appointees commanding a regiment, imposed a regular drill schedule for the Confederate Fourth Alabama. Reveille sounded at 4:00 A.M. each day, incurring the wrath of his men. A petition for his removal was signed by six companies, and seven captains sent word that his resignation would be both welcome and appropriate. Jones consulted General Joseph Johnston, who advised him to return the petition and tell his men to file a formal complaint or stop griping. Jones assembled his men and offered to resign right after the upcoming battle if they were still dissatisfied with his leadership—and kept on drilling them.[16]

The Fourth's major, Scott, was known by everyone to be unfamiliar with military procedures, but, as was common, most apparently considered that a minor problem, believing he was going to acquire the knowledge he needed because he was intelligent.[17]

The Southern agrarian lifestyle in which most of these men participated, whether rich or poor, did not follow the same regimentation as the business and factory work schedules of the North.

> They were hardy lovers of field sports, accustomed to outdoor life, and in all physical respects excellent material of which to make an army. But they were not used to control of any sort, and were not disposed to obey anybody except for good and sufficient reason given.[18]

It may have been harder for these men initially to cope with the exigencies of army life. In this, they more resembled the men who fought in the Revolutionary War, when all America was agrarian.

In Georgia, a group of men were volunteering for the army who were to have a huge impact on the reputation of Sullivan Ballou, and an even bigger impact on Sarah and her children. The road to war for the Twenty-first Georgia Regiment could hardly have been more different than the organization and departure of the Second Rhode Island Regiment. From the outset, the Twenty-first was beset by contention, controversy, and conflict, which delayed its completion, resulting in its men missing their chance to fight in the first glorious battle.

Back in April 1861, the First Rhode Island had sailed from Providence within one week of President Lincoln's call, accompanied by Governor Sprague and expedited by a task force of business leaders. By contrast, in those early months, patriotic Georgians loyal to the Southern cause found it was hard for a red-blooded fighting man to get into the Civil War. A wealthy planter, James J. Morrison, traveled to the provisional Southern capital to personally obtain authority from Jefferson Davis to raise a regiment of cavalry for the Confederacy. Davis refused, telling Morrison that he preferred the cavalry to come from Virginia, where the fighting was going to take place; he gave permission to raise a battalion of infantry instead.

However, once raised, infantry companies found that the governor of Georgia, Joseph Brown, placed further roadblocks in their way, refusing to release arms, weapons, and munitions. Putting Georgia first, he wanted to keep Georgia troops and weapons in

Georgia defending Georgians. Naturally, this viewpoint was not appreciated by Davis, who was under pressure to assemble armies strong enough to hold off the anticipated Northern invasion. A feud was inevitable. Brown and Francis Bartow publicly exchanged barbs in the newspapers about thievery and personal cowardice, when Bartow's Oglethorpe Rifles left Georgia carrying state-owned muskets.[19]

In the midst of this considerable political turmoil, as it became known that James J. Morrison had direct authority from President Davis to raise a regiment of infantry, officers of other rejected units met with him in Rome, Georgia. These gentlemen agreed on a plan to merge their units into a new battalion-strength force and, through grit and ingenuity, to somehow get the companies of this paper battalion armed, clothed, and individually transported to Richmond, 600 miles away. One lone officer went ahead to prepare a camp at the fairgrounds; the difficulties of transportation and acquisition of uniforms delayed the arrival of the companies in Richmond for six weeks. The units at their dates of muster were:

Company/County	Muster Date in 1861	Commanding Officer
A: Campbell County Guards	June 6	Dr. Thomas C. Glover
B: Floyd [County] Sharpshooters	June 24	Algernon S. Hamilton
C: Buck Waddail's Regiment [Fulton County]	June 26	J. S. Waddail
D: Cedartown Guards [Polk County]	June 27	S. A. Borders

E: Concord Rangers [Floyd County]	June 24	Rev. John R. Hart
F: Ben Hill Infantry [Troup County]	July 9	J. T. Boykin
G: Dabney Rifles [Gordon County]	July 4	Wesley Kinman
H: Silver Grays [Dade County]	July 2	James Cooper Nisbet
J: Stewart [County] Infantry	July 17	Mike Lynch
K: Bartow's Avengers [Chattanooga County]	August 28	J. B. Ackridge

The men in these companies came from the sparsely settled mountainous counties of the northwestern Georgia highlands.

Compared to the Second Rhode Islanders, who had traveled to war in the lap of luxury, with prepaid passage as a whole regiment on steamship and train, uniformed at state cost, and armed with weapons manufactured at the company owned by their commanding officer, these Georgia companies were thrown back on their own resources to make arrangements. Algernon Hamilton and James Nisbet personally paid for the uniforms of their companies; Company H was outfitted with Bowie knives, scabbards, and belts by the owner of the local general store, and had neither muskets nor ammunition, nor even train fare to reach Richmond.

Nisbet took his troops by railroad, clutching his telegram from Confederate Vice President Stephens that read "Report at once with your Company to Richmond, very urgent."[20] By showing this to railroad conductors, Nisbet was able to get his men far enough along the road to reach Bristol Station, where he could get army vouchers for the train fare onward and reimbursement for that just concluded. Company E traveled to Richmond by rail via Atlanta, Augusta, across the Carolinas to Wilmington and Walden in North Carolina. The 730-mile journey took them thirteen days and at times they rode in freight boxcars.[21]

It was at Bristol that the country boys met members of Bartow's Brigade from the Seventh and Eighth Georgia, on their way home to recuperate from wounds received at First Manassas, a very powerful, emotional moment for these new recruits.[22] Most soldiers reported being deeply touched by their first sight of wounded comrades in arms; it was something burned into their memories and commented on in diaries.

By July 17, 1861, enough men were present in Richmond to offer the Georgia regiment to President Davis. He accepted the men but not their officers. Jefferson Davis insisted on appointing his own, not only another slap in the face to the men who had worked so hard to raise, train, and equip the regiment; but, in this instance, he also chose as colonel a man overly fond of the bottle and too often under its influence.[23] A first lieutenant in the First Dragoons, Regular Army Cavalry, a graduate of the West Point Class of 1854, John T. Mercer spent seven years in the Regular Army without promotion, meaning his superiors, among whom was Richard Ewell, noted some social, personal or command weakness.[24] Perhaps because of Mercer's reputation, this regiment had trouble finding a major; several men declined who would serve elsewhere with distinction.

All of these delays lost the men their chance to fight in the opening battle of the war. They began drilling with many other companies on the New Fair Grounds (Fairfield Racetrack) some 2.5 miles from the downtown area of Richmond. Company E camped in the stables of the racetrack.[25] Captain Nisbet recalled a sergeant from the First Kentucky Infantry was seconded to drill Company H.

> He was a big, fine looking fellow, on to his job and a strict disciplinarian. My country boys held him in great awe. . . . afterwards I heard them say that never at any time did they feel half as scared of the "Yanks" as they were of that redoubtable sergeant who would slap a raw recruit on the stomach with his sword. . . . And oh, the fierceness of his eye when he caught a man in the ranks slyly scratching and knocking mosquitoes off his nose . . .[26]

The amenities of Richmond may have offered the best training academy for the Southern Army, but the sector around the critical northeast railway junction at Manassas began receiving increasing numbers of troops as well. The state government therefore began assembling their own militia forces near Manassas in early May, under the enlightened direction of Philip St. George Cocke, the first general to lead the Virginia state forces. A wealthy planter, Cocke owned 658 slaves, 375 at his two Mississippi cotton plantations and the balance at his two Virginia grain plantations. Out of the fifty elite plantation owners in the South with more than five hundred slaves, he ranked number fifteen overall and second in Virginia.[27]

Cocke had been trained at West Point, as had many sons of the South's finest families—it offered an unparalleled education and was the preeminent engineering school in the Western Hemisphere—but he had left the military soon after. Despite almost thirty years spent as a planter and agrarian author, this fifty-two-year-old civilian was nonetheless an innovative strategist. Together, he and Robert E. Lee began planning the strategy to resist the anticipated invasion of Virginia, and by May 6, had settled on the junction of several railroads in eastern Virginia known as Manassas Junction as the place to begin concentrating the Confederacy's military forces.[28] After a personal inspection tour of the terrain, Cocke concluded that the lack of roads was going to hamper Union attack capabilities in that quadrant of the state. The topography of this location supported his initial guerrilla strategy—a replay of the American Revolution—in which small bands of men firing from the woods ambushed armies of marching troops.

On about May 15, Cocke suggested to Lee that Manassas Gap Railroad could be used to move troops around for initial deployment, and especially for rapid reinforcements. This was a truly innovative idea, and was the Confederacy's major contribution to the development of military strategy. When Virginia ratified the Confederate Constitution, Cocke was transferred to command the army of the Confederate States of America, and Robert E. Lee named his successor in charge of Virginia's militia. The Confederate government concurred with that of Virginia in their assessment that the strike zone composed of Fairfax, Prince William, and Loudoun counties needed special attention. To command the multistate forces soon to be deployed to this hot spot, Jefferson Davis assigned the hero with the greatest track record so far, General Beauregard.

Beauregard arrived June 1, and set up his first headquarters in Fairfax Court House. At this stage of the war, his hair was still dark colored; eventually the blockade interfered with the availability of

A youthful, fiery image of Brigadier General Pierre Gustave Toutant Beauregard, with dark hair, photographed by Matthew Brady, probably just before he resigned his commission as commandant of the United States Military Academy. *From author's collection.*

the imported French hair dye he used to cover the gray. His early arrival and occupation of the Bull Run area allowed him to personally inspect much of the territory in the expected area of combat. An army engineer by training, the Creole general analyzed the topography and geography, and factored both into his battle planning with the exacting eye of an engineer. Beauregard's volunteer aide-de-camp, Colonel James Chesnut of South Carolina, wrote to his wife, the diarist Mary Chesnut,

> I have been in the saddle for two days, all day, with the General; to become familiar with the topography of the country, the posts he intends to assume, and the communications between them.[29]

Inland, in that part of northeastern Virginia that Sullivan was going to come to know, small settlements were the rule—a few houses, a tavern, a church built of stone to prove its permanence, with a dirt path serving as Main Street. These tiny villages were scattered across the countryside, where land had been cleared for farming amid remaining stands of woods. Scarcely one hundred years before, the forests had been so dense here that a youthful George Washington had to wait for wintertime to transverse them for his surveying job. Even so, humankind had trod gently on the Virginia countryside up to this point.

Comfortable two-story farmhouses, often with a name to grace a villa of Italian nobility, like Portici or Liberia, crowned the tops of some of these small hills and their two hundred acres of farmlands and woods. Indeed, some were named for places their builders had visited on the Grand Tour. These homes were owned by the more wealthy residents, and from their high points, the graceful silhouette of a blue-toned mountain range could be seen far off to the west.

Named the Blue Ridge Mountains, they were mimicked by ever

smaller, parallel rows moving east. Rainfall from these elevations found its way eastward to the Potomac River through dozens of creeks, runs, and streams.

Men wrote of the plains of Manassas, but these were not the wide-open prairies of Kansas. This landscape was composed of broad meadows less than a mile wide, bounded by woods and brooks, interspersed with fields of tall corn, undulated by swales that blocked the sight of anything on the other side.

The maze of narrow waterways were unsuited to commercial use, so goods and people moved by roads that thread their way inland. Narrow and ill suited to major traffic, these roads rarely enjoyed any great length before they were interrupted by another river, but this the Union commanders did not know, and there were no maps to tell them. Even between towns, most of the roads were dirt. Only turnpikes, or main roads to major destinations, might be "macadamized"—laid with a gravel surface. Some arched stone or suspension bridge transversed wide streams; even these were miles apart, so shallow spots in the stream beds were designated, formally or informally, as "fords." Major fords were usually known by the names of the adjacent landowners, such as Blackburn's Ford, and yet other crossing places were used and known primarily by the locals, sometimes barely a track through the dense summer undergrowth.

This area was at the time largely unknown to the North. The South that Olmstead and Opdyke had written about for the New York newspapers was the large cotton plantations, which required hundreds of slaves as a labor force. Such large plantations were found almost exclusively farther south. Sullivan Ballou and his men were not to encounter fancy plantations with oak-shaded entrance corridors and separate slave villages; this was not the land of "Tara." While no less insidious, the scale of slavery was different here. In northern Virginia, while the inland hilltop magnates of Portici and Liberia owned a few slaves, the smaller grain and corn farms in the interior did not require hordes of workers to operate. Slaves made up only a small portion of the population of northeastern Virginia region, and free Blacks were well established here at the time of the Civil War.

Moreover, the large number of farms on the market, averaging between 150 and 200 acres, were attractive to Northern farmers and recent immigrants, and by the early 1850s about two hundred Northern families had moved to Fairfax and invested more than $200,000 [now $5 million] in land, which they set about improving with a vigor and ingenuity that impressed their Virginia neighbors. Some of the earliest emigrants were from Dutchess County, where Poughkeepsie was located. In 1850, roughly one in three adult white males in Fairfax hailed from the Northern states or European countries. These Yankee newcomers, including many Pennsylvania and New Jersey Quakers, were inherently antislavery, though not aggressively so. They did not own slaves, but might hire free Black laborers. Primarily, family labor and white hired hands worked the land. By improving their farms with free and white labor, the Northerners hoped to show Southerners that slavery was not simply immoral, but also economically unsound.[30]

Finding Yankee farmers well established in the region was just one of several surprises waiting for Confederates and Rhode Island troops alike once they went into northern Virginia. As the Confederates developed a militarized zone around Manassas, they complained that in Fairfax County, "not one man in ten" was helpful to the Confederate cause. That 90 percent were, "traitors . . . not native Virginians but Yankees who have settled in here. And they are not a few."[31]

The Confederates relied on loyal natives of the area to assist the cause, like those cavalrymen of Bonham's Brigade who lived right there in Prince William County and knew the byways and secret places to ford the local runs. In June, Major James Longstreet was hoping for promotion to brigadier general, at which point he wanted "to organize a command, and have it composed of Texans."[32] He got the promotion on June 17, but not the Texans, the bulk of whom were delayed for a host of reasons. But by July 1, Longstreet had a squad of "independent Texas Rangers," including Thomas Goree and Benjamin Franklin Terry, "acting as scouts for this division of the army." These intrepid men ranged all over northeastern Virginia, spying on the Yankees. "Every day nearly, we are within a mile or two of their camp."[33]

The so-called Black Horse Cavalry had been raised during the spring from standing cavalry units of the various county militias. In May 1861, Robert E. Lee, while head of the Virginia Militia, put Lieutenant Colonel J. E. B. Stuart in charge of their training. These young men all rode well but knew nothing about warfare. Stuart, who had resigned his commission in the United States Cavalry to join the Confederacy, used dramatic methods to teach them that "a good man on a horse can never be caught." His men learned that "cavalry can trot away from anything, and a gallop is a gait unbecoming a soldier." Stuart emphasized that cavalry "gallops at the enemy," but trots away.

Stuart's teaching methods made an impression on both sides. He would take companies out of camp and go in search of parties of

Lieutenant Colonel J. E. B. Stuart. *From author's collection.*

Yankee troops camped west of Alexandria. He and the men would gallop at them at full speed, shooting with their shotguns and creating consternation and panic in the Yankee ranks before trotting away, sometimes with prisoners.[34] While Stuart's men trained, the Yankees came to believe that this infernally brave horse troop was lurking everywhere, ready to attack them.

Traditionally, cavalry rode out ahead of the infantry units to scout the ground and determine the presence and strength of the enemy forces. Once this was reported back to the infantry commanders, they could plan their battle strategy. As the most mobile of forces, cavalry could protect encampments of infantry by patrolling nearby as the outermost layer of security, intercepting attack parties and warning the camp. Cavalry could also harass and capture wagon trains of supplies, ride into towns and secure them for their infantry, and disrupt pickets and enemy patrols.

Only rarely did cavalry charge regiments of infantry and fight them from horseback. Most frequently, the cavalry dismounted, left one man in four to hold the reins of the horses, and fought on the ground, firing their rifles at the enemy. Because of their ability to dash in and out of tight spots, they added a level of flexible firepower. Engagements with enemy cavalry were fought mounted.

In addition to scouting the terrain, erecting defenses, and organizing their cavalry and transportation services, the Confederates were also very attentive to communications. On June 3, Edward Porter Alexander was "ordered to start in Richmond a little factory of signal apparatus, such as torches, poles and flags."[35] Beauregard was establishing a signal corps, and wanted the men to start training promptly to improve their proficiency. By July 2, his chief communications officer, Alexander, had laid out four signal stations: one, a mile east of Manassas on "a high rocky point having a good outlook over a valley to the north and west," the other three fanning out between Centreville and the Stone Bridge. The "rocky point" was only some six to eight feet above grade, but after a little judicious tree trimming, the line of sight was six clear miles between these stations. "Intelligent privates" were trained in the signals, assigned to camp at the four stations and set to practice signaling "by and day night."[36] The Confederates set other communication systems in place as well. General Beauregard confided,

> Arrangements were made which enabled me to receive regularly, from private persons at the Federal capital, most accurate information, of which politicians high in council, as well as War Department clerks, were the unconscious ducts.[37]

The Union did not have equivalent means to penetrate Southern military circles, which further placed them at a disadvantage. One of Longstreet's scouts noted, "Our plans are all kept very secret, and it is impossible to tell what the movements are to be until they are about to be executed."[38]

Knowing the terrain, the waterways, the path of the roads, meant Beauregard could foretell the likely approach routes of his foe. He knew, long before did Irvin McDowell, that the miry roads near the Occoquan, south of Manassas did not permit passage of an army, and that McDowell was going to be forced to use a more northerly track for his attack.

To gain further control, he ordered his troops to work to create additional obstacles to funnel the advance of the Union troops into his trap. He set the South Carolinians to work, using axes to fell trees across roadways so the army would need to stop while their men cleared the roadway. The first such set of hurdles was just beyond a major road junction at Fairfax Court House, all or some of which roads McDowell needed to use. In all directions, the work went on for days. Chestnuts, hickories, oaks, and pines were all cut and left to fall on the roadway like so many pickup sticks. The military term for this type of obstacle is "abatis," from the Latin root word meaning "to slaughter."

The Virginians of James Longstreet's Brigade were urban folk, "more familiar with the amenities of city life than with the axe, pick, spade, or shovel." Beauregard first had them spend two days felling trees at Blackburn's Ford on Bull Run, but then decided that this was not the best position and pulled him back. When some of the men objected to the strenuous work, and that they, as gentlemen, had not enlisted to work like Blacks, Beauregard got Blacks. He persuaded local planters to lend him their slaves for much of the work.[39]

> I regret my inability to mention the names of those patriotic gentleman of Virginia by the gratuitous labor of whose slaves the entrenched camp at Manassas had been mainly constructed, relieving the troops from that laborious service, and giving opportunity for military instruction.[40]

All of this supported Beauregard's general strategy in the upcoming campaign, to draw the Union forces deep enough into Virginia so it was going to be difficult to maintain supply lines, communicate with Washington, and receive reinforcements, but not so deeply as to threaten Manassas Junction itself. Beauregard then identified the best ground from which his armies were to mount an all-out attack to totally defeat the Union Army.

In addition to trying to influence McDowell's itinerary, Beauregard intended to delay him whenever possible. In many a Civil War battle, a skirmish or diversion fought in the early hours of a battle made all the difference in the final outcome because it allowed reinforcements to arrive just in the nick of time, or permitted a canny commander to revise his battle formation in light of new intelligence. What Beauregard did based on general principles was going to pay off magnificently for him in the specific circumstance of his battle with McDowell.

Near Fairfax Court House, an earthwork was built to mimic a

fort. Advancing forces dared not risk moving onward until they first wasted time capturing the false fort. Also, key genuine units were strategically placed in the most forward areas to report on the timing and strength of the enemy's advance. Their orders were limited to delaying and harassing the enemy before pulling back to join the main body of troops.

With the personality of a true engineer, Beauregard analyzed the physical site, drew his conclusions, designed a solution, and expected everything to work out just as he planned it. It never really occurred to the Louisianan that the behavior of human beings could be in any way contrary to his perfect plan, that McDowell's main force might choose to cross Bull Run at a ford different than the one Beauregard planned for him to use. His careful preparations and courtliness to his soldiers made him a popular commander, and the adulation reinforced his own opinions of his talents.

> Our men are very impatient and anxious for a fight. They don't think of a defeat. In Genl Beauregard they have the greatest confidence, and they believe him invincible.[41]

So did Beauregard. Convinced that he was going to administer a knock-out punch to this army, he went on to develop a grandiose plan to wipe out other Union forces and attack Washington via Baltimore. His colleagues and superiors politely ignored this flight of fancy when he submitted it.

America had been a nation at peace for so long that her people held romanticized viewpoints about the nature of warfare. Despite the length of the Revolutionary War, only the last decisive battle, Yorktown, lived in popular recall. For nineteen years, Napoleon had fought across the length and breadth of Europe and the Mediterranean, but the only battle Americans remembered was Waterloo, fought in 1815. The people, newspapers, politicians, and generals of both the North and South had it figured out that the Civil War was just going straight to Waterloo—one decisive battle was going to wipe out the enemy and secure the desired outcome. Jacob Dolson Cox, an Ohio State senator and lawyer, commissioned Union brigadier general on May 17, 1861, said, "I believe that three-fourths of us still cherished the belief that a single campaign would end the war."[42]

CHAPTER TWELVE

"In the Watch Fires of a Hundred Circling Camps"*

Becoming a Union Officer and Soldier

July 1861

As June turned into July, each side still believed their own men, who dressed so snappily, who drilled so well, who were imbued with the hopes of a patriotic nation, would cause the other side to run off in panic if confronted. Sullivan Ballou himself echoed these thoughts in various letters home: "Scott is clenching his fingers and fist so closely around the Confederates that they must jump and run or be caught, and of course they will run rather than be caught."[1] Private Albert Greene of the Second wrote home to South County his overnight impressions from talking to friends in Camp Sprague: "The first regiment marched 25 miles in track of the enemy but could not catch them. They were at harpers ferry. . . . they fled like so many sheep."[2]

* From the Civil War song "The Battle Hymn of the Republic."

If only the blessings of homefolk had bestowed competence, each army would have been invincible.

> To the praise of those who have gone out from us, the flower of our youth and the prime of our manhood—there is a greatness in such action, worthy of the very highest commendation, and it is all the more worthy, in that it has been done, with an unconsciousness of aught but duty. War is terrible, terrible in its anticipation, terrible in its reality. But there is something even more terrible—the sense of humiliation and defeat in a rightful enterprise, and the sense of dishonor in a failure of duty.[3]

Immersed in this superpositive atmosphere, eager to do their duty, the men in the camps ringing Washington wondered if and when they would get a chance to fight their enemy. Sullivan wrote: "After hanging round camp for a few weeks it is wonderful how the men wish for the excitement of a battle."[4] Expectations were high in both armies, and legends began to be born:

> As part of their equipment, the men of the 13th Brooklyn were issued a length of rope so each could bind up and bring home a rebel prisoner. The men tied these to their musket barrels, where they fluttered like streamers while they marched.[5]

This may have been the origin of the urban legend that the Northern troops were bringing thousands of pairs of handcuffs to Virginia, to take hostages and captives. As the days of June passed, a great comet grew ever brighter in the evening sky. It outshone "every star and planet except for Venus," and its tail stretched in a hundred-degree arc across the night sky. In popular mythology, comets were associated with dire events—the murder of Julius

Caesar, the volcanic destruction of Pompeii, the conquest of England, the Great Fire and Plague of London, and the slaughter of the defenders of the Alamo. Born while one was in the sky, Napoleon fought several of his sixty battles with comets overhead, and made his disastrous decision to invade Russia "under the influence" of one. As the soldiers gathered around their campfires each night before lights out, they looked skyward and wondered for which side this one prophesied disaster.

Once settled into their base camp, named for Bishop Clark in honor of his many services to the regiments,* it was time for the Second Rhode Island to learn more about soldiering.[6] Utilizing his former military experience, Colonel Slocum set extremely high standards for his men, striving to produce a crack regiment, one in which the folks back home could know extreme pride, and "won the affection and esteem of his men in a remarkable degree."[6] Chaplain Woodbury noted their routine,

> Life in camp, though afterwards sufficiently familiar to become monotonous, had then all the charm and variety of a novel experience. The daily drill, the evening parade and prayers . . . inspections, reviews, and the usual routine of the school of the soldier, occupied the time.[7]

The "school of the soldier," to which the chaplain referred, was a key building block in training. Coming from many backgrounds and occupations, the men of the volunteer forces had to be taught the language, the habit of obedience to orders, and the main skills they needed to perform their duties and stay alive. Their common tool was: *Hardee's Rifle and Light Infantry Tactics, for the Instruction, exercises and Manoeuvers of Riflemen and Light Infantry including*

* The bishop wrote his wife: "this is something new under the sun, a camp called after a bishop."

School of the Soldier School of the Company by Brevet Lt. W. J. Hardee.

This was a paperback book, conveniently small enough to be carried in a pocket, and was a best seller in the North and South, from 1861 onward. Everyone studied it diligently. As many officers were themselves so green, they read the manual one step ahead of their men. Colonel Francis Bartow, a Savannah politician in charge of the Second Brigade, which included the Seventh and Eighth Georgia regiments, reputedly worked nineteen-hour days to teach himself tactics from this manual.[8]

The most dominant factor of the volunteers' life, and their biggest learning curve, was their physical training, begun in Rhode Island but now intensified. To be able to execute directions in the field, under fire, men had to have practiced various moves until they were automatic and required no thought to tell their left foot from their right. Private Warren Goss, a New Englander in another regiment, noted an early mistake he would not repeat,

> The first day I went out to drill, getting tired of doing the same things over and over, I said to the drill-sergeant: "let's stop this fooling and go over to the grocery." His only reply was addressed to a corporal: "Corporal, take this man out and drill him like h—l!"; and the corporal did![9]

All regiments needed to drill morning and night, enduring the repetition and taunts of their drill masters. They had to know how to move at the same pace so they could stay together as a company, so the first lessons from *Hardee's Manual* included explanation and practice of the marching cadences: common time—90 steps per minute, quick time—110 steps per minute, and the double quick—165 steps per minute. Of course, like Sullivan's hike to Brown University, or Corporal Rhodes' to his mother's house, most men walked long distances in their daily lives, five or six miles a day being nothing special, but they rarely had to carry gear, packs, or a thirteen-pound rifle on their trek.

A typical day in the camp consisted of reveille and morning parade to see if any man was sick, then breakfast and morning drill. The midday meal provided a break, but was normally followed by afternoon drill. The workday concluded with evening religious services before the evening meal. In between, the band practiced, and the men washed clothes, wrote letters, and did camp chores. The closest some of the Rhode Island boys ever came to having personal servants like their Southern counterparts had was when some of the artillery corporals in Battery A worked out a scheme whereby all of the men in the detachments contributed money "to hire Negroes to polish their boots." In reality, the servants spent more time waiting on the corporals, and the plan was soon abandoned, leaving everyone to shift for themselves.[10] Work parties "policed" the camp, correcting any lapses in behavior where men failed to use the latrines or dumped garbage outside their tent. A tidy camp reduced illness significantly. Thousands of soldiers, North and South, wrote home to tell of this routine, as did Sullivan.

On June 25, he wrote his law partner, Charles Brownell, the least emotional letter in the series:

> Dear Brownell
> I need not offer you any excuse for not remembering you by letter before this—you know my time thus far must have been occupied. The Hurry & bustle of our journey and Camp are now over and I expect we shall now settle down. . . . today by general order were united in the R. I. Brigade—Burnside commanding. We hope he will be made a Brigadier and if he is not it will be because he has no one to take command of his regiment. Pitman you have seen probably before this. He was insane here—and worthless on that account. It is a great

misfortune—but the excitement was too much for him; He had in Mexico a short spell of the same difficulty. This is the sole cause of his difficulties here.

We hope you hear us well spoken of in the papers, for we think we deserve it. There is a most marked difference between our troops & all the others I have seen, and I have seen them all except the Massachusetts troops. The "phisique" and "morale" of our boys are greatly above them all. . . . I think of you often & should be glad to see you. I look in upon you in the office every day and examine every thing there even to the papers in my desk. Does Hart work as hard as ever? Remember me to him & to all on the flat. How comes on my Life Assurance? I forgot two little bills when I came away, Gladding & bro—about $10.50 and Seth Scott about 7 or 8 dollars or perhaps 12 or 13. If you hear from them, please tell them I will send home the money to pay them in about six weeks.

When you see any one coming here, and you can think of it, I wish you would send me some Magnum [illegible]—pens and a few pen handles. After reading this letter, I suppose it will be of little use to you and I wish much you would send it to my wife. I shall be glad to hear from you often and hoping you will commence soon.

I remain
Yours with much regard

S. Ballou[11]

Sullivan had carried a life insurance policy for at least four years; most were invalidated by going to war, and it is possible that Brownell was working on converting it to one that covered soldiering. There is no record if this was accomplished. Perhaps pressured by taking on the full weight of the joint law practice, Brownell never did find time to write back.

At this point in time, Union preparations presented two faces to the world. The militarization of the national capital, the training of the troops, were deliberately, blatantly obvious. The ring of fortifications around the capital continued to grow visibly, with the Union soldiers, especially the Irish boys, not protesting about digging and constructing but just getting on with it. General Mansfield, as commandant of the city, issued a pass to Virginia so the bishop and distinguished visitors could travel out to Arlington on June 25 to see General Lee's house and the new Union fortifications. They returned to Washington promptly toward evening, where Bishop Clark stood to President Lincoln's right under the portico of the White House, to review the Rhode Island troops. Often, the historian correlates different accounts of the same event to obtain a full picture of what happened, for each person usually writes only about what matters to them. In this case, Lieutenant Ames wrote his parents,

> [At] 5 P.M. set out, a proud day for little Rhody . . . marched through Pennsylvania Avenue to the White House. The column passed in at one gate, round the semicircle passing the portico, where stood the President with a few friends, and out the other gate. Thence the march was continued a few squares to the west, to the residence of Gen. Scott. Standing at the curb-stone, with head uncovered, surrounded by his staff, the veteran gazed with pride upon our sturdy battalions as men to be trusted in a perilous hour.

Ames had seen Lincoln when he campaigned in Providence, and commented on his new beard. And he thought the aged general looked " a little the worse for wear" but still "very fine looking" for one "in his old age."[12] Corporal Rhodes was also in the marching ranks:

Monday June 24, 1861—today we brushed up and marched into Washington and were reviewed by the President. As we passed the White House I had my first view of Abraham Lincoln. He looks like a good honest man, and I trust that with God's help he can bring our country safely out of its peril. I was not well pleased with the appearance of the city, but was struck with the magnitude of the public buildings. The Capitol, although unfinished, is a magnificent structure and every American should be proud of it. After the review we returned to camp.[13]

Sullivan reported to his law partner,

Yesterday the whole Brigade & both Batteries marched down to the White House & was reviewed by Abraham. The papers will tell you how we appeared. The whole first Regiment marched as the American Infantry used to in its palmiest days. I was very proud of them & so was everybody else. But Burnside was too careful of their reputation to try any movements. But Slocum, when *we* turned the corner between Willard's and the Treasury building put us into company front stretching our serried ranks abreast across the Avenue. I trembled for our reputation when I heard the command but our men did it *splendidly;* and we swept down towards the Capitol as proud as soldiers could be.[14]

Private Green furnished a slightly more prosaic version:

I am well but rather tired today after marching all over the city of Washington. . . . President Lincoln, his wife and two children were in our camp Sunday evening last. Governor Sprague looked like a baby by his side. . . . Washington is a nasty place, it is verry dirty. When we were marching through

> the streets the dust was awful. We could not see the platoon in front of us, no air at all, the dust arose right in our faces. We could scarcely breathe. . . . We can see three camps besides our own.[15]

Despite the open display of the troops, calculated to let secessionist sympathizers realize just how many troops were now on hand, spies tried to penetrate the camps to learn invasion plans. Since the Rhode Island camp was not fenced in, it was necessary to patrol its perimeters to minimize the infiltration. Officers took turns doing the grand round, the midnight inspection of the camp to check on the efficiency of the sentinels, a task Major Ballou had to learn, and one in which the bishop was an interested tourist.

> Almost every night there are one or more spies taken in some of the camps around here. NH [New Hampshire] shot one and captured 3, some nearby regiments under arms for the past week now putting whole companies on guard duty at one time, then they have the next day off.[16]

On June 25, General McDowell announced the brigade partnerships for those regiments under his command, news of great importance to the Rhode Island commanders. Burnside's Brigade was now to consist of both Rhode Island regiments, the Seventy-first New York, and the Second New Hampshire. Had all four been at full strength, this would have totaled over four thousand men. More likely the total approached 3,250. McDowell shared his thoughts on the process:

> I think it of great consequence that, as for the most part our regiment are exceedingly raw and the best of them, with few exceptions, not over steady in line, they be organized into as many small fixed brigades as the number of regular colonels

will admit, . . . so that the men may have as fair a chance as the nature of things and the comparative inexperience of most will allow.

That same day, Sullivan noted the regiment "marched into Washington to the Arsenal to exchange arms. It was very warm and the march six miles. Two of our men dropped in the line but they are not seriously affected."[17] The guns could have been brought to the men, but the show was important. The men were very unhappy to receive nonrifled muskets—far inferior to the newly manufactured rifled guns which the First Regiment had brought from home. The First Regiment had far superior firepower going into any battle.[18]

His next letter on June 26 was to complain to his wife that she was failing to write him.

My Dear Sarah
I hoped for a letter from you tonight—but am disappointed. I wrote you last Saturday—and again on Sunday and on Tuesday I wrote Brownell with instructions to hand the letter to you. That is really 3 letters to you in four days and this makes the *fourth* letter on the *fifth* day after our arrival. You wanted I should write you every day—Sarah I fear you will not write *me* once a week. I beg of you do not let me suffer and complain as I have in years gone by, about your letters. . . . I sleep as well in my tent as I should at home; only I sometimes yearn so much to hold my dear wife and my little boys in my arms. O! Sarah, guard them well that I may find them both when I come home.

What think you of meeting me in New York or Englewood in a few weeks? I cannot go many weeks without seeing you, and must come home or you must come to me. After Congress meets there will be a change in affairs and if we continue

> here I shall get a furlough for a week and come home. If I cannot you must come to me. There are many things I would ask you but I hope you will answer many of them in your letter (when I get it) and I will not write them. I shall write a letter to Edgar in a few days.* Does he & Willie miss me? Talk to them often about me and tell them how much I love them. Turn them outdoors all you can and bear with their roguery and waywardness. It seems to me if I could only be with them once more I would never complain of them but be a model of patience and forbearance towards them. You and these children Sarah bind me to this world like cables of iron. I never dream of them breaking—but when they do, this world is no world for me.

Away from home only two weeks, Sullivan was worried about the support Sarah and his boys would be receiving from the folks back home. While he had total confidence in her abilities, he was concerned about her support network, living in Cranston, far from Pawtucket, Woonsocket, and her own family. Whatever happened, he was doing his practical best to surround her with protection. Sullivan was very impressed with Bishop Clark's approachability, his loving nature that reached out to all men, whether Abraham Lincoln, or a private or major of the Second Regiment. In his letter to Sarah, he shares the news almost casually that he has asked the bishop to call on her with tidbits of news, almost as if to spare her the surprise of the visit.

> Bishop Clark left us this morning much to our regret. I asked him to call and see you & tell you about our situation here and he promised to do so. We are all filled with admiration for him. He is so little crusted over with formal religion—is a

* If he did, this letter has never been found.

> man of such genial humor generous heart and manly sympathy and noble learning, that we forget his apostolic character and instinctively call him a trump.

Yet the bishop remembers Sullivan's entreaty differently. Just a month later, he spoke of an emotional major bidding him farewell and making a very poignant request:

> The accomplished Ballou, so genial and yet so brave, so tenderly attached to his household, and yet so willing to leave all behind at the call of his country, sacrificing so much in a profession which he promised to adorn by his skills and his acquirements; who, as if he had a presentiment of the evil which might come to him, said to me, with a gush of feeling, just as I left camp, "you are a stranger to my family, but I ask permission to commend them to your care."

But the letter Sullivan wrote to Sarah was wrapped up with a prosaic description of some things he needed, and a glimpse into the hygienic standards of the army.

> There are a number of little things I should like to have by & by and I wish you would be getting them ready. Two more calico shirts—perhaps three more. Two more pairs of drawers. Riding as much as I do perspire freely and have to change my underclothes twice a week—I take a bath twice a week and oftener in case I ride more than usual.

There was much discussion about the availability of bathing—and drinking—water in the twin Rhode Island camps, for all that the map shows a stream or two. Lieutenant William Ames, a Regular Army man now serving with the Rhode Island regiments, who had a criticism ready for almost everyone and everything, wrote to this mother that their, "stream is miserable and suited only to washing dirty shirts; not deep enough to bathe in."[19] Camps Sprague and Clark at least had the merit of not using contaminated drinking water from the Potomac. The regimental surgeon of the Third Michigan Volunteers complained,

> The water of the Potomac, always muddy and dirty, is at this point pretty well mixed with the drains of sewers and filth of every kind from Washington, which at the present time, between citizens and to the civilians and soldiers, must have a population over 100,000. This was the only water our men had to drink from the time we embarked, and in less than twelve hours it began to show its effect in diarrhea and dysentery.[20]

The other face of war was private, still secretive, reserved for the president, the Cabinet, and the top generals. On June 3, Scott had directed McDowell to prepare a plan for the southern half of a joint action against the Confederates. Patterson was to fight at Harper's Ferry, and McDowell at Manassas Junction. McClellan was also exerting pressure in western Virginia, but it was decided staging an attack along triple fronts was too complicated. The plan McDowell submitted immediately was altered during June by Patterson's passivity in attacking Winchester, and by reconnaissance and new intelligence on Rebel troop strength. On June 21, the target changed to Leesburg, and by the end of the week, changed back. In the interim, on June 25, Lincoln met with three of his generals and expressed a strong desire to bag General Thomas J. Jackson.[21]

McDowell next presented Scott a revised plan detailing five different ways to attack Manassas, recommending that three of these routes be used simultaneously to strike so hard a blow that the Confederates would evacuate northeastern Virginia and withdraw forty miles away to the safety of distant Fredericksburg. He planned to send columns through Fairfax Court House, Vienna, and along the Orange and Alexandria railroad, hoping to move fast enough to pick off the Confederate regiments assigned to defend these locations. No one in the camps knew anything about these plans, but that did not stop the grapevine from working overtime with rumors. Sullivan repeats one in his June 26 letter, and though he continued to repeat them, he eventually came to distrust them entirely:

> Genl Scott says he shall finish the whole thing up by next spring—and I think he will manage it so as to have no pitched battles. At any rate the South will avoid them by any means in their power.

Three important things happened on June 29. The first was that generals Scott and McDowell went to the White House to attend a special cabinet meeting and present the battle plan to Lincoln and the Cabinet. Also present were generals John Frémont, Montgomery Meigs, the new army quartermaster, and Scott's protégé, Mansfield.[22] McDowell's plan was soundly reasoned and well developed—he already knew which divisions were assigned to which roads—and no one present offered any corrections or objections. McDowell discussed the plan with his colonels the same night, with the same basic result.

The same day as this still secret decision was reached at this still secret meeting, Major Sullivan Ballou had his first major interface with the Union command structure, "the first break in the general dullness." He described it in great detail to Sarah the next day, carefully omitting from his letter any exact details that might assist the enemy.

> It came my turn under orders from Genl Mansfield to act as Officer of the day over about one half of the City of Washington. I rode in to Head Quarters at 1/2 past 5 yesterday

> afternoon and received my instructions and was ordered to report myself there again at 9 o'clock last night when an orderly Sergeant would be detailed as my guide. I reported accordingly at nine and found in front of Head Quarters a long line of horses all saddled and equipped for sudden service in all directions. A Sergeant having been detailed for my guide it became my duty to visit the camps of about 15,000 men on this side of the Potomac—to try their sentinels—see if they had the proper countersign—to ride through their camp & see if they were in a proper state of Discipline and properly guarded against surprise by an enemy.

From the War Department, they rode southeast toward the Potomac.

> We started for the Head of Long bridge first to see if it was properly guarded and found the sentinels promptly on the alert and furnished with the countersign. We then passed out beyond the Capitol to the various Camps—the Minnesota New Jersey Wisconsin New York Vermont and these Regiments passing over lots & estates in order to search the sentinels in obscure and quiet places to see if they were at all negligent or remiss. The mode of procedures is something like this. As we rode on to the line of sentinels—the latter, the moment he saw us would say "Halt! Who comes there" My orderly then replied "Field Officer of the Day" Sentinel "Advance Sergeant and give the countersign." The orderly then advances and whispers the countersign—the sentinel however keeping him constantly on the point of his bayonet so that if he proves an enemy or a spy or attempts to force the line he may shoot him at once. The countersign being correct the sentinel says "the Countersign is correct! Pass on." We

> three pass in the lines—and the Sentinel shouts "—Form out the Guard: Field Officer of the day." This cry all the sentinels repeat all round the camp, when the guard are all called up and ordered into line at the present arms. In the mean time I examine & ride thro the Camp as I best can in the dark—see if the men are asleep lights out & no disturbances—ride off & try some of the other sentinels—then ride to the guard house review the guard—leave any orders I think fit for the better protection of the camp and then try the next. I thus continue for seven hours without getting out of my saddle. If any one had told me a month ago I could have stayed in a saddle that time, I think I should have given them the lie. I expected to be used up today; but I am in camp phrase—tip top. It was a terrible shaking up and I expected a sore stomach for a week and chafed legs besides; but when I got back into camp this morning I found myself only very tired and after a good sleep till the middle of this forenoon and a good bath I find myself ready for another ride.[23]

From his twenty years experience in the militia, Sullivan knew many basics, but life in the federal army was new. Even then, the army had a form for everything that mattered, and a few that did not. The Regular Army, after all, had been around for many years, and its preprinted forms came along with its officers. These, Sullivan was now learning, and developing the contacts to keep them moving along the chain of command—properly completed.

These forms included the morning report, to show how many men were present for duty, how many on leave, how many sick, how many absent without leave. There were passes to places, passes to go on leave, and passes to go forage for food in the surrounding countryside, thereby separating official supply parties from looters. There were casualty report forms to record the dead and missing after battles, and property damage forms to compensate civilians for foraging transgressions. There were receipts to sign when a regiment received supplies or gear. It was all probably nowhere near as challenging to Sullivan as practicing law.

> Camp life has been very dull for me—it is so destitute of all intellectual effort and offers so few opportunities for intellectual or social pleasure that I feel very sensitively my great change in life.[24]

Sullivan's constant reassurances to Sarah about his state of health seem to indicate this was her greatest concern for him. His references to use of liquor below indicate that he had sworn a vow of temperance, for this journey at least—whether he abstained at home is not known—but that Sullivan had stretched the rules to permit the taking of brandy for medicinal purposes.

> My health is still all that even you would wish; and I see no deprivations or duties ahead that need give you any fuss for it so far as dirt; clothing cleanliness, sleeping in my tent & is concerned. When I came in this morning however, feeling that everything in me had had a constant shaking for seven hours, I opened my brandy bottle and took a swig—the first drop I have swallowed since my resolution; and I think it was that brandy that kept me from lameness today. I believe my resolution excepted cases like that.
>
> Every body here in the army drinks liquor and I am a source of great surprise to all I meet because I do not. Capt Reynolds of the Light Battery & myself are the only two I know of. Capt Reynolds by the way is a noble fellow & much beloved by his men he is a gentleman a Christian and a soldier and I mean to be even more intimately acquainted with him.

Sullivan continues with some choice gossip concerning their landlord,

> It is curious here to see how strangely men are developed by a military life. There is Captain Tompkins for instance—would you believe that he is hated by his men. They hold him in the utmost contempt and have groaned him in public. It is said that if his battery ever goes into battle some of his own men will dispose of him. This will no doubt surprise you much and I need not caution you to maintain silence. But the truth is, he is a mere brainless fop who cares more for the admiration of Ladies while he is in parade than he does for his men. Soldiers want men to command them—whose ability and power they can rely on and respect and Capt T. is the most miserable failure as a military man that I have ever heard of. Of course you will be cautious with this information in your intercourse with his wife.[25]

As an officer, Sullivan was sitting on top of the food chain in camp as the summer abundance of fruits and vegetables were harvested at the farms surrounding the capital.

> We officers board ourselves & we get the best the market affords. Besides I keep lemons always by me and suck a great many of them—sometimes one a day. They are excellent to keep off bilious fevers—assuage thirst—consequently ward off the temptation to drink much of this lime water. . . .[26]
>
> Yesterday Capt Dexter invited me up to his quarters to dine with him. We had pork and beans, fried liver, boiled potatoes, pickles, lettuce, bread and butter and two kinds of pie & cheese. Oh! Yes and green peas. That will do for camp life wont it. . . . I have just been to dinner in the Col's tent. We had a nice leg of veal, roast, green peas, potatoes & bread and butter.[27]

The enlisted men of the Second soon learned the camp food was very good indeed, and could be supplemented from local vendors, as the enterprising Black women of the town stepped up their baking and sold pies and cakes, and others sold produce from their yards and farms to the ready customers.

> The commissariat was under the charge of a noted caterer of our own State, whose rotundity of person was a good evidence of his skill in cookery. He had under his charge a detachment of cooks who were busy morning to night . . . .When our two regiments were encamped together . . . nine hundred and sixty gallons of coffee barely sufficed for the morning and evening draught.

The regimental bakery, a large brick building in camp, used eight to ten barrels of four each day to turn out bread, and the 180 pounds of gingerbread sometimes served in the evening. The regiments consumed thirteen hundred pounds of meat each day. The men supplemented their diet with quantities of seasonal fresh produce—at this time cherries and strawberries "which in their season were daily for sale within the camp."[28]

Lacking any real news about military things, several of Sullivan's letters focus on the development of the Second Regiment as they learn the art of soldiering. In this letter he makes a comparison to the gentlemen soldiers of the New York Seventh Regiment, the ones with the splendid indoor armory:

> We get the Providence Journal here the night of the day after publication and it is from that I get all my general information. We know nothing of what is going on in Harpers Ferry or Fortress Munroe or even in Washington any more than you do; and what seems strange to me is; that nobody cares what is going on. The utmost confidence is felt in Scott & the

Government; and all expect to be called in when wanted and to go where they are sent without asking any questions. There is a rumor today that the first Regiment is ordered off tomorrow, but nobody takes any interest in it and I don't believe it. When they get their orders & start they will doubtless be very eager & excited for the fray—but until they do, they don't care for rumors. There is one feature in the camp life here you don't see when looking through the spectacles of the Providence Journal. The first Regiment has been highly flattered here—and deservedly so. But since we have come they are the most jealous set of fellows you ever saw. Their two months drill here has made them splendid soldiers and I have no doubt they would surpass the 7th New York Regiment today. But our men are larger—stronger and better men every way—they look much more soldierly on parade . . . One month drill here has wrought a wonderful change in us; and the whole first regiment see plainly that we shall be their acknowledged rivals in less than a month. The intercourse between the camps is on this account rather cool. If the term of enlistment for the first Rgt were not so soon out I should fear there might be ill feeling between the 2 regiments. Whatever comes of it our boys are very ambitious to surpass them and I have confidence that they will.

Parts of this letter are nearly unintelligible—along the crease lines—but in addition to encouraging his wife, Sullivan seems to be recalling some incidents that happened in their home in Cranston, which was only a few blocks from a road animals were herded along to a slaughterhouse to become meat for the tables of Providence. The long line of cattle seemed to have been an irresistible lure to his oldest son:

Your second letter I received Friday night and opened it

eagerly & read it with joy. I was glad to have you write me little things about your domestic affairs and about the children. I wish you might fill in pages of little things that might seem to you nonsense perhaps—but to me would be of the deepest interest. In the many hours of the Day and night in which I think of you all, I want something more than the domestications of home that I have thought over and over again. The children running away to the slaughter house afforded me great pleasure as I thought of Edgar's great blue eyes while he talked about it and poor Willies tumble down stairs only proved to me how much I loved him when I heard him bumping falling down and the tears rushing to my eyes.

As to your domestic affairs I know you will fill all your stations in life, and have the self reliance the occasion requires. And I am glad to feel when I think of you, that you are so self reliant . . . I can at any time when I turn my thought homeward see you all about the house, and every thing in it. I can look through all the rooms and out of the windows, and recall almost every trifle that goes to make up the "tout ensemble." Through this faculty I derive great pleasure in looking at you. I notice your dress, your pin, your hair your collar—scan every feature and then awake with a sharp pang to think I cannot put my lips to yours. My dear Sarah I scarcely dare to put upon paper my ardent love for you: it has been so many years since I used to express it upon paper, that it seems strange to have to do so now, I have so long clasped you in my arms and told it to you with my own lips and seen your warm return of it in your own eyes and felt your responsive heart on my own bosom that I cannot wait to put it upon paper. And when it seems so tantalizing to wait to put it down word by word, when, if I was only with you, a thousand closely written pages of love could be enjoyed in a moment. Sarah you will never forget that I love you, but can

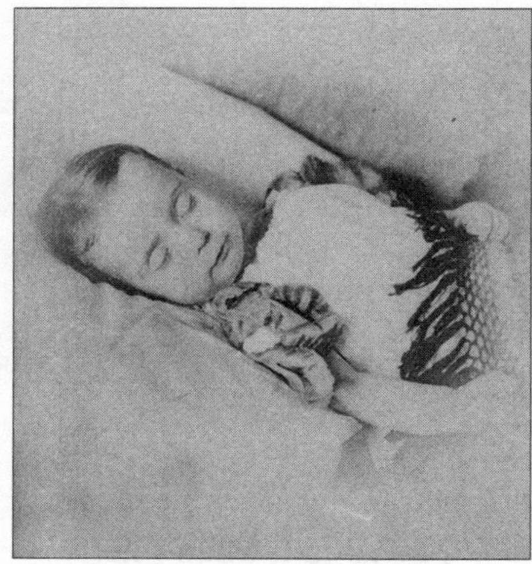

Knowing that children were subject to so many dreadful diseases, Sullivan worried about his boys while away from them. If a child had been ill, parents often rushed to have a photo taken—just in case. If they were too late, post mortem photos, like this one were common. *Photo by C. Seaves, Jr., from the author's collection.*

you always remember how much I love you. No you cannot. I cannot tell myself. The more I am called upon to fathom the depths of my love for you—the more vast they seem—the whole world could be drowned in it. Now my little boys—what another world of affection I have for them. O! Sarah—guard those priceless jewels for my sake—there are none others in the world like them. You know nothing of the almost desperate yearning I feel toward them. Your short absence from them for a day, when you can easily reach them, can give you no idea whatever of your emotions if you should lay down on the tented field miles and miles away, and feel that you could not step to their bedsides and kiss their little cheeks for many long weeks. But I cannot bear such thoughts long, and I always turn from them to the fond anticipation of my joyful return home when I can clasp you in my arms and gambol with my children once more. That fond meeting I can dwell upon for hours until it almost seems real. May God soon make it a joyful reality. You are writing me today—I have seen you several times doing so—write me much of yourself and your affairs even if you repeat them—tell me often that you love me and that my little boys still talk of me.

> My love to your mother. I am glad she has been to Pawtucket & hope you will go often. Write me about my mother & their affairs. Do not wait for my letters to answer them, but write as often as you can & believe me
>
> Your affectionate Sully[29]

This and every other letter written from Camp Clarke contained a line revealing Sullivan's fears that his children might die while he was away; when he implores his wife to "guard those priceless jewels," he is not only using a traditional Victorian phrase for children, but acknowledging the dreadful reality that 40 percent of all deaths were children under five, and hoping his own did not become such a statistic.

The next set of lessons was the manual of arms. First, the men were taught the care of the gun and ammo, and to keep their powder dry when crossing streams and rivers or marching in the rain. The soldiers learned basic manipulation of the rifle, or as Hardee called it, "the piece." This involved moving the twelve-pound, five-foot-long rifle and bayonet from its resting position against the shoulder into a position to begin its use. Sullivan had begun to learn this at age fourteen, when he was the youngest man in his militia company—when he and the gun were almost the same height! The new generation of citified men may never have been hunting or used any kind of musket. One recruit grumbled,

> I was taught my facings, and at the time I thought the drill-master needlessly fussy about shouldering, ordering and presenting arms.[30]

The basic physics of firing a gun has not changed since their invention around 1450 when they were known as "hand cannon." The same principles applied to large cannon, or artillery, which were simply cannon on wheels. An inert metallic projectile was needed. This bullet could be round, normally for a hand gun, or longer, with a pointed dome, for a rifle. At the time of the Civil War, a French-designed bullet named for its inventor was most popular. Made of lead, the so-called Minie ball (the men pronounced it minny) was not round. To guide the bullet forward in the desired direction, a long tube, called a barrel, was needed on the weapon.

An explosive substance was required to create the heat, gas, and air flow to propel the bullet the only direction it could normally go, down the barrel and out the open end. In the Civil War, as in the Revolutionary War of their grandfathers, that substance was black gunpowder,* which must be ignited by a spark of fire behind it. This was accomplished by inserting a small cap of gunpowder on to the strike plate underneath the hammer, which spontaneously exploded when struck. Pulling the trigger caused the cocked hammer to strike the cap, igniting it first, and then the gunpowder. These were the scientific principles behind the operation of the weapon.

There were about a dozen steps required to prepare the muzzle-loading Civil War–era rifle for firing each single bullet. First, the soldier shifted the cartridge box attached to his belt to the front of his body, and placed the rifle butt on the ground in front of his feet. Unfastening the cartridge box, he withdrew the newest technological advance in military armaments, a little packet that contained *both* powder and the soft lead bullet. Using his front teeth, he ripped open the paper covering, tasting a little black powder as he did so, no matter. The powder was poured down the muzzle of the rifle barrel and then the bullet was manipulated free of the paper and placed, pointed end up, in the muzzle.

* Gunpowder, originally invented by the Chinese, is a mixture of sulphur, carbon, and potassium nitrate (saltpeter).

The soldier then withdrew, in two long sweeping motions, the ramrod fastened alongside his gun barrel. He twirled the ramrod so the correct end faced the gun barrel, inserted it, and rammed the bullet down the barrel as far as it went. He next reversed the procedure, withdrawing the rammer and returning it into its "pipes" on the barrel. Specific hand positions were required for each move, and the manual detailed the position of the back of the hand, the thumb, and even the little finger. Failure to master a flowing set of movements here could result in a soldier getting all tangled up or failing to seat the bullet properly. If he lost the ramrod, the gun was useless and he practically defenseless.

Only once he had loaded it could the soldier hoist the weapon up to eye level before bringing it back to rest against his chest. But it still could not be fired. He had to half-cock it, pry loose the old firing cap, grasp a new one from his pouch, insert it, and press it down firmly.

Now, he was ready to shoulder his weapon, and begin the firing sequence. On the command of "ready," the soldier spread his feet apart to steady himself to aim and to receive the recoil of the weapon. The piece was brought into position, and the strike hammer, which Hardee calls the cock, fully opened. Next came the command to aim—the man looking down the barrel through the sites and choosing his target. "Fire!" The soldier squeezed the trigger, and the spark from the cap ignited the black powder, which blasted the bullet down the muzzle at a good velocity and out toward the enemy.

After firing his first shot, the soldier was now ready to repeat all these steps to fire another round—and they were expected to be able to fire three rounds per minute.* It was a difficult sequence of steps to perform accurately and quickly and under the stress of

* The excellent Civil War movie *Glory,* has a set of realistic scenes showing the Fifty-fourth Massachussets being trained to use their rifles. Disregard the last part of the training sequence where the second line seemingly fires their guns right into the line of men in front of them!

incoming bullets and shells. Sometimes men under fire needed to perform all these steps lying on the ground, and so the soldiers practiced all the rifle techniques in different positions. With the exception of sharpshooters who might indeed take precise aim, the aiming was inaccurate. The whole battle technique consisted of a straight line of men firing volleys of bullets into the enemy at close enough range to hit many of them at random and stop their advance.

Every piece came with a bayonet, a long, knifelike blade, attached to the musket barrel with clips. These could be turned around to protrude off the top of the rifle barrel, creating a long pike with which the soldier could parry a sword blow struck by a cavalryman, slash at the horse, or stick into an opponent. The soldiers had to be taught to attach these, move, march, and run with them in place without impaling their comrades, and to lunge with the full weight of their body behind them when attacking. The foreigners who had fought with Garibaldi in the Italian Revolution of 1848–9, knew that one of his bayonet charges was worth four to five hours of firing—especially the 2:00 A.M. attacks! Although bayonet charges were infrequent in the Civil War, soldiers were nonetheless trained in these techniques.

In battle of course, the officers did not call out each step or weapon as they did in camp drill. Sullivan, in command of the left flank as major, and the lieutenant colonel in command of the right, lined the men up in the proper formation and gave the order to fire. After that, it was up to the men to keep it up until ordered to halt. For all their training, amidst the turmoil of battle, a soldier might forget to withdraw his ramrod, thereby firing it at the enemy rather like the bolt from a crossbow. Or he might forget to actually fire the gun, and just reload it with, say, five bullets. Battle conditions were very challenging, even for men who had been excellent shots at home. The marksman who might have been an expert squirrel hunter—as the Georgia boys were reported to be—never had to cope with the squirrel firing back!

During this period of weapons training, Sullivan mentioned to Sarah his admiration for Captain William Reynolds, the commander of the Rhode Island Battery, and his intention to spend more time with him; perhaps through this association, Sullivan honed his knowledge of the third branch of the service, the light (cannon) artillery. In peacetime, back home, these had little to do except fire salutes on holidays, but during war, they supported the infantry on the battlefield, often working in close coordination with them. Ideally, in battle, an artillery barrage—or duel—preceded any clash of infantry. The cannon were supposed to "soften up" the enemy, interfere with his assemblage and movement of lines of troops, and frighten and demoralize his men. By the time of the Civil War, however, if the infantry was equipped with rifled muskets, they had the advantage over smooth bore guns and could shoot down artillery crews. Therefore the rules of engagement, the paradigm of cannonades, was shifting, but this was not yet recognized by the commanders.

Such guns weighed anywhere from 1,500 to 1,800 pounds, but were designated by the weight of the cannonball they fired, i.e., a

A cannon, limber, and caisson in traveling mode. *Author's photo.*

twelve-pounder fires twelve-pound ball. Mounted on a two-wheeled frame, hitched to, and towed muzzle backward behind a two-wheeled gun carriage called a limber, the whole was pulled by six horses. Each gun crew was made up of eight men, including a sergeant and corporal, some of whom rode on the ammunition storage chests, rather like coachmen. In a pinch, especially for fast getaways, they were able to ride the horses in the team. Forage for the horses, battery tools, and gear were also loaded onto the caisson. Gear included the ramrod, a repair kit, a bucket of grease and another for water. Water was necessary to cool the cannon, so a barrel of water might be carried if the battle was not known to be near a stream. Each gun was supported by a second caisson and limber with six horses. Two guns made a section, commanded by a lieutenant and was the minimum deployment; even two guns made a difference on a section of a battlefront.

On the battlefield, the gun could not just dash into place and fire. "Going into battery," required the team of horses to be unhitched, tethered some distance away, the gun "unlimbered" or uncoupled from the limber, after which the men pushed the gun into a position facing the enemy. The officer began to aim the gun, ordering the desired form of ammunition be brought. A sighting device was inserted, and the angle of the gun adjusted by turn screws, so its projectiles would fall where desired, though it normally took a practice round or two before the "range" was found. In an infantry battle, the guns were not aimed at people or targets, just at the overall assemblage of the enemy's men, who once within range, if they were unlucky, were in the wrong place at the wrong time when the ball landed. After each shot, a recoil of four to five feet was usual, and each gun needed to be repositioned.

Artillery work was very dangerous, as the Rhode Islanders found out during training in camp on

Thursday July 9, a sad incident occurred today . . . through

> some unknown cause, the limber-chest of Lieutenant Vaughn's section, filled with cartridges, exploded, while the gunner Morris, and privates Bourne and Freeman were mounted. They were thrown some 20 feet up in the air. Morris and Bourne died within the space of an hour. Freeman, being badly injured, recovered after a lingering sickness. Two drivers were slightly wounded, and two horses injured. We escorted the bodies of Morris and Bourne to the depot, to be sent to Rhode Island.[31]

Now, the devil was in the details as the army began to prepare for actual battle. Perhaps a well-equipped army of some standing, with experienced staff, could have performed without difficulty, but no such animal existed, so the troubles started immediately. As one of the military instruction books said,

> Civilians will find themselves greatly deceived if they indulge the belief that a knowledge of the tactics of their arm of service is all that is required of them. To feed, clothe, transport and govern troops is the great labor to be performed, and the drill and training in Companies is only an exercise. Administration is the grand task to be mastered before he has fairly acquired his profession.[32]

Weaknesses in any of these areas might be overcome by surprise, the ability to improvise on the spot—or a great deal of luck.

McDowell, from his humble headquarters consisting of four tents on the front lawn of Arlington House, riding back over the bridge into Washington to plead for resources, told the inside story,

> I was on the other side a long while without anything. No additions were made to the force at all. With difficulty could

> I get any officers. I had begged of the Secretary of War and the Secretary of the Treasury . . . that I should not be obliged to organize and discipline and march and fight all at the same time. I said that it was too much for any person to do. But they could not help it, or did not help it, and the thing went on . . . I got everything with great difficulty. Some of my regiments came over very late; some of them not till the very day I was to move the army.[33]

Of course, the top commanders were keeping the Union plans as secret as possible, along with the snafus, because no military command can succeed if it airs all its dirty laundry.

For a battle in northern Virginia, McDowell had to get his men—and their supplies—to the battle site on foot. He had to walk them in over roads that were one to ten horses wide, which meant keeping them on parallel roads until just before they had to fight.

> I had difficulty in getting transportation. In fact, I started out with no baggage train, with nothing at all for the tents, simply transportation for the sick and wounded and the munitions. The supplies were to go on afterwards. I expected the men to

An abundant number of wagons were available later in the war, but not when McDowell needed them to move his army. *Library of Congress Prints and Photographs Division.*

> carry supplies for three days in their haversacks. If I went to General Mansfield for troops, he said: 'I have no transportation.' I went to General Meigs and he said he had transportation, but General Mansfield did not want any to be given until the troops should move.[34]

Transportation was a very real issue, for army gear had to move on army wagons. The army needed hundreds of wagons to move rations, forage for the horses, gear, munitions, and medical supplies—far more than what was for sale in the small capital. They could not be readily driven in through the surrounding hostile states, and the regiments traveling by boat and train were unable to bring their own.

The quartermaster, Montgomery Meigs,* from the Regular Army, an exceptionally talented and organized man still struggling to get up to speed in this assignment, did his best, but wound up buying many derelict wagons "in a very incomplete condition for the road." The horses were "new" and "very few . . . shod; a large number of teamsters and wagon-masters very inexperienced; . . . My whole attention was directed to putting them in proper condition, neglecting for a time my legitimate duties in the subsistence department.[35]

Housing and food remained problems in the camps on the Virginia side. In clear violation of the Constitution they were fighting to protect and honor, the Yankees were camping in farmers' fields, officers moving into farmhouses, and the men starting to live off trespassed land for food.** One regiment chartered its own private

* The Meigs remained a professional military family; one commanded in Desert Storm.

** The third amendment to the U.S. Constitution reads: No soldier shall, in time of peace be quartered in any house, without the consent of the Owner, nor in time of war, but in a manner to be prescribed by law.

freight wagons to bring in food.[36] Not all of them enjoyed the benefits of business communities back home chartering a ship laden with ice to deliver a cargo of shellfish as a treat for the men.*

There were eighteen thousand men in the army at Harper's Ferry, where an anxious General Robert Patterson "often called for batteries and rifled cannon beyond our capacity to supply . . . and . . . one or more regiments. He might as well have asked for a brigade of elephants."[37] Undersupply generally ruled the day. McDowell also continued to believe that his commanding officer did not give him sufficient support to build up his department. How much of this was due to the general inefficiency of an army gearing up for its first war in thirteen years, and how much to personal animosity hiding behind military snafus, is unclear.

McDowell's battle plan called for an excessive concentration of men in a narrow corridor of countryside, a very difficult scenario to manage. His army needed time to practice together in large groups, if for no other reason than to learn to keep out of each other's way on the roads.

In their respective camps, the men had now diligently worked their way through many sections of *Hardee's Manual* and were now practicing the drills in the later chapters. These taught the new soldiers how to maneuver as a group in the field so they could go where directed across any configuration of terrain to attack, or to move out of harm's way. They were taught to hold the line, and keep their ranks closed up by matching the length of their strides.

* The shellfish sent to the First Rhode Island was spoiled by the time it reached camp, but the ice was very welcome and put to good use. The squads had taken "great pride in the embellishment of their huts; and flowers, books, . . . hangings . . . of patriotic colors of various fabrics, and musical instruments were not uncommon. A little cellar occupied the centre of the hut, and served as a refrigerator, well supplied with ice by the generosity of our friends at home."

They learned to "face about," march backward, and proceed at an oblique—or diagonal—course by first making a forty-five-degree turn to the right or left. Here again, the savvy recruit

> found that suggestions were not so well appreciated in the army as in private life, and that no wisdom was equal to a drill-masters "Right face," "Left wheel," and "Right, oblique, march."[38]

Especially important was the flank march, which required the men to make a ninety degree turn right or left, step into two columns, and march in the indicated direction at the indicated pace. By keeping their elbows touching, and their shoulders squared in the direction they were marching, a body of men could cross ditches, crest hills, and tramp through pastures of cow dung without losing formation. Once their objective was reached, they widened out into a battle line, normally two men deep. Of course, no one expected them to march in perfect cadence in the field—although when some regiments did when coming into battle, the sight was utterly breathtaking and caused the enemy to stare in admiration. The purpose was to cause an awareness of the movements of comrades, to instill good listening skills to the commands of officers, unquestioning and unhesitating obedience to the same, and to keep the basic battle unit, the companies of one hundred men, together.

> It takes a raw recruit some time to learn that he is not to think or suggest, but obey. Some never do learn. I acquired it at last, in humility and mud, but it was tough.[39]

The final fancy move that the troops learned was to wheel their line. A pivot man anchored the line, while the rest of the men took measured steps and swung the line, staying rigidly straight, like a gate on its hinges.* This was practiced at all three cadences, and while its practical use in the field might be limited, it looked awesome at dress parade, never failing to impress the spectators. It also served as an analogy for positioning adjacent regiments to attack and sweep an enemy before them on the battlefield. Such a move had a whiff of Napoleonic grandeur about it, and General Pierre Beauregard, newly assigned from Fort Sumter to field command in the Virginia theater of war, a man who counted himself among the great general's apprentices, was going to try to find a way to use it.

Although Sullivan had—as did every field officer—a vested interest in having his men perform all these tasks in the School of the Soldier competently, he did not have to personally partake in their drill. His duty was to bring the men to the desired level of competency, but he used drill masters, sergeants, or lieutenants to accomplish it. Often Regular Army men were assigned to drill various regiments, and even members of the newest class to graduate and depart the West Point Military Academy, in June 1861, taught drill.[40] The enlisted men who had come out of the militia units could help the new boys to learn the drills, as could the "old soldiers" like Thomas Parker, a veteran of the British Army and Crimean War serving in Company D. Sullivan had practiced marching with the militia back home for many years; what was new for him was giving the proper commands at the critical moment. So when Lieutenant Ames sized up the Second Rhode Island's commanders, and noted,

> Major Ballou was a man out of his place. He had no knowledge of field movements which made him less efficient as an officer. We all liked him as a man, and he was a brave man upon the field.[41]

Sullivan was in good company with many other officers.

* The move used by Joshua Lawrence Chamberlain commanding the Twenty-first Maine on Little Round Top at Gettysburg.

The next phase of the soldiers' education from *Hardee's Manual* was the School of the Company. This set of drills enabled the men to move out of range quickly when shells were falling in their midst, or to charge the enemy.

A regiment moving through the field passed through different terrain, going from narrow roads to broad fields. They might climb over fences or run through thickets. To stay together in some semblance of order, the men needed to learn the various commands for moving forward or obliquely, for going from narrow columns to the broad lines of an attack formation. In their field maneuvers, they were guided by the "directing" sergeant, who was out in front of the company line as it went into battle. Their captain, too, marched in the front of the line, at the very right, protected by the "covering" sergeant right behind him. Behind the lines of each company came the assigned "file closers," the lieutenants and sergeants whose job it was to make sure the line stayed even and moving in the correct direction—and that no one ran away from his duty.

The ten companies comprising the full regiment drilled as a whole in Gale's Woods, where the surgeons, hospital stewards, band, and regimental staff each had a defined position behind the advancing line. The colonel positioned himself in the middle, and tradition held that the lieutenant colonel marched with the right wing, and the major with the left. The Second Rhode Island followed this procedure.

At some point, the commanding general might call a battalion drill, in which a multitude of regiments were drilled and inspected together, to permit the general to see how they performed. Although an accepted technique discussed in the manual, McDowell was criticized when he held one with two full brigades. Given the fact that none of this set of commanders had ever maneuvered large bodies of troops in the field, battalion drills would have been most useful, but here the interpersonal dynamics, the jealousies, and competitiveness, reared its head and interfered with what was best for this army. Scott chastised the brigadier for "trying to make some show" when McDowell brought the eight regiments together for a review, a tame way of seeing if they could maneuver in force. "I had no opportunity to test my machinery, to move it around and see whether it would work smoothly or not."[42]

General Irvin McDowell, although promoted from a staff-level desk job, knew neither he nor his army were ready to fight a major battle. At the start of the war, a pool of 940 West Point graduates were available for service, almost equally divided between currently serving officers and those who had resigned over the last fifteen years. Thirty-six percent of those, predominantly current officers, went with the Confederacy. Twelve percent remained in the Regular Army, and the remaining forty-eight percent took positions, usually promotions, with the volunteer regiments. The majority of these had never commanded more than one hundred men during the Mexican War, thirteen years ago. To bridge the gap, many of McDowell's commanders were political appointees, given commissions for their ability to organize the mobilization. The company officers were the neighbors and prominent figures from the hometowns of the recruits; the men trusted these local authority figures more than they did some unknown lieutenant absent in the Indian Wars for many years.

Regardless of his inexperience, McDowell had a month or two to build an army, and he had to use the resources at hand. The men available for assignment as colonels to this first campaign in Virginia were: Ohioan Robert Schenk had been a Latin teacher, a lawyer, an ex-minister to Brazil, a congressman, and Republican campaigner. Erasmus Darwin Keyes had been fired from Scott's staff; he then helped the governor of New York dispatch the thousands of troops sent from that state; then McDowell took him in and gave him a command. Despite fourteen years' earlier service, David Hunter's Mexican War experience had been as paymaster, and he had just spent a month organizing a new cavalry troop for

Mansfield; his command was probably awarded because Lincoln trusted his energy and integrity. Andrew Porter, a Pennsylvanian and West Point graduate, had gone from regular army captain to colonel, in May, and brigadier general three days later; he had served in the Southwest. William Franklin, another Pennsylvanian whose background was military engineering, similar to Beauregard's, graduated first in his class at West Point; he, too, jumped from captain to brigadier general in May 1861. Samuel Heintzelman had graduated from West Point and served in the Mexican War and on Indian patrols; though personally brave and gallant, the kind of man who would personally lead his troops into battle, he was not a major military talent. Israel "Fighting Dick" Richardson, from Vermont, another West Pointer, had fought in the Seminole wars in Florida and the war with Mexico, then resigned in 1855 to become a farmer in Michigan. Orlando Willcox had much the same experience as Richardson, but had resigned in 1857 to practice law. Oliver Howard, a Mainer, had graduated near the top of his class at West Point, served on the frontier, and was back at the military academy as a mathematics professor when the war broke out; after seven years in the service, he was still a first lieutenant. Daniel Tyler, from Connecticut, was an 1819 graduate of the U.S. Military Academy, had done ordnance and garrison duty, been sent to France, translated an artillery manual, and then resigned his commission in 1834; a civil engineer, he had been president of a railroad in Georgia. Thomas Davies, from New York, served only two years before resigning his military commission to become a merchant, and had no fighting experience at all.[43] Louis Blenker, another New York merchant after his flight from Germany, had at least participated in the combat of the revolution of 1848 there, but he commanded reserves unlikely to see any action at all.[44] Dixon S. Miles, from Maryland, had an uninterrupted career in the Regular Army after graduating West Point in 1824; in the Seminole wars in Florida, he had served as a recruiter and quartermaster;

during the Mexican War, he had won praise and a promotion to major for distinguished conduct in combat; after a year on duty in Missouri, he was sent to New Mexico and Arizona for five years, where his main activity was chasing Navajos without catching them, before recall and promotion to colonel.[45] Theodore Runyon, of New Jersey, was a Yale graduate, city attorney and later city councilman of Newark.[46] With the notable exception of William Tecumseh Sherman and Ambrose Burnside, who will be discussed in detail later, none of these men ever played major military roles in the Civil War. By midwar, most of them had been transferred to minor administrative roles in the army.

On the Confederate side, with the exception of Jubal Early who had resigned his commission in 1838 in favor of the law and politics, the other Southern brigade commanders, and major players who survived Bull Run—Richard Ewell, James Longstreet, E. Porter Alexander, J. E. B. Stuart, Kirby Smith, P. T. Beauregard and Joseph E. Johnston—had all remained in the U.S. Army their whole careers. Jubal Early was one of the Virginians who did not favor secession, feeling it "unnecessary and imprudent. . . . offered no remedy for existing or possible ills, and . . . opposed it with all their might . . . as suicidal," but "believed it their duty to side with their State" when it came.[47]

With the exception of career politician Milledge Bonham, who resigned his commission for elected office; D. R. Jones, who died from a heart attack; and Philip St. George Cocke, who killed himself before the year was out, all the other Confederate commanders involved in First Manassas went on to become superstars in the Confederate Army.

CHAPTER THIRTEEN

"Rally Round the Flag Boys"*

A Look at Union Preparations for Battle

First Half of July 1861

The war needed to go forward swiftly for many reasons. The martial atmosphere in the nation's capital and other big cities, for one, was contagious, and instead of supporting the systematic organization of the army, worked against it. The government was being carried along by the tide of political opinion: "public opinion," as William Tecumseh Sherman observed in a letter to his wife, "is a more terrible tyrant than Napoleon."[1]

Northern newspapers were clamoring for victory, led by Horace Greeley's *New York Tribune*, whose repetitive shilling of "On to Richmond!" made it the slogan of the day. Throughout the North, everyone wanted to get the war over with and bring the men home, a sentiment that was as unrealistic in this war as in all others. The

* From the Civil War song "The Battle Cry of Freedom."

New York bankers who were providing the loans to Lincoln's government to finance the early war efforts, also believed an early victory would contain the formidable costs. They, too, hoped for Waterloo.

In 1861, the U.S. government was experiencing a financial crisis. The stagnation of the economy, lingering from the Panic of 1857, meant the Buchanan administration had been borrowing to meet expenses; the nation was $60 million in debt when Fort Sumter was attacked. Some $12.6 million of that debt was in short-term bonds, which the government had pledged to redeem in 1862. Worse yet, "the nation is now in debt for money applied to the benefit of these so called seceding States" whose territorial debts the federal government had assumed on their behalf when they were granted statehood.[2] Florida's debt alone was $100 million, but only Alabama had offered to pay its prorated share of the national debt. Even worse for the bankers was that, with secession, individual Southern businessmen not only defaulted on their personal debts to banks in the North, but compounded the impact by withdrawing any funds on deposit. Bank failures were once again a real possibility, and Northern banks hesitated about making further loans. In June, when the Treasury had tried to sell bonds, there were no takers—an unheard-of situation. Lincoln planned to point out that the only way bankers could recover the outstanding defaulted loans was by a Union victory.

However, the financial crisis that Lincoln faced that spring was not confined to the debt alone. The financing system for the federal government had also basically terminated with the outbreak of the Civil War. Tariffs on imported goods—goods bought predominately by Southerners who did not manufacture their own—made up 92 percent of the nation's income. The Confederacy had kept for its own use most of the revenue collected to date in 1861 at ports like Richmond, Charleston, Mobile, and New Orleans; that, and all such future revenue, was lost to the United States Treasury.

"The treasury was empty. There was not enough money even to pay the Members of Congress." Secretary Chase needed to head to New York to see if the banks would cooperate and keep the Union's government functioning.

Lincoln and his Cabinet therefore faced two financial challenges: One was to invent a new system to fund government in the long term. The second, and most immediate, was to raise the extra money needed to finance the war—to equip, arm, and pay the troops. Secretary Chase had estimated the war would cost $320 million and wanted Congress to approve the sale of $240 million in long-term, twenty-year bonds. He figured the government could raise another $80 million from land sales on the frontier, and from new taxes. Lincoln prepared to deliver that message to Congress in late June; he had gotten on well with Bishop Thomas Clark, and invited him back to the White House the day after the review, for the first of many appointments. As Clark recounted,

> I called at his private office, soon after breakfast, and found him at his writing desk with a loose dressing gown about him. After one or two general remarks, he said, "I can hardly tell you how relieved I am this morning. I have just finished my message to Congress, and now that is off my mind."

Clark told the president it was a pity he had to call this special session for "no body could tell what mischief it might do."

> Lincoln confided, "I have called this Congress because I must have money. There is Chase, Secretary of the Treasury: sometimes he calls for a million of dollars in twenty-four hours, and I can assure you that it is not an easy matter to raise that amount in a day." The president then continued. "This war is a matter of resources. That side will win, in the end, where the money holds out longest."

Lincoln was confident that a developed America could repay the $500 million debt the war might cost.[3]

In view of the financial situation, a short war was essential, and that could only happen if quick military action knocked out the Confederacy. Having lost Fort Sumter, the Union that summer had to demonstrate to its financial backers that it was capable of winning such a war. As the president said, "A right result, at this time, will be worth more to the world, than ten times the men, and ten times the money." As his options narrowed, Lincoln decided to risk throwing his army into battle before it was fully supported and trained. When McDowell regretted, "I wanted very much a little time. All of us wanted it. We did not have a bit of it," it was because Lincoln ordered the attack, telling him, "You are green, it is true; but they are green, also; you are all green alike."[4]

As Independence Day dawned, the Rhode Island Battery north of the city fired a salute, which was echoed by other batteries from entrenchments across the river.[5] Later that morning, the members of Congress convened in the Capitol Building, which had been scoured clean after its use as regimental barracks of last resort, for a critically important emergency session of Congress. The chambers had been given a fresh coat of paint, and the carpets taken up, cleaned, and put back down. Requested by the president, who with his Cabinet shaped this agenda, the members had returned to that "City of Magnificent Intentions" in its most unpleasant season, when the city was hot, humid, and odiferous. Its stinking canals, sewers, and privies were at their most aromatic in summer, while at night the streets were patrolled by far fewer policemen than armies of mosquitoes.

The Senate convened with the vice president in the chair overlooking the twenty-one empty desks of seceded senators. The chaplain reminded God that "disasters have befallen us and darkness broods in the land," and asked, "May the angel of Thy presence walk in the Cabinet and in the Congress and in the camp . . ."[6] The

Senate swore in the two members from the new state of Kansas, and awaited the reception of the president's message. It was read aloud the following day; Lincoln did not attend. In the months since he had called the session,

> the Executive found the duty of employing the war-power, in defense of the government, forced upon him. He could but perform this duty, or surrender the existence of the government.

However, since the legality of some of the president's actions had been challenged, President Lincoln needed the Congress to ratify his actions.

For example, the Constitution specifically stated that "the privilege of the writ of habeas corpus, shall not be suspended unless when, in cases of rebellion or invasion, the public safety may require it." But the Constitution did not specify which branch of government could do so. Lincoln assumed the powers so the nation would "not . . . perish" but, after stinging criticism from the Chief Justice Roger Taney that only the Congress had that specific power, the president wanted Congress to sustain the action.

In this message to Congress, Lincoln avoided high-flying rhetoric in favor of simple logic, writing what was basically an attorney's closing argument about the indivisibility of the nation, contending that "some dependent colonies made the Union," which is "older than any of the States; and, in fact, it created them as States."

He ran down the list of hostile actions taken even before her secession by Virginia, which "received—perhaps invited—into their state, large bodies of troops, with their warlike appointments, from the so-called seceded States." His warning to Virginia was crystal clear: "The people of Virginia have thus allowed this giant insurrection to make its nest within her borders; and this government has no choice left but to deal with it."

He had equally stern words for the border states and their policy of "armed neutrality" and denial of passage to the troops of both sides, which created a wall of protection for the Confederacy, which was "treason in effect."[7]

The new Speaker of the House, Pennsylvanian Galusha Grow, received lengthy "vociferous applause upon the floor and in the galleries," for the closing words of his fiery speech that followed, which characterized the deep emotions in the government:

> No flag alien to the sources of the Mississippi river will ever float permanently over its mouth till its waters are crimsoned in human gore, and not one foot of American soil can ever be wrenched from the jurisdiction of the Constitution . . . until it is baptised in fire and blood.[8]

The members of Congress had been to visit their constituents in their respective camps. They came away mighty impressed with the size and caliber of the armies in Washington, and, talking themselves into believing them invincible, came out in favor of immediate military action. British journalist William Howard Russell drolly observed, "They think that an army is like a round of canister which can be fired off whenever the match is applied."[9] After lengthy discussion, Congress authorized $250 million in loans at 7 percent, 500,000 troops—to be disbanded at the end of the war, and the temporary increase of the navy.[10] General McDowell, who knew his army was not ready, and General Scott, who preferred not to fight in Virginia, were no match for the combined executive and legislative branches—and the press.

This year's Fourth of July celebrations in Washington were very different for the city's residents, whose usual activity of picnicking outside the city was forestalled now that army regiments were camped in all the picnic grounds. Celebrants instead thronged the Avenue, Lafayette Square, and President's Park to watch the largest parade ever seen in Washington, D.C. New York State had so far supplied most of the regiments, and on this day, by order of Major General Sandford, those twenty thousand men still encamped in the District paraded the length of the Avenue. Protected from the hot sun by a viewing stand, President Lincoln, General Scott, the Cabinet, and most of the army staff reviewed the parade and took the salutes of the regiments.

With the Fire Zouaves now deployed in Virginia, the most exotic New York regiment presently in the District was the Thirty-ninth New York Volunteers, the Garibaldi Guards. The first three-year regiment to be fielded from the state, these men were experienced fighters from various European revolutionary wars. The regiment was named in honor of Giuseppe Garibaldi, who had led the 1860 uprising in Naples. Their recruiting poster was quintilingual, in English, Italian, French, German, and Hungarian, and called upon men to rally to their adopted country to form a regiment of "Riflemen, Bersaglieri, Horsedek, Chasseurs, and Scharfachatmen." Their uniforms were a similar hybrid: red wool Garibaldi shirts,* dark blue French trousers, black leather leggings, a dark blue Hungarian coat, all topped off with wide brimmed Bersaglieri hats with a cutout eagle emblem and jaunty cockades of iridescent green feathers.[11]

Naturally, this "foreign legion" was not content to offer a conventional salute to the president when something more dramatic might be done instead. Early that morning, they had stripped the flower gardens of homes near their encampment, so that as they marched past the reviewing stand, each soldier threw sprays "of flowers or evergreens" at the feet of Lincoln and Scott, "each company officer a bouquet."[12]

A rather more ominous Fourth of July event involved Beauregard's enterprising

* Full-sleeved Garibaldi shirts became very fashionable for ladies during the war. They were often trimmed with braid.

> intelligent pickets [who] were watchfully kept in the closest possible proximity to General McDowell's headquarters, and by a stroke of good fortune on the fourth of July, happened upon and captured a sergeant and soldier of the regulars, who were leisurely riding for recreation not far outside their lines. The soldier, an intelligent, educated Scotchman, proved to be a clerk in the Adjutant-General's office of General McDowell, in trusted with the special duty of compiling returns of his army—a work he confessed, without reluctance, he had just executed, showing the forces under McDowell about the first of July. His statement of the strength and composition of that force tallied so closely with that which had been acquired through my Washington agencies, already mentioned, as well as through the leading newspapers of New York and Washington, Philadelphia and Baltimore, regular files of which were also transmitted to my headquarters from the Federal capital, that I could not doubt them.[13]

Back home in Providence, drums and cannons also heralded the morning of this especially important Independence Day holiday. At 5:30 A.M. "the Providence Drum Band marched through the principal streets of the town, playing National Airs." For anyone not yet awake at 6:00 A.M., church bells rang for thirty-four minutes during which a national salute was fired off by the Providence Artillery Company.* Well publicized by the newspapers, the longest continuously running Fourth of July parade in America began at 8:30 A.M., downtown at Exchange Place, exactly where the photo had been taken of Ambrose Burnside and the First Regiment marching splendidly off to war. Flags displayed throughout the city made a patriotic background as the parade moved through the business district and up the truly steep hill leading to the Benefit

* Presumably one minute for every state in the true Union.

Street Armory, where the soldiers had enrolled, and down North Main Street to the First Baptist Church.

Music from Shepard's Cornet Band and the Drum Band escorted all the militia and artillery units still at home, veterans of past wars, and a flock of municipal and state politicians, headed by the mayor and governor, along the route. The Sprague Zouaves marched, thirty-eight privates strong, wearing their dashing red Turkish caps with tassels, white shirts, dark pants, and a blue sash. About this time, clothing for little boys began to imitate Zouave uniforms, with curved jackets outlined in braid. Willie and Edgar Ballou may have been dressed thus as they watched the extravaganza.

One theme strongly represented by the many student groups in the parade was the commitment to sustaining the nation the Revolution had made. The Northern commitment to educating daughters was also prominently touted, "One of the most interesting features of the procession was the young ladies and misses from the public schools. . . ."

> Thirty-four young ladies from the High School, emblematical of the States, occupied a carriage decorated with wreathes, flowers and flags; a banner was conspicuously displayed having for a legend the following: "Our Fathers Planted; We'll Nourish and Protect." . . . Upon the carriage of the Prospect street school was the inscription, "The Nursery of the Republic." There was also a portrait of Washington surrounded by the legend, "He still lives in our Hearts."

Following the young ladies were representatives of such well-known civic organizations as the Odd Fellows, the Sons of Temperance, . . . and 235 members of the Providence Hibernian Benevolent Sick and Burial Association, who "carried an elegant banner inscribed with various devices indicative of the objects of the Association." Those readers of the *Providence Journal* not present could indulge their imaginations regarding the emblems of a burial society. The Providence Fire Department was the final official group, after which anyone might tag along.

Following the parade, church services began promptly at 11:00 A.M., probably in the city's largest church structure, often used for civic events, the First Baptist. With the odd gallantry that made women with children climb three stories of stairs to the "safety" of the choir loft where they escaped being jostled by strange men, the

> doors to the galleries reserved for ladies and scholars open [ed] at 10 AM. There the program commenced with more sweetly harmonized singing by the young ladies choir, an opening benediction, and a reading of the Declaration of Independence by the principal of the Benefit Street Grammar School.

This was followed by a patriotic oration, the length of which was severely constrained by the fact that

> at noon, church bells pealed for a solid hour, during which the Old Guard Artillery fired a two hundred gun salute in the park. During the afternoon, the various companies continued to parade through town individually before rendezvousing in the park at 6 PM for a dress parade of fancy marching, while another half hour of bell pealing and a hundred gun salute took place.[14]

Finishing the day in this state, which was the "first to begin revolution, last to enter the Union," some families hosted outdoor parties, and many picnicked in the park. Anyone wishing to enjoy fireworks had a good selection from which to choose. One newspaper in

Connecticut advertised for sale "rockets of all sizes, blue lights, roman candles, wheels, stars, fancy pieces, chasers, Chinese crackers, torpedos."[15]

Up in the healthful air of the cooler hills above Washington, in Camp Sprague and Camp Clark, Major Sullivan Ballou had been put in charge of the Rhode Island regiment's celebration there, and in a letter to Sarah spanning two days, he described how he spent this "civil Sabbath of the patriot."

July 3 1861

My dear Sarah
Your letters have all reached me and you can fully appreciate the joy and comfort they have been to me. Tell me in your next if Bishop Clark has called to see you yet, & if Brownell sent you my letter to him. . . .

Yesterday being 4th of July we extemporized a celebration. We made a platform on some whiskey barrels in front of the Col's tent & surmounted it with our flags. On the table we put two champagne (empty) bottles and in the necks, two splendid boquetts. Our Regiment was assembled around it; and I acted as President of the Day. Chaplin Woodbury read the declaration of Independence—Chaplain Jameson made the prayer, Father Quinn of the first Regiment made a capitol address, and Capt Dyer of 2d Regiment read a good poem, & our band discoursed national music. It was a very successful affair.

Corporal Rhodes had a good time, calling it "a grand celebration. . . . At 12 noon a national salute was fired by the Light Battery and we were invited to a fine dinner," furnished by the folks back home.[16] That afternoon, Rhode Island certainly captured the market on the most unusual entertainment of the day, when tightrope artist Professor Benoni Sweet, "a private in the Second

Regiment, delighted a numerous assembly of spectators with his famous, brain-bewildering "Callacoes" and "Pancraticals."[17] No wonder Rhodes was able to write about the dignitaries his camp attracted:

> Our camp has been full of people all day. In fact we are in the habit of seeing many distinguished men at our parade. Night before last (July 2nd) there were present the Honorable Salmon P. Chase, Secretary of the Treasury, Colonel John C. Fremont the great path finder, James F. Smith Esq. of Rhode Island and others.[18]

The enlisted men bragged about the V.I.P.s. Private Sholes waxed eloquent when noting their "dress parade at evening . . . attracted an audience of the great, the gallant and the beautiful."[19] But Sullivan, who routinely worked with top-level officials, was happier to see homefolk:

Evening dress parade in the Rhode Island camp attracted "the great, the gallant and the beautiful." The unfinished dome of the Capitol could be clearly seen. *Courtesy of the Anne S. K. Brown Military Collection, Brown University.*

> We have had a great many R.I. people here within the last few days and it has been very pleasant to meet them. Congress brings a great many of them here, and they are very constant in their visits to us.[20]

Sullivan recorded that "in the afternoon our Col treated all the officers to Ice Cream and Raspberries."[21]

In an effort to cheer up Sarah, Sullivan began to sound a bit like Abraham Lincoln, relating anecdotes from camp life:

> Camp life goes on rather dull; and we have very little to relieve the monotony of constant drilling. Night before last however one of our horses got loose and wandered around in the dark he got near one of the sentinels, who challenged him 3 times. But the poor old horse not having the countersign; and the sentinel not being able to distinguish him from a man, shot him. . . . I was very much amused at your anxiety about the man that attempted to poizen our spring. It was the first time I had heard that we *had* a spring in the camp; and as for the attempted poisoning it was all a hoax. If you can catch the man that started the story you had better hang him.

Talk of the July 8 advance of the army was now an ill-kept secret throughout the District, and it must be presumed, in Richmond and Manassas. Sullivan mentioned the date to Sarah.

> I have no news whatever to write you unless it be as to the movement of our regiment. It is said that we are to unite with the 1st Rhode Island—the New York 71st and the 2d New Hampshire in a Brigade under Burnside and to move over into Virginia next Sunday noon. We are to leave all our Camp equipage and Baggage here and take nothing with us but our blankets and four days rations. If this should turn out correct

> it is probable the Genls Patterson & McClellan will move on the rear of Manassas Gap and Genl McDowell will move from here in the front. I cannot make up my mind that there will be any fighting. The rebels will retire. It is of no earthly use for them to fight when a superior force is taking them in front and rear. By leaving everything here in camp and a few men to guard it, it is evident we are to return here and it is possible we may make this our headquarters all summer. If we do I shall see you this month or next. The amount of troops pouring in here is perfectly enormous and in course of a few months they will be disciplined into fine troops whom the South cannot resist. Col Slocum has just returned from the city and says the report there is, that the rebels are retreating from Manassas gap junction. This is just what I have expected; and our expedition will be fruitless. We shall probably start on a line of march next Sunday noon, as Col Slocum has just assured me: but if the Rebels are retreating now, we shall see no fighting, and have to come back without it. . . . I suppose you will be glad of this. . . .

The Rebels were not retreating, the intelligence was bad. The repositioning of some unit might have been misinterpreted. George McClellan, brigadier general of the Volunteers from Ohio, in command of the Union forces in western Virginia, was moving into position for a battle at Rich Mountain. As Sullivan explained,

> Sunday morning. I have delayed my letter that I might tell you about our movement. The order is countermanded and we are not to move for some days. I presume Genl McClellan & Patterson have not moved fast enough or got close enough in the rear of Manassas Gap for the forward movement from Washington; and therefore we must wait a few days.

Sullivan next reassured Sarah about the protections he was going to take if deployed to the field. A mosquito net was hardly practical in the field, though a good many men did use nightcaps.

> When we go I shall carry strapped to my saddle my two heavy blankets—an india rubber blanket—a mosquito net—havelock india rubber covering for my cap and a few trifles for my toilet like hair & a tooth brush. At night I shall lay on the ground on my rubber blanket—wrap myself up in my heavy woolen blankets take my saddle for a pillow—and put on my silk night cap. My horse will be hitched beside me. In pleasant weather it will be very comfortable there is so little dew here and if it rains I anticipate no trouble.

In this letter, it becomes clear that both Sullivan and Sarah are beginning to come to grips with managing the details of life apart after three weeks. Given Sullivan's inattention to details about money, Sarah emerges as the family banker who has obviously been analyzing her financial position. Sullivan is, however, prudent as concerns his watch.

> This morning our Lt. Col Robbins the Cashier of the Merchants Bank went home; and by him I sent you my watch and chain. Experience has taught me that it is too nice an establishment to have laying round in my tent; and it is too much trouble to lock it up in my chest every night. I am going to send to Brownell to get me a cheap Wattram watch with silver case. It will cost about 30 dollars and I can sell it when I get home. You keep my gold one very choicely. Keep it running all the time—wind it up every night or morning just as will be most convenient for you—and if any thing ever ails it or it gets out of time, don't touch it yourself but take it to Famingtons & they will fix it. You know I an very proud of that

watch—it has been my constant companion for about eight years and I am sorry to give it up.* When you lay it down, always lay it with the face up. Never *hang* it up. . . .

As for my tent in camp I really sleep as well as I do at home—sleep all night soundly—no wind blows on me and no rain touches me. I have in my tent all I need for my personal comfort, and I get along as well as I could wish to or expect to alone. But I begin to feel the loss of your society and every night as I lay down I think of you & Willie and sigh to touch your cheeks. I see you sleeping on your pillows as I used to see you; and at last go to sleep dreaming of you. How come on your financial matters. How much money have you & how many debts do you owe? Suppose Tompkins could take off 50 doll[ar]s from the rent—could you put up stoves in place of the furnace & stay there this winter: You can do as you like but I suggest it because you speak of being sorry to leave. You had better sell the cow if you can get any where near what you speak of for her. Send me in your next letter the scrip for the 40 shares of the Hancock Mining Co. Stock. It is in my pocket book. I want to sign it and send it to Latimer W. Ballou for him to sell it whenever he thinks best. I cannot look after it & would be glad to have it sold. Your letters so full of tenderness and affection have come very promptly and are a great solace in my loneliness. Do not let me go long without them. I will try to write Uncle Henry soon. My love to Aunt Sarah and her children—kiss my little boys for me and believe me yours ever

Sullivan

* The watch was likely acquired in conjunction with Sullivan's admission to the Rhode Island Bar in 1853.

Sarah had informed Sullivan she was going to visit the Henry Ballous in Bristol. Their aunt Sarah was now six months pregnant, at the age of thirty-eight, and would have been grateful to have such agreeable and useful company. By custom, and for convenience, she was not going out much in public in her condition.

July 8, originally the first departure date for the Union offensive, found the army far from ready. Regiments were still being assigned to McDowell's command, and basic equipment like ambulances remained to be issued. Departure was delayed until the army became organized. McDowell formed five divisions of varying sizes, according to the role they were to play in the campaign, an innovative and useful idea.

On July 10, Confederate spy Bette Duvall rode out to Milledge Bonham's camp in Virginia, where Bonham agreed to receive her. In his presence, she took out her hairpins, let down her long black hair—a shockingly intimate thing to do in front of a strange man—and, removing a black silk bag from her tresses, extracted a message written on a piece of paper and handed it to him. It contained the plans of the Union attack on Manassas. The hiding place was a safe one; etiquette guaranteed that even had she been captured, she would have not been searched in such a way that the message could have been found. Along with the information elicited from the men captured July 4, Beauregard now had confirmation of the Union battle plans.[22]

Also by July 10, the Confederates in northern Virginia had completed their communications system. They now had an operative telegraph line. They also had a series of crude wooden platforms, made out of fence rails lashed together, which they could use as watch towers and flag semaphore platforms. Towers were located at the highest knolls in the area, rising some six to eight feet above their bases. The height sounds inadequate, but was actually sufficient for the terrain of the greater Bull Run valley at the time.

First Division
Brigadier General Daniel Tyler
First Brigade Colonel Erasmus Keyes
Second Maine Infantry
First, Second, and Third Connecticut Infantry
Second Brigade Brig. General Robert Schenck
Second New York Infantry
First and Second Ohio Infantry
Artillery: Company E, Second US Artillery (7)
Third Brigade Col William Tecumseh Sherman
Thirteenth, Sixty-ninth, and Seventy-ninth New York Infantry
Second Wisconsin Infantry
Artillery: Company E, Fifth U. S. Artillery
Fourth Brigade Colonel Israel Richardson
First Massachusetts Infantry
Twelfth New York Infantry
Second and Third Michigan Infantry
Artillery: Company M, Second U. S. Artillery (4)
Company G, First U. S. Artillery (2)

Second Division
Colonel David Hunter, succeeded by Colonel Andrew Porter
First Brigade Colonel Andrew Porter
Eighth New York Militia
Fourteenth Brooklyn Militia
Twenty-seventh New York Infantry
United States Regular Army
Infantry Battalion (8 cos.)
U. S. Marine Corps Battalion
US Cavalry Battalion (7 cos.)
Artillery: Company D, Fifth U. S. Army (6)
Second Brigade Colonel Ambrose Burnside
Second New Hampshire Infantry
First Rhode Island Infantry
Second Rhode Island Infantry
Rhode Island Artillery Battery (6)
Seventy-first New York Infantry
Boat Howitzer detail (2)

Third Division
Colonel Samuel Heintzelman
First Brigade Colonel William Franklin
Fifth and Eleventh Massachusetts Infantry
First Minnesota Infantry
Artillery: Company I, First U. S. Army
Second Brigade
Colonel Orlando Willcox succeeded by Colonel J. H. Hobart Ward
Eleventh New York Infantry (Fire Zouaves)
Thirty-eighth New York Infantry
First and Fourth Michigan Infantry
Artillery: Company D, Second US Army (4)
Third Brigade Colonel Oliver Howard
Third, Fourth, and Fifth Maine Infantry
Second Vermont Infantry

Fourth Division
Brigadier General Theodore Runyon Militia
First, Second, Third, and Fourth New Jersey Infantry
Volunteers
First, Second, and Third New Jersey Infantry
Forty-first New York Infantry

Fifth Division
Colonel Dixon Miles
First Brigade Colonel Lewis Blenker
Eighth, Twenty-ninth, and Thirty-ninth New York Infantry
Twenty-seventh Pennsylvania Infantry
Artillery: Company A, Second U. S. Army (4)
Brookwood's New York (6)
Second Brigade Colonel Thomas Davies
Sixteenth, Eighteenth, Thirty-first, and Thirty-second New York Infantry
Artillery: Company G, Second US Army

Regiments sent in relief on July 22, 1861
Twenty-fifth and Thirty-seventh New York Infantry
Fourth Michigan

The Confederate Armies under

General Pierre Beauregard
Army of the Potomac

First Brigade
Brigadier General Milledge Bonham
11th North Carolina Infantry
2nd & 3rd & 7th South Carolina Infantry
8th Louisiana Infantry
Artillery: 1st Company Richmond Howitzers (4); Alexandria Light Artillery under the Cavalry: 30th Virginia (4)

Second Brigade
Brigadier General Richard Ewell
5th & 6th Alabama Infantry
6th Louisiana Infantry
Artillery: Washington (4)
Cavalry: 1 Battalion

Third Brigade
Brigadier General David Jones
17th & 18th Mississippi Infantry
5th South Carolina Infantry
Artillery: Washington (2)
Cavalry: Flood's Company 30th Virginia

Fourth Brigade
Brigadier General James Longstreet
5th North Carolina Infantry
1st & 11th & 17th & 24th Virginia Infantry
Artillery: Washington (2)
Cavalry: Company E, 30th Virginia

Fifth Brigade
Colonel Phillip St. George Cocke
8th & 18th & 19th & 28th & 49th Virginia Infantry
Artillery: Loudoun (4) & Lynchburg (4)

Sixth Brigade
Colonel Jubal Early
7th Louisiana Infantry
13th Mississippi Infantry
7th Virginia Infantry
Artillery: Washington (5)

Seventh Brigade
Colonel Nathan Evans
1st Special Louisiana Brigade (Wheat's Tigers)
4th South Carolina Infantry
Cavalry: Alexander's Troop, Terry's Troop of the 30th Virginia

General Joseph Johnston
Army of the Shenandoah

Reserve Brigade
Brigadier General Theophilus Holmes
1st Arkansas Infantry
2nd Tennessee Infantry
Artillery: Purcell (6)
Camp Pickens (15)
(Col. Wade) Hampton's Legion (6 companies)

First Brigade
Brigadier General Thomas J. Jackson
1st & 2nd & 4th & 5th & 27th Virginia Infantry
33rd Virginia Infantry (8 companies)
Artillery: Rockbridge, Virginia (4)

Second Brigade
Colonel Francis Bartow
7th & 8th Georgia Infantry
Artillery: Wise (Alburtis) (4)

Third Brigade
Brigadier General Barnard Bee
4th Alabama Infantry
2nd & 11th Mississippi Infantry (2 companies)
6th North Carolina Infantry
Artillery: Staunton (4)

Fourth Brigade
Brigadier General Edmund Kirby Smith succeeded by Colonel Arnold Elzey
1st Maryland Infantry Battalion
3rd Tennessee Infantry
10th Virginia Infantry
Artillery: Culpepper (4)

Not brigaded
1st Virginia Cavalry, Colonel J. E. B. Stuart
Companies Present for Battle
A Newtown Troop
B Berkeley Troop
C Rockbridge Dragoons
H Loudoun Light Horse
I Harrisonburg Cavalry
K Rockingham Cavalry a.k.a River Rangers
L (a.k.a D2nd) Washington Mounted Rifles
M (a.k.a K2nd) Howard Dragoons Maryland
Thomas Artillery (Stanard's Battery) (4)

Communications were flowing well between Rhode Island and Camp Clark, and Sullivan was the happier for it. Perhaps as a visitor in someone else's house Sarah had more free time than when managing her own home, for she wrote him a long, chatty letter. Either his requests for a more intimate tone finally overcame her deeply rooted modesty, or perhaps Aunt Sarah encouraged the younger woman to loosen up her pen and finally write what her husband wanted to hear. In any event, the letter was affectionate enough to please him, and he responded warmly.

July 10 1861

My dear Sarah

I have just received your letter from Bristol and hope you have also rec'd mine written last Sunday. You know I need to be in some fault with your letters—because they were so short and told me too little of your everyday thoughts & feelings—But I find a happy change in your style now; and I know when the mail comes I shall find a missive full of tenderness and affection—and something to tell me how all your domestic affairs go on and how my dear little children get along. Knowing how you must depend entirely on yourself I feel as though I must hear of everything you do in almost every hour of the day. Then too in my deprivation of all objects of affection I love to read new words that your own dear hand has written, and which tell me of our love and affection. Absence from loved ones is very hard to bear and if we never heard from those we love, how hard it would be to depend upon our own thoughts alone to satisfy the cravings of love. In fact ones thoughts are the poorest kind of food for love to live upon, and it would surely die if it were not for faith and hope and confidence. How joyous it is then to read every few days some new page that love has [three illegible words] some new words that tell us we are still loved as dearly

> and fondly as the most jealous heart could ask. Your letters are indeed very dear to me and I file them all numbered and dated so I can read them over and over again and recur to them long afterwards and receive the exquisite emotion I have felt before. You speak of feeling my loss as never before and I assure you I pray most heartily that God and my country will never call me from your side again. . . . Keep up good courage and have my little Edgar praying for me; for I believe God will answer his prayer and not let the soldiers hurt his dear papa.[23]

At this point, Sarah probably had her whole little family praying not only for their papa but for their uncle John as well. Sarah's "little" brother, John Fowler Shumway, six feet tall, dark haired, and twenty-three years old, had joined the Union Navy on June 7. He enlisted from Massachusetts as a seaman for a one-year term of service, and was now in Boston Harbor on the receiving ship *Ohio*, where new sailors were trained.[24] He was unlikely to get into much danger during the first three months of his training, but once he was posted to a ship doing active service on the blockade of the Southern states, Sarah and Catherine had another reason to worry. While John was off "seeing the elephant," Sullivan, doing two sets of duties, had no opportunity for sightseeing.

> I have scarcely been out of camp since I have been here. The Capitol is in plain sight; no farther off than from our house to the Hoyle Tavern on High St yet I have not been there. If we stay here I mean to push myself in among the notables and enjoy more society than Camp affords. We occasionally see some of the public men out here at our dress parades for it is becoming quite fashionable for the city people to drive out here and look at our two Regiments. And it really is worth seeing. They say there are no regiments that begin to compare with ours. Mr. Breckenridge and Mr. Crittenden were both

here the night before last; and last night Genl Coombs of Kentucky. Fremont has also been out to see us. Lincoln & different members of the Cabinet come occasionally and every night the ground is lined with ladies and carriages.

I have considerable more care than I have had heretofore because we have no Lieutenant Colonel and I am therefore second in command. When we come back from Virginia (if we go) I am going to claim promotion to that place and I think I can get it. I have become quite well acquainted with Gov Sprague as he has taken up his quarters in our Camp—occupying a tent not very far from mine. I shall improve the acquaintance and make it serviceable to me if I can. He is a very unassuming man and a very agreeable man. I think if he stays here long I can advance myself in his good opinion.

A contemporary sketch of the tents of Burnside and Sprague, close to officers' row in the camp of the Second Regiment, where Sullivan and the other field officers lived. Sullivan told Sarah how his mare, Jenny, was "hitched" nearby. *Courtesy of the Rhode Island Historical Society, anonymous soldier/artist, June 27, 1861.*

This was an interesting concession for Sullivan, who apparently held no grudges against the man whose ticket had defeated him in his run for state office. The war had changed politics in the North forever, and Sullivan was enough of a pragmatist to work on forming a new and useful coalition with the men in power in Rhode Island, men who could be useful to him in the postwar world.

> Gov Sprague has just come up from town saying he *thinks* we shall move Saturday but I told him I did not believe it & should not till I saw the order. We shall not be gone however many days though we may go through severe service.

Sullivan meant to reassure Sarah about his travails in the hot Southern sun when he wrote: "I have a nice linen Havelock if they will do any good." Surely he knew by this time the soldiers had universally determined the havelocks only made them hotter in the sweltering humidity, but were reluctant to tell the sisters, mothers, and sweethearts who had spent all spring diligently sewing them to protect their dear men from sunstroke, and sending them by post to the camps. In the meantime, the soldiers had found a use for them after all by turning them into coffee strainers, which were in short supply in the camps. One soldier of the Second reported his father had come down to check on the progress of the regiment and, discovering there was a real need for a device to strain the grinds, was going home to invent and manufacture some for army use for when the havelocks wore out.

The closing line of Sullivan's letter is very revealing about his relationship with Sarah:

> I shall send you some money in a few days to pay the one bill I left home and also for the last two tons of coal I got. Enclosed you will find the receipt for rent I forgot to leave at home—put it in my little drawer in the library. I shall send

home some Congressional globes to fill up my set in a few days.* If you can sell the cow for money—do so & put it in the bank. Buy those 2 daguerreotypes of Goddard and give one to mother. Have the children taken two of them in a double case & send me one and your own with it. Direct your letters to Washington as before till you are written to the contrary. I will write you again before we leave—and Sunday at farthest. Write me my dear Sarah as often & promptly as before and I will try to be as punctual with you. You know how my Hope towers above all misfortune and doubts—and you must know therefore how ardently I look forward to meeting you & my children again and enjoying anew and with a thousand times the zest I have ever done before—your and their love. Few men can boast a wife's love as I can; and it is a pride I can feed upon in secret and never be sated.

Yours as ever
Sullivan[25]

At this time, Corporal Rhodes bragged about more distinguished visitors to the Rhode Island camp.

Camp Clark, July 11, 1861—President Lincoln and wife paid our camp a visit to day and received a fine reception from the troops. In the afternoon both regiments have a dress parade after which we passed before the President to review. We begin to hear rumors of a movement by the army but we do not know much about it.

As developments made it more certain that the Union forces were to leave camp to go into battle, Sullivan stepped up his efforts

* The early version of the Congressional Record.

to provide security for Sarah if anything should happen to him. His experiences as a fatherless boy seemed to be driving him to shield his sons from hardship and emotional deprivation, and to diminish the hardships endured by a widowed wife. About this time, Sullivan penned another letter, this one to "Charlie," perhaps to Charles Parkhurst, his former law partner, because its tone is more intimate than the known letter to his current law partner, Charles Brownell. Only part of this letter survives:

> It would stimulate your State pride very much, if you were here, and could see the action and know the reputation of the Rhode Island troops. At the present time our camp is about the only fashionable resort in Washington. The ground is crowded with the elite of the city; while we are reviewed almost every night by Mr. Lincoln, some member of the Cabinet, the Speaker of the House, or some other distinguished personage. Some of the enemy also have had the curiosity to look at us—such as Breckinridge, Buckner of Kentucky, and others. The officers of other regiments flock to see us, and the universal exclamation is not one merely of praise, but of astonishment. . . . Camp life begins to grow rather dull, and all of us sigh for active service. . . . The patriotism of the troops is by no means abated. . . .
>
> If we do not move South this summer, I hope to get a furlough for a week and come home and see you all. I want to see my dear little boys, around whom the tendrils of my heart cling so powerfully. And I assure you, it is a stern conflict between my affection and duty to my country, when I give up my children and take the battle-field in defence of the great principles of American civilization. Do not suspect me, however, of any hesitancy or misgivings;—the world has never yet seen nobler institutions in peril than ours, and men were never yet called upon to die in a nobler cause. I shall do my duty with

> all my might and mind, and to my latest breath; and if I cannot remain here to care for my children, I shall leave them a name of which they will not be ashamed. But I do not deem it inconsistent with true courage for a soldier, before stepping upon the battlefield, to give some affectionate thoughts to the loved ones at home; and though this is the first time such thoughts have dropped from my pen, yet they fall without reserve to you. I have great confidence, Charlie, in the strength of the foundation on which your character is laid, and know that you will not only honor the institutions which I have pledged my life to sustain, but will have both mind and heart to cherish an obligation for the posterity of those who have fallen in their country's service. Let me ask you, therefore, Charlie, if it is my fate to fall on the field, to be a brother to my little boys. I need not enlarge upon the sacred obligation I thus impose upon you, nor labor to impress it upon your heart.[26]

As the now inevitable clash of arms approached, each side stepped up its efforts to learn about the actions of the other. On July 13, with the Union battle plans in his tent, and rumors of McDowell bringing the last of his forces over the Potomac intensifying, General Beauregard wrote to General Joseph E. Johnston up at Winchester, urging him to move south to merge the two armies. Beauregard also sent a copy of his battle plans to Richmond for final approval.

In Washington, President Lincoln and the War Department decided against further delay. The enlistments of the three-month regiments, mustered in the third week of April, were due to run out the third week of July and the men planned to return to homes, families, farms, mills, and businesses. These were the most seasoned and best drilled units in the army; the First Rhode Island was the best equipped. If the Union Army did not move now to engage the Confederacy, they would have to wait another two to three months for new men to arrive and be trained.

Scott preferred, and originally proposed a plan to slowly strangle the South into submission by surrounding it, blockading it, and closing in from all sides. The political and financial realities did not admit such a strategy. An anaconda might slowly strangle its prey, but the Union was instead going to try to eviscerate the Confederacy with a slashing strike from a giant, three-clawed hand, aimed straight at the railway junction at Manassas. To strike this blow, McDowell needed to move his force

> on four lines that had no communication with each other from the very nature of the country. But I thought I made each column strong enough to hold its own. If it could not penetrate it could stand still, and if attacked it could hold its own, while the other columns were pressing forward and trying to get behind the enemy. The roads from Alexandria radiate. One goes out to Vienna, one goes to Fairfax Court House, one to Fairfax Station, and one further south to

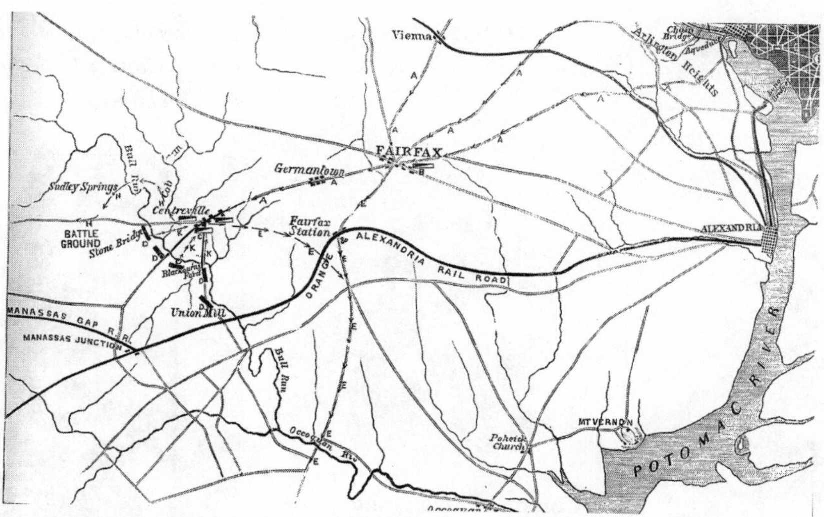

Northern Virginia, showing Fairfax and Prince William counties and the main routes of McDowell's army in this campaign. Washington, D.C., is at the upper right. *From* Harper's Pictoral History of the Civil War.

Captain Nelson Viall. *From the B. William Henry Collection, courtesy of the U.S. Army Military History Institute.*

Captain Charles H. Tompkins rose through the ranks during the war, but Sullivan was appalled at his landlord's womanizing. *From the Roger D. Hunt Collection, courtesy of the U.S. Army Military History Institute.*

Sergeant Henry Prescott. *Courtesy of the Anne S. K. Brown Military Collection, Brown University.*

Officers, Second Rhode Island Regiment.

Colonel John Slocum. *Courtesy of the Anne S. K. Brown Military Collection, Brown University.*

Lieutenant Colonel Frank Wheaton. *From author's collection..*

Corporal Elisha Hunt Rhodes, the great diarist of the Second, as he appeared later in the war. *Courtesy of the Anne S. K. Brown Military Collection, Brown University.*

Captain Levi Tower. *Courtesy of the Anne S. K. Brown Military Collection, Brown University.*

Captain Samuel James Smith. *Courtesy of Bill Gladstone, U.S. Army Military History Institute.*

> Pohick church. . . . General Hunter, who commanded what I intended to be a sort of reserve, composed of General Burnside's command and General Porter's command, were to go on the Little River turnpike to Annandale.[27]

The tempo of regimental paperwork picked up as the departure date neared, and Sullivan remained busy performing the duties of major and lieutenant colonel, in absence of anyone in the latter position. This situation was not to continue much longer, for while home on bereavement leave, Colonel John Slocum apparently persuaded Captain Frank Wheaton to join the regiment, literally stealing him away from a command with the First Cavalry in Arkansas on the eve of his departure for that post. With the concurrence of Governor Sprague, Wheaton filled this vacant key position just before the march, and Sullivan Ballou lost what he no doubt saw as an eventual promotion. Rhodes wrote in his journal that Frank Wheaton "is the son of our surgeon Frances D. Wheaton . . . he is a handsome fellow and looks as if he would fight."[28]

Wheaton had years of experience fighting the Apache, Comanche, and many other tribes. One of the most traveled men in the United States, after graduating Brown as an engineer Wheaton had journeyed through Utah and the Northwest, but especially through Texas and New Mexico with topographical expeditions. America needed to survey its long southern border with Mexico after its victory over that country, and as the tribes of the Southwest resisted the growing American presence, hostilities broke out and the topographical engineers found themselves fighting on more than one occasion. His base of operations in Texas was often San Antonio De Bexar, where that constant reminder of American fighting spirit and valor, the Alamo, sat on a small hill at the edge of town. Wheaton was recruited at officer level into the cavalry for his valor and meritorious service. New York's mobilization effort for this war was so massive that they brought in officers to help; Wheaton worked with Erasmus Keyes in that task during the spring, and probably knew David Hunter from their days at Fort Leavenworth. Here was a man with a decade's experience in field organization and command, and he sprang into action.[29] On July 14, Surgeon Wheaton signed an army form noting the Second had received fourteen ambulances and harnesses.[30]

Despite the bustle of preparing for imminent battle, Sullivan allocated time to write Sarah a lengthy and detailed letter, full of hope for their future, and once again referencing the visions his intuitive powers gave him. This letter in later months and years probably caused tears to fall, for its ironies and tenderness. He also began to organize their communication process for his upcoming time in the field.

My Dear Sarah.

Here we are still at Camp Clark. It is quite probable we shall move into Virginia before long and I have no doubt it will be sudden because the government are getting so cautious about their movements no one knows anything until they see it done. . . . You must not be surprised if you do not receive letters very regularly from me for a little while for if we go into Virginia only a few miles—there being no post roads or mails—it will be difficult to send or receive letters. I shall however send you a *few* lines, as often as possible. In the meantime do not waiver in the promptness and constancy of your letters. The post office at Washington will undoubtedly use the means they can to send forward letters to us wherever we are, and I shall eventually receive all you write. . . . I think being in the open air improves my health and saving balls and bullets I have no doubt my general health will be permanently improved by the campaign. Again let me assure you by the love you know I bear you that I shall not neglect my health. I am looking with too many fond hopes to our happy meeting and enjoying even more exquisite bliss than ever. . . .

There have been many times since we were first acquainted where I have been separated from you, and longed to see & be with you with all the deepest fervor of my heart. These same feelings now pervade my breast with increased power and in greater volume, if that can be! but I have new emotions now—like Osea piled upon Pelion.* I was never separated from my children before. I never knew the longing of a father for his children before. And you can scarcely imagine how my blood—my nerves thrill and my brain almost whirls, when with eyes wide open the world all becomes blank to me, and I see my little boys going through their childish pranks, and hear their singing voices, and even stretch my arms to catch them, and awake to touch the white walls of my tent. O Sarah how often do I think of them, and remember and recall their whole existence; and then heave the deepest sighs that all such imaginings are worthless compared with one actual embrace of them. You have them with you Sarah—may you never be separated from them.

For all Sullivan's blandishments about a short war, Sarah seems to be readying herself, their sons, and their budget for him to be absent a year or so, as detailed in his responses to things she proposed for her domestic arrangements. There is no hint of her combining residences with her mother.

As for your house I want you to get a good one—and not scrimp yourself with little rooms or a few of them. Of course

* Pelion is a mountain in Thessalonica in Greece; the reference is to making it larger. Its significance in this letter is that it is a very minor point of Greek mythology. That both understood its context reveals their level of education in the classics.

you will have to get a cottage to be alone—and I am much opposed to my children living with any others constantly or being where they cannot play out doors. And I want you to pay 250 dol[lar]s [$6725 per year] rather than not have a house to suit you. Then too if I should be able to get home this fall or winter or even next spring (and I have every confidence this war will be over by that time) I want a house we will be content to remain in. And I want you to fit me up a little library just as though I was at home now, and always keep it waiting for me. I think I have never written you about my pay. It is $175 dollars per month or 2100 doll[ar]s per year. [$56,700] Out of that it will cost me about 25 doll[ar]s per month for my horse & man. Then I must pay for my own living & necessaries. I shall send you at least One Hundred Dollars each month and perhaps more. Of course if I remain in the service long we shall not want. I shall have a months pay next week when I will send to you the above sum.

He wrapped up by reviving again his plan of rendezvousing with her, this time by having her come to camp, and by teasing her about her reticence to commit her own passion to paper.

Everything goes pleasantly with me in the regiment. Am on good terms with my brother officers and with the men. As long as our camp remains here though we leave it for a short time, I shall live in hope of having you here. Our Quartermaster, J. Aborn & Capt Smith of Woonsocket and I had all formed a plan to bring our 3 wives down here, and we have not yet given it up.

My love to your Mother and kiss my little boys for me. Talk to them about me often. Tell my little Edgar how much I love him and that I kiss this very line for him. Tell little Willie he is my jewell, and papa wants to lay him on a pillow and whistle him to sleep.

You are writing me to day I suppose. Be sure and write me that you love me as of old, True, I might have suspected it from all your letters but try if you can to tell me so, so as to satisfy and assuage my burning love for you. No, you cannot. I am glad you have a little care for my mother. God Bless you.

Ever your Sullivan[31]

He wrote a second letter that night. Before July 14 ended, something happened to him that compelled him to sit down and write Sarah another, very different kind of letter, one that was meant to be read by her eyes only in the event of his death. His mood changed profoundly, perhaps from the knowledge of impending orders to march and leave the safety of the camp, or perhaps from one of his visions or dreams.

Civil War folklore is replete with examples of prescience. There are many tales told by soldiers about comrades who intuited or prophesied their own deaths in the next battle, and made their final arrangements, disposing of property or writing one last letter home. Victorian mysticism respected the supernatural.[32] Abraham Lincoln, while president, had symbolic visions while he was sleeping, one of which foretold his own death. However it was triggered for him, several of Sullivan's letters reveal that he experienced a trance-like state on occasion, as visions related to people dear to him.

It appeared that after supper on July 14, as peaceful darkness settled over the camp, Sullivan Ballou had a premonition that he would not survive the forthcoming battle. Men did not shrink from going into combat as a result of their precognition; brave Sullivan did not. Honor and duty carried them forward, fire in the soul, ice in the veins.[33] The second letter of July 14 may have taken some time to write, perhaps even requiring a draft to get the elegant language flowing across the page. Full of the same type of sentimental endearments he used in earlier letters, employing familiar themes, resplendent with eloquence, this letter was a masterpiece. It was without doubt the handiwork of a master of the art of rhetoric, it was a speech on paper. It contained all the requisite elements of a fine oration:

> American eloquence is directed chiefly to the *feelings* of those to whom it is addressed, and to the sense of national honor. The strongest and noblest sentiments in man to which the appeals of eloquence can be addressed are, first, the sense of right and wrong, and next, the love of country and of kindred.[34]

Even though the original letter in his handwriting is no longer extant, there can be no doubt he was the author, conspiracy buffs not withstanding. Sarah did not write it to herself, and the very few other men in Rhode Island so trained were unlikely to have the time, motivation, or anything to gain by its forgery. Copies in other handwriting—none of them Sarah's—exist because that was the only way to copy anything in the 1860s.

Because this second letter Sullivan Ballou wrote to Sarah on the fourteenth was meant to be received by her only in the event of his death, once it was completed and sealed, the safest place to leave the letter to ensure its reaching Sarah was to lock it in his chest—the one he was leaving safely behind in camp. If anything happened to him, these personal effects would be escorted to Sarah by a member of his regiment. Should he himself return to his own tent, safe and whole after battle, he could burn it—or save it for next time. It made no sense to carry it on his person, subject to getting soaked crossing a stream or saturated by that more viscous fluid whose loss drained away life.

In any event, there was little time to think of it the next morning as the camp bustled with men scurrying to complete tasks. Finally, on July 15, after days of rumors and anticipation, Brigadier General Irvin McDowell finally issued the order—his divisions based on the eastern bank of the Potomac, in and about Washington, were to move out the next day.

Corporal Rhodes reflected,

> We have orders to be ready to move, but where no one can tell. Rations are being cooked and we expect to march very soon. It begins to look warlike, and we shall probably have a chance to pay our southern brethren a visit upon the sacred soil of Virginia very soon. Well I hope we shall be successful and give the Rebels a good pounding.[35]

The men of Battery A likewise reported, "great excitement in camp; order was received to get ready for a forward movement; ammunition packed; haversacks and canteens were issued."[36] There was an immediate flurry of activity in the camps ringing the city. Almost everyone in the specified regiments was leaving. Only those men on sick call were left behind with comrades to tend them; they got to fight another day—although "men who had been under the surgeon's care for weeks buckled on their armor and obstinately refused to be left behind while the death blow was given to the rebellion."[37]

When a regiment left its base camp to march to battle, all nonessential gear was left behind under a guard detailed to remain in camp. The few wagons available were needed to transport food and ammunition. Especially on such a short campaign—one intended to last just a few days—all that was needed was clothing, blankets, haversack, weapons, and ammunition. Each man carried all his immediate needs—about thirty-five pounds' worth. Many also had tin cups, a plate, fork, and knife hanging off them, so they clanked when they walked. The haversack contained three to four pound of salt beef or pork, thirty "crackers," and some coffee and sugar—three days' rations. Any personal effects, like bibles, family pictures, or inkwells, just increased the load. For the enlisted men, this meant leaving their Sibley tents pitched right where they were, and locking up any of their valuables in the company storage chest. Of course, members of the guard, like Corporal Rhodes, were not happy to be left behind:

> This morning my Captain [Steere] sent for me and said: "corporal . . . You are detailed to remain in camp with a guard to look after the tents and Company property while the Regiment is absent." I objected to this plan and finally told my Captain that if he left me in camp I would run away and join the Regiment on the road as soon as it became dark. He tried to convince me that I was too slight built to march, but I insisted that I would go orders or no orders, and he finally told me to go to my tent and pack up my traps, and that he would detail another corporal to remain in camp. I packed up such things as I thought I should need and left my treasures that have accumulated in the company chest. Our large felt hats with a blue cord and brass eagle were left in the First Sergeants tents.[38]

For the officers, who had much more gear in camp, it meant leaving behind tents, beds, tables, chairs, lamps, quilts from home, and their own personal campaign chests, into which they locked any valuables like excess money or important personal papers. The officers had saddlebags in which they could store a few items like pen, ink, and paper; they took their pocket watches—useful for timing attacks—and sufficient funds to buy meals along the way.

The band took their instruments but left their only "weapon," their ceremonial swords, in camp; they would only get in the way on the march, or when carrying the stretchers. They went to the battlefield unarmed.

The surgeons were also mounted and carried their own medical bags. A divisional wagon toted a field tent, personal kit, campaign desk, and some modest furniture for a general. Wagons managed by the army—not under the control of the regiments in any way—carried ammunition for the muskets and guns, rations for the men, and forage for the horses. The artillery was, in most cases, self-sufficient, with its own wagons hauling the necessary cannonballs, powder, and gear, and its own teams pulling the gun assemblies.

The company's wagon—if already procured—carried the band instruments, the axes and shovels of the "pioneer" squads, about two dozen heavy cast-iron frying pans and cooking pots for the messes, as well as the lighterweight coffeepots. They might carry any of the surgeon's gear that could not be accommodated elsewhere. As happened with the Third Maine, whose wagons moved four days behind them, lack of such wagons meant that the cast-iron cooking pots were left behind, so if the men could not cook or consume any rations like rice or beans, they went hungry. The coffeepots, often made of tin, were lighter and could be carried by the marching men.

At last, it was time to go and Corporal Rhodes rejoiced,

> *Camp Clark, July 16, 1861*—Hurrah! We are all packed and waiting to move. Our haversacks are filled with salt pork and hard bread and our canteens with water.[39]

It was just as well the army moved as unencumbered as possible, because there was no staging area within Washington, D.C., large enough to assemble so many troops. The Second Division had to assemble itself using the streets themselves, and it took quite a bit of planning. Pennsylvania Avenue was the main assembly point, with units using side streets to approach the Avenue and holding in place until they could assume their assigned positions. Even so, this task was easy compared to what awaited them on the narrow roads of Virginia.

Because the camp of the Rhode Island troops was at the far northeastern part of city, the First and Second regiments had to march across the whole city to get to their assigned place in line. Since they had been honored with leading the march, other units had to wait to fall in place behind the 3,700 men of Burnside's Brigade.

Never had the capital seen this magnitude of military spectacle. For a month, regiments had been going to Virginia. Sometimes they marched at night, awakening residents with their tread. But today, Washingtonians now accustomed to the drilling of a regiment or two, could not remain blasé about the force of ten thousand men marching down Pennsylvania Avenue. Rhodes wrote, "Excitement ran high in the streets, and as we moved through the city we were loudly cheered by the people.[40]

Though the excited spectators on the Avenue could not see it all, the men marching smartly past them were joining with other divisions already in Virginia to form the largest army ever raised on the North American continent: 35,000 troops. This was double the manpower of the combined French/Continental Army force at Yorktown, and triple the size of George Washington's Continental Army when he took control.

This army was composed of units of volunteers from thirteen states—from Ohio, Michigan, Minnesota, Wisconsin, Maine, Connecticut, Rhode Island, Massachusetts, Vermont, New Hampshire, New Jersey, and Pennsylvania, plus the predominant state at this point, New York. Not every man in the march was one; some were women—like Canadian Sarah Emma Edmonds, disguised as nurse "Frank Thompson"—who were going to do their patriotic duty on the battlefield. If every account of "disguised females" found in various regiments published in Civil War–era newspapers were to be believed, hundreds of women on both sides served as soldiers, teamsters, and company officers. These women risked social ostracism for cross-dressing and "unsexing themselves" to fight for their country.

Some women were not disguised, but marched proudly with some of the units going to battle. Mrs. Chaplain "B," with the

Second Michigan, and Miss Harriet Patience Dame, the hospital matron of the Second New Hampshire, who had badgered the state authorities into transferring her to the field medical unit from the hospital in the state capital, accompanied them into battle. Of the latter, Colonel Gilman Marston said,

> Wherever the regiment went she went, often going on foot, and sometimes camping on the field without tent . . . She was truly an angel of mercy, the bravest woman I ever knew.[41]

Yet another Napoleonic adaptation, vivandières, who were also known as cantinières, had quasi-official status with their regiments. They each carried an oversize canteen filled with water or reviving spirits. In recognition that rough comrades often did not get it right while trying to tend to a wounded or ill comrade, the vivandières nurtured the men in a variety of ways. They might fill the men's canteen at a nearby spring while the men were busy fighting, or kneel down and help a wounded man to drink. They soothed the dying and severely wounded, and bandaged minor wounds, providing that touch of female sympathy that men and boys remembered getting from their mothers. They carried food from the cook station to the wounded, sewed up rips in shirts and trousers, and sometimes did laundry. They were also a kind of mascot, whose example of bravely bearing up under the rigors of camp life, the march, and battle inspired the men to quit complaining and get on with it. One was described by a male comrade as

> with us in storm and sunshine. . . . never pouting or passionate, with a kind word for every one, and every one a kind word for her.[42]

There are instances where they encouraged the men in battle, rescued flags, or helped rally the men around the flag.

Though each side disparaged each other's "daughters of the regiment" as mere "camp followers," the genuine vivandières did not provide sexual services to their regiments. Most encampments had no trouble attracting genuine prostitutes for those men so inclined to use them. Most vivandières had official sanction, and some served under the protection of fathers, brothers, husbands, or fiancés, and wore a feminized version of the regiment's uniform:

The vivandières marched into Virginia and into battle alongside men who passed out from the heat—but the women wore twice the fabric. Of course, they wore corsets but, since they were so active physically, they did not lace as tightly as a society belle striving for a wasp waist. Over that, they wore a shirt, jacket, and trousers for practicality, but their trousers were full, a kind of Turkish-style bloomer, fitted at the waist. Over this, they wore a shortened skirt and apparently petticoats to make it stand out in the fashion silhouette of the period. The skirt used only four yards of fabric and most pictures show a length just below the knee. The overall ensemble was decorated with braid or lace, and often reflected the dress of their militia regiment. They might wear an apron on top; stockings and sturdy boots completed their uniform. These outfits were not very different from the bathing and gymnastic fashions shown in ladies's magazines of the period. Their hair was worn up as any other lady's in public, which also kept it clean. They wore a hat with or without a brim, often with military insignia and whatever fashion statement they could make with feathers and trim. Some carried musicians' swords, some pistols, some both. Going into battle, they marched in with the file closers at the back of the unit.

Not every regiment had vivandières,* but Kady Brownell marched with the Second Rhode Island, and Martha Francis and Sarah

* A ballet pas de six, *La Vivandiere*, debuted in London in 1844. As the Civil War progressed, and marches became more prolonged, most generals ordered women nurses to remain at fixed location hospitals.

Beasley with the First. Augusta Foster went to war with the Second Maine, and six vivandières accompanied the Garibaldi Guards.

At least one other woman played a key role this day. Southern spy Rose Greenhow sent a coded message from her Washington mansion, which supplied the final piece of data the Confederate command was missing—the date of McDowell's march out of D.C. It appeared to be an ill-kept secret: twenty-seven-year-old Mary Henry, a loyal Union girl, knew, as did many others. The daughter of the secretary of the Smithsonian Institution, her family lived in the museum and moved in the highest circles, counting among their closest friends Generals Winfield Scott and David Hunter. On July 16 and 17, Mary was able to record in her diary the plans for the attack on Fairfax Courthouse, which she had heard from girlfriends, friends she met while out walking, and contacts who had been at the War Department, although she noted, "General Scott is in constant communication with the army by

The afternoon of July 16, the last brigades of the Union Army marched across Long Bridge to complete McDowell's army in Virginia. Despite being a night view, this drawing provides the best view of the length of the span across the Potomac. *From* Harper's Weekly.

telegraph but he keeps his own counsel." Within twelve hours, the coded message Rose Greenhow had written, "Order issued for McDowell to march upon Manassas tonight," was placed in Beauregard's hands.[43] The Confederate commanding general knew when to expect the Union Army.

In D.C. the sidewalks were crowded, and still more people watched from the windows, outside stairwells, and balconies of the houses along the route feeling joyful or resentful, according to their politics. Flags and handkerchiefs waved, and the onlookers shouted accolades to home state boys as they marched past.

The men and the crowd fed off each other's enthusiasm in that peculiar bonding that takes place when warriors parade within arms' reach of the populace they defend. The writer Upton Sinclair described this dynamic in his novel *Manassas*,

> It was a marvelously uncomfortable thing—this army; a thing newly born, and green, very much aware of itself, palpitating, thin-skinned, sensitive. Every man there was a-tremble with excitement, burning up with the consciousness that humanity was counting on him.[44]

The order of march was symbolic and meant to convey honor to the regiment chosen to lead it—Rhode Island. General McDowell had gone back into D.C. from his command post in Arlington to escort his army, and rode proudly next to General Hunter. The regimental officers—Slocum, Wheaton, and Sullivan Ballou—rode right behind them, along with the general's staff.

Riding as he was at the front of the march, Sullivan had a panoramic view. Ahead, he saw the general of the army and the shores of Virginia. Behind him exuberant ranks of men filled the total width of the streets as far as the eye could see. What a heady moment for a man who had come from being the poorest boy in his family, struggling to get an education. This may have been the

This magnificent panorama evokes the thrill and pageantry of the march out of Washington, when the Union was sure of a victory. (The Ellsworth Zouaves, already stationed in Virginia, were not part of the parade.) *From the West Point Museum Collection, United States Military Academy.*

proudest, most inspiring moment of his professional life. Here he was, a thirty-three year old lawyer from the Ballou Neighborhood in Cumberland—way up in the North—parading down Pennsylvania Avenue in his nation's capital, just a few feet behind famous generals and at the head of a vast army, going forth to preserve America—and liberty.

- CHAPTER FOURTEEN -

"The Most Glorious Scene"*

The March into Virginia

July 16–20, 1861

Mounted on his mare, Jennie, Sullivan Ballou continued with the procession as it marched down the length of Pennsylvania Avenue, past the president's mansion, down to the Long Bridge, and over the wide Potomac River into Virginia, where able adversaries—men from the Carolinas, Georgia, Louisiana, Mississippi, Alabama, Maryland, Tennessee, and, above all, Virginia—awaited them. Rhodes followed about five hundred persons behind Sullivan:

> We moved through Washington with crowds of people looking at us from the sidewalks and houses and at last reached Long Bridge and crossed into Virginia. It is my first visit to the Old Dominion and every object is of interest. At

* From the Civil War Song "The Boys That Wore the Green."

> the head of the bridge on the Virginia side is a large fort called Fort Runyon. We saw several forts on the hills and soldiers in all directions. It was nearly dark when we crossed the river, so our march has been short.[1]

Upon reaching the Virginia side of Long Bridge, the Second New Hampshire band struck up "Dixie," to the cheers of their men. At that point in the war, "Dixie" was not yet the unofficial ballad of the Confederacy. More marching songs followed as the Second Division passed the toll gate on the Columbia Turnpike, their mood still euphoric, joking about paying no tolls.

On this day, the men marched no more than the distance they were used to walking had they been on an errand back in their hometowns. However, the sights were new and gratifying, and the location exotic. The men perceived this new land through the filter of their own experiences, and found both positives and negatives. For months, the Southern papers had made such a slogan out of defending Virginia's "sacred soil" that it was inevitable the Northern soldiers took up the term and used it derisively. Now that they trod it, the New Englanders saw for themselves that the color of the soil was that of a ginger cat.

No sooner had the Yankees marched into Virginia than a universal, never-ending condemnation of Southern roads started. "The column marched over a narrow and miserable road (one of the chief features of the barbarism of Virginia)."[2] The Yankees reacted as if these bad roads were personal insults and the stream of ceaseless complaints became almost humorous.

Yet the road pattern itself was a problem for the invaders; because not all led toward Manassas Junction, the generals had to split apart their divisions and then try to regroup. Hunter's Second Division came over one bridge, Richardson's Fourth Brigade came across the Chain Bridge.[3] When Richardson had asked McDowell, "Are there any cross-roads to communicate from the right of the line to the left, so that if one of these columns is attacked . . . they can come to each other's support?" the general did not know.[4] The Rhode Island soldiers, who heretofore had depended on their own officers, John Slocum and Sullivan Ballou, and relied on their own cleverness, were now part of a much bigger, less organized, more slowly responding organism.

The assigned route for the Rhode Islanders was to use the Little River Turnpike, go across the Loudoun and Hampshire Railroad to Bailey's Crossroads. Hunter's Division stopped here briefly for supper, the men eating heartily from their haversacks' rations, before resuming their march to their assigned bivouac, which they reached about 10:00 P.M.

> We camp at a little place called Annandale and our regiment stacked arms in a large meadow. Rail fences were plenty and we soon had fires burning and coffee cooking in our cups. The novelty of this scene interested me very much, and I enjoyed the evening sitting by the fire and speculating on what might happen on tomorrow. As we have no tents with us, we lay upon our rubber blankets spread upon the ground and slept soundly.[5]

This was the first time many regiments camped together, and their drum corps began to beat the tattoo one after the other, the echo of the drums rolling over the men as they bedded down in the fields.[6] Sullivan received a letter from Sarah that night, and in one he wrote to her later, he gave a brief account:

> We left Washington last Tuesday & marched across Long bridge with thousands upon thousands of other troops. Tuesday night we encamped in the open fields—I was lucky enough to get into an ambulance waggon and had a very good rest.[7]

On this day, being first had its advantages, as Corporal Sam English of the Second Rhode Island noted in a letter home. "Nothing occurred of importance to disturb our slumbers except the passing of troops bound on the same expedition."[8]

The troops he referred to were the 9,500 men of Heintzelman's Third Division, now moving into place behind the Rhode Islanders, come from their camp in Alexandria. With only two divisions sharing a turnpike, traffic jams were already becoming a problem, delaying the forward movement of men pouring into the combat zone. "Our progress was extremely slow after sunset; and the column for seven hours advanced, at irregular intervals of time, five, twenty, or one hundred feet."[9]

While the Rhode Islanders were snoring away in their camp, other soldiers from the Fifth Maine were still waiting in line to cross Pohick Creek, a knee-high brook with steep sides, spanned by a single felled tree. In the darkness, each man was removing his shoes and socks, and treading the log, one by one. The adjutant of the Fifth Maine noted, "An axe, a little muscle and some common sense, might have erected a passable bridge in a few moments."[10] One officer came upon this sheeplike scene, cursed the stupidity, and ordered his men straight in and across. This simple tale spoke volumes about leadership, responsibility, and common sense; virtues too often in short supply on this campaign.

"The last of the division did not get into camp until one hour before daylight."[11] The Eleventh Massachusetts got to their assigned bivouac so late the men were allowed only one hour's sleep upon the ground, at 3:45 A.M. the morning of the seventeenth, after which time they were roused and marched off road and across country another twelve hours without food or water until a halt was called at Sangster's Station. Stragglers who could not keep up the pace of this march kept coming into the Eleventh's camp until the evening.[12] The colonels commanding brigades knew of these delays, assumed they were transitory, and took no action to compensate for or fix them. Their failure to address this problem badly foreshadowed future events.

That same night, at the White House, President and Mrs. Lincoln gave a levee. General Scott attended and was mobbed by the faithful. When he left early, the rumor spread that he was leaving to go to Virginia to lead the charge in person.[13] The evening of July 16, as [London] *Times* correspondent William Howard Russell returned to Washington on the train from Annapolis, he encountered General McDowell at the depot, alone, going along the platform inspecting the empty cars.

> He was in search of two batteries of artillery and was obliged to look after them himself, for his small staff was engaged at his headquarters. "You are aware that I have advanced?" he asked.

Russell had been offered a seat in the general's carriage, and noted that while McDowell spoke confidently, he did not seem in high spirits. Russell learned more in his interview.

> It would scarcely be credited, were I not told it by General McDowell, that there is no such thing procurable as a decent map of Virginia. He knows little or nothing of the country before him, more than the general direction of the main roads, . . . and he can obtain no information, inasmuch as the enemy are in full force and he has not a cavalry officer capable of conducting a reconnaissance.[14]

As July 17 dawned, sunny and hot, McDowell now had a full army on one side of the Potomac River. His plan for this Tuesday called for the divisions of this army to link up, using all available roads on this beachhead wedged against the bank of the Potomac, move forward and engage the Confederate forces around Fairfax

Court House around midday, then push onward. To this end, all his divisions were ordered to rendezvous in a ring surrounding that objective, from where they could sweep into the Confederate forces on several flanks.

Once those Confederates had been routed and disposed of, McDowell intended to choose the most expedient route to the junction, defeat any other rebel troops still in the area, and capture the railroad junction. It was a reasonable plan, so long as its two key premises held—that he could surprise the Confederates, and that Patterson held Johnston's Army of the Shenandoah up north so it could not swoop down on McDowell's troops at Manassas Junction. He had no way of knowing that the female spies, Bette Duvall and Rose Greenhow, had transmitted all the details of his master plan and timetable to General Beauregard, who had adjusted his forces accordingly and was eagerly waiting his old school chum.

Beauregard kept just enough men in the area to convince the invading army that the Confederates were indeed there. Bonham's brigade and other advance units stayed at their posts till the last possible minute, the better to estimate the strength and intentions of the approaching foe, before withdrawing. They used their cavalry scouts in the classic way—they rode forward, noted enemy details, turned around, and trotted out of harm's way. Beauregard's successful withdrawal of his troops from each successive village just before federal forces arrived deprived McDowell of any opportunity to pick off his forces.

The Union troops started out gladly enough that Wednesday morning, their spirits high, even rowdy, as "word passes along the line that the enemy are falling back before our advance."[15] Some of the Connecticuters made plans: after winning at Manassas, they would go by train to Richmond, capture the city, and "hang Jeff Davis from a sour apple tree,"[16] The boys from Maine fantasized as they marched along, about the "ideal of lovely villas and gorgeous residences" that might become their "future residences" once confiscated from the defeated Secessionists.[17] They had not passed many such dwellings thus far on their march, the Massachusetts men noting,

> The houses, or, to speak truly, hovels, upon the road, were small in number and dimension, and the country was thickly wooded. The population that was visible comprised aged men, women with their children, and the negroes.[18]

Miles's Division started first and ran into felled trees and pickets: "next morning at 5_ started, marched very slowly toward Germantown."[19] David Hunter had to wait for Miles to get out of the way so his division could march to Fairfax Court House. Brigadier General Daniel Tyler opined,

> The road was obstructed by fallen timber but no signs of an armed opposition we found at Germantown an Earth parapet thrown across the road, but very poor. The axe-men of one of our Maine regiments cut it out in the course of fifteen minutes, so that our brigade passed right on. . . . they were the meanest, most miserable works ever got up by military men.[20]

Burnside's New Hampshiremen chopped on through as well, clearing a quarter mile of felled trees in half an hour, and "the long line of soldiers with their bright gun barrels, with now and then a battery moving between two regiments," pressed forward.[21]

Captain Thomas Francis Meagher wrote about the impact of the sacred soil on his men: "The sun was fierce—the dust blinding and stifling—we had been tramping it since a little after sunrise."[22] He commanded the Sixty-ninth New York, and was the same Meagher whose book of speeches Sullivan had purchased not so long ago for the Carrington library in Woonsocket; when they camped nearby in another couple days, Ballou might have sought out the Irishman. The army was much slower than anticipated, the men tired and not in condition. Unused to a diet of salt pork, the men found not only it produced a great, "mutinous thirst," but that there was scarcity of water along the route of march, which sent the men running off into the farm yards they passed, "not merely disregarding, but defying, every effort of their officers to restrain them," hoping to fill their canteens at the farm wells. But,

> the retreating Southerners had cut the ropes which held the buckets in the wells, or broken the chains, as the case might be. It was enough to force hot tears from the sternest eye to see the sufferers, panting and breathless almost after their wild race, looking hopelessly down those dark, deep wells, the forbidden water glimmering sixty feet or more below, and the fevered and crusted lip quivering with a redoubled pang.[23]

Some found another way to assuage their thirst: "On the way we found an old railroad embankment, and I never saw black berries more plenty. We stopped and ate what we wanted and then moved on."[24]

General McDowell perceived a lack of discipline in his troops—"They would not keep in the ranks, order as much as you pleased"—but never wrote about the serious logistical issue of lack of water for his army.[25] The lack of maps of the area he was invading might have made him unaware that water sources for twenty thousand men were few and far between.

Other factors were debilitating his men before they went into battle—things the nurses, like Sarah Edmonds a.k.a. Frank Thompson, observed if McDowell did not.

> Several regiments had been supplied with new shoes the day before leaving camp, and they found by sad experience, that

they were not the most comfortable things to march in, as their poor blistered feet testified; in many cases their feet were literally raw, the thick woolen stockings having chafed the skin off. Mrs. B. and I, having provided ourselves before leaving camp, with a quantity of linen, bandages, lint, ointment, etc., found it very convenient now, [to use these supplies for the men] even before a shot had been fired by the enemy.[26]

The planned engagement of the day was to take place at the village ahead of them, Fairfax Court House. About noon, "when within half a mile of the village . . . word was sent that the rebels' battery was directly in our line of march. There seemed to be eight cannon.[27] The Second Rhode Island advanced cautiously. Families began to get a sample of the lingo the men had learned in training, as when Sullivan described the action to Sarah,

> Wednesday we expected a fight at Fairfax. And we approached with extreme caution—we sent out skirmishers on each side for a mile that we might march onto no masked batteries. I commanded the skirmishers on the left.[28]

Corporal Samuel English of the Second Rhode Island was even more explicit in his letter home:

> Co. K. acting as advance on the left. Co. C as flankers and Co. G. as rear guard. I cannot state exactly the strength of our forces at the time, but should judge there were seven or eight thousand including 1500 cavalry and two Batteries of artillery with two howitzers belonging to the New York 71st Regt.[29]

Command of the left portion of the regiment was the traditional role of the major, so that the pattern of companies advancing looked like this:

K A
C D
G F
main body:
B
E
H
I
J

Sullivan's letter continued:

I never knew what labor was till then—with the Weight of my pistols and sword & commanding men extending in line nearly a mile & in hourly expectation of coming upon the enemy—in fact ordered to march in that way until we *did* meet him—the Sun pouring down its hottest rays—I was nearly exhausted when at the head of my men & in advance of our whole force I observed the entrenchments around Fairfax hill built by the enemy. I shall not claim any great bravery for I soon saw the embrasures were without cannon & I saw no one on the walls or ramparts. At first I thought their guns were withdrawn for a ruse and I advanced with my men with caution. At length when within about 600 feet I felt sure they had fled & I ran in advance and mounted the works and waived my sword & gave the Narragansett shout—my men soon followed & we all yelled like demons. The main column with Col Slocum & Gen Sprague McDowell xc [etc.] soon came up. Capt Dyer tried to claim that he was in the other side as soon as I. But he has had to give it up. Col. playfully dubbed me Lieut Genl. From Fairfax all but the blacks had fled. . . .[30]

After the earthworks outside of town were "conquered," the next move was into the town itself, devoid of all Confederate troops. The Union soldiers converged from various directions, meeting in the center of the town, which was built in a typical rural pattern: a small wooden church, an ordinary country tavern, perhaps fifty or sixty houses, and a courthouse flying the "secession flag," which stood in a green park square in the center.[31] Sergeant Duffy, the color sergeant of the Second, used the roof of a barn when ordered to hoist the Stars and Stripes

> from the top of one of the buildings in the outskirts of the village, as an indication to General Tyler's column, which was advancing upon another road, that the place was in our hands . . . Its garrison would also have been ours, if General Tyler . . . had started an hour or two earlier.[32]

Once again, being first seemed to pay off, as the Second Rhode Island claimed the best camping spot near town, "in the yard of the mansion formerly occupied by the rebel General Beauregard."[33]

The Union troops took over this mansion in Fairfax Court House; the Second Rhode Island camped around the house. *Courtesy of the Library of Congress Prints and Photographs Division.*

The men were not confined to camp but permitted to roam the town. The Confederates had left so recently that meat was still roasting over campfires, and Burnside's boys lost no time in chowing down on the goodies. "The houses were deserted and in some places the tables were set for dinner and coffee warm on the stove."[34]

What started out as foraging for food escalated into rummaging through supplies the retreating army had left behind. "The streets were strewn with the knapsacks, haversacks, canteens, blankets, shirts and most every article pertaining to camp life."[35] The sight of the rebel flag, "the defenceless state of the town," the sabotaged water wells, and their ire over Beauregard's proclamation to the population of northern Virginia warning that the Yankees were coming to ravish the women of Virginia, triggered a loss of control. The Rhode Islanders went plundering, "much to the mortification of the better disciplined part of the command," who were out in the streets trying to curb the acquisitive urges of their men.[36] After all, what was a man on the march going to be able to do with unwieldy booty? How would he transport anything even the size of a teapot? Nonetheless, relic hunters were "indefatigable."[37] When

> Private Thomas Parker, of our Company "D." an old English soldier who had served in the Crimea, came down the street with a large Bible under one arm and a picture of General Washington under the other, Captain Viall saw him and sent him back to the house and made him restore them.[38]

Far from ravishing Southern ladies, the Northern men seemed more intent on impersonating them:

> Toward the close of the day, when the rage of acquisition had subsided, the place wore the softened aspect of a carnival; and

Sullivan wrote Sarah that he slept on a lounge; most likely it was in the boudoir of the mistress of the house. This photo was taken in a restored house in Louisiana. *From author's collection.*

> soldiers, appareled in crinoline and silk, walked with their bearded gallants up and down, replying with affected gab to the rather racy compliments tendered them from every side. This . . . gave the scene rather a merry show; but I notice that the shuddering inhabitants regarded it with fear and undisguised abhorrence. One female, hearing me condemn the conduct of the soldiers, as a fellow passed by with a pair of ladies' ruffled drawers hauled up over his pantaloons, said she "thought it was it was really too bad the clothes of Mr. Smith's poor dead mother . . . should be desecrated in that coarse, vulgar way."[39]

Also popular were the stores of homemade jams, pickles, and fruit. Edibles were practical booty, because once these eaten or sold, the soldier had nothing to lug along. Corporal Rhodes also stole: "the only thing I took was an old rooster and I had a lively time catching him." After boiling him in a kettle, "we tried to eat him. But he was tough, and we had to give it up."[40] While Rhodes joked "that I knew very little about boiling roosters," General McDowell was especially indignant and issued a stringent order in condemnation of such practices.[41] Once the men were under control, a weary Sullivan penned a hasty letter to his wife to let her know how they had fared in the day's "battle."

> Thursday 18 July/1861
>
> My dear Wife
> We are about a mile beyond Fairfax Court House on the way to Manassas We entered Fairfax yesterday about noon. I had command of the left wing of Skirmish & was then first man of our whole army to mount the breastworks of the enemy. We however found them deserted in great haste about one hour & one half before. They left their camp equipage & tents & fled in confusion. I am still perfectly well. Our Regiment is well & in advance. They expect to fight at Manassas. I rather think they will run.
>
> Got your letter night before last
> Goodby
>
> Sullivan

While the men were camped in the grounds of a mansion that had been occupied by the rebel commanding general," the officers had the use of the house.[42] A photo of the building, nestled among a grove of a dozen old, tall trees, and surrounded by lawn, was taken by Alexander Gardner, a famous photographer of the era. It showed a magnificent brick plantation-style house with four massive front pillars, and a first- and second-story porch. In such a large house, the mistress normally had her own suite of rooms, which furniture commonly included a chaise longue; Sullivan mentioned one when he wrote Sarah a longer letter:

> The enemy had retreated in great haste leaving most everything—our boys could hardly be restrained from

> sacking the place: and as it *was,* destroyed considerable property. I slept in a lounge that night in a deserted house of a notorious *Seceshionist.*[43]

Most likely, the Ballous' own home was not so grand that Sarah, the busy wife and mother, had either a chaise lounge or the time to use it.

The South Carolininans had pulled out in haste around at 11:00 A.M.; by not getting there until 3:00 P.M., they "slipped through our hands." One by one, the Union brigades linked up, reporting to each other that no Confederates were to be found. In the distance, they could see the smoke from burning bridges the Confederates had torched behind them.[44]

Those units at Fairfax set up camp around the town. Heintzelman halted his division at Elzey's Farm, and sent out reconnaissance parties. Colonel Willcox sent back word that before the Rebels had retreated from Fairfax Station, they had sabotaged some two hundred feet of track on the Orange and Alexandria railway by piling dirt and logs ten to twelve feet high. This obstruction made it impossible for the Union troops to use the railway to send food or reinforcements to McDowell, but no effort was made over the next few days to clear the tracks.[45] Yet there was some hot action there later that day:

> Firing being heard in the direction of Fairfax Station, we rushed on about half way towards that place, but found the ground occupied by Miles' division, & the shots were from Garibaldi's [39th NY, Blenker's Brigade] men, who were foraging after turkeys.[46]

For both the North and South, the seventeenth of July was full of lost opportunities. McDowell had hoped to surprise the Confederates, obliterate at least one brigade to make the later odds more favorable, perhaps force a battle on the eastern side of Bull Run, even get all the way to Centreville before nightfall. None of it happened. Beauregard telegraphed Richmond to inform the Confederate government that the Union attack was taking place on his front, and requesting all possible reinforcements be sent to him, including Johnston's Army of the Shenandoah. He got no answer that day; Richmond needed to verify there was no attack on Johnston's front before committing all their forces at any single front. In the meantime, neither army moved.[47]

Poor communications contributed to this stalemate. The more dynamic, changing positions of the divisions were not served by the telegraph. Communications within both armies had to rely on mounted couriers, because the device worked only in a linear as opposed to multifocal mode. The telegraph was able to relay messages from Fairfax to Washington to Harper's Ferry, and from Manassas to Richmond to Harper's Ferry for the South, but that was the best that technology could offer at that moment in the war; it was a clumsy system that was to result in disastrous surprises at the fronts for the Union. When the *Providence Journal* reported, "Telegraphic wires are rapidly following the army, and an office was opened this morning at Fairfax Court House," it meant only that it was slightly faster for McDowell to send messages to his stationary invalid general in chief, who stayed home on his couch. At the same time, Colonel Orlando Willcox, Second Brigade, sent this plea:

> Please forward the inclosed. Can I have a small mounted party of soldiers for carrying dispatches? I have to communicate with yourself, Colonel Heintzelman, and Alexandria, and the horses have to be taken from the teams
> Respectfully, &c.
> O. B. W.[48]

Northern field communications remained inadequate and worse than those of the South, due in part to the spread out external lines of the Union divisions that had insufficient cavalry—and horses—assigned. When Colonel Heintzelman moved his forces to Sangster's Station late on the seventeenth, he never bothered to notify General McDowell where he was camped; the result the next morning was that McDowell lost three hours of time searching for him.

McDowell could not communicate directly at all with General Patterson in the North—all messages had to be relayed through Scott in Washington over lines that were not secure. Friday night, McDowell and two aides reportedly rode all the way back to the capital to meet with Scott and ascertain whether Patterson had succeeded in keeping the Army of the Shenandoah at Harper's Ferry.[49]

As the clock hands passed midnight into July 18, army command in Washington, D.C., had not heard from General Patterson in three days and Scott had been reduced to reading the *Philadelphia Ledger* for information on his general.[50] Around 1:00 A.M., in response to some previous prod by Scott, Patterson queried by telegraph: "Shall I attack?"[51] Scott's reply later in the morning wondered why he had not already beaten his opponent, and asked if Johnston had secretly departed for the Southern front. Patterson's obvious timidity and passivity no longer fooled the Confederates because, also at 1:00 A.M., the Confederate government in Richmond ordered General Joe Johnston to immediately redeploy his troops to Manassas.

Within twelve hours, Johnston arranged railroad transport to speed his men the fifty miles to Manassas, already had Thomas J. Jackson's brigade of Virginians en route, and others waiting at the Piedmont* railway station for their locomotive. Johnston only left

* Modern day Delaplane, Virginia.

behind three troops of cavalry totaling no more than six hundred men, but Stuart's horsemen kept Patterson convinced the full army remained. A victim of his own weak intelligence, the general telegraphed Scott before noon to say, "The enemy has stolen no march upon me. I have caused him to be reenforced." Even if Patterson had staged an attack that morning, he would have interfered with the withdrawal and forced Johnston's army to stay and fight—at a minimum to protect its rear. Johnston would have been unable to convey them as promptly as he had to Manassas Junction to reinforce Beauregard's army. As Johnston was pulling out of Winchester, the oblivious Patterson telegraphed Scott again to report: "I have succeeded . . . in keeping General Johnston's force at Winchester."[52]

All the activity on the Union side on July 18 occurred under McDowell's command. He needed to find his divisions which had not reported in, find the delinquent wagon trains bringing food and supplies for his hungry men, and reconnoiter those routes which still appeared open to him. These were south over the Occoquan River, north around Sudley Springs, and directly ahead where there were several promising fords which he might use if the Confederates were not defending them. Maps might have told him, but having none, he had to devote a full day to reconnaissance. In order to give the appearance of moving masterfully forward toward an objective—instead of skulking desperately around the countryside trying to find useful roads—McDowell ordered one division to make a forward movement.

> Brigadier General Tyler—General: I have information which leads me to believe you will find no force at Centreville, and will meet with no resistance in getting there. Observe well the road to Bull Run and to Warrenton. Do not bring on any engagement but keep up the impression that we are moving on Manassas. I go to Heintzelman to arrange about the plan we have talked over.[53]

If Beauregard could be made to think this was the main attack route of the entire Union Army, he might shift his attention southward, giving McDowell a badly needed advantage in the element of surprise at whatever point of attack he chose. McDowell and Beauregard had been classmates at West Point in 1834 and knew something of each other's style. No master of improvisation, Beauregard was obsessed with the execution of the perfect battle plan he had crafted, to draw McDowell straight into the spider's web he had set up on the western bank. Keeping Beauregard excited, preoccupied, and off-balance could create additional advantages.

While the air was "still damp and raw, a squadron of United States dragoons trotted briskly down the road to Centreville." Tyler and his division followed, and two hours later, they beheld "the dingy, aged, miserable little handful of houses" that comprised the town.[54] Hunter's Brigade came up next, taking a position on the left, and drew up in line, as every one awaited the reports of the dragoons on the state of affairs in the "formidable earthworks" that "frowned upon the advancing troops. . . . A shout, hearty and prolonged, soon told us that Centreville, alas, had been vacated."[55] About 9:00 A.M. Tyler moved through easily with part of his brigade toward Bull Run. The balance of the men rigged blankets over rail fences and muskets to provide some shade, and settled in to await events. By "noon, the 18th of July, the Stars and Stripes were flying over Centreville."[56] Meanwhile, the balance of the regiments were finding their third day on the road harder than the previous two.

> After a slight breakfast from our haversacks the march was resumed. The day was very hot, and we found great difficulty in obtaining water, the want of which caused the troops much suffering. Many of the men were sunstruck, and others began to drop out of the ranks from exhaustion. All such as were not able to march were put into ambulances and sent back to

> Washington . . . considerable excitement prevailed throughout the day, as we were every hour in expectation of meeting the enemy.[57]

About 8:00 A.M. that same morning, McDowell rode off to find Heintzelman, to accompany him on a reconnaissance. When he found him, around 11:00 A.M., they rode to inspect the junction of Bull Run and Occoquan Creek, one of its tributaries; to their dismay, the roads were too narrow to permit passage of the army. The option of the more southerly route to the junction had to be ruled out. McDowell now knew what Beauregard knew.[58]

Beauregard's commanders had performed their early assignments well, with verve and precision, setting up a mind game, luring the Union onward with a sense of false security that the Southern men were too "afeared" to stand up to them and fight. There was both hope and expectation that the Union forces might become cocky and take unnecessary risks. Captain Meagher quipped that it was the Confederate plan "to entice us headlong, breathless and breadless almost to destruction."[59]

On July 18, Tyler took the psychological bait the Southerners had laid; he began to think he could get his army across Bull Run and grab Manassas Junction single-handedly before the commander of either army could react. These dreams of glory and fame overcame whatever nascent good sense he might have had about riding straight into a trap; even years later, he continued to assert: "I think my four brigades could have whipped Beauregard before sundown."[60]

If McDowell had owned a map, Bull Run would have rambled diagonally across the paper from top left to bottom right; the fords were strung along it like jewels in a necklace. The creek was up to thirty feet wide in some places. The Warrenton Turnpike would have run straight across the middle of the piece of paper; each of the fords below the turnpike was currently defended by a Confederate brigade to prevent the Yankees from crossing. As McDowell noted in a report to Scott, "Bull Run, though not a wide stream, is only to be crossed at certain places, owing to its precipitous, rocky banks."[61]

General Beauregard had picked out Blackburn's Ford as the one they were most likely to use and, ironically, Tyler went straight for it. He marched his men through a "thousand yards of perfectly open country," from where "we had a very good view of Manassas," and "closed on the ford through pine under brush very thick, ahead of us and as we had marched into them about 1 or 2 rods,* not thinking of danger quite so near, the bushes seemed to be alive with the rebels (judging from the firing for we never saw one of them at any time)."[62]

For an hour, the two sides exchanged gunfire, the rebels never coming out of their pine thicket into the open. At this point, McDowell's objectives had been accomplished. The Union had gathered valuable intelligence that could have been the centerpiece of any headquarter's debriefing, discussion, and integration into the morrow's battle planning, complete with advice from the engineers. They knew this and the next ford over, where they could see troops, were defended. If Tyler had intended to obey McDowell's orders, this was the point at which he ought to have withdrawn.

Instead, he ignored them, and involved two complete brigades in a long attack, sustaining eighty-three casualties. Part of his command was pushed back in disarray bordering on panic, leaving behind their rifles, canteens, blankets, and a load of other gear, all later claimed gleefully by the Confederates. Colonel "Fighting Dick" Richardson, one of Tyler's brigade commanders, mounted two more unsuccessful charges. Tyler continued to refuse to heed the advice from McDowell's staff, who kept coming to urge him to break off the engagement, and when Tyler ordered Sherman's Brigade to come in from Centreville to support his

* A rod is 16.5 feet

assault at Blackburn's, another courier rode to headquarters to summon McDowell.

This courier interrupted a critically important meeting going on between chief of engineers Major John Barnard and a local man who knew the layout of the few remaining routes open to McDowell.

> Whilst I was awaiting Captain Alexander [another engineer gone with Tyler], I encountered Matthew C. Mitchell, who was secured as a guide. Representing himself as a Union man and a resident of that vicinity, I was engaged questioning him, when . . .[63]

the messenger interrupted their discussion to report that Tyler was further escalating his attack.

Barnard broke off the meeting, leaving important things unsaid, and went to Tyler, with whom he, too, had no influence.[64] At a time when no supply trains were in motion to bring up new cannonballs, Tyler wasted 415 of them by shooting them over the creek for hours in a wildly unaimed artillery barrage, whose only casualty was the dinner of the Southern generals.[65]* McDowell finally arrived in person about 4:00 P.M. to fetch Tyler off the battlefield during the fifth hour of engagement. Tyler argued, but was directly ordered to disengage, and complied. Losing control of himself and his two brigades at Blackburn's Ford, which the Confederates called the Battle of Bull Run, did not auger well.

The rout of Union regiments at Blackburn's Ford confirmed for McDowell his opinion that his raw troops could not attack

* No one was injured when the shell crashed into the dining room of the McLean farmhouse that Beauregard was using for his headquarters. The McLeans themselves had previously evacuated.

Confederate positions head on, but should "turn" them, i.e., attack on their flanks.[66] Given the constraints of the topography, the only way he could get to the sides of the Confederate positions was by devising a plan of attack so complicated that his green troops and commanders were to have difficulty executing it, a violation of an important principle of military strategy.

Another incident that happened that day did not get the attention it deserved, lost in the hyperbole of the skirmish. When the gray-clad Union soldiers from the First Massachusetts were fired upon by both Confederate skirmishers hiding in farm buildings along the road and fellow Union troops wearing blue uniforms, it was obvious that confusion was going to be a problem on the battlefield until each nation's troops adopted standard colors for their uniforms.

Ordered by McDowell to withdraw north and hold the base of the Centreville-Manassas Road, Tyler instead camped west of Centreville on the turnpike, where he "dug for water and found it."[67] There, he was a sitting duck, jutting forward out ahead of the rest of the army, some still camped at Fairfax Court House, where any Confederate troops brought up in response to his attack earlier in the day could annihilate the isolated division.

McDowell's hand was forced again, and he moved the whole army forward to protect Tyler, stringing their camps out along the turnpike, where they were to remain for the next three days. The supply trains had not caught up with the army; the inexperienced troops had gobbled up their three-day supply of rations designed to last through July 19–20 and were already hungry. The deeper into Virginia that McDowell moved his men, the greater the delay in feeding them, and the greater the risk of their capture, as the plodding wagon train attempted to catch up.

Meanwhile, on the chessboard of the Warrenton turnpike, the Rhode Islanders and the rest of Hunter's Division were moved up a few squares, the Rhode Islanders marching up near through Centreville and bivouacked at sunset about a mile to the east of it. Their tents left behind in camp, they needed to devise some method of sheltering from the hot summer sun while encamped for these three days. Corporal Rhodes noted: "Here we built shelters with pine and cedar boughs and called the camp 'Bush Camp.' Here we have heard our first hostile shot, and we wonder what is to follow." Walt Whitman described "Shebangs," as "the little huts of green boughs, pine or what not, put up for the impromptu shelter of soldiers in Virginia &c."[68]

Heintzelman's division was ordered up to Centreville to wait for rations and support Tyler. They left bivouac at 5:00 P.M. on Thursday the eighteenth, and got to Centreville about dark. "I had sent out to get beef, but could get nothing but an old cow."[69] Heintzelman took the initiative to send an officer to check on the supply train and learned, that owing to lack of wagons, it had not even left Alexandria until July 18, then took the road to Occoquan.[70] Redirected and urged forward, they moved on to Centreville the evening of July 19. Meanwhile, the men foraged, and murmured "many questionable blessings upon quarter-masters, in particular and general."[71] For the next couple of days, "lazily and stupidly waiting," watching "the Blue Ridge glowing and melting on the horizon," the hungry army spent two "wearisome, hot, drawling, idle" days with little to do but gossip and have the demoralization felt by the First Division spread through the entire army.[72]

> Numerous stories and rumors about the bayoneting of the wounded, and the terrible scene of carnage which had been enacted, all of which were retailed with considerable exaggeration. "There had been 1000 killed and wounded"—"Our men had broken and run like sheep"—"The enemy was outgeneraling us,". . . found eager listeners."[73]

The psychological advantage still remained with the Southern Army.

No regiment camped within Centreville itself, about which Captain Meagher complained,

> I wager there is not a village of shabbier aspect and such reduced resources as that of Centreville. It looks, for all the world, as though it had done its business, whatever it was, if it every had any, full eight years ago, and since then had bolted its doors, put out its fires and gone to sleep.[74]

Colonel Franklin felt that once fed, the army should have repositioned itself closer to the battlefield.

> We ought to have encamped on the fine hills there and waited there over night, and then got up early the next morning, when we would have whipped them. . . . We should have fought on our own ground. . . . We could have had a beautiful position there."[75]

Struggling to prepare, the Rebels pronounced themselves glad of the Union delays. "An attack in force by the Federals had been expected each morning and its non-occurrence gratefully appreciated."[76] Holmes' brigade came up from Aquia Creek on the nineteenth with 1,265 men and six pieces of artillery.[77] Better still, as the sun set that afternoon, Johnston's forces were marching across the Blue Ridge Mountains to a train station.[78]

In Centreville, where he had made his headquarters adjacent to the Rhode Island troops and Tyler, McDowell was as busy as his men were idle. Still plotting his strategy on the principle that Johnston's army was not joining the Army of the Potomac to overwhelm him, Irvin McDowell continued searching for the keyhole to unlock the Plains of Manassas. His quest was growing curiouser and curiouser. His original plan of taking the most direct route to

Manassas Junction was doomed beyond salvage. Through delays, he had lost most of his element of surprise and had few choices of positions from which to strike his original objective. The Confederates were assuredly in front of him, and he now knew he could not turn left—south—to slip under them and get to Manassas through Occoquan. One chance alone remained to surprise them: to swing up to the right and use an apparent eight-mile detour to go against their right flank.

McDowell began to formulate that if he could keep the Rebels focused on a full-strength attack at Centreville, he might be able to sneak one division northward, cross at Sudley, take the Rebels by surprise, punch through at the Stone Bridge, and then use the Sudley-Manassas, also called the Sudley–New Market Road to make a mad dash five miles south to capture the railroad. Before he could commit to this plan, he needed more knowledge of the farms, byways, and positions of Confederate units in the area through which his eight-mile detour was to move, and so he sent out scouting parties.

While waiting for the results, there was time to analyze success or failure to date. The performance of the commanders and troops during the march into Virginia, and the battle of Blackburn's Ford, offered many lessons for planning the main battle if the command structure had been open to them and not been too distracted to focus. Union units marched confidently up through a place that looked good—and hidden artillery and infantry raked them with heavy fire. But the Confederates used old-style Revolutionary War tactics, not the Napoleonic tactics in which West Point had trained its cadets in the 1830s. The Southerners did not come forth, line up, and do battle; so far that week, they had fired on infantry advances from such unexpected places as abandoned houses, brier patches, pine thickets, and stands of trees.

The Union deployed piecemeal, failing to deliver a major blow to their opponents, giving them time to bring in reinforcements while the Union could not. Had such problems been discussed, they might not have been made again three days later in the main battle. However, McDowell held no tactical conference after Blackburn's Ford. In all fairness, few commanders had collaborative management styles in the early days of the war, and McDowell was unfortunately busy with many petty details of the deployment. Analyzing the situation alone, he found no reason to deviate from his preconceived notion that he could never attack head on because the Confederates were too strong.

McDowell was not the only general facing uncertainty on July 19. Beauregard had the Union Army on his doorstep yet could not frame his final battle plan because he was uncertain whether Johnston was moving to join up with him and, if so, when he might arrive. The two generals could not communicate directly, and Beauregard felt time was of the essence if the Southerners were to "sell our lives as dearly as possible."[79] Johnston's last known position was fifty miles away at Winchester, and volunteer aide Colonel Alexander Chisholm offered to ride out to try and find him in order to deliver a note from Beauregard. Chisholm saddled up and rode off into the night alone, at a gallop, headed for the Blue Ridge Mountains.

After the first eighteen miles, he exchanged his worn out horse with one he found in a pasture, and rode for another fifteen miles. Near midnight, the activity at Piedmont Railway Station, the first station on the eastern side of Blue Ridge, caused him to ride over there, where he found General Johnston supervising the loading of Thomas J. Jackson's First Brigade of the Army of the Shenandoah onto a train headed south.

Chisholm and his mount enjoyed a brief rest and nourishment while Johnston formulated a response to some of the less useful advice in Beauregard's missive. Declining a bed for the night, the colonel remounted and headed back through the perilous mountain pass to bring the good news that Johnston's troops were to start pulling into Manassas that day and the next. It was so dark, "I could not see the reins in my hand." Exhausted from his long hours in the saddle, he galloped periodically to stay awake, despite the danger after the moon had set. Just before daylight he returned to his own horse, and left a dirty and tired horse back in its original pasture for its no-doubt puzzled farmer to find later, then hastened back to Beauregard's camp. If the Union had communicated as aggressively with Patterson, outcomes might have altered. Surprised at Chisholm's prompt return, and satisfied that Johnston was moving to Manassas, Beauregard apparently construed that only part of the Army of the Shenandoah was moving by train and configured a battle plan accordingly.

Late in the afternoon of July 19, while addressing his brigade commanders in the McLean parlor about the next day's strategy, Beauregard was surprised when Thomas Jackson walked in the door. The Virginian's timing was impeccable, for Beauregard had just finished describing Jackson's assigned position in the next day's battle plan, after they had marched along the route he had suggested. Recovering his poise as quickly as possible, Beauregard asked which units were marching overland, and lost it again when told *all* were coming by train. Dismissing that intelligence as noncredible, he went on describing his "perfect Waterloo."[80]

Key to the reenactment of Waterloo was a grand right wheel that Beauregard's army would make, from the lower fords up to the turnpike where Johnston's army was to pin the Union. This move relied on McDowell striking straight for Manassas, along the most direct, *diagonal* route, terrain defended to the maximum, the road from Centreville to Manassas Junction, which Beauregard had every confidence Irvin McDowell would do.

The Union troops remained hungry and peckish during the early hours of July 19. Sullivan was one of those hungry men but, while waiting for food, used the time to write Sarah a detailed letter about his personal role in the events of the last few days, most of which has already been quoted. What follows are the personal details:

Friday July 19 1861

My dear Sarah

We are about five miles from Manassas. I am sitting under a few green boughs writing on a drum head. A man is going to Washington & I haste to send you a few lines. . . . Yesterday we marched here & are still in the open fields. I am very tired but perfectly well; and would give a hundred dollars if I could get a good meal of victuals. The streams are muddy & water very poor—however I am able to get a little vinegar to put in it and that is all. Hard bread & joints of meat are all we can get to eat, and that goes hard 3 times a day. We can get scarcely any thing from the people here, they are all against us. They all live miserably I think, and the slaves are to me more filthy than our Irish.

We shall remain here, I think till all our troops can collect around Manassas, and then we shall have a big fight if they don't retreat. I rec'd your letter on the night before last—a messenger staying in Washington to bring them out. You must read the New York papers for particulars of all our movements, Genl McDowell publicly complimented our skirmishing—write me often Sarah. I get no letters except from you & they are a great joy & comfort. It is a great deprivation not to be able to tell you how much I still love you & my dear children but I cannot express it in this hasty errand, we left Washington too hurriedly to get any pay & I [can?] send you no money. But I will soon. My dear Sarah I should become crazy if I should see you—at least for an hour! My darling wife goodbye

Ever your

Sullivan[81]

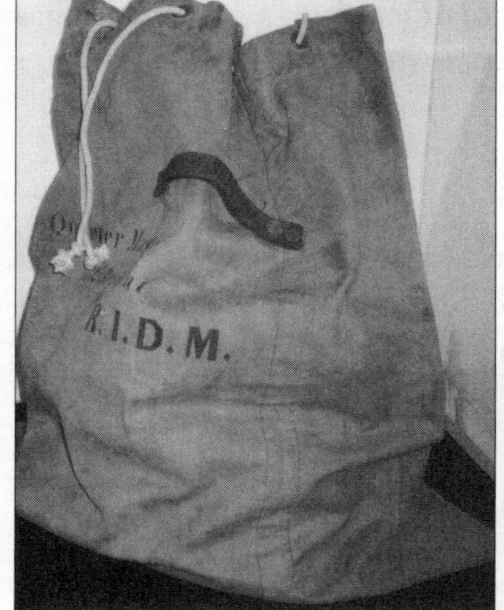

(left) The large leather mailbag of the Second Regiment Detached Militia. *Author's photo at the Museum of Work and Culture, Woonsocket.*

(below) Hardtack and a haversack. Author's photo.

(above) A patriotic envelope sold in Rhode Island for writing to the troops. Sarah's letters may have been posted in such an envelope. *From author's collection.*

Savvy and experienced Regular Army officers like Sherman knew to draw pay before leaving town: "I have drawn my pay to embrace June 30,"[82] but Sarah was apparently expected somehow to cope with the lack of further cash. Luckily, in 1861, merchants routinely allowed their regular customers to shop on credit.

Sullivan had asked his wife to send him three more shirts and to have the children's photos taken and sent to him. Hers had been taken already, so she had to either get a small print of that to send him, or get a new one made. During his absence she probably made daily trips to the post office to post or pick up letters from her husband, because in those days mail was not yet delivered to homes. She did not learn of her husband's going hungry until around July 22, so she had not yet found it necessary to join the thousands of Northern families sending crates of food to their soldiers.

Johnston's army, en route to Manassas, was not going hungry. In 1861, the countryside and farms of Virginia were unspoilt. They poured forth an abundance of fruits, vegetables, and grain; and the many farms and plantations provided baked and dairy goods, and meat. One story illustrates the hospitality and care lavished on the Southern troops preparing for the battle in Manassas. One of Bartow's Georgians, Berien McPherson Zettler, wrote,

> After a march of two hours, and covering a distance of perhaps five miles, we came to a place where a carriage gate on our left opened and a circular driveway led to a large brick residence with a long veranda. A negro in a white apron stood in the gateway and, with intense earnestness, kept saying, "Missus says come up to breakfast. Come right up, Missus says, all of you come right up." . . . The boys hurrahed, saying: "The fool thinks we are officers."* . . . The head of the column turned into the gateway and up the drive. When we approached the house a lady standing on the front veranda said, "Glad to see you dear boys; just pass round the house to the dining-room." We passed; we came to the dining room;

* "Company A, the Rome Light Guards, wore a handsome grey uniform with frock coats, and Company B, the Oglethorpe, followed in a handsome blue-black uniform, and not only frock coats but with eqaulet straps on our shoulders, giving us much the appearance of officers."

> we entered . . . and . . . I saw on that dining room table: biscuits by the bushel, sliced bread and ham in stacks two feet high, cakes and doughnuts of all sizes and shapes and each side of the exit door innumerable tubs and cans of hot coffee. . . . But we were not allowed to tarry. A half dozen or more ladies were posted along the sides of the long table and they literally passed us along, at the same time stuffing our haversacks as we proceeded, and saying, "You haven't time to stop to eat; you are going to Manassas to help Beauregard; the Yankees attacked him yesterday and were repulsed. You must get there to help him."
>
> This was out first knowledge that we were going to Manassas . . . and . . . the news. . . filled us with joy and gladness little short of ecstasy. As we passed down the circular driveway to the other gate and out to the turnpike, I saw the stream of men still moving up toward that dining room.[83]

At the Union camps, food supplies were finally distributed on Saturday the twentieth. The supply train was not delivering ready-to-eat meals; this was do-it-yourself food. The cattle had to be slaughtered, butchered, and cooked; the barrels of flour made into bread—but at least hot coffee could be quickly brewed. Spirits rose. The Union camp at Centreville became aromatic, noisy and lively. Poet and journalist Walt Whitman, who was a volunteer nurse, remarked on

> the fenced enclosure in the midst of the woods, for butchering the beef, the just quartered cattle in huge pieces lying around, the men with rolled up sleeves and stained arms.[84]

Other smells of war and the farmyard—latrines, coffee, smoke from campfires, sweaty men, pipe tobacco, and the cologne of the politicians—mingled together. Adjutant Fry noted,

> During the 19th and 20th, the bivouacs of McDowell's army around Centreville, almost within cannon range of the enemy, were thronged by visitors, official and unofficial, who came in carriages from Washington. They were under no military restraint, and passed to and fro among the troops as they pleased, giving the appearance of a monster military picnic—and gathering whatever intelligence they could.[85]

At relative leisure, Sullivan perhaps saw some of the nationally famous personages as well as persons he knew from home. As Jack Davis described,

> To add to the confusion, there seemed to be a phenomenal number of private citizens from Washington in the camps without authorization. Congressmen and senators, businessmen, and even ladies from the capital were following in the wake of the army as it advanced, all wanting to be present to see the first and last battle of the war. By Saturday morning, July 20, the crowd of onlookers swelled to several hundred as they came out from Washington in their buggies, picnic hampers at the ready, many attended by their coachmen. The Secretary of War, Simon Cameron, came to visit his brother who commanded the 79th New York Highlanders; senators and congressmen prowled around, making speeches and handing out cigars.[86]

To impress the visitors and keep up the morale of their men, the regimental bands were playing tunes alternately cheery and martial. In the background, distant railroad whistles could be heard coming from the direction of Manassas Junction, and the air was ripe with speculation about which Southern troops were on the trains. Colonel Israel Richardson, who reported to Brigadier General Tyler, a former railroad president, said,

A German-born soldier sketched some of the men with whom he marched into Virginia

An officer, possibly Heintzelman. *Courtesy of the Anne S. K. Brown Military Collection, Brown University.*

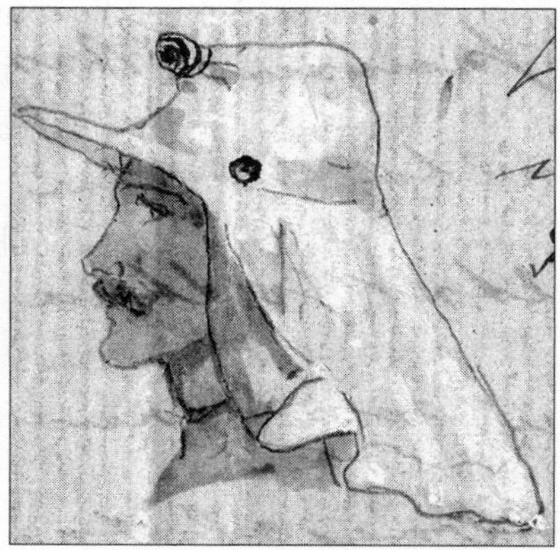

The havelock, adapted from British uniforms in India, and lovingly sewn in great numbers in early 1861 by the women of the North, proved so uncomfortable that the men soon stopped wearing them and used them as coffee filters. *Courtesy of the Anne S. K. Brown Military Collection, Brown University.*

> Friday and Saturday we heard the cars running all night. The next morning we spoke of it, and concluded that 50 car-loads had come.[87]

Out of sight of the Union, screened by the mountains, a strategy the Confederates were to continue to use over the next few years, thousands more troops had indeed come by rail into Manassas. General Johnston reported,

> I reached Manassas about noon on the 20th, preceded by the Seventh and Eighth Georgia Regiments and by Jackson's

The men made "shebangs" to shelter themselves from the hot July sun; usually, several men shared one hut—having "the whole shebang" would have been a luxury. *Author's photo at the Yorktown Victory Center.*

> brigade, consisting of the Second, Fourth, Fifth, Twenty-seventh, and Thirty-third Virginia Regiments. I was accompanied by General Bee, with the Fourth Alabama, the Second, and two companies of the Eleventh Mississippi. The president of the railroad company had assured me that the remaining troops should arrive during the day.[88]

Bee's and Bartow's Second and Third brigades had followed Jackson's First Brigade. Colonel Egbert Jones's Fourth Alabamians had volunteered to board the trains without waiting for rations to catch up with them. When they arrived at Manassas Junction, Private George Anderson reported they: "moved about two miles and camped in the woods, when some bread and meat soon reached us, and we walked right into it like a starved hound eats," and then slept all day.[89] McDowell just missed out on learning they had arrived.

One of the hallmarks of the Northern conduct of the war was the invention of new technology to use in the war effort and, in July 1861, the Union Army was attempting to pioneer a brand-new surveillance methodology. On June 17, President Lincoln had attended, and was impressed by, a hot-air balloon demonstration by Professor Thaddeus Lowe, who sent Lincoln a telegraph while aloft in his balloon *Enterprise*. As a result, the Aeronautics Corps was established in the War Department.[90] Two Rhode Islanders, "James Allen from the Light Battery, and William C. Holmes of Company C, were authorized to act as aeronauts," most likely under Lowe's auspices. The plan was for them to ascend in hot-air balloons to reconnoiter the Confederate positions around Bull Run.* Unfortunately, the two balloons in their possession were damaged, rendered useless, and "the commanding general was deprived of information which would have been of great advantage on the day of the battle."[91]

Without the balloon reconnaissance, Union patrols were still sneaking around the fords, trying not to be discovered by their rebel counterparts, whose dozen troops of cavalry were so constantly patrolling the roads and country lanes that a Union boy could hardly sneeze outside of camp without Confederate patrols knowing about it. Still, McDowell needed to know if more than a farm wagon could use the northern route road, if he could move artillery and an army of thirteen thousand men up to and through that ford at Sudley.

> Thus far these efforts, five of them, have not been successful, the enemy being in such force on this side of the run as to make it impossible to ascertain. I wished yesterday to make the reconnaissance in force, but deferred to the better judgment of others—to try and get it by observation and stealth.[92]

* Lowe made his first successful trip for the Union the last week of July, after the battle; intelligence gathered by balloon flights became more precise through late 1863, when the practice fell out of use.

On two separate occasions, engineer Barnard had to withdraw from the Sudley route after hearing Rebel patrols, so it was never fully reconnoitered.

> On Friday in going over the ground as far as we could . . . we fell upon the enemy's patrol, and, not liking to attract their attention that way, we did not explore the ground up to the ford.[93]

The Confederate forces knew where the Union camps were, and harassed them. Picket firing could be heard nearby and sometimes a stray shot whizzed through the camps or the animal paddocks. Neither was it unusual for some irritated volunteer soldier to return fire in the general direction of that first shot—without noting who might be in between. Colonel Sherman was

> uneasy at the fact that the Volunteers do pretty much as they please, and on the Slightest provocation bang away—the danger from this desultory firing is greater than from the Enemy as they are always so close whilst the latter keep a respectful distance.[94]

One officer needed to order his soldiers to lie down when stray bullets flew through the camp.

Press correspondents roamed freely as well, conducting interviews amid the obvious hardships of life in the field, which they were only too happy to let their readers know they were enduring:

> Corresponding under difficulties certainly, with a cartridge box for a table, and forty five drops of ink, all in the country, as the limit of my material, the drum likely to beat at any moment for an advance.[95]

They filed their reports from the Fairfax Court House telegraph office to towns across America, where the stories were published in the newspaper whatever day they arrived, often right next to contradictory reports. On July 22, Sarah read a mélange of conflicting reports in the *Providence Journal*, such as this headline from their correspondent who was: ON THE WAY TO MANASSAS—FOUR MILES WEST OF FAIRFAX—FRIDAY JULY 19 1861.[96] There was no real-time news, and the jumble of reports left only the certainty that her husband was heading into, and perhaps had already fought in, a major battle.

The enlistment terms of those ninety-day regiments raised the third week of April were expiring this week, many on the twentieth. McDowell wrote Scott,

> The Fourth Pennsylvania goes out to-day, and others succeed rapidly. I have made a request to the regiment to remain a few days longer, but do not hope for much success. In a few days I shall lose many thousands of the best of this force. Will it suit the views of the General and the Government that they shall be replaced by long-service regiments?[97]

The battery of the Eighth New York left, but the First Rhode Island and the Irish Brigade, the Sixty-ninth New York, mustered from the streets of Lower Manhattan around (Old) Saint Patrick's Cathedral, gallantly volunteered to stay on for the battle. The longer the fighting was put off, the more ninety-day regiments terms expired; the Union feared trying to send to the field men who had only gotten off their trains a week ago. They also needed to step up preparations to handle the inevitable injured or dead. Sara Edmonds, disguised as nurse Frank Thompson, watched as

> our surgeons began to prepare for the coming battle, by appropriating several buildings and fitting them up to for the wounded—among others the stone church in Centreville—a church which many a soldier will remember, as long as memory lasts.[98]

In the midst of this hullabaloo, the high command of the army was trying to do business. At this point, General Patterson, who had withdrawn back an additional seven miles from Johnston's last known position, still did not realize that Johnston had slipped away.

On Saturday the twentieth at noon, McDowell's intrepid engineers completed their surreptitious surveys and reported that the movement north through Sudley was possible.[99] McDowell issued the first version of General Order Number 22 around midday and readied his army to march out at 6:00 P.M., to advance part of the way, bivouac and rest the men, and then to cover the remaining few miles in the morning when the men were rested. It said in part,

> The enemy has planted a battery on the Warrenton turnpike to defend the passage of Bull Run, has mined the stone bridge, and made a heavy abatis on the right bank to oppose our advance in that direction. The ford above the bridge is also guarded, whether with artillery or not is not positively known.[100]

Sometime that afternoon, Sherman and Burnside prevailed upon McDowell to change the order, start later, and march straight through without a rest. McDowell "yielded to it at once, as it was only on account of the men that I wanted to stop." The general reissued his order just before 6:00 P.M., delaying the march until 2:30 A.M.

McDowell's original instincts had not been bad. All anyone had to do was check the distance and analyze the marching time. A departure in the evening seemed to be the best alternative to not having camped on the highlands near Bull Run. The men could have traveled the turnpike in daylight mellowing into twilight, and continued along the farm roads while the full moon was still in the sky, giving them some light. The Union Army brigades would also have had some flexibility. If the regiments became tangled up on the road—as usual—they would have had time to sort it out, as well as an opportunity to regroup after the inevitable delays. Even if the march went badly, McDowell would still have had a chance to launch his coordinated attack before the rising of the hot July sun desiccated his troops. The original timetable for starting the battle might be met.

Instead, this was going to be like crossing the log over Pohick Creek all over again, and Burnside was about to have his first experience with the potent creek curse that dogged him throughout the war. The revised plan left no margin for error, and was to wreak debilitating hardship on the men by forcing them to commence a long, uninterrupted march twelve hours after they had eaten. After their journey, they still had to fight. Any part of this action that occurred during the full heat of the day was going to amplify the difficulties of troops not yet field hardened.

The march rescheduled, McDowell called for a meeting for 8:00 P.M. in his tent. Regrettably, the delay allowed time for a proper dinner to be served to the general and his staff, and, by all accounts, McDowell went on one of his famous binges, packing down a prodigious quantity of food. A man of no other vices, perhaps McDowell found security and reassurance in gorging when under stress. Tonight, it also brought on a stomachache. Consequently, the "council of war," as some called it, the staff meeting, called for eight o'clock, did not start until eleven o'clock All the division and brigade commanders—colonels and above—who had been summoned to attend, waited for him for three hours. The devout Rhode Islanders used the time to hold one last evening prayer service: "On the evening of that day the service was repeated, with the certainty that before another sun would set we would not all be present to answer to roll-call."[101]

The field commanders crowded into the headquarters' tent, where the regiments were assigned their positions in the attack plan with the use of an inaccurate map. Colonel Slocum attended, Major Ballou did not. The gist of the meeting was that the Union was to turn the enemy's left, force him from his defensive position, and "if possible, destroy the railroad leading from Manassas to the Valley of Virginia."[102] Once it took place, Colonel Keyes noted, "it was a mere specification of the line in which we should all proceed the next day. The plans appeared to have been digested and matured before that meeting was called."[103] McDowell did not hold a council of war, for he was not a general who believed in candid discussions of options: "I myself never have inclined towards them; and . . . I do not think well of them." He believed they "have always proved to be of little account, even if they have not been injurious."[104]

Johnston's location, if mentioned, was not discussed. Colonel Keyes reported, "I do not think a word was said about it at the meeting the night before the battle."[105] McDowell mentioned to Scott in a report, "I learn from a person who represents himself as having just come from General Patterson that he has fallen back. There are rumors that Johnston has joined Beauregard," but Scott was unable to confirm this.[106] Apparently McDowell expected Johnston's army to enter the battle on the Union's right flank, in "that direction," after marching in from Harper's Ferry. But he only admitted this to Colonel Richardson later, privately, when the latter came in from reconnaissance after the meeting.[107] Despite having received the report about Johnston from someone he did not know if he could trust, McDowell had publicly maintained,

"Great God! I heard every rumor in the world, and I put them all aside unless a man spoke of his own personal knowledge."[108]

Some discussion was reported on whether or not the troops could assemble within the allotted hour but reveille was not moved up. Others were disturbed about the reveille time, and Richardson told his own superior, Tyler,

> It is impossible, general, to move an army of regular troops under two hours, and you will take at least that time to move volunteers; and if reveille is not beaten before two o'clock in the morning, you cannot get into action at daylight; it is impossible. . . . If you beat reveille at 12 o'clock, with volunteer troops, you may get into action at daylight, but not before; that is the best you can do.[109]

For the early part of the march, the plan called for all three attacking divisions to share the same main road, the Warrenton Turnpike, for somewhere between 2.4 to 2.75 miles, all of them crossing the wooden suspension bridge at Cub Run, a potential bottleneck. Then, Hunter and Heintzelman were to branch off at one of the two routes that lead north to commence their 6-mile detour through Sudley. Because they had the longest, most difficult march, *and* their camp was the easternmost of the Union forces headed for battle, another 1.4 miles further east of Centreville, it made the most sense to start them first.

Instead, Tyler's First Division, the closest, with the shortest distance to march, straight to the Stone Bridge, and led by a man who had not yet gotten his division anyplace on time, was ordered to proceed first. McDowell's brand new artillery chief, Major Barry, another recipient of a meteoric promotion, recalled McDowell, "was very particular giving directions about General Tyler's division being out of the way, as his division was the first to take the road, so as not to stop up the road for the others."[110]

> Tyler will move precisely at 2:30 A.M. The Second Division, Hunter's, will move from its camp at 2 A.M. precisely.[111]

McDowell later explained that he planned for Tyler's forces to be able to protect Hunter's rear in case of a 4:00 A.M. attack by the Confederates, a scenario neither likely nor convincing. The Third Brigade, led by Heintzelman, was now to go at 2:30 A.M., from their spot south of Centreville. Hunter's Division was expected to clear .75 miles in thirty minutes, after which Heintzelman's troops were to step smartly in behind them. While 1.75 miles per hour is a good speed for an army on the march in the field in daylight, the officers failed to factor in that the *last* marching man in a large division will not pass the starting point as soon as the *first*.[112] Nor was it apparently put forth that Hunter's Second Brigade should have first crack at the empty road, and so the colonels adjourned, each to return to their regiments and brigades and respective fates.

Meanwhile, Runyon's Fourth Division, 5,700 men, was held in reserve, but near Alexandria, so far from the line that it was said the Queen's Guards in London were closer.[113] It was impossible to bring those men into action at Manassas in a one-day battle, but they would be able to intervene if the Confederates made a surprise move on Washington, D.C. The odds of this were astronomical on July 21, but keeping a force between the Virginia-based enemy and the capital was necessary throughout the whole war. Miles's Fifth Division of 6,100 soldiers was also placed in reserve at Centreville, theoretically close enough to respond as needed to any portion of the battlefield. However, had Beauregard been able to launch his grand right wheel unobstructed, they would have been players in the battle along the turnpike.

The editor of the *New York Times* was not privy to the politically disastrous goings-on in the command tent, and wrote to his paper glowingly about what he could see of the men in camp:

> This is one of the most beautiful nights that the imagination can conceive. The sky is perfectly clear, the moon is full and bright, and the air as still as if it were not within a few hours to be disturbed by the roar of cannon and the shouts of contending men. . . . An hour ago I rode back to General McDowell's headquarters. As I rose over the crest of the hill, and caught a view of the scene in front, it seemed a picture of enchantment. The bright moon cast the woods which bound the field into deep shadows, through which the camp fires shed a clear and brilliant glow. On the extreme right, in the neighbourhood of the Fire Zouaves, a party were singing "The Star Spangled Banner," and from the left rose the sweet strains of a magnificent band intermingling opera airs with patriotic bursts of "Hail Columbia" and "Yankee Doodle."[114]

- CHAPTER FIFTEEN -

"How Many Miles to the Junction?"*

Rhode Island Leads the Union Army to Success

2:00 A.M. to 10:00 A.M., July 21, 1861

Hundreds of campfires dotted the darkened plains of Manassas north and south of Bull Run, and within reach of their glow, more than fifty thousand soldiers tensed in anticipation of their first battle. The educated among them had studied Homer's words to soldiers on the eve of battle in the *Iliad:* "anger now be thy song."[1] But these soldiers were not angry men. They were one people, for whom courage and honor were important, but divided by two conflicting interpretations of common American values like liberty. For the Union boys, the role of the government was to intervene to protect liberty. For the Rebel boys, the role of the government was to leave things alone in order not to interfere with liberty. The next day they were going to fight to see which philosophy might prevail. And this night, they had all

* From the Civil War Song "Nine Miles to the Junction."

talked themselves into the frame of mind, "to silently gather up one's resources of character, to be in readiness for the great assault."[2] They tapped into the unshakeable belief in their own ability to face and transcend danger, instilled by many hours of training in their military camps.[3]

The men rested or slept, awaiting their orders. When Colonel Slocum returned from the staff meeting, he briefed them on the details of the march: Hunter's Division was assigned to take the northern salient through Sudley, escorted by a local guide and two engineers, and Heintzelman's Third Division was to follow behind them for part of the distance, but was then to branch off at a fork in the road and infiltrate the countryside just above the Stone Bridge. In a coordinated attack, the fifteen thousand men of the two divisions were to take out any Rebel troops in the area, before moving in on their main objective, Manassas Railway Junction, about four miles south of the turnpike. The Second Rhode Island Regiment was to lead the Union movement.

Slocum then visited Chaplain Woodbury, who recorded that

> he had with me a serious and earnest conversation. He was usually bright, eager, full of spirits and sometimes jocular. But that time I noticed that he was somber and somewhat pre-engaged. We spoke of the possibilities of the morrow. I suggested that possibly we might not meet with much opposition to our movement. He looked at me in silence for moment, and then said: "It will be the hottest kind of a fight. You'll never want to see a severer battle." I do not suppose that any clouded gloomy presentiment was resting upon his mind. But he knew the temper of the foe better than any of us.

Woodbury knew Slocum for a realist, not a coward, and was duly impressed with his opinion that "the contest would be such as would call for the exercise of the greatest endurance and strength. He bade me good-night and returned to his own quarters."[4]

Ranging in age from sixteen to fifty-nine, the men and boys from Rhode Island did not know their colonel's concerns, but had to now deal with their own. Each needed to conquer his personal fear in his own way factor as he prepared for the upcoming battle. Many soldiers were

> engaged in writing by the glimmering light of the camp-fire . . . Some were reading their bibles, perhaps with more than usual interest; while others sat in groups, conversing in low earnest tones; but the great mass were stretched upon the ground, wrapped in their blankets, fast asleep, and all unconscious of the dangers of the morrow.[5]

Sullivan, too, must have grappled with his own personal fears, especially given his premonition, which may have been strong upon him that night. If he wrote any letter to Sarah, it would have been impossible to post it then, and there is no evidence that such a missive existed.

Across Bull Run, the Confederate brigadiers were encamped at their assigned fords. Texan Thomas Jewett Goree wrote to his mother,

> Our headquarters are in the open air in a pine thicket. I write on my saddlebags, my seat on the ground, the Genl and balance of the staff on the ground around. . . . I am very tired. Have been on my horse almost all the time since the commencement of the retreat from Fairfax. . . . Have not had a chance to wash my face for more than three days. . . . We fully expected an attack all day on Saturday, the 20th, but the day passed off without any.[6]

These Southerners were also preparing for battle, in ways little different than their enemy. Here, too, the men hoped they would be brave and make the home folks proud. Their commanders were also making the rounds:

> Just after dark, Colonel Bartow came down to the company, his Savannah boys, the Oglethorpe Light Infantry now known as Company B—and gave us a fatherly talk. . . . His last words somewhat saddened me. He said, "But remember boys, that battle and fighting mean death, and probably before sunrise some of us will be dead."[7]

There were other premonitions of tragedy. Congressman Elihu Washburne, whose district in Illinois included Ulysses Grant's hometown, headed out of the capital Saturday night for the camps at Centreville. He does not define at what hour he

> went to the tent of Genl. McDowell and had quite a conversation with him. I never had much of an opinion of him as a General, and I left his tent with a feeling of great sadness and a sort of a prescience of coming disaster. He seemed discouraged and in low spirits, and appeared very doubtful of the result of the approaching conflict. That was a bad symptom.[8]

McDowell had ample reason to feel uneasy about the day to come. There was likely no more insecure, hounded, or fatalistic man in America that night. His unbloodied men were still civilians on loan to the military. The enemy was dug in and had many advantages. He'd deduced that the trains he'd heard were bringing in reinforcements, but whether they were platoons of militia or Johnston's army he had no way of knowing; and, without confirmation, he was unable to alter or delay his plans. His knowledge about the countryside and the enemy was incomplete because his reconnaissance patrols had been unable to penetrate the area. The ground he did know about was bad: mile upon mile of presumptive Confederate positions behind steep riverbanks.

To overcome the lack of Union intelligence of the locale, engineer Barnard had hired a local guide "on the spot," one Mathias (Matthew) C. Mitchell, a twenty-one-year-old farm laborer. Born in New Jersey, Mitchell had lived in this area of Virginia for at least a year. He is shown in the 1860 census as living with and working for the Albert Flagler family. The Flaglers were New Yorkers who had bought a good-sized farm in Fairfax County between 1850 and 1860. Keeping no slaves, they farmed it themselves, with the help of Mitchell, and likely the eight-member Jesse Murphy clan, also from New Jersey. Although they lived on the east side of Bull Run, they moved back and forth over the various fords, trading, perhaps patronizing the mill, and possibly visiting the Van Pelts at their farm on the west bank. The elderly Van Pelt family was also from New Jersey. Mitchell was the right age to have been a son or nephew of the George Mitchell family, New Jerseyites who farmed nearby. In any event, he was probably working away from home to earn cash or independence.[9]

Probably with the permission of his employer, Mitchell went to the Union camp to offer his services, full of twenty-one-year-old assurance and earnestness. Energetic, able to ride a horse, speaking with a Northern accent, he was undoubtedly a convincing and believable representative of these many Northern families whose interests and sentiments lay with the Union Army.

Meanwhile, McDowell's own staff had not yet had time to develop cohesion or relationships among themselves, so he was sometimes badly served. McDowell had been in command only fifty-five days and had developed little rapport with his new team, some of whom did not give him the respect his position merited. He had not had the time to drill it into them either. A key position, his chief of artillery, was filled on July 18 with the promotion

Brigadier General Irvin McDowell, commanding the Union Army. *Courtesy of the Library of Congress Prints and Photographs Division.*

of William Farquar Barry to major.[10] Porter and Burnside's egos clashed, and the New Yorkers were not overfond of Sherman's brusqueness; Richardson despised Miles as a drunkard, and Miles hated Richardson for knowing it. McDowell had to have personally questioned the capabilities of some, though he kept his own counsel in the political vortex that made and unmade field officers in mid-1861. Tyler's ego made it questionable if he would obey orders, and McDowell had likely heard enough allusions to Colonel Miles's capacity for drink that he choose to place Miles's Brigade out of action as a reserve force behind the front lines. That cocky governor of Rhode Island, William Sprague, was omnipresent and endeavoring to be helpful as an aide. The cohesion of the Rhode Islanders caused McDowell to switch their role: the division previously referred to by McDowell as a "a kind of reserve," was now going to lead the attack, although the commanders still planned to hold the regiments of ninety-day men in reserve and out of harm's way.

Regiments within a brigade were expected to support one another, but McDowell's units were still being brigaded as they marched into Virginia and had not established relationships, except perhaps between the Rhode Islanders and the New Yorkers, who even attended each other's church services. In contrast, the Confederates had completed brigading a month ago, on June twentieth.

McDowell had two crack units of artillery, "Griffin's and Ricketts' splendid companies of regulars."[11] His others were commanded by green, newly assigned officers, like Lieutenant Peter Haines, a nineteen-year-old lad who had just graduated West Point Military Academy twenty-seven days earlier.[12] McDowell's cavalry was universally ridiculed; Colonel Thomas Davies, commanding the Second Brigade of the Fifth Division (Miles) called them "good for nothing."[13] (London) *Times* war correspondent William Howard Russell had written in his paper, "They have no cavalry, only a few scarecrow men, who would dissolve partnership with their steeds at the first serious combined movement."[14] With all these impediments, McDowell could only hope and pray that he had patched together enough bits and pieces to prevail on the morrow. Chaos theory had not yet been invented to analyze the flow of events, but it was nonetheless at work here.

> Things that didn't seem particularly like a particularly serious thing at the time would end up being one of many little things a slow accrual, compounding steadily and imperceptibly toward critical mass.[15]

McDowell did not fall asleep until late. Indeed, as he later reported, "I was sick during the night and morning."[16] Some units seemed to have gotten no sleep at all. The Eleventh Massachusetts cooked rations until midnight, issued them, and then lined the men up at 1:00 A.M. to await the 2:30 departure.[17]

> Through the hazy valley and on hill-slope, miles apart, were burning the fires at which forty regiments had prepared their midnight meal. In the vistas opening along a dozen lines of view, thousands of men were moving among the fitful beacons, horses were harnessing to artillery, white army waggons were in motion with the ambulances—whose black covering, when one thought about it, seemed as appropriate as that of the coffin which accompanies a condemned man to the death before him. All was silent confusion. . . .[18]

The *New York Tribune* reported the common experience of eighteen thousand men that morning:

> We were awakened quietly, and the whole regiment told to sling their blankets and haversacks and fall in light marching order, with as little noise as possible. As it still wanted an hour or two of daylight, the air was remarkably chilly; and it was after some little yawning and stretching and shivering that our men gathered the half-numb limbs from the wet grass where they had been lying, and proceeded to arrange their equipment and fall in their places, all breakfast less, for the march.[19]

At 2:30 A.M., as the Rhode Island vanguard prepared to depart, "the moon was just sinking in the west; a cool wind had sprung up in the night made the morning chilly."[20] In the chill and damp, everyone had slept fully clothed. Sullivan wore two shirts—one silk, one calico—underneath his knee-length wool officer's tunic. His trousers were tucked into his boots, his revolvers loaded, his canteen full—a detail had gone to a nearby spring. He now put on his hat, strapped on his sword, and waited for his horse. Candles and fires were put out, and lanterns extinguished. The horses were brought forward, and the officers put on their gauntlets and mounted. They rode to the front of the line and surveyed their men. The fateful moment had arrived.

The division assigned priority access to the common road this morning had the shortest distance to travel of any—a mere three miles. McDowell sent Tyler out on the road first because his position was the most forward and the commanding general saw no point in rearranging positions.[21]

Hunter's Division got itself on the road in its allotted time and marched west toward the traffic jam. Two miles ahead of them, the road was already blocked by Tyler's First Division was almost thirteen thousand soldiers in four brigades led by Colonel William Tecumseh Sherman, Colonel Israel Richardson, Brigadier General Robert Schenck, and Colonel Erasmus Keyes. Corporal Rhodes reported, "About two o'clock this morning we left 'Bush Camp,'. . . We started without breakfast and only a little hard bread in our haversacks."[22] Once again the Rhode Islanders led, the Second followed by the First. Following on their heels were balance of their brigade, the Second New Hampshire Infantry and the Seventy-first New York, all volunteers. Young Mathias Mitchell, the guide, escorted Hunter's Division. At first he probably rode up front with Hunter, but men reported talking with the amiable guide at various times, so he may have moved along the line. Engineer Woodbury, no relation to the chaplain, also rode with the Second Division.

Next came the units of the First Brigade commanded by Colonel Andrew Porter, led by the United States Cavalry Battalion, protected and useless in the midst of infantry. In addition to the Eighty-fourth and Twenty-seventh New York Volunteer Infantry Regiments, Porter had a battalion of U.S. Marines, many of them new recruits, and one battalion of U.S. Army Regulars. Griffin's Battery, which had been brought down from West Point to assist with capital security some months earlier, completed his brigade.

Heintzelman's Third Division, 7,200 strong, followed, his brigades led by colonels Orlando Willcox, William Franklin, and Oliver

Howard. The nurses, too, were ready; Sarah Edmonds described one who accompanied her husband, a regimental chaplain:

> She stood there, looking as brave as possible, with her narrow brimmed leghorn hat, black cloth riding habit, shortened to walking length by the use of page, a silver-mounted seven-shooter in her belt, a canteen of water swung over one shoulder and a flask of brandy over the other, and a haversack with provision, lint, bandages, adhesive plaster, etc. hanging by her side.

The full moon was to remain in the sky for another couple hours—moonset was not until 4:30 A.M.—though before that it was lost behind the hills and trees. For now, it continued to illuminate

> a magnificent spectacle, as column after column wound its way over the green hills and through the hazy valleys, with the soft moonlight falling on the long lines of shining steel. Not a drum or bugle was heard during the march, and the deep silence was only broken by the rumbling of artillery, the muffled tread of infantry, or the low hum of thousands of subdued voices.[23]

Surprising the Rebels was going to be unlikely under any circumstances, for the Confederates had indeed heard things going bump in the night. By 3:00 A.M., pickets of the Fourth South Carolina, at the Stone Bridge, reported hearing muffled commands in the nearby woods. By 4:00 A.M., these same pickets, who reported to Colonel Nathan Evans, had fired on Tyler's vanguard approaching the Stone Bridge. The Carolinians deployed their sleeping men, apprised the Louisianans, put their artillery in place, and notified Beauregard. Still, in the darkness, they were unsure if this was a reconnaissance party, a reconnaissance in force, a feint, or an attack.

General in Chief Winfield Scott had briefly thought about being taken along into battle in a carriage or other conveyance, but correctly decided that was too impractical. Even McDowell did not march out with any of his divisions in the darkness of the twenty-first:

> I was sick during the night and morning and did not leave my quarters, east of Centreville—until I thought all the divisions were fully in motion, so as to give myself as much rest as possible."[24]

When he did ride out with his staff at about four or four-thirty in the morning, they were surprised to find "columns standing in the road waiting for one of Tyler's brigades to get out of camp and under motion."[25] Here, right at the outset, the inevitable traffic jam had happened, causing a two-hour delay. The last units in Tyler's line of march were unable to leave camp because the flow of traffic on the road was moving too slowly to let them onto it.

It was bad enough not to have sent cavalry patrols down the moonlit road, but to use an entire brigade for reconnaissance instead of dispatching advance infantry patrols was stupid.

> The country between Cub Run and Bull Run was supposed to be occupied by the enemy, and it became indispensable for the leading division, being without cavalry, and with no knowledge of the country, to move slowly, in order to protect themselves against any surprise on the part of the enemy.[26]

Tyler's lead brigade, Schenck's, was not in position until moonset, and the unfamiliar country was dark, dark, dark. Schenck's soldiers inched along at half a mile per hour, assisted by their skirmishers, who groped their way down the roadways, verges, and fields, orienting themselves to the main body only by the sound of the voice of each man next to them. It was a break for the Union Army to have a wide turnpike with a gravel surface for its use, but the lack of visibility negated any advantage. Captain George Finch of the Second Ohio reported,

> We never knew where a fence or a tree was located in front of us until we ran slap against it. Many of the skirmishers had bloody noses and bruised limbs from such collisions.[27]

At 4:30 A.M., General McDowell was observed on the turnpike, urging Schenk to hurry up.[28] Porter, coming into line just behind Burnside's Brigade, was caught in it too, and spoke of it in his usual stinging tone of voice,

> We got out into the road and were delayed a great while there. We were formed on the road in front of my camp. I had the reserve brigade in the rear. After some delay we then moved on some distance and halted again and we kept pottering along, pottering along in that way, instead of being fairly on the road. It was intended that we should turn their position at daylight, as we could have done very easily but for the delay. There was a great deal of delay—very vexatious delay. . . . The whole affair was extremely disagree able to me. I was disgusted with the whole thing, and I asked no questions, and I did not want to know who was to blame.[29]

Alarmed by the delay, Colonel Keyes held his own brigade off the road and did not join with the three others until midmorning morning.[30] Keyes had no artillery, so it was possible for his men to leave the road and march parallel to it, leaving the road clear for Hunter.[31] Had he not done so, it might have taken even longer than three hours to get to Cub Run. Augustus Woodbury moaned,

> Another halt. Across one narrow bridge which spanned the river, this whole army was to file. Our division was obliged to wait till all of Tyler's division, eleven regiments, and artillery, had passed. . . . When we actually crossed the bridge, men were at work staying and propping the structure, to sustain the weight of our passage.[32]

Not only was this decrepit-looking, old wooden suspension bridge narrower than the roadbed, so the men had to realign themselves to cross it, but Tyler's forces were lugging along the biggest piece of artillery in Virginia, a behemoth siege cannon weighing three tons, known as a thirty-pounder Parrot rifle. Its gun barrel was as long as the height of one man standing on the shoulders of another; it fired an elongated projectile weighing thirty pounds. By comparison, the "average" field gun fired a ten- or twelve-pound ball that was sufficient to kill infantry and cavalry. A "thirty-pounder" was more appropriate to siege warfare like at Fort Sumter, and was hardly needed to blast through the kind of dirt-mound fortifications the Confederates had built near Manassas. Nicknamed "Lincoln's Baby Waker," it was assigned the "sacred duty" of firing the opening shot of the battle.[33] Yet, they left fourteen more useful guns behind with the reserve units—almost one-third of their cannon. It took a half hour to get this single gun across the Cub Run Bridge, while Hunter's Division stood idly in the road, waiting.

All this while, trains continued bringing more units of Johnston's Army into Manassas Junction. McHenry Howard, First Maryland Infantry Battalion said,*

> At 2 A.M. Sunday, July 21, we were aroused by the shrill whistle of the locomotive and marched down from our

* Although Maryland as a state did not secede from the Union, loyal secessionist men wishing to fight for the Confederacy formed their own unit in the Confederate Army.

> somewhat elevated position to take the train, but delays ensued as usual and it was daybreak before we started. The cars were filled to their utmost capacity and I rode part of the way on the platform and part on top of a car. The engine made slow time and there were frequent stops. . . .[34]

Sunrise was at 5:01 A.M. but it was 5:30 A.M. before the Cub Run bridge was clear and Sullivan Ballou and his men, as the lead regiment of Hunter's Division, could cross over. Once over the bridge, the congestion ahead of them still impeded their progress getting to their turnoff, which was one mile away. According to their battle plans, they should have already completed the northern hook through Sudley Springs by 4:00 A.M., and been ready to strike a surprise blow at the enemy as dawn broke. Even if they could now achieve 1.5 miles per hour on a clear, sunlit road, they were still 2.5 hours away—which would put them on the battle line about 8:00 A.M., four hours late. The congestion on the turnpike may have been behind a decision to take another route entirely.

The stated reason for the change was to allow the troops to travel under cover of the woods now that the sun had risen. The guide, Mathias Mitchell, warned the command staff that the original route traversed land that could be shelled by Confederate artillery in daylight. As no commander ever accepted responsibility for authorizing the change, much about it remains an unsolved mystery today. It is unclear if anyone in the army fully understood at the time they approved it, that the new route through the woods was several miles longer than the former one. That might have been an equable trade-off, however, for waiting interminably on the turnpike for Tyler's men to get out of their way. However, because this more camouflaged farm road served a smaller geographic area and fewer farms, it was less traveled and unmaintained. It also had no water sources after the first half mile. Historians have always assumed the Second Division took their originally assigned turnoff and then took a detour. An analysis of the maps makes that seem highly unlikely. Instead, it reveals they turned off the main road at a junction closer than planned. Then as now, a shortcut out of a traffic jam often saved no time.*

By 6:00 A.M. the lead units of Hunter's Division were marching past Grigsby's Farm. These troops formed a four-mile-long procession on a narrow road, led by Hunter, his staff, Burnside, and Governor Sprague. Immediately following were a unit of the Second Rhode Island acting as pioneers,** followed by a wagon filled with shovels, axes, and entrenching tools, guarded by a company of engineers from the Seventy-first. Next came Reynolds's Rhode Island Battery, the First Rhode Island, the Second New Hampshire, and then the balance of the Seventy-first New York. The national guard men trudged behind them, pulling their boat howitzers by hand.[35] Porter's Brigade completed Hunter's Division. Heintzelman's division traveled behind them. From this last division, Colonel Oliver O. Howard's Brigade had been ordered to remain behind until sent forward, to act as a reserve at the fork in the road.[36] By some reports, General McDowell sat there on his horse at the blacksmith shop, watching. Surely the commanding general must have known which road they were to take. Others came to observe as well.

As the Eleventh Massachusetts crossed "the bridge that spans Cub Run," Captain Nathan Butler

> noticed about twenty barouches and carriages that contained members of Congress and their friends, who had left Washington for the purpose of witnessing the approaching conflict.[37]

* For a complete analysis, see Appendix Two.

** In the Civil War "pioneers" broke down fences, abatis, and breastworks, clearing the way for troops that followed.

The civilians were in search of a good view and of officers who could explain what was happening. Except for a few especially aggressive visitors, they remained on the eastern bank of the run. Still more came later in the day, among them Congressman Ely who had gone to support the Thirteenth New York, raised from his home district in Rochester.

On the farm road, the Rhode Islanders soon passed a tiny house where a dirty old crone "who so loved the sacred soil of Virginia that she bore much of it on her person" told the men that "there were enough Confederates ahead to wipe us all out and that her old man was among them." After a mile or so, her curse seemed to take substance: the road deteriorated into a "much obstructed" pathway overgrown by woods.[38] Only then did the Union commanders find out what a bad road it was. At first, it was "so dark each man followed his file leader blindly."[39]

The exuberant summer growth of a free-growing forest—tree branches, brush, weeds like goldenrod and Queen Anne's lace, the tentacles of fragrant wild honeysuckle vines and the brambles of blackberry, not to mention noxious vines of poison ivy—reduced the road to a narrow path that grabbed at the men as they passed through. Barnard himself called it "not a beaten, traveled road, but a mere country path."[40] Mitchell, the guide, who never had to take more than a wagon or horse down this road, clearly overestimated its usefulness to an army.

However, the New Englanders rose to the challenge, and two groups of men claimed the honor of clearing the path, the pioneers of the Second Rhode Island and the New Hampshire axe men. "As we led the Brigade the task of clearing the road fell to us, and hard work we found it."[41] "Twenty five axemen of the Second New Hampshire helped chop a passage for the . . . men of the division."[42] While the virgin forests of New England were vigorous, they never attained the lushness of the mature forests of the more temperate Southern climate:

> Dawn found us in the midst of a forest, such as few if any of us had ever before seen. Giant trees were on every hand, while all about us other giants had grown to maturity, lived their day, decayed and fallen to earth. We could almost image the genie of the forest peering out upon us and saying, "Who be these who thus disturb us? Surely their like never passed this way before."[43]

Not for all the years that trail had been in existence, had it cumulatively known so many commuters as it did that morning when Hunter's Division crept along it. Private Sholes recalled, "clambering over the fallen trunks of trees, pushing through heavy growths of underbrush, we presently emerged into the open ground."[44] There, the unforgiving sun waited to scorch them. "An open space of fifteen acres sometimes intervened, but it was always enclosed by dense woods."[45] The denseness of the woods "shut out the breeze and made the heat almost intolerable" as the men marched along.[46]

Hunter's Brigade made very good time despite the difficulties. Lieutenant Colonel Francis S. Fiske, Second New Hampshire, treasured a Thoreau moment he shared with other officers:

> I wish I could adequately describe the loveliness of this summer Sabbath morning. In the midst of war we were in peace. There was not a cloud in the sky; a gentle breeze rustled the foliage over our heads, mingling its murmurs with the soft notes of the wood-birds; the thick carpet of leaves under our feet deadened the sound of the artillery wheels and of the tramp of men. Everybody felt the influence of the scene, and the men, marching on their leafy path, spoke in subdued tones. A Rhode Island officer riding beside me quoted some lines from Wordsworth fitting the morning, which I am sorry I cannot recall. Colonel Slocum of the Second Rhode Island rode up

> and joined in our talk about the peaceful aspect of nature around us. [Cannon fire in the distance spoiled the peaceful moment] Men ceased speaking and without orders closed their ranks, and only the sullen rumble of the artillery wheels was to be heard; the influence of our peaceful surroundings was gone, and men were reminded that the time which was to test their manhood had come.[47]

Likely those men clearing the growth of brush from the road or pulling the boat howitzers along by hand were waxing less poetic. The dust choked them, and their endeavors in the heat soon caused the men to drink the last drop from their canteens without knowing how soon they could refill them.

The change in route eliminated the road junction at which Heintzelman's Division was to have turned left to head for Poplar Ford. Along the original route near the Spindle Farm, his troops should have angled westerly and turned off at a hard-to-miss farm road at a 90-degree angle that lead to the Poplar Ford crossing of Bull Run.

> I had orders not to cross until Hunter had crossed at Sudley's Church and come down opposite to me on the other side of Bull Run. Then I was to cross, and we were to follow on down opposite the Stone Bridge, and turn that.[48]

Not only were there four streams on that route to water men and horses, but the very presence of his brigade north of the Stone Bridge would have hampered the sending of Confederate reinforcements to the northern fords. But the elimination of the two-pronged attack by the change in route was neither recognized nor explained to him.

> Major Wright, of the engineers, went with Hunter's column.

> He was to stop with the guide, where the road turned off to this second ford I spoke of. He could not find the road, and of course, we kept on. . . .[49]

And so his column trudged along in Hunter's dust as they continued up past Richard Weir's Mountain View Farm and joined the Sudley Road just above the Cushing's at Sudley Mansion, making a left turn onto the Sudley–New Market Road to come down into Sudley.

> The day was one of the hottest of the year: there was no friendly cloud to obstruct the rays of the sun; and it was impossible for the army to march a long distance with unusual speed. Nevertheless, for twelve miles, the men were pushed forward at an unnatural gait, generally walking as rapidly as possible, and double-quicking one-fourth of the time, to keep the different regiments in the column within supporting distance of each other. Nearly every man impatiently asked, "How far is it to the junction?" whenever the loyal citizen residing in the vicinity, who acted as a guide, rode along the line. He always answered the question in a good natured manner by saying, 'six miles.' The Brigade Commander never attempted to secure a rest for the soldiers; and some of them sank upon the ground, wholly overcome by faintness, which was produced by the intolerable heat and the furious pace at which they were marched.[50]

The only way McDowell had figured out to coordinate a simultaneous attack on three fronts miles apart was to have the Baby Waker cannon fired to signal commencement of hostilities. Tyler arrived at his assigned position on the turnpike close in front of the Stone Bridge no later than 6:30 A.M., only an hour late, and fired the gun. Of course, with the northern salient running over three hours late, all this accomplished was to let General Beauregard know beyond a doubt that McDowell had arrived to do battle.

As the sun rose further in the cloudless sky, everyone knew a battle was about to take place somewhere, but no one knew where. Scott was in Washington, McDowell near Centreville, and Beauregard at Mitchell's Ford. From this moment on, these generals were not really in control any more. The battle became what Lieutenant Dangerfield Parker identified as "minor armies continually interchanging their position."[51] With their forces scattered around beyond their range of effective communication, command had shifted down to the level of division, brigade, and regimental officers.

Once the cannon had been fired, Tyler sat back and lobbed shells over Bull Run, giving a rather unconvincing performance of a commander about to storm over and attack. He skirmished for two hours and fired his artillery for three, demolishing the tent of E. Porter Alexander, in charge of the Confederate signal men.

Facing Tyler at the Stone Bridge was thirty-seven-year-old West Point graduate Nathan Evans, who had been left to hold this key promontory between the two crossings with the tiny Seventh Brigade. An experienced Indian fighter in the regular U.S. Army, South Carolina–born Captain Evans was a hard-talking, hard-swearing, hard-drinking, and hard-fighting man. In the cool damp of that morning, Evans strode around wearing his khaki cape with leopard-print fabric lining.[52]

Evans had two military objectives that morning: to let the Union know he was there, but to conceal that he only had eleven hundred men. The Fourth South Carolina, the First Louisiana Special Infantry Battalion, two companies of Virginia cavalry and a section of the Lynchburg Artillery constituted his entire command, but by pivoting them around from his lair in the bushes, he kept up appearances of more men. Periodically his men fired their muskets, especially if some Yankee was darn fool enough to show himself. Colonel Sherman was one such, and noted some badly aimed bullets whizzing around him. Sherman also provoked Major Chatham Roberdeau Wheat, (or a member of the cavalry,) into riding out into the water of the run to taunt him. "Come get us, you damned abolitionist!" Wheat yelled at the red head on the opposite bank; Sherman did not reply, but noted that the Southern heckler's horse splashed through shallow water, revealing a ford previously unknown to Union forces.[53]

Evans was attended by his personal orderly, a huge Prussian fellow whose job it was to carry around a gallon jug of whiskey and keep it close at hand so Evans could take frequent swigs. If Evans had imbibed that morning, it did not impair his judgment or ingenuity.

McDowell, who had stayed close to Tyler that morning, recognized that he had failed to engage the main body of the Confederate Army, when they did not march out to do battle. He remained on the turnpike, awaiting developments, hoping to direct operations from there. Edmund Stedman, correspondent for the *New York World*, reported, "the general was lying on the ground, having been ill during the night, but at once mounted his horse and rode on to join the column," when he received a message from Hunter.[54]

Brigadier General Milledge Bonham, camped way south on Mitchell's Ford, reported to headquarters before daylight that he had the enemy in force near his sector. Beauregard was unsure how to interpret these federal movements and shared his consternation with General Johnston, who, after arriving at headquarters, had

> found Gen. Beauregard's position too extensive, and the ground too densely wooded and intricate, to be learned in the brief time at my disposal and therefore determined to rely upon his knowledge of it and of the enemy's positions. This I did readily from full confidence in his capacity.[55]

In the forty-eight hours in which they collaborated on this battle, they worked effectively together; egos seemed not to have surfaced until later. Johnston urged the reinforcement of their left flank above the Stone Bridge, an area wholly undefended, with the Second and Third brigades of the Army of the Shenandoah in case the Union opened a front there.[56] Raised, funded, trained, and commanded by General Barnard Bee and colonels Francis Bartow and Wade Hampton, these regiments had tremendous cohesion and loyalty. General Thomas J. Jackson's First Brigade of Virginians was to be placed in reserve until they knew where best to deploy it.

General Beauregard may have garbled some written orders that morning, but he did one thing right when he ordered his chief signalman, Captain Edward Porter Alexander, to personally man one of the signal stations.*[57] He took the farthest one, near the junction, and trained his telescope on the station near Stone Bridge, and watched for developments. From his vantage point, the valley beyond this station near the Van Pelt house flattened out

> into a narrow band of green. While watching the flag of this station with a good glass, when I had been there about half an hour, the sun being low in the east . . . my eye was caught by a glitter in the narrow band of green. . . . It was about 8 miles from me in an air line and was but a faint gleam, indescribably quick, but I had a fine glass and well trained eyes, and I knew at once what it was. And careful observation also detected the glitter of bayonets all along a road crossing the valley, and I was sure I was "on to" McDowell's plan. . . . First I signaled to Evans as of most immediate consequence, "Look out for your left. You are flanked."[58]

* Alexander's assignment to the station atop Wilcoxen's Hill probably saved his life—the second or third shot fired by Lincoln's Baby Waker crashed into and collapsed his tent.

His next message went to Beauregard:

> I see a column crossing Bull Run about two miles above Stone Bridge. Head of it is in woods on this side; tail of it in woods on other side. About a quarter of a mile length of column visible in the opening. Artillery forms part of it.[59]

By 9:00 A.M. the game was up; the Confederates had discovered the whereabouts of Hunter's Division. Porter explained,

> Evans . . . told me that a picket, which he had had at Sudley, being driven in by the enemy's advance guard, had sent a courier, and the two couriers, one with my signal message and one with the report of the picket, reached him together. The simultaneous reports from different sources impressed him, and he acted at once and with sound judgment. . . . He marched to oppose and delay the turning column, at the same time notifying Cocke on his right, of his movement.[60]

Evans sent all but 200 men to the left flank, telling the South Carolinians to remain hidden in the bushes. His withdrawal went unnoticed, and these 200 held Tyler's 7,100 in place for hours. Relying on his scouts, Evans kept relocating his men and guns to the north to keep his enemy in range. The country was so dry that great clouds of dust rose from the footfalls of man and beast. It rose up into the sky, broadcasting the movements of the armies. The greater the cloud, the larger the body of men moving under it.

Unaware that their dust cloud had been spotted, Chaplain Woodbury

> rode with him [Slocum] at the head of the brigade as the Second Regiment was in front, for a considerable distance, after we had come out into the open fields of which I have

> before spoken, and we chatted pleasantly and cheerfully as we went along the road. The somber mood had passed away. I recall his saying that the flank march which we were making was a somewhat hazardous operation. If it succeeded, it was a brilliant thing to do; if it failed, it was disastrous.[61]

By now, other Confederate observers noted a telltale dust cloud rising from the dirt road the Union Army was using.[62] Until they realized it was only Johnston's guns and cavalry wagons catching up with the men come by train, the Confederates had taken alarm from a second immense cloud of dust, this one ten miles to the northwest, fearing it was Patterson's army coming upon them.

The Northerners had set out in the cool of the night, but now the heat of the day was building and was especially intense whenever they came out of the woods. They were dehydrated, tired, and hungry. They had been on the move for seven hours with no solid food. Sweat poured off them. Sullivan Ballou may have regretted wearing the calico shirt on top of his silk one. The men moved within this fog of dust, so thick it seemed almost a biblical plague here on the plains named for the eldest son of Moses. It coated their faces, eyes, noses, and mouths, choking them and increasing their thirst. Uniforms turned a common shade of brown as the dust settled over them. This march was the hardest thing any of them had done in their entire time in the army, and they still had to fight the enemy.

First Lieutenant J. Albert Monroe, Reynolds' battery, Second Rhode Island, developed such a thirst that he was willing to approach a local house for water. It turned into a memorable encounter with one of the locals on that

> exceedingly hot day; at least it appeared to be so by all who had not been accustomed to violent exercise in a warm climate. On the way to the battle ground in the morning, before

> reaching Sudley church, I went up to a large white house at one of the windows of which, a lady was standing, watching the passing troops, and I politely asked for some water. She gave me a gruff and insolent answer, and I turned away with feelings not the kindliest imaginable.[63]

Young Lieutenant Monroe and his empty canteen went back to the road and continued south. Unbeknown to him, water was just ahead and he could get his own drink for himself. The large white house he had approached was Sudley Mansion, the only house of that description in the area, and the woman most likely sixty-year-old Mrs. Eleanor Cushing, whom he was to meet again that day. Mrs. Cushing was a native Virginian, and brought the property and slaves into her marriage with her Massachusetts-born husband, Crawford, now a devoted Southerner. Walking past her door that day were more Massachusetts men than she had ever seen in her life.

Finally, about 9:30 A.M. Burnside's Brigade arrived at Sudley Ford, where "Bull Run was twenty yards in width. . . . The water was yellow with mud, and flowed between banks of red earth that showed the abundance of the sandstone in the soil.[64] The men crossed steadily through, and were kept on moving out the other side, not yet allowed to drink, climbing onto the sandy flats on the western side. Led by Slocum, Wheaton, and Ballou, the Second Rhode Island followed the road as it curved sharply south, continuing onward for another quarter mile or so, until they reached the second ford, the one over Catharpin Run, a tributary of Bull Run. This was known as Sudley Springs Ford because of its proximity to the little hamlet of the same name.

Led by Company D, the Second Rhode Island forded Catharpin Run between 9:00 and 10:00 A.M. Their passage turned the water cloudy with the mud churned up by thousands of feet, human and equine, but the four thousand men and fifty-odd horses of Hunter's Division needed to draw water here.

Again, the Second Rhode Island crossed the stream, then "General Hunter halted his command for about a half hour," to an hour.[65] (All times approximate to within twenty minutes.)

The men eagerly spread out along the village lanes of the west bank, broke ranks, drank, filled their canteens, and rested. Again lucky to be first, the Second Rhode Island enjoyed a forty-five minute break.[66] Their hunger was another matter. Those men who had any hardtack left had to soften it in water before eating it; the biscuits were so solid they could break a man's teeth if he bit into one dry.

The officers had been mounted for six hours now—this was a good opportunity for them to dismount and stretch their legs. Aides watered the horses of Colonels Burnside and Hunter, who sat down together to eat a lunch that was most likely not hardtack biscuits.

The mounts of the other officers were watered alongside the canteen details, and then the horses were tethered to trees or bushes, the reins left long enough so they could lower their heads to graze. Most of the horses, including those of the cavalry, were "in a starved condition" because the few wagons had no room to carry bags of oats or corn. Even Burnside complained about it, so likely Sullivan's Jennie was also hungry. "Colonel Corcoran's was greedily eating newspapers, in front of his hut, before he mounted him, the morning of the 21st," to lead the Sixty-ninth into battle.[67] However, the artillery horses were allowed to drink as they forded the run, because unharnessing them was not only time consuming, but left the guns vulnerable in the event of a surprise attack. Major Sullivan Ballou rode Jennie into the run to allow her to drink, handing down his own canteen to a soldier to fill for him, then dismounted along the pathway.

If he went off to join fellow officers in speculative banter, he would have found most of them spying into enemy territory from a nearby hill, which rose propitiously above the ford. About 10:00 A.M., Colonel Porter, Captain Griffin, and a cluster of Union officers had gone up there for a look at the plains of Manassas on the other side of the run. Their luck continued, for at the top of the hill was one of those typical farm fence made of split rails. These fences could be as many layers high as the terrain and type of farm animals required, from five to nine rails tall. Stacked horizontally and wedged between X-shaped endposts, they were stalwart and strong enough to keep a bull and cows in their own pastures. They were useful to a soldier as a ladder to gain a few extra feet of height for observation—and great death traps for units of soldiers slowed down clambering up one side and down the other while advancing into battle under enemy fire.

This morning, on this hill by Bull Run, some of the Union officers climbed this convenient fence to gain a few more feet of height over the treetops enclosing the run, and thereby noted a dust cloud rising in the distance on the plains. One officer pulled out a telescope and reported the most horrible sight—troops headed toward them, banners fluttering, the telltale sun now glinting on their musket barrels.[68] Colonel Porter saw,

A wooden rail fence. Note the two hills behind the fence. *Author's photo.*

> two columns of dust . . . we saw it coming but did not know whether it was General Heintzelman coming in from above or whether it was the enemy. We rather thought it was Heintzelman, as we expected him there if he was successful. We could see some blue pantaloons. We could distinguish this, when Major Woodbury came to me and said we had got now to Bull Run, and suppose we go down and have a consultation.[69]

Porter probably saw the First Louisiana Special Battalion moving in with Evans, some of whom wore Zouave-style uniforms, which included baggy, blue-and-white-striped pantaloons. At the distance of a mile or more, these may have appeared solid blue. Heintzelman's Minnesotans and Massachusetts men did not wear such uniforms. Porter hurried forward to inform Hunter and Burnside. "I mentioned what I had seen to them. They had not observed it before."[70]

Apparently, Sullivan and the colonels conferring at the head of Hunter's column did not even know Heintzelman's division had failed to find their assigned side road—Heintzelman apparently had not thought to send word forward to Hunter, Burnside, or Porter.

As the two colonels were digesting the news and their lunch, General McDowell arrived and traded much the same news with Hunter and Burnside. Having come all the way up the line, he should have known Heintzelman's position. The only conclusion to make at the moment was that General Beauregard had discerned the Union flank march on the northerly end of his battle line and was sending troops to his left flank to stop them. Clearly dismay was expressed over the detour and their guide—some said he was a Southern agent—but the decision had not been his to make, only the recommendation of it. It had added four miles and two hours to their march, further delayed the attack, and dangerously exhausted the troops. McDowell and his aides arrived and directed Hunter to move onward.

> During our halt to rest and fill canteens at the Sudlay spring, [*sic*]Captain . . . H. G. Wright of the engineers, and Lieut. Frank Armstrong with General Hunter's body guard and twenty well mounted men of the Second Dragoons, went forward on our line of march reconnoitering for more than a mile, encountering no enemy. . . .[71]

Colonel Porter, by some reports, rode with them. A few mounted Rebel pickets were seen doing an about-face, probably also cavalry, but these were to be expected and they aroused little concern. The main object of interest was the "heavy columns of dust within three miles of us," which "indicated the approach of the Rebel Infantry" moving in to meet them.[72] At "about 10:30 A.M. General Hunter ordered the advance to be sounded, and we renewed our march along the Sudley road." Sullivan and the other officers quickly remounted. It took some minutes to reform the men and get the column underway. At the run, the skirmishers were increased to five companies, all taken from the Second Regiment.[73]

> Gov. Sprague and Capt. Woodbury then went forward to reconnoiter but could learn nothing. McDowell and staff rode by. "As he passed, he said, "in a few moments you will be in action."[74]

Hunter himself rode out at the head of his division, and invited Slocum and Wheaton "to ride with him a few yards in advance of the leading Company." This party was "moving briskly along looking ahead for an enemy," sure that they would meet them in battle a couple of miles ahead, lined up in a proper text book formation once Hunter's column and the dust cloud met up on the Sudley–New Market Road, south of the turnpike, auspiciously nearer to Manassas.[75] Companies F and D were among the skirmishers, who today contrary to the custom of throwing them well in advance, ". . . moved directly on the flanks of the column."[76]

From the low point of the ford at Catharpin Run, the road rose up a gentle hill to higher ground and the hamlet of Sudley. Sudley Methodist Church sat on higher ground to the right, and was a simple country church of rectangular shape, a modest and straightforward building that had neither steeple, parsonage, cemetery, nor wall enclosing the church yard. It had a gabled roof, and a single arched entry door on the side nearest the road, twelve windows to let in the light and a single hearth and chimney. Built sometime between 1822 and 1845 on land deeded from the Sudley plantation of the Carters, it was set on a small knoll above the flood level of the runs. When the land for the church was cleared out of the oak forests on the hillside, some trees were left to shade the church. It was the only brick building for miles around, and its front facade had been white-washed at some point.

> It was Sunday, and, as we approached the field of battle the villagers appeared making their way to the chapel, which was afterwards used for a hospital, surprised to see the large body of armed men that were invading their peaceful hamlet. How quiet our march had been through the woods, in the early morning! How bright the sunshine, as we came out into the open fields of waving corn and grain! In another hour all was changed.[77]

The congregation was well aware that Union troops were as close as Fairfax County, and some residents had already taken refuge with relatives deeper into the county. But as far as they knew, all the combatants were down below the turnpike—the Confederate headquarters area—or at the Union camps surrounding Centreville. Those who stayed thought it was safe enough to make their way to the church for the Sunday services. Despite strong rumors of an imminent battle, they must have been horrified to find the Union Army going past their door!

Accompanied by teams of horses pulling artillery carriages, the procession must have seemed endless, the army enormous. Passing through was one Yankee soldier for every man, woman, and child, White and Black, in the entire county. By the time Heintzelman's Division came through, *double* the population of the 8,565-person county had passed, every one of them an invader! Among those watching were Amos Benson, his wife Margaret Newman Benson, and the twelve year old orphan niece they were raising, Molly Benson Dogan. Their farm, Christian Hill, was on Sudley Road, just south of the church. Young Molly was very impressed, "It made a memory on me. It was a beautiful sight to see the sun glistening on the sabers, but it was a scary sight."[78]

Most of the Civil War was fought on Southern land, much of it in Virginia, but whether there, in border states, or Pennsylvania, the marching armies gave no advance notice to civilians. It became a pattern for civilians to hide in the basements of their homes or flee to the nearest strong stone building that hopefully remained out of the direct center of the battle. Many civilian residents of Sudley Springs went to Sudley Mill and Hotel, which flanked the ford.[79] Sudley Methodist Church might have been used as a shelter—except that it had another fate that warm summer's day: the army surgeons traveling with Hunter's column had noted: "a stone church, pleasantly situated in a grove of timber, directly on the side and to the right of the road we had passed on advancing to the attack."[80]

Many Rhode Islanders recalled less bellicose Sundays spent back home. The more devout—on both sides—felt a battle on the

Sabbath was profane and unlucky. The Northern Army now moved down a better and wider road, one used regularly by carts going to and from Sudley Mill. Corporal Rhodes said, "we now took a side road that skirted a piece of woods and marched for some distance, the men amusing themselves with laughter and jokes, with occasional stops for berries."[81] This was the Sudley–New Market Road, a local thoroughfare that led them south through farm country, past "a few comfortable-looking houses" on farms owned by longtime settlers, it intersected the turnpike a couple miles farther down.[82]

> [This] road leading from Sudley Springs south, and over which Burnside's brigade marched, was, for about a mile from the ford, thickly wooded whilst on the right of the road for about the same distance the country was divided between fields and woods. About a mile from the ford the country on both sides of the road is open, and for nearly a mile farther large rolling fields extend down to the Warrenton Turnpike.[83]

Evans was at this time hurrying to arrive first in the area, to gain the prize of the choice of ground. As he shadowed the Union troops, his men moving up along farmland, it was not hard to conclude the enemy column was making for the twin fords at Sudley.

Evans perceptively chose the first open hilltop south of the Sudley Ford on which to establish his defensive position. The battlefront this day was to be eight miles long. Matthews Hill, named for the four siblings who lived in the farmhouse at its crest, sat at the uppermost end of this front. Whoever sat on top of this hill controlled all the roads below. Not only did these roads lead to the rear of all Southern positions on the west bank of Bull Run, but one led straight to Manassas Junction, only five miles away. The Confederates had to hold the hill at all costs or have thousands of Yankees pouring into their midst, demolishing their lines.

He deployed six companies of the Fourth South Carolina, plus the Louisiana First Special Battalion, a tough unit recruited from the dock and jails of New Orleans. Known at this point as Wheat's Battalion, the unit became known to history as the Louisiana Tigers. Company B, the Tiger Rifles, whose name came to represent the entire battalion due to their notoriety, wore the distinctive Algerian-inspired Zouave uniform: a red shirt, a soft fez-style hat with a foot-long tassel, and the blue-striped pantaloons seen in the telescope.

For the second time today, Evans deployed like a man afraid that his small force would be swarmed by the enemy if they ever saw just how modest it really was, and gambled that would go undetected in the initial confusion. The more usual deployment would have been right on the top of the crest of a hill—but there he could be seen. Instead, he placed the hillcrest between him and the Union forces—and positioned his troops, on its far side, about 250 yards from, and 30 feet below, its summit.

Directly behind Evans's position on Matthews Hill were two more hills. The second was known as Buck Hill, and had no dwelling. It dropped sharply down into the valley bisected by the turnpike. At the road junction stood the Stone House occupied by another, unrelated family named Matthew. A brook known as Young's Branch, after a nearby farmer, had etched its way along the course of this valley, meandering down the rear slope of Buck Hill, its steep banks cutting across the intersection of the turnpike and Sudley Road. The slopes of these hills undulated with swales and rises that impeded clear lines of view.

Farther south, the third hill had two dwellings. Flatter on its summit than the others, it was called Henry Hill, named for navy surgeon Dr. Isaac Henry. Henry House occupied its summit; to the northeast and closer to the Warrenton Turnpike was a drover's tavern, serving the teamsters traveling along the pike to Alexandria, operated by Jim Robinson, a free black half-related to Judith Carter-Henry and

Robinson's house. Evans planned to fight from his position on the reverse slope of the first hill, while his reinforcements slipped in behind him from their staging area on the third hill. This area of northeast Prince William County was to become the focus of the daylong battle of First Manassas.

Evans began the battle with only the two guns of the Lynchburg (Virginia) Artillery supporting him, commanded by Lieutenant Davidson and his gun crew on the right, along the turnpike near the entrance to Robinson's lane, and Lieutenant Leftwich, with the second gun, to the left on Buck Hill. They, too, were in place and waiting for the arrival of Hunter's troops. By using spherical case shot in an upward angle, the gunners could reach the unsuspecting Union soldiers when they came onto the fields. The gunners were to earn a reputation as some of the enemy's "most annoying batteries."[84]

Other nearby hills were higher, and Evans and his men could be fired upon from those hills—but the Union troops were not yet on those hills. Most important, he was in place fifteen to thirty minutes before the Union troops arrived. Ten regiments, only three miles or so away, were already en route to him: General Bee and Colonel Bartow were moving their brigades at the double quick, expected within the hour.

> About eight o'clock . . . [Bartow] dashed up and exclaimed, "Get ready, men! The battle has been raging for two hours on our extreme left, and we must go there at once." Soon we were in line and off at a double quick for our left. . . . Frequently Colonel Bartow would gallop up to troops or artillery in position as we passed along in their rear and inquire, "Is this our extreme left?" He was told it was not, and on we trotted. My! how tired I was and how the perspiration oozed from every pore![85]

Hampton's Legion was following, and behind it was Jackson's brigade.[86]

A Union unit was in a position to note what Evans was doing, but they had some trouble interpreting it: Colonel Richardson had a great view from his observation point at a log house high on a hill further east and south of the turnpike. He noted "three bodies of men" coming into battle position with the Confederates. "One body was probably two regiments, and the others were one regiment each, as much as that." Yet, he did not send word of these troop movements to McDowell. About noon, his commanding officer, "Colonel Miles showed himself to us. . . . I showed him, with a glass I had, the bayonets of some of the men coming in front of us on the road—the last detachment." Miles also did not believe it was the enemy, and so did not report it to McDowell, either.[87]

Hunter and McDowell were therefore on their own when it came down to assessing what they had just glimpsed themselves. One of the few advantages they had had in this battle was the element of surprise—and now it appeared they had lost it. If they could not reach the Warrenton Turnpike before the Confederates gathered there en masse, their entire thrust would be useless.

Aware that the enemy was advancing to meet them, and moreover that they could not see over the rolling hills or through the trees to know just where the Rebels were, the Second Division went into battle formation. Hunter ordered his lead regiment, the Second Rhode Island, to divide in half; he kept five companies on the road and sent five companies on ahead to act as skirmishers, fanning out through the woods on both sides of the road.

Fate had led Sullivan Ballou and the Second Rhode Island Volunteer Infantry right to the most pivotal point of the four-square-mile battlefield—Matthews Hill—the keystone of this battle for both sides. This first full battle of the Civil War could be won or lost based on its opening moments, affecting the entire future of the war.

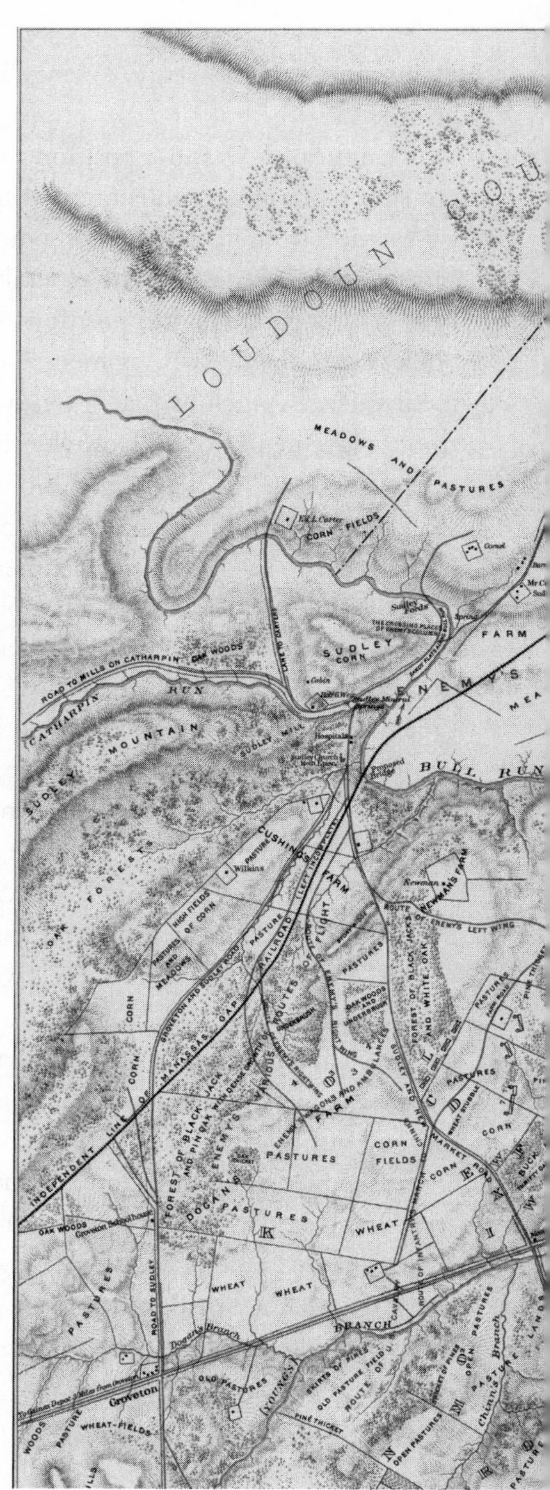

This map of the battlefield is a copy of one drawn for General Beauregard. He occupied the area from June 1861 to March 1862, which allowed ample time for detailed surveys. The map presents in detail the terrain traversed by both armies in preparing their attacks, and the morning and afternoon phases of the battle. *From author's collection.*

2.

N
Magnetic Meridian
W
E
S
ENEMY'S WAGON ROUTE
OF ENEMY ON THE NIGHT OF JULY 20
OAK FOREST
PASTURE LANDS
OF FLIGHT
G.E.Carter
MOUNTAIN VIEW
RED HILL FARM
Poplar Ford
PRIVATE ROAD OF FARMS
Barn
Geo.W.Lee
CORN
ENEMY'S ROUTE OF FLIGHT
BROOM SEDGE AND BRUSH
GRIGSBY'S FARM
CUB RUN
OLD PASTURE FIELDS
Mr. Grigsby
GRIGSBY'S LANE
Old Shop
OLD PASTURE FIELDS
OAK LEVEL FARM
Simpson Pomeroy
POMEROY'S FARM
Mrs. Spindle
Orchard
PASTURE
HILLWOOD
WHEAT
CORN
WARRENTON TURNPIKE
CULTIVATED FIELDS
THICKETS
Van Pelt
CORN FIELD
OAK WOODS
BEST'S FARM
ROAD FROM LEWIS FORD
Mrs. E. CARTER'S FARM
CORN
FLAT LANDS PASTURE
PINE WOODS
OAK WOODS
Lewis' Ford
BULL RUN
Ball's Ford
ROLLING
Portici
CORN FIELDS
ALEXANDRIA AND WASHINGTON
MEMORANDA
Surveys were made of the roads leading viz:
From New Market to Sudley,
From Groveton to Sudley,
From Groveton to Mrs. Spindles (West of Cub Run)
(Warrenton Turnpike)
Surveys also were made of cross lines connecting
fields, woods, roads &c. of Chinns, Mrs. Henry's,
Bogans, Lewis Carter's, Matthew Lee's & Sudley places.
No survey was made of enemy's route of
ingress by road through forest. It was taken
only from general observation.

CHAPTER SIXTEEN

"A Cannonball Don't Pay No Mind"*

Major Sullivan Ballou Is Badly Wounded

10:00 A.M. to Noon July 21, 1861

Sarah Ballou and the rest of Rhode Island craved accurate news about their men, but it was not readily available. On July 19, the *Providence Press* became the first paper to break a century-old tradition and put the war news—instead of advertisements—on its first page. The *Providence Journal* put out an extraordinary Sunday edition, on July 21, but its news was days old—between the time correspondents spent getting to the telegraph and the time required to set the type at the print shop, there was no real-time news. That Sunday edition published a blend of meaningless gossip, wrong information, and accurate facts. Far away in the North, it was hard to judge if the skirmish at Blackburn's Ford was the "real" battle that had been expected, or something else.

Conflicting newspaper reports notwithstanding, on the small

* From the Civil War song "Two Brothers."

country road leading out of Sudley Springs, the stage was being set for the fighting debut of Sullivan Ballou. On the morning of the twenty-first, the Confederates were defining the terms on which the opening action would be fought, and choosing the ground which gave them best advantage.

While the brass rode on ahead, Sullivan Ballou remained with his men, leading the eleven hundred civilian soldiers of the Second Rhode Island along a country road, bounded by woods that did not allow their column to deploy into a battle line of any breadth or depth, and blocked their view of what lay alongside them. Each step forward was a surprise to these strangers to Prince William County. With the column moving so briskly, the skirmishers were not able to get out very far in advance. When the Second Rhode Island ultimately "debouched," or came to the point in the road where the trees were replaced by the farmlands of the Benson, Watkins/Cushing, Newman, and Matthews properties, they would be totally exposed and vulnerable to attack. If anything untoward happened along this road they would also be virtually alone. It did not matter that, at this moment, thousands of troops were in the pipeline behind them, because only the ones in front could be first to confront the enemy. They were led that day by one of the more interesting brigade commanders in the Union Army.

Brigade Commander Ambrose Burnside, an Indianan whom Rhode Island chose to lead its First Regiment because of his arms-manufacturing background, had studied at West Point in the class of 1847. After service in the Mexican and Indian wars he, like so many others, left the army for a civilian career. In 1852, he settled in Rhode Island and began manufacturing breechloading rifles* of his own design.[1]

* Breechloading rifles, including the carbines used by the cavalry, did not require their cartridges to be rammed down the barrel with a ramrod; their cartridges were loaded at the firing point, midgun.

In an age of ostentatious male facial hair, he wore and gave his name to a particularly flamboyant set of "side burns." In other ways, he did little to call attention to his person, wearing no scarves, feathers or sashes. His men noted he had "no low desire for effect."

> He sought from this service no personal glory, no mere military distinction, which has such charms for weaker men. He desired no pomp, no parade, no flattery, no preferment. He simply wished to do his duty to the men under his command; to the parents, sisters, wives and friends who had entrusted these precious lives to his keeping; to the State which had recognized his abilities, and had sent him forth; to the country which needed his counsels and his arm; to God.[2]

A deeply religious man who knelt in prayer each night before going to bed, he also had boundless, unwarranted trust in the "goodness and honesty of others," which may not have served him well in the political cauldron of the Union Army.

> This sense of responsibility was marked in his care for his men when in command of the First Regiment. . . . The regiment was required to do everything which it had to do, and was not spared in the hour of extremity. But in all the details of its life, in camp and field, its Colonel was very particular in his personal supervision and knowledge of every officer and man. "How does the first Rhode Island succeed in getting transportation, food and shelter so easily?" was sometimes asked by members of other regiments who were left on the road without forage, rations and tents. The reply at the department headquarters was: "Because the First Rhode Island has a Colonel that knows how to take care of his men."[3]

Care and compassion have been among the hallmarks of Rhode Island social values, from the founding of the colony to the present day. Rhode Islanders valued public-spirited citizens who volunteered at critical times, accepted the burdens of accomplishment without seeking honors, and were faithful in applying themselves to the responsibilities they had accepted. Burnside fit this model perfectly, and it was for this he was loved and revered—not his military genius.

The skirmishers and the party of riders had already moved a mile or more down the road, when Burnside and the mounted officers realized that the left hand group of "skirmishers had become hopelessly entangled in the woods and undergrowth." To make matters worse, they were also "impeded . . . greatly by a wide and winding creek with very steep banks." This slowed the skirmishers down so much that "the head of the main column had passed them." The officers conferred and agreed to move on, "two or three hundred yards further . . . pass these woods, and reach open ground where we could deploy readily, and readjust our old or establish a new skirmish line.[4] They were unaware the Rebels were only thirty yards away, concealed in the woods.

> Two volleys of musketry were heard in the distance, and soon after Col. Porter of the 2nd Brigade, who was in advance, returned to Col. Hunter and reported the enemy in front.[5]

It seemed somebody had shot at the Dragoons. Private Greene reported the men in the ranks were "as unconcerned as though nothing but a drill was going on, picking black berrys along through the pastures and chatting to ourselves."[6] But the officers had a greater sense of urgency.

> We were hurrying forward to an indicated point, for a halt, when we received from the Rebels, secreted in the woods left of us, the most suddenly unexpected attack I ever new [*sic*] them to make.[7]

The hills and depressions of the area south of Sudley Springs created a deceptive landscape that was used to advantage by the Confederates in establishing defensive positions. This view looks south to Henry Hill from Matthews Hill. The house in the distance is Henry House, where the afternoon battle took shape. The tall trees were planted in the twentieth century. *Author's photo.*

In this photo, only the treetop in the distance reveals that the land drops off ahead. Both Evans and Jackson deployed their units on the opposite side of such hills, from which they mounted surprise attacks. The pine thickets scattered around completed the cloaking of the Confederate forces. Another ridge is visible in the distance. *Author's photo.*

Officers and men alike reacted, all the way back down the line.

> Our troops could hardly have been more astonished if they had been attacked at night while asleep in camp. So utterly unlooked for were the terrific volies we received from woods we never imagined in the enemy had had time to reach![8]

Sullivan looked far down the road to figure out what was occurring. Rhode Island responded in three stages. Their artillery accelerated its pace: "Our battery, after passing Sudley's church, commenced to trot in great haste to the place of combat."[9] The men on the road took cover. Corporal Rhodes reported,

> On reaching a clearing, separated from our left flank by a rail fence, we were saluted with a volley of musketry, which, however, was fired so high that all the bullets went over our heads. I remember that my first sensation was one of astonishment at the peculiar whir of the bullets, and that the Regiment immediately laid down without waiting for orders.[10]

The Union soldiers already in the woods crashed on through and out the other side, and began chasing the Southerners they saw; these Confederate skirmishers were the Catahoula Guerrillas, a company of Wheat's Battalion. The Confederates withdrew back up the hill and down the far side, rejoining their unit—as planned. The five hundred Rhode Island skirmishers were ordered to climb over a fence that bordered the field at the roadside, and charge up the hill. Among them was Corporal Samuel English of Company D, who gave his own inexact calculations of the size of the enemy:

> We advanced double quick time yelling like so many devils. On our arrival into the open field I saw I should judge three

> or four thousand rebels retreating for a dense woods firing as they retreated.[11]

> The regt was at once ordered to charge on them which they did and of all noises that was ever made was made there. They started with a furious yell and them bloody Georgians fled in all directions. Those were the ones that wanted to meet the RI boys face to face and I guess they did meet them face to face but they did not stay there long.[12]

Taking stock of their situation, heeding the direction from which the bullets came, the startled Rhode Islanders saw a group of men firing at them from the crest of a hill on their left. Standing behind a rail fence, firing their muskets down at the Rhode Islanders, was the full Louisiana Special Battalion. The Louisianans may have been firing high, as nervous, green soldiers often did—none of the Yankees was hit—and the Rhode Islanders likely did the same when they shot back. The accuracy of the firing mattered little at this point, for the whole purpose of this demonstration was to provoke the Yankees to charge the hill, to do battle here, and abandon their push south. Evans was buying time for the reinforcements coming up behind him, including additional artillery.

The Yankees had to defend themselves, and the balance of the regiment behind the skirmishers could not parade down the road under fire. They knew not where more forces might be concealed further down the road; there was little choice, it seemed, but to engage. This meant the Northern commanders had to improvise tactics well before their anticipated battle at Manassas.

Colonel Hunter chose at this time to go up the open field with the skirmishers without leaving orders for the rest of his division. The balance of Burnside's brigade, "in the confusion incident to the first sudden attack," continued their march down the Sudley Road.[13] The First Rhode Island had the good sense to halt in the

Rhode Island vs. Louisiana

A Tiger from the Louisiana Special Battalion in a Zouave uniform. His cartridge box and bowie knife can be seen at his belt, his haversack and canteen at his sides. His bayonet is fixed. *Courtesy of the Anne S. K. Brown Military Collection, Brown University.*

A Rhode Island soldier wearing the Burnside blouse belted tight, with red blanket, canteen, and haversack. *Courtesy of the Anne S. K. Brown Military Collection, Brown University.*

The battle flag used by the Confederates at First Manassas closely resembled the Union flag, especially when hanging still; it was later redesigned. *Courtesy of the Anne S. K. Brown Military Collection, Brown University.*

Members of the American Brass Band of the First Rhode Island Regiment acted as medics, stretcher bearers, and ambulance drivers during the battle. *Courtesy of the Rhode Island Historical Society, photographer unknown.*

The national colors of the First Rhode Island. *Courtesy of the U.S. Army Military History Institute.*

open land where the brigade had planned to regroup and to form a battle line at the bottom of the field, way on the far right of the action as seen from the road. Lacking orders though, they stood idle for "nearly three quarters of an hour" while the Second "maintained alone an unequal contest, with the Rebel brigade in position."[14]

Seeing the Rebels fall back under pressure, Hunter ordered in the balance of the Second Rhode Island, "and the Battle of Bull Run or Manassas began in earnest."[15] The men on the road "hurried forward, rounded a small piece of forest that concealed the crest of the hill . . . and came out on an open field beyond. To the left side of the hill, the men could see a house with outbuildings surrounded by a farmyard. Colonel Slocum gallantly led into action the balance of the Second Regiment—five companies that had been posted on the left in a small clearing.[16] Sullivan Ballou brought his men forward. Rhodes said,

> Colonel Slocum gave the command: "by the left flank—MARCH!" And we commenced crossing the field. One of our boys by the name of Webb fell off the fence and broke his bayonet. This caused some amusement. . . .[17]

The men quick-timed across the field four abreast in the flank march they had practiced in camp. The men of Battery A watched the infantry deployment with interest: "Every man seemed to move at once. And all threw off their haversacks and blankets and away they went on a quick run over the hill—after they had climbed over the rail fence."[18]

Just as they had done on the ramparts of the earthen fort at Fairfax, the Rhode Islanders gave the Narragansett shout as they charged, described as a long, drawn out "Hurrah," "a fierce, loud, shout. Such a yell . . . has seldom been heard since the Indian war whoop has become extinct."[19] "It was afterwards ascertained from a prisoner that the rebels thought we numbered 20 or 30 thousand from the noise made by us while making the charge."[20]

Evans's artillery waited until the Yankees had gained the hill before firing in an arc high above the heads of their own troops, over the crest of the hill, and down on the Rhode Islanders, who nonetheless, "formed under full fire, and marched past the Confederate battery as coolly as they did on a dress parade."[21] It seemed that the hours of drilling had paid off; the men exceeded the officer's expectations. Lieutenant Colonel Wheaton enthused,

> It was a severe ordeal for troops who had never in battle smelled burnt powder, or witnessed the frightful scenes and bloody carnage of actual war! It was new to all of us and if our men were dumb founded to find the enemy just where we did not believe it possible for him to be, their officers were as much astonished and delighted to see the cool bearing with which the troops withstood the withering [*sic*] fire of the enemy and the dashing gallantry with which they followed their officers in charging into the woods, speedily routing the rebels and driving them through and quite a distance beyond. . . .[22]

It was hardly cause for rejoicing, however, when the officers realized that the Confederate skirmishers had retreated into a battleline on the opposite side of the hill, near where a "large corn-field" sloped down to "a piece of woods in front."[23]

> We found the Rebel main line established in a cultivated field some one hundred yards in front of the position or crest on which the Second Rhode Island was halted. The enemy laid low in a ridge of undergrowth on the edge of the field, and though both sides maintained a continuous and to us a very destructive fire, the Rebels were very little exposed while our troops whenever they raised to fire over the crest became fair targets to the enemy.[24]

It was tough gauging what the Confederate's strength really was when their battle line faded off into pine thickets. The only way seemed to be to probe them. Rhodes reported,

> We marched to the brow of the hill and fired. . . . The enemy opened fire from several masked forts and cut down our men in great numbers. We loaded and fired as fast as we could. This was the time that Wm. Aborn was shot. He was fighting bravely when he was shot through the back. He fell into a dry ditch and then got out and crawled into the woods. He no doubt died immediately* as the wound was a bad one.[25]

The Second also lost the first of their officers in the charge up the hill—Lieutenant Levi Tower, Company F, fell gravely wounded.

> As the Second Rhode Island Regiment advanced . . . the fronting thicket held by Evan's South Carolinians poured forth its sudden volleys, while the two howitzers flung their grape-shot upon the attacking line. . . .[26]

Hunter had only this single regiment on the field, and no others coming into the fight. Whether by his order or someone else's, Burnside's units, which had marched on down the road, seemed to have returned and lined up in front of the First Rhode Island on the west side of the road. No one called for them to take the field within a time frame that might have made any difference to the fate of Sullivan Ballou or the battle. Everyone knew the First Rhode Island was to be held in reserve; there were no plans to deploy them in a first strike. In front of them were "the Seventy-First New York, [which] formed in line in a field, through which

* In fact, Private Aborn survived his would, his imprisonment, lived to fight again, and died in 1919.

ran an abandoned railroad embankment, behind the woods." Also deployed in front of them, the New Hampshire men were still further to the right.[27]

By the time Porter's Brigade arrived in the rear at Sudley, there was real concern and "orders were sent back to the heads of the regiments to break from the column, and come forward separately as fast as possible."[28] The artillery, too, was urged forward, Major Barry reported,

> As soon as the column came in presence of the enemy, after crossing Bull Run, I received from General McDowell, in person, directions to superintend the posting of the batteries as they severally debouched from the road and arrived upon the field.[29]

Porter, however, once he gained the Sudley–New Market Road, rushed his troops past the clearing and the battle, continued on down the road, and deployed west, on open land, behind Burnside's Brigade, a location from which his troops could not readily reach the present battleground.[30] So when Hunter sent down orders for Porter to bring up his brigade and go to the support of the Second Rhode Island, this brigade could not respond. Up on the field, Hunter could not know how tangled up the brigades were back on the road, out of his sight. At this point, both brigade commanders were occupied with disentangling their brigades.

Hunter was "endeavoring to induce my advanced guard to charge the enemy with the bayonet," when he himself took a bullet or shrapnel in the neck and left cheek, flesh wounds that bled so profusely as to cause concern about the jugular vein being damaged.[31] He may have been too far forward with his men, too close to danger in an exposed situation. A small flurry of action occurred as some of his men took him back down the hill for medical treatment. Chaplain Woodbury was a witness:

> Col. Hunter, the division commander, came down the road wounded and supported by his aides. As he saw Colonels Burnside and Porter he said to them, "I leave the matter in your hands. Slocum has gone bravely in* and is driving the scoundrels."[32]

Hunter's wounding required the command staff to reorganize themselves. Sullivan Ballou, Frank Wheaton, John Slocum, and their Rhode Islanders had the misfortune to be left alone with their men, taking fire without reinforcements or orders, while the prolonged change of command was effected.

One unit at least knew the infantry needed help. Hearing the firing ahead, the Rhode Island Battery knew its business and moved forward through the line, scattering men out of its way on the narrow Sudley road.

> At once we were in motion. Have you ever seen a battery move into action? It is a spirited sight. Cannoneers swing to their seats on the limber chests, horses are spurred and lashed into a gallop, officers draw their sabers and shout their orders in ringing tones.[33]

Certainly the Union deployment was not moving quickly enough to suit McDowell:

> At this moment General McDowell rode up in great excitement shouting to Captain Reynolds: "forward with your light battery." This was entirely needless, as we were going at high speed for all were anxious to come to the rescue of our Second regiment.[34]

* Another description says "went in handsomely" (Hennessy p. 53).

Infantry jumped forward to assist the battery, breaking down a section of wooden fence so the cannons could enter the field.[35] Spotting the guns approaching, Colonel Burnside issued the next order, to Reynolds. "Forward the Battery!" Reynolds inquired, "In what position?" "Forward the Battery!" Burnside repeated. A battery must, of course, be placed in proximity to infantry who can protect its gun crews while they go about their business. "No position being assigned the Battery, Gov. Sprague posted it on the right of the 2nd Regiment."[36] "In quick time we arrived in the open space where the conflict was raging already in its greatest fury. The guns were unlimbered, with or without command; no matter, it was done."[37]

The Rhode Island Battery immediately came under heavy fire, and suffered casualties. Still, the men persevered and got the guns to the proper position on top of the hill, where they began the complicated process of unlimbering them. They could not immediately open fire.

> When we reached the open field the air seemed to be filled with myriads of serpents, such was the sound of the bullets passing through it. Above us and around us on every side, they seemed to be hissing, writhing and twisting.[38]

The early hours of the Battle of First Manassas resembled a chess game, in which each deployment of force by one side was met by its match on the other. On the Confederate side of the battlefield, the Staunton (Virginia) Artillery commanded by Captain John Imboden, had ridden ahead of the infantry of General Barnard Bee's brigade. Just as the Rhode Island Battery galloped onto the field, Captain Imboden was positioning his guns to participate in the attack against the Rhode Islanders, and was watching Reynolds from atop Henry Hill, two hills behind Evans's. He noted,

> We went into position none too soon; for, by the time we had unlimbered, Captain Ricketts [should be Reynold's] battery appearing on the crest of the opposite hill, came beautifully and gallantly into battery at a gallop, a short distance from the Matthews house on our side of the Sudley road, and about fifteen hundred yards to our front. I wanted to open on him while he was unlimbering, but General Bee objected till we had received a fire, and had thus ascertained the character and caliber of the enemy's guns. Mine, four in number, were all brass smoothbore 6-pounders.[39]

The Rhode Island Battery hurried to open fire first, without adjusting the range of the guns. It might not have mattered all that much since they had neither a clear view nor knowledge of where in all the smoke the enemy was positioned in front of them. A shot or two would give them their range while announcing their battle presence to the enemy soldiers who had so far enjoyed all the advantage. It also buoyed the morale of the infantry: "Never did better music sound to the ears of the Second Regiment, than the quick reports of our guns, driving back the advancing foe" and "hurling destruction among the rebels," from a position on "our right."[40]

Imboden's Staunton Artillery wasted no time either:

> The first round or two from the enemy went high over us. Seeing this, General Bee directed us to fire low and ricochet our shot and shrapnel on the hard, smooth, open field that sloped toward the Warrenton turnpike in the valley between us. We did this, and the effect was very destructive to the enemy. . . . So long as Bee, Bartow, Evans and Wheat were on that side we were firing over their heads.[41]

Imboden's cannons had a deadly effect on the Rhode Island infantry, as "a perfect hail storm of bullets, round shot and shell

An artillery crew in action, loading their gun. *Author's collection.*

was poured into us, tearing through the ranks and scattering death and confusion everywhere."[42] As the only Union artillery functioning at that moment,

> the Rhode Island Battery . . . was immediately exposed to a sharp fire from the enemy's skirmishers and infantry, . . . and to a well-sustained fire of shot and shell from the enemy's batteries posted behind the crest of the range of hills about one thousand yards distant. This battery sustained in a very gallant manner the whole force of this fire for nearly half an hour.

All hands pitched in to help. "After Frederic Bub, a gunner of the 2d battery was killed, Reeder, the well known colored servant of Capt. Reynolds, took his place and worked bravely."[43]

The much-debated question, to dodge or not to dodge, now took on real meaning to the men. Seasoned combat troops who had a clear line of sight to the muzzle flashes of firing cannons, learned to visually track their trajectory and, whenever possible, dodge the cannonballs. Perhaps outfielders had an advantage? This method worked only for solid shot—regular cannonballs—not for canister or cluster rounds, which exploded midair into many pieces of shrapnel that did not fall predictably and could be neither tracked by sound nor dodged. While the booming of the powder charge expelling the shell from a cannon could be heard, the whistling sound could only be heard once the projectile passed by a soldier's ears. As James Cooper Nisbet of the Twenty-first Georgia put it, "you never hear the one that hits you."

When Imboden's Staunton Artillery ricocheted its solid shot off the hill top, the Rhode Islanders did not have a clear line of sight to the Confederate guns. It was dangerous for officers of rank who could not duck and dodge while on horseback and who might not do so for pride of setting a bold example to their men. Officers also had to watch both the battleground in front of them, and also check behind themselves to see how their men were responding to orders. It was harder and more dangerous to position their troops to fight in front of artillery.

In a line hundreds of feet long, men blazed at each other with muskets and cannon from only two hundred feet apart. The Louisiana Tigers fired an estimated five volleys into the Second Rhode Island—that was several thousand bullets—though many went high and others wild.

After the Rhode Island Battery had been firing at the Confederates for about a half-hour, at just after 11:00 A.M., Evans and Wheat decided to try and capture it. The first charge of the Tigers was reported by some to have coincided with a period of inactivity on the Union side, perhaps related to the removal of Hunter from the battlefield. The Second was ordered to the right to stop the charge.

> Next orders were given for us to fall back and protect our battery as the enemy were charging upon it from another quarter, and then we saw with dismay that the second R. I. regiment

> were the only troops in the fight; the others having lagged so far behind that we had to stand the fight alone for 30 minutes; 1100 against 7 or 8 thousand.[44]

The charge was repulsed, the battery saved and prisoners taken, Rhodes noted,

> About this time, Private Thomas Parker, an Englishman in Company "D." captured a prisoner, a member of the Louisiana Tigers Regiment [Battalion], and as he brought him back to the line was spoken to by Colonel Slocum.

Each side was learning just how tough the other was.

> This battle will always occupy a prominent place in the memory of every man of the battery. They all expected to find a disorganized mob, that would disburse at our mere appearance; while, to the general surprise, they not only were better disciplined, but also better officered than our troops. . . .[45]

The battle line of a single regiment could inflict random death upon the Southern men, but it was insufficient to drive them from their position. Although Evans was sorely pressed, the Confederates reinforced their line quickly: Reinforcements, from the Second and Third Brigades of the Army of the Shenandoah, arrived in supporting distance in the nick of time.

General Bee, the senior officer, had command of two brigades in the column that had followed him from the railway junction to the battle. The unit at the head of the column was the spunky Fourth Alabama, commanded by Colonel Egbert Jones. Only 558 of their men were fit to fight—measles had hit the regiment hard—and some of them were engaging in this battle against the orders of their surgeon.[46] When they had earlier received word that a major

Union force was moving toward Sudley, they "ran through pine thickets and cedar hammocks, over ditches, gullies and briar patches, fences, swamps, hills and valleys [in order to have a] chance to get a dab at the Yankees."[47] Completely unobserved by the Union command, the Fourth Alabama formed into their battle line formation on Henry Hill, loaded their weapons, and waited for further orders.[48]

Next to arrive on Henry Hill was a smaller force, the Seventh and Eighth Georgia, which made up the Second Brigade commanded by Colonel Francis Bartow.

> Presently from an officer of an artillery company that we were passing, Colonel Bartow received the answer that he was at the extreme left. We had come four or five miles . . . we passed through a skirt of woods, then into a cornfield, the stalks being about waist high. We were halted, and Lieutenant Colonel Gardner said, "Let the men load their guns and lie down."[49]

The Confederates, further reinforced by the rest of Bee's Third Brigade, the Second Mississippi, and two companies of the Eleventh Mississippi, now had troops on three consecutive hills, Matthews, Buck, and Henry, and the valleys in between. Evans fought on the first, Matthews, with Buck Hill at his back. He could be rapidly reinforced from the rear by the troops on Henry Hill. If Evans was pushed back further, he could retreat to Henry, join up with fresh troops, and make a stand. If the Union troops pursued Evans down the back slopes of Buck, over the next hill, crossed the stream, and started up the front slopes of Henry, they would be raked by the Confederate artillery above and surprised from below by regiments newly arrived by railroad.

These were General Joe Johnston's men, the ones he had cannily held in reserve for deployment to the left flank. Already in the first hour of the battle, the troops from this second Confederate army that Union General Patterson failed to divert, were beginning to improve the odds of victory for the South. The Confederates had brought these men from Winchester, over sixty miles away, and were already using them to shore up their line, while McDowell had not yet gotten all his primary attacking divisions to the battlefield.

Tyler's 7,100 men were still on the far side of the Stone Bridge, where had the commander of the First Division mounted a more convincing diversion, he might have easily routed and panicked the two hundred tired Carolinians into retreat, punched through at the Stone Bridge without opposition, come right up behind the Southerners at Matthews Hill, caught them in a squeeze play with Hunter's Division and forced a surrender. But his assigned role was to stay on the eastern side of the run, and McDowell's permission was required before he crossed the bridge. Today, when his initiative might have counted for something, he was obeying orders to the letter. Meanwhile, Keyes was just catching up to the rest of his division, after deferring to Hunter's and Heintzelman's divisions on the turnpike.

Beauregard's attack plan failed because three of his brigades either never received their orders, the courier too afraid to deliver it, or they had received confusing orders about the placement of their troops before "the orders to attack would be given by the Commander-in-Chief."[50] Neither Generals Longstreet nor Jubal Early was able to figure out his meaning, so they held their existing positions pending clarification. It seems grammar does matter, even in the middle of a battle.

Evans had been "fighting for time and he had managed to delay the Federal advance for about an hour. The fighting was not bad for beginners. . . . It was doubtless influenced by the morale gained on the 18th."[51] When Evans knew he could hold out no longer, he went for help, galloping back to the next hill to bring reinforcements back with him.

In response to Evans's pleas, General Bee rode up to his brigade and ordered the Fourth Alabama into battle with the cry, "Up Alabamians!" Major Egbert Jones, six feet three inches tall, recently a state senator, led his men toward the fray. The Alabamians were shelled as they ran down the northern slope of Henry Hill, then were protected as they crossed Young's Branch creek. They ran up Buck's Hill and came into the battlefield arena, but went into the center of Evans's line onto very bad ground. Fired upon, the Alabamian line stopped. Colonel Jones ordered them to lie down and fire. They held a miserable position, however, which prevented them from immediately entering the fray. With no clear line of sight at any target this ground was very untenable to try to hold. Some men reckoned that the reason their colonel held this position so tenaciously, "with severe bearing," and holding them there "against great odds," was to prove wrong the men who had insinuated he would avoid battle.[52]

General Bee next sent the Seventh and Eighth Georgia toward the front of the line. Bartow led them to the rear of Alabamians, where they were held in a cornfield while their exact placement was determined.

Captain Griffin's West Point Battery had roared down the Sudley–New Market Road at a gallop, and "drove through the ranks" of the Seventy-first, scattering the men, before coming into battery about 150 yards to the right of the Rhode Island and New York batteries, just south of Porter's position.[53] This gave them excellent range over most Confederate operations on the east side of the road. The Union gunners were now dropping too many shells into the Georgians' midst—Bartow galloped back and told their colonel to send the Eighth forward to the right of the Alabamians, to extend the Confederate line.

Continuing forward, the Confederate regiments used available cover, until they were sent toward the right flank on Matthews Hill by Bee, who was not accompanying each regiment to its place but, like a traffic cop, was sending them in the direction in which they were needed. The Seventh, he still held back.

The Eighth Georgia did a right-flank march at the double quick, a route which took them to the northeast, flanking Rhode Island lines. They described being "led to the extreme right of the attacking force, going under the cover of woods, between us and the enemy's artillery. We were led up and deployed in a pine thicket."[54]

> We entered a pine sapling thicket, and were halted directly north of the house. Then we faced to the left and started forward. A few steps brought us to the edge of the thicket and, looking up the hillside, we saw the "Bluecoats" literally covering the earth. They were in the shrubbery in the front yard, down through the horse lot, behind the stables and barns and haystacks.[55]

Sullivan Ballou "was in charge of the left wing of the Regiment," the most dangerous place on the battlefield. While Union troops down on the road were "forming to the right rear" of the Second Rhode Island's battlefield, where access to the hill was unobstructed, none were deploying toward the left, where thickets edged the road. It was obvious no troops were positioned to support the left of the Rhode Island line, where Ballou was, "which was in an open field and utterly exposed to a flank attack . . . and the enemy saw that. . . ."

Lieutenant Colonel Wheaton was in charge of the right wing; Colonel Slocum was not commanding troops per se but rather was analyzing the situation. "Some movement of the enemy attracted his attention and he went to a little rise in the rear of our left." After "looking intently to the left" and observing the enemy a few minutes, Slocum called out to Wheaton and beckoned him over to join him. "This I did exchanging a word with Ballou as I passed him!" Sullivan was now the only field-grade officer commanding the fighting of the entire Second Rhode Island battle line, because the others were scouting.

What Slocum saw in the woods perhaps "some two hundred and fifty yards" away, was ominous:

> Mainly hidden by the undulation and slope left of us, . . . a continuous line of Rebel troops filing past our left flank to a position perfectly enfilading our line and which if they could maintain or even have time to form on for an attack rendered our position not only fatally defective but absolutely untenable.

Although "a man's head could only occasionally be seen, it was evident the enemy was making a movement in that direction." Slocum had no way of knowing that Evans was not deployed that far east—that his force was too small to spread out that way. The troops Slocum's eagle eyes had spotted creeping silently through the woods were the Eighth Georgia, the second regiment of General Bee's reinforcements deploying.

And so the two top officers of the Second Rhode Island Regiment were standing in an exposed position where, under different circumstances, they could have been picked off by well-aimed rifle shots. They were temporarily safe only because the Eighth Georgia were still coming into position and had not been given the order to fire. "Slocum and myself were greatly disturbed at this discovery fearing an immediate attack before any preparation could be made to meet it. There were no reinforcements at hand," Wheaton recalled.[56]

Porter claimed to have relinquished command of his brigade to his senior officer when Hunter left the battlefield because, as senior colonel, command of the division fell to him.[57] However, he appeared not to leave his brigade until he had moved them where he wanted them, a high spot on a ridge on the west side of the road. Porter's actions showed he was more focused on intercepting the dust cloud than in participating in the engagement already underway on the hill, to which he gave no attention at this point. His attitude seemed to be that Burnside's troops had gotten themselves into this little scrape and they could get themselves out of it. The Southern commanders, however, were working as a team, swiftly sending in more and more reinforcements. Burnside, an emotional man under normal circumstances, seemed to be in high tide, bounding about the battlefield so much that he is placed by eyewitnesses in many locations, just minutes apart.

Neither Burnside, McDowell, nor Porter realized the Union Army line was close to being overwhelmed from the left. But McDowell had reason to be preoccupied, since a telegram from Scott had been brought to him on the field.

> It is known that a strong reinforcement left Winchester on the afternoon of the 18th, which you will also have to beat. Four new regiments will leave to-day to be at Fairfax Station.[58]

Once he read the telegram, McDowell acted swiftly. He ordered Tyler to immediately break through at the Stone Bridge and link up with Hunter. This would increase the ranks of the attacking divisions to 26,000 men.

> I ordered over the 69th and 79th New York, a Wisconsin and another regiment, with orders to come into line on the right of the troops that we saw attacked, which we supposed, from the appearance of them, to be Hunter's Division.[59]

At the edge of the pine forest, Slocum and Wheaton knew they had very little time to act. "There probably would not be time to call the reserve regiments to aid us in this very critical situation of affairs," Wheaton later recalled.[60] He meant of course, the ones just down the road, not Runyon's or Miles's divisions.

The 4,500 men sitting idle on the verges of the road below them had yet to experience battle. All morning long, only one or two regiments at a time would come off that road and charge up that hill. The inexperienced Union commanders, green in combat, failed to bring up enough men to overwhelm the enemy. This lack of judgment, which had left one regiment and battery to battle three of the enemy's for forty-five minutes, was just about to cost the Union the battle.

The Union troops were barely holding on facing the enemy in front. They knew an attack from the left might shatter the line held so long and so bravely, resulting in "defeat and disaster."[61] "A Rebel . . . battery on our right front had damaged us considerably killing and wounding many men, its range so accurate, that two of its shots passed through our Regimental Flag."[62]

Wheaton said, "Both Slocum and myself considered the situation alarming" and decided to do what they could to be ready to receive and repulse, or delay such an attack. To meet the new threat growing on its left, Rhode Island had to change its line. "Minutes seemed to be hours" while Wheaton "ran to the left of the regiment to tell Ballou our Major that Slocum wanted our two left companies reformed and thrown back at an angle to meet a flank attack."

Sullivan was placed in charge of executing a critical maneuver upon which the fate of the battle—and his regiment—now rested. Wheaton noted, "To attempt to reform or throw back our own left Companies was a very difficult matter, and under fire a movement the oldest veterans can hardly be expected to form without confusion."[63] Redeploying a battle line under fire was tough enough, but pulling it *backward* at an angle was vastly more difficult, and risked giving the appearance of an opening the enemy could rush in to exploit. Yet, if the men could accomplish it, they would present part of a hollow square, or phalanx, one of the oldest and most effective defensive infantry postures ever invented. In such a position, the Eighth Georgia could not rush them from the side or from behind. But that would be at best a temporary solution. When Slocum cried, "Wheaton, I am afraid two Companies might not be enough . . ." he was stating the obvious—they could only play for time, hoping reinforcements could come up to their assistance before they were overwhelmed.

It was critical that Company C, led by Captain Nelson Viall, the color company, receive and understand the order to create a new formation, so they could lead with the flag. Just like medieval knights, Civil War soldiers rallied on their flag, following its movement around the battlefield if they were unable to hear verbal commands. In the heat of battle, it was a communications device as well as a symbol of allegiance. The color sergeant of the Second Rhode Island Regiment, John M. Duffy, was "a very brave young fellow who stood like a man of iron in the face of the hottest fire." Duffy did not relinquish the flag even when "a cannon ball came rushing through the silken folds of our banner." His comrades said "that fellow alone is worth a thousand men."*[64]

The Rhode Island line was several hundred feet long, and even a practiced orator like Sullivan could not expect his shouted commands to be heard over such a great distance, above the roar of cannon and musket fire. Like actors on a stage, officers needed to be able to make large gestures, reinforced by a sword, a hat in the hand, or a hat on a sword to be seen and understood. Moreover, the officer executing such instructions needed to be out in front of his troops, and normally at a right angle to them, so he could be seen by as many of them as possible. It helped if he remained on his horse—not only was he more easily seen by his men, but he gained a few extra feet of height to let him see further.

* Duffy was promoted to lieutenant on July 22 for bravery on the field.

It is probable that Sullivan urged his men to hurry into their new position by moving back and forth in front of his line, on horseback, guiding Jennie with his knees, and by neck rein held with one hand, while the other pointed the way. Although the cannonade was constant, his sense of duty overrode his concerns for his own safety out in front of the line. Whatever fears or presentiments he took privately into battle, "Ballou showed himself among the bravest of the brave. He was constantly in the thickest of the fight, cheering the men by his voice and by his example, to yet greater valor."[65]

Jennie, too, proved a brave battle horse—she was not one who spooked or bolted at the sound of gun or cannon fire as some mounts did.* This was a lucky thing for Sullivan, for the shower of iron projectiles was steady. "One ball struck in front of our first platoon and bounded over their heads; another struck in front of our platoon, and covered us with dust."[66] Cannonballs that "bound" and "bounce" are smooth bores. Rifled projectiles, traveling at a faster velocity, burrow into the earth when they land. The Rhode Islanders were at that moment being shelled by the four smooth-bore guns of Captain Imboden's Staunton Artillery, as well as Leftwich's gun, all of which were firing six-pound shot.

Sullivan had been lucky so far not to be hit by any of the thousands of bullets whizzing past him, but at this point, his luck ran out. His premonition was about to come true.

One of the Confederate guns fired a six-pound ball of death in an arc over the hill and into the Rhode Island line. There it found a victim too busy to notice its arrival. "Major Sullivan Ballou, while bravely assisting in changing the position of our center, was struck

* Just over a year later, General Robert E. Lee was thrown from a borrowed horse when it spooked at cannon fire. He sprained his hands so badly that he could not ride, and went to the battle of Antietam in an ambulance.

from his horse by a ball from a . . . cannon, and also left unconscious and dying."[67] "He was shot in the leg close below the knee, the ball blasting through and killing the horse."[68] From other accounts by men severely wounded in battle, it is possible to infer his reactions. Two wounded soldiers eloquently described the sequences of sensations after being hit. Wrote one,

> The loss of so much blood had made me cold. I shook until I almost feared that I would shake in pieces. . . . My limbs were as cold as ice and still I wanted water. . . . I did not at the moment feel any pain, only a numbness all over the body. I felt as if someone had given me an awful jar, and fell as limber as a drunken man. I could not even tell where I was hit.[69]

The other felt

> a sharp, electric pain in the lower part of the body, and then a sinking sensation to the earth; and falling, all things growing dark, the one and last idea passing through the mind was: "This is the last of earth."[70]

Ballou's men ran to help their fallen major. "The soldier who raised him says he merely said 'Oh,' once or twice, prolonging the sound as the horse fell on him."[71] A horse falling heavily on a man can injure him, too. They withdrew him as gently as possible from the dying Jennie. Someone immediately applied a tourniquet above the knee to stop the hemorrhaging or else he would have bled out within ten minutes. They placed him near the fence, which offered little shelter, but kept him from being run over during troop movements.

Private Clifford Fuller of Company C of the Second Rhode Island reported being within ten feet of their "commanding

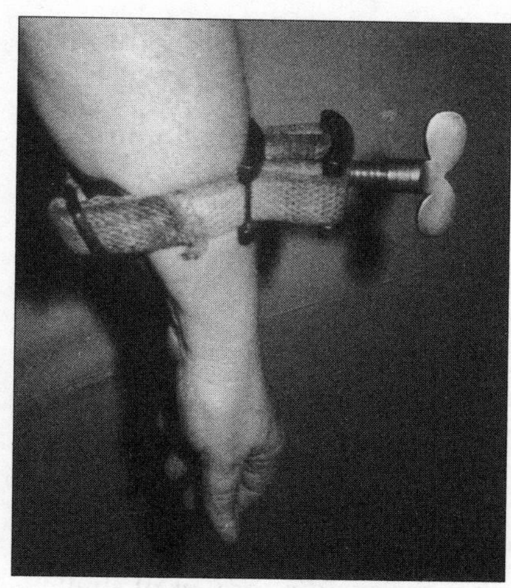

The thumb-screw tourniquet changed little between the Revolutionary and Civil wars. A canvas band held the device on the limb and, when the thumbscrew was correctly positioned over a bone and tightened, the clamp stopped the flow of blood. *Author's photo at the Yorktown Victory Center.*

officer" who was shot and fell from his horse.* A crowd of officers gathered around their leader. "Even after his fall, he continued to shout to the men to press onward," and the Ballou legend commenced.[72] Certainly he knew his wound was severe, and by telling his helpers to leave him, he may have been expressing fulfillment of his premonition. His own blood was comingled with that of Jennie's, so he must have looked even worse off than he was. This may account for those witnesses who reported seeing him dead on the battlefield at this point. Lieutenant Ames reported "I saw his horse laying [*sic*] upon the field with a hole in his side as large round as the top of a hat,** made by the ball that killed the Major."[73]

His leg, however, had not been severed, but "crushed."[74] A six-pound cannonball is three and one half inches in diameter and, had it hit him full on the leg, the limb would have been blown completely off. Soldiers of both armies lost limbs that way in this

* Although Fuller named him as Colonel Slocum, the circumstances match Ballou, under whose command Company C was.

** The crown of a top hat measures six to seven inches.

battle. Sullivan must have been hit only by the edge of the ball, striking his booted calf just below the knee and shattering the twin bones of his lower leg, the tibia and fibula. Poor Jennie caught most of the impact.

When Sullivan went down, Sergeant Albert W. Chappell from Company I, a twenty-seven-year-old painter from Woonsocket, helped him. Several men would have pitched in, perhaps making a litter from their muskets or jackets. Chappell wrote home a few days later,

> Major Ballou received a cannon shot through the leg, I was close to him and carried him to the rear amid a shower of shell and bullets. As he fell he was forming the Companies in line of battle. He suffered much, but said to me "O it is magnificent cause. O if I could only hear the cry of victory, I would be content."[75]

Slocum knew, but could not absent himself from his post at this critical juncture. He shouted over to Wheaton, "Poor Ballou has fallen!" Wheaton took over the left side of the division and started giving the "necessary orders for this change in our left Companies." Around this time, Lieutenant Colonel William Gardner ordered the men from Rome, Georgia, to charge and open fire. They were now close enough to see that "the enemy were about 100 yards, and many of them protected by stables and stacks of straw and hay, and all by a fence."[76] This volley may well have been part of a coordinated charge ordered by Evans and Bee at about this time.

The Rhode Islanders were taking fire on their left flank, but they were giving it, too. Private Virgil Stewart of Company A Eighth Georgia, mourned,

> Among our dead [was] perhaps the most beloved young man in the town: Charles B. Norton, a clothing merchant. . . .

> when [he] was shot, he pitched forward and fell across me, for I was on my knees firing. He was the first Light Guard Member to be killed. It was a horrible sight; men falling all around, some dying quickly and the others making the day hideous with their groans. Considering that so many were our boyhood friends, it was all the harder to bear. . . .[77]

Wheaton said, "we were already enfiladed and our left squarely turned." At this grim and desperate moment, Wheaton "heard voices in the woods in our rear, and looking back to my delight saw what I supposed to be the head of a regiment coming to our support at this most trying moment." He raced over to greet them and lead them in.

> I was quite out of breath an[d] greatly exhausted when I reached the officer at the head of the troops coming out of the woods behind us. The officer was Captain Francis W. Goddard followed by his Company of R.I. Carabineers. Any reinforcements would have been considered a Godsend at that juncture, but I was more than gratified to find that they were commanded by an old schoolmate and boyhood intimate. . . . We hastily shook hands . . . and ran as we conversed to the left of our regimental line, where I pointed out to him the enemies position, and the slope behind which he was undoubtedly preparing his advance for an attack we could not without the newly arrived aid have met.

The enemy most assuredly was. Melvin Dwinnell described how the Georgians second charge was stopped by the Carabineers.

> After falling back about 200 yards we halted, faced about, loaded, and again rallied upon the enemy, at the same place as the first charge. After firing one or two rounds, we discovered a

> large, heavy column on our right, that we had supposed to be a portion of General Bee's command, were enemies and were carrying the stars and stripes; just then they opened fire upon us, and we were obliged to fall back again, out of this cross fire.[78]

The Georgians began taking heavy losses. Zettler noted, "I saw a line of Federal soldiers coming through the thick undergrowth not more than fifty steps distant. They fired a volley down our line.[79] Melvin Dwinell of Company A wrote, "The balls whizzed about us like hail in a thick storm. There were probably 6000 men firing upon our force of 600. Most of Col. Gardner's command loaded lying down and rose up to fire." He noted how men just five steps apart from each other were felled.[80] In the second charge, Colonel Gardner, shot in the ankle, told his men to shoot on, but it soon became obvious the position was now too hot to hold:

> Everyone around me seemed to be dead or wounded, I determined to take my chances of saving myself by getting away as fast as I could. I had not heard an order to retreat, but I felt that was the thing to do. . . .[81]

Rhode Island Captain Goddard's intuitive grasp of the situation and quick deployment of his men in just the right position blocked the enemy's forward movement. The Carabineers were a special-operations team formed out of men already in the First Regiment, men who were good shots and had trained together in camp, doing extra rifle drill to perfect their skills. They used new Burnside breech-loading carbines with a greater range, accuracy, and rate of fire than anything the Georgians had, and the men of the Eighth thought a whole regiment was coming up against them. The Georgians were expert shots, but the rifled carbines gained the upper hand: "After twenty minutes, we were ordered to fall back to a place where the intervening ground would protect us from the enemy's fire."[82] They left some dead and wounded behind, among them Private R. DeJournette of Company A, the Rome Light Guards.

Wheaton rejoined the Second Rhode Island Regiment, joined Slocum now commanding the left, and continued back to the right. Regimental reinforcements were finally coming up and he wanted to position them on the Rhode Island right flank. Colonel Slocum decided to move forward one more time, probably to check on the withdrawal of the Rebel forces in front of them. He apparently climbed the rail fence in the Matthew's pasture to get a better view. Like Major Ballou, this time his luck ran out.

Georgian private DeJournette had managed to escape detection by Union troops by staying quiet and hiding in some bushes. From his vantage point atop the fence,

> Colonel Slocum . . . discovered him in the bushes. Attempting to draw his pistol, he said, "Your life, you rebel!" For some reason, he could not get out his pistol easily, and seeing DeJournette level his musket at him, he cried out, "don't shoot." But the Georgian did shoot and killed him too.[83]

The colonel had not been killed outright, but the combination of his losing consciousness from a bullet wound to the head and so much bleeding made him appear to be a goner to DeJournette, who somehow made good his escape and lived to tell the tale. Corporal Rhodes saw him fall and rushed to his aid.

Slocum became the next Rhode Island officer to be carried to the triage center set up in the Matthews farmhouse, which was now farther behind the lines. Dr. Harris was there, already attending Ballou, Tower, and various enlisted men.

In the early days of the Civil War, a memorable patriotic quote guaranteed to swell the hearts of sympathetic readers when read in the hometown newspaper was attributed to every dying officer above the rank of captain. When Captain Tower was hit as the Second first assaulted the hill, he said, "Turn me over on my back boys and go in."[84] Slocum was no exception, with his "Leave me and avenge my death" attributed to both Mayor Ballou and Slocum, though given the latter's well-documented inability to speak right after the injury, it is likely apocryphal. Regardless, melodramatic Northern press accounts of his death were avidly read by receptive audiences on the Rebel side, who vowed not to forget the heavy death toll inflicted on their troops by the Rhode Islanders and began formulating plans for revenge.

At the time of Slocum's removal from the battlefield, the Second Regiment and Reynolds' Battery on top of Matthews Hill had been exposed to the whole fire of the enemy for nearly an hour, and were sustaining more casualties.[85] "We were in full relief on top of the hill, while they were a little behind the crest of the hill. We presented a better mark for them than they did for us."[86] Private Green of Levi Tower's company wrote home,

> The first man that I saw fall was shot through the head . . . but in less than 10 minutes 20 lives were taken for his but when our gallant Slocum fell that tried our hearts and we rushed madly on and when Gov Spragues horse was shot from under him and he rushed for a dead mans rifle and rushed to the front it was then we showed them Rhode Island force. Major Ballou was shot from his horse. they picked our officers of[f] dreadfully and we picked theirs to[o]. . . . One old gray headed man that was in most of the battles of Mexico left his body in the field at bull run.[87]

Burnside, struggling against Murphy's Law to get reinforcements up on Matthews Hill, ordered the rest of his brigade—the Second New Hampshire and the Seventy-first New York—to leave the road and support the Second Rhode Island. For all their practice on the streets of Washington, the former struggled to extricate themselves from the logjam of troops on and around the road, and could not form up as promptly as required. The latter, still scattered from Griffin's Battery galloping through their position, took too long.

Disgusted, Burnside ordered them to lie down in place, and bellowed for the First Rhode Island to run through them and onto the field.[88]

> They did so most unwillingly, and we marched through and over them with a front almost as straight and steady as on dress parade.[89]

Or, as another more droll diarist noted, "We were to be kept as a reserve. But the first thing we knew the lion had his jaws open and we walking in like flies."[90] Burnside, who likely did not yet know Ballou and Slocum were down, shouted out,

The Second New Hampshire and Seventy-first New York struggled to achieve a battle line after their forces had been scattered along the Sudley Road. Note how the sun glints off these rifles, the very thing that gave away the secret advance the morning of the battle. *Author's photo of a reenactment.*

> "Forward, First Rhode Island!!" We moved out of the woods to the brow of the hill . . . passing on the way the dead body of Captain Tower, of our 2d, and many others. . . . Soon from the hill above we saw Burnside beckoning to us "forward, over the fence." To the fence we went. How the shot did drop around us.[91]

Everyone on that hill faced "death on the right, death on the left, and in front."[92] The Confederates' situation was also growing desperate. Evans and Major Roberdeau Wheat, the commander of the Tigers, decided to make a final charge against the Rhode Islanders to see if they would break. It is certain that both the Eighth Georgia and the Tigers charged, and the Fourth Alabama at the very least repositioned. Brandishing their hugely impressive Bowie knives, yelling like the Irishmen they were, the Tigers bolted out of their lair and swarmed toward the weary Rhode Islanders, led by their six-foot-tall, three-hundred-pound commander, Major Wheat. They came close to succeeding, and "had advanced within twenty paces of our lines." The soldiers of the Second desperately struggled to repel them.[93]

> While preparing to make our final effort to keep our battery out of their hands, the 1st R.I. regiment then came filing over the fence and poured a volley out to them that drove them under cover again.[94]

The wounded still had not been evacuated, and one soldier deploying with the First reported, "We passed Major Ballou lying wounded by the fence."[95] Chappell said, "As we were bearing him through the wood our First Regiment came up, and Major Ballou urged them onward. They went forward with a shout."[96]

The Tigers were repulsed, suffering heavy casualties and now pulled back and withdrew toward the Sudley Road. The

Alabamians took the field next, passing dead, wounded and retreating Louisianans. Running up the lower, southerly shoulder of Matthews, past Evans' old position, they came under fire again. They veered into woods, where they had to step over the bodies of dead and wounded Tigers as Jones led them forward into the open. As they neared the crest of the hill, they met Wheat's men falling back. The First Rhode Island and Fourth Alabama faced each other across a cornfield.

The Seventh Georgia were still held back behind them as a reserve. Through the smoke, Georgians and Rhode Islanders peered at each over their muskets. Bee put the rest of his own brigade, the Mississippians, between the Alabamians and Evans. This way he could shore up Evans, whose men had been fighting the longest.

On the left, in military terminology, it was the Confederate right facing the Union left. On the other side of the line, the Confederate left facing the Union right, Alabama had repositioned and was waiting to welcome the First Rhode Island. Fighting under their major, Joseph Balch, the latter

> arrived at the edge of the hill we were greeted by a storm of musket balls from a large body of men, Alabaman troops, drawn up in a corn field in front, which whistled past our ears, each minute dropping one of our brave fellows, for about half an hour, though I cannot speak with any certainty of the lapse of time. We returned it with interest, every man advancing to the front, firing and falling back to load as quick as possible.[97]

There was so much smoke in that little valley that it was hard to see where to go. When the First Rhode Island color guard moved to help establish the readjusted line, it became a target.

> Our color sergeant had been wounded. One of the guard who had taken the flag had also been struck. Still another who had taken it from him, had been disabled. Yet the flag was there, waving defiantly in the front and center of our line.[98]

"Most of the men were as cool as cucumbers—each would load, pick his man, and take deliberate aim."[99] The man shooting at the color bearer was thirty-year-old Private John Fowler from Company D, Fourth Alabama:

> I am proud to say that I fired the first shot, that was fired in the ranks of the "Cane-brake rifles.". . . I waited until I saw him good. . . . I drew as fine a bede [*sic*] on him as any one can with a rifle, and pulled trigger, and down went the stars and stripes.[100]

For the next hour, the Alabamians held on. The men ran forward to get a view of the enemy, fired their muskets, then ran back, laid down and reloaded. Colonel Jones choreographed their advances and retreats, sitting on his horse, Old Battalion, one leg thrown over the pommel of the saddle, until the horse was wounded and Jones had to dismount.[101] "Gallant Col. [Egbert] Jones . . . during the hottest of the engagement, sat conspicuously on his horse, as calm as a statue giving orders as they came."[102]

Frank Wheaton coordinated the deployment of the Seventy-first New York adjoining the Rhode Island battle line, where they "fought well and bravely by our side." Presently someone cried, "Hold, we are firing on our own men!" This slackened our fire for a moment, when "the Colonel* rode up and told us to keep up the fire"; this was the day's first documented episode of uniform color

* Wheaton is referred to as colonel in accounts about the later part of the battle even though his promotion occurred the next day.

confusion.[103] "Together we drove them down the hill, and concealed in the bushes they blowed away at us, who, exposed on the summit of the hill, returned the fire."[104]

The Union was beginning to bring more artillery to bear on the Confederate line, in hopes of breaking it. The Seventy-first New York Militia's howitzers had followed them onto the battlefield, positioning to their left, the men now glad they had hauled them all this way. Captain James B. Ricketts' battery came up less than half an hour afterwards, and was posted to the left of and immediately adjoining Griffin's over on Dogan's Hill.[105] These two new batteries had a good vantage point over the battlefield and could turn their guns onto any new troops climbing up Matthews Hill from the turnpike.

Things were looking up for the Union as Burnside's final regiment now took the line at about 11:30 A.M. New Hampshire's original position was untenable, so they formed a protective horseshoe around the Rhode Island Battery, which proved to be a very wise move.[106]

The Eighth Georgia continued to battle on the right of the Fourth Alabama, trying to take the Yankees in flank, the Georgians scattering in a thicket, in the shrubbery in the front yard, down through the horse lot, behind the stables and barns and haystacks. "Seemingly a thousand rifles were flashing and the air was alive with whistling bullets."[107] Corporal Rhodes felt the fury of the battle intensify for the Yankees:

> There was a hay stack in front of our line and some of the boys sheltered themselves behind it. A shell from the enemy struck and covered the men with hay from which they emerged and retook their places in line.

Unfortunately for Major Sullivan Ballou and the others who had been wounded, this maelstrom of battle raged for another half hour, and the Union ambulances were unable to remove anyone from this section of the battlefield.[108]

Both sides suffered casualties. The battle itself seemed to be at an impasse. Burnside decided to seek a detachment of Regular Army Infantry, and rode back to Colonel Porter in person because he did not think an aide could induce Porter to hand over his regular troops. Although Porter felt Burnside was panicky when he galloped up crying, "For God's sake, my men are being cut to pieces!" he agreed to divert his Regulars and send them to the aid of the Rhode Islanders.

> They sweep up the hill where Burnside's exhausted, shattered brigade still lingers, and are greeted with a shout of joy, such as none but soldiers, who are almost overpowered by a fierce enemy, and are reinforced by their brave comrades, can give. Onward they go, close up to the cloud of flame and smoke rolling from the hill upon which the rebel batteries are placed—their muskets are leveled—there is a click, click—a sheet of flame—a deep roll like that of thunder, and the rebel gunners are seen to stagger and fall.[109]

The Regulars delivered the death blow to the remaining Georgia boys on the left, and the Confederate position on Matthews Hill began to fail, as their line broke and units pulled back unevenly. Colonel Jones was on foot when an artillery projectile (possibly canister) from the Rhode Island Battery hit him in the leg. "Jones fell wounded, gasping, he yelled 'Men don't run,' but they left him behind in the retreat."[110] Jones then sustained a second wound, the odd angle of which suggested he may have been hit again once he had fallen. A bullet struck him in the hip and then burrowed down the flesh of his leg. His men unable to come back for him, enfeebled from loss of blood, "surrounded only with the dead and wounded, supporting himself with his arm thrown across his saddle," Jones remained alone in this valley of death.[111]

Burnside galloped in front of the reinforcements he had obtained from Colonel Porter, leading the Regular forces onto the field at a double quick, to the accompaniment of loud cheers. *From author's collection.*

Colonel Egbert Jones, a lawyer and state legislator, commanded the Fourth Alabama, but fell wounded in late morning. *Courtesy of the State of Alabama Department of Archives and History.*

With the pullback of the rebel line, "the order was given to cease firing."[112] Burnside requested permission to withdraw his brigade to the rear to replenish ammunition. Captain William W. Brown of the First Rhode Island said, "After two hours fight we were allowed to stack arms for a brief rest. . . . About this time a shout of victory went up."[113]

Even their own mothers would scarcely have recognized these begrimed and bloodied men. When they grinned, upon seeing friends alive, their teeth and lips were smeared black with powder from ripping open the cartridges. The weary Union soldiers flung themselves on the ground underneath the trees, grateful to be out of the broiling sun and concentrated on tending to two things only: their thirst and their injured. "On all sides, from wounded and unwounded, the cry went up, 'water, water, water.' "[114]

Rhose Island Casualties[115]

Killed	Wounded	POW	Missing
First	12	33	1
	13	39	
Second	19	64	410
	23	49	

less than 10% of regiment

Men who had now been on the march and in action for twenty-two hours straight, now helped their walking wounded along. Litter bearers carried out the seriously injured down to the waiting ambulances. Private Albert Sholes, First Rhode Island, was sitting in the shade next to his friend Irving Haskins when, "here to us came the news of the wounding of Colonel Slocum, Major Ballou and Captain Tower, and that they had been borne to the little house at the rear of our line of battle."

Securing permission from Captain Van Slyck, I at once went to the cabin especially to know if I could render services to the man whom I had always loved and honored Colonel Slocum.

No physician or attendant was with them when I entered. Colonel Slocum, Major Ballou and I think a third man lay on the floor at the side of a room, while I passed Captain Tower lying in the yard near the door of the cabin with the pallor of death on his face. I gave utterance to some expression of sorrow when the Colonel said, "I am glad you came, Albert; can't you get us some water?" I removed their canteens, cutting the tapes and went to the old sweep well nearly up on the line of battle.

Shoals apparently visited the officers at the Matthew's House, the triage center, where the men were probably awaiting ambulance transport to the field hospital down the road, for he does not describe them as having received surgical care. The lack of attendants is puzzling, but the doctors and chaplains who worked at this house during the day may have been out on the field assisting newly discovered wounded. The ambulances did come up the hill to this house later in the day, when the battle had moved a mile away. There were precious few ambulances and it may have been too risky to have them trundling up and down the hill while shells were still flying. So it may well be that Elisha Hunt Rhodes returned later to make his door litter to carry Slocum down to one waiting on the road. The sweep well may have been used to water the farm animals. It had a balance arm to raise the bucket and would be labor saving if the hilltop well were deep. Still, it remained a dangerous place to get a drink.

As I drew up the bucket, a man waiting by the well at my side, fell dead, as he was struck by a fragment of shell. The canteens

> were filled and returning, I gently raised the head first of Captain Tower in the yard, then of Major Ballou, and finally of the Colonel, gave them to drink and moistened their faces with my handkerchief. When I had helped Colonel Slocum, I eased his position as best I could and then sat or half lay beside him with his head upon my arm, while I wiped the blood away as it slowly oozed to his lips, til he suggested that I return to my company. He bade me goodbye and as the tears ran down my face he said, "Never mind, Albert, it's all right." Captain Tower's mind was wandering and he was near death as I left, but the voices of both Colonel Slocum and Major Ballou were comparatively clear and their eyes not unsteady, so that I hoped to see them again.[116]

Young Sholes, whose writings are not well known, is the only eyewitness who reported Slocum speaking, and his testimony comes the latest in the sequence of caregivers who wrote down their experiences. Perhaps Slocum's earlier inability to speak came from being dazed from the concussion of the bullet, which "plowed a furrow in his head." Although his wistful account was written years after the fact, and is almost apocryphal in its reverential wish-fulfillment, Sholes is very explicit about all other details. The blood oozing to the lips of his dear colonel did not bode well.

Shortly after the battle stopped, Corporal Rhodes apparently returned to help.

> When it was decided to place the Colonel in an ambulance, I took the door from its hinges with my gun screw driver, and assisted in carrying him on this door to the ambulance. . . . When we left I brought his spurs and delivered them to the Lieu. Col. He thanked me very kindly for them.[117]

Slocum may have been accompanied by the regimental surgeon.

The new colonel, Frank Wheaton, who received field promotion from Governor Sprague the next day, noted wistfully, "my father surgeon F. L. Wheaton carried him from the field."

But where was the ambulance going? The inexperienced Union Army medical director had thought casualties would be so few that they did not commandeer in advance any buildings in the army's rear for use as a field hospital. Even though they expected to be fighting in a more forward location, main hospitals were always located outside the combat zone itself. On this day, William S. King, medical director of the army, calmly noted how they had to scurry to catch up with the grim reaper.

> After the action had fairly commenced and the wounded and the dead were seen lying on the field in every direction, I dispatched Assist. Surg. D. L. Magruder to the rear, with directions to prepare a church (which I had observed as we passed before arriving at the scene of action) for the reception of our wounded, and also to send the ambulances forward as rapidly as possible to pick up the wounded and the dead. In a very few minutes the ambulances made their appearance, and continued throughout the day to visit every part of the ground which was accessible, so as to be within reach of those parts of the field where the fighting was going on and wounded were to be found.[118]

Slocum's transport in a jostling ambulance, over rutted dirt roads to Sudley Church field hospital, down the hill and over a mile away, might have jostled bullet or bone fragments, doing more damage. There may have been bleeding in the brain. At the field hospital, Slocum received tender if hasty care, the doctor being unable to offer suitable life support for such a serious injury. The regiment had reason to regret "our gallant little Col.—now no more."[119] Lieutenant Tower may have expired by now, for he was later buried nearby.

Sullivan, too, had high priority for evacuation, though he was concerned that other wounded with a greater chance of survival be treated first. Likely the men called out to their popular major with encouragement as he was carried past and put into the ambulance about 12:30 P.M. He knew the vehicle well—just a few nights before, he had slept in one overnight, thinking himself lucky to get off the hard ground.

By now, Colonel Sherman had ridden up to Matthews Hill, where he joined McDowell, Burnside, and Porter. There he found an atmosphere of euphoria that the Union had won the battle by taking the hill. Happy officers were practically doing a dance of victory on horseback. General Tyler, too, shared the same impression:

> I saw Captain Fry, of General McDowell's staff, standing by the fence, crying out 'Victory! Victory! We have done it! We have done it!' He supposed, and I supposed, and General McDowell at that time supposed, that the victory was substantially won.[120]

Inexperienced in the ebb and flow of field combat, the Union command mistook a tactical withdrawal to align with reinforcements as a retreat.[121]

The battle had ended none too soon for the Second Rhode soldiers, who had used all their ammunition and were scrounging from the cartridge boxes of the dead: "I filled the box of one of our men from a dead man's. When this was gone we were helpless."[122] They had to replenish their cartridges and for this, they had to wait for the quartermaster to grind into action. Apparently, the ammunition wagons had not been brought up close to the battlefield for fear of capture. Also, Heintzelman's troops were inbound now on the road, and the ambulances moved back and forth, delaying the munitions wagons. When it did arrive, "the ammunition brought would not fit our rifles and the wagons had been sent back."[123] Criticized by some for not returning to battle that afternoon, the simple answer was these regiments, with two different models of guns, still had no ammunition. Lieutenant Ames noted, "The lack of ammunition was one of the greatest oversights on the part of those who commanded the expedition that could have been made."[124]

Yet, the Rhode Islanders had accomplished more than normally credited. Had these soldiers panicked, buckled, failed to hold, fled back down the hill, or surrendered, the Southerners would have swept the battlefield immediately. McDowell's northern salient would have failed, in death and confusion, and gained him no advantage.

Not much effort was made to organize further action on behalf of the Union for the next couple of hours. The Regulars continued to marched down the slope, stepping over the dead bodies of Tigers, Mississippians, and Alabamians, hearing the groans of the dying, and the everpresent calls for "water" from the wounded. Lieutenant Eugene Carter, Eighth U.S. Infantry Regiment, led one patrol. Moving alertly, watchful for a pistol shot that could end their own lives, they,

> got to the edge of the wood [where] we observed a white flag upon a sword, held by someone lying down. We went to the spot and found Colonel Jones of one of the Alabama regiments mortally wounded. He asked for a drink of water, which we gave him. He asked what we intended to do, and we told him to whip them. He said "Gentlemen, you have got me, but a hundred thousand more await you."[125]

The soldiers were unfazed. They arranged for this Alabama colonel to be carried to the road, placed in an ambulance, and evacuated to Sudley Church field hospital.

CHAPTER SEVENTEEN

"The Murdering Cannons Roar"*

Sullivan Ballou is Taken to the Field Hospital

Noon to 4:00 P.M. July 21, 1861

As the ambulance carrying Sullivan Ballou made slow but steady progress up the Sudley Road, it was an agonizing journey for the major and the other wounded men in the little procession. Neither the two-wheeled nor the four-wheeled vehicles had springs, so each time one hit a rut in the heavily pot-holed road, which could make the conveyance bounce six inches or more, the men were abruptly jostled. Such sharp motions could cause bullets to move deeper into flesh or reopen bound wounds. Men were known to bleed to death on the way to the hospital. And crying out in pain was considered bad form for officers.

An ambulance was itself no guarantee of safety. Captain Hiram Rollins of the Second New Hampshire, lying wounded under a fence by the Sudley–New Market Road, was found by another

* From the Civil War song "Paddy's Lament."

A Zouave unit conducts an ambulance drill, showing the transport and treatment of patients. *Courtesy of the Library of Congress, Prints and Photographs Division.*

captain from his regiment, who hailed a passing ambulance and hoisted Rollins aboard. "A few moments after," when the ambulance hit a rut, Rollins was thrown out onto the road. "Almost immediately afterward a cannonball struck the ambulance, shattering it and scattering the pieces in a fearful manner." Rollins was picked up by another wagon shortly thereafter and made it to his destination.[1]

Each ambulance had only a driver, a member of the regimental band, steering his horse through the congestion on the narrow lane. No attendant rode inside although sometimes comrades "detailed to look after one of the wounded," followed the hospital wagon "to the hospital to help remove him."[2] Sergeant Chappell, who had tended Sullivan on the battlefield when he fell, accompanied him to the hospital. "There I was obliged to leave him and return to the regiment."[3]

The walking wounded going in for treatment limped their way

slowly along the edges, often carried or supported by two or more friends. Others, unable to wait their turn for the single ambulance issued to some regiments, were carried on stretchers, official, or ones improvised by fastening blankets or buttoning jackets over poles cut from trees.[4] About half past one o'clock in the afternoon those on their way to the hospital passed the remaining two regiments of Willcox's Brigade, the Eleventh and Thirty-eighth New York, who were trotting down the middle of the Sudley Road toward the battle scene. The arriving New Yorkers realized the Rebels had not run away as forecast.

Meanwhile, the Seventy-first New York was resting in the woods, not far from the Second Rhode Island, but "all the time we were resting we were within reach of the enemies guns."[5] As Lieutenant Edward Doherty of I Company watched, "a shell . . . rebounded upon the foot of Private Wm. N. Smith of Brooklyn, tearing it open. He threw his arms around my neck, and I assisted in carrying him to the hospital."[6]

The dead never made it there at all. In the frenzy of the battle, most were left where they fell, except for Lieutenant Levi Tower. A letter published in the *Pawtucket Gazette* said,

> Second Lieut. Shaw, of company F, took the body of Capt. Tower on his shoulders and carried it to a farm house about two miles distant from the battlefield. He represents him to have looked as if in a quiet sleep. He was not disfigured in the slightest degree. Lieut. Shaw took from his pockets his watch and other valuables and they will be restored to his family in Pawtucket.[7*]

The battlefield was now quiet—neither volleys of musketry nor fusillades of cannon carried through the air. The civilian spectators,

* A later witness saw Tower on the point of death, so he may only have been unconscious when Shaw carried him.

nearly all five miles off near Centreville, did not know what conclusions to draw. The placidly picnicking sightseers gleaned what news they could from passing messengers.

On the actual battlefield, after pushing the Rebels off Matthews Hill and sending patrols down toward the turnpike to reconnoiter and bring in prisoners, the Union forces had not advanced. Sherman had brought over two of his regiments, now positioned on Matthews Hill, and the three brigades of Heintzelman's Third Division, though coming in from an originally unintended direction, would soon be available to fight if not worn out from double quicking for three to six miles in the heat. Sergeant Abner Small of the Third Maine reported,

> About noon a mounted officer came dashing out of the woods and drew rein where Colonel Howard was fidgeting. There was a sudden stir, a shouting of orders, and we started up the forest track. . . . We went on at the double quick. . . . Another mile, and another, we hurried on. When we got to Bull Run at Sudley's Ford many stopped to drink; scooped up muddy water in their hands, their hats, their shoes; drank too much; were lost to service for that day. Not half the brigade, nor half the regiment, crossed the run.
>
> Beyond the stream, we went up through a scattering of trees and came out into cleared lands. We passed a . . . hospital near Sudley Church. I . . . saw . . . the dead and hurt men lying limp on the ground.[8]

Designated field hospitals were normally housed in structures the regiment had passed on their march into battle; soldiers were normally taken back behind their own lines to receive medical treatment, where the surgeons could work on their patients away from flying lead. Whenever possible, soldiers were taken to the surgeons of their own regiments, men whose competency the soldiers had already evaluated, and in whose hands they felt safer. Churches were especially good for this purpose. The largest buildings in most rural areas, their interior space could be organized more efficiently than the small rooms of farmhouses.

The Rhode Islanders of the First and Second regiments received treatment at two primary locations on July 21, the Matthews farmhouse on Matthews Hill, and the Methodist Church at Sudley Springs. The fragrant smell of the beeswax used on the pews must have still been in the air at the church, now converted to Sudley Field Hospital, when assistant surgeon of the U.S. Army, D. S. Magruder, rode into the churchyard an hour or so after the battle began.

> Upon taking possession of the church, I set men to work at removing the seats from the body of the church, with as little injury to them as practicable; had the floor covered with what blankets could be found, buckets of water brought, instruments and dressings placed in convenient places for use, and operating table improvised, and sent off the men to the fields nearby to bring hay for bedding.[9]

The reason for removing furniture or pews was to line up soldiers along the walls, and in rows down the middle, so that many more could fit inside. The readily available hay softened the hard floor and absorbed blood.

There was a small contingent of Rhode Islanders at Sudley Field Hospital. Dr. John Harris, the First Regiment's surgeon, and Dr. Henry Rivers, the Second's, were there. Private Josiah Richardson, of the First, along with privates Joseph Eldridge and James Collins from the Second, stayed on to help as orderlies. These men were untrained—Richardson was an ambrotypist, a photographer—but they knew something of compassion and opted to fetch water and sooth their wounded brethren.[10]

This one small church building had to suffice for more than ten thousand fighting men. Here, doctors from the Regular Army, the Fifth Massachusetts, the Eighth and Seventy-first New York, Fourteenth Brooklyn, First Minnesota, and Fourth Maine were all documented as having joined the Rhode Islanders in making this hospital their base of operations.[11] As such, it was undersupplied. By 1:00 P.M., the doctors had already been using the supplies in their personal field medical chests for a couple of hours.

The majority of the wounds the doctors saw were from musket balls and Minie bullets. Although weighing less than two ounces, molded out of soft lead, their weight and velocity created a destructive force that skin and bone could not withstand. If a bullet entered soft flesh and passed out again, its victim was pained and inconvenienced, but if he did not die from an infection, or shock from loss of blood, recovery was assured. Similarly, if a bullet remained lodged in flesh, its removal, even by an unsterile probe, usually resulted in survival. The further a bullet burrowed, however, the more the spherical or conical lead shape flattened out, destroying tissue and organs in its tumbling path. Once stomach acids, or bowel contents, or organ enzymes were let loose into a trauma area filling with blood, the outcome was nearly always fatal. Surgeons could do little for gut-shot men, and normally did not bother to treat them, beyond keeping them as comfortable as possible in the hospital until they died.

When a bullet struck bone, the results were disastrous. A simple broken bone was well within the capabilities of medical personnel of the time to set and heal. But a shattered or "splintered" bone was not. Survivors might have sharp splinters, called "spicules," working their way through their body for months. If these bone fragments rammed a nerve, paralysis could result; if they struck a blood vessel, the victim would bleed to death internally. Hence, amputation became the standard treatment. Strong men could survive this if the surgeon did a credible procedure, cleaned out the wound, and created proper

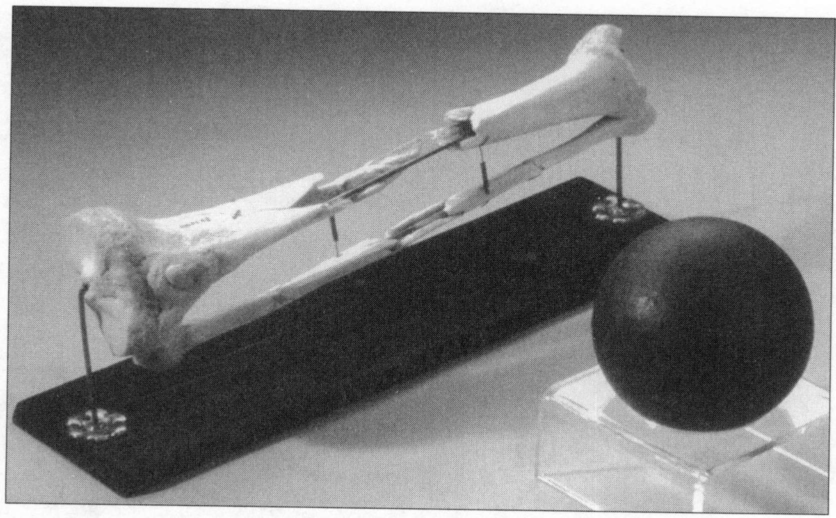

At Gettysburg, Union General Daniel Sickles of New York received an injury similar to Sullivan's. At the time, such shattered bone was irreparable. Sickles donated the amputated limb to the government and visited it periodically during his life. Here pictured with a six-pound cannonball, it can still be seen at a museum in Washington, D.C. *Courtesy of the National Museum of Health and Medicine, Armed Forces Institute of Pathology.*

skin flaps in his initial incision to cover the stump while suturing the flesh closed. The further away from the main torso an amputation took place, the better the chance of survival for the soldier. Feet and hands did best; knees and elbows next best; anything near the pelvis or shoulder, not well at all. Bullets taken directly in the complex joints of the shoulders or thighs were often fatal.

The scalpels, probes, forceps, clamps, and saws, which had already seen some action, were about to be in such constant use there would hardly be time for the blood of one patient to coagulate on an unwashed, not to mention unsterilized, instrument before it was used on another.

William Croffut, a reporter for the *New York Tribune*, was embedded with Company E of the First Minnesota. He found a role more important than journalist that day:

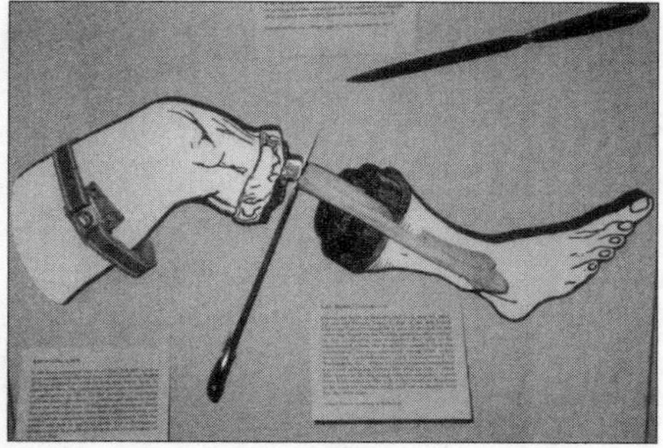

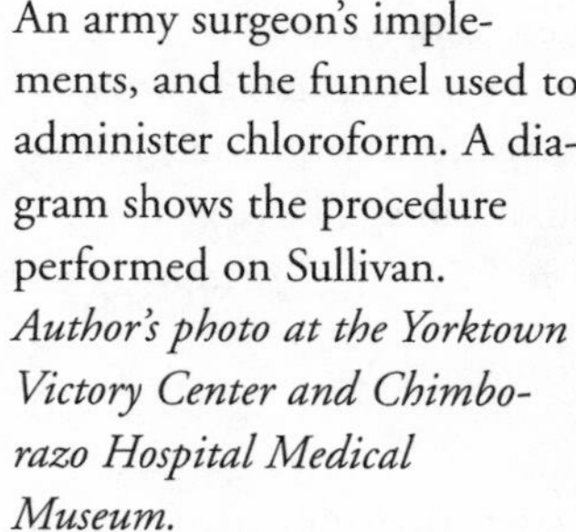

An army surgeon's implements, and the funnel used to administer chloroform. A diagram shows the procedure performed on Sullivan. *Author's photo at the Yorktown Victory Center and Chimborazo Hospital Medical Museum.*

Before noon I . . . was engaged in carrying our wounded back to the hospital . . . in the old Sudley Church. There was a sickening spectacle. The pulpit had put on the appearance of a drug store, and the communion table had become the horrible amputation table, while the floor was covered so thickly with wounded and dying that it was difficult to get across it by stepping carefully. For hours we made rapid trips between the battlefield and the hospital, and still the carnage went on.[12]

Within two hours, the field hospital was filled, upstairs and down. A witness noted,

> It was a scene too frightful and sickening to witness, much more describe. There were in it, scattered thickly upon the floor and in the galleries, 60 or 70 wounded in every possible way—arms and legs shot off, some dead, and scores gasping for water and aid. The pulpit was appropriated for a surgeon's room, and the communion table of pious ancestry became an amputation table baptized in willing blood and consecrated to the holy uses of Liberty and Law! The road and woods, on either side and all around, are strewed with maimed and mutilated heroes, and the balls from rifles go over us like winged devils.—There sits a Col. with his arm bound up, asking to be put on his horse and led back to his regiment; here lies a captain with a grape shot through his head, and blood and brain oozing out as we touched him tenderly to see if he is dead; . . . Oh God! What a hideous sight![13]

As the wounded were brought in, "blood trickled from the ambulances like water from an ice cart, and directly in front of the church door was a large puddle of blood."[14]

Drawn to the rich nutrient promise of blood, blow flies from every stable and pigsty in the area came to lay their eggs in open wounds. Within two to six hours, these hatched into legless larvae known as maggots. Doctors everywhere complained, "The flies were exceedingly troublesome after the battle, maggots forming in the wounds in less than an hour after dressing them, and also upon any clothing or bedding soiled by blood or pus."[15]

This was the state of affairs when the ambulance bearing Sullivan Ballou arrived. Most wounded were offloaded and placed wherever space was available amidst a jumble of casualties waiting their turn for treatment. Not so a high-ranking officer like Sullivan.

It took only a moment to assess the urgency and method of treatment needed for him, and he was immediately carried to the front of the church where the light was best and the surgeons were at work.

It was Sullivan's great good luck to have Dr. Henry Rivers for his surgeon. Dr. Rivers had far more experience in mangled limbs than did the average practitioner. Rivers had been the surgeon of the United States Marine Hospital in Providence, where injured mariners were treated; and for more than twenty years, his patients had included the mill workers of Providence, for whom he all too frequently had to amputate hands, arms, or legs caught and crushed in machinery. In the mid-nineteenth century, the sophisticated nerve, blood vessel, muscle suturing, bone setting, and drainage we now know are required for crush injuries could not be accomplished, so amputation was the standard treatment, even for this.

In addition to being someone from home whom Sullivan trusted, Rivers was a very smart, intuitive, and visionary physician, years ahead of his time. In 1845, he had written a practical guidebook called *Accidents: Popular Directions for Their Immediate Treatment*, illustrating tourniquet techniques, outlining the steps of mouth-to-mouth resuscitation, and speculating about the use of electricity, or galvanism, to restart a stopped heart.[16] Such a first-aid manual would have been very useful on a ship at sea, where sailors had to treat their own.

Sullivan's initial sighting of Dr. Rivers in that dim church interior must have been poignant, for Rivers's elaborate set of Burnside-style whiskers was flecked with blood, and his apron and rolled up shirt sleeves bore ample evidence of his morning's work. There are multiple reports of Sullivan instructing the doctors not to waste their time on him but to instead treat those who could still be helped. "To the surgeon who amputated his leg, he said, 'I am mortally wounded; give your attention to those whom your skill may save.'"[17]

It was a noble and generous gesture, but the doctors had no intention of complying. Still, Sullivan had to have felt reassured when Dr. Rivers assured him that he could survive this wound.[18] Why, a lost leg was nothing compared to being gut shot. Perhaps Sullivan felt a flame of hope kindle in his heart after hearing this, that he might in truth recover and return home to Sarah, Edgar, and William. Perhaps he was content to leave his fate in the caring hands of his doctor and his God.

If he was lucky, the communion table that served as an operating table was sloshed off with a bucket of water, or wiped down with a rag before he was lifted onto it and the stretcher taken away to be used by others. What remained of his trouser leg was cut off near the hip to give the doctor a good look at the limb.

At that point in the busy day, the doctors still had anesthetics among their dwindling supplies, and Sullivan received chloroform. His shirt collar was loosened, and his mouth and nostrils "anointed" with grease to prevent burning from the chloroform. Less than an ounce was poured into a cone held half an inch above his face, again to prevent blistering, and allow him to inhale air at the same time.* The surgeon, if not the attendant administering the cone, was trained to pay strict attention to "the respiration, pulse and countenance" of the patient, who might become excited, agitated, yell, cry out, or even sing patriotic songs while first going under.[19] The cone was held in place throughout the major part of the surgery, unless the patient became ashen and his skin cold.[20]

Doctor Rivers probably applied his own tourniquet up near the groin. The most effective of these belted around the leg and had a thumb screw that Rivers would have tightened to press a pad down on the major leg artery to compress it firmly against the bone below. With the femoral artery thus controlled, the flow of blood to the knee area minimized.

Experienced doctors knew that, the higher up on the leg and closer to the hip joint that they operated, the less chance of survival

* An ounce or two could anesthetize a full-grown cow.

the patient had—by 30 percent. Also, after recovery, the more of the leg that remained, the easier it was to fit the patient with a wooden leg.

Ballou was tall and his long leg bones worked in his favor, allowing the cut to be made well below the hip joint, leaving his lymph glands in place to fight infection—though, with germs then unrecognized as a source of infection, it was not traditional to sterilize the surgical area.

Rivers inspected the femur, the long bone of the upper leg, to check for hidden fractures. Finding none, he selected an amputation knife appropriate to leg surgery and began to map out the contours of the skin flaps he would first cut so he could successfully close the wound at the end of the operation.

While his assistant held the skin flaps back out of the way, Doctor Rivers sawed a straight cut across the femur, then filed off any rough edges and removed any splinters.

Next, the doctor needed to suture the blood vessels in the leg stump. Cat-gut was preferred for internal sutures, since it was absorbed eventually by the body. If Rivers had run out of these, he would have substituted linen or silk threads, and left a tail end hanging out of the wound. Each artery was identified, grasped with locking artery forceps, and stitched. Veins normally collapsed and did not require sutures, so the next step was to loosen the tourniquet to see if any thing oozed blood. Tiny bleeders might be cauterized with hot metal.

At this point, the anesthetic cone would have been removed as Doctor Rivers prepared to close the wound with an adhesive plaster. Depending on his original technique, he may also have used a set of needles to make a series of individually knotted stitches to neatly fasten the flaps and create a well-sealed incision. A leg amputation was sometimes closed with only five or six sutures. Cotton, or a wad of cotton threads called lint, held in place by a rolled bandage, was placed over the incision to absorb any drainage.

Rivers had done his very best for the prominent Rhode Islander, believed the surgery had been successful, and felt Sullivan would recover if he received postoperative care. The statistical odds were fifty-fifty, but Rivers was an excellent surgeon, and Sullivan was young, healthy, and in good condition, all of which might improve his chances. There was no recovery room: Sullivan was lifted onto a litter, carried outdoors, and laid on the ground—or possibly on one of the removed pews—in the shade of the small grove of trees near the church. It was believed that fresh air helped patients come out of anesthesia more quickly and they were probably safer outside the fetid hospital. "After the operation he was easy but very weak, and he was held up to send the blood to his heart, as he very calmly said, 'Turn me on this side, now on that.' "[21]

A short time later, Dr. Rivers completed surgery on Colonel Jones of the Fourth Alabama and he too was placed under the trees next to Sullivan, and the same attendants cared for both men.[22] Jones actually was more at risk of death than Ballou, from a secondary wound, a bullet that had burrowed along the length of his leg. This type of wound was especially susceptible to infection and almost impossible to clean out. Without his own attendants, Jones benefited from the kindness of the Rhode Islanders, who nursed him well.

There is ample evidence Sullivan and the colonel were clear headed and chatted amiably, not as enemies, as the afternoon wore on. Perhaps they discussed how intense the fighting had been as the Yankees pushed back the Rebels. At this point, while the guns were still silent, Sullivan Ballou rested comfortably enough, believing the battle had been won, the Union its victor.

General McDowell knew differently, or should have. It was true the Confederates had pulled back, but was it surrender or were they regrouping to fight again? For McDowell to assume his fondest wish, a general retreat, was especially puzzling since he now had both Scott's telegram and admissions from POWs that Johnston's Confederate reinforcements had joined Beauregard on the field. It was also a mistake not to direct his reserves at Fairfax Court House, ten miles away, to edge closer.

On the right hand, or eastern, side of the battlefield, after holding Sherman back for hours, Tyler had allowed him to take his men across Bull Run at the ford he had found. Sherman had taken the initiative to place his brigade under McDowell's command, but the rest of Tyler's forces acted independently and failed to communicate with McDowell. Keyes's brigade had come over, too, and veered south, where they stumbled onto something whose importance they failed to fully recognize or communicate.

In the only live action during the two-hour lull, when his First, Second, and Third Connecticut and Second Maine regiments moved up the slope of Henry Hill, up to the Robinson's yard, they encountered a small Confederate force already on that hill. Bee and Evans saw no need in sacrificing the remnants of the Seventh Georgia and Hampton's Legion, South Carolinians who had been almost annihilated in earlier fighting while covering the retreat of Bee's and Bartow's forces from Matthews Hill. They withdrew them under covering fire provided by the Fifth Virginia, on Jackson's extreme left flank. By the standards of that day, the New Englanders had encountered only "modest fire," but Keyes pulled them out of the fight, back to the shelter of Young's Branch.

Although the depth of the Confederate deployment on the hill could not be ascertained, Keyes was now the only Union commander who knew definitively that the Rebels were on the hill at all—and that information was too valuable not to communicate, to assume other commanders already knew. Once again, the lack of coordination cost the Union a chance to gain an advantage. Had they been able to assault Jackson en masse before he was reinforced, they might have gained that hill. Instead, Keyes stopped his assault and did not engage his troops in any further action—the whole day. Later, Tyler pulled him back even further to guard the Stone Bridge, by then rendered tactically useless. As E. Porter Alexander later noted, Keyes's brigade

> was out of touch with everything. McDowell did not even know where it was. Had it advanced . . . had it communicated . . . had it, in short, tried *anything*, it might have accomplished important results.[23]

His brigade sustained the lightest casualties of any that saw action that day.

Tyler also let McDowell down again, by not mounting a more convincing diversion that morning at the Stone Bridge. Tyler's failure to attack convinced the Southern command that he was just a straw man; they turned their attention—and their steadily arriving reinforcements—northward. McDowell had less flexibility in his application of combat power because he was never able to utilize Tyler's troops.

On the western side of the battlefield, Porter's forces solidly held Dogan's Ridge, a westerly extension of Matthews Hill across the Sudley–New Market Road and northwest from Henry Hill, which let them observe certain Confederate operations. The two batteries in his front were posted where they could effectively shell two-thirds of the ground then held by the Confederates, although Ricketts was close enough to receive incoming fire: "It killed some horses and wounded some few of my men; I myself saw one man struck on the arm."[24] Griffin, deployed more securely, noted his cannon's "fuses were set for a thousand yards and they were pretty accurate [and] did most murderous execution."[25]

At this point in the day, on the eastern side of the battlefield, Burnside's brigade was resting in the woods, while the Regulars and others prowled the slopes toward Young's branch, harassing Confederate stragglers. Some of Heintzelman's regiments waited on

Matthews Hill, while others hurried forward, at what Blake of the Eleventh Massachusetts called a "furious rate" on a "day [that] was one of the hottest of the year," with "no friendly cloud to obstruct the rays of the sun." The men were dehydrated and suffered badly from thirst, but since they were inbound during the battle for Matthews Hill,

> the cannonading inspired the men with a patriotism, and gave them a physical strength which they could not have possessed under similar circumstances in the avocations of a peaceful life. They . . . beheld the long clouds of dust in the south, which showed that the rebels were moving in the same direction: and it required no deep knowledge of mathematics to demonstrate that the two lines of march, if extended, would soon intersect.[26]

The Fifth Maine, the second-to-last regiment in the long parade, was obliged to run six to seven miles, at huge cost. Adjutant Bicknell described their travails,

> Our thinning ranks began to show the effects of overexertion. Men seemed to fall in squads by the roadside, some sunstruck, some bleeding at nose, mouth, ears; others were windbroken, while others were exhausted to such a degree, that the threatening muzzle of the officers' pistol, failed to induce them a step further.[27]

As a result, some of these later arriving regiments could not deploy at full strength. The Fifth Maine lost a full half of its men to this march, but only one to actual combat.[28]

A curious dynamic overcame Heintzelman's regiments after they paused for water at Catharpin Run. Beginning with the Eleventh Massachusetts, who "marched up a hilly road by the church, in front of which the men threw off their overcoats & blankets & many their jackets," others did the same thing.[29] "Throwing away their blankets and rations to facilitate their progress, [they] merely retained their muskets and ammunition."[30] The plan was to pick up their items on the march back, and maybe they felt they were safe left at a church held by Union forces. "For miles the road was strewed with blankets, haversacks, coats, thrown aside by the almost exhausted soldiers."[31] The Irishmen of the Sixty-ninth New York took things the furthest later that afternoon, when many threw off their shirts and fought bare chested.

The Confederates were also deciding their next move. Beauregard had initially deployed his own army in a broad swath, while holding Johnston's in reserve. A well-connected observer, a Southern physician visiting at headquarters, Dr. Josiah Nott, noted,

> Not knowing at what point of a semicircle of ten miles around Manassas the enemy would attack, his forces had to be scattered in such a way as to guard all points, prevent a flank movement on either side, and guard his intrenchments and supplies in the centre.[32]

Beauregard had kept his focus south of Bull Run, still committed to an attack on the Union left near Centreville. Given the failure of his specific orders to reach his commanders, and the clumsy wording of his general orders, that attack never came together.

Prudently not reacting to the first few cannon shots in the early hours of the day, both Johnston and Beauregard established a field headquarters near Mitchell's Ford on Lookout Hill, from where they could see the aerial dust and smoke patterns, and try to decipher the Union's intentions and the course of battle. When they left it, they went first toward the Stone Bridge:

> to determine if an attack was being made there. At eleven, the batteries boomed up at Matthews Hill, and they knew this had been a feint. They galloped three miles north to observe.[33]

As Dr. Nott understood it,

> I never had any idea of military science before. Beauregard and Johnston played it like a game of chess without seeing the board—when a messenger came and told the enemy's move, a move was immediately ordered to put him in check.[34]

The South used the lull to rally and redeploy men scattered by the noontime retreat. Beauregard needed to use the partial regiments hanging around the fringes of the battlefield to shore up his line. As Sergeant Blake wryly put it "in the mean time, the rebel leaders had rallied their stragglers and fugitives."[35] Each Confederate regiment on Matthews Hill had held out until the last possible moment, before withdrawing one at a time, their survivors now clustered in scattered groups on the south side of Young's Branch, near farm buildings. Private George Barnsley, Eighth Georgia, stopped for a moment "to gather the half ripe blackberries, for my lips were cracked and bleeding from the powder of the cartridges and my tongue and mouth dry as a chip of pine lying in the sun."[36]

For these men, and others later in the day, Beauregard, by staying on the battlefield and rallying the men, who were highly motivated by his attention and complements, played a vital role. A certain amount of theater was helpful out there, officers putting themselves into a group of men retreating unordered, sitting astride their horses, waving their swords, yelling encouragements and, when those failed, quotable deprecations. Sometimes they took up the regimental colors and waved them high to create a visual rallying point.

The toll on officers was high in this battle because the green troops had to be led by example. At one point, Beauregard had a horse killed underneath him "by a bursting shell, a fragment of which carried away part of the heel" of his boot.[37] He was six inches luckier than Sullivan Ballou.

Ordered to form up a line of resistance to any new Union probe, Colonel Bartow began

> to rally his men. Frenzied at his heavy loss, he seized a flag from the hand of a color bearer. It happened that these were the colors of a South Carolina unit under Bee. The incident was noticed by Bee, who rushed up and snatched the colors from Bartow. . . . Had he and Bartow been spared, it is quite likely they would have fought a duel.[38]

At least a quarter of the Eighth's thousand Georgians had fallen dead or wounded, or were captured or lost. The Fourth Alabama was also well decimated and had been taken over by Lieutenant Colonel Evander McIver Law, but with their major also wounded, the regiment could not be reformed after its retreat. Captain Tracey made a rousing rallying speech, which was interrupted by the arrival of General Bee, seeking troops to redeploy his line. Bee also wanted to take the colors of the Fourth, but its color sergeant refused to hand over their flag, offering instead to "place it wherever you command."[39]

Pointing at the Twenty-seventh Virginia, Bee gave what was to become an immortal reply. Sergeant Major Robert Coles of the Fourth Alabama, heard Bee say,

> "Come with me and go yonder where Jackson stands like a stonewall." As soon as the water detail which had been sent out returned and the men had satisfied their thirst, the regiment fell into line and followed General Bee to the support of General Jackson.[40]

Stonewall Jackson before he was wounded at Henry Hill. The man with his cap off is presumably General Bee attempting to rally his brigade. *Drawing by H. Gordon, from the Library of Congress Prints and Photographs Division.*

As the Fourth marched toward Jackson, it was split up by a repositioning artillery battery racing down the road through their midst. General Bee took the smaller group, those who had jumped off the road to the right, and lead them and assorted others forward toward the Union batteries. He rode in front of his men, cheering them to follow him, but such bravery often had its price. Bee was shot in the lower abdomen, and carried into the shade by two of his men—an uncle and nephew fighting together—who made him comfortable. The mortally wounded Bee was later borne from the field in a litter, and later still taken by ambulance to a field hospital.[41] He took to his grave the exact meaning of his simile regarding Jackson. Was it a compliment for bravery while his troops held their position as shells flew overhead, or a jibe at Jackson's refusal to come to the aid of regiments he saw being cut to pieces in front of him?

Beauregard's units, assigned to the attack that never came off, were available for redeployment from any of the fords below the turnpike, in addition to Thomas J. Jackson's Virginians now stealthily hugging the ground on the reverse slope of Henry Hill. And more men were still coming off the trains at the junction—so many that Beauregard and Johnston divided their workloads to coalesce their fighting force more quickly. Just after noon that day, after a line of resistance to further federal attack was stabilized, they bifurcated the command, keeping Beauregard on the battlefield and sending Johnston to direct and speed up the positioning of the reinforcements.[42] Whether it happened amicably or not, that decision greatly improved the Confederate's odds of success.

In reality, the battle of First Manassas was fought by two Confederate armies combined; President Jefferson Davis had, in effect, given joint command of the battle to his two army commanders generals Beauregard and Johnston. While this caused some jockeying for position between them, they did attempt to work together and conferred on strategies, deployment, and the roles they would play. They balanced each other—the even-tempered, more experienced Johnston steadying the flamboyant, mercurial Beauregard. Both men had large egos; however, Johnston was savvy enough to put Beauregard's in-depth knowledge of the battlefield terrain to the best use. At this point in the battle, Johnston withdrew one-half mile away, to the Portici mansion from which he had a commanding view of the countryside.

Portici, a fine, two-storied country house, became the Confederate command post for the afternoon phase of the battle. The Lewis family who owned it had evacuated earlier, alerted to the danger of the proximity of the battle. Mrs. Fannie Lewis was nine months pregnant, and the stress of evacuating toward her father-in-law's house was too much. As they made their way to safety, she went into labor and delivered her baby in a ravine with the assistance of her house slaves. She apparently held no grudge, for she named the child John Beauregard Lewis.

Not only could Johnston see the battle in front of him, but all reinforcements from his own army arriving by railroad came past him, and he could direct them to the most-needed place on the battlefield where Beauregard commanded. Johnston's relocation to Portici was timely, for the last troop train transporting his army from the Shenandoah was pulling into Manassas Junction, and the units and officers coming off the cars needed orders. McHenry Howard, of the First Maryland, one of the last units to arrive by train, reported,

> As we neared Manassas Junction we distinctly heard the booming of cannon at intervals and could even see the smoke from some of the discharges a few miles to the left, but we had no Idea that a general engagement was then actually going on. We arrived at the railroad junction, a few hundred yards west of the station, about 1 P.M. and immediately disembarking, threw off our knapsacks into a pile and formed in line. Colonel Elzey galloped down the front. . . . and I now suddenly realized that we were going straight into our first battle. . . . We were marched north, partly across the country, towards the firing. We took a quick step at first, but presently in our excitement broke into a double quick, with a cheer, . . . the whole distance passed over being about five miles. The dust was most distressing, so thick at times that it was impossible to see more than a few feet ahead of one.[43]

Until these men completed their march, the Confederates had only a few new regiments—the Eighth and three companies of the Forty-ninth Virginia—to add to the conglomeration of partial regiments come back together after the morning's carnage. Nevertheless, by 1:00 P.M., a line of some seven thousand men was in place. Morale was strong, the men were eager to repay the North for the losses they had suffered that morning.[44] On Henry Hill,

> Beauregard's task . . . was to hold his line of battle until some of these bodies of reinforcements could reach him. It was his

> last chance. And to do it, he had about 3000 fresh infantry, and about as much more which had been engaged and driven back, and he had about 16 guns, mostly 6 pounders.[45]

On the other hand, McDowell's task that afternoon was to crush Beauregard's line before reinforcements could reach it—his last chance, actually. The job of the Union Army this afternoon was very similar to their opponent's, including putting its own troops in the best possible place in the field and arranging effective artillery placement and support. No one understood why McDowell had waited, why he issued no orders for two hours. His aide indicated they all knew the only new troops they would ever have were Heintzelman's division now on the Sudley Road:

> General Scott's report that Beauregard had been re-enforced, the information that four regiments had been sent to McDowell, and the promise that twice the number would be sent *if necessary*, all came too late—and Patterson came not at all.[46]

McDowell technically had eight brigades, about eighteen thousand men, though only half that number were engaged, and twenty-four guns, mostly long-range, rifled ten-pounders. Even though he was now on the battlefield in person, he took his time preparing the next phase of his attack in an intelligence vacuum, perhaps still feeling ill.

The Yankee soldiers were chafing, and individual commanders were irritated with the army's "hurry up and wait" conduct: "18,000 men spent the better part of two hours standing around with nothing to do."[47] Blake of the Eleventh Massachusetts rued the inactivity:

> The men that were unoccupied should have attacked the

> rebels, who were enabled by this blundering delay to re-organize their shattered ranks, and offer a firm resistance when the offensive was assumed. These were the precious moments when a small fraction of the larger reserve should have been ordered to complete the triumph that had already been won.[48]

Another difference was that McDowell was responsible for playing both the Johnston and Beauregard roles at the same time. This may explain why there were periods of time he could not be found, which caused consternation because nobody seemed to know how to reach him. As one officer complained, "there was a want of a headquarters somewhere on the field." All the staff officers who knew anything about the position of the enemy had to act without orders.[49]

With McDowell "lost" on the battlefield, some of the junior officers on location were reacting to the situation on his behalf. Engineer Barnard reported,

> I had got separated from General McDowell, and I hunted up the adjutant, who was behind attending to some duty, and requested him to order up the brigade at Centreville to the stone Bridge, in order to support us.[50]

Lieutenant William Woods Averell, a Regular Army man and West Point graduate who served formerly on the frontier and now as Colonel Porter's adjutant, had been placed in charge of Porter's brigade, instead of any of the regimental colonels. Averill had observed the ebb and flow of the morning's action on the eastern side of the Sudley–New Market Road from a vantage point on Dogan's Ridge on the western side. The key point of control of that terrain was now Henry Hill. It took its name from the Henry family who occupied the Spring Hill farmhouse. The widow Henry was now in her mid-eighties, bedridden, and tended by a slave named

Lucy Griffiths. Her daughter Ellen was present, as was her son John, a teacher, come for a Sunday visit.

Her nearest neighbor, at the bottom of the hill along the turnpike, was her half-brother, a free Black, James Robinson, who was the third largest landowner among free Blacks in Prince William County. He was sixty-two years old when the war came to his doorstep.[51]

General Beauregard described Henry Hill as being one hundred feet high,

> furrowed by ravines of irregular directions and length,—studded with clumps and patches of young pines and oaks. . . . Around the eastern and southern brow of the plateau an almost unbroken fringe of second-growth pines gave excellent shelter for our marksmen, who availed themselves of it with the most satisfactory skill. . . . To the east, a broad belt of oaks extends directly across the crest on both sides of the Sudley road.[52]

E. Porter Alexander added a description of the position Jackson's forces occupied:

> The hill was really a ridge, with a plateau like top, some 200 yards more across. The inner edge of such a ridge is a fairly good position for a defensive line of battle. It affords some cover both from view and from fire. If the enemy bring their artillery to the front edge of it, they are within musket range, and are also near enough to be charged.[53]

Averell understood this was key ground and believed it was unoccupied. Aware that broken Confederate regiments had left the immediate area, concerned that the Confederates might gain its heights while Union troops stood idle, Averell wanted to get his own troops up on top of Henry Hill to hold it for the Union. He started two units, the Eighth New York and Fourteenth Brooklyn Militia, in that direction, but they took a wrong turn.*

> They went down fine, perfectly cool and in good order. They were going so rapidly that the enemy could not keep the[ir] range. [By] some misunderstanding, an order was sent to them . . . and they were diverted to the left [down the turnpike].

Lieutenant Averell sprang into action to assist them, and finding no ranking officers on his area of the field, conferred with Lieutenant Whipple, of Second Division staff.

> We talked over the position of affairs, and came to the conclusion that the hill in front of us was the key-point of the enemy's position, and must be taken before the battle would be given up. We felt we had won the battle; but in order to make it decisive and hold the position, we would have to take that hill. We agreed upon a plan which was to collect the regiments in the centre of the field: the fifth and eleventh Massachusetts, the second Minnesota, the thirty-eighth New York, and, I think, Colonel Coffer's regiment, sixty-ninth, I think—five or six regiments—and to send them up on the hill in line. Put the fourteenth on the right, with the marines and zouaves [Eleventh New York], and then move them all up together with Griffin's battery in the centre. That would make an embrasure of troops for the battery to fire through, and they never could take the battery as long as these supports were on its flanks, neither could their cavalry ever charge upon the infantry line as long as the battery was there. . . . I

* This unit was at this point known by its prewar militia designation, and shortly afterwards became the Eighty-fourth New York.

had gone to Griffin and notified him of this plan, telling him these troops were going to move up.

This plan was the single most solid tactical decision made since 9:30 A.M. and it came from two lieutenants! It was in fact collaborative: They brainstormed the moves with the colonels commanding all the regiments involved, and with the battery commanders. Everyone knew what everyone else was doing, for a change. "We went over to the center and succeeded in getting these five regiments started. I found Colonel Franklin and two or three other officers there who assisted me . . ."

They were unaware that McDowell had resumed command about 2:00 P.M., bringing his chief of artillery, Major Barry, and had issued counter orders to execute a typical Napoleonic tactic. "Just about this time . . . we saw the battery moving up the hill . . . without any support except the marines and the zouaves. . . ." The commanding general wanted his artillery to bombard the Confederate position and soften it up for an infantry charge. Newly arrived on the scene and apparently poorly briefed, for he did not realize how close the enemy was, McDowell knew less about the situation than did Averell, who had been there longer.

Major William Farquar Barry, McDowell's newly promoted chief of artillery, had ordered Griffin's and Ricketts' batteries to move up the flanks of Henry Hill. Griffin had argued back, protesting the lack of infantry support for the exposed position, and predicting the Zouave unit, which had been rowdy in camp, could not hold together under hot fire. Ricketts faced exactly the same situation. A square-jawed, large-boned giant of a man, Barry was adamant and prevailed, "It is General McDowell's order to go there."[54] The other infantry units remained undeployed because of this change of plans, and the guns went forward alone.

McDowell and Barry made two profound miscalculations. The first was in sending the two largest artillery units, six guns each, to such an extreme, forward position so close to the enemy line. True, they could better see Confederate targets from there, but if he wanted to use Napoleon's tactics, McDowell needed to remember the other half of the rules—that guns crews must be protected by an iron ring of infantry. Seeing these tempting targets dangling within their reach, the Confederates made their capture an immediate tactical goal. The afternoon phase of that day's combat became the battle for the batteries. The second mistake was in forgetting to apply the knowledge that the new rifled guns did not have to move in close to shell the enemy.* Ricketts, Griffin, their gun crews, and all the horses were jeopardized needlessly that afternoon.

Dismayed, and obliged to follow what they knew was a bad order, the guns crews had no alternative but to go for it as fast as possible. They dashed across the hillside under heavy fire, jounced into the ravine, and as luck had it, one of Ricketts' caissons broke a wheel. They replaced it on the spot, under fire, got underway again, took down the fence and ascended the hill near the Henry House.

There, soldiers of the North and South deployed around the fences of both families, their outbuildings, their ice houses and haystacks. Captain Ricketts noted, the Henry House

> was at that time filled with sharpshooters. I had scarcely got into battery before I saw some of my horses fall and some of my men wounded by the sharpshooters. I turned my guns upon the house and literally riddled it.[55]

The Henry family was trapped. As the bullets and balls whizzed around them, the family first carried the widow Judith Henry on

* From this battle forward, tactics were never adjusted to the reality of the rifled guns, and the outmoded strategies doomed tens of thousands of men to needless deaths during the war.

her mattress out to the spring house. Petrified, the old lady pleaded to be returned to her bed. No sooner had they complied with her wishes than a shell crashed into the room, exploded, and threw her out of bed with wounds in her neck and side. A foot was "almost entirely blown off," and Mrs. Henry soon died.[56] Lucy Griffiths, a hired slave hiding under the bed, was slightly wounded, but able to walk home to the Comptons later.[57] Daughter Ellen sought safety in the large fireplace, whose chimney reverberated the noise of the shelling, damaging her hearing. Son John escaped unscathed—it was thought he may have remained outside.

But Ricketts was up on this hill without protection, and, down below, McDowell had countermanded the order to send adequate support to Griffin. Colonel Jackson had been watching all this and had his Virginians ready. Lieutenant Averell had gone in search of McDowell, but before he could reach him, the general "called out to the colonel of the 14th" and told them to change their direction, sending them ineffectively to the rear of the battery. Averell implored him to recall the battery and redirect the Fourteenth, providing information about the location of the enemy that he knew from his personal observations of the battlefield over the last few hours. McDowell agreed to Averell's request to reposition the Fourteenth, and the lieutenant rode off to accomplish this, and then continued up the hill to join Griffin.

Averell found the battery unlimbering, the marines sitting on the ground, the Eleventh New York Fire Zouaves still coming up in the rear, the First Minnesota next to them, and Colonel Heintzelman, who led all his units into battle personally, sitting on his horse, surveying the ground, apparently trying to determine if the men in front of them were Union or Confederate. From this position, on the side of Henry Hill, it was impossible to see who or what was above them.

> The day had been very dusty, and all uniforms, blue and gray, were now of the same dusty color. All over the field, and on both sides, cases of confusion had occurred, but the most important of all took place now.[58]

Averell, too, spotted a regiment of men about one hundred yards off, and, dropping his reins, picked up his binoculars to try and identify them.

> Just at that moment, down came their pieces, rifles and muskets, and probably there never was such a destructive fire for a few minutes. It seemed as though every man and horse of that battery just laid right down and died right off.[59]

The fusillade had been fired by the Thirty-third Virginians of Jackson's brigade. Averell escaped and tried to rally the infantry behind the battery, along with Heintzelman and one of McDowell's aides, "but the destruction of the battery was so complete that the marines and zouaves seemed to be struck with such astonishment, such consternation, that they could not do anything."[60]

Maybe a hundred men fired back, but since the enemy could not be seen on the ridge above, there was no way to target them, and anyway, the men fired high. Their brigade commander fought with them, but realized the noise of the battle was so great that the men could not hear his shouted orders.[61]

The New York firefighters were plucky and not given to panic. Their years of firefighting experience had taught them to recognize when a situation was doomed, and withdrawal the only prudent course of action. Their situation on Henry Hill that afternoon certainly seemed like such a situation—the closest thing to a collapsing, burning, multistory building that could be found in rural Virginia. The Union infantry "began to break and run down the hill and nothing could stop them, and then the enemy rushed right over there like a lowering cloud—right over the hill."[62] At one gun, only a single artilleryman remained to do the work of eight.[63]

With federal units probing both his flanks, Jackson had asked his cavalry commander, J. E. B. Stuart, to keep a sharp eye out for incursions. Stuart had three hundred well-mounted men, and simply divided them in half to watch each flank. When the Zouaves retreated, Stuart saw an opportunity. The Confederate cavalry charged through the ranks of the New Yorkers, bludgeoning them with carbine butts, slicing them with their sabers. Ellsworth had drilled these men to form a line triple-deep, kneeling, semikneeling, and standing. As the cavalry came at them, the Zouaves formed a line, though some say it did not hold and only half the men fired their muskets.[64] The horsemen raced through the Zouaves, who remained surrounded by the cloud of smoke from their muskets and did not see the cavalry rein in near the fence, turn around, and charge back. They struck the men of the Eleventh New York from another angle; this time the combat was hand to hand, with some of the firemen fixing bayonets.

The cavalry "wheeled to return" on a third charge, when a Union battery opened fire on them with canister shot, killing more horses, and sending some of Stuart's men running for Manassas. Broken as a regiment, many of the Zouaves "joined other regiments and did good service as skirmishers."[65] Heintzelman held back the cavalry, "the ground being unfavorable" apparently only to Union cavalrymen.*[66]

Henry Hill was a nasty place for every one that day, a whirling vortex of death for man, woman and beast alike that eventually claimed hundreds of lives. Newly wounded men in the distinctive

* Averell saw Barry galloping away near him, as both fled "the general wreck." Barry lamented, "I am to blame for the loss of that battery. I put Griffin there myself."

uniforms of many different regiments now began to be carried off Henry Hill and conveyed to Sudley Field Hospital. Each wave of wounded soldiers reported new developments, so the men at Sudley Church heard news less than an hour old.

In Washington, D.C., the president was not getting real-time reports. Washington kept in touch with the battle's progress by means of a mounted courier service that Andrew Carnegie had organized to ride between McDowell and the closest telegraph station at Fairfax Courthouse. Even on a fast horse, it took the rider some time to transit the lines and the distance. These telegrams were received at a station on the first floor landing of the War Office Building, and the telegraph operator reported,

> All the morning and well along into the afternoon, McDowell's telegrams were more or less encouraging, and Lincoln and his advisers waited with eager hope, believing that Beauregard had been pushed back to Manassas Junction; but all at once the despatches ceased coming. At first this was taken to mean that McDowell was moving farther away from the telegraph, and then, as the silence became prolonged, a strange fear seized upon the assembled watchers that perhaps all was not well.[67]

It was probable that McDowell became too busy to send telegrams once he mounted the afternoon attack after 2:00 P.M. The suspense was palpable Sunday afternoon, and all of Washington held its breath.

> It may well be supposed that President Lincoln suffered great anxiety during that eventful Sunday; but General Scott talked confidently of success, and Lincoln bore his impatience without any visible sign, and quietly went to church at eleven o'clock.[68]

After his return to the White House, copies of later telegrams were sent over by the War Department but, as they came only from the telegraph operator at Fairfax Court House, reporting what he heard at a distance, they were deemed of little use.

In Providence, there was, as yet, no news whatsoever. Sarah Ballou most likely had received Sullivan's early letter of July 14 written when he was still in camp, but probably did not yet have his six-line note from July 18, or anything written after that. She who worried lest he catch a cold was now confronted by his silence, with the most terrible of her fears for him. Like everyone else, she could only wait for another letter—or a telegram to bring news.

As the little Methodist church filled up, overflowing with casualties, Assistant Surgeon D. S. Magruder

> was obliged to take possession of three other unoccupied buildings, which are situated about seventy-five paces farther down and on the opposite side of the road towards the creek. As soon as I could get them cleared out, wounded men were carried into them until they were filled also. For want of other buildings, I was obliged to order many of the wounded to be laid under the trees, in a grove immediately around the church.[69]

These three nearby buildings were part of the complex leased from Sudley Mill by John Thornberry, a carpenter, wheelwright, coffin maker, and, by default, undertaker. His shop—which the medical personnel seemed not to use—was built close to the road so that damaged wagons could easily be driven into his yard.

Besides the shop, which was readily visible from the road, his house, where he lived with his wife, Martha, and five children, was built farther back off the road on a knoll facing the church. His two female slaves lived in one of the domestic outbuildings, and a second was a detached kitchen with a root cellar underneath for storing food. In hot climates, detached kitchens prevented the house from becoming even hotter from cooking and baking activities, and reduced the risk of fire to the main house. There was also an outhouse and an icehouse, neither useful for hospital purposes. These domestic buildings were visible from, but off, the road, affording his family some measure of privacy from the teamsters.[70]

Thornberry was away from home fighting with Company A of the Forty-ninth Virginia Infantry Battalion under Cocke, who were even now disengaging from their defense of Lewis Ford and heading for Henry Hill. Martha Thornberry and her five children, and their two slaves had evacuated the previous night, so the living quarters were unoccupied when Dr. Magruder took over the buildings as an extension of the hospital.

As with the church, he likely ordered Union troops to clear out the family house, the slave house and the kitchen buildings, to accommodate wounded officers in more privacy than was possible in the open space of the church. This was likely accomplished with little regard for the possessions the family had left behind and unguarded. The Thornberry family suffered a real economic loss from this occupation. Even their towels, bedsheets, and clothing were appropriated to use as bandages for the wounded.

The medical personnel normally tried to cluster or shelter wounded field and staff level officers together, away from the wounded masses where one or two attendants could provide nursing care. This is certainly what happened with Ballou and Jones on the grass outside the church, and the same principle was probably followed when Sullivan and Slocum were moved into the Thornberry complex before darkness fell. Repeated references to "the shanty" in which Sullivan Ballou was housed might be interpreted to mean either the Thornberry dwelling did not meet Yankee standards, or that he and Slocum were carried to the slave quarters.

By that time, Slocum had slipped into a comatose state from

which he never regained consciousness. Because bone shatters *around* an impact, small blood vessels in the brain, ruptured by small fractures, bleed freely.

Up on Henry Hill, the North and South began a series of charges and counterattacks, all focused on eleven Union guns, control of which seesawed back and forth for the next two hours in roughly fifteen-minute intervals. The Union sent in thirteen regiments, the Confederates deployed eight-plus. The North was determined not to allow their own guns to be used against themselves.

The need to rescue his guns thus dominated McDowell's options that afternoon, preventing him from going on the offensive. Just as he had done in the morning, when the "nature of the ground" reportedly " rendered a united advance impossible," he threw one regiment at a time into the fight.[71] This may have been as far as his vision and experience took him—he was, after all, a general who had never commanded so many troops in battle or drill.

McDowell threw twelve Regiments onto Henry Hill in multiple unsuccessful attempts to rescue his two batteries:

5th Massachusetts
11th Massachusetts
1st Michigan
1st Minnesota
11th New York
13th New York
14th New York State Militia
38th New York
69th New York
79th New York
2nd Wisconsin
U.S. Marine BN.

Together, they sustained 1,500 casualties:

270 killed
613 wounded
617 missing

The Confederates deployed eight full regiments and parts of others:

2nd Virginia
4th Virginia
5th Virginia
6th Virginia
8th Virginia
18th Virginia
27th Virginia
33rd Virginia
49th Virginia (3 Colorado)
7th Georgia
8th Georgia
6th North Carolina
Hampton's Legion (6 Colorado)

One of the most thrilling scenes of the battle occurred as the Fourteenth Brooklyn moved into battle position.* They formed and executed a picture-perfect battle line that would have made Hardee proud. This spectacle was recounted in numerous diaries and countless letters home by admiring Confederates:

* Often mistaken for the Zouaves of the Eleventh New York in laudatory contemporary reports, the "Red Legged Devils" wore chasseur uniforms (no pantaloons, no stocking hat).

> In strong relief against the smoke beyond, stretched a brilliant line of scarlet—a regiment of New York Zouaves in column of fours, marching out of the Sudley Road to attack the flank of our line of battle. Dressed in scarlet caps and trousers, blue jackets with quantities of gilt buttons, and white gaiters, with a fringe of bayonets swaying above them as they moved, their appearance was indeed magnificent.[72]

The attack of the Fourteenth achieved some success, caving in Jackson's left flank. The Thirty-third soon found itself too far from home to maintain its position, and it had to leave its trophies and fall back. Thus ended the first Confederate custody of the guns. However, instead of securing their battery, the Fourteenth went streaming across the field to attempt to capture a Confederate battery, and were repulsed. They remained on the hill, along with remnants of the First Minnesota, and finally the Confederates opened on them with canister shot.[73] Its colonel down, the gallant Fourteenth went back three times, but their ranks were now so decimated they lacked the power to seize the guns.[74]

With the hilltop cleared of Yankees, Jackson ordered a charge and told his men to yell. For the first time, the celebrated Rebel yell—woh who-ey—was heard in battle.

In the firefight over the two sets of Union guns that afternoon, the only constant was death. Dr. Nott stated,

> The cannon were roaring and the musketry sounded like a large bundle of fire crackers, and the constant roaring of the big guns, the sharp sound of rifled cannons, Minie rifles and muskets, with the bursting of shells made one feel that death was doing his work with fearful rapidity.[75]

The plateau around Henry House now swarmed with bits of troops from both sides—regimental remnants hiding behind haystacks, sniping at each other from fences. The smoke was so dense that battle flags were needed to form up the men and direct their movement. Colonel Bartow and the color sergeant of the Seventh Georgia bore the regimental flag forward, leading a charge toward the Union guns. As always, the color bearers were in special jeopardy as targets, and Bartow was shot in his left breast above the heart. Dr. H. V. Miller rushed to his aid, but the wound was mortal. Colonel Bartow just had time for a few last words: "They have killed me, but boys, never give it up."[76] The body of the man who had urgently raced his troops to the fight earlier that morning was carried off the field. As the scattered bands of his men learned of his death, they expressed great sorrow at the loss of their popular, brave commander.

At some point during the day, through his field glasses, Heintzelman clearly recognized Major Charles L. Scott of the Fourth Alabama, a close friend. Charles Scott had been a congressman from California while Heintzelman was stationed there.[77] This was one of the first instances of many to occur during the Civil War where two "warm friends" faced each other on the battlefield. Scott was wounded quite severely, and Heintzelman took a bullet in the arm; a surgeon removed the bullet while the colonel remained on his horse.

The next Union commander ordered to assault the hill was Sherman, and he, too, sent a single regiment at a time into the fray after McDowell told him to pursue the enemy, an order that implied the enemy was in flight.[78] Advancing over this portion of the Sudley–New Market Road had become gruesome. The Union dead were stacked like cord wood, three and four deep in some places. The noise of the battle was still so loud that the men could not hear the orders of their officers. Sergeant Nathaniel Rollins wrote his homefolk that, "by sort of mutual consent, we rushed over the dead men, climbed up the bank, over the fence, and up the hill . . . to the guns."[79]

The attack of the Second Wisconsin faltered in another episode of uniform confusion; they drew friendly fire because of their gray uniforms. The Seventy-ninth New York Highlanders went in to an unhappy fate; as the men withdrew, one noted their colonel, James Cameron, brother to the secretary of war, "lying still in the hands of death."[80]

The Sixty-ninth New York, the next regiment to go in, had better luck. The Thirty-eighth New York joined them. These two regiments, supported by part of the Rhode Island battery, were able to drive the Confederates back to the far side of Henry Hill. Admittedly, these latter were worn-out fragments of Confederate regiments, but a concerted forty-minute action paid off. McDowell himself rode up to Henry Hill to congratulate Colonel Corcoran of the Sixty-ninth. Once again, the Union seemed victorious, and not a moment too soon, for McDowell had no more soldiers left for Henry Hill; he now planned to extend the Union line and outflank the Confederate left.

Once again though, the time he had wasted came to haunt McDowell and steal his victory. The railroad at Manassas Junction had delivered one more load of Southern troops by 1:00 P.M., and the last of these had now completed their five-mile march to the battlefield. General Johnston had also been working effectively to call in troops no longer needed to guard the string of fords along Bull Run. As the Irishmen struggled for supremacy atop Henry Hill, seven thousand fresh Confederate troops became available to Johnston to deploy from Portici.

McDowell had more men than Beauregard and Johnston, but could not deploy them to his purposes as effectively. Eighteen thousand out of thirty-three thousand crossed Bull Run and fought.

At this hour, the Southern forces were approaching their peak deployment level. The arrival of Cocke's brigade had been delayed, a precaution over yet another ambiguous dust cloud, but now they came in from Lewis and Ball's fords, surged up Henry Hill, and smacked into the New York regimental positions. "First one regiment and then another and another were forced back, not by the bayonet but by a musketry and rifle fire, which it seemed impossible to push our men through."[81] In the face of this assault, Sherman's brigade lost its fighting effectiveness.

McDowell sent preemptive orders to Colonel Miles at Centreville to prepare to cover a retreat if necessary, also dispatching a courier to telegraph Washington to send all available troops to the front, even though they could not possibly arrive for two days.

Now that he had almost no troops left to execute the maneuver, McDowell deployed the "fresh" troops available to him, Howard's brigade, consisting of the Second Vermont and the Third, Fourth, and Fifth Maine. But these units had been decimated by their forced march in the heat, and were at only 15 percent of their strength. McDowell needed more men if he was to outflank the ever-extending Confederate line and launch a new attack, but one-fifth of the army remained at Fairfax Court House, ten miles away.[82] At 4:00 P.M., Howard's brigade marched out from Matthews Hill, across the road, along Dogan's Ridge, heading for Chinn's Ridge, a ridge top on the west of Sudley Road, a slightly larger twin to Henry Hill. Chinn's was longer and, because it extended further south, was a perfect place for Union artillery to shell the Confederate line, but the Union brought no artillery up to counter the Confederates. Unfortunately, Howard's brigade arrived simultaneously with the Second and Eighth South Carolina regiments and the Alexandria Artillery, who began to shell them. Adjutant Bicknell reported the Fifth Maine advanced up to "a belt of woods" into which "we poured our volleys" with "not a Johnny in sight," "wholly ignorant whether our efforts were of any use or note: but still we worked with a will."

As they battled, Johnston's Fourth Brigade arrived from the

railroad. The Culpepper Artillery, the Third Tennessee, Tenth Virginia, and First Maryland Special Battalion were taken into battle by Colonel Arnold Elzey.*

What happened next was both ironic and poignant. "Col. Elzey cried 'Stars and Stripes' give it to them boys!" and Sergeant McHenry Howard, grandson of Frances Scott Key (who had written the words to "The Star-Spangled Banner," not yet the national anthem) led the attack on the flag. He described the scene: Ordered to fire, "a rolling volley was poured into the enemy," who were only "a skirmish line of New York Zouaves." "Once or twice we loaded and fired, or many did, and we had the satisfaction of seeing the line disappear behind the crest in confusion."[83]

Johnston next directed the Sixth Brigade of the Army of the Potomac under Jubal Early to go find the flank and extend the Confederate line. After waiting all day to play a role in the battle, once they received firm orders, Colonel Jubal Early's men hastened to the Confederate left, arriving sooner than expected.** In this battle, Early was early. Dr. Nott excitedly described,

> At this juncture I saw our reinforcements pouring in with the rapidity and eagerness of a fox chase, and was satisfied that they would drive every thing before them. No one can imagine such a grand, glorious picture as these patriots presented, rushing to the field through the masses of wounded bodies which strewed the roadside as they passed along. I could see a regiment of infantry coming in a trot, with their bright muskets glittering in the sun; then would come a battery of artillery,

* After the wounding of its commander, Brigadier E. Kirby Smith.

** Early said that he could take no special credit for the Union retreat, as his line had only deployed when the retreat commenced. (Early letter in Baltimore paper.)

> each gun carriage crowded with men and drawn by four horses in full gallop. Next came troops of cavalry, . . . after these followed, with almost equal speed, wagons loaded with ammunition, &c, screaming all the while, "push ahead boys," "pitch into the d—d Yankees," "drive them into the Potomac." This keep up from about midday till dark, and I felt as if the Alps themselves could not withstand such a rush.[84]

Just as these troops came up, Beauregard charged his whole line of battle. McDowell, preoccupied with his own newest flanking movement, did not catch on in time. Confederate pressure was inexorable. Another observer, author, poet, and soldier, Thomas Cooper De Leon, was impressed:

> On they came, their yells piercing the woods before they are yet visible; and, as if by magic, the tide of battle turned! . . . Regiment after regiment hears the yell, and echoes it with a wild swelling chorus! And ever on rush the fresh troops—past their weary brothers, into the hottest of the deadly rain of fire—wherever the blue coats are thickest! . . . Like a fire in the prairie spreads the contagion of fear—line after line melts before the hot blast of the charge. . . .[85]

The Union troops were pushed back by a Confederate line that just kept growing longer and longer, and wrapping around them on Chinn's Ridge. Not all of the Union regiments could be rallied by their inexperienced officers, but those that did were often only a shadow of their former selves; they could not be further pressed to hold the tide on the left. Confusion prevailed everywhere; Beauregard's description of the battlefield dynamics and the difficulty of commanding men applied to both sides:

> More than two thousand men were shouting each some sug-

gestion to his neighbor, their voices mingling with the noise of the shells hurtling through the trees overhead, and all word of command drowned in the confusion and uproar.[86]

About this time, Colonel Oliver Howard commanding Third Brigade, Third Division, withdrew his Second Vermonters to his rear, so he could redeploy them as his engagement developed. Their companion unit, the Fourth Maine, thought they were meant to go too, and followed. It turned into a spontaneous withdrawal.

North or South, soldiers usually rallied only to familiar or charismatic figures, their own officers, or generals who had courted their loyalty for weeks like a politician running for office. So when Major Barry reported how, "General McDowell and myself took regimental flags . . . and begged the troops to rally around them; and a few did, but not a sufficient number," it was because they were relative unknowns.[87] Heintzelman lamented,

> Finding it impossible to rally any of the regiments, we commenced our retreat about 4:30 P.M. There was a fine position a short distance in rear, where I hoped to make a stand with a section of Arnold's battery and the U.S. cavalry, if I could rally a few regiments of infantry. In this I utterly failed, and we continued our retreat on the road we had before advanced in the morning. I sent forward my staff officers to rally some troops beyond the run, but not a company would form.[88]

Almost every man fighting for the Union that day had pushed himself way beyond his personal limits, had performed beyond his wildest imagination in the face of horror and privation. By 4:00 P.M., without the adrenaline surge of a victory, they could perform no longer. Each man found he had run out of energy—about the same time the man next to him discovered the same thing.

Scattered, lost from officers and comrades, the men of the badly battered units caught the fever and started pulling back. McDowell's adjutant, Fry, over at Henry Hill, noted that "the men walked quietly off. . . . There was no special excitement, except that arising from the frantic efforts of the officers to stop [the] men."[88] Not knowing the geography of the battlefield, without officers to control their movements, the Union soldiers went home the only way they knew, the way they had come in, the Second and Third divisions again taking along the long, looping country path back to the Warrenton Turnpike and Cub Run, the First retracing their steps along the turnpike. There was general consensus among the men that they were to meet up at their camps in Centreville, the camps they had left just fourteen hours ago. McDowell now had a general retreat on his hands.

CHAPTER EIGHTEEN

"Yankee Doodle Wheeled About and Scampered Off at Full Run, and Such a Race Was Never Seen as that He Made at Bull Run"*

The Union Retreats from Bull Run

July 21, 5:00 P.M. to Noon July 22, 1861

For many in the rear, the retreat was a total surprise. Although the main battle had just stopped,[1] there was to be sporadic fighting for the next few hours in the "only campaign in which three distinct organizations were represented—regulars,

* From the Civil War song "Confederate Yankee Doodle." This song was a parody using the traditional tune. Parodies were common and popular on both sides during the war.

volunteers and militia."[2] The ordeal of the men was not yet over and, in some respects, Sullivan Ballou's was just starting.

Finding a retreat forming up outside their front door, and with takeover by Confederate troops imminent, the surgeons, orderlies, and patients were dumbfounded, and rushed to organize what they could in what little time was left. The most serious cases could not be moved. Sullivan's sutures were too fragile to attempt to move him on a rutted road—he had to stay, as did Colonel Slocum, as well as anyone still awaiting surgery. The surgeons had some quick thinking to do, for available transportation was insufficient to evacuate the wounded and the hospital staff with the retreating army. Patients unable to walk only got away if they were very lucky, like Captain Julius Ellis of F Company, Seventy-first New York, who had scarcely joined Sullivan Ballou at the Thornberry house before he fled. Ellis, who had been treated at the hospital,

> was brought out of the building & wished to be taken to a small house nearby, in which we assisted [Thornberry], we had hardly got him there when the 8th Regt. came along on a run. I asked what was the matter they said the whole Army was on a retreat. I told Capt. Ellis and asked him what I should do get him on ambulance or leave him there he told me to get the ambulance which I did & helped his brother Sam [private Samuel C. Ellis] put him into it.[3]

Some wounded exhibited remarkable endurance in making their way to safety, so determined were they to avoid capture. His arm amputated above the elbow, one soldier walked all the way to the capital, twenty-five miles from his starting point. Another walked the same distance "with a large hole through both thighs and the scrotum," while yet another was able to make it with "a hole through both cheeks, a broken jaw and his tongue nearly out."[4] One Rhode Islander was apparently shot in the buttocks yet walked all the way back to Camp Sprague, where he was later interviewed, "sitting outside the hospital-barracks, coolly smoking his pipe."[5] Others were apparently less lucky, despite the devotion of comrades. Private John Rice of the Second New Hampshire took a bullet through the lung and his comrades carried him up the Sudley Road, intending to take him to the hospital. To their eyes, he appeared to have died along the way, so they tucked him under a fence and hastened to make good their escape.[6] Many other wounded lay where they had fallen, among the dead, in the fields, pastures, roadsides, and woods.

As Union troops passed Sudley Church Hospital, many men darted over to bid farewell to friends, "Upward of 150–250 [of whom were] left there at the end of the day, all of them serious cases."[7]

Each caregiver quickly searched his conscience, and reviewed his options; the Union surgeons held a hurried conference among themselves. From a medical standpoint, a hundred or more men still awaited treatment and surgery, postoperative patients like Sullivan Ballou needed follow-up, and they expected more wounded troops to wander in from the woods for help. If the hospital staff left, their patients would be totally at the mercy of the enemy. As officers, surgeons could intervene for mercy on behalf of their patients, and, while no formal legal agreements protected surgeons, armies traditionally did not take them prisoner. If they stayed, they might reasonably expect to be sent home shortly.

Yet doctors needed to accompany the retreat, for once the regiments returned to their temporary camps back near Centreville, any wounded who had walked or ridden away would still require treatment, as would any injured during the retreat itself. Those doctors who opted not to trust the mercies of the enemy quickly grabbed their gear, imparted crucial information on seriously ill patients, mounted their horses, and joined the retreating army. Dr. Henry Rivers was among those who left, and the last patient he checked on was Sullivan Ballou. Rivers later reported that he left him, "*alive, the last one* and that he was *brave, brave, brave.*" Dr. Rivers said his last words to him were:

> "Go, Doctor, as you have done all you can for me, and there is but little chance for me, and save those of the wounded that you can." A brave man was Sullivan Ballou.[8]

A core group representing most of the regiments whose men were at the hospital opted to remain behind. Doctors Eugene Peugnet of the Seventy-first New York; George Sternberg and Charles Gray of the Regular Army; W. W. Keen of the Fifth Massachusetts; Charles DeGraw, Foster Swift,* and Gustavus Winston of the Eighth New York; Joseph Homeston and William Swalm of the Fourteenth Brooklyn; and Jacob H. Stewart of the First Minnesota were "on staff" as well.[9] Doctor John Harris of Rhode Island stayed, as did Privates Josiah Richardson of the First, and Joseph Eldridge and James Collins from the Second Regiment, the men who had tended Colonel Egbert Jones and Sullivan. Chaplain John Mines from Maine abided with the men, as did a great many other nameless volunteers. Some wounded men were being cared for by relatives—brothers or cousins—who chose not to leave them.

A few men who dashed in to say good-bye were overwhelmed with empathy for the sufferers calling for water, and decided, on the spot, to remain. Lieutenant Charles J. Murphy from the Thirty-eighth New York felt his duty to the wounded overcame the personal risk of being taken prisoner by the Confederates. Sitting atop one of his quartermaster's wagons, which were lined up to join the retreat, repeatedly urged to get out while he could, Murphy stepped down and let the wagons leave without him. He maintained that not one man could be spared from the care of the

* Swift had been let go from the Thirty-ninth New York when he had failed to revive a drowned man. He was immediately hired by the Eighth.

wounded, and told his comrades he would rather risk death or capture than leave the wounded to die without care.* Murphy then helped care for Sullivan for two days.[10] Just before the Confederates arrived, Doctor Stewart persuaded journalist William Croffut to leave before he could be captured.[11]

For the most part, the men injured on Henry Hill just before the retreat were not evacuated, but left on the field. The nurses tried to assist them as best they could, concentrating on forming a canteen detail to bring water for the wounded. One of them, with about fifty canteens hanging off the pommel of the saddle, "running her horse with all possible speed," the other nurses gathered up the empty canteens lying about the field and went to a spring a mile off, near Centreville, braved sharpshooters to fill them, and brought them back to the men.[12] But the female nurses also left the field before they could be captured by Confederate patrols, and the men were then truly alone.

Some died from lack of care; others were picked up as much as a day or two later, and brought into the Stone House or Stone Church hospitals closer to Henry Hill. Burnside's brigade formed up just across the run, and then marched off in columns, artillery and cavalry following them, leaving Sullivan Ballou and thirty-four other Rhode Island wounded behind them.**

As the road looped up into Fairfax County and past Sudley Mansion, Lieutenant Munroe had a very different encounter with the lady in the white house as the troops retreated past it. Munroe had received a scalp wound earlier, but had refused to leave the field. On his way out of Sudley, he decided to take another chance at getting a drink of water.

* For this act of bravery, he later received the Medal of Honor. See appendix 3.

** Forty-four men of the Second Rhode Island were taken prisoner, 68 percent of them wounded. Roughly half of the wounded were captured while the other half got away in the retreat. For the First Rhode Island, twenty-one men became POWs, 25 percent of them wounded. (Analysis by author, from Civil War Database information.)

> On our way back in the afternoon, after our apparent signal defeat, I saw the same lady standing at the same window, with a tin cup in her hand, from which she was dispensing water to a goodly sized crowd of our thirsty men. I rode through the crowd and asked her for a drink. She passed the cup to me with a very little water in it, and I found it deliciously cold and refreshing. As she handed the cup, she remarked, "I can only give this to the wounded, for my ice is almost out, and I want very much to look out for them." My acrimonious feelings of the morning were entirely dispelled, for her heart, stubborn with the well and strong, had melted to the mostly kindly sympathy with those whose sufferings required a refreshing draught, though they were enemies to the cause she evidently was devoted to.[13]

The women of Sudley Springs and their neighbors soon began to assist with the care of the wounded the retreating army left behind, as well as with the Confederate injured.

The Confederates had not anticipated a general retreat at this moment, and needed time to formulate a response. Their bifurcated command had worked effectively all afternoon, sending men in one direction into an ever-widening battlefront on Henry Hill. Now that this battlefront had evaporated, improvising a plan to send men in all directions as the sun was setting would just dissipate the command of the army, which might be needed on the morrow if the Union regrouped at Centreville. Once again, there were clouds of dust toward the west and Beauregard could not discount that Patterson's army might have marched on him at last. Neither he nor Johnston were in any position to send away a portion of their two armies. In the disorganization of sudden victory, with nightfall nearing, pockets of enemy troops still a threat, and units of Rebel troops probing and galloping in new directions Rebel army communications and command faltered.

Another complication for the exhausted but exhilarated-with-victory Confederate commanders was the presence of President Jefferson Davis on the battlefield. Davis, a former soldier, had not been content to sit in his capital and wait for telegrams, so earlier in the day he had set out by train for Manassas. When stragglers met the train about a half mile south of Manassas Junction with news of the Union victory on Matthews Hill, the engineer refused to take the train into the station, afraid the cars would be captured. A compromise was reached: only the engine chugged northward, carrying Davis, who stared at the horizon, trying to read the portents from the smoke rising from the battlefield. By the time he arrived, accompanied by a single aide, the tide of events had turned. Davis was then everywhere, buttonholing officers for news, urging the wounded to seek medical care, congratulating colonels, and issuing impromptu battlefield promotions.[14] Neither general could ignore his presence in their midst.

With the battle on Henry Hill over, Jackson's artillery withdrew to the hilltop of Portici from where "part of this artillery fired on the retreating enemy."[15] Other artillery was on the field, and the Union's own captured guns may indeed have been turned on the "skedaddling" Yanks.* Some of the Rhode Islanders believed Sudley Field Hospital was shelled, and so reported to the press: "Lieut. Sears thinks the house was shelled, but Dr. Rivers says 'No.'"[16] Sudley Church did lose a chunk of wall, blown out by a shell sometime between the summers of 1861 and 1862, but just when it happened is unknown.[17]

Imboden, whose battery may have fired the shot that claimed Sullivan's leg, did not himself leave the field unscathed that day. Personally firing the last round of his ammunition, he forgot to

* A term whose origin dates to this event. For all its homegrown-sounding flavor, it is possibly derived from the Greek verb meaning to disperse or retire tumultuously. (Partridge, *Historical Slang*)

stand away from the gun muzzle. He was blown twenty feet by the blast, and had his left eardrum ruptured. This caused permanent deafness on his left side. Later that day he received various superficial wounds from shrapnel, and in trying to prevent some spooked soldiers from running away from the battlefield, had his left arm slit open from wrist to elbow by the bayonet of one of them.[18]

Although several Southern units and batteries claimed the honor of being the first to fire the best-aimed of these important salvos, and debated the fact in memoirs and the *Confederate Veteran* for the next twenty years, the fact was, there was enough shelling to go around. The fire was so concentrated that while pursuing the retreat, Stuart had to put his troopers into a gallop to dodge some Southern cannonballs whizzing through their ranks.[19] The Confederates not only fired on Centreville, but aimed for the farm roads leading to the Spindle and Grigsby farms, from which the men of the Second and Third divisions would emerge onto the turnpike.

> When within two miles of the road, in an open space, the enemy poured in upon us from an eminence to the right a raking fire. The troops sought shelter in the woods to the left and were finally led into the road which they had left in the morning. Here again the enemy opened fire upon us. This was very destructive. We had expected to meet here the reserve ready to protect us. Everything was in confusion.[20]

Adjutant George Bicknell of the Fifth Maine experienced the same thing.

> We reached the road, and here all discipline was at an end. Our regiment, like every other, was entirely broken up. Strike for the camp of last night the best you can, was the last direction any

> one heard. A more heterogeneous complication of regiments could not be conceived.[21]

The Union battery commanders were most concerned about evacuating their guns for future use, so only Arnolds' and Ayres' paused to shoot back. The most inviting target was the bottleneck of the morning, the bridge over Cub Run. This bombardment not only damaged and blocked the bridge, but caused a panic among the civilian carriages and the military competing to leave the area. The bridge was blocked to further vehicular traffic, and human traffic remained well within cannon range. Lieutenant Munroe was puzzled by the hotness of the Confederate attack.

> Just as I rode alongside him (Captain Reynolds), a shot from the enemy's artillery struck the ground only a few feet from us. Unsophisticated as I was, I could not understand why they should continue to fire upon us when we were doing the best we could to let them alone, and I said to Captain Reynolds: "what do you suppose they're trying to do?" His reply was a characteristic one: "they are trying to kill every mother's son of us: that is what they're trying to do!"[22]

The ongoing barrage killed some Rhode Island men, most notably Captain Samuel James Smith from Woonsocket, one of the officers with whom Sullivan had made the plan to bring their wives down to camp to visit. Corporal English of Company D, Second Rhode Island was involved:

> As we neared the bridge, the rebels opened a very destructive fire upon us, mowing down our men like grass, and caused even greater confusion than before. Our artillery and baggage wagons became fouled with each other, completely blocking the bridge, while the mob shells bursting on the bridge make

> it "rather unhealthy" to be around. As I crossed on my hands and knees, Capt [Samuel J.] Smith who was crossing by my side at the same time was struck by a round shot at the same time and completely cut in two.[23]

Corporal English said, "At Cub Run the bridge was rendered impassable by the wrecks of several baggage wagons," and for many soldiers, it was every man for himself in the struggle to get to the east bank of Bull Run.[24] Corporal Rhodes

> looked for a place to cross the stream, not daring to try the bridge. I jumped into the run and holding my gun above my head struggled across with the water up to my waist. After crossing, the Regiment gradually formed again.[25]

Lieutenant Munroe described how the artillerymen got away,

> The leading team of the battery had to halt; and as it was impossible to stop the rear carriages on the hill, the column became a jumbled heap of horses, limbers, caissons, and gun carriages . . . at this moment a rebel battery in our rear opened fire, and it seemed as if every one of their shots came into our very midst. The men immediately set to work taking the horses from their harnesses, after doing so they mounted upon them in the most lively manner. Some horses carried only a single passenger, others had doublets and triplets on their backs.[26]

While many of the Union men took it amiss that the South was still trying to kill them, the South still had a purpose to accomplish this day. If the Union could be humiliated badly enough, the war might end that month. If enough homes in the North lost their men, they might press the federal government to end the war. The

South still hoped to achieve a key war goal, succession without interference. If they might be let alone to set up their government, they expected Britain to recognize them to guarantee the flow of cotton to British mills, and the Confederate States of America would flourish.

Beauregard did send cavalry along the turnpike and Sudley Road to reconnoiter and harass the retreat and take prisoners—including ambulances evaluating the wounded. Infantrymen from Cocke's and Early's brigades swept up the Sudley Road and east side fields as far as the Matthews House, taking mostly wounded as prisoners.

Assigned to move north along the Sudley Road, Stuart's First Virginia Cavalry found so many severely wounded along the road that they did not bother to capture them, for they were neither going anywhere nor did they pose any threat. Stuart noted,

> The enemy being now in full retreat, I followed with the cavalry as rapidly as possible, but was so much encumbered with prisoners, whom I sent as fast as possible back to the infantry, that my command was soon too much reduced to encounter any odds.[27]

J. E. B. Stuart reported,

> I have no idea how many prisoners were taken. . . . In the pursuit Lieut. William Taylor alone captured six of the enemy with arms in their hands. A large number of arms, quantities of clothing and hospital stores, and means of transportation were found abandoned on the road.[28]

One of the prisoners they took was Lieutenant Doherty, who after taking a wounded man to Sudley Church

> returned from the hospital towards my regiment, and met other troops retreating, who informed me that my regiment

> had gone across the fields. I ran back past Sudley Church, . . . up the hill, saw a regiment about half a mile ahead which I supposed was the Seventy-first; took a short cut across the fields when the cavalry galloped up and arrested me.[29]

When Stuart's men arrived at Sudley Church hospital, however, their forward movement stopped dead in its tracks. The Union surgeons had been on the lookout for the arrival of the Confederate forces and did the only thing they could under the circumstances: surrender.

> Dr. Harris, who had gone down the hill in front, returned to the church and remained there, sending back a man with a white handkerchief for a flag of truce, to surrender the wounded men we had been compelled to abandon. That was the only flag of truce sent to the enemy from our wing, and that was an act of humanity.[30]

Harris sent one of the Rhode Island orderlies, Private Joseph Eldridge, a fifer with the band of the Second; there were no officers on their feet to conduct the parley, and the surgeons were too busy.

Here, the Confederates found hundreds of severely wounded prisoners spread out over the ground around the church. Many of them were Southerners who would need to be transferred to Confederate care as soon as it could be arranged. There were also dozens of able-bodied soldiers assisting the dozen or so physicians and chaplains. Encumbered with prisoners and the responsibility for the hospital, Stuart could go no further. "I encamped that night on Sudley farm, where was a large church, used as a hospital by the enemy, containing about 300 wounded, the majority mortally."[31] Sudley Church hospital had just become a Southern prison camp.

With darkness falling, and Stuart short of men, all Yankees captured in the fields, farmyards, and hedges along that quadrant of the battlefield were now brought to the church and detained, including Lieutenant Doherty. "They took me back to the hospital, where, during the confusion, I managed to conceal myself under a blanket, which was saturated with blood."

It is unclear whether Colonel Jones had been moved to the "officer's quarters," or was left outside the church to await the change of command. Either way, Jones made it clear to the Confederate cavalry that he had been well treated by Dr. Rivers, and tenderly nursed by Private Josiah Richardson and the other Rhode Island volunteer orderlies. Colonel Jones received priority transport to Manassas Junction for transfer to a Southern hospital, but before he left Sudley church, he negotiated special treatment for the men who had succored him and, it appears likely, for Major Sullivan Ballou as well, completing a circle of kindness.

There had been a news blackout on the battle, due to the fact that the reporters could not get to the field. Five miles away on Centreville heights, the journalists and spectators had seen bits of movements in the distance, but between the dust and smoke, and the ambivalence of the uniforms, had barely distinguished which side was doing what to the other at any given moment.[32] Even so experienced a battle reporter as the London *Times* correspondent William Howard Russell, who had covered the Crimean War, had to content himself with getting glimpses in the distance, if he used field glasses. He, too, was unable to tell one side from the other.[33] After getting a late start because his colleague had overslept, Russell rested his horse, picnicked, and got no closer to the battle than the intersection of the turnpike and the forest road by Mrs. Spindle's, where Hunter's Division had turned northward. He did see shelling and one dust cloud.[34]

During the day, the only military personnel most reporters found to interview were inbound and knew nothing, yet these were the men who would supply the initial news reports upon which

Sarah Ballou, and others in the hometowns across New England, Ohio, Michigan, and Minnesota, would have to rely. Personal reports from actual combatants were to come in much later. Hiking on toward Centreville, publisher George Putnam and colleagues, moving through Fairfax Station, a town of a single structure, "found a Lt. sitting on the track and taking notes which he sent every half hour to Scott."[35] Next, on the turnpike, they were overtaken by

> two soldiers and a doctorial looking companion . . . from the Second Rhode Island. "That's Greene," says the surgeon, nodding toward the gentlemanly-looking soldier ahead of us. "He was in the hospital at Washington; positive orders not to stir from it; but heard there was to be a battle, tumbled on his uniform, seized his musket, walked twenty miles, and here he is." It was a grandson of the great general of our first revolution, and a cousin of our friend.

This happenstance meeting had special meaning for Putnam, himself the grandson of General Israel Putnam. Both their grandfathers had commanded troops in the same battles of the Revolutionary War.[36]

Things remained ambiguous to the observers as late as "half past three to four, carriages of spectators who had seen enough returning to Washington calmly, thinking the battle won."[37] Suddenly though, the pattern began to change, and the reporters' instincts prickled.

> Then an army-officer on horseback, apparently on special business, and riding much faster than those who had passed, whirled by in such hot haste as wouldn't stay question. He looked any thing but jubilant, and we just managed to entice from him four muttered words: "Bad as can be!" Away he galloped.[38]

Russell then observed the wagons inbound to battlefield via Cub Run—baggage wagons he thought—suddenly turned around and reversed course. This, too, tied up traffic, because wagons have a large turning radius.[39] Stedman, the correspondent for the *New York World,* realized that Hunter's munition trains were coming onto the turnpike, when the shelling began, cut the traces of their teams and rode off on the horses.[40]

Putnam, who published *Putnam's Monthly Magazine of American Literature, Science and Art,* wrote,

> The first indication of disturbed nerves met us in the shape of a soldier, musket less and coatless, clinging to the bare back of a great, bony, wagon-horse—sans reins, sans everything. Man and beast came panting along, each looking exhausted, and just as they pass us, the horse tumbles down helpless in the road, and his rider tumbles off and hobbles away.[41]

The Confederates reported "by five o'clock there was not a Union soldier except the dead, wounded and prisoners on the south side of Bull Run."[42]

Russell started traveling east, and got a scoop when he was able to report that he "had left Hunter with men in a cart seven miles west of Long Bridge." The senior aide with him was drunk and proclaimed to all who would listen, "We've been licked into a cocked hat!"[43] Russell hurried homeward to file his report on the battle he never saw, a caustic article castigating the Union war effort, which was to make him persona non grata for years in the North.

Putnam and the colleague who remained with him, known only as "T," stayed near Centreville and were at least able report the details of the retreat, and to intercept soldiers for interviews on what had occurred. They observed Brigadier General Runyon's forces deploying to intercept, a mile east of Centreville at half past four, the First New Jersey Regiment under Colonel Montgomery coming up at the double quick from Vienna. The reporters went and sat on a nearby hill to watch them take a position across the turnpike, turning back the vanguard of the retreat.

> In less than twenty minutes the road was cleared and regulated, the army-wagons halted, still in line, on one side of the road; the civilians were permitted to drive on as fast as they pleased toward Washington; the regiment deployed into a field on the opposite hill and formed in line of battle commanding the road; a detachment was sent out to "clear the track" to Centreville; and presently the regiment itself marched up the road in the direction of the field of conflict. It was now about half past five.[44]

They interviewed some "men from different parts of the field. . . . before they could have compared notes among themselves," and a got a decent summary of what happened to report to the readers back home. They learned, "Our men held their ground sturdily until 3 o' clock; and whenever they came in actual contact with the rebels they drove them back . . . and many of our officers were grossly inefficient." The spoke with men who said, "The greatest mistake on our side was want of cavalry. The next was making us fight on empty stomachs, tired out, and without any water to taste except mud-puddles."[45]

By 5:45 P.M., General McDowell had reached Centreville, given orders for the retreat to be covered, and discovered that Colonel Dixon Miles had withdrawn regiments intended to block the Confederates from using multiple fords in their pursuit of the Union forces. "Fighting Dick" Richardson's troops were among them. "General McDowell rode up to me. Said he, 'Great God, Colonel Richardson, why didn't you hold on to the position at Blackburn's Ford?'" Richardson replied,

> "Colonel Miles ordered me to retreat to Centreville, and I obeyed the order. Colonel Miles is continually interfering with me, and he is drunk, and is not fit to command." At that time, he could hardly sit his horse. I could see from his reeling in the saddle, from his incoherent language, and from his general appearance, that he was drunk. I had been acquainted with Colonel Miles long before.[46]

Many others in the reserves confirmed Miles's behavior and smelled liquor on him. Miles, reportedly ill and told by his physician to drink brandy, was apparently an alcoholic for whom this was the wrong medicine. McDowell promptly relieved Miles from duty, and authorized Richardson to redeploy.*

As the sunburnt, grimy, thirsty soldiers who had been in the hottest of battle all day long encountered the reserves at Centreville, they became angry. Here were federal soldiers with no more than the dust of the road on them, hundreds, no, thousands of men. Two divisions and a brigade who obviously had not fought, whose presence on the battlefield might have made a difference to the outcome. As Henry Blake told it,

> The appearance of so many full regiments at Centreville, that had been unemployed during the day, caused much excitement; and the troops that had undergone the perils of the fight were very severe in their comments upon the ability and loyalty of the commanding general. "We have been sold," was a common remark in their conversation.[47]

* At a hearing preliminary to a full court-martial, in August 1861, the panel found it "would not be in the interests of the service to convene a court in this case" due to the "greatest inconvenience at present."

The reporters waited two more hours, and then went to a farm well to help themselves to water; there, they were "joined by many men, some wounded, some just exhausted. "Their first word of all was 'water! Is there any water here?'" Revived by a drink, the men "rested, washed, breathed long and well, and trudged on toward Fairfax."[48] Here, they were told by an eighteen-year-old that he had been in a hospital that was shelled; he also told stories of the wounded being bayoneted on the field, a story whose universal veracity was hard to verify. Putnam and "T" concluded there may have been isolated incidents of this on the battlefield, but that it was neither a condoned policy nor something that happened after the battle was over. They fed the soldiers from their own haversack.[49]

"It was now nearly seven o'clock and the sun about a half-hour high," and the men of both sides were reeling from "the terrors of this battle."[50] One soldier from the Fourth South Carolina, which began fighting with Evans since early that morning, wrote to his wife,

> For ten long hours it literally rained balls, shells and other missiles of destruction. The firing did not cease for a moment. . . . It was truly terrific. . . . The sight of the dead, the cries of the wounded, the thundering noise of battle can never be put on paper. The dead, the dying and wounded, all mixed up together; friend and foe embraced in death; some crying for water; some praying their last prayers; some trying to whisper to a friend their last farewell message to the loved ones at home. It is heartrending. . . . Mine eyes are damp with tears.[51]

Women like Sarah Ballou, mothers like Emeline Ballou, sisters like Hannah Frances Bogle, who had nervously sent their men off for months of outdoor living and a demonstration against the enemy, never imagined the horror that their husbands, sons, and brothers had lived through this day. Mercifully, they did not yet know of it.

Neither did the president nor the army command. Toward three o'clock, ever more frequent telegrams were received at the War Office in Washington; they reported considerable fluctuation in the apparent course and progress of the cannonade. The president went to call on General Scott at his home; the general had to be awakened from a long nap around 4:00 P.M. to talk to him. It is unclear whether Scott had read the full set of messages, but told the president that the changes in the currents of wind and the variation of the echoes made it impossible for a distant listener to determine the course of a battle. What Scott said was true enough but, ironically in hindsight, these messages were accurate enough regarding the movement of the battle.

The general in chief then went back to sleep, and the president, himself, went over to the telegraph office to read the messages that now came in every ten or fifteen minutes.[52] They reported that "the battle had extended over nearly the whole line; that there had been considerable loss," but that the Union had successfully driven the Southern forces back, some dispatches said to the Junction.[53]

Scott read a positive spin into the message to "send on immediately all troops," and sent a messenger to Lincoln with the interpretation that McDowell was about to attack and capture the Junction. "Deeming all doubt at an end, President Lincoln ordered his carriage and went out to take his usual evening drive."[54]

At 5:45 P.M., McDowell telegraphed an understated battle report, noting, "We passed Bull Run. Engaged the enemy, who, it seems, had just be re-enforced by General Johnston." It ended with the news that his army had been "driven from the position we had gained overlooking Manassas. After this the men could not be rallied, but slowly left the field." He reported the death of the politically well-connected Colonel Cameron, and told Scott that Miles's Division was going to hold Centreville "so the our men can get behind it."[55]

However, about that time, another, more candid telegram was

received from Captain B. S. Alexander of the Corps of Engineers. It was both coherent and alarming:

> General McDowell's army in full retreat through Centreville. The day is lost. Save Washington and the remnants of this army. All available troops ought to be thrown forward in one body. General McDowell is doing all that he can to cover the retreat. Colonel Miles is forming for that purpose. He was in reserve at Centreville. The routed troops will not reform.[56]

While the news was incredible, the author of the telegram displayed inside knowledge of the Union troop dispositions, recommended a course of action, and conveyed a good sense of developments—Scott still remained unconvinced.

The Union soldiers on the turnpike running for their lives might just as well have been a million miles away from the wounded prisoners left behind at the field hospitals, for whom no rescue was coming. Lieutenant Edward Doherty created a chronicle of events at Sudley Church hospital, which he published in the *New York Post* once he got home, not only to inform people what happened, but to assist families in learning the fate of their missing men. Lieutenant Charles Murphy, later awarded the Medal of Honor for his valor with the wounded, wrote one by request many years later. Their accounts differ only in the name of a cavalry captain. By correlating their timetables with reports found in letters from other men, and the time of day various units went into battle, it is possible to establish for the first time a picture of life at Sudley hospital over the next few days. Doherty starts his account after the cavalry was in command at the hospital, after he came out from under his bloody blanket:

> Col. Barker [Parker] of the Virginia Cavalry, then galloped up, and ordered all the unwounded prisoners to be driven to the Junction.

I should think there were about 50 prisoners in all at that point. They left me, supposing I was wounded. A guard was left to guard the hospital. I arose to go in quest of Dr. Peugnet, and found him engaged in amputating the arm of Harry Rockafellow. . . . Dr. Peugnet requested me to assist him, and he having completed his operation, then amputated the arm at the shoulder joint of a sergeant of a Maine . . . Regiment who had a brother, about 17 years of age, who had remained behind to take care of him. This man died under the amputation. The next operation was that of my friend Sm. Smith of Brooklyn, whom I had conveyed to the hospital. His foot was amputated.[57]

Rockafellow had waited six to seven hours for surgery, Smith about two, yet the doctors worked without cease on the men of their own regiments and others.

Genl. Beauregard and Col. Barker [Parker] came up about 7 1/2- o'clock that evening with 10 prisoners of different regiments, most of whom were Fire Zouaves. He stopped and inquired how our wounded were getting along, while the prisoners were driven toward the Junction by the cavalry. During the night a number of prisoners were brought in and on Monday morning were sent on. . . . with Manila rope, among them [the soldier] of 17, from Maine, who plead bitterly to be left to see his brother buried, but was refused.[58]

Stuart was managing all of this with just a small squad of men, for his cavalry was not yet at full strength. Meanwhile, the flood tide of men surged toward Centreville. George Bicknell gave a good description that covers his own Fifth Maine and the Rhode Islanders:

> It was about eight o'clock in the evening when most of the men arrived at the place of our camp the previous night. Here we took supper, talked over the incidents of the day . . . and lay down upon the ground to rest, terribly tired. . . . Scarcely had we got into a good position to sleep, before we were suddenly awakened to obey the order to move at once. . . . A great many evil thoughts entered our brains, as we viewed in semi-wakeful condition, the prospect of a night-march. . . . The sky had become overcast, and there was every indication of an approaching storm, as though the elements were desirous of dampening our clothes . . . even as . . . indisputable defeat, had dampened our spirits. . . . A little after ten o'clock at night our line was again formed, and, under the valiant charge of officers more frightened than hurt, we moved out onto the turnpike, the column heading toward Fairfax Courthouse.[59]

Rhode Island which, of course, had the easternmost camp, had the longest distance to go before reaching their camp. They had to pass through Blenker's troops, "posted across the road to protect the retreat, before entering "Bush Camp." They thought this was their final destination for the evening, and were "preparing to make a stand against the enemy." "The order to retreat from Centreville was very unexpected."[60] Rhodes grumbled about being roused from sleep about 11:00 P.M. to march to Washington "in the midst of a rain storm."[61] The rain clouds blocked the moon as the men of many regiments converged on the little town of Fairfax Court House, already full of reserve troops like the Fourth Michigan, who were stationed there.

> "Who are these?" cried out some of the 69th New York, as we were nearing Fairfax Court House on the retreat and had come to the fork of the road at which they were halting. "The

> First and Second Rhode Island" was the reply. Quick as thought came back the response, "wherever Rhode Island leads we are ready to follow"—so soon was the valor of our men recognized. We certainly had done no dishonor to the State that had sent us forth, and the cause which she had entrusted to our defence. Some of our comrades had sealed their devotion with their blood and left an honorable memory for us to cherish as a dear possession.[62]

Once within its confines, the streets were crowded with men and wagons, and the regiments became comingled as little groups took their rest on lawns and porches and the streets themselves, in the rain. Men who during the battle longed for a little water were now being drenched with it.* William Russell noted as he passed through, "the residents of Fairfax Courthouse at their doorways, anxious."[63] During the night, the tentative plan to reform the army at Fairfax Court House was abandoned, and the men were all pushed on towards the Potomac. Private Rhodes bemoaned,

> Of the horrors of that night, I can give you no adequate idea. I suffered . . . from thirst and fatigue but struggled on, clinging to my gun and cartridge box. Many times I sat down in the mud determined to go no further, and willing to die to end my misery. But soon a friend would pass and urge me to make another effort, and I would stagger on a mile further.[64]

* E. Porter Alexander, who was to become very experienced in artillery working for Robert E. Lee, remarked on the curious fact that heavy rainstorms followed many large battles: "At dawn the next morning it was pouring rain and it continued most of the day. This heavy precipitation has often been appealed to by the rain-makers as confirmation of their theories than rain may be induced by heavy cannonading."

Meanwhile, at 6:00 P.M., even before Lincoln returned from his drive, Secretary Seward had hastened to the Executive Mansion, "pale and haggard," and inquiring for the president in a hoarse voice. When told by John Hay and John Nicolay that he had gone out after reading the optimistic telegrams, Seward swore them to secrecy and told them the opposite was now known to be true. They were to tell the president,

> The battle is lost. The telegraph says that McDowell is in full retreat, and calls on General Scott to save the capital. Find the President and tell him to come immediately to General Scott's.

When they did, Lincoln received the news "in silence, without the slightest change of feature or expression, and walked away to army headquarters."[65] He returned to the White House at 7:00 P.M., after meetings with Scott and Dahlgren.

The conflicting reports seemed preposterous to Scott, but the president summoned the Cabinet and they joined him "in feverish suspense," assembled in Scott's quarters, and sat grimly listening to the worsening situation. Messengers ran the telegrams across the street from the War Department and were read aloud by Colonel Townsend. In hushed whispers, the secretary of war learned of the death of his brother, commanding the Seventy-ninth New York.[66] At seven, Scott telegraphed Baltimore to put troops on the alert there, just in case, though he concluded, "bad news from McDowell's army not credited by me." An hour later, he telegraphed Brigadier General Theodore Runyon to hold Alexandria against any Confederate onslaught. At this moment, the thought seems to have been to hold the western bank of the Potomac and make a stand there against the Confederates storming Washington, D.C.[67]

McDowell's first telegram said he would hold Centreville. His second indicated that "the larger part of the men are a confused mob, entirely disorganized," but that he would try to rally them for a stand at Fairfax Court House even though "we are without artillery ammunition." His third reported that the men did not wait around long enough for orders, and were "in a state of utter disorganization"; and the most prudent course of action, as agreed upon by his commanders when he discussed it with them at Centreville, was to make a stand at the Potomac.[68] After midnight he reported they had not been attacked, were drawing in the stragglers and "now trying to get matters a little organized over here."[69]

Once again, the Lincoln administration began a new round of preparations to defend the national capital. John Hay noted,

> All available troops were hurried forward to McDowell's support; Baltimore was put on the alert; telegrams were sent to the recruiting stations of the nearest Northern States to lose no time in sending all their organized regiments to Washington; McClellan was ordered to "come down to the Shenandoah Valley with such troops as can be spared from Western Virginia."[70]

The plan seemed to be to keep any battle for Washington on the western shore of the Potomac. Colonel Erasmus Keyes believed,

> The troops then were not in a sufficient state of discipline to enable any man living to have had an absolute command of them. The next point was to balance all the probabilities in regard to this capital; that is, was it more probable that the capital would fall into the hands of the enemy by retreating than by remaining there?[71]

To that end, that evening, Scott had telegraphed McDowell care of Fairfax Court House that three regiments including the Fourth

Michigan were at Fairfax Station but he was holding the trains. At that point, the two hundred feet of obstructed tracks had not been cleared to enable the train to move closer. At 9:00 P.M., Scott had sent a second telegram to McDowell, informing him that four additional regiments have been sent across the Potomac River, and "we are not discouraged." Colonel John McCunn, commanding the Thirty-seventh New York, also telegraphed McDowell, noting, "Scouts report trees felled on road to Alexandria. Things looking ugly here." McCunn had set his men to work removing the landslide at Fairfax Station and, not having heard back from McDowell, he telegraphed Scott at 11:05 P.M. to report the tracks cleared. He asked, "What shall I do?" Scott was up late and tending to business, because he telegraphed back forty minutes later to tell McCunn that McDowell was at Fairfax Court House, implying he should work directly with McDowell. Once again, far too much work and responsibility was placed on McDowell's shoulders; he had now been without sleep for over forty hours.[72]

Thomas J. Scott, president of the Pennsylvania Railroad, began sending an increasingly urgent volley of telegrams to Governor Curtin of Pennsylvania, urging him to rush on any troops presently in Philadelphia and Harrisburg; the last telegram urged, "Press forward all available forces. Start before daylight." His messages contained injunctions to the telegraph operators to keep the news strictly secret.[73] These troops were later ordered diverted "to Baltimore, which is liable to revolt." General Mansfield ordered the navy to tow a small ship, the brig *Perry,* to Alexandria, to provide an extra battery should the Confederates attack there as expected. Scott telegraphed McDowell that the equivalent of a new division was on the way to him, but apparently left it up to him to coordinate it, even though McDowell seemed to be incommunicado for much of this time and his staff scattered about, dealing with issues of the retreat.

A Confederate counterattack was hardly a figment of McDowell's imagination, for another president was up late making decisions that night: Between 10:00 and 11:00 P.M., Davis and Beauregard arrived at Confederate headquarters, and had supper on the upper floor. At midnight, a messenger arrived to report that the Union had not held Centreville, and a discussion went on into the wee hours of the morning, about whether an attack toward the Potomac should be organized.[74]

In Richmond, Mrs. Varina Davis was shown the report her husband had telegraphed, reporting the victory and the deaths. Mrs. Davis called personally on the wife of Francis Bartow to tell her gently of her husband's death. Thomas Cooper De Leon described the mood of the Southern capital. At the railway, in the heart of downtown,

> the first arrivals were the ominous ones—splashed and muddy hospital stewards and quartermaster's men, who wanted more stretchers and instruments, more tourniquets and stimulants; and their stories threw a deeper gloom over the crowds. . . . There was no sleep in Richmond that night. Men and women gathered in knots and huddled into groups on the corners and doorsteps, and the black shadow of some dreadful calamity seemed brooding over every rooftree.[75]

At 4:00 A.M., in a house near Manassas Junction, General Bee died from his groin wound, as Captain Imboden held his hand.[76]

Given the rain, the exhaustion and hunger of the men and horses and the lack of supplies the Confederates decided not to pursue the Union forces in the morning. Washington escaped again, but there was perhaps a greater threat on its doorstep. The swiftest of the general army had gained Alexandria, where they milled around in disarray, hungry and confused. Colonel Kerrigan of the Twenty-fifth New York telegraphed the secretary of war: "Sir: There are about 7000 men here without officers. Nothing but confusion. Please tell me what I shall do with my regiment."[77] It was decided to shut down the ferries and close off Long Bridge, in order to "prevent soldiers from crossing over to the city; their arrival here would produce panic on this side and cause more trouble."[78] Sherman called them "an armed mob."[79]

As July 21 waned, the advance guard of the retreat had arrived in Washington on horseback. David Hunter's carriage arrived. Burnside galloped across town to Willard's, his emotions showing plainly. Russell made good time back to Washington, arriving at Willard's just as a clock struck 11:00 P.M.[80] Senator Wilson of Massachusetts arrived on a stray mule he had captured. Carriages fleeing the bombardment at Cub Run Bridge also came into town with tales of the rout. The citizenry feared Confederate invasion at any moment.

Lincoln was to become well known to the telegraph operators during the war, for on this night, he started a pattern that was to become familiar—he haunted the telegraph office. This night, he

The Union retreat was orderly until the Confederates shelled the Stone Bridge the Yankees had to cross to go home. Then it turned into "the Great Skedaddle." *From the Library of Congress Prints and Photographs Division.*

kept returning to the telegraph office until after midnight, when the line went down at Fairfax.[81]

Deprived of further telegrams for the present, Lincoln stayed up the rest of the night "on a lounge in the Cabinet room" where he received senators and congressmen returned from Virginia and listened to their hair-raising stories of escape and soldiers turned fugitives.[82] At 2:00 A.M. General Scott called at the White House to insist that Mrs. Lincoln and the boys be sent north out of danger, but Mrs. Lincoln refused to leave. At 3:00 A.M., the president had a long talk with General Meigs, "just returned."[83]

The closure of the bridge meant the regiments would have to reform their men into some semblance of order in Virginia before being permitted to cross back into town. The moon and its light was obscured by thickening clouds, and rain started to fall. The men were famished and their horses were in even worse shape.

The last miles of the march took their toll, one Edwin Barrett reporting, "The cords of my legs worked like rusty wires, giving me great pain at every step."[84] Corporal Rhodes, the young man thought too slight of build to survive army life, suffered on the marathon:

> At daylight, we could see the spires of Washington, and a welcome sight it was. About eight o' clock I reached Fort Runyon, earn Long Bridge, and giving my gun to an officer who was collecting them, I entered a tent and was soon asleep. Towards noon I awoke and, with my Company, endeavored to cross Long Bridge, but fell exhausted before reaching the Washington side. My officers kindly placed me in an army wagon and I was carried to camp, where with rest and proper care, I soon recovered and went on duty.[85]

In the early morning, only wagons and disabled men were allowed into town.[86] Putnam and friend "reached the 7 A.M., (first) boat for Washington," which they shared with "fugitive soldiers . . . some of them slightly disabled." The ferry passengers piled onto two omnibuses waiting at the dock, and "rumbled up the avenue" to Willard's.[87]

Burnside returned to Long Bridge about dawn, where Lieutenant Munroe saw him pacing in the early morning light. "That model of an American volunteer, Burnside" was there to see that his men got across and back into the city—one of those gestures that endeared him to his soldiers.[88] About 10:00 A.M., the bulk of his brigade crossed over under his orders, with the stragglers coming over later as they caught up.[89] Although individual soldiers had come through the city since dawn, as a brigade Burnside's were "the first to have the privilege of returning to the camps they have left."

As those first troops gained the city, wild rumors swept the town. Near hysteria again reigned. Congressman Julian of Indiana reported the Avenue was solidly packed with people from the Capitol to the Treasury. By noon, Long Bridge was solidly jammed with returning soldiers, and the cries of the wounded rent the air.[90] Hungry soldiers knocked on the doors of strangers, asking for food. Exhausted soldiers slept on porches, lawns, and against streetlamp posts. Mary Henry, the daughter of the secretary of the Smithsonian Institution recorded in her diary,

> The Rhode Island Regiment was the only one that retreated in good order we saw them come into the city about 10 A.M. It was a pitiable sight. Many of the men were without shoes or stockings jaded & terribly dirty, some had yielded to exhaustion & were borne upon the shoulders of others who seemed scarcely less weary than themselves they formed a sad contrast to the enthusiastic well dressed military looking men who left us on [the 16th][91]

The people of Washington reacted according to their political sentiments, and those who backed the Union turned out to offer aid to the wet, weary men. Corporal English recorded the welcome they received:

> We arrived about 2 o'clock Monday noon more dead than alive, having been on our feet for 36 hours without a mouthful to eat, and traveled a distance of 60 miles without twenty minutes halt. The last five miles of the march was perfect misery, none of us having scarce strength to put one foot before the other, but I tell you the cheers we rec'd going through the streets of Washington seemed to put new life into the men for they rallied and marched to our camps and every man dropped on the ground and in one moment the greater part of them were asleep.[92]

Another reported the Washington sidewalks along the route to Camp Clark "were lined with people, many of whom furnished us with refreshments." Lieutenant Munroe was not too weary to notice that one such offering came "from the hands of two very intelligent looking and attractive young ladies," whom in later days he went back to thank.[93] Walt Whitman, then a correspondent for the *Brooklyn Standard*, reported,

> The sidewalks of Pennsylvania Avenue, Fourteenth Street &c. were jammed with citizens, darkies, clerks, everybody, lookers-on; women in the windows, curious expressions from faces, as those swarms of dirt-cover'd return'd soldiers there (will they never end?) move by; but nothing said, no comments. . . . During the forenoon Washington gets all over motley with these defeated soldiers . . . strange eyes and faces, drench'd (the steady rain drizzles on all day) and fearfully worn, hungry, haggard, blister'd in the feet. Good people (but not over-many of them either,) hurry up something for their grub. They put wash-kettles on the fire, for soup, for coffee. They set tables on the sidewalks-wagon—loads of bread are purchased, swiftly

> cut in stout chunks. Here are two aged ladies. . . . They stand with store of eating and drink at an improvis'd table of rough plank, and give food, and have the store replenished from their house every half hour all that day; and there in the rain they stand, active, silent, white hair'd and give food, though the tears stream down their checks, almost without intermission the whole time.[94]

Young Mary Henry's tender heart empathized with those who were crying:

> I have heard of the death of several of our friends but I am happy to learn Col Hunter & his young aid are safe. The former is quite severely wounded but is not in danger at present. . . . It is terrible to think of the hearts bleeding tonight, of the thousands weeping for sons husbands & brothers falling unknown & unnoticed except to swell the number . . . of the country's loss.[95]

The battle had ended about eighteen hours earlier, "the last shot was fired a few minutes before sunset; and the armies no longer heard . . . the cannonade. The shells and bullets ceased to sing their songs of death in the forests of Manassas, but rushed in silence, until they struck the homes of their victims, in the peaceful villages of the north.[96] So devastating was the news that followed this and other battles, that Henry Wadsworth Longfellow immortalized it in a poem, "Killed at the Ford":

> And I saw in a vision how far and fleet
> That fatal bullet went speeding forth
> Til it reached a town in the distant North,
> Till it reached a house in a sunny street,
> Till it reached a heart that ceased to beat.[97]

CHAPTER NINETEEN

"Weeping Sad and Lonely"*

Sarah Ballou Hears Conflicting Reports on Her Husband

Late July 1861

The deaths of Colonel Slocum and Major Ballou made headlines in the Rhode Island newspapers. The *New York Times*, *Providence Journal*, and *Woonsocket Patriot* reported them as dying on the day of the battle, as part of the first reports from Manassas. The trouble was, neither was actually dead when the articles first appeared.

Rhode Island was far removed from the seat of war and, while there was great confusion about the exact sequence of events in general, this was especially the case as concerned Sullivan Ballou, who was still alive at the Thornberrys'. The failure to evacuate the wounded; the capture of the field hospital; the routing of the Union Army, whose men took three days to straggle back into Washington, D.C., which had telegraph offices open for business;

* From the Civil War song of the same name.

the deaths and injuries of so many in the Rhode Island chain of command—all made it unlikely that anyone was telegraphing the families promptly or directly with news of their wounded and dead.

Beginning around July 17, the Rhode Island newspapers had printed the news that its two regiments had marched into Virginia and that a major battle was expected. On July 19 and 20, families were still receiving letters mailed from Camp Clark, telling of a peaceful life in a secure, pastoral camp or sightseeing in town; but based on the newspapers, they stepped up their worrying. All week, the papers printed speculation about when and where that battle would be. The news from Blackburn's Ford, overhyped as it was, made it sound as if the war had begun on the eighteenth.

At Sunday services in churches all over the state on the twenty-first, congregations prayed for their men. With over two thousand soldiers in the field, everybody knew someone who had been sent to Virginia. Breaking with tradition, the *Journal* published a Sunday edition, which told its readers, "Scott . . . said the Union is strong enough," and "Dispatches were sent to McDowell at 2 o'clock this morning. McDowell was to have moved on the enemy at 6 last evening." Startlingly, it also announced,

> The orders to move last evening were countermanded till early this morning. Our troops meantime are cutting a road through the woods to flank the enemy's batteries.[1]

All Sunday, Rhode Island was holding its breath for additional news about their regiments, but that night Sarah and Emeline and everyone else went to bed none the wiser. The Monday paper ran with the story of a Union victory, likely based on a morning telegram sent before the Fairfax Court House telegraph office had shut down during the retreat:

> The greatest battle ever fought upon this continent took place yesterday near Manassas Junction and resulted, it appears, in a brilliant victory of the national army.[2]

In supplying its readers with such information, the *Providence Journal*, *Pawtucket Gazette*, *Woonsocket Patriot*, and other newspapers throughout the state relied on news from its own correspondents, and from reports mailed in by Rhode Islanders located in Washington, D.C. They also picked up stories from the New York papers, and one another. Some were telegraphed, but some came by regular mail service and thus were several days getting north on the trains. Trying to be helpful, many families turned their personal letters over to the newspaper to print to enlighten the community. The papers printed it all, side by side, with no attempt at reconciliation of the details. When reports contradicted each other, it was hard for readers to know what to believe.

Some of the more dramatic false disclosures the week after the battle included: "General Jackson was killed," "Gov. Sprague had his horse's head shot off," and "Colonel Slocum was pierced by two balls, after which he lived two hours." The only retractions came with regard to the status of the state's soldiers: "Frances C. Greene, reported dead, was only wounded in the leg, but he is still missing."[3] The trouble with the publication of private letters was that so often did they misreport living men dead that the papers finally embargoed those passages, and printed a warning to contributors to be absolutely sure of their facts, lest they cause needless distress.

However, sometime Monday, those in Rhode Island government and their confidants knew what had truly happened. It is not known with precision when or how this occurred: the White House and War Department kept a careful log of when telegrams were received, but if such a log was kept in Providence, it has not come to light. There is no way to know if Burnside or Sprague telegraphed private messages to family or key government figures in the wee hours of the morning, or waited until daybreak, or if any of these were leaked to the press. Once word got out, however, news of the defeat spread. The merchant tailors in the towns immediately began sewing black armbands for the men, black dresses for the women and girls, and the white suits worn by young boys.

The Victorians had refined the etiquette of dealing with death, and, if the war was new, the process of notifying a widow was not. Behind the scenes, things were set in motion for a distinguished personage, accompanied by one or two females, to call at the homes of the about-to-be bereaved. Bishop Clark later wrote that he had paid visits to console the families, but it is unclear if he was the one delivering the initial news. In view of his promise to Sullivan to stay in touch with his family, he certainly went to the Ballous at some point.

By rigid custom, Monday was laundry day for the women of America and, in the month of July, was best done before the heat peaked. Women often had their laundry hanging on the line by the forenoon, and this may have been the occupation at which the little delegation found Sarah when they came to call. Her precise reaction is unknown; however, as the war progressed, images of the just-notified widow, weeping with her head on a table, her skirts billowed out around her chair, became iconic to the sentimental Victorians of North and South.

While Sarah may have still been too numb to notice any of it, a support network would have quietly begun to form around her, people offering to notify her mother and other relatives, and tend the boys. As the news made its way through the business district Providence, Sullivan's current and past law partners would soon learn of it and know they must call to render all assistance. The neighborhood grapevine on Sarah's street in Cranston would have gone instantly to work, friends and neighbor women slipped in the door to offer comfort, smelling salts, medicinal brandy, and the loan of any black garments she might lack. Again, according to the

Black clothing, including collar and cuffs, was traditional for the first year of widowhood. *From author's collection.*

As the war progressed, images of the just-notified widow, weeping with her head on a table, her skirts billowed out around her chair, became iconic to the sentimental Victorians of North and South. *From author's collection.*

rigid social convention of the time, Sarah would have been expected to be assume the most extreme formal mourning, that of a wife for her husband, by Tuesday. Women frequently loaned bonnets, shawls, gloves, and other accessories until the wardrobe of the new widow could achieve conformity.

Sarah was isolated—far from her mother, eight miles from the Bogles and Emeline, even more from Uncle Henry and Aunt Sarah. Just twenty-six years old, living in this neighborhood for a little over a year, she was also far from her close friends in Woonsocket and the Ballou Neighborhood. Until Catherine could arrive, she had only her maid, Mary Block, to see her through this most dreadful of times. Thirty-six years old, the Irishwoman had the skills to care for her mistress and keep the household from falling apart as they coped with the sudden death of the master of the house, something the sixteen-year-old maid employed by the Tompkins could not have managed. As was proper for those times, an atmosphere of decorous silence descended over the house at Peace and Elmwood in Cranston that day.

On the roads to Washington, and within the city itself, the scene was anything but calm. In fact, chaos reigned.

The Rhode Island regiments, thanks to Burnside's arrangements, had been the first to reenter the District as a group, but many of its men were still in Virginia. Of those now prisoners, 68 percent were wounded troops who could not retreat; most of the able-bodied men had gotten out, but confusion reigned as far as tallies went. One officer in Company C of the First mused, "The men come in languid and late, exhausted with their hardship, and I find they have straggled along the road and been reported among the missing."[4]

Private Albert Sholes, for example, had dropped out of the march, fallen asleep on the side of the road, and awakened to a teamster cursing his mules, which had gotten tangled as "only army mules could." Sholes helped him reposition the animals and, for his assistance, was given a ride. He later had breakfast at the Marshall House in Alexandria, after which he hooked up with another soldier, Will Berrian from the Seventy-first New York, at the pier in Alexandria, where the New Yorkers were awaiting the arrival of a boat sent out from the Navy Yard to bring them back to Washington. The officers were doing their best to prevent men from other units from boarding their boat but, with the connivance of his friends, Sholes snuck on board. They landed at the Navy Yard at seven o'clock. Monday night, and the weary private spent his last two dollars on a carriage ride back to Camp Sprague. His comrades, who had listed him as missing, gave him a hearty welcome. He crawled into his tent and slept through until noon the next day.[5]

That night, Private Charles V. Scott brought into the Rhode Island camp one of their new James rifle artillery pieces that Lieutenant Munroe had sent off the field for lack of ammunition. Scott said that, while he was walking through the woods after losing contact with his company, he found the gun with horses still hitched to it. Calling upon some infantrymen who were also astray, "Scott mounted one horse himself and directed them to mount the other horses; and together they took the piece to Centreville. Its advent was hailed with special joy by every member of the battery."[6]

Sergeant Henry Blake of the Eleventh Massachusetts had also gotten separated from his regiment, and slept the night in a clump of bushes. When he awoke at dawn, he walked to Centreville, where he "expected to find the army established upon the heights." Instead, he found,

> The houses along the public way, and especially those of Centreville, were filled with the wounded who could not walk: there were no surgeons or nurses to dress and bandage their injuries; and they implored all the able-bodied person to tell the general to send doctors and ambulances. Squads of

stragglers, and slightly wounded men, with bandaged heads, arms in slings, and limping upon sticks, were walking to overtake the army. . . . Upon the line of retreat, the natives, comprising old men and the female portion of the community openly expressed their joy at the result of the conflict, and misled the soldiers by willfully deceiving them about the direction of the roads. . . . The Irish settlers near the railroad in every way assisted the stragglers. . . . [In] Centreville at half past seven o'clock in the morning, a loyal man . . . adorned with the white hair of age, stood at the intersection of the streets, pointed out to all that which led to Fairfax Court House, and earnestly advised them to hurry as much as possible, because the rebel cavalry could cut them off as soon as they knew that the troops had marched to Alexandria.[7]

The hundreds of Union men making their way east noted the commissary wagons, which had been bringing the next meal to the Union troops and grain for the horses; the baggage wagons catching up with the cooking pots; and those carrying munitions, all abandoned by their teamsters, many in Centreville itself, through which fleeing wagons could not make good time

up and down two or three little hills and hollows, over a road . . . which has ruts and rocks, boulders and pit-falls in it, enough to shake the shoes from off a thousand horses, and more than enough to rattle to pieces and disable a thousand wagons.[8]

Many personal belongings were abandoned by the fleeing civilian spectators and soldiers:

Blankets, rifles and equipments of many descriptions were scattered in the road, and the woods that bordered upon it. . . .

> Crowds of women and negroes, like wreckers in a stranded ship, were taking flour and provisions from the deserted wagons.[9]

Blake arrived at Alexandria the night of the twenty-second, completely saturated from the heavy rain that continued to fall steadily through Tuesday.

All day Monday, units kept arriving, their condition pitifully changed from when Captain Fry noted at their departure, "brilliantly uniformed . . . the silken banners . . . unsoiled and untorn."[10] Mary Henry described the experience of civilians waiting for news:

> All last night ambulances were passing the house & we expected every moment one would stop at our door. As we were seated at the breakfast table this morning a violent pull at the door bell made us all start to our feet. Two soldiers entered bloodstained & dusty. Poor little Fanny threw herself on the floor at my feet covering her ears fearing to hear the terrible news they might bring.

They were messengers of good tidings for her, however, as the men brought news her fiancé was safe. They told of a fierce battle. "Three times our narrator a strong man burst into tears & cried like a child."[11*]

The streets of Washington were full of soldiers separated from their units, all with a story to tell. Crowds of spectators gathered around to hear the tales, and the press took notes as the men described how, in the open field, the Confederates had been driven

* Fanny Gurley's fiancé, Second Lieutenant William Elderkin, arrived at noon. "He had not tasted food for twenty-four hours," but, attached to Rickett's Battery, he was fortunate to be alive at all.

Period cartoons lampooned everyone. Here, a giant Zoauve stands taller than the top hats of the gentlemen hearing his tale of how he fought the Black Horse Cavalry and lived to tell of it. A planter, at right, in the flat hat, listens, as do two Black servants. *From* Harper's Weekly.

back but their cavalry and hidden batteries had been their chief success.[12] The most quoted and most impressive of these raconteurs were individual Fire Zouaves, now thrown back on their own resources since they had not retreated as a unit. Their prewar base had been Alexandria, but many had fled farther, into the safety of the capital, from which a few reportedly took trains straight back to New York City.

These men put the best possible spin on their role in the battle, and their tales of bravery and exaggerated descriptions of annihilating the "Black Horse Cavalry" during its charge against them were widely quoted in the press and in letters home. William H. Pierce, visiting from Rhode Island, wrote home noting that those whom he met yesterday and today, "are a fine set of fellows," who acted "heroically," especially since "they were to be the special marks of the enemy as they were known to the rebels by their dress . . . and dreaded by them as the Devil hates holy water."

As Washingtonians learned that there were stragglers, they began sending their own carriages and wagons over the bridge to bring the wounded back into the capital for care. A few days after the battle, medical director King went out toward Bull Run with a train of thirty-nine ambulances, in an attempt to rescue the wounded but, after wandering around the countryside for a while, these were compelled to return empty when McDowell could not secure the necessary permission from the Confederate authorities to enter land under their control.[13]

The exhausted Confederates had not hastened to seize Centreville that Monday morning, which allowed many Union men to escape. Those who did remain became prisoners when the Southerners reoccupied the town, but the Southern Army did not pursue the retreat into Fairfax Court House until

> two days after the battle we were literally starved out of Manassas, and were forced to advance to Fairfax Court House in order to get the supplies which the Union army had left in abundance . . ."[14]

The Confederate government opted not to throw its tired and hungry men into a battle against the ring of forts the Union had constructed around Alexandria. Though its occupants did not know it, the capital was safe for the time being, if still vulnerable.

The Senate and House were in session that morning. In the former, G. P. Putnam observed "About thirty Senators were present, looking as calm as if the Battle of New Orleans had been the last on the continent." Senator Wilson apparently having gone straight to work, was protesting the idea of returning contraband slaves to their owners so they could be put to work to build more fortifications from which to shell and kill Union soldiers.[15] The members of Lincoln's cabinet were somber men on July 22. Secretary Cameron had lost his brother, and Secretary Chase realized this defeat now propelled the federal government into a longer, costlier war that would exceed the Congressional budgetary allocations of July 4.

Lincoln's secretaries recorded that, starting the twenty-second, the president began making notes on a tablet, listing action steps to take, already planning the next phase of the war. The exertions, the glory, the sacrifices of the past week had just brought the nation full circle, back to where it had been in April, back to the first phase of the war plan, the defense of Washington, D.C., from Confederate attack. Lincoln's bold gamble with his green army, his attempt to shorten the conflict, had failed. The political repercussions would come quickly. The newspapers noted, "The tone of feeling today in Washington is rising very fast. General Scott will not acknowledge that we have suffered a defeat." While people speculated on what the government might be planning next, General Robert Patterson was promptly relieved of command of his army. Mary Henry wrote in her diary:

> The excitement after the Battle is intense. Gen. McDowell is very much blamed. Gen Scott declares he [is] washing his hands of the affair & hope now he may be allowed to carry out his plans without molestation. He is said to have declared to the President that he must be commander in chief in reality, as well as in name or he must resign. . . . Reports are so contradictis it is impossible to know the number of the killed and wounded.[16]

But Walt Whitman praised Lincoln's businesslike approach to the crisis:

> The hour, the day, the night pass'd, and whatever returns, an hour, a day, a night like that can never again return. The President, recovering himself, begins that very night—sternly, rapidly sets about the task of reorganizing his forces, and

> placing himself in positions for future and surer work. If there were nothing else of Abraham Lincoln for history to stamp him with, it is enough to send him with his wreath to memory of all future time, that he endured that hell that day, bitterer than gall—indeed a crucifixion day—that it did not conquer him—that he unflinchingly stemm'd it, and resolv'd to lift himself and the Union out of it.[17]

Still struggling to report the news of the battle, and lacking accurate information from the army, as days passed the newspapers continued to waver on casualty lists—"Col. Jameson and Lt. Col. Roberts of the second Maine were not killed as reported." At the same time, they alarmed soldiers' families by printing reports of the Confederates "giving no quarter to wounded." Stedman of the *World* was at least candid: "Nine tenths of our killed and wounded were perforce left on the field, and in the hospitals at either end; and as the enemy retains possession of the ground, we can get no accurate details."[18] Yet the papers did one great service to a Union, struggling to accept the idea of a defeat, as Whitman noted,

> Then the great New York papers at once appear'd, (commencing that evening, and following it up the next morning and incessantly through many days after wards,) with leaders [headlines] that rang out over the land with the loudest, most reverberating ring of clearest bugles, full of encouragement, hope, inspiration, unfaltering defiance. Those magnificent editorials! They never flagged for a moment.[19]

In Providence, the newspaper announced a mass meeting was to be held at Market Square in the forenoon of the twenty-third, its purpose

> that we may know and feel that we are all governed by a common purpose. . . . That our public servants should know

> if they are sustained in their arduous labors by a zealous and united people. The lesson though bought at great price, will not be without value.[20]

The paper declared that Rhode Island had,

> new patience, new determination, . . . and with the zeal that draws strength out of defeat itself, the loyal millions are again rallying to the support of the glorious old standard. "Advance!" is their watchword. They will send a legion for every man who has fallen. They will never flinch or abate their efforts in the least until this matter is settled. They are in earnest—the rebels may rely upon that—and never so much in earnest and since the repulse at Manassas.[21]

Out around Centreville, where the Confederate commanders had never expected to have responsibility for large numbers of enemy wounded, they were struggling to organize their postbattle operations. Assistant surgeon Gray, attached to Porter's Cavalry where he was not needed, was ordered to assist at Sudley Hospital between 2:00 and 5:00 P.M. He observed that at the time the hospital was captured, "no more than a tenth of the wounded had received attention." Gray had the misfortune to be arrested that night and, from then onward, worked under the supervision of the Confederate chief medical officer, Dr. Gaston.[22]

A plethora of miscommunications resulted in the needless death and temporarily inhumane treatment of the Union wounded who remained behind. There is no evidence to indicate this was either deliberate or punitive, but rather demonstrated the inefficiency of an equally green army responding to an unexpected situation. For that matter, no comprehensive list of names of any of the prisoners seems to have been made. In a list appended to a report by Beauregard, Sullivan appears as a footnote:

> A list appended exhibits some 1,460 of their wounded and others who fell into our hands and were sent to Richmond.* Some were sent to other points, so that the number of prisoners, including wounded who did not die, may be set down as not less than 1,600. Besides these a considerable number who could not be removed from the field died at several farmhouses and field hospitals within ten days following the battle.

The Confederates were dismayed that the Union did not evacuate their wounded. "The cowardly dogs left wounded and dead to be taken care of by our troops," On Monday, some effort was apparently made to send parties of Union prisoners out to bring in their own injured:

> In the morning, Dr. Gaston sent me, with Dr. Lewis of the Wisconsin Volunteers, with a captured two wheel ambulance . . . to assist in collecting and caring for wounded on the field. It was raining, and on reaching the battleground, we found these unfortunates suffering from much cold. . . . We were obliged to select such for immediate removal as it seem possible to save by treatment and shelter. We . . . bore most of the patients to a farmhouse called the Lewis House, already nearly full of Rebel wounded. . . . The house's out buildings were soon packed with wounded, and still many were left on the field, the numbers doubtless died for want of timely assistance.[23]

Here, surgeon Gray continued to report the how the doctors faced severe handicaps in treating their patients:

* Namely: 3 colonels, 1 major, 13 captains, 36 lieutenants, 5 surgeons, 7 assistant surgeons, 2 chaplains, 15 citizens, and 1,376 enlisted men.

> We were unable to operate in many cases urgently requiring, as our instruments had been taken from us. We suffered much for want of food, water, and blankets. For the first, we were dependent upon the . . . knapsacks of the dead; for the second, upon a small muddy spring half-mile distant, a broken pitcher being our best means of transportation. We had blankets for but five or six men. We found a large supply of linen in a chest of drawers, and turned it to account for dressings.[24]

The hospital at Sudley Church benefited from the quirky behavior of Heintzelman's overstressed, tired, and thirsty troops on the afternoon of the battle, when they had deposited their knapsacks and blanket rolls in front of the church as they passed: Not wanting such encumbrance when going into battle, they figured to pick them up again on the way home, but in the haste of the retreat did not stop to retrieve them. Now, this pile of supplies provided the hospital with woolen blankets, jackets, biscuits, and other basic items, although it must be assumed the booty of war along this roadway was every bit as tempting to the Rebel soldiers and local poor as it was over on the turnpike. The band of the Second Rhode Island had taken their role of caregivers seriously enough to leave all their woolen and rubber blankets directly with the wounded before retreating.

Water was plentiful from Catharpin Run for the church, and not only did Bull Run itself ran back of the house but the water level at the Thornberrys' was high enough that the well would not run dry with heavy use. Murphy was adamant about the standards of care while he was at Sudley.

> I afterward saw it stated in the Northern paper "that the Confederates on guard there are refused to let our men to catch the water that fell from the eaves of the house to drink." All of which is untrue.

Within the context of all available sites to be administering care, Sullivan Ballou was very fortunate to be at the Thornberry House. However, food was in very short supply. The makeshift hospital housed some 350 wounded plus hospital staff. Union assistant surgeon G. Sternberg reported that on Monday,

> A small quantity of cornmeal was obtained from a house near the church, and some gruel was made. A portion of this was given to nearly every man, and this was all the food we were able to obtain for them till Monday evening.[25]

Murphy was moving back and forth between the Thornberry compound and the hospital:

> Towards dusk we had twenty-eight dead bodies which we placed in a row in front of the church, who had died during the night and that day, and the amputated limbs and pieces of flesh accumulated to such a degree that they were almost on a level with the table used for amputating under the pulpit of the church, and the stench arising therefrom was beginning to be terribly offensive to the living wounded men lying crowded together on the floor of that charnel house, and we began to be alarmed for the sake of the living as to the disposition of bodies, as we had no force to bury them.
>
> I at last hit on the expediency of ensuring them in a small ice house connected with one of the buildings, and had just broken the lock of the door, when we were summoned by Captain White, of the Confederate cavalry, who, with a small squad of men, had charge of us.[26]

The morning of July 22, one or both of the generals issued an order that all captured Union troops should be sent behind the lines for transport out of the area. Manassas Junction served as the embarkation point for a prison that was hastily being prepared in Richmond. The multistory warehouse of a wealthy New England ship chandler, Luther Libby, located near his wharves on in the Shako Bottom district of Richmond, was seized and hastily converted to receive Northern prisoners of war.

At Sudley hospital, "an order was issued by" either Captain Patrick (Doherty), or Captain White (Murphy), of the cavalry (the two differ on the name) for all prisoners but the wounded to leave for Manassas Junction.

> We expostulated with him and tried to prove that the order did not intend to include the surgeons, and pointed out to the enormity of such an unparalleled act of inhumanity, to abandon nearly three hundred wounded men to their fate, many of whose wounds were not even examined; but to all our entreaties he turned a deaf ear. He answered that he was very sorry, but he must obey his orders, when we told him that we would yield only to force. Nothing would satisfy him.[27]

Murphy, whom the men were calling "doc," was understood by the Confederates to be one, and accordingly was sent away with the real ones, while Doherty stayed. "All who were not wounded were taken under a tree and tied, as an attack was anticipated. . . . We were seized . . . hands bound, except the doctors who were in ambulances."[28] Murphy continued,

> Go we must. So we had to submit to the inevitable, and prepared to start off at once, and in a drenching rain. We hurriedly entered the church and the other buildings to bid our poor disabled comrades goodbye, and the scene at parting beggars all description. God spare me from ever witnessing such a dreadful spectacle again. I have seen service in Mexico in many of the great battles of the war since, but nothing has

ever been so indelibly impressed on my memory as the solemn, heart-rending leave-taking with those brave, patient and suffering men. They lay there in their agony on those bare floors, with naught on which to rest their weary heads but the hard boards, with no friendly hand near to give succor, no dear mother nor kindly sister to tenderly and affectionately care for and soothe their last moments in that supreme hour of their affliction, and no good priest to pour the consolations of religion in the hearts of those who were about to wing their way into eternity.

When they came to realize that we were about to abandon them, their lamentations and cries were heart rending to listen to; but go we must. I will never forget the look of anguish on the face of brave Major Ballou, when I took his cold clammy hand in mine to bid him farewell. He was the last one of whom I took leave.[29]

Though many had reported Sullivan dead on the battlefield on Sunday morning, he was clearly alive on Monday. The clammy hand, on a sultry July day, indicated he was still in some degree of shock. Murphy recorded what happened next:

> On our arrival at Manassas at eleven o'clock that night, we reported to the surgeon in charge, and informed him of the condition of the men left at Sudley church, when he expressed great surprise and indignation at our being ordered away, which he said was never intended, as the order only related to able-bodied prisoners, and left it optional with us to return at once, or remain until morning; it was near midnight, our clothing was thoroughly drenched, and the surgeons have been up the previous night and most of the night before the battle, and were utterly exhausted and needed some rest, and knowing they were in a condition to be of little service that

> night, we concluded to wait until daylight, and start back then without delay.[30]

Doctor Sternberg reported, "at Manassas we were lodged in the barn with some 30 or 40 other prisoners, officers and privates, under guard." In an article written later for *Century Magazine*, Beauregard noted,

> We captured also many prisoners, including a number of surgeons, whom (the first time in war), were treated not as prisoners, but as guests. Calling attention to their brave devotion to their wounded, I recommended to the War Department that they be sent home without exchange, together with some other prisoners, who had shown personal kindness to Colonel Jones, of the Fourth Alabama, who had been mortally wounded early in the day.[31]

At the hospital, "It was then raining in torrents and some 80 of the wounded were laying in the vicinity of the church and blacksmith shop without any shelter excepting a blanket." Gradually, Doherty and other Union officers began asserting themselves.

> We waited till 1 o'clock at night in the rain, awaiting orders, when I requested Capt. Patrick to let me go down to the hospital to see a relative who was severely/mortally wounded, telling him it would be better to shoot our wounded at once than to allow them to die off by inches; they were all calling for water, and no one there to give it to them. He then said, "Well, my man, choose another man with you and go down: I chose Smith, of Company H, Seventy-first Regiment. Captain Patrick then asked if there were any more men who had brothers or relatives among the wounded. A general rush took place among the prisoners—they all stepping forward. He then allowed Atwood

> Crosby of Maine to take care of his brother, Augustine, who was wounded in the back, and five others, [including] a young boy of the Second Rhode Island, about 17 years old.*

For the wounded men lying outside the church in this rain, a detail "erected a frame shelter" covered with the rubber blankets discarded by the Eleventh New York and others on their way to battle. The rest of the able-bodied prisoners were kept out in the rain all night, and the following morning were sent to Richmond.[32]

Before being allowed to return the next day, July 23, the doctors were asked to give their word of honor "as an officer and gentleman," not to participate in further hostilities against the South. The parole system was based on the French system of a *parole d'honneur,* and "is a pledge or oath under which a prisoner of war is released with the understanding that he will not bear arms again until exchanged."[33] This was a similar situation to the parole given to Sullivan Ballou's grandfather, Joseph Bowen, when released from the prison ship, *Jersey,* as part of a delegation to General George Washington. If the doctors at Sudley Church Hospital agreed, they were to be allowed to go home when the field hospitals closed. Those who refused were given five-day paroles, in recognition of the need to treat so many patients. No written records of paroles were kept at this early date, but it was understood by all involved that the promise had meaning. Most accepted the paroles but those physicians who refused were incarcerated later in the month. Even so, during the hours medical personnel were traveling or otherwise called away, men died because "doctors were not there to amputate."

> On Tuesday evening, six of the Doctors came back on parole, Drs. Peugnet, Swift, Winston, DeGraw, Burton and Stewart—

* The Crosby brothers got out of this scrape, but both had the bad luck to be again captured at the Second Battle of Manassas in 1862, and eventually released.

> and immediately commenced attending to the wounded. Their exertions were unremitting; their time day and night was given to the wounded until all the wounded were properly dressed and all cared for.[34]

It is not recorded which doctor went over to the Thornberry compound to check on Sullivan. Murphy, who did not return, tried to find out what happened to his patients, probably by asking incoming prisoners at Libby Prison what they knew. Out of all the patients he assisted, he seemed especially taken with the major and regretted learning—incorrectly—that "the noble fellow was called to his final account next morning." He was closer to the truth with the Second's commander, whose death is correlated to the early part of the week: "Col. Slocum also breathed his last during that night. Cursed be the causes that led to the cruel and fratricidal war."[35]

The officers' "ward" seemed to be under special protection, arranged by Colonel Jones in recognition of the kind treatment he received. Josiah Richardson attended Sullivan the rest of the week, and Rhode Islanders Collins and Eldridge also continued to assist at the hospital, though undoubtedly helping with other patients as well.

Lieutenant Doherty did not learn the names of all the men he helped nurse, but wrote a descriptive list of men in a poignant effort to help their families recognize them. One such entry read,

> A boy about 18 years old, dressed in the uniform of the Eighth Regiment, about 5 feet 10 inches in height, sandy complexion, shot in the head; had $21 in his pocketbook, and a white silk badge, marked "Parker Guard," died Monday night.

Men far younger than Sullivan were now in charge of the hospital. Dr. Peugnet was just twenty-four years old, newly promoted to surgeon on July 15 from paymaster of the Seventy-first. That same age, Canadian-born Doherty continued,

> On Wednesday morning, Dr. Peugnet put me in charge of the hospital, and allowed me to chose 20 from the prisoners and wounded, who were able to take care of the wounded to assist me. The same morning, a lady of the neighborhood brought us a bottle of wine and two dozen eggs, and we bought at noon twelve dozen of eggs. . . . Thursday morning a number of secession doctors made their appearance, bringing with them some luxuries which they gave to our doctors. . . . This day a number of ladies and farmers of the surrounding country visited our hospitals, bringing with them milk, soup and cakes.[36]

Three days after his surgery, there was at last food for Sullivan to eat. His body needed nourishment if it was to produce new blood to replace what he had lost. In this sparsely settled area, any milk and eggs brought to the hospital meant the local people gave up their own portion to bring to the wounded. Neighbors also began nursing duties at the hospital, helping "an enemy whom might slay justly in honest combat, but whom as Christians, they felt it their duty to minister to." They performed typical tasks like providing water, fanning the men, putting wet compresses on fevered brows, and changing bandages.

One couple in particular was exemplary in their service: Amos and Margaret Benson, who lived nearby at Christian Hill farm and had been among those who had watched the invading army march in on Sunday morning. On Tuesday, the husband and wife were walking home together after a full day's service at Sudley Hospital, when they heard Private John Rice of the Second New Hampshire, Burnside's Brigade, moaning under a fence. Shot through the lungs, his comrades thought he died while they were carrying him to the hospital, and laid him beneath the fence before joining the retreat. He was unconscious for two days, during which time maggots had entered his wounds and were wriggling under his clothing. The Bensons brought "an overworked surgeon from the Church, who . . . turned away with the remark that he had no time to waste on so hopeless a case."

While Margaret Benson went home to bring food and water, Amos "removed my clothing and scraped away the vermin that was preying on me." For ten days, in addition to their duties at the hospital, the Bensons cared for Rice outside, until he was so much improved that the surgeons were compelled to take him to Manassas Junction with other wounded in early August. By mid-August he was sent on to Libby Prison, from which he was later exchanged. The Bensons' steady kindness was remembered by uncounted men whom they nursed in this, and the Second Battle of Manassas in 1862, "men who took our names and promised to write us." At least one of their patients had tears streaming down his face as he departed, asking to take Mrs. Benson's hand "one more time," and assuring her that his mother would pray for her. Rice noted that,

> had it not been for the efforts of the Bensons and the few other living in the vicinity . . . our wounded would have had little food or attention during the first few days following the battle.[37]

Surely, Margaret visited the Thornberry house and had some occasion to meet Sullivan. His conduct while in the hospital sufficiently impressed many to the point that it was remarked upon specifically by those who were with him then, so he cannot have failed to have touched Margaret Benson's compassionate heart. This week provided the first opportunity for her to show kindness to Sullivan Ballou. She was to have one, possibly two such opportunities in the future.

CHAPTER TWENTY

"Life's Tide Is Ebbing Out So Fast"*

Prisoner-of-War Sullivan Ballou Struggles to Survive

The Last Week of July 1861

On Tuesday, July 23, the capital was still chaotic and reeling with the after effects of the "Great Skedaddle," or as some wags among Mary Henry's circle called it, the "Southern Races."

> The streets are still crowded with soldiers, every few steps almost we encounter crowds collected around some of the Bull's Run adventurers listening with mouth & eyes wide open.[1]

Friends, relatives, and comrades crisscrossed the town, searching for each other and trying to establish the fate of those not yet reported returned. With missing men still coming in, it was no easy

* From the Civil War song "Lorena."

task for the regiments to report their casualties. The Rhode Island contingent at Camp Clark relied on information from Rhode Island soldiers trickling back from Virginia. Each told what he had heard or seen—but because each soldier had witnessed different parts of the scenario at different times, an exact chronology remained elusive. Conflicting information on Sullivan Ballou persisted for several days. As late as July 26, Captain Nelson Viall was still unaccounted for in the hometown papers, as were many of the enlisted men of the Second Rhode Island, though the *Journal* could proclaim,

> We are happy to announce the safety of the American Brass band. We learn that they were in the most exposed situation on the battlefield, and during the entire engagement, devoted themselves to the removal of the dead and wounded.[2]

In a report prepared July 23, Lieutenant Colonel Frank Wheaton gave the names of the major personnel killed and indicated the current tally of losses:

> SIR: . . . I have the honor to submit . . . the following report of the killed, wounded, and missing in the Second Regiment Rhode Island Volunteers in the late battle with the secession forces near Bull Run, Va. A more detailed report, giving the names of all killed, &c., is now being prepared, and will be submitted at the earliest possible moment.
>
> It is my mournful duty to record as amongst the first killed, as he was first in the fight, our gallant colonel, John S. Slocum, who was three times wounded, and left in a dying condition. Major Sullivan Ballou, while bravely assisting in changing the position of our center, was struck from his horse by a ball from a rifled cannon, and also left unconscious and dying.

The total loss of my command is 114 killed, wounded, and missing. . . .The total number killed, wounded, and missing is 114; total number killed, 28; total Number wounded, 56; total number missing, 30. A carefully corrected list of the names in full of all who are among the above will accompany my detailed report . . . as also a list of arms, &c., destroyed or lost in action.

Thanking you for the compliment bestowed us on the field, and for having assigned us the advance on our way to meet the enemy and the lead in the fight and the rear in the retreat, I am, very respectfully, your obedient servant,

FRANK WHEATON,
Captain, U.S. Army,
Lieutenant Colonel Second Rhode Island Vols.[3]

Later in the war, casualty lists from battles, relayed by telegraph to local newspaper offices, were often a family's first source of information on the fate of their brother, son, or husband. The kindly letter from the commanding officer, coming by regular mail, even if written promptly, could not outrace the telegraph.

Soon after the battle, while the governor remained with the regiments, the Second reorganized. "Wheaton was advanced to the colonelcy. Captain Steere of Company D was promoted to lieutenant colonel, and Captain Viall of C to major."[4] Viall had taken over as acting major during the battle after Sullivan was shot. All appointments were backdated to July 22.

Not only was it one of the duties of the major to take custody of the personal belongings of deceased soldiers and arrange their return to their families, but Nelson Viall now moved into Sullivan's tent, and Sullivan's things had to be inventoried and packed. He had several choices for transporting Sullivan's belongings and camp trunk, which, probably unknown to anyone, contained his last letter to Sarah, the one written the evening of July 14. There were a number of visiting Rhode Islanders to whom it might be entrusted, or it could accompany the First Regiment when it returned home in a few days.

William H. Pierce of Providence was visiting in Washington, D.C., and wrote an excited letter to his father at home which contained interesting details. The letter is written in two parts. It begins on July 24 and is interrupted when Pierce goes out to dinner.

> I have just come from the Senate Chamber where Andrew Johnson was expected to speak, but he was not ready and the speech was postponed until Friday—the troops are getting organized from the scattering of the battle—the loss is not near as great as was at first reported, they have been coming in from the woods to the City ever since Sunday, it appears by all the accounts that the enemy were as badly whipped as we were for they did not follow our army at all from the field in its retreat—There is no doubt but they lost two men to our one. . . . I saw and conversed with Dr. Rivers yesterday, he amputated Major Ballou's leg and thought if he should have care he would likely recover—He was left in a yard upon the field with other wounded. About the time Ballou was wounded, an Alabama Col was also wounded and brought to him for treatment, he dressed his wounds and placed him by the side of Ballou and when he was obliged to retreat, the Col promised that our wounded would be taken care of—It has since been reported that our hospital and yard containing the wounded was shelled by the enemy and perhaps all therein killed—I am now going to dinner, after which I shall ride out to Camp Sprague and see the boys—

Pierce resumes his narrative at "10 o'clock PM," reporting that he has seen many friends "and hundreds of others all in poor spirits. . . .

I saw Capt Reynolds, he felt very low about losing all the guns of his battery but one." One of his friends "told me he saw Ballou after he was dead in the Hospital." Possibly this was when the still-anesthetized Sullivan was laid outside on the grass to revive; he further reported,

> Simon Henry-Greene was at Camp finding out about his son who was left on the field wounded and Charles Brownell Partner of Ballou is here trying to have Ballou's body recovered, which will very likely be done.[5]

To be there on the twenty-fourth, Charles Brownell had to have immediately closed up the law office after receiving Sarah's consent to act on her behalf, told his friends in the building about his errand, and taken the next train south for Washington, D.C., a two-day journey if he traveled with interruption. Once there, he went immediately to the Rhode Island camp off New York Avenue to find out how to bring Sullivan's body home. There, depending on to whom he spoke, he learned that Sullivan might still be alive, or might have died. Regardless, he would have wanted to personally reach him. To do this, the young lawyer needed to know what protocols had been established between the two armies to exchange prisoners and the honored dead. It was harsh news indeed to find out the two armies had none, and moreover were not communicating, and that the border around Alexandria was rigidly sealed. With the Confederates arresting civilians, even congressmen, it was unsafe to try to trespass; there was no way Brownell was getting out there. He was not alone in his frustration. Mary Henry reported,

> Yesterday a poor man came to father to know if he could obtain permission to visit the battle field. He wished to look for the body of his son. He heard of him through a companion by whose side he was shot down. . . . The unhappy

> father was over [come] with grief we could hear his groans from one end of the house to the other.[6]

Report after report confirmed the same thing: "Have just returned from Alexandria, Could not get out of the line of the pickets in the vicinity."

> No persons are allowed to pass beyond the lines, which seem to extend out four or five miles. So stringent is this regulation that a lady in the perils of childbirth was refused permission to go to her home in Fairfax county, where she had left her children.

Pawtucket sent its own emissary to Washington to check on their soldiers but, while he had access to the men in camps Clark and Sprague, he could not enter Virginia:

> Dr. Morton . . . arrived home Saturday morning. His report of the dead, wounded and missing among our Pawtucket men, corresponded closely with the report published Saturday, though it is rather more specific. It was impossible for him to obtain a pass to the battlefield. . . . Dr. Morton said there is no doubt that Major Ballou is dead.[7]

Perhaps Brownell wired home his lack of progress and departed, or perhaps he remained a few more days to see if the situation would change, before reluctantly going home empty handed to apologetically explain the stalemate.

One extremely forceful woman did make her way through the sealed border to go to the aid of her husband, James Ricketts, generating immense publicity at the time, and setting a precedent for other wives to follow throughout the war. Fanny Ricketts, a beautiful woman whose sweet face belied the strength within, had joined her husband for three years at his artillery posting on the Rio Grande, during which time she learned army ways and made friends among the officer corps. Not permitted to accompany him to the battlefield this July, she waited anxiously in Washington, where she first heard the news of his death. Presently, his aides came to deliver his sword and his dying message, and to confirm his demise. Soon afterward, however, General Wadsworth telegraphed her that "an officer who had met his flag of truce informed him that Captain Ricketts was alive, but dangerously wounded and a prisoner."

She immediately began to persistently chivy and persuade her way to his side. First, she cajoled the subsistence department into providing her with a two-horse carriage and a driver with secessionist sympathies, willing to go into Virginia. General Scott provided her with a pass to cross the Union lines, which she did without incident. When she was stopped by Southern pickets, she insisted on a note being taken to J. E. B. Stuart, with whom her husband had served in Texas. He allowed her to travel as far as Fairfax, where he met her and asked her to sign a parole not to act as a spy. She tore it up, told him she would go as his prisoner, and insisted on a safe conduct and escort to General Johnston's headquarters. Former Senator Wigfall, who had been so keen to kidnap president-elect Lincoln, intervened for her, and Stuart rudely allowed her to travel onward, by some reports confiscating her carriage.

Johnston sent her on to the Stone House at the intersection of the Sudley–New Market Road and the Warrenton Turnpike. The conditions there were appallingly bad, as it was only an unofficial hospital. Dr. Lewis, from Michigan, was present, and urged her to maintain her self-control in the blood-drenched surroundings whose very ceilings were stained with spurted blood, the porch piled high with amputated limbs. Mrs. Ricketts began taking care of her husband and the other officers sharing his room, and bringing water to men scattered throughout the house. She cleaned things up, organized what little food they had, nursed her husband, and remained their constant advocate with the Confederate command and medical corps. Ricketts' worst wound was a bone shattered from a bullet below the knee. Normally, his lower leg should have been amputated, but between no anesthetic and the unsanitary conditions, it had not seemed a prudent course of action, and they opted instead to see if it might heal. He remained in pain, with a badly swollen leg, in constant danger of gangrene.[8]

Fanny Ricketts had blazed a trail not open to Sarah Ballou in July 1861, for all that Sarah must have retrospectively wished it had been. Later in the war, urgent telegrams often summoned officers' wives to the bedsides of their wounded husbands. If the victim could hold on for a day or two more, the swift Northern train network could reunite a wife with her husband in time to hear his last whispered words, or, if the omens were more auspicious, assume his nursing. In crude field hospitals, in the houses and churches of the town nearest the battle, or if evacuated to a proper hospital, wives were then welcomed. It was not unusual for a commander on either side to arrange for safe passage through the lines for the wife of an injured old colleague with whom he had trained at West Point.

Lacking concrete information and Fanny's connections, Sarah had not been able to rush to Sullivan's side, nurse him, fuss over him, plead with him to live, try to infuse her own strength into him or even sit by him, watching him ebb away while she anticipated his death. She had no opportunity to bargain with God for his life to be spared. She had no chance to kiss him one more time, to tell him she loved him, to hold his hand, to say farewell.

In Elmwood, in Cranston, Sarah mourned her husband as dead; she had not yet received his instructions not to. During the next week, she received two more letters from Sullivan, those describing the action at Fairfax Court House. These, and the loving words of his other letters, she could read over and over again for comfort.

They held no forebodings of death, only his little health reports, reassuring her of his well being. Sarah had a hundred questions that only time would answer. What had happened in the battle? How had he been wounded? How had he died, did he suffer? How would she pay his funeral expenses? How would she manage her household now? Emeline and Catherine, her models in the rocky course of widowhood, advised her that most of these would be answered in time. The First Regiment was coming home any day now, and its men and officers could tell them much. Meanwhile, tributes to Sullivan commenced.

The night Pierce wrote home, a group of Sullivan's longtime friends gathered to honor and pay tribute to their dead comrade in Woonsocket.

> At a Special meeting of the Woonsocket Guards on Wednesday evening, July 24th, 1861, the following resolutions unanimously passed:
>
> Whereas, the Woonsocket Guards have learned with deep sorrow the death of Major Sullivan Ballou, late of the Second Regiment, Rhode Island Volunteers, who was mortally wounded in the Battle at Bull Run, near Manassas, in Virginia, while nobly fighting in defense of our flag,
>
> And Whereas Major Ballou has been connected with this corps since its organization at first, too young to carry a musket, acting as marker, afterwards filling the offices successively of Orderly and Lieutenant: and whereas, we were much attached to him, thorough our high appreciation of his military abilities and moral worth, Therefore, Resolved. That while we bow in submission to this decree of Divine Providence, we extend to his family, to the widow and her orphan children our deep and heartfelt sympathy.
>
> Resolved. That in token of respect for his memory we wear the usual badge of mourning. Resolved. That the above

> resolution be entered on our books and published in the Woonsocket Patriot.
>
> Resolved that a copy of the above resolutions, signed by the Commandant, be sent, by special messenger, to the widow of the deceased.
>
> William Lindsey, Col
> Commanding, Woonsocket Guards

Although Washington, D.C., had so far escaped Confederate invasion, and managed to stave off the onslaught of thousands of fleeing soldiers on the twenty-second, the capital was still destabilized by what nurse Emma Edmonds, quoting Captain Noyes, described as hundreds of

> stragglers sneaking along through the mud inquiring for their regiments, wanderers driven in by the pickets, some with guns and some without. . . . Every barroom and groggery seemed filled to overflowing with officers and men, and military discipline was nearly . . . forgotten for a time in the army of the Potomac.[9]

On the twenty-third, Private Sholes, displaying the resilience of youth, headed back down New York Avenue to go into town to see some friends and compare notes. As he grew near to town, a carriage passed him going the other way—to the Rhode Island camp—and he was hailed by Colonel Burnside, who recognized his uniform. Burnside told Sholes it was too dangerous to be on streets of the capital that day, and asked him to reconsider. Sholes argued back, but the brigade commander finally convinced him, and the young man climbed into the carriage for the trip back. By the time they arrived, Burnside

> had all my pedigree, knew several of my kindred and had

> permanently established himself in a very warm place in my heart. He thanked me, implying by his manner that in obeying his request, I had conferred on him a special favor.[10]

Burnside had been in town, arranging details of the return of the First Regiment to Rhode Island, and, with all he had on his mind that day, it was characteristically compassionate of him to take a hand in the fate of this young private. Soon, the capital would institute a virtual lockdown, confining soldiers of all ranks to their camps, in order to regain control and army discipline.

On July 25, the Second Regiment received their "first government pay in gold." They also swapped muskets with the First, sending the smooth bores back home, keeping the more powerful rifled muskets in camp. Burnside had spent several hectic days making the arrangements to transport home all the survivors of the First Regiment, whose enlistment had expired before the battle. That Wednesday, the men of the two regiments visited back and forth saying farewells. In the evening, as the First marched by the artillery camp as they headed for New York Avenue and the depot, "Captain Reynolds proposed cheers for every company, which was spontaneously replied to."[11]

The First Regiment embarked late, almost at midnight on the twenty-fifth, and arrived early Sunday the twenty-eighth. In the towns of Rhode Island, the excitement was palpable. Even Sunday morning church services were curtailed so families could meet the train, which arrived first in Providence, where the men from other towns transferred to local trains. The *Providence Journal* captured the mood in Woonsocket:

> Sunday was a happy day with us. All were glad, with the exception of the few whose dear ones had perished that day week. Company K are coming was on every lip. As the hour of 1 P.M. approached, Railroad Square and the windows and

> heights overlooking it were densely crowded with people. Soon the train appeared with its precious freight of brave volunteers. They were received with a salute. A procession . . . escorted them to the Mechanics hotel where addresses of welcome were briefly made . . . then escorted the volunteers to the Guards' Armory, where they were dismissed to meet the "loved ones at home." Along their route the suppressed hurrah of the densely packed masses of people told what wild demonstrations their respect for the Sabbath restrained.
>
> Yet in our joy at the return of the 1st regiment we are sad for Capt. Smith of the 2d. None knew him but loved him. Not Smith alone do we mourn. The gallant Ballou was our former townsman. With us he spent the greater part of his life. He had hosts of friends here. He deserved them. Both were brave men, and like brave men they met their deaths.[12]

The men of the First Regiment fanned out through the towns and, after visiting their own loved ones, paid calls on the families of the dead of both regiments, extending their condolences and sharing their firsthand accounts of how the man had died. Each soldier offered his own description and interpretation of the battle, though one common refrain was "the guide was supposed to be treacherous." They mustered out on August 2 as the men of the next regiment, forming on order of Lieutenant Governor Arnold rushed to enlist.

Trains pulled into the Southern capital of Richmond that week, too, the most widely reported of which bore Jefferson Davis and the dead heroes of the Confederate Army. Though Bartow was a Georgian, the sorrow for his loss was very real in Virginia. Thomas Cooper De Leon observed and reported the events of July 23:

> At night the President returned; and on the train with him were the bodies of the dead generals, with their garde d'honneur.

> These proceeded to the Capitol . . . while President Davis went on to address a vast crowd. An hour after Davis finished speaking, the rain descending in torrents, the first ambulance train arrived.
>
> First came forth the slightly wounded, with bandaged heads, arms in slings, or with painful limp.
>
> Then came ugly, narrow boxes of rough plank. These were tenderly handled, and the soldiers who bore them upon their shoulders carried sad faces, too; . . . And lastly—lifted so gently, and suffering so patiently—came the ghastly burdens of the stretcher. Strong men, maimed and torn, their muscular hands straining the handles of the litter with the bitter effort to repress complaint . . . It was a strange crowd that stood there in the driving storm, lit up by the fitful flashes of the moving lanterns. The whole city was there. . . .

And occasionally, "the wild, wordless wail of sudden widowhood was torn from the inmost heart of some stricken creature who had hoped in vain!"[13]

The gravity of the situation as perceived on the Southern side, helped to explain the harsh sentiments towards the invading forces from the Union, reinforcing the Confederate Army's disinclination to confer with the Union command on exchange of prisoners or access to the wounded. In reality, after this battle, both sides reviewed and strengthened their moral ground, much as they did just after Fort Sumter in April. The "war meeting" held in Providence

> proved a very enthusiastic one. . . . The speeches were bold and patriotic. Bishop Clark referred to Edward Harris of Woonsocket as saying that he "Would divide his fortune, if necessary and divide it again, and again, in behalf of the war, till it is all gone."[14]

Just as in April, more regiments were formed. Woonsocket called

> a grand meeting of all citizens in favor of suppressing the wicked Southern Rebellion and of sustaining the Government in any and all circumstances at 5[rule] Sat afternoon. Col Sinnott of the RI Vol Irish Regiment will be present and accept such volunteers as may offer their services for the war. This Regiment already numbers six or seven hundred men.[15]

As civic and military events swirled around them, the Ballou families remained closeted with their grief. In Pawtucket, according to the customs of the time, a mourning wreath was hung on the front doors of the three families living "almost within a stone's throw of" Emeline, the mothers of Lieutenant Levi Tower and Colonel Slocum. These three neighbors were now further bonded by their grief over their respective losses.[16] The wreaths signaled to all would-be callers that the inhabitants within were observing the rituals of mourning. Emeline was shocked that her son was among the first of the war's casualties, that he had died the very first day, that her prayers had not kept him safe. Emeline sadly recalled the many sacrifices made to educate her only son, to enable him to achieve his dream of a professional career, ambitions now interred with him in some hasty grave in Virginia.

On July 27, when the *New York Tribune* ran a "local interest" type story on mothers whose officer sons had been slain, it picked up from the *Pawtucket Chronicle.* Mrs. Tower's son was certifiably dead, his limp body carried off the field by one of his men for a long distance; Mrs. Ballou's son was yet alive; and Mrs. Slocum's son had passed away on July 23 or 24.

Slocum's cause of death was not easy to verify, given the state of nineteenth-century medicine. A depressed skull fracture might have exerted pressure on the brain, causing gradual brain death; or a variety of injuries secondary to trauma, concussion, or skull fracture also could have been fatal.

His mortal remains had been packed into a large, non-coffin-shaped, squarish wooden box whose proportions most likely made for a rather unconventional posture. Probably an empty munitions chest left behind on the nearby battlefield, possibly a shipping crate from some machinery shipped to Sudley Mill, it would have been expediently at hand when the Southerners unexpectedly needed some semblance of a coffin to bury the highest-ranking Union officer at the hospital. In this first battle, neither army had yet realized the practicality of traveling with coffins and undertakers in tow. Given the warm summer weather, waiting the arrival of either was impractical.

As the newspapers of the nation wrung the last details out of the story of the Battle of Manassas, as it was then called by all, stories noted that Slocum uniquely was buried in a coffin. "Colonel Slocum [lingered] three days, and was the only officer buried in a coffin." Because the people of both sides not only read each other's newspapers, but those of North and South also ran stories lifted from those on the other side, Slocum's burial arrangements were well known to Rebel soldiers. His gravesite in the Thornberry garden, along with those who became his companions in death, even became something of a minor tourist attraction after the battle, at least until the Thornberry family reoccupied their premises.

Lieutenant Levi Tower did not experience the same dignified burial as his distinguished Revolutionary War grandfather, or Slocum. Tower and Sergeant Prescott were each wrapped in a blanket and put straight into the ground—lying face down. Such a burial position was reserved for cowards, and the gesture by the Southern burial detail was deliberately insulting to the two Union officers. The unmistakable message of this position would not be lost on any Northerners who might later come to claim them for reburial up north.[17]

Dr. Rivers came home with First Regiment, for he had elected to join the retreat and had not been taken prisoner. His may have been the first credible information that Sullivan survived the operation and might still be alive. Charles Brownell returned home about the same time, having talked to many others who may have shared other opinions. Sarah hardly knew what to believe: first her husband was dead, then he was not but was not expected to live. Then he was dead, but—not really. It was an awful time for her. Everyone was powerless to affect the outcome of his life, and his family despondently realized they might not know the full truth until the POWs came home.

Approximately the twenty-sixth of July, Sullivan's trunk was delivered to Sarah's home in Cranston; it contained everything tangible that was left of his war experience. His officer's sword would not hang proudly over the mantel of this or any other Ballou home, for it had been surrendered as required, along with his person, at the hospital. But inside the trunk, she found her own letters to him, numbered and tied neatly, just as he had said. She found yet one other envelope, addressed to her in his handwriting, containing a letter to her dated July 14—a bit odd, since she already had one he had written on that same date.

July 14, 1861
Camp Clark, Washington

My dear Sarah,

The indications are very strong that we shall move in a few days—perhaps tomorrow. Lest I should not be able to write again, I feel impelled to write a few lines which will fall under your eye when I shall be no more. Our movement may be one of a few days duration and full of pleasure—and it may be one of severe conflict and death to me. Not my will but thine O God be done. If it is necessary that I should fall on the battlefield for my country, I am ready. I have no misgivings about, or lack of confidence in the cause in which I am engaged, and my courage does not halt or falter. I know how strongly American Civilization now leans on the triumph of the Government and how great a debt we owe to those who went before us through the blood and sufferings of the Revolution. And I am willing—perfectly willing—to lay down all my joys in this life, to help maintain this Government and to pay that debt. But, my dear wife, when I know that with my own joys I lay down nearly all of yours, and replace them in this life with cares and sorrows—when, after having eaten for long years the bitter fruits of orphanage myself, I must offer it as their only sustenance to my dear little children—is it weak or dishonorable, while the banner of my purpose floats calmly and proudly in the breeze, that my unbounded love for you, my darling wife and children, should struggle in fierce, though useless, contest with my love of country?

I cannot describe to you my feelings on this calm summer night, when two thousand men are sleeping around me, many of them enjoying the last, perhaps, before that of death—and I, suspicious that Death is creeping behind me with his fatal dart, am communing with God, my country and thee.

I have sought most closely and diligently, and often in my breast, for a wrong motive in thus hazarding the happiness of those I loved and I could not find one. A pure love of country and of the principles I have often advocated before the people and "the name of honor that I love more than I fear Death" have called upon me and I have obeyed.

Sarah, my love for you is deathless, it seems to bind me with mighty cables that nothing but Omnipotence could break. And yet my love of Country comes over me like a strong wind and bears me irresistibly on with all those chains, to the battlefield.

The memories of all the blissful moments I have enjoyed

with you come creeping over me, and I feel most grateful to God and you that I've enjoyed them for so long. And how hard it is for me to give them up and burn to ashes the hopes of the future years, when, God willing, we might still have lived and loved together and see our boys grown up to honorable manhood around us. I have, I know, but few and small claims upon Divine Providence, but something whispers to me—perhaps it is the wafted prayer of my little Edgar, that I shall return to my loved ones unharmed. If I do not, my dear Sarah, never forget how much I love you, and as my last breath escapes me on the battlefield, it will whisper your name. Forgive my many faults, and the many pains I have caused you. How thoughtless, how foolish I have often times been! How gladly I would wash out with my tears every little spot upon your happiness and struggle with all the misfortunes of this world to shield you, and your children from harm. But I cannot. I must watch you from the Spirit-land and hover near you, while you buffit the storm, with your precious little freight, and wait with sad patience, till we meet to part no more.

But O Sarah! if the dead can come back to this earth and flit unseen around those they loved, I shall always be near you—in the garish days and the darkest nights . . . amidst your happiest scenes and gloomiest hours—always, always, and if there be a soft breeze upon your cheek, it shall be my breath, or if the cool air fans your throbbing temple, it shall be my spirit passing by. Sarah, do not mourn me dead—think I am gone and wait for thee—for we shall meet again.

As for my little boys, they will grow as I have done, and never know a father's love and care. Little Willie is too young to remember me long, and my blue eyed Edgar will keep my frolics with him among the dimmest memories of his childhood. Sarah, I have unlimited confidence in your maternal care and your development of their characters, and feel that God will bless you in your holy work. Tell my two mothers, his and hers, I call God's blessing upon them. O Sarah, I wait for you there! Come to me and lead thither my children.

Sullivan[18]

Sullivan's tender letter had accomplished his purpose, enveloping Sarah with consolation, infusing her with strength, soothing her anger over his death for his country in army service, and surrounding her with deep love as tangibly as he could given his physical absence. Given his spiritual connection with her, perhaps he even knew when she read it.

Down in Virginia, the week dragged on for Sullivan, despite visits from the chaplain of the Second Maine, and Charles Wesley Andrews, a visiting Southern Methodist minister who mentioned how "I spent more time with them than with our own as they were far from home & friends & I now regret . . . I did not stay with them longer.[19] They encouraged him to bear up like a noble Christian under his pain, but could not lessen it. Sullivan's recovery now rested solely on his body's own ability to recuperate from the surgery.

One dangerous complication might have been bone fragments. If pottery is dropped upon a hard floor, it shatters into large and small pieces. These small pieces, often irregular, jagged and sharp, are called "spicules." Bone shatters in much the same way, and Civil War surgeons had no technology to locate and remove such fragments. Left in the flesh, they could work their way out painfully, or, if the patient was unlucky, cause internal bleeding. No evidence exist to suggest Sullivan's wound became infected, or that he suffered from gangrene.

Meanwhile, it was inevitable that an organizational decision would be made by the Confederate government and army to consolidate the wounded. None of the temporary field hospitals were well suited to their purpose, and supplying these scattered farmhouses and churches with food, water, and guards was difficult. Some Southerners grumbled that care of the Union prisoners was detracting from their own, although most remained compassionate to their fallen opponents.[20] The entire battlefield was unhealthy and noxious in the days after the battle, and the Southern Medical Corps was overextended trying to manage so many scattered sites. Lacking any understanding of the dynamics of germs and wound contamination, medical personnel believed that gangrene was a contagious condition resulting from the noxious miasma of a battlefield, and that removing soldiers from the site was the best way to reduce outbreaks.[21] Food supplies were low for all the forces at Manassas in the week after the battle: Beauregard wrote Davis not to send any more men to the Virginia front as "some regiments are nearly starving."[22]

For all these reasons, orders went out to transfer the wounded prisoners of war. Beginning July 25, and stretching into August 2, 550 Union wounded, officers and enlisted men alike, were loaded into wagons and ambulances that jolted across the rutted and rocky country lanes to the railroad junction at Manassas.[23] Doherty reported the first group left Sudley Church Hospital on July 26.

> On Friday, they commenced removing the prisoners and wounded, among them Capt Gordon, of the Eleventh Massachusetts; Lieut. Hamlen, Scot Life Guard, and all the Non-Commissioned Officers, leaving instructions with us to be prepared to follow the ambulances containing the wounded, who had undergone operations, on Saturday.[24]

Lieutenant Doherty, allowed to ride on the battlefield on the twenty-fourth, had the lay of the land and knew, with the closure of the hospital, his future lay in Libby Prison. He and several other attendants plotted their escape. Along with Captain William C.

Allen, Company G, Eighth Massachusetts, and one of the Waldorf brothers from Company C of the Second Wisconsin Infantry, they donned disguises, crawled away on their hands and knees in the dead of night and embarked upon a two-day odyssey of evasion. Using the roads and avoiding pickets, they eventually posed as members of the Fourth Alabama Regiment when stopping to ask directions of local farmers. Buying food from farmhouses, eluding horsemen, sneaking through the woods, they climbed a tree out of sight of a posse of vigilantes who were on their tail. The farmers fired their rifles in a 360-degree circle, trying to smoke them out of the thickets. Luckily for the trio of Yankees, nobody fired upward. The escapees would shake one set of pursuers only to acquire another.

Unable to search out a ford, they finally swam the Potomac River and arrived in Maryland seventeen miles north of the District of Columbia, near Great Falls. Further hiking brought them to the picket post of the Second Vermont Regiment, who fed them and loaned them beds. After a few hours' sleep, they hurried on to Washington to telegraph their safe arrival to family and friends.[25] Their adventure was pretty typical of other medical orderlies, doctors, and escapees. Doherty promptly prepared his accounting of Sudley Hospital for the *New York Post*, which published it July 29. On July 30, the *Providence Journal* published it, and Sarah learned the harsh realities of life at the hospital.[26]

On Saturday, July 27, the command of the Southern Army transferred almost all remaining wounded prisoners southward to Libby Prison. The journey was agonizing and took a terrible toll in lives of the wounded men. Overcrowded, springless ambulances bounced and jostled their passengers around, opening wounds and leaving trails of blood on the roads. With no painkillers, no medicine, no nursing, the wounded helped each other as best they could while trying to survive the trip.

The first of the Geneva Conventions was three years away, and, as they had in the Revolutionary War, the antagonists were slow in meeting to organize protocols for prisoner exchanges and care. Some of the harsh treatment was deliberate—prisoners were not to be coddled, but neither was either side striving for inhumanity at this point. In reality, both governments were improvising the care of their own wounded at this stage of the war, and did such a poor job of it that an outraged citizenry mobilized massive civilian-run medical projects. Known in the North as the Christian Commission and the Sanitary Commission, in the South they were less centralized. Individual states and hometown supporters of many units also organized relief societies, sent ambulance services to the front, built and staffed hospitals, and succored the impoverished families of wounded and dead soldiers. The Manassas prisoners did not experience these advantages.

Surgeon Gray suggested that the field officers were moved last. "In a week all of our surviving patients [at the Stone House field hospital], excepting Col. Willcox and Capt. Ricketts, had been sent to Manassas Junction." Was this why Sullivan still remained at the Thornberrys', or was there another reason? Had it perhaps been evident for a day or so that he was sinking, was unlikely to survive the trip to the junction, and it was pointless to move him? The last of the Union deaths recorded at the hospital complex took place between July 28 and 31; the last was Rhode Islander Jesse Comstock. It is possible the hopeless cases were left behind to quietly expire, tended by the neighbors and their nurses. Doctors accompanied each shipment of men to the railway, and gradually, none of the Union physicians were left.*

* Imprisoned, some were paroled quickly, surgeon Harris within Richmond on August 13 and to freedom September 13; while others like assistant surgeon Gray, remained incarcerated for over a year. Murphy escaped from Richmond that fall, enduring hardships like Doherty's during his trek to freedom.

> On Sunday, July 28, I accompanied the last load to the depot. At Manassas, I met surgeon Thomas H. Williams, medical director of General Beauregard's army, and was informed by him that I should remain at the Station and assist in placing our wounded, as they arrived, upon the cars destined to transport them to Richmond. . . . Our wounded arrived from the field, from which they came crowded in rough army wagons, and under a scorching sun, had to be thrust into freight cars, in which they were obliged to lie on the bare floor. Often they had been a whole day without food, and time was barely allowed us to furnish them with water. These railroad cars, having no right of track, were sometimes two days in reaching Richmond. Numbers died on the road. . . . I proceeded to Richmond on a train with Col. Willcox [on August 2] and about sixty wounded privates. Two of the latter died, exhausted, before reaching the end of the journey, the trip taking twenty-four hours; neither food, water, nor medicine were provided.[27]

Sullivan was spared this last hardship and indignity. Chaplain Mines wrote, "I soothed the last days of Major Sullivan Ballou," implying that Sullivan was uncomfortable or distressed before death.[28] At 4:00 P.M. on Sunday, July 28, a week after becoming a POW, Sullivan died. The official cause of death in the municipal records of Providence is "'exhaustion' following surgery."[29] The most likely explanation is that he was unable to recover from the loss of blood that occurred either at the time of the wound or from later internal bleeding. Without proper blood volume, his internal organs eventually began shutting down, and his system failed. Josiah Richardson was with him until the end.[30]

CHAPTER TWENTY-ONE

"And Our Hopes in Ruin Lie"*

Developments After the Battle

August 1861

A coffin was a profound luxury in the Manassas area that last week of July 1861. Yet during the afternoon of July 29, Sullivan Ballou was buried in one in the rich red soil of Virginia, close to Sudley Church "within a few feet from the spot where he breathed his last," at the Thornberry complex.[1] As far as is recorded, he is the only Union officer from this battle to have been so honored. Most were buried wrapped only in a blanket.

Perhaps someone washed his face if there was water, perhaps not. The faithful Private Richardson probably closed his eyes. Probably Chaplain Mines prayed over his departed spirit. He was buried in the same clothes he wore into battle, the same clothes in which he was wounded: his silk shirt, his striped calico shirt, his blue wool trousers covering his single remaining leg. His shroud was a

* From the Civil War song "The Vacant Chair."

blanket.[2] His boots had been removed, one in connection with the amputation and the other at some point in his hospital stay, so it was unlikely that they rejoined him for the burial. Footwear was at a premium on every battlefield during the entire war, and soldiers who died with their boots on, like Captain Levi Tower, rarely wore them into the afterlife.[3]

Richardson superintended the burial, but it is hard to know who dug the grave in the Thornberry's cabbage patch. This late in the week, most of the able-bodied prisoners were gone, but three Rhode Island attendants remained, and undoubtedly labor was for hire among the local free Blacks. Sullivan was almost the last Union casualty to be buried from this field hospital, certainly the last officer of rank.

Some from the neighborhood, embittered, would have noted with satisfaction that there was now one less Yankee oppressor alive on the sacred soil. Perhaps one or two kindhearted members of the parish attended the burial, in place of family who could not be there. Friend and foe alike had sympathy for a soldier dying far away from his home and loved ones. It remained a strong motif of Civil War poetry, songs, letters, and etiquette.

The song "Somebody's Darling"* describes the sentiments of death during wartime:

> Cross his white hands on his broad bosom now,
> Somebody's darling is still and cold. . . .
>
> Give him a kiss, but for somebody's sake,
> Murmur a prayer for him, soft and low;
> One little curl from his golden mates take,
> Somebody's pride they were once you know;

* This song may be heard on the Web site, www.sullivanballou.info

Somebody's watching and waiting for him,
Yearning to hold him again to her breast;
Yet, there he lies with his blue eyes so dim, . . .
Tenderly bury the fair, unknown dead,
Pausing to drop on his grave a tear;
Carve on the wooden slab over his head,
"Somebody's darling is slumbering here"

Some Union graves in the woods around Sudley were marked with crosses fashioned from thin branches. At the beginning, Slocum and Ballou's graves would have been marked with their names etched on a board, but these would not last the winter, too tempting a choice for firewood. As early as the first week of August, Southerners were visiting their gravesites at the Thornberry's. The young brother-in-law of Captain Fitzhugh of the First Virginia Cavalry, who was visiting Beauregard's headquarters, wrote: "I saw Slocum's grave today in a little cabbage garden by the roadside, and also found there Major Ballou, of the same regiment, who had his leg shot off."[4] Unmarked graves, two among so many hundreds, would have proved more difficult to visit. Southern graves near other field hospitals were marked with names and unit numbers, courtesy of comrades on site.

Yet it is remarkable that someone procured, or commissioned, a coffin. John Thornberry, the local carpenter, wheelwright, and undertaker on whose property Sullivan Ballou had died, could not have made one. He had joined Company A, Forty-ninth Virginia, a Confederate battalion that had assisted in the charge on Ricketts' Battery on Henry Hill. Wounded, Thornberry had been taken away to the house of his father-in-law, where he remained for eight weeks, recuperating from wound fever or possibly typhoid fever.[5]

Did Thornberry have some stockpile of coffins? The death rate in the area was not so intense that the undertaker would need to keep a stock of coffins on hand. There had been 118 deaths in

Prince William County in the previous year, but only about twelve of them occurred in the Groveton/Sudley area. These included the Thornton's baby son from dysentery and their sixty-five-year-old father from heart failure, as well as Sudley Methodist lay minister Alexander Compton's sixteen-year-old daughter, Elizabeth from bronchitis.[6] The carpenter would have time to assemble the correct size coffin for each from lumber on hand. There is always the likelihood that any stock on hand July 21 or 22 was immediately secured by the Confederates for their own heroes, Brigadier General Bee and Colonels Bartow and Charles Fisher of the Sixth North Carolina. Had coffins been available on July 23 or 24 when Colonel Slocum died, he would have been buried in one, instead of in a packing case.

Centreville and Sudley Springs were the first of many communities in the nation forced by war to deal with the unwelcome, unwanted, repulsive task of disposal of large numbers of dead men and horses. In the week since the battle, the army was forced to become more organized about acquiring sufficient coffins. By August 25, the Confederate quartermaster had established a supply of them at Manassas Junction from which a coffin could be requisitioned for a Confederate burial, but just how much earlier they were available is a matter of conjecture.[7] In theory, in the twenty-four hours of elapsed time between Sullivan's death and burial, a coffin could have been brought for him from such a depot.

Or, possibly the Virginians of the little community around Sudley Church came forward in Christian charity and self-interest to assist the occupying Southern Army with the means of decently burying the dead. Thornberry's tools were still at his house, along with a supply of lumber, and a coffin could have been made up by locals or soldiers of either side. Helping the army clear the battlefield of dead soldiers became an art Virginians practiced for the next several years as armies moved back and forth over the heartland of northern Virginia.

What was obvious was that Sullivan Ballou, during the week preceding his death, touched the hearts of some person or persons who had intervened to secure a coffin for this "good Christian man," despite his being a Yankee. Perhaps, since they had gotten to know him in the days he had been their patient, there was a bond, maybe cemented by talk and photos of his wife and children at home. To bury him in a coffin was to give him that last little bit of honor and dignity, and to make it easier for his remains to be sent home eventually to the family who loved him. This would have provided an opportunity for Margaret Benson's hypothetical second act of kindness.

The men of the overworked Southern burial details were, at the time, exacting petty revenge on the remains of some of the Rhode Island officers, burying them face-down in the grave, an insult that connoted cowardice. By interring the earthly remains of Major Ballou in a coffin, his protectors thought they were guaranteeing his dignity. Nonetheless, it was a humble grave for a man who, had the war not claimed his life, most likely would have been governor of his state and United States senator.

On the day of Sullivan's burial, the *Providence Journal* printed a report of services held the day of his death, during which he was mentioned. The main Episcopal church of Providence was mourning only its own parishioners that day, and the Ballous were not among them, but Sullivan had so impressed the bishop that he mentioned him anyway, speaking from a pulpit draped in black cloth:

> There are many others, of whom I would like to speak, if the time allowed. The accomplished Ballou, so genial and yet so brave, so tenderly attached to his household, and yet so willing to leave all behind at the call of his country, sacrificing so much in a profession which he promised to adorn by his skills and his acquirements; who, as if he had a presentiment

Sarah Ballou was among the first widows of the war, but many others were to follow. Small reproductions of sentimental paintings like these were often used to fill blank slots in photo albums. Titled "Hopes and Fears," a picture of father in uniform hangs over the piano, as the family reads the casualty report from a major battle. *Painted by G. Fish, from the author's collection.*

of the evil which might come to him, said to me, with a gush of feeling, just as I left camp, "You are a stranger to my family, but I ask permission to commend them to your care." How noble his last words: "Go, Doctor, as you have done all you can for me—there's but little chance for me,—save those of the wounded that you can."

Clark issued a challenge to his listeners that Sunday evening:

It is very easy to say "God's will be done" when it accords with our own will. It requires no effort to acknowledge the general right of the Almighty to have His way among the armies of heaven and the inhabitants of earth; and if His dispensations bring sorrow to a people far off from us and with whom we have no special concern, we are ready enough to submit to the affective providence. But when the blow falls upon our own

> head and crushes us, when the darkness descends upon our own dwellings and we are left desolate, when the choicest treasure that we clung to is suddenly wrenched from us, then to say from the very depths the heart, "Thy will be done," is the noblest triumph of Christian grace.

His talk, commiserating with and acknowledging the pain of the mourners, went on to tell them what to expect to be feeling, and acknowledged the Victorian belief that the dead are not really parted from the living. Similar orations would have echoed through many churches of the North and South as parishioners grieved for their dead. Said Bishop Clark,

> And now I must say one word to the fathers and mothers, the widows and children, the brothers and sisters, the friends and companions of the noble dead. God has afflicted you very heavily. The world will in your eyes never again wear the same bright aspect as in days gone by. There will be long hours . . . when you will feel as though your heart must break. There is a familiar voice whose tones you will miss in the morning, at noon day and in the evening. There is a place at your fireside which will be vacant forever. But time will bring with it a healing influence on you, so seek communion with God. He will give you a peace which passeth human understanding. You will begin to feel that your departed friends are not so far off: the bands of sympathy between you and them are not really broken, that they are not extinct but only passed out of the day. You will begin to feel that now it becomes you to put your house in order that you may be ready to go where they have gone before whenever the Master calls you.[8]

Sullivan had made the greatest of all transitions that week but, a week after the battle, many other lives were changing in the

Sudley-Manassas area. Colonel Willcox was finally transported to Richmond, in the greater comfort of a hospital car, where he was met by General Winder, superintendent of prisons, who had him transported in a cushioned carriage to a private room in Dr. Gibson's hospital. Colonel Ricketts' party arrived a day or two later, as Sullivan might have done had he lived.[9]

The Southern wounded were dispersed in many directions. Once the surgeon had done his best, recuperation often was accomplished more efficiently in a private family home, under the tender ministrations of the ladies of the house, who had the patience to drizzle drops of water down fevered throats or cook bland foods that an invalid's palate could tolerate. The wounded from Virginia regiments might be sent to their own homes if they were near the railway; those from the southernmost states could not withstand the long journey home and were cared for by volunteer families in Virginia. Southern—and some Union—wounded from this battle were sent by railroad to Haymarket Church, Culpeper Courthouse, even the dormitories at the University of Virginia at Charlotte. A few remained in local farmhouses in the Manassas area.

Colonel Egbert Jones of the Fourth Alabama was taken by wagon the late afternoon of the twenty-first to Manassas Junction. He, too, had to endure the jolting ride to Manassas Junction, but then went by way of the Orange and Alexandria railroad to the Confederate field hospital at Orange Court House, some sixty-five miles away.

The Fourth Alabama became state heroes for the role they played, and their fallen colonel suddenly become popular and vaunted, his men forgiving him their earlier grievances about overdrilling them. "A resolution expressing the regiment's sentiment" was sent to him in hospital in Orange Court House, as were warm individual messages from individual soldiers. Dr. Josiah Nott, a physician from Mobile who had ridden with Beauregard during the battle, was dispatched to treat Jones on July 23.

Old Battalion had also been treated for his wounds and recovered. Jones did not; he died at 1:00 A.M. on Sept. 3, 1861. His remains were sent home to Huntsville by train, Old Battalion accompanying his rider. A large crowd saw Jones to his final resting place three days later and witnessed a hero's burial with full military honors. It was noted many lawyers and judges were present at his large funeral.[10]

The medical care issues arising from the first battle galvanized civilian relief efforts in the North and South—but neither government nor war department responded. The Confederate military forces continued to do an extremely poor job of caring for their own wounded and prisoners. On October 22, the *Richmond Daily Dispatch* told the plight of hundreds of sick soldiers transiting Manassas Junction. They were unloaded in the rain, and received neither shelter, care, nor food. Their thin blankets did little to prevent them from getting soaked. They were then loaded into a Richmond-bound train without any rations. No one expected them at Richmond either, where they were unloaded like cargo and waited pitifully at the depot for hospital authorities to react. A few ambulatory cases went out into the streets of Richmond to beg for help.[11] If a dispatch did announce their coming, more wounded were often transported than predicted, again overwhelming the medical services. The frustration and anger was great on all sides.

> They had been thrown into cattle cars, without straw or hay for bedding—those with broken and amputated limbs must have suffered most terribly. The fractured limbs had not been placed in splints in the majority of cases, and the bones generally had worked their way through the wound and protruded through. The cases of amputation was still worse. The sutures had cut through the flesh leaving the muscles and bones bare, and the majority of wounds were alive with maggots—almost every case of amputation resulted fatally.[12]

After enduring the journey, the Union soldiers had to endure the fate of most captives—harassment. Huge crowds of curious bystanders at the Richmond Depot jeered at the Union wounded, so that the *Richmond Dispatch* counseled: "If all who have no business there would stay away, it would be great deal better."[13]

The Southern physicians began analyzing their experiences and concluded, "Those that have been early operated on by timely amputation have done best."[14] If Sullivan had lost less blood, he might well have survived the operation and his wound. The delayed removal of the wounded from the battlefield, caused by the lack of ambulances and constant heavy fire on Matthews Hill meant that many men "were actually in a dying state from the want of operations which should have been performed immediately" to reduce blood loss from seeping wounds.[15]

Yet the death of Sullivan and his fellow soldiers apparently had an impact on medical policy. Thomas H. Williams, surgeon and medical director, Army of the Potomac, directed his surgeons henceforth to:

> Perform their amputations and other surgical operations upon the field, and not as was the case in the battles of the 18th and 21st July, send their wounded to Manassas, and other places distant from the field, for operations to be performed, thus causing unnecessary suffering and increasing the mortality.[16]

Sullivan was part of a large group of soldiers who would not be leaving Manassas—the 847 "officially" dead men. Along with countless other soldiers who, though tallied as "officially missing," were also dead, and dozens of dead horses, these presented a logistical challenge of epic proportions. To the victors went the task of collecting and burying everyone who had died within the four-square-mile battlefield. Begun soon after the battle ended, it rapidly became a hideous task. The same shovels used in building the original entrenchments were now employed digging graves. The rain on July 22 had turned some areas into mud.

Lieutenant Doherty went for a grisly ride with a captain of the Virginia cavalry:

> On Wednesday [July 24] I visited the field of battle on horseback, . . . I saw there a number of our comrades, unburied, principally in the uniforms of the Fourteenth Brooklyn and Ellsworth Zouaves. I asked the reason; the reply was they had not yet reached them. The smell was very offensive. I galloped up to count their number, but was obliged to turn back on this account. I counted 14 of the Fourteenth Regiment in one spot.[17]

Minister Joseph A. Higginbotham testified to the travails of the people of Sudley and Centreville:

> As to the dead, they were being buried this Monday & Tuesday—piled up in waggons-some carried to long trenches, some to ravines—wh[ich] from their numbers & the heat of [the] weather was all that c[oul] be done. As late as the fifth day I rode among [the]dead . . . lying in every posture of agony.[18]

On August 1, the correspondent to *New York Tribune* wrote bluntly, "Manassas is one of the most stinking spots on the face of the globe."[19] The procedures taken for granted in hometown burials for the last two hundred years could not be achieved with the large number of interments occasioned by battle. Battlefield burials were rarely the standard six-foot depth of normal cemeteries because of the massive scale of the interments performed by weary and hungry enlisted men. Shallow graves of two feet in depth, however, did not well resist heavy rain or the depredations of farm hogs running loose after their pens were destroyed.

For some years afterward, it was unexceptional to come across bones, skeletons, and skulls on the surface at Manassas battlefield. The James Robinson family found them on their farm for the next fifty years. Nurse Frank Thompson a.k.a. Emma Edmonds, crossing the battlefield later in the war shuddered,

> But how shall I describe the sites which I saw and the impressions which I had as I rode over those fields! There were men and horses thrown together in heaps, and some clay thrown on them above ground; others lay where they had fallen, their limbs bleaching in the sun without the appearance of burial. There was one in particular—a cavalry man: he and his horse both lay together, nothing but the buttons and clothing remained; but one of his arms stood straight up.[20]

By the standards of July 1861, Sullivan Ballou had indeed been well buried. As the field hospitals cleared out at the end of July, homes and barns which had been commandeered by the military of both sides came back into the custody of their owners in a much altered state. Several young women wrote of the devastation to their homes. Laura Thornberry, then only six years old, recalled at age eighty-two,

> my mother went to our home. It was desolate. . . . We had lived in it for . . . twenty years . . . and there was not an article of anything in it. Ten men had bled to death in mothers bedroom. . . . Carpets and all furniture were out and gone. We never saw any of it again, or anything else. The old farm well in the back yard was almost full of everything that would go in it. Such as china ware, cooking utensils, flat irons, and every thing you can image used in a family was

> thrown in it. Of course, everything was broken. How we all cried over it.[21]

Another local girl recalled her own return home: "Amputated legs and arms seemed everywhere. We saw a foot that had just been cut off lying on one of our dinner plates."[22]

For Sarah, and the rest of Sullivan's loved ones, July and early August were given over to grief and the desperate quest to find out the truth about his death. By July 25, the *Woonsocket Patriot* had a comprehensive report on the battle for its readers. Its headlines read,

> The Great Battle At Bull Run On Sunday Last
> Terrible Fighting and Great Slaughter . . . .
> Col. Slocum, Major Ballou and Capt. Smith of the Rhode Island Second Regiment, among those Slain!
> Interesting but Mournful Particulars[23]

So great was the mystery about Sullivan that the *Providence Journal* apparently assigned some of its anonymous correspondents to do some detective work. On Friday, August 2, they ran several stories:

> THE DEATH OF MAJOR BALLOU
>
> I have exerted myself to know the facts of Major Ballou. He was shot in the leg close below the knee, the ball blasting through and killing the horse. The soldier who raised him says he merely said "Oh," once or twice, prolonging the sound as the horse fell on him. He was carried to a house with others says Dr. Wheaton, and then removed to the yard of a small school house (as the last place was shelled) and placed on the seats, where he took chloroform and his leg was amputated above the knee.

> After the operation he was easy but very weak, and he was held up to send the blood to his heart, as he very calmly said, "Turn me on this side, now on that." Lieut. Sears thinks the house was shelled, but Dr. Rivers says "No." He left him, *alive, the last one* and that he was *brave, brave, brave.* Dr. Rivers says his last words to him were: "Go, Doctor, as you have done all you can for me, and there is but little chance for me, and save those of the wounded that you can." A brave man was Sullivan Ballou."[24]

From another correspondent:

> Ballou showed himself among the bravest of the brave. He was constantly in the thickest of the fight, cheering the men by his voice and by his example, to yet greater valor. Even after his fall, he continued to shout to the men to press onward. He was, as we know, a gentleman of most amiable character and high culture, and has now crowned his distinguished life by a heroic fall. He was yet alive when the army retreated, but no hope was entertained by Dr. Wheaton that he would survive.[25]

Once her mother arrived, Sarah had the benefit of her experience and wisdom in widowhood, and followed a similar course of action as Catherine had in 1845, when she found it necessary to act very promptly to secure her livelihood and protect her children's future.

By August, with the assistance of Charles Brownell and Charles Parkhurst, Sarah initiated a number of actions. Forty days of a major's pay was due his estate, and a number of people owed Sullivan money for legal work. Initiating collection of these assets was the fastest way to put cash in Sarah's hand, as was selling the cow, if she still owned it. Selling his watch was another way to raise money, but it had great symbolic value and was likely preserved for Edgar as the eldest son. Although in their correspondence Sarah had been discussing household economies and the possibility of moving to another house, until she knew her financial position she had to continue living where she was.

The General Assembly, convening in special session that August, voted on the eighth to send all the families a

> resolution of sympathy with the families of the officers and men who lost their lives in the late battle in Virginia.
>
> Resolved that we tender our sympathies to the families of Col Slocum, Major Ballou, Captain Tower, Captain Smith, Lieut Prescott and the other officers and privates, who lost their lives in the late battle near Manassas in Virginia, and that the Governor be requested to communicate this to them, in such manner as he may deem proper.
>
> I hereby certify the above to be true copy of a resolution passed at the Special August session A.D. 1861. In testimony where of I have hereunto placed my hand and affixed the seal of the State this twenty first day of August. A.D. 1861.
>
> Henry A. Bartlett
> Deputy Secry of State[26]

The second most important development for Sarah that month, after the receipt of Sullivan's last letter, was the return to Providence on August 17 of thirty-eight-year-old Private Josiah W. Richardson of the First Regiment. He, Eldridge, and Collins had remained at Sudley Church hospital until the last wounded Union soldier departed, and Jesse Comstock of the Second died of his wounds on July 31. They had moved in a unique aura of protection and civility, at a time when the governments and commanders remained unbendingly uncivil to each other; a prominent member of Sudley Parish, Margaret Benson's father, reassured them, "'You are all right; it is understood that you are to be released.'" On that date, under the terms of the bargain made by Colonel Jones, their transfer home was arranged, via Richmond and Norfolk. At the latter depot, a mob threatened and reviled them. Acting more like a politician than a photographer, Richardson spoke to the crowd from the car's platform, telling them how he and his companions had

> remained behind to administer to the dying and distressed, not only of the federal but of their own soldiers, and asked if for this they were to be molested or ill treated?

The crowd hushed, some cheered, and the Southerners fell back to let them pass. Richardson and the others were repatriated at Fortress Monroe on the coast of Virginia and sent on to Washington, where they found a new Rhode Island camp.[27] Immediately upon the departure of the First, the Second had moved into Camp Sprague, then were reassigned to a new site about four miles away, in Maryland on the Rockville-Bladensburg Road. After a brief visit they then continued to Providence.*

Once home, Richardson informed the *Providence Journal* that he had

> the names of the prisoner who were at Manassas and also at Richmond. He took their names and residences, also the nature of their wounds, and is able to communicate full information respecting them. . . . He was with Colonel Slocum and Major Ballou. They were buried under his superintendence, and he can find their remains whenever they shall be accessible.[28]

* This fort secured the same approach to the capital the British had used to burn the town in 1814.

The latter information, he had privately communicated to Sarah and Mrs. Slocum, when he called upon them to give them full details of the last hours of their respective husbands.

Only now, twenty-seven days after the battle, did Sarah get the answers to her questions. Her anguish at hearing how long Sullivan had lingered on in pain was somewhat tempered by the knowledge that so many people with him at Sudley Hospital gave him comfort, care, and spiritual consolation. She now had hope that, when the war was over, he could be brought home to a cemetery near her home, where she and their sons could pay him proper respect. A gesture of kindness had now come full circle, helping her at the time of her greatest emotional need: the Rhode Island medical staff had helped the Confederate wounded, and Colonel Jones's reciprocation had allowed her husband to receive attentive care during his last days and a decent burial, and had sent Richardson home with vital information.

Among the many beneficences Richardson gave her in that visit was a fixed date of death for her husband, which now made it possible for her to apply for a widow's pension from the federal government under the legal provision that "pensions of widows and minors will commence from the death of the officer, soldier, or seaman on whose service the claim is based."[29]

Within the next week, with the assistance of both Charles Brownell, who prepared the claim, and Charles Parkhurst, who notarized statements from Richardson and her mother, Sarah obtained copies of birth records for her sons from the town clerk; and an application under the Federal Pension Act of 1836 was submitted to Washington on August 23, 1861. They had moved fast, it was logged in as Claim Number 27. Now, she waited for the gears of the federal bureaucracy in Washington to turn.[30]

Her last action that August was to file Sullivan's will for probate. The court examined the document, found it to be valid, and admitted it to probate. Only three short paragraphs in length, it directed the payment of his just debts and funeral expenses, and "constituted" and "appointed" Sarah as "Sole Executrix." He left to:

> my wife, Sarah H. Ballou, her heirs and assigns, all the rest, residue and remainder of my all Estate, Real Personal and mixed and wherever or however the same may be situated, whether in possession or action reversion or remainder of which I may be seized and possess or to which I maybe entitled at the time of my death.[31]

The only request which the Probate Court did not honor was that Sarah serve without posting any bond. On August 31, the court required her to post a $1,000 bond, probably to guarantee payment of outstanding debts, like that coal bill Sullivan had sent home to her. Charles Brownell and Uncle Henry were named as sureties to guarantee "the payment of funeral charges, debts and legacies."*[32]

No further probate records exist for them for the next year. No guardians were assigned for his sons at that time. Unaccountably, no inventory of their household goods was taken. With no records describing the cash on hand or debts owed, it is hard to determine the family's exact financial situation.

As the dust from the battle finally settled, there were no lack of pundits offering opinions on all aspects of the Union's performance in battle. Lyrics to such popular Southern songs as "The Flight of Doodles," and "Richmond Is a Hard Road to Travel," mocked Scott, Lincoln, McDowell, and the fleet-footed troops. The *Richmond Examiner* quoted the *Philadelphia Ledger*,

* Legacies in this case was misplaced boilerplate language, for Sullivan did not bequeath sums of money to anyone.

> The moral effect of this disaster is more dreaded even than its physical results. Merchants and business men fear that its first result abroad will be the recognition of the rebel government by England and France.[33]

Europe did not yet know the news, and would not until the steamer *Canada* arrived in August, she being the first ship to sail for Europe, on July 24.

Lieutenant Ames wrote such scathing letters home, undermining everybody else's performance but his own, that he eventually cautioned his mother not to repeat such tidbits as how he regretted the appointment of

> [Charles H.] Tompkins as Major of the Light Artillery. He was despised by all of his men and was even driven all around the cannons one night by one of the men who was just drunk enough to show his spite to his Captain. Tompkins never noticed it as he should have done. . . . Capt Cyrus Dyer is accused of not making his appearance in good season and when he was seen was under the influence of liquor. . . . [Arnold] Dexter of the 1st was not at all anxious to get into harms way but laid on his stomach in a hollow clawing the earth as if he had a bad belly ache. . . . Frank Goddard fought well on his own part but had no command over his men—the Carabineers, Co K.[34]

While it was to be expected that the hometown newspapers heaped accolades on their men from Newport, Greenwich, Providence, and Pawtucket, the men of Rhode Island had truly accomplished critically important things with their life's blood during the Manassas battle. As first into the fray, they had demonstrated to the Southerners that Yankee troops were neither afraid to fight nor would they run away under fire, exploding one myth, just as Evans's forces had done for the Yankees.

Second, by remaining in the field, Rhode Island had saved the lives of thousands of men of the three divisions deployed to the battlefield that day. If the first troops on the field had broken and retreated down the hill, back to the Sudley–New Market Road, Evans's reinforcements coming swiftly on the field could have pursued them right into the narrow country road, turning it into a slaughter pen. The Union Army was bottlenecked in this lane between 9:30 A.M. and 1:30 P.M., hemmed in by fences and trees. Had the Rebels attacked down the lane, or from the cover of the thickets alongside it, they could have broken up as many as five brigades. During such an attack, the Southerners could have mowed down the ranks of the Second and Third divisions like ducks in a row. There would be no way to mass these Union men into a counterattack, or reinforce them. There was no way out, except for the farmland up at Sudley Manor, where it would have been be easy to control any Union breakout northeast of Bull Run by pivoting Southern units. Given Tyler's reluctance to give battle that day, many Union troops would have died before McDowell could respond.

The slaughter might not have been total, but the death toll, POW count, and number of wounded would have increased dramatically. The psychological impact on the Northern public of so many casualties might well have undermined Union willingness to fight, and might have assisted the South in achieving its goal of causing the Union to abandon the cause and leave them to their independence. The war might have stopped right there in the first bloody lane. The political damage to the Lincoln administration would have been considerable, and Southern independence might have cost Lincoln his second term. The future of America might have been very different indeed if Rhode Island had run that morning.

In the capital, the lockdown continued as the government prevented open movement by its own troops, deserters—scores of the Fourteenth Brooklyn deserted during August—and Southern agitators or agents. When General Irvin McDowell had been relieved of command—later reinstated commanding his own single division—General George McClellan was appointed to command of the Division of the Potomac. This was part of his plan to restore discipline. The army being the army, the officers of the Second continued to complete paperwork on material lost in the battle.

The Rhode Island Second Regimental Band
Manifest of Equipment lost the day of the battle.
One man William Ryan
1 E flat Alto Horn
2 E flat Bass Tubas
1 B flat Cornett
1 small drum & sticks
1 pair cymbals with man missing
Several instruments badly damaged
1 complete set music books
2 pair shoes
18 blankets all left with the wounded men
15 rubber coats all left with the wounded men
6 lanterns
10 cups
1 cap
4 belts
7 haversacks
2 mouthpieces

Signed P. Kalkmann Bandmaster

The band trudged home in the rainstorm without their rubber coats or blankets, so they suffered more than the average soldier. The missing belts may have been used as tourniquets, and the cups left with the wounded.[35]

Mary Henry reported that, on August 17,

> The city has been very quiet for the last two weeks. Most of the soldiers are encamped beyond the limits of the city and are not allowed to leave their quarters. Even the officers are arrested if they appear in the streets without a pass.[36]

In the immediate months following his death, the mortal shell of Sullivan Ballou slumbered in the little makeshift cemetery in Sudley, as his spirit commenced its protective watch over Sarah and his boys. Meanwhile, developments were underway not far from Sullivan's grave—in Manassas and across the Potomac in Washington—that would have a profound impact on the Ballous' lives.

- CHAPTER TWENTY-TWO -

"Though We Live in Winter Quarters Now, We're but Waiting for the Hour"*

Rebel Revels in the Graveyard

August 1861–February 1962

The Confederates did not win the war on July 21, 1861, as many in the South had hoped; nor did the Yankees go home. Nevertheless, their victory in the Battle of First Manassas was sweet, and worth savoring; and the new Secession government, still hoping to convince the North to drop their objections to secession, publicized the triumph to the hilt. The victorious generals issued compliments:

> Soldiers: We congratulate you on glorious, triumphant, and complete victory. We thank you for doing your whole duty in the service of your Country.[1]
>
> J. E. Johnston, Gen. C. S. A.
> G. T. Beauregard, Gen. C. S. A.

* From the Civil War song "The Army of the Free."

For the next eight months following First Manassas, from July 1861 until March 1862, the opposing armies eyeballed each other uneasily from their deployments along a line that extended from Centreville down the Occoquan River to the Potomac. Each army was training, organizing, becoming more professional; neither believed itself ready for another big fight.

The Union kept a toehold in Virginia and there, along the District border with Maryland, completed a ring of forts to protect the national capital. These forts were built so the ranges of their guns overlapped, to ensure a complete and steady fire could be brought to bear on any force attacking the capital. Fort Slocum, which the Rhode Islanders built that fall, was part of this overall security plan for the capital, which could then be garrisoned with fewer men. With the exception of two Connecticut regiments that volunteered to extend their enlistments an extra thirty days, the three-month regiments all went home. Rhode Island, which had equipped its men more fully than most other states, had spent $258,000 [$7 million] on the First Regiment, from its enlistment through its return home.[2] New units were raised in response to the defeat, creating an army committed for three years, one that General McClellan could train to high standards. The next battles would still be fought with combat novices, but they would not be as "green" in military skills as the brave men who fought on July 18 and 21.

As did the military camps, the general population of the District of Columbia swelled in size as the federal infrastructure began to respond to the needs of organizing a war. The people of the District came to terms with the nearness of the foe, and the Secessionist stranglehold on the capital did not seem so threatening as long as access through Maryland remained secure. Military communications improved, and Andrew Carnegie, working for Tom Scott of the Pennsylvania Railroad, liaised with army officials to mesh the railroad system with their needs.

The Confederates never left the bloody battlefields, continuing to occupy Manassas Junction and arming their men with weapons and ammunition they had seized from Union sources there. By early August, Beauregard's lines stretched back to Fairfax Court House, reclaiming the fortifications joyously captured by Sullivan Ballou and the boys from the Second Rhode Island a month earlier. More Southern troops poured into Prince William County by railroad to reinforce the armies of Beauregard and Johnston. The pastures and fields from Sudley to Manassas Junction looked like a gold rush was in progress, everyone putting up a tent or cabin to stake his claim.

The Confederate encampments were all named for various Southern warriors. Of course there was a Camp Bartow for, with his death on Henry Hill when some miscreant's ball pierced his brave heart, Colonel Francis Stebbins Bartow had become a folk hero and martyr, doing for the Southern cause what Elmer Ellsworth had for the North a few months before.[3]

A popular lawyer, militia officer, state legislator, and charismatic Confederate senator, Bartow cut a wide swath through the popular consciousness of his native Georgia. A failed candidate for the U.S.

The plucky Bartow had rushed his Oglethorpe Rifles off to war to defend Southern rights and died in the first battle. The popular state legislator instantly became a martyr and many units were raised in his name. Company K of the Twenty-first Georgia was named "Bartow's Avengers" and seemingly figured out a way to live up to their name prior to combat. *From the Brian Pohanka Collection, courtesy of the U.S. Army Military History Institute.*

Congress in 1854, he became disenchanted with the prevailing political parties and evolved into a passionate, outspoken leader in the secession movement. As chairman of the Military Affairs Committee of the Confederate Congress, he guided the choice of the very emblems under which the South gave its lifeblood over the next four years: the gray uniform, the national flag, and the Confederate seal. He raised and trained the Oglethorpe Rifles from a militia unit at the outset of the war. His photo captured the image of a balding, well-dressed, middle-aged man impatiently sitting for the photographer, long-fingered, elegant hands temporarily at rest. In death he was lionized and played a larger-than-life role as an early hero of the Confederacy.

Bartow's remains laid in state in the Confederate capital city before they were returned to Georgia for burial. The *Richmond Dispatch* reported, under the headline THE DISTINGUISHED DEAD.

Georgians responded with an outpouring of sentiment to honor his memory. The very first battlefield monument ever erected was dedicated to his memory on September 4, 1861, by his men. Counties, forts, military companies, and babies were named for him. Captain Ujanirtus Cincinnatus Allen of the Twenty-first Georgia, named for a Roman general, and generally called Ugie, was a new father, and like Ziba Ballou, had apparently decided not to encumber his sons with his own name. He mused, "I had rather name him Bartow than after any other patriot hero that this war has developed.[4]

Bartow was also the most popular name for Georgia army units—at least twenty-one companies named themselves after him. Several of these companies styled themselves "Bartow's Avengers," among them Company K of the Twenty-first Georgia.

As companies of the Twenty-first Georgia arrived in Manassas, they took the scenic route at least once, touring the battlefield as if on a staff ride, noting where various commanders and units had come into action.* They halted to view the hillock where Thomas Jonathan Jackson and his Virginia Brigade awaited the right moment to move into action to reinforce the Georgians, earning the soubriquet "Stonewall Jackson." They reverently noted the spots where "Bee was killed and Bartow fell," and where the Northern batteries were captured, for example:

> I saw the ground where Bartow fell. Noble son of my native State, posterity will crown you with the laurels that thou has so bravely won.[5]

With the federal army in control of the best attractions in northeast Virginia—Alexandria, Mount Vernon, and Arlington—the battlefield was the only place off-duty soldiers could tour. Private Otis Smith of the Sixth Alabama described his sightseeing trip:

> The graves of the enemy could be distinguished from ours by the manner of burial. The enemy were buried by throwing dirt upon them just as they fell, sufficient to cover them, while ours were put in graves and generally marked by some means of recognition. The severe rains had washed the dirt from many of the lightly covered bodies, exposing protruding limbs and grinning skulls to view in all their horror."[6]

This relatively easy availability of skeletal material, combined with steadily increasing vitriol towards the North, seemed to occasion a loosening of traditional societal taboos on the uses of human remains. While a letter saying, "Hurrah for Georgia! Bring me a

* A training practice continued even in today's military, in which a leader narrates a tour of a battlefield so officers may study terrain, deployment, attack patterns, and strategy. For example, the U.S. Army in 2005 still studies the Gettysburg battlefield.

scalp when you come back," might be discounted as verbal excess, there were repeated references to a grisly souvenir trade.[7] Phoebe Yates Pember, a well-educated, well-traveled, and sophisticated woman who was to become the matron at Chimborazo Hospital in Richmond, wrote,

> The feelings here against the Yankees exceeds anything I could imagine, particularly among the good Christians. . . . One lady said she had a pile of Yankee bones lying around her pump so that the first glance on evening her eyes would rest upon them. Another begged me to get her a Yankee Skull to keep her toilet trinkets in.[8]

Once witnessed, the glories of the battlefield, of "Yankee Run" as the stream was called, faded into the background of daily life in camp. Deprived of the excitement and manliness of combat, the men settled into eight months of routine camp life, little mitigated by frequent relocations of their camp site. It was a disappointing and inglorious start to an expected life of conquest and fame, with little to brag about in letters to the ladies back home. One period song, written by Stephen Foster in 1854, "Hard Times Come Again No More," was especially popular during the Civil War as a lamentation. It could have been the theme song of the Twenty-first Georgia, a real hard-luck outfit that now endured a series of non-stop misfortunes.

The first of these was sickness and death among its men. By August 1861 a typhoid epidemic raged in the Manassas area; it continued until the snows of December. The natural occurrence of the disease was amplified by twenty thousand newly inducted men, largely ignorant of camp hygiene, clustered together in the camps.

In 1860, Prince William County had been a relatively healthy place, with only 118 deaths, out of a population of 8,565, a death rate of only 1.4 percent. By 1861, Prince William County was the most diseased place in America because the military camps acted as a transfer amplifier for the spread of childhood diseases like mumps. Contagious diseases like typhoid and measles raged, and infection threatened to spill over into Washington, D.C. The disease curve kept on getting worse for the Confederates; Sudley Church Hospital remained open for the next six months, caring not for wounded Southern soldiers but those who were ill.

Date	Total command	Number ill	Percentage ill	Reporting General[9]
August 17	18,178	4,809	27%	Joseph E. Johnston
December 31	91,998	37,984	41%	A. S. Johnston

The average Southern soldier was sick or wounded six times during the length of his enlistment. Sickness occurred five times more frequently than a battle wound, and the death rate was three to one, sickness to wound.[10]

The diseases that ravaged the armies of the North and South left few camps untouched. Statistics showed that during the first year and a half of the war, the Union lost 2 percent of its forces from disease and sickness. The figures for the Confederate forces were higher—3.81 percent. The Twenty-first Regiment had the twelfth highest rate of "death by disease" rate of sixty-three volunteer infantry units from Georgia, some of which served in more unhealthy climates. Within the entire Twenty-first itself, the average rate of "death by disease" for the first eight months of service was 9 percent, more than double the average. Within Company K, Bartow's Avengers, the death rate from disease was 19 percent, the highest in the regiment, and 500 percent higher than the army average.[11]

The sick soldiers could not always count on assistance from their comrades. One Georgian, E. B. Stiles, expressed his unhappiness:

> I did not believe men could be so selfish and indifferent as they have been in our regiment. Two thirds of them would not wait on the sick if they were not made to do it they would let them lie and suffer.[12]

On October 14, 1861, another soldier wrote his father, "it scares a man to death to get sick down here."[13]

But the North and South continued to lose men in other ways, too. During the stalemate of the late summer and fall of 1861, both armies took advantage of the lull in fighting to conduct general medical fitness examinations of their troops, whose enlistment examinations back home, if conducted at all, had varied in thoroughness. In the full flush of patriotism, seventy- and eighty-year-old men, epileptics, underage boys, tuberculosis sufferers, and men with hearts damaged by rheumatic fever, had rushed to join up and been passed into service, only to fall ill in the field or be unable to withstand the rigors of forced marches.[14]

If the number of men dead from disease was combined with those discharged for disability, one man out of every four in camp would die or leave the unit impaired, without ever having fought any battle. The Twenty-first lost still more personnel through what might be termed "disaffection discharges," as many of its commissioned and noncommissioned officers resigned or transferred.

Another problem was boredom. If he stayed well, camp routine for the average soldier was monotonous and boring. Napier Bartlett, a corporal from Louisiana, described Manassas Junction as "the most uninteresting place on earth."[15] Sullivan Ballou's regiment had rushed to muster, then rushed from training and staging to battle within five weeks. Now, for seven months, in all kinds of weather, the Georgians followed their routine, alleviated only by two grand reviews in October, one on the third for Jefferson Davis, the other at the end of the month for the governor of Virginia.[16]

During early autumn, reasonably certain the Union was not going to attack again in northeastern Virginia, the Confederate Army of Northern Virginia began preparing to pull out of Fairfax Court House on October 5. Under cover of darkness on the evening of October 16, the Rebel armies pulled in their pickets and retreated from Fairfax Court House to Centreville, whose heights provided excellent ground for observation and defense, especially once the forests were chopped down and the logs left in place to form a barrier to the movement of troops. A ring of earthworks—rifle pits, redoubts, and lunettes—was constructed, each angled and within firing range to cover one another to prevent penetration of the line.[17] The pastoral countryside was despoiled. The men could see the hot-air balloons of Dr. Thaddeus Lowe or La Mountain rising to spy on them, from bases near Alexandria.[17] The Twenty-first moved their camp to Centreville, adjacent to Bartow's Georgia Brigade, from whom they learned the full details of Matthew's and Henry Hill and cousins newly dead from wounds.

During the third week of October, the Union feint at Ball's Bluff resulted in another Yankee defeat, when Confederate forces used a bayonet charge to push Union troops back down a steep bluff overlooking a branch of the Potomac. Many prisoners were taken, and many Union troops drowned while jumping from the bluff into the swift current to avoid capture. Newspapers fomented over a thousand new federal casualties and another 155 Southern dead. No further military action was taken in Virginia in 1861.

November was ushered in, not with the still, smoky atmosphere that betokens the coming Indian Summer, but as a roaring lion bringing destruction and confusion in its wake to many a well-kept camping ground.[18]

Winter came early and, because major engagements were rarely undertaken then, armies went into a semihibernation, known politely as "winter quarters." With winter approaching, the commanding general tried to select a locale with adequate water, drainage, timber, and access to transportation, so far as the location of the army allowed. General Joseph E. Johnston tried to get barracks built around Manassas in 1861, but delays and misunderstandings prevented it.[19] As it turned out, the soldiers were left to their own resources to build huts that provided them some comfort until they came out of hibernation in March or April.

At the end of October, general in chief Winfield Scott just faded away. Not wanting to fire the old hero of the Mexican War after the disappointing performance of his army at First Manassas, Lincoln left him alone—literally. At first so jealous of McClellan when he came to town that he kidnapped him one evening to prevent him from attending a levee at the White House, a gesture that amused Lincoln, Scott was maneuvered out of power by the president, the cabinet, and McClellan. Realizing he was being increasingly circumvented, Scott offered his resignation to the White House; it was not refused. Now fully in charge, McClellan had an army of three-year men, which during that winter he organized, supplied, trained, drilled, and turned into a competent fighting machine ready to be unleashed on the Confederacy after the spring thaw.

In Rhode Island that fall, Sarah Ballou continued to adjust to life without Sullivan. Edgar had begun school, which gave him a new focus in his life.

The letter of condolence that the General Assembly had requested in August that the governor to write to the families of the war dead took two months to happen: Sprague was out of the state a great deal during that period. It was a most impersonal letter, likely the same one written, to every family, by a clerk or assistant but signed by the governor.

It was addressed to Sarah in Pawtucket, either a clerical error assuming she lived with Sullivan's mother, or that accurately reflected she was indeed on a visit to Emeline.

State of Rhode Island and Providence Plantations
Executive Department
Providence, October 4, 1861

Madam:

I derive a melancholy pleasure from the duty which devolves upon me, of transmitting to you an official copy of certain resolutions adopted by the General Assembly at its recent special session.

I need not assure you that the whole State mourns with you the loss of some of her best and bravest citizens; and that, in this hour of your deep affliction, it offers no unmeaning ceremony of condolence and sympathy. We also loved him whom you so deeply mourn, and shall forever cherish his memory and the memory of the other gallant officers and soldiers who fell with him, as an inheritance worthy of a brave, self sacrificing, and patriotic people. They fell in a richeous [righteous] cause, while encouraging their associates in the discharge of a high duty; and if mortality can be immortalized, they have been made immortal—for it is indeed a glorious thing to die for one's country. Allow me to offer you, in this moment of your grief, my own personal sympathy, and to express the hope that while the State and the Nation shall care for the good name of him who has fallen and for the interest of those who were bound to him by ties more tender than those which bind the government to the citizen or the soldier, the God of the widow and the fatherless may remember you in the dispensation of his choicest blessings, and heal the wounds which this affliction has caused.

I am, Madam, very truly,
Your friend and ob't ser't

Wm Sprague[20]

To:
Mrs. Sullivan Ballou
Pawtucket
R.I.

On November 7, 1861, the Office of Pensions in the Department of the Interior, after confirming Sullivan's existence with the adjutant general's office, certifying the credibility of the claimant and witnesses, and authenticating the papers, sent notice that Sarah had been approved for Pension Number 25, which entitled her to $35 [now $945] per month for a period of five years. Under a pension act originally designed for Revolutionary War widows, which had been modified multiple times after the Mexican War to cover widows of later conflicts, Sarah evidently did not qualify for the half-pay provisions that would have provided $56 [$1512] per month, with no provisions for minors. There is also no telling how promptly payments began; it is known that at one point in her record, the government was running four to five months late.[21]

The pension gave her a guaranteed income of $420 a year. In his first letter of July 14, Sullivan had expressed his wishes that she have a house with a yard for the boys to play outside, which he indicated might cost $250 a year in rent. If she paid that for a house, clearly, the remaining $180, a pittance averaging $15 a month, would not cover much. Despite their hopes for a better life for their sons, it appeared William and Edgar might now have to experience "the bitter fruits of orphanage."

The happiest news for the Ballous that fall was the birth of Aunt Sarah's and Uncle Henry's new baby on October 30. They named their youngest son Sullivan Ballou. Uncle Henry had helped raise his namesake, and now the family had another Sullivan. As the years passed, this boy was often referred to as Sullivan Junior.[22]

That November, the Twenty-first Georgia went into winter quarters two miles from Manassas Junction.[23] This location put them approximately three miles south of the Bartow Monument on the battlefield, and four to five miles from Sudley Methodist Church Hospital, an easy stroll for mountain boys. The lucky ones won the race to dismantle abandoned homes, sheds, and barns in the demilitarized zone around Centreville and reconstruct them in their camps. Otherwise, mess mates set about building their shelters together, and took their axes into the nearby stands of blackjack, oak, pine, and thrifty oak. These logs, trimmed and cut on site to the proper length, were then hauled back to camp—dragged by horses if the men were lucky, otherwise by manpower—where they had their ends notched, and were stacked to construct cabins.[24] Sarah "Sallie" Summers Clarke, who lived nearby at Level Green Farm grew distressed:

> There was enough firewood on our farm to last us for hundreds of years. But during the winter the Southern troops had their winter quarters there and cut down every last bit of it. They built log houses to live in and they even used our logs to corduroy the road from Centreville to Manassas (to help against the Virginia mud.) And all during the war they burned out trees for firewood. We were beginning to worry what we were going to do for wood for ourselves the next winter.

About eight feet high, these cabins had a roof that might be shingles or most often canvas, and a chimney made from river

A stereoscopic photograph of the winter quarters built in the Manassas area by the Southern Army in 1861. *From the Library of Congress Prints and Photographs Division.*

stone. Their furnishings were improvised from boxes, barrels, and leftover timber.[25] The men took pride in these dwellings—"We have the best fire place and chimney in the company"—and gave them names reminiscent of home or the fraternity within: "No. 4 Carondolet," or "Growlers."[26]

The frigid weather and deep snow, in addition to their new housing arrangements, kept these men isolated not only from the local community and the outside world but from their own officers. These winter cabins were set out with wide streets between them, and the officers' quarters were "some distance away." While it was standard to separate troops from field officers, normally company officers were not far away from their men. In this setting, lack of any supervision was troublesome, as Captain Nisbet confirmed in his description of his camp:

> One snowy day I was reading by a comfortable fire in my quarters when I heard a tremendous racket down in the company quarters. On looking out, I saw a fight going on between ten or twelve Zouaves and men of my company. I ran down there and commanded the peace, which the sergeants restored after much difficulty. Several of Wheat's Tiger Rifles

> of Taylor's Brigade were lying on the ground, having been knocked down by my men. They said they had been robbed of their whiskey, by some boys of that company . . . that they had followed them to get satisfaction. . . . I ordered the Sergeant to take them to my quarters and give them water and towels and after they had washed [bloody heads] I gave them a drink all round and said I was sorry they had been robbed; that if such disorders were reported to me I would punish the perpetrators, but to come into that company for a row was a dangerous business. "These men would have killed some of you if I had not stopped 'em," said I. And they went off, saying: "We are much obliged, sor, but Wheat's Battalion kin clean up the whole damn Twenty-first Georgia any time." They were Irish and, of course, love a scrap.[27]

Neither drill nor church services were conducted in snow drifts, and without a Union foe at hand, impromptu snowball fights transitioned into "snowball wars" as the Rebels formed regiments and brigades from their own ranks, recruited opposing companies to serve as "the enemy," yowled the Rebel yell, and "charged with a realism that quickened the pulse of participants and spectators." Such escapades were sometimes written up in letters and diaries as if they had been actual military engagements. Even General Longstreet participated with his aides.[28]

With the snow, however, came shortages in various basic foodstuffs and other supplies. Ugie Allen complained, "I could not get a candle if I were to be hung."[29] While all regiments suffered equally, the crack regiments with good officers kept up their morale and toughed it out, while those with the lowest morale descended into "the universal slouch and depression . . . overcome by an enervating moldiness."[30] The third week of December, a foraging party of four regiments and cavalry were intercepted by Union forces in Loudoun County, resulting in almost two hundred Confederate deaths. Burying comrades at Christmastime added to the Southern troops' miseries of homesickness and loneliness.[31]

The weather became brutal. Captain Nisbet described the unusual parade of snowstorms that swept over northeastern Virginia that year:

> It was the coldest winter known to the inhabitants of those regions. . . . The storm king ruled in all his majesty and power. Snow, rain, sleet and tempest, seemed to ride, laugh, shriek, howl, moan and groan in all their fury. . . . The zig-zag lightnings began to flare and flash, sheet after sheet of flames seemed to burst right over our heads, and were hissing around us. . . . Streak after streak of lightning pierced each other. . . . The white clouds rolled up, looking like huge snow-balls encircled with living fire. . . . I remember that storm now as the grandest picture that every made any impression on my memory. As soon as it quit lightening, the most blinding snow-storm was on, . . . I was freezing.[32]

The men from the deeper South were not all equipped for this kind of weather, and many officers wrote home frantically trying to get family members to obtain warm clothing and more blankets. The army had its own strategies for keeping the troops warm:

> Rations of whiskey were issued as a tonic, and as a preventive of colds. . . . There was no visible reluctance in according it a prompt and cordial reception; and . . . in the shadows of night, a large proportion of the rank and file of the army was—well, certainly not frozen. . . . It was apparent their Christmas festival had begun in real, if not sober earnest.[33]

A correspondent to the *Richmond Dispatch*, writing under a

pseudonym, confided, "You will be surprised and mortified to learn that this army is not free from the vice of intemperance."

Early in 1862, the Confederate War Department issued a general order instructing commanders to use every means at their disposal to suppress drunkenness.[34] However, the lack of sufficient supervision within the camps allowed the troops to find many ways to get intoxicated despite the embargo, whether by regular whiskey or moonshine. Teetotalers sold their share of holiday liquor rations to drinking men; contraband liquids were smuggled into camp in musket barrels, and Wheat's Tigers had arranged a steady supply from Richmond.[35]

Gloomy news further dampened the spirits of the army. Their "beloved commander" General Beauregard, whose political relationship with Jefferson Davis had deteriorated over the fall, was persuaded to leave Virginia. On January 30, 1862, he accepted a transfer to the western theater. His men took it as a "severe blow . . . as they had learned to look up to him and reverence him as a great general."[36] They gave him a valiant sendoff, with much waving of hats and hearty shouts, before returning morosely to their huts. Then, the next day, news circulated that Stonewall Jackson had tendered his resignation, widely believed by the troops to be due to political interference. He was convinced to withdraw it, but such rumors lowered the soldiers' morale still more.

As new fronts opened up throughout the South and West, the government in Richmond began reassigning other generals: General Crittenden was promoted out, and the Twenty-first moved to the Seventh Brigade of the Army of Northern Virginia under Brigadier General Isaac Trimble. The division commander, however, was General Richard Ewell, a veteran of the First Dragoons, Regular Army, from which he knew John Mercer and his fondness for the bottle. Mercer's men were getting fed up with his alcoholism. Captain Nisbet was accused of being absent without leave and,

> was put under arrest for going to Manassas Depot to get boxes of clothing which had been sent to my men from home. Colonel Mercer gave me verbal permission. . . . Colonel Mercer said he did not remember giving me permission to leave camp, which may have been true, as he was under the influence of the "rosy" at the time. This and other misunderstandings with line officers caused a measure of estrangement continuing until his death.[37]

In January, many company-level officers of the Twenty-first were furloughed or detailed to recruiting duties back home. They needed to replace the men who had died or been discharged, to bring their units back up to strength.

If these men had officers, any officers, to set them a good example, to lead them, care about them, and make their lot easier, like the Rhode Islanders had, the morale of the men of the Twenty-first might have been entirely different. With both field and company in flux or officers absent, self-discipline began to break down. The troops began to demonstrate a lack of respect for one another, for example, refusing to build winter cabins for men and officers who had been away on furlough, who had to shiver in tents in the snow until they could build their own in late January.

During their trips home, or from their contacts with civilians back home, these men were exposed to a growing climate of hatred for the Yankee invaders. The war on the battlefield may have been at a standstill but, on the home front, it was fought through rhetoric and propaganda, in daily conversation, books, and newspapers. Textbooks taught math posing such problems as, "If one confederate soldier kills 90 Yankees, how many Yankees can 10 confederate soldiers kill?"[38] The death and suffering caused by the first battle, and the realization that the war was going to be lengthy, inflamed the animosity felt toward the North. This viewpoint began festering in the military encampments at Manassas. Georgia soldier T. W. Monfort wrote to his wife in 1862,

> Teach my children to hate them with that bitter hatred that will never permit them to meet under any circumstances without seeking to destroy each other.[39]

Soldiers near Manassas, with easy access to bones, whittled finger rings from them to send home as unique souvenirs.[40]

Living in isolation from the finer influences that had stabilized their lives and morals in their prewar world: home and family, church, work, and a sense of community, many men gave in to their baser instincts in varying degrees. Gripes over rain, mud, rancid beef, and weevil-infested flour, arrogant adjutants and quirky quartermasters, damp clothing, and cheap shoes that fell apart, were never ending.

> You have no idea how demoralizing camp life is. Oaths, blasphemies, imprecations, obscenity, are hourly heard ringing in your ears until your mind is almost filled with them.[41]

Wiley noted,

> As weeks lengthened into months most Rebs tired of the inactivity and confinement. Small mannerisms that had once seemed amusing now provoked irritation, jokes and stories no longer entertained, and conversation became dull. Discipline, once accepted as a matter of course, now began to irk and offend. Officers who were followed gladly on the battlefield now became the subject of gossip and criticism. Resentments deepened, tempers quickened, quarreling and fighting increased.[42]

From their perspective, the damn Yankees, who had killed their cousins and boyhood chums, were responsible for the misery and hard times these Georgians now endured, for it was only to fight the Yankee invaders these men had left their homes. The focus of their bias was, of course, the Rhode Islanders, believed to have killed Bartow. It mattered not that by the time Bartow received his mortal wound, the Rhode Islanders were all a mile and a half up the road sitting in the shade or taking their wounded to the hospital, that they fought only on Matthews Hill, not on Henry Hill. The myths surrounding Bartow's death did not distinguish that the men fighting on Henry Hill were from Massachusetts, New York, Michigan, and Minnesota; the prevailing conviction was that a Rhode Islander had shot a musket round into Francis Bartow's heart.

Bartow's Avengers had gone to war to get revenge, and had so far had no chance, given that the nearest live Rhode Island soldiers were in Washington, D.C. However, the nearest *dead* Rhode Islanders, indeed the very officers who had led the fight against the Georgians, were well known to be buried nearby, by Sudley Church.

In one of these winter cabins, a group of men from the Twenty-first Georgia hatched a plan to go up to Sudley Church and to find the grave of Colonel John Slocum of the Second Rhode Island.[43]

⁃ CHAPTER TWENTY-THREE ⁃

"With Tender Care"*

A Team of Rhode Islanders Recover Their Dead

March 1862

The grieving widows and mothers of Rhode Island, "not regarding secession soil as sacred," wished for their soldiers to be brought home and laid to rest in New England soil, but the opportunity was denied them through the fall of 1861 and winter of 1862, while the Rebels remained in, and emphatically asserted their control over, the turf where the battle had been fought.[1]

After the battle, a friend of War Secretary Cameron had gone through the lines to recover the body of the secretary's brother, a colonel, but was taken prisoner and sent to Richmond for four or

* Excerpted from Abraham Lincoln's proclamation to observe a day of prayer August 6, 1863, inviting "the people of the United States . . . to invoke the influence of His Holy Spirit . . . to visit with tender care and consolation . . . all those who . . . have been brought to suffer in mind, body or estate."

five months.[2] Sergeant John Kane, acting orderly to Colonel Cameron, also went out under a flag of truce, with a written request to obtain Cameron's body. Alas, it had been addressed "to whom it may concern" and, after twenty-four hours, a reply came back from J. E. B. Stuart's headquarters "that it did not concern them at all," and that they would not recognize any papers not officially addressed to them.[3]

It was obvious Union families were going to have to bide their time and wait on developments that, to them, as well as the Northern bankers, the president, and the men in the camps, seemed slow in coming.

Winter in and about the District was harsh that year, with rain, sleet, snow, wind, hail, and even a nor'easter continuing to make the men of both armies miserable through February. On the sixth of that month, Washington, D.C., was on the edge of an unstable weather front passing over the Great Lakes, during which the temperature oscillated 160 degrees over three days. The winds were so intense that one of the derricks being used to finish the work on the Capitol dome blew over, in front of a huge crowd that had braved the high winds to see if the unfinished dome itself would fail.[4] A second gale came through on the twenty-fourth, which blew down a church on Thirteenth Street, and caused water to slosh over the roadway of the Long Bridge.[5] The *Richmond Daily Dispatch* noted that, at Camp Bartow, "there is scarcely a man you meet that can speak plainly, in consequence of colds, and the frequent barking of nights would remind one of a pack of hounds in full chase."[6]

In January, the first group of Rhode Island prisoners were released from Libby Prison in Richmond, and made their way back to Washington on their way home. There, Corporal Rhodes met a man he had given up for dead:

> Jany 24/62—Walking down street today a soldier in a Zouave uniform spoke to me, and it proved to be William W. Aborn of

> Pawtucket, R.I. a private in my company "D" 2nd R.I. Vols. Aborn was severely wounded at the Battle of Bull Run Jul. 21st 1861 and left for dead upon the field. He was carried to Richmond as a prisoner and had just been released. I took him to the office with me and shall send him home in a few days.[7]

In February, passes were again issued for the soldiers to visit the capital.[8] Some of the boys of the Fifth Maine were sent into town to help prepare the regimental payroll and were told they could tour around afterward. They completed the work promptly, and,

> sauntered out upon a tour of observation. We turned first toward the White House, feeling that could we only get a glimpse of "Uncle Abe," we should be amply repaid for the labor we had already performed. Approaching the door to the public entrance, hat in hand, we were met at the threshold by some burly officer, who wanted to know what we wanted. Conscious of our position—soldiers, only common soldiers, we hardly dared to explain that we came only out of curiosity, but yet ventured to remark that we were very desirous of seeing the White House. Immediately we were told that we had better leave; when, at that moment, who should appear but the president himself, passing out toward the street. Perceiving us, humble as we were, a smile seemed to overspread his features, and slightly bowing, he said, "How do you do, my boys?" Giving us each a shake of the hand, accompanied by a look which seemed to say that we might enter. Suffice it to say, that we did see the green and the reception rooms. It was some such little acts of President Lincoln which endeared him to the hearts of the soldiery.

The Northern blockade of Southern ports had begun to take effect, and the Southerners in turn, blockaded Washington, D.C., by interrupting traffic on the Baltimore and Ohio canal north of Harper's Ferry, and establishing batteries around Aquia Creek on the Potomac, "so none of our supply vessels below Aquia Creek dare come up without risk of capture."[9] Every night for an hour or so, the Union batteries of Hooker and Sickles, on the east bank, would shell the Confederates on the west, on either side of Possum Nose Point, who would fire back. Although the sounds of the guns could be heard for miles, little was accomplished.

To counter the blockade, the Southerners also reinstituted a old practice, privateering. Many small ships began operating off the North Carolina coastline, so in the fall of 1861, a series of successful naval operations, in which Sarah's younger brother, John Fowler Shumway participated, captured Fort Hatteras and Fort Clark and put a Union presence on the ground. John participated as a landsman, a sailor who operated onshore until Union troops under General Butler came in to secure the territory. He also participated, aboard the *Preble*, in another important naval operation to secure offshore islands off the mouth of the Mississippi River, preparatory to staging an attack to capture New Orleans. John came through these adventures unscathed.[10]

On land, the war for the Union had not gone as well. The disastrous affair at Ball's Bluff had resulted in seven hundred Union prisoners and three hundred deaths, among them a grandson of Paul Revere, a son of Oliver Wendell Holmes, and Senator Edward Baker of Oregon. Convinced the executive branch was not prosecuting the war vigorously enough, Congress sought a role to play in directing the war effort, and formed its own investigating committee, the Joint Committee on the Conduct of the War. It met in the Capitol basement and was chaired by abolitionist Ohio senator Benjamin Wade. Although it kept political pressure on the Lincoln administration, the committee never ran the war. However, its examination of military leaders in a typical congressional hearing setting, with opening statements followed by questions, was widely covered in the newspapers of the North and South. A general had only to read his predecessor's mistakes over his morning eggs to learn what pitfalls to avoid in his own upcoming campaign.

McClellan, a tireless administrator, had an ever-growing army at his disposal. On November 20, he put seventy thousand of them through their paces in a grand review at Bailey's Crossroads in Virginia, but Lincoln could not get him to use them in battle before the winter made operations impossible. Searching for victory wherever he could find it, the president looked west.

In the western theater, where the Confederates fielded an inadequate force to guard the five-hundred-mile border of Kentucky, Tennessee, and Missouri, the Union discussed using ironclad gunboats and a joint infantry action to capture the forts guarding the Tennessee and Cumberland Rivers. With these forts, and their connecting railroad in their hands, the Union could penetrate Tennessee, secure navigation along the upper Mississippi, and threaten Alabama. When intelligence was received from a Southern deserter that Beauregard's departure from Manassas in late January meant he was headed for Kentucky with reinforcements, Union commanders in the Trans-Mississippi District hesitated no longer and launched an attack before the Confederates grew stronger. Ulysses Grant and Commodore Foote captured the first fort on February 6, and news reached the Union soldiers camped around Washington three days later, boosting morale. On February 10, Private Joseph Martin wrote in his diary, "We are looking for the war to be over again the fourth of July next." On February 17, after two days of rumors, official confirmation was received that Fort Donaldson was taken. The forts around the city fired a salute and there was "great cheering" in the camps.[11]

There was more good news in the capital that week, again from amphibious operations. Building on the successes on the Carolina Coast, including later operations at Hilton Head, which captured Fort Walker and Fort Beauregard, Ambrose Burnside had planned and trained troops for another landing in North Carolina. He was supported by sixty-five naval vessels, and the Fourth and Fifth Rhode Island regiments were under his command.[12] In February, he captured Elisabeth, Roanoke Island, and prepared to attack New Bern.

The men were itching to fight. Corporal Rhodes wrote,

> Still packed up and ready to move, but the orders are countermanded almost as soon as received. I want to go, I want to get out of Washington, and I want the war to end.[13]

McClellan now commanded an army grown from 50,000 after Manassas to 168,000. Persuaded by bad intelligence that Johnston had fortified the plains of Manassas against him with numerous forts and 90,000 crack troops, McClellan abandoned plans to attack Richmond from that front, and developed instead a plan to move his army by sea below Richmond and attack up the swampy peninsula on which were located Williamsburg and Yorktown. Just as he was getting ready to leave, news came in that Johnston had left Manassas. Private Robert Snedon of the Fortieth New York, a mapmaker seconded to Heintzelman, wrote on March 9,

> [The Rebels] suddenly evacuated all their batteries and moved their whole army from the front of Washington, destroying all their camps, burning all the bridges from Munson's Hill to Centreville, Manassas to Gordonsville. Thus doing of their own accord what McClellan thought his whole army of 80,000 fighting men was unable to make them do. So "McClellan stock" now is very low.[14]

Johnston had pulled his troops and part of his enormous store of supplies out of Manassas, and redeployed them around Orange Court House and as far north as Fredericksburg, to facilitate linkage with other Confederate armies and better repel McClellan's expected advance.

Nurse Emma Edmonds/Frank Thompson remembered that on the fourteenth of March, [1862] General McClellan issued an address to the army of the Potomac, "announcing the reasons why they had been so long unemployed":

> Soldiers of the Army of the Potomac: For a long time I have kept you inactive, but not without a purpose. You were to be disciplined, armed and instructed. The formidable artillery you now have had to be created. Other armies were to move and accomplish certain results [in the West].
>
> I have held you back that you might fire the death-blow to the rebellion that has distracted our once happy country. The patience you have shown, and your confidence in your General, are worth a dozen victories. These preliminary results are now accomplished. I feel that the patient labors of many months have produced their fruit. The army of the Potomac is now a real army, magnificent in material, admirable in discipline and instruction, excellently equipped and armed. Your commanders are all that I could wish. The moment for action has arrived, and I know that I can trust in you to save our country. The period of inaction has passed. I will bring you now face to face with the rebels, and only pray that God may defend the right.[15]

One deficiency in his army that McClellan had needed to remedy was sufficient cavalry, well-enough trained, to play a role in any spring campaign; Rhode Island had began recruiting the First Rhode Island Cavalry in the fall. These cavalrymen mustered first into a camp in Cranston, so that from October to December, there were many horsemen moving past the picket fences of the houses in that quiet neighborhood. In December, the cavalry moved to the riding park in Pawtucket where they were joined by a battalion from New Hampshire, and obtained their horses. These Morgans, reared in Canada and northern New England, known for their maneuverability, even tempers, and intelligence, went all through the war with their riders. The regiment spent the winter months drilling and training in horse care, manueuvers, the use of their sabers, and the carbine, the lightweight gun used by mounted men.[16]

Once the unexpected pullback of the Confederates was noted, and all of northeastern Virginia lay open to the Union forces, "though their scouts still infested and threatened the region just abandoned," it was imperative to send cavalry in to scout the area for traps, and report back conditions.[17] Three days after the Confederate retreat, the First Cavalry was ordered to Washington, D.C., one battalion given only two hours' notice. It took five days to transport the twelve hundred horses and thousand men, on "monster trains" in a heavy rain storm, through "the city of brotherly love," where the men were fed "at the famous Cooper Shop Volunteer Refreshment Saloon," through "semi-loyal" Baltimore, into Washington, where they arrived "seriously numbed."

They found the capital was a vortex of military movement. Reverend Frederic Denison, the chaplain to the regiment, recorded his impressions:

> Bugles, drums, fifes, flags, guidons; reports of arms; the rush of horsemen; the wheeling of artillery; the maneuvering squads, squadrons, battalions, and regiments; the dashing hither and yon of aids, quartermasters, surgeons and field officers, gave to the District of Columbia a most lively but serious aspect, in strange contrast with its purpose of legislation.[18]

The cavalry had reached the city on a momentous day. The main war goal was still the capture of Richmond, which McClellan and the government now proposed to accomplish by staging out of Fortress Monroe, by Hampton Roads. Over the ten days, McClellan's "Potomac Fleet," 330 steamers, ferried ninety thousand men down to begin the Peninsula campaign. Sailing with the Fiftieth New York Regiment as surgeon was Sullivan's uncle by marriage to his Aunt Louisa Ballou, Dr. Hazard A. Potter, a graduate of Bowdoin College in Maine, who joined up from the Rochester area. "Troops were pressing to the front from all the Northern and Middle States" to bolster positions in the capital, western Virginia, the western theater, and the attack on Richmond. The hustle and bustle somewhat camouflaged the fact that Lincoln had removed McClellan from overall command on March 8, because of his procrastination. The armies had again been reorganized. The War Department could not have been busier.

However, the Confederate pullback had now created the opportunity for which Rhode Island had been waiting, and "Gov. Sprague, now in Washington, caring for the Rhode Island soldiers and aiding the federal government, obtained consent of the War Department to select a detachment" from the First Rhode Island Cavalry to mount a recovery operation. A military escort was required because federal troops had advanced only as far as Fairfax Court House.[19] Such a recovery operation was unprecedented, and that it was led in person by a sitting governor was even more amazing.

Sprague's team included two aides recruited for the mission, Private Olney Arnold, on loan from the Rhode Island First Light Artillery, and Tristam Burgess, a prominent Rhode Island attorney. The rest of the group came from the First Cavalry: Chaplain Denison, a minister from Pawtucket, and their assistant surgeon, James Bonaparte Greeley, from New Hampshire. Major Willard Sayles commanded the detachment from the cavalry, "sixty picked men from Troop D," headed by their captain, Robert Anthony, both from Providence.[20] Chaplain Denison provided a lively commentary on this mission in his history of the regiment, *Sabers and Spurs.*

> Anthony had charge of the detachment and the accompanying train of wagons. Mr. J. Richardson, who was in the Battle of Bull line, acted as our guide. Two baggage wagons carried forage, rations, and empty coffins. The governor had a private two-horse wagon, with supplies for his staff, under the management of his private secretary.[21]

Josiah Richardson, no longer in the military, had traveled down from Providence to accompany the party to identify the burial site of Colonel Slocum and Major Ballou. An undertaker, Mr. Coleman, also accompanied the party. As it turned out, the first mission of the First Cavalry

> upon the soil of Virginia was two days after our arrival at the capital, and in the discharge of a very tender duty . . . we were unwilling that our martyred dead of the First and 2nd Infantry Regiments of Rhode Island, who fell in the Battle of Bull Run, July 21, 1861, should remain in the rude graves into which they were cast by rebel hands. They were lying in the trenches and side graves on the gory fields where they fell, up about 14 miles west of the capital.[22]

On March 19, ten days after Johnston removed his army, Sprague and the Rhode Islanders

> left Washington at 5:00 P.M., while the clouds were making ready copious showers for us, that we might have a fair experience of Virginia roads and fields in the months of spring. Crossing Long Bridge at six o'clock, we pressed on by the principal road towards Fairfax Court House.[23]

The weather had been rainy for the past six weeks, and another storm broke over them as they rode on. "However, our horses were good, and we were fresh in muscle. The roads were literally horrible, and delays to our train were inevitable." The governor and his staff rode until midnight, reaching the safety, if not the shelter, of General Blenker's encampment at Fairfax Court House. Blenker, leading a division of German-speaking brigades raised in the Midwest and East, was on his way to join Frémont in West Virginia. Hastily dispatched, without basic supplies, maps, or tents, his men slept out in the rain, enduring the first privations of an infamous six-week march. Blenker was occupying a farmhouse, and the Rhode Island command staff were given the hospitality of its parlor floor and warm fire, the chaplain using the general's boots as his pillow.[24]

> The remainder of our party, wet, weary, and retarded by the wagons, was obliged to halt and bivouac in the deep darkness, seven miles back on the road. The soldiers occupied the grand apartments of nature.[25]

The morning of March 20, the party pressed further into Virginia, but the intensity of the storm forced them to take shelter in the "stripped and peeled" town of Centreville, forsaken by all but a few of its residents, "in desolate houses and the deserted log barracks of rebel regiments."

Many trees had been felled to create log cabins to shelter the officers, men, and "business offices" of this army. Still more trees had been used to strengthen the palisades and earthen entrenchments constructed over some eighty square miles of Prince William and Fairfax counties, and others which blocked the view from Centreville, chopped down into a giant moat of an abatis. Scarcely a tree was seen for miles around, excepting those that shaded a hospital or the house of a secessionist. Logs also served another purpose:

> In front of the place were six well constructed earth forts, connected by good trenches and rifle pits. In some of the embrasures the rebels had mounted painted logs, like cannon, looking defiance towards Washington. In one of them was mounted the smokestack of an old locomotive.[26]

These phony guns, known as "Quaker guns," since they did not fire, had so awed McClellan from afar that he declined to mount an attack. Denison concluded,

> Beauregard, as his works in and around Manassas testified, was a splendid engineer; but neither the Confederacy nor England supplied him with the guns he expected.[27]

These Rhode Islanders were the vanguard of the federal reoccupation of Fairfax County. Only that evening did Union cavalry ride in to secure the place where the troops had built their "shebangs" in the summer heat. The storm compelled them to stay in Centreville overnight, some paying room and board to sleep in the house of a Dr. Alexander, who had hidden his saber and its belt under his sofa cushions to escape notice. The Rhode Islander who discovered the items while lying down to sleep on the sofa choose not to make an issue of the householder masquerading as a good Union man, now that the balance of power had shifted.

The weather cleared and, the next morning, the band of seventy-five again moved beyond federal protection, noting "disrupted corduroy roads and broken timber bridges," the transportation infrastructure destroyed to frustrate the Yankees. After two days of heavy rain Bull Run was "overflowing its banks and utterly impassable." They headed north,

> through ruined forests and evacuated rebel camps, up the stream till we reached a hopeful ford where the river was but

> three hundred feet broad and ten feet deep in the middle, but running with great velocity. We had no time for hesitancy.[28]

With dexterity worthy of the Ellsworth Zouaves in their finest moments, someone in the party knew how, and rigged up a system of safety ropes.

> Surgeon Greeley was the first to swim the swift, cold stream, followed by his orderly, who took over the end of joined lariat ropes borrowed from our saddles, and to the extremity of which was attached a large picket rope found nearby in the debris of a Georgia regiment.* The next swimmer was Hon. T. Burgess, followed by the detached lead horses from one of our wagons. These were attached to the further end of the picket rope, while the hither end was tied to the neap of the wagons with the wheel horses. Now, with shout and whip, the spans on both sides of the river were put to their best metal [mettle]. Up the bank went the leaders; into the river plunged the wheel horses and wagon. That was animated and exciting swimming. The opposite bank was reached without loss.[29]

The wagons were the trickiest to get across, and the seventy or so men gathered on the banks watched the proceedings with interest, while the officers passed around a bottle of whiskey from the governor's private reserve to brace themselves for the cold dip.

> Then in dashed the Governor and staff and troop. Only one man was unhorsed in the torrent, but he and his beast were rescued. We always regarded this cold Virginia bath as a fair initiation into field service.

* In camp, the reins or bridle ropes of horses were attached a picket rope, a long rope stretched between trees.

> Starting on our way, we think there was some good riding done to shake off the chills of Cub Run. Reaching the Warrenton Turnpike, the Governor, Col. Arnold, Mr. Burgess, Surgeon Greeley and the Chaplain tried the best speed of their animals. Mud and small stones flew merrily to the rear. Some thought the ration of whiskey, medically administered before swimming the run, had something to do with this speed. As it was, one soldier did not rally from the cold shock of the stream.[30]

Obviously, this chaplain was not a temperance man, and Governor Sprague, who in later life was to become a chronic alcoholic, either imbibed so much, or was so upset by later developments, that his recollections of certain occurrences later that day were blurred. By a twist of fate, the Rhode Islanders were forced to travel up the original route Hunter was to have taken to Sudley Ford the morning of the battle.

> Reaching the Stone Bridge at Bull Run, we found it had been blown up by the retreating Confederates. Turning to the right, up the stream, we advanced, over fields and through woods, to the ford nearly opposite Sudley Church, where we crossed, barely wetting our girths. . . . Now beyond the federal lines, we moved cautiously and together . . . and gazed for a moment with intense curiosity upon the torn acres, scarred trees, and rude graves.[31]

At the church, they seemed to split up. Some rode inside to see the derelict church, while surgeon Greeley noticed a Black girl at a nearby stream and went to ask directions to the battlefield, after which they got lost for about twenty minutes before retracing their steps.[32] A squad appeared to remain near the church, and a security patrol was dispatched to guard the exterior perimeter around

Sudley church and hospital were once pleasantly located in a grove of trees, but this photo, taken by Barnard and Gibson in March 1862, shows stumps left when trees were cut for firewood and cabin construction. *From the Library of Congress Prints and Photographs Division.*

the Thornberry complex, where Richardson had taken his team, "near the little house to the left of the church." The undertaker, the star of his own narrative, described what happened next:

> Mr. Richardson at once recognized the spot, and pointed out the graves of the heroes, and the preparations for exhuming were at once commenced under the direction of Mr. Coleman.
>
> The party had but just commenced digging, the troopers had lifted out but one or two shovels full of earth, when a negro girl came down through the woods from a house near by on the hill, and watched the proceedings. Suddenly she came up by the side of the grave . . .[33]

The girl—or young woman—with whom Greeley had spoken, worked in a house nearby, and might have been any one of numerous slaves or hired servants from the area. The description is insufficient to identify her further. Although appearing somewhat afraid of the troops, she now made a very important contribution to their work. Fumbling with the name, whom the key players heard as either Slinkum, Slogan, or Sloke, she inquired if they were searching for the body of this colonel. When the name was properly supplied, she said, "Yes, sir, that is the name; you won't find him."[34] She continued, "You're too late; the Georgia Regiment have dug him up a good many weeks ago to procure his bones for trophies."[35] She stunned them by adding, they "first cut off his head and then burned his body in the little hollow there," pointing to it. Governor Sprague reported, "We stopped digging and went to the place thus designated, where we found coals, ashes and bones mingled together."[36] Surgeon Greeley observed with clinical precision that on arriving, they found "partly burned" bones, including "some of the vertebrae, or back bone."

> I examined the remains in the ashes very carefully. . . . I examined them through my own hands. I examined especially for teeth, for I knew if the head had been there, the teeth would have been the last to have been destroyed. I found the femur, or thigh bone. . . . The angle at the neck of it indicated a man at least thirty years of age. The body was proved to be a man by the pelvis bone that was found; but we found no portion of the skull.[37]

Chaplain Denison likewise "looked particularly among the ashes, but saw nothing that to my eye looked like any portion of the skull," and observed,

In modern times, the forest has returned to the banks of Bull Run. Located near the Thornberry House, this may be the spot where Sullivan's remains were transported, where his shirt was floating, caught on branches in the stream. *Author's photo at Manassas National Battlefield Park.*

> Words may not describe the indignation revealed in the face of the Governor, and of all who gazed upon that rifled grave and those bones protruding from the ashes and dead coals. Was this . . . Southern chivalry?[38]

Mr. Coleman, the undertaker, called them "cannibal rites," and noted,

> She also guided the party to a spot a little further down on the banks of the brook, and in the water, stopped by a little clump of bushes, the blanket and shirt stripped from the body were floating in the current.[39]

This area had apparently been the site to which the Georgians had first carried the coffin, opened it, and removed the body. The blanket had "large quantities of hair upon it."[40] This was obviously the blanket that had shrouded the corpse, and the separation of the hair was a natural occurrence. The coffin itself had been left in the stream, and, some time later, local people had fished it out to use for the burial of a "colored pauper."[41]

The shirts provided two sets of further clues to the astonished Rhode Island men, "who had proceeded thus far with the full conviction that the body thus burned had been that of Colonel Slocum."[42] First, they noted the collar buttons were still fastened, while the wrist buttons had been opened. From this, they inferred "the head had been cut off," like the young woman said.[43] There were two shirts, one plain-colored silk, the other striped. Governor Sprague asserted that Colonel Slocum never wore such a shirt, but that he "recognized [it] as one belonging to Major Ballou, as I had been very intimate with him."*[44]

There was one way to verify this conclusion, but first "all the remaining bones of the body were found and gathered," "sacredly," along with "the ashes containing portions of his remains that were left and put them in a coffin, together with his shirt, and the blanket and the hair found upon it."[45]

Surgeon Greeley was perplexed. "We could not believe it possible and went back to the graves to examine them." When they showed the shirt to Richardson, he also verified it as Sullivan's.[46] At the gravesite, the men had not made good progress with the

* Quaint wording aside, Sullivan had written to Sarah on July 10, "I have become quite well acquainted with Gov Sprague as he has taken up his quarters in our Camp—occupying a tent not very far from mine. I shall improve the acquaintance and make it serviceable to me if I can. He is a very unassuming man and a very agreeable man. I think if he stays here long I can advance myself in his good opinion." On June 26, he asked her to send "Two more calico shirts—perhaps three more."

slippery mud, which filled in the hole as soon as they shifted some dirt out, and only "had dug down nearly a foot" by the time the governor returned. Eager to learn the truth, for "before we had arrived there, Mr. Richardson had described to us the relative positions of the graves," Dr. Greeley took a saber and thrust it into the dirt where Sullivan's coffin should have been. It hit nothing. Next, he tried the spot where Slocum was supposed to be and "we struck a coffin not more than two feet below the surface."[47]

This was exhumed, and found to be "an oblong box—a square box."[48] When the top was removed, the colonel was recognizable by his enormous, distinctive moustache and uniform. Dr. Greeley then recalled they had found the bones of only one leg in the ashes, and remembered that "Major Ballou had lost a limb."[49] Slocum, too, was placed into one of the coffins the Rhode Islanders had brought, and it was labeled, as were each of the others. The party concluded that "the Ghouls had mistaken the object of their vengeance, and that the fate intended for the remains of Col. S. was received by those of the heroic and unfortunate Major B."[50]

Again, the party split up, some to complete the recovery mission, others to question local inhabitants about what they knew about this crime. Doctor Greeley headed the team that went to search for the location from which they needed to recover Lieutenant Levi Tower, accompanied by a man named Clark, who had been receiving medical treatment inside the Matthew's House and had watched through the window as Tower was buried.

> We continued our search for the dead, and found the trenches containing them in a concave portion of the field, very wet, near the log cabin of Mr. Matthew. [but then] we returned to the crest of the hill on the margin of the battlefield, and made arrangements to remain till the following morning, for our work was not yet to complete.[51]

Dr. Greeley and Major Sayles questioned a

> lad there, about fourteen years of age, I should judge. . . . Major Sayles . . . questioned the boy very closely, but the boy stood the examination very well. The boy said that it was the 21st Georgia regiment who came there, and he saw the body burned. He said they put the fire out afterwards because it made such a horrible stench. He said that he knew, several days before, that they were going to do it. After they did it, it was talked about a great deal in the neighborhood and they all condemned it.[52]

Two white boys of that age lived in the area, neither of them right at the run but close enough. One was James Compton, son of the lay minister of the church; the other was Lucinda Dogan's son, William. Unfortunately, no one in the recovery party, not even the undertaker, acted the good detective and took names of anyone other than mature white males:

> Mr. Coleman also made inquiries at another house in the neighborhood and had a long conversation with a white woman on the premises who had nursed our wounded at Sudley Church. She assured me she herself had witnessed the whole affair and had expostulated, begged and entreated that the dead should be held sacred but the savages mocked at her and finding all endeavors useless she had saved a lock of his hair and preserved it for his friends who she was confident someday would appear and the lock of hair she gave to Mr. Coleman. The men who had performed this hellish deed were members of the Twenty-first Georgia Regiment and it will be remembered that it was the Georgia regiments that the Second Rhode Island had met and vanquished on the battlefield.[53]

It took great courage for this lone woman to confront such repugnant soldiers, and great faith to argue with them and berate them to leave the dead alone. It required great compassion to overcome natural reluctance to pick up a lock of hair that had been in a coffin to rescue it to save it for a loved one of this officer. It maybe took some knowledge of this officer to know that someone far away would treasure this lock of hair. Described as living near the church—some four hundred yards southeast—and as a woman who had nursed the wounded there, this woman was almost certainly Margaret Benson, doing her third good deed for Sullivan Ballou. She was alone because Amos Benson had enlisted as a private in the Fourth Virginia Cavalry on December 3, 1861, and was likely already on the peninsula where military records show his horse was killed in April.[54] The woman who had been tough enough to nurse a maggoty Private John Rice under the fence by the road was strong enough to perform this act of mercy.

The chaplain accompanied the governor to the house of Burkett Newman, an "old gentleman who seemed to be a man highly esteemed by all who knew him." While not present when it happened, Newman knew of the deed, its perpetrators, and had himself gone down to the spot a few days later to check things out. Newman not only took him down there to corroborate the place, but came to visit them the next morning, so he certainly got around well for an octogenarian. The chaplain misjudged Newman to be "sixty years of age."[55] According to the Prince William County census, he was eighty-one, and a recent father twice over, having fathered a son in 1859 by his slave Emily, and a daughter the same year, named Harriet for her mother, another slave girl. It is possible, but not wholly certain, based on a reference by the undertaker, that the woman who tipped them off to the grave robbing had emerged from the Newman house.

> Mr. Newman spoke a great deal of this matter of exhuming, beheading and burning the body of Major Ballou. He called it Colonel Slocum, as that was what he had all along understood. He was very emphatic in his declarations that it could not have been done by Virginians. He seemed to think it a very barbaric thing, and wished to exculpate Virginians.[56]

Barbaric enough, perhaps, to be the handiwork of a few renegade members of Bartow's Avengers, men from Chatooga County, where the veneer of civilization lay thin upon people just coming out of decades of lawlessness? Were these men veterans of the Georgia Guards, the same ones who had brutalized the Cherokees a generation earlier and took their proclivities to war against the Yankees? All witnesses independently agreed it was men from the Twenty-first, who were not camped close to Sudley. It fit the pattern of soldiers so unsupervised that they wandered the countryside, familiar to the locals. Of course, they may have been visiting sick comrades in the nearby hospital. Two witnesses said the skull was taken home a souvenir, and one said the act was premeditated, not a single drunken binge. Several witnesses repeated the Georgians were bitter against Slocum for Georgian deaths during the battle. Significantly, while the neighborhood did not approve of the behavior, no one went to the colonel of that regiment, or the Confederate commanding officer, General Johnston, to report the act. Did they fear retribution from its perpetrators?

While robbing the pockets of dead men was nothing special on a battlefield—Colonel Cameron was not yet cold when his pockets were turned inside out—this act could only have been accomplished by soldiers who were very drunk—or very determined, or both. They had not sought advice from other soldiers involved in processing less high-ranking bones for drumsticks or finger rings, who might have told them burning was the wrong technique. They were patently inexperienced in the business of grave robbing, for although they carried the coffin to the stream, realizing they might have to rinse off the skull and bones, they must have experienced a really big shock.

After death, a body undergoes four stages of decomposition, the last of which is little more than a skeleton. Even some of the men buried straight in the dirt on the battlefield had not totally achieved that final stage, given the early onset and severity of the winter, but they were much farther along than someone buried in a coffin. Modern forensic science is able to calculate that an individual buried in a more protected way, in a coffin, would still be in stage three after six months. That meant there was still some skin, muscle, tissue, and brain matter present, and, once removed from the coffin, decomposition accelerated. To persist in dealing with a body in that state required unique perseverance, even to the point of finding enough dry firewood after a winter of rain and snow to start a roaring and sustained blaze. A clean skull weighs six pounds, so whoever took that South as his personal trophy had to have a means of transporting it other than bouncing it on his hip in his haversack. That implied a man going on furlough who was taking a satchel, or someone with a horse. As Douglas Freeman explained, mounted men were always envied for their ability to carry away more booty than the foot soldier:

> The boy on foot had his haversack and his pockets—no more; the trooper had an animal that could carry much loot. The advantage enjoyed by an officer who had two horses was scandalous.[57]

Even men so determined would not be fool enough to stand around in a blizzard or major rainstorm to do their evil deed, nor would nearby civilians go out in the same to watch them. A private in the 102nd Pennsylvania stationed not far away, Joseph Martin, kept excellent weather logs in his diary, as did Robert Knox Sneden, and even Elisha Hunt Rhodes with the Second Rhode Island. Correlating these reports of "shirt sleeve" days, hard frosts, and gales which blew over the sutler's tents and the preaching tent of the 102nd, the longest spell of good weather took place from January 22 to 29 (with the exception of January 25 and 28) just when the officers of the Twenty-first were on furlough or worrying about building their own cabins. The Twenty-first were not camped at Sudley, though they may have visited sick comrades in the hospital there. For them to be well known in that hamlet meant they had roamed, unsupervised, outside the boundaries of their camp.

In this time frame, in the mornings, there was enough of a hard frost on the ground to firm up the surface of "the lake of mud" and make walking the distance easy.[58] Otherwise, Snedon noted how wagon wheels driving over the wet clay soil "churn it into filthy red paste. All the cavalry who return home from picket are splashed with this filthy, vile smelling compost." Many a soldier griped,

> The mud was at least two feet deep . . . so deep that a horse would sink up to his belly, or in walking a square on foot, one would have his boots pulled off his feet, at least a half dozen times.[59]

Yet by midday, the frost was gone, allowing shovels to penetrate the soil. After two months of rain, the clay soil in the Thornberry's garden had flowed back over the empty hole and restored a natural contour, masking the fact that one coffin was missing.

> For the night, most of our men found a shelter in a house near the gory fields. Our horses stood out in the wind and the rain, that had returned. Seventeen of us accepted the roof and hospitalities of Mr. Matthew. Eating his hoe-cake and drinking his aromatic rye coffee, we lay down on his cabin floor, with our feet to the log fire. The Governor and his staff

> laughed at their military plight, till short and strange dreams came over them.[60]

The next morning, neighbors Burkett Newman and Abraham Van Pelt came to call, and told "doleful stories of their experiences and losses." The morning of the twenty-second, the recovery party hoped to find two men, Tower and Prescott. They found the lieutenant in a mass grave, everyone buried face downward, considered a great insult. On top of the tangled bodies was an unexploded artillery shell, which the chaplain confiscated. It took great internal fortitude for these men to separate the lieutenant from the embrace of those with whom he had shared a grave. Like his comrades, Tower was transferred to the greater dignity of his own casket. "His orderly was positive that when Captain Tower died he had on a very fine pair of boots; they were not on his body when we found him."[61]

> While opening the graves and pits, rebel scouts and spies, in the disguise of farmers, appeared in the vicinity. But we were on our guard. Once our sentinels fired an alarm, which brought our troop to the crown of the field ready for a dash.[62]

Perhaps nervous, concerned about the time, or deterred by the probability of disentangling more remains, they desisted from opening the second pit where they thought Prescott might be.

> Our work on the battlefield ended, we turned our faces, about noon, towards Washington. Dashing again across the runs, over plains and ruined plantations, we passed Centreville and reached Fairfax Court House about dark. We only paused to care for our hungry and lame horses. With the night, came another heavy rain. By the Alexandria and Columbia roads we pushed forward, till, after fourteen hours in the saddle, over full forty miles, wet, weary and hungry, we entered our camp,

> east of the Capitol, at two o'clock Sunday morning, (March 23d) bringing with us the precious dead.[63]

Chaplain Denison was so "wet and chilled," so stiff in his saddle, that he could not dismount when he got to camp, but had to be "taken from his saddle."[64]

> In the expedition we lost but one horse, though several were injured. The health of our men continued good. William Brown (Troop G,) died of congestive fever, March 26th and was suitably buried the next day, at the Soldiers' Home.*[65]

This trooper, possibly the one who fell into the stream and was retrieved, seemed to have caught a cold which developed into pneumonia; he gave his life so that the trio of officers could be recovered.

> On the same day Colonel Lawton, with his staff and a squadron, escorted the bodies to Camp Brightwood, and gave them, with fitting ceremony, to the Second Regiment Rhode Island Volunteers, from whose ranks they fell. The regiment received them with touching funeral honors. The Governor and many friends were present at the solemnities. Due thanks were rendered to the Governor and his staff, and to Troop D, for their venturesome but successful mission.[66]

While various Yankee skulls were recovered throughout the war, and some displayed as war curiosities or as examples of the depth to which human nature can sink, no correlation of these was ever made with specific individuals.** Sullivan Ballou's skull was never found, but what was left of him was going home to his family.

* The Soldiers' Home, north of the District, now open to the public, was Lincoln's weekend White House.

** Something that modern forensic and DNA testing might now be able to do.

CHAPTER TWENTY-FOUR

"Wreaths of Glory"*

The Funerals of Sullivan Ballou

Late March to Early April 1862

Major Sullivan Ballou, Colonel John Slocum, and Captain Levi Tower were about to start their posthumous journey home. No one could have predicted that the progress of this small cortege was to become an odyssey of national importance, avidly reported and tracked across the nation and even attracting the official attention of the United States Senate.

That Sunday morning, as the exhausted members of the recovery team began clambering out their tent flaps, word of the savage treatment of the popular and respected Major Ballou had started spreading around Camp Brightwood, where the Second Rhode Island Regiment had established its winter quarters on the Maryland side of its border with the District.

* From the Civil War song "The Vacant Chair."

The military immediately began organizing their portion of the funeral arrangements—to get the honored dead back to Rhode Island. Knowing the details of the insults to Ballou, the governor and the commanding officer felt a great obligation to observe strict military etiquette, for the sake of the families and the honor of the regiment and state. The arrangements for their reception in Providence could be confidently left to the kind hearts and capable hands of the home folks.

Providence knew nothing until a haggard William Sprague called an aide into his tent and gave him messages to take to the telegraph office. Telegraph messengers urgently interrupted the Sunday dinners of important clerics, militia commanders, and political figures in Rhode Island. Key people at the state and city level started discussing arrangements for the homecoming, Bishop Clark again chosen as the messenger of faith to the families, with Mayor Jabez Knight in charge of civic arrangements.

Between Rhode Islanders north and south that day, there developed a shared, intuitive sense of entrustment, of the need to restore balance, and of the need to put right a great wrong. This sense inspired much of what was to happen.

The coffins remained in camp all day Sunday. The first people to pay their respects were the men of the Second Regiment, who assembled at attention on the parade ground. Now a sergeant major, Elisha Hunt Rhodes wrote in his diary,

> *Sunday March 23rd/62-* This afternoon we received the bodies of Col. John S. Slocum, Major Sullivan Ballou and Lieutenant Levi Tower, officers of the 2nd R. I. killed at the Battle of Bull Run, Va., July 21/61. The remains were escorted by Gov. Sprague. The regiment presented arms as the procession passed, and the remains were placed in the surgeon's quarters. I have before me a statement signed by Gov. Sprague and read upon Dress Parade as follows: "the rebels supposing the

> remains of Major Ballou to be Col. Slocum disinterred the body, removed the clothing, and burned the body to ashes." The Governor collected all remains he could and brought them to camp. The other bodies were buried lying upon their faces. This to us is horrible, and the 2nd Rhode Island will remember it when they meet the foe again.[1]

That same quiet spring afternoon, Sarah Ballou again received unexpected callers at her house bearing unanticipated news from the regiment in Washington, eerily reminiscent of the day she learned Sullivan was dead. Kind people had deemed it most urgent that Major Ballou's brave widow immediately receive the news, and details, of the recovery of her husband's remains. As before, everyone advanced into the good parlor and seated themselves.

Sarah's reaction was complicated. The first thing she understood was that his body was coming home for burial. It was now nine months since she lost her husband and her original raw, wild grief had subsided into a daily dullness. To have Sullivan home and properly buried was the very thing she had wanted. To lay him to rest in a grave that she and the boys could visit and place flowers on was the missing piece in her mourning. After the pace of the war picked up, in 1862, many more families would experience this extra heartache, but for now, Sarah Ballou was one of the few widows who had to deal with a missing body and delayed funeral.

For Sarah, the desecration of her husband's grave was one last, awful thing she had to endure. Now, she stood irrevocably apart from the Slocums and the Towers, struggling to take in the worst possible scenario, experiencing a new wave of heartache for her husband's plight. It was understood that not every casualty in combat even received burial, but digging up the dead was among the oldest and most strict of societal taboos; for any family to be victimized by such an act of unutterable evil would cause a sensation. It took no prescience to know this story was soon to run in the newspapers, and the notoriety and publicity were her burden to bear. Even though the newspapers of the time tried to protect women by not printing their names, or mentioning them, she would become known, as would he, for this terrible desecration, which might even overshadow the memory of Sullivan's brave death. Everyone would know her heartache—there was to be no privacy, though the courtesies of the time forbade strangers to speak to her about the terrible deed.

Indeed, the story was soon carried in newspapers around the nation. At some point during their stay in Washington, members of the recovery team had told a reporter the vivid details of their adventures in Virginia, the journey home, and the "fiendish outrage" of the desecration of Sullivan's grave. The newly formed Associated Press organization allowed member newspapers to reprint each other's stories, with accreditation, thereby reducing the high costs of covering so many battles and fronts. The telegraph sped this story across the nation the same day and so, in late March 1862, with no major military campaigns to report, the big story was the vandalism of the remains of Sullivan Ballou, printed almost simultaneously in the *Belvidere Press* in Illinois, the *New York Times,* and the *Philadelphia Public Ledger.*

Even after family, friends, and ministers assured Sarah that her husband's spirit had been far away from his body when his mortal remains suffered those deprecations, her dismay and anguish were incalculable. Despite the story in the papers, society denied her any opportunity to denounce Sullivan's tormenters publicly; a lady never issued a public statement. Whatever feelings she had were never recorded; Sarah could in propriety only express them to family, minister, or friends, her sons being too young. Much remained between her and God. Undoubtedly, the military promised her they would remember these deeds when next they met Georgians in battle. For comfort, she could only return to Sullivan's farewell letter, in which his spirit soared above all earthly concerns except those for her and their sons, a letter, in which love and goodness overcame all.

Practical concerns tugged at her, too, and she had no choice but to get involved in the little distracting tasks of getting ready for the awful thrill of welcoming home her beloved. After wearing two or three black mourning outfits steadily for nine months, they were shabby and no longer fit to wear at the public ceremony Rhode Island was planning for the three officers. Sarah could have made do with her mourning wear for the remaining three months of the required year—until July 1862—when etiquette would allow her to wear less severe clothing. Now she had no money to buy new clothes, and she, Emeline, and Hannah Frances had to find the time and money to sew new dresses or turn* and refurbish old ones.

Back at Camp Brightwood, the colonel and the governor's staffs began coordinating the journey home. In February, Lieutenant Colonel Steere of the Second Rhode Island Regiment had decorated his quarters with banners honoring Slocum and Ballou for the regimental celebration of Washington's birthday. Now he found himself in charge of getting them home. He was detached from all other duties and detailed to arrange a simple and straightforward trip to Rhode Island, honorably escorted by soldiers of the Second Regiment.

It was to proceed in stages, mostly by rail: through Baltimore, still teeming with Secession sympathies, staunchly Union Philadelphia, influential New York, and then by ship up to New England, connecting with the boat train into Providence. Once underway, the transport through Baltimore needed to be very low key because that city had never fully settled down after the anti-Union riots of the previous year.

* *Turning* was a common way to reuse fabric that had become worn, snagged, or stained. The seams were picked apart and the fabric turned over and the garment restitched back together.

However, the next stop, Philadelphia, a major railroad hub for the northern states, was wholeheartedly a Union city and one that prided itself on providing hot meals and hearty welcomes for transiting troops. Here, the Rhode Islanders had the first indication that people were keenly interested in Sullivan Ballou and his two companions.

Although the city lamented that "the notice of the arrival . . . was so short as to preclude any particular demonstration," it offered a heartfelt spontaneous reception. The entire newly formed Sixty-seventh Pennsylvania Regiment was ordered to parade to the Baltimore Depot at 12:30 P.M. to receive the caskets and escort them to Independence Hall. They were accompanied by "a fine band of music. . . . A large crowd surrounded the Hall during the day."[2] Many handkerchiefs were dampened as kind hearted ladies wept as Sullivan's flag-covered casket passed. Many prayers were likely whispered that God might preserve Ballou's family—and their own.

People in the last major stopover were awaiting their turn to honor Sullivan and his comrades. The *New York Times,* which had began reporting the story to its readers from its inception, contributed this insight into the behind-the-scenes organization of the journey home:

> Letter to Mr. Stetson, Astor House, New York City
> Washington, March 26, 1862
>
> Sir: I am instructed by Hon. William Sprague, Governor of State Rhode Island, to request you to prepare a suitable room for the bodies of Col. Slocum, Major Ballou, and Capt. Tower.
>
> I leave here this A.M. Shall arrive in New-York by Friday, second train from Philadelphia, if not the first. I have a guard of ten men, who will be on duty in the room with said bodies.
>
> Gov. Sprague and Suite will arrive during the day, but, I presume, will himself advise you of his own arrival.

> I will telegraph you from Philadelphia some time to-day.
>
> Also, make preparations for transporting the bodies from ferry to hotel. Three boxes, each 24 inches wide, 7 feet 2 inches long, probably. Will have to have two teams, as they must not be placed on top each other. Very respectfully yours,
>
> W. H. P. Steere
> Lieutenant Colonel Second Regiment Rhode Island Volunteers, Commanding escort of detail from said regiment.[3]

Despite its coverage of Philadelphia's tribute, there was no hint that New York planned anything special. The first report, in the General News column of the *New York Times,* was the briefest mention alongside the news from Wall Street:

> The Stock Market was dull through the dealings of yesterday, prices closing steady in the afternoon. . . . Flour was rather more freely purchased yesterday, in part for export. . . . Very limited movements transpired in Candles, Metals, Oils, Pork, . . . Cotton was less active. Logwood, codfish, Hay, Clover Seed, Cassia, Teas and Whalebone were in moderate request.[4]

Overnight, however, the story assumed heroic proportions. By the next day, March 28, when the cortege departed Independence Hall at 8:00 A.M., bound for the Philadelphia and Trenton Railway Depot, it was becoming apparent that its overnight stay in New York City would be something very special. New Yorkers love heroes, and were not about to let these pass quietly through town for all that they were already dead.

On the spur of the moment, the city's social, military, and political elite mobilized to plan a magnificent ceremonial event, with a prominent role given to New York's own Seventy-first Regiment that had bonded, bled, and died with the Rhode Islanders on Matthews Hill last July 21. These men had passed the wounded Sullivan lying by the fence as they had taken the field to fight alongside the Second Rhode Island.

The *Times* and other papers assisted in the organization of the event by rushing military orders and details into print for their readers. Now, far from avoiding the newspaper, Uncle Henry, the two Sarahs, and Emeline read these developments with astonishment. The faithful Brownell, whose early efforts to recover and return his law partner to his hometown met with failure, must have been extremely gratified by this turn of events. For the many politicians who had known Sullivan, the tribute quite overshadowed the upcoming state elections.

The Yankee sense of kinship came into play as New Englanders living in New York City found themselves moved by the story of Sullivan Ballou and decided to participate in the rites, to show solidarity with Rhode Island and to honor those men who paid the ultimate price after answering the call of duty. The *Times* also printed their call to arms:

> The Sons of Massachusetts will meet at the Astor House this afternoon at 3 o'clock, to join in the obsequies of Col. Slocum, Major Ballou and Capt. Tower. . . . Gov. Sprague, of Rhode Island, and Staff, will be present. . . . The Sons of Vermont and Connecticut will likewise join in the ceremonies.[5]

So many New Yorkers expressed an interest in personally honoring Sullivan and his comrades that arrangements were made to allow members of the general public an opportunity to pay their respects at a wake. The bodies were now to lie in state with all the full-blown trappings of Victorian funerary symbolism. Had anyone anticipated this, the families might have been able to come down from Providence to witness and experience the homage, but given the spontaneity of developments in New York, there was not enough time for Sarah or the other wives to catch a train.

In 1862, the train tracks from Philadelphia did not run all the way into New York City, so the cortege had to switch at Jersey City to a ferryboat to cross the Hudson River. Neither parade nor tribute was planned by the State of Jersey, but still people came to observe the transfer. "A large number of persons in the railroad depot . . . witnessed . . . in respectful silence . . . the removal" of the trio from the cars and their transfer onto three hearses, drawn by teams of two or four horses, each horse "appropriately caparisoned in crape,* with sable plumes" on its head.[6]

Over and over, the stories commented emphatically on the "appropriateness" of everything—as if everywhere people shared the urge to put right the great wrong.

Sullivan Ballou entered New York history on Cortlandt Street, where the waiting crowd was so "immense" that the hearses halted because the street was blocked by spectators.

"A space was only made for the procession by the united exertions of detachments of police from the 27th Precinct, Capt. Bogert, and the 4th and 6th precincts." The *New York Express* continues the story: "Company A of the 71st regiment, in accordance with orders, were promptly on hand, with the Regimental band, to escort the remains." Emotions running high, they marched with their arms reversed, a military honorific for missing comrades.[7] The *New York Times* reported in under its new headline, THE HONORED DEAD:

> During the whole of yesterday the flags on the public buildings, hotels and the principal business establishments, were displayed at half-mast in honor of the dead heroes. Cortlandt-street and

*An alternative spelling for crepe fabric, which, dyed black, was used for mourning.

Broadway from thence to the Astor House was thronged with people to watch the mournful procession pass.[8]

The busiest thoroughfare in Lower Manhattan, Broadway—normally clogged with horse-drawn trolleys and cabs, and thronged with pedestrians—was closed to make way for the cortege, whose destination was the Astor House, the most fashionable hotel in New York City, directly across the street from the City Hall, the park, and Park Row.

Dodsworth's Band, playing the march from Handel's oratorio, *Saul,* written in 1739 and played on state occasions, such as the death of a sovereign, serenaded the onlookers, who jostled each other for a better look.[9] The first glass hearse to come into view was that of Captain Tower. It was followed by Major Ballou's and finally Colonel Slocum's—in military hierarchy. Each was escorted by

The Astor House, the preeminent New York Hotel of the era, where Lincoln stayed before his Cooper Union address, was the overnight resting place for the cortege. *Photo by Currier and Ives.*

With the mayor of New York participating, Sullivan's funeral procession surpassed even the one drawn here, that of Colonel Vosburgh of the Seventy-First, who died from illness in May 1861. *From* Harper's Weekly, *June 8, 1861.*

three noncommissioned officers of the Second Rhode Island Regiment, representing each company of the soldiers of the regiment.[10]

In the street between City Hall and the hotel, the police were again called upon to create room to move. With several thousand persons watching, the police rapidly formed a hollow square, and the procession halted and maneuvered the hearses into the center.

The military marched over in front of the entrance to the Astor House and lined up, while the band played more solemn dirges. Next, the Rhode Island noncommissioned officers lined the steps of the hotel and presented arms. Only then were the caskets lifted off their conveyances, hefted to the shoulders of the pallbearers, and carried past the line of soldiers into the hotel.

Inside, guests and visitors respectfully made room as the caskets were carried through vestibules and hallways to two large public meeting rooms, parlors nine and ten. Civilian gentlemen inside the hotel removed their top hats in salute as the caskets were carried past. Another newspaper report assured its readers that:

> Every arrangement that could honor the remains was made at the Astor House for their reception and disposition. The parlor where they were placed was draped in mourning. The various articles of furniture—mirrors, side-board, centre-tables—and window and door cornices were covered with crape. At the southern end of the parlor was a canopy, about eighteen feet long by sixteen feet in breadth, and some twelve feet in height, covered with mourning, the stars of an American flag being festooned in the centre, and the stripes ornamenting either side. Under this canopy the coffins were laid on tressels.[11]

The newspapers confided to their readers that each officer was in double coffins, the inner coffin was zinc lined as "the remains were much decomposed."

The military honor guard stood by while the coffins were draped with American flags and strewn with flowers by "the ladies of the Astor House." Nameplates to identify each soldier were placed on their respective coffins, Ballou's read,

Major Sullivan Ballou
2d Regiment RIV
Killed at the Battle of Bull Run
July 21st, 1861

Floral wreaths formed of camellias, lilies, heliotropes and violets encircled the name plate, and head and foot of each coffin, and other decorations were added, in harmony with the mournful occasion.[12]

Now, appropriately bedecked with every symbol of an emotional, patriotic, and flamboyant age, attended by a military honor guard, the bodies were ready to receive callers, lying in state the balance of the day and until midafternoon of the following. "All morning and up to the time for the removal of the corpses, there was a constant stream of people passing in and out of the Astor House" entering by the main columned entrance on Broadway and exiting through the side doors on Vesey Street. "Thousands" visited. Policemen from the Third Precinct kept watch in the vestibule against "unnecessary intrusions."[13]

The Sons of the various New England States had engaged various parlors in the hotel for the use of their members attending the obsequies. Several additional parlors were occupied by the assembled officers of the regiments of Hunter's Second Division.

Governor Sprague, Mayor Cranston of Newport, Father Quinn, former chaplain of the First Regiment, and Colonel Van Zandt, were among the more recognizable names present in the Rhode Island contingent of dignitaries. When Major Bagley, representing the Sixty-ninth New York State, appeared at the hotel, he was questioned sharply by visitors as to why the Sixty-ninth was not also escorting the procession. He replied that they had "expected to be called out" to participate, a remark that created "much feeling." It was later reported that the regiment's commanding officer had received an order calling out his troops, but had decided they were "not prepared to parade."[14] Such was the jockeying of regiments competing for the opportunity to pay tribute.

After Bagley it was easy to understand the interest of the New Englanders, but that of the New Yorkers was more puzzling. Some of it may have been triggered by the lurid stories of the Rebel revels in the graveyard now appearing in the press. However, the official expression of sympathy more likely had political motivations.

In early 1862, the first Republican mayor of New York, George Opdyke, had replaced Confederate sympathizer Fernando Wood in that office. Wood had proposed New York City's own secession from the United States in 1861. The *New York Daily News,* which Wood had purchased for his brother to run, at times found its offices under siege by rioting crowds protesting its antiwar, anti-Union editorials.

Under Wood's administration, and despite it, in April 1861, the first New York regiments to depart for the war had marched down Broadway on their way to defend Washington, a splendid, showy, gallant parade in their new uniforms. However, in the year since then, there had been no victories, no triumphs, nothing to bring New Yorkers together in continued support for the Union side of the war.

To the military and political leaders of New York, Slocum, Ballou, and Tower were sent from heaven: symbols of heroism and sacrifice that could be used to rally support for the war at a critical time in the city, to increase enlistments and strengthen resolve. Sullivan's experience in particular personified everything Northern propaganda believed the war to be about—good patriotic men fighting to preserve the Union and the blessings of liberty against moral reprobates who not only did not revere common American ideals but enslaved Negroes, raped their slave women, sold off their half-breed children for cash, and—to confirm their villainy—dug up the dead!

In the desperate months of early 1862, when no victories came from the muddy peninsula or the western theater, politicians wasted no time in capitalizing on the opportunity of lauding fallen heroes. As a patriot and fellow politician, Sullivan would have understood.

These politics even determined the route to the boat dock, when it was time to leave town. The hearses only needed to go from the hotel straight south to the nearby Battery. Instead, it was decided to orchestrate a ceremonial procession that passed through the key streets in a huge square before heading south to the pier. Building

The portico and porch of City Hall were "black with spectators" watching Sullivan's procession pass down Broadway. *From author's collection.*

owners along the way got into the spirit of the event by draping their facades in the black crepe of mourning, or patriotic red, white, and blue banners, flags, and bunting.

Mayor Opdyke decided on a personal tribute of great political and symbolic significance—he personally joined the cortege. The hearse containing the former Speaker of the House of the Rhode Island General Assembly, as well as those of his colleagues, was now to be followed on foot by the mayor and City Council of New York City.[15]

The crowd outside the hotel began assembling at 12:30 P.M., a full three hours ahead of the time announced for the procession to depart. By three o'clock, when the military escort arrived a half hour late because of the traffic jam, the crowd had grown to ten thousand.* The portico and porch of City Hall were "black with spectators."

* The population of New York at the time was 1.2 million.

After lining up in the park, the military paraded down Park Row and formed up on the east side of Broadway, the City Hall at their back, facing the Astor House. Police superintendent Carpenter had the crowd cleared off the roadway and three biers were erected on the sidewalk in front of the main entrance to receive the coffins. Pallbearers bore out the coffins, still covered with their American flags. Additional fresh flowers were provided:

> Beautiful wreaths of immortelles,* and unstrung flowers adorned the coffins of the gallant dead, furnished by Mrs. C. M. Connolly of Fort Washington, Mrs. John Jacob Astor of this city, Mrs. George W. Benson of Brooklyn, and Mrs. Stetson of the Astor House. Muffled drums beat a salute and the gentlemen in the crowd respectfully removed their hats. The band of the 37th Regiment played a dirge as the caskets were placed in the hearses.

Detachments from the Seventy-first, Thirty-seventh and, at last, the Sixty-ninth regiments formed the escort.[16]

> The line of march of the procession. . . . [was] up Park-row to Chambers-street, up Chatham-street to the Bowery, up the Bowery to Canal-street, through Canal to Broadway and down Broadway to the [Battery] Groton boat. Great crowds witnessed the cortege in all the streets through which it passed.

* Immortelles resemble daisies in having multiple petals around a yellow center. They dry well to a silvery color, hence their name and use in Victorian dried flower arrangements and funerals. Mrs. Stetson is the wife of the man who bought the Astor House from the Astors in the late 1850s. Fort Washington is up near the site of the present day George Washington Bridge. Assuming this is the wife of John Jacob Astor IV, she was Southern-born, from Carolina.

At the pier, the hired hearses were left behind as the caskets were loaded onto the steamer, the *Commonwealth.* Once on board, likely everyone who still could breathed a sigh of relief at being out of the public eye for a few hours and retired to their cabins. The boat sailed for Groton, Connecticut, and there, yet another transfer was accomplished, this time to a train bound for Providence Railroad Station, where Sarah was waiting.

Much behind-the-scenes organizing had gone on between military, church, and civic leaders. By March 26, the Providence newspapers were printing muster orders for the various home guard units to prepare for a role in welcoming the men home. Days before the bodies were north of the Mason-Dixon Line, Mayor Jabez Knight issued a directive via the press that persons attending the ceremonies must not obstruct the route with their parked carriages. Grace Church agreed to provide burial space for all the men in the receiving tomb at their new graveyard south of the city. A feature in Northern cemeteries, where frozen ground made it impossible to dig graves for several months each year, receiving tombs stored caskets until burials were resumed. Made of stone and resembling small temples, they were normally placed at the front entrance to cemeteries.

Its engine draped in mourning colors, the boat train arrived at 4:30 A.M. and was met by the Burnside Zouaves. The churches of Providence canceled services that Sunday morning—something unheard of in 215 years of New England worship—so their parishioners could participate in the ceremonies.

From the depot, the bodies were escorted to the walled and turreted infantry armory—where the regiment had first trained in those optimistic days of the spring of 1861—to lie in state into the next day.

A huge black canopy was spread out in the South Hall, its four corners draping down to the ground, American flags festooning the middle and each corner. Mrs. Benson's wreath from New York City

The Armory on Benefit Street in Providence. Sullivan shuttled between various armories as he helped recruit the First Regiment. *Author's photo.*

was still displayed on the Slocum coffin, along with her note that she was a former pupil [or classmate] and wished to pay her respects. The nameplates traveling with the coffins were again displayed in wreaths, into which were interwoven symbolic flowers. To the Victorians, camellias conveyed admiration. Lilies bore silent, fragrant witness to the restored innocence of the soul at death.[17] (Strong-smelling flowers were preferred for funerals for obvious reasons.)

The streets leading to the armory were draped in mourning. Black crepe and shrouded American flags were everywhere. In some streets, flags stretched overhead. Flags on flagpoles were at half mast and two businessmen suspended "the largest flag ever raised in this city."[18]

Rhode Islanders converged to pay their respects to these men whom they had known as their business colleagues, schoolmates, neighbors, friends, and relatives. The streets were so crowded that "the labors of the guard were very arduous to keep the multitude in check." Between 9:00 A.M. to 5:00 P.M., ten thousand people visited.

At one point, a line of carriages pulled up in front of the armory, and the guards stopped the line of the mournful and the curious from entering. The doors were temporarily closed to the public so the family members could at last have private time with their long-lost men.

Each carriage discharged its black-clad passengers, those in top hats alighting first to help those in hoop skirts. Strong male arms lifted little children down into the protective cocoon of family members. For this occasion, everyone had reverted to the garb of heaviest mourning. The widows' red-rimmed eyes were hidden from view by their large, heavy black veils, which covered bonnet, face, and shoulders. Each widow was surrounded by a circle of family members as the parties walked into the armory.

Their honored loved ones were swaddled in flags, in closed off wooden boxes, close yet distant, their presence satisfying yet not quite so. The mourners strove to bless and commune with them. It was so unlike the traditional New England wake, in which the deceased was seen. "Death here is different than at home" a soldier in the Second Regiment had observed.[19]

It was still the mournful Lenten season, with few flowers yet in bloom this far north; still the families set their own wreathes and floral tributes on and about the caskets. Tears flowed in the privacy of the vast room as the families grieved. In Virginia, the undertaker had taken possession of the lock of hair preserved by brave Mrs. Benson, and may have taken this first possible opportunity to present this little packet to Sarah. (Victorians especially prized locks of hair as mementos of the dear departed, often wearing them in lockets or brooches, or if the length was sufficient, weaving them into ovals or squares, which could be incorporated into jewelry.)

This humble lock of hair was therefore a great treasure to Sarah. They embraced and departed. There was a possibility that baby Sullivan, only six months old, had been brought just so he could be told when he was older that he shared a moment, however melancholy, in the same room with his namesake.

When the families' private time drew to a close, there was a crowd waiting to enter and pay their respects. Back in their carriages, Sarah and the other widows were relieved to return home and rest up for tomorrow's obsequies. Only one more duty remained, and it would be Sarah who experienced the greatest relief that her husband's mortal remains had at last reached a place of relative safety and honor, just as she believed his soul had in heaven.

The armory closed at 5:00 P.M. and the guard remained with the bodies overnight. The weather on the day of burial was "unpropitious" but it did not diminish "the tribute [that] was a most impressive exhibition of popular respect."[20] At 9:00 A.M. Monday morning, the guard reformed to escort the bodies to their burial place. There was to be no additional funeral service after the rites held last year. The route would now transverse a different part of the city and here, too, "emblems" of mourning were on display. Places of business were generally closed, flags were universally displayed at half mast on the route of the procession, and homes and businesses hung out mourning banners. Such banners were normally used to announce a death in the family. On this day, all Providence proudly claimed Sullivan Ballou, John Slocum, and Levi Tower as family.

Each hearse was drawn by four horses led by grooms in uniform. "The American flag was festooned on in crape on the sides of the hearses, and they were flanked by the American flag shrouded to the staff."

In Providence, the line of march of the procession also followed military etiquette. It was again led by the lesser-ranking officer,

Captain Tower, whose pallbearers were all fellow captains. As in life he had commanded a company of men, he was escorted to his final resting place by a company of 108 members of the Pawtucket Light Guard.

Next came Major Ballou, attended by six majors and a battalion-size honor guard of two hundred, including two companies from Pawtucket, where his mother and sister lived, and another from Slatersville, from the northern part of Providence County, near the Ballou Neighborhood settled by his ancestors. His own Woonsocket Guards, the unit he had joined at age fourteen when he was hardly big enough to shoulder a rifle, completed his escort.

Included with the host of Rhode Island units comprising the regimental size force of eight hundred men and six colonels escorting Colonel John Slocum, were a detachment of Ellsworth Zouaves, the unit of New York fireman so badly devastated in the afternoon phase of the battle, who had come north expressly for this ceremony. A detail of noncommissioned officers, the corporals and sergeants of the Second Rhode Island, made up further escort. Colonel Slocum's former groom, John Dexter, lead a riderless horse with its stirrups reversed.*

The parade moved down Dorrance Street, through Exchange Place where the famous photograph of the regimental departure was taken, across Steeple Street, along North Main, through Market Square, down Westminster where the photographers and lawyers had their offices, and down Summer, Broad, and Greenwich [Elmwood] Streets to Grace Church Cemetery. It had been decided the men would be buried here, at this newly founded cemetery, out of charity, gratitude, expediency and efficiency.

* The riderless horse is a powerful military image evoking the lost leader. The stirrups are reversed because no rider can take his place; literally, no one can fill his shoes. It also commemorates the bond between horse and rider, with each keeping the other safe in battle.

Grace Church had not acquired downtown land for an adjacent cemetery and this location served the burgeoning southern end of town near Cranston. It did not matter that all were not Episcopalians; they were buried with the full majesty of the Episcopal burial rites conducted by Bishop Clark himself and a full military salute.[21]

At last all that could be done had been done. The *Providence Journal* reported with satisfaction that the recovered bodies were "entombed with the honored rites of Christian burial. They rest where no rude hand can profane their remains."[22]

They had come full circle, these men who had gone off to demonstrate the importance of preserving liberty and the American union. They were now at the end stage of an amazing journey in which they had experienced the best and worst that a nation at war had to offer. All along their journey home,

> the hearts of entire communities spontaneously poured forth the deepest feelings of respect and reverence. Everywhere the tribute was worthy of the heroes who gave themselves to their country, and in the plentitude of their powers and in the vigor of their manhood, patriotically resigned their lives in the cause of law, constitutional order and good government.[23]

Major Sullivan Ballou, who died so far from home, in a quiet, humble house on a narrow country lane, practically the last prisoner of war left in the hospital, went to the second of his three graves with the homage of a hundred thousand people.

Sarah Ballou went home grateful to everyone who had done so much to honor him and to help her family. The strength she had gained over the last year saw her through this painfully difficult week, and the cycle of what was owed her husband was at last complete. Sullivan had always praised her self-reliance and, working with a network of friends and family, she would emerge from this tragedy to remake her life and raise their boys as he would have wanted.

CHAPTER TWENTY-FIVE

"The Eagle of Freedom Shrieks"*

From Sullivan's Return through the End of the War

May 1862–May 1865

Had Sullivan's grave not been robbed, and the three Rhode Island officers uneventfully recovered and taken home, the story would have merited only a few lines in the newspapers, and it is doubtful whether the tributes along their route home would have been so extensive, lacking the need to show a nation united against Southern misdeeds. The coast-to-coast newspaper coverage of the desecration of Sullivan's body not only inflamed the public but roused the politicians, who were not far behind in expressing their own outrage and scrambling to capture the moral high ground.

On April 1, Senator Charles Sumner of Massachusetts rose on the floor of the United States Senate, to introduce a motion:

* From a version of the Civil war song "The Irish Volunteer."

> That the select committee on the conduct of the war be directed to collect the evidence with regard to the barbarous treatment by the rebels, at Manassas, of the remains of officers and soldiers of the United States killed in battle there.[1]

On April 2, the first witnesses were the closest at hand, and most promptly summoned from their camp north of the city: assistant surgeon James Bonaparte Greeley, followed by Reverend Frederic Denison. Governor Sprague was unable to speak to the committee until April 11. Their detailed testimony, covering six single-spaced pages in the Congressional Record, provided the information on Sullivan's disinterment. The committee met for a total of six days spread out over the month of April, taking twenty-two pages of testimony, which they summarized in a seven-page report for Congress. It seemed the Rhode Islanders were not the only persons who had gone to recover bodies; several New Yorkers also went to reclaim the bodies of brothers or commanding officers, and two of the New York surgeons who had been at Sudley Church were also interviewed.[2]

For the first time, the people of the nation learned about the extreme dichotomy of sentiment that existed after a battle. The contrast was eloquently expressed in the letters written home to his wife from Sudley, on July 22 to 23, by Peter Hairston, First Virginia Cavalry, who first discussed the sympathy felt:*

> Within a few hundred yards of where we are now is a church wh[ich] they took possession of for a hospital. In and around

* Hairston had been J. E. B. Stuart's brother-in-law and remained close enough to him to assist him in organizing the First Virginia Cavalry. Hairston's first wife, Columbia Lafayette Stuart, had died four years before the war, and Hairston wrote this description of the Sudley Church Field Hospital to his second wife, Fanny.

> are 279 dead and wounded—many out in the drenching rain will die before morning—around are arms and legs. . . . To pass by it was enough to soften and sicken the hardest heart. . . . I will not dwell on the awful scene. The Battle was nothing to this afterpiece. The excitement of the contest, the cheering of the soldiers the triumph of victory hid the battlefield of many of its terrors. *Nothing—Nothing* could lessen the horrors of the field by moonlight.

He next mentioned the other dynamic, "Our troops have been busily engaged in appropriating everything they might possibly need, from a pincushion to the finest army tent."[3] This acquisition of booty normally extended to removing money or military items the dead could no longer use, although most soldiers enjoyed reading pilfered letters. All muskets were picked up and most turned in to the Confederate command, which used them to equip its own regiments. Boots and shoes were generally kept by the scavengers, as were pistols, watches, and useful items of clothing. In the hometowns of the North and South, no civilian family member was interred wearing good shoes or clothing, which were too valuable to spare; rather, they were dressed in grave clothes. The taking of this booty on the field was a ruder extension of that tradition. The Forty-ninth Virginia, who had gone into battle with their cartridges in the pockets of their trousers because they lacked cartridge boxes, were likely to welcome any that came their way, whatever the state's initials stamped on the leather. Normally however, such booty was taken before burial.

What soon became clear from the testimony of these witnesses before the Congress, was a sequence of events following the Union abandonment of the battlefield, and the knowledge that the desecration of Sullivan's grave was the pinnacle of an unchecked spiral of violence that was stopped only by the withdrawal to the

Rappahannock. The nation now had both detail and context. Witnesses reported speaking with Benjamin F. Lewis, related to the Lewis family at Portici who, fearing a "pestilence" in the neighborhood, had by the Tuesday after the battle sent word around to his neighbors to promptly bury such bodies as were on their own property, and sent his own Negroes out to do just that.

But, often no sooner had the soldiers been decently, albeit shallowly, buried than roving bands of Southern soldiers came through, pushing rails under the body to raise the mid part so they could take the brass buttons of the coats for souvenirs. This quickly progressed to behavior outside the accepted norm—taking bones for various purposes. Frederick Scholes of Brooklyn testified that, while searching for his brother on April 4, whom he never did find, we

> were digging there, a party of soldiers came up and showed us a part of a shin-bone five or six inches long, which had the end sawed off. They said they had found it among many other pieces in one of the cabins that the rebels had deserted. From the appearance of it, pieces had been sawed off out of which to make finger-rings. As soon as the Negroes saw it, they said that the rebels had had rings made of the bones of our dead that they had dug up; that they had had them for sale in the camps.[4]

Surgeon Swalm corroborated it as a shin bone. Further testimony quoted Mrs. Pierce Butler who lived near Blackburn's Ford:

> She had seen the rebels boiling portions of the bodies of our dead in order to obtain their bones as relics, the rebels not waiting for them to decay. . . . She had seen drum sticks made of "Yankee shin bone,". . . and . . . a skull that one of the New Orleans artillery had, which he said he was going to send

> home and have mounted, and was going to drink a brandy punch out of it the day he was married.[5]

Scholes testified that Benjamin Lewis identified a few out-of-control men as the perpetrators. He said they belonged to the Louisiana Tigers, known to be troublemakers in camp, and he emphasized that the entire army should not be blamed.[6] Mr. Lewis was wholly correct; despite the later establishment of the Geneva Conventions, which stipulated appropriate behavior toward captured and dead soldiers, armies forever struggle to control aberrant behavior among a distinct minority of soldiers.

For six weeks, throughout April and May, the Southern papers printed the congressional testimony, all the better to deny it, under headings like MORE FEDERAL LIES. The commentary ran from general disbelief and rebuttal, to statements that the burned bodies were really Confederate soldiers who had been buried in a hospital that later burned down. The *Richmond Dispatch* said on April 9, 1861,

> The Yankee papers, since the evacuation of Manassas by the Confederates, have been entertaining their readers with all sorts of legends, which they profess to have derived from Virginia farmers and old ladies in the neighborhood.[7]

That part of the testimony regarding harsh treatment of Union prisoners, on the battlefield and in Richmond, stung, as generally the best available care had been provided to the wounded of both armies. Given that when the war began, only six hundred physicians in the United States had ever performed an operation, and triple that number went to war as regimental surgeons, there were bound to be inexperienced doctors "learning" on unfortunate victims. The case of Prescott of the Fourteenth Brooklyn, well discussed in papers of the North and South, may have illuminated the need for training in amputation techniques; Prescott had died after inexperienced Southern physicians performed additional surgeries in unsuccessful attempts to suture the skin closed.[8] Again, it highlighted how extremely fortunate Sullivan had been to have a surgeon with twenty years' experience in amputations, for that gave him his only chance.

The *Boston Traveller*, quoted in the *Richmond Dispatch*, hit the right note when it said,

> An isolated case of brutality and barbarism is magnified and applied to a great mass of people. It was these bloody and brutal stories in the North about the South, and in the South about the North, circulated first by fools and then used by designing knaves, which produced this bloody revolutionary movement. In the name of Heaven, let us now discountenance them forever.[9]

The select committee noted in its own report,

> that during the last two weeks, the skull of a Union soldier has been exhibited in the office of the Sergeant-at-arms of the House of Representatives, which had been converted to such a purpose, and which had been found on the person of one of the rebel prisoners taken in a recent conflict.[10]

The Union government was still negotiating with the nations of Europe not to recognize the Confederacy as an independent nation, and the committee report used a powerful and bone-chilling analogy well understood in the 1860s in suggesting that

> foreign nations must, with one accord, however they have hesitated heretofore, consign to lasting odium the authors of

> crimes, which in all their details, exceed the worst excesses of the Sepoys of India.*[11]

Society rushed to support and ennoble widows and other relatives of the dead, making them co-warriors. Chaplain Woodbury, in a speech delivered July 2, 1862, equated the efforts of

> the men of the nation on the field of battle, the women of the nation in the hospital and at their homes, are alike contending for civilization, loyalty and freedom, against barbarism, treason and slavery.

Beginning in 1861, women picked up two new roles. The first was "celebrating and sanctifying the martyrdom of others," and the second was "the mitigation of the soldier's lot."[12] The first—that of being a public widow—was more or less forced on Sarah, who was not only the widow of a prominent, newsworthy officer but also one of the first women in black. The second—that of becoming a co-warrior in the Northern war effort—included making medical

*During the yearlong Sepoy Mutiny in British India in 1857, triggered by issues of religious ritual purity, native soldiers known as Sepoys, formerly in the British occupying army, fought the occupiers and seized two forts on the Ganges: Cawnpore and Lucknow. At Cawnpore, after weeks of shelling, starvation, and lack of water and medicine, over a hundred women and children were herded into the Indian part of town and locked up in the Bibigar, a harem building, where they were shot and hacked at en masse; the living, the dead, and the wounded thrown down a well together, where their remains were discovered when a British relief column retook the city some days later. The British response to the massacre of Cawnpore was savage. The mutineers were arrested, dragged to the Bibigar where they were forced to lick the dried blood off the walls and floors. Now ritually polluted, neither Hindu nor Moslem could enter paradise after the British hanged them and blew their bodies apart with cannon fire after finding them guilty at trial.

supplies, sewing, cooking, or organizing the shipment of what had been sewn or cooked. Initially, nursing anyone outside of a woman's own immediate family was considered deviant behavior, but necessity eventually overwhelmed the available male nurses.

Much of the early relief work came from women already organized in groups like the sewing circles of Worcester, a town with a tradition of activism. The length and breadth of the war, however, soon trained countless other women in community and social organization skills. While it is not known if Sarah participated in war work, she certainly had many opportunities to do so if she chose.

Sarah still had one special man in the war to worry about, her brother John. In the fall of 1862, John Shumway's enlistment in the navy ran out, and he left his ship, the U.S.S. *Preble,* still part of the Gulf Blockading Squadron. The hottest action seen by this, the second navy ship named for Commodore Preble, who had commanded the U.S.S. *Constitution* against the Barbary Pirates in 1803, during John's time aboard, was in a sea lane called the Head of Passes, near the mouth of the Mississippi. It happened when the Confederate ram C.S.S. *Manassas* attacked the *Vincennes*, and the *Preble* came to her support. John also spent time on the ground in North Carolina, as previously mentioned. Sarah's brother did not reenlist in that branch of service, and he was lucky to be off the *Preble*, when it sank off Pensacola after burning to the water line in April 1863.[13]

Once he left the navy, Catherine, Sarah, and his nephews seemed only to have the briefest chance of the pleasure of John's company, because he promptly joined the army. Most fellows just joined the local infantry regiment, but John chose more unique and adventurous ways to serve the Union, perhaps truly a young man "out to see the elephant." On October 8, 1862, he enlisted in Company K of the Second New York Cavalry, whose men mustered from the Poughkeepsie area and saw action all over Virginia. If Company K was with the full regiment from November 3–6 of that year, when they were camped at Sudley Church, John had a chance to see where his brother-in-law had fought and died.

To make ends meet, Sarah began to dismantle the library, which Sullivan had built for himself, selling off the kinds of books for which she and her sons had no use, especially some of the legal reference books that Sullivan had used in his work. At its May 1862 session in Newport, the General Assembly passed the following resolution:

> Resolved that the Secretary of State be authorized to purchase of the widow of the late Major Sullivan Ballou, a sett of the Schedules of the General Assembly of the State of Rhode Island, from the year 1764 to the year 1820; that he cause the same to be bound and deposited for safe keeping in the Rhode Island Historical Society; and that the State Auditor be directed to pay Mrs. Ballou one hundred dollars for the same, upon the certificate of the Secretary of State.[14]

The first law in a general trend to expand pension benefits to widows and orphans began in 1862 when, to encourage recruitment, the government extended the length of the widow's pension from five years to life. Perhaps in updating her file, the Pension Office noted she had been paid at the improper rate. The highest rate was only $30—for colonels. Accordingly, on September 25, 1862, the Pension Office notified Sarah that her pension had been reduced to $25 monthly. To make matters worse, they declared she must repay the extra $10 per month, which they were to begin deducting from her upcoming payments. No payment schedule is part of the pension record at the National Archives, so it is not possible to determine if they took it gradually, perhaps at the rate of $5 or $10 a month, or sent nothing for as long as four months until the overpayment, which may have been as much as $100 [now $2,700] was recovered.[15] Any income she made in addition to her pension would now be taxed, for in need of more money to fight the war, Lincoln signed a bill creating the first income tax in America on July 1, 1862.

Sarah made two important decisions between this time period and her actions' certain documentation in 1865. First, she and her mother combined their households and moved in together, taking in a third woman as a boarder, back in Woonsocket, which was to remain Sarah's home for many years. Second, with the options for women working outside the home still as restricted as those her mother-in-law faced thirty years earlier, Sarah choose to become a music teacher and give piano lessons in her home, using the piano Sullivan had bought for her enjoyment before the war. With the income she received from this genteel occupation, the rent paid by the boarder, the contribution her mother provided, and her pension, Sarah was able to raise her sons outside the reaches of poverty.

It was hard to count on other male friends and supporters during the war years. Death and the war had removed many from the immediate circle of Sarah's protectors, requiring her to rely more than ever on her own resources and strengths. Others may have provided assistance, but the little Ballou family was not dependent on their generosity. Indeed, as events turned out, Uncle Henry and Latimer Ballou were about the only two constant stars left in her constellation, although Sullivan's former guardian Uncle Clovis should not be wholly disregarded.

After Sullivan's death, Charles Brownell took as his law partner Lucius Ashley, and both men worked out of the office he had shared with Sullivan.[16] Unlucky office that, for again, the senior partner died, of a diseased spleen, a rare occurrence.[17] In May 1863, the newspapers sadly reported,

> Mr. Charles F. Brownell, one of the most promising of the younger members of the our bar, died Sunday morning at one o'clock, after an illness of several months, from which it had long been supposed that recovery was impossible. Mr. Brownell

> was the son of Dr. Richmond Brownell of this city, and was thirty-two years of age. He graduated at Brown University in 1851. He took a high position in College, as he afterwards did at the bar. He was a young man of pure character and lofty aims and decided talent, and was rapidly acquiring a conspicuous position in his profession. His loss will be deeply regretted by his professional brethren and by his numerous friends.[18]

On Tuesday, May 5, the Providence Bar met and issued a resolution of respect and regret for Sullivan Ballou's law partner to be sent to Dr. Richmond Brownell. It recalled his

> clearness of mind, the love of laborious legal research and acquirement, and the enthusiastic devotion alike to the labors of the office and the forum. . . . His obliging, yet unassuming, readiness to impart to us the suggestions of his sound, practical judgment, and the treasures of his various and accurate professional information.

It went on to commemorate how he had been a good example to the other lawyers in town in his

> gentlemanly manners, in his pure moral character, in his amiability of disposition, in his faithfulness to duty, and in that singularly liberal spirit which led him to love his profession rather for the distinctions and opportunities than for the emoluments which flow from its successful practice.[19]

Sarah had lost a youthful, energetic friend and champion, one who had not hesitated to assist in her hour of greatest need. If he was the "Dear Charlie" whom Sullivan had asked to "be a father" to his sons, then the boys lost another male who cared about them.

At this time, the "other" Charles, Charles Parkhurst, was also out of Sarah's life, serving as a captain with the Eleventh Rhode Island. They mustered out in July 1863, lucky to avoid the bloodbath of Gettysburg, but he was shortly thereafter commissioned lieutenant colonel of the Third Rhode Island Cavalry and left again. Sullivan's other close friend, attorney Horatio Rogers, Jr., had joined an artillery battalion about a month after Sullivan's death and remained out of Rhode Island for several years, earning the rank of brevet brigadier general.[20] Their friend, Christopher Robinson, had departed in the fall of 1861 for South America after the Senate had confirmed President Lincoln's nomination of him as ambassador to Peru, and did not return home until 1866.[21]

Dr. Harris reenlisted with the Seventh Rhode Island in 1862, eventually being elevated to surgeon in chief and medical director of the Ninth Army Corps. He was away until the summer of 1865. Dr. Rivers spent only two months at home before joining the Fourth Rhode Island Infantry as their surgeon. He, too, served as a medical director, in Seventh Corps, and returned to Rhode Island in the fall of 1864.[22]

Sarah's friends and relatives marched in and out of the state during the four-year period that Rhode Island sent thousands of men to war in twenty-one separate units. If she had wanted to avoid the sight and sound of militias, armies, and marching men, she could never have done so. Unlike the Revolutionary War, in which Rhode Island was under threat from the enemy for so many years, this war was fought far away, but its effects continued to devastate the hearths and hearts of the town.

In July 1863, the Second New York Cavalry was engaged in the cavalry battles and skirmishes around Hanover, Pennsylvania, which prevented J. E. B. Stuart's cavalry from rejoining Robert E. Lee. During the battle, they patrolled the countryside around Gettysburg and then pursued the retreating Confederate Army, capturing Ewell's wagon train and two thousand prisoners headed south through

Maryland. John Shumway came down with typhoid fever in mid-August, and was hospitalized until the end of October.[23]

By 1864, John had transferred to Company B, and was fortunate not to be among the one hundred men chosen to participate in a daring cavalry raid on Richmond, led by Colonel Judson Kilpatrick and Ulrich Dahlgren. Their three goals were to capture major Confederate leaders, emancipate the Union prisoners from Belle Island prison camp, and distribute amnesty proclamations. The Confederate capital was unprepared for such a sneak attack, and it might have succeeded if the raiders had not destroyed property in their path as they rode in. Their high-profile approach gave the government time to organize resistance, and when the two attacking columns failed to link up, they were captured. Friends and acquaintances of John's were first imprisoned in Belle Isle, then sent to the notorious death camp in Georgia, garrisoned by the Georgia Guards, Andersonville. Among these men was Dorrance Atwater, who when assigned the work of a clerk in the prison office, braved great danger to keep a secret detailed log of all dead soldiers and their burial locations. Despite government attempts to block its publication for fear of a backlash, his log became the impetus for the development of the Red Cross and its services of notifying and assisting the families of deceased soldiers. John's friend Atwater became modestly famous after the war before dying of undermined health, but the Red Cross prospered and provided much needed services. Military widows like Sarah Ballou never again needed to wonder about the fate, location, health status, death date, and burial location of their husbands.

In April 1865, Robert E. Lee was losing ground rapidly, trying to prevent total encirclement of the main Confederate Army by Union forces gaining strength near Appomattox Court House. His men had not received rations for several days, and Lee was endeavoring to link up with a supply train loaded with food. The Second Cavalry, under Division Commander General George Custer, captured this train after sunset on April 8, as rations were being offloaded. The loss of these rations forced Lee into a hard decision.

Among his troops were the Twenty-first Georgia—like other units, proud, severely undernourished, and barefoot. These men had fought at Front Royal, Chickahominy, Cold Harbor, Malvern Hill, Bristow Station, Second Manassas, Antietam, Fredericksburg, Chancellorsville, Spottsylvania, Gettysburg, and Petersburg. There were sixty-nine men from the Twenty-first Georgia who fought the whole length of the war and mustered out at Appomattox. These 9 percent of the original regiment froze, starved, endured countless ailments, marched many leagues with bare, bruised feet. It would be a great tribulation to their souls to surrender after such sacrifice, but Lee saw little point in spending their lives without reason. All but surrounded, Lee decided against ordering his army to fight one last desperate battle to break out of the closing trap when to do so would have meant another delay of several more days in issuing rations to the men.

As negotiations for a truce seesawed back and forth on the morning of the ninth, the Second Cavalry, which had been skirmishing with concentrations of Rebel troops in the area, was about to mount an all-out charge on what appeared to be a modest force of Rebel infantry directly in front of them, when a flag of truce was carried forward. The truce came just in the nick of time for John Shumway and his comrades, for hidden behind the screening brush was a full brigade of Rebels with emplaced batteries, and a creek between the combatants. The Second New York Cavalry would have been "swept into eternity" according to their colonel.[24] Sarah and Catherine would have had another funeral to attend. Instead, the troops were just in time to assemble along the road and see General Lee ride away from Appomattox Court House. John and his fellow soldiers were among those who raised their caps in salute to General Lee, and were saluted in return. John and his comrades were among the Union troops who then gave their rations to the starving Rebs.

On the ninth of April, the church bells began ringing at midnight throughout Rhode Island. In Pawtucket, a hundred people promptly assembled on Main Street, shouting to each other, "General Lee has surrendered! The war is over!" Barrels, boxes, and trash were gathered and set alight to build a bonfire so huge it filled the entire intersection of Mill and High Streets, and cracked the glass windows of nearby houses. Next, the celebration moved to the bridge that Sullivan had helped dedicate in 1858. A participant enthused,

> We rushed to the Armory of the Tower Light Battery and hauled out two brass cannon. Took them to Main Street Bridge and began to fire with the ammunition on hand. Messengers were sent to Providence for 100 rounds more. This arrived at four A.M. We continued to fire for about two hours and the guns were so hot when we finished that we could not put our hands on them. . . . Hundreds of panes of glass were broken on both sides of the river and one unpatriotic citizen sent a bill to the Tower Light Battery for glass broken. After the bill reached the company they voted unanimously to refer it to the Confederate government. There was a whole week of celebration and rejoicing. Nearly all of the manufacturers were shut down for a few days.[25]

In Washington, crowds of people celebrated in the streets and gathered around the White House, calling for their president to address them. Lincoln, foreswearing the role of laureled conqueror, worked quietly inside on his clement policies for rebuilding the South and reuniting the nation. He also had oddly prescient dreams of himself lying on a funeral bier in the White House. The president and his wife put together a small theater party and went to see a popular comedy being performed at Ford's Theater. There, Lincoln, whose life had been in danger since 1860, finally succumbed to a successful assassination plot executed by actor John Wilkes Booth. Lax security at the theater had failed to prevent Booth from sabotaging the box, shooting Lincoln in the head with a pistol bullet, jumping to the stage to escape, and creating an uproar in the audience as he fled the theater he knew so well. A doctor in the house attended Mr. Lincoln, observed the wound to be mortal, and a party of volunteers carried the dying president and his hysterical wife to a house directly across the street.

News spread through the town like a shock wave, its transmission making so much noise outside the windows of Senator Sumner that he came to listen. Stunned by the news that the man he revered had been struck down, Sumner alone had the presence of mind to hurry in a carriage to the White House to inform twenty-one-year-old Robert Lincoln, and bring him to his father's deathbed. Sumner sat all night beside Lincoln, holding his hand, until the president's death was pronounced Saturday morning.

The shockwave then rolled across the entire nation, carried by the telegraph through North and South. When news of it reached Rhode Island, all celebrations of the end of the war arrested "in sad gloom."[26] People mourned the loss of their president, a man who was also a great national leader, but because Lincoln had personally touched the lives of so many people by his accessibility and travels around the nation, many, like those who had heard him speak in Harris Hall and Providence five years before, felt a personal sense of loss.

Augustus Woodbury preached one of the sermons in Providence after the death of Lincoln, in which he linked the death of the president to those soldiers who had died in the war, noting Lincoln had made it clear even before his inauguration that "if it was necessary for him to die for the people . . . he was fully prepared." Even after a long, costly war, the people of Providence viewed Lincoln as a leader

> who in the day of compromises, stood faithful to justice; in the day of treason, was always loyal to liberty; and, in the day

> of national distress, preserved his country from destruction and saved her from the sin of slavery!

Woodbury, and Northern public opinion, believed that with the successful end of the war, the nation had come back "to a brave, generous, just and true life, full of vigor and full of promise for the future." His next remarks, however, foreshadowed the change in policy that followed the assassination of the one man who might have forced consensus on the policy of conciliation to the vanquished South:

> The abettors of the rebellion,—wherever they may be, whoever they may be,—hereafter become accessories of this great crime, and are to be so marked, by a just and indignant people.[27]

After the surrender of the remaining Confederate military units in the west, a nation ever alert to the dangers of a permanent military force prepared to send its soldiers home to "take up the threads of small ambitions," to return to farms and businesses, to families if they had them, or to start them if they did not. One last grand review of the victorious armies was arranged, some said to placate the thousands of men camped around the capital, who some feared if not recognized, might pose a threat to the five-week-old administration of Andrew Johnson.

The capital threw off its swathes of black mourning, and festooned itself in the national colors. Stands were set up all along the Avenue, the fanciest before the White House, for the use of the new president, General Grant, and the corps commanders

> in company with the Cabinet members, the diplomatic corps and other notables. Just across the Avenue was a large stand for governors, members of Congress and the Supreme Court

judges. Other stands afforded space for officers of army and navy, the press, invited guests, State delegations and disabled soldiers, and there were ranks of seats extending down both sides of the Avenue.[28]

Spectators gathered at dawn, and from 9:00 A.M. until late afternoon on May 23, the Army of the Potomac paraded past, corps by corps, displaying battle flags torn at Antietam, Gettysburg, and Fredericksburg. "People wept as the battle flags went by, and many rushed into the street to kiss their shredded folds." They also sang along with the military bands, all the familiar songs of the last four years, as Zouaves, and Irishmen with green sprigs in their hats, marched past, sixty abreast. They cheered General Meade on his garlanded horse, and General Custer in his buckskins as he galloped past the presidential stand brandishing his sword in salute. The Second New York Cavalry—including Private John Fowler Shumway—followed after Custer at regulation speed.

The next day, on May 24, the Army of the West paraded, rougher, less spit and polish, some without shoes. The legendary Sherman led his army—men who had triumphed at Fort Donelson, Vicksburg, and Atlanta—past the throngs of spectators. Everyone who had contributed to their victory participated, from Mother Bickerdyke, who had organized their medical aid services, to the brigade of foragers who had marched through Georgia, boasting they could kill, skin, gut, and butcher a hog while on the move, not missing a step. "The last rush of the receding tide" of the war, 150,000 men, marched through the streets of Washington those two spring days, before dispersing back into a single nation determined to put war in its past and look to its future.

CHAPTER TWENTY-SIX

"We Shall Win the Day"*

Sarah, Edgar, and William into the Twentieth Century

1865–1972

At war's end, Sarah's home was once again in Woonsocket. She had returned to that little corner of New England where she had known the greatest happiness with her husband, and where her last son was born. The 1865 Rhode Island mid-decennial census listed her as the head of household in her earning capacity of music teacher, her mother listed as housekeeper for their home on Bernon Street. Both boys were in public school, and their quarters were shared with Lucy Smith, a thirty-four-year-old schoolteacher.

They were living in a wooden frame house owned by John Worall and his wife, both age fifty-two. A third family, that of blacksmith Lyman Southerich, shared the dwelling and they had a baby son. No live-in servant was employed by any of the families.

* From the Civil War song "The Southern Soldier Boy."

Far from luxury living, this crowded domicile, with three families sharing the ground-floor kitchen and outdoor privy, seemed to represent the nadir of Sarah's fortunes. Had they been more than just scraping by, they would not have lived doubled- and tripled-up in the bedrooms on their allotted floor of the three-story house.

The Civil War had brought a boom of prosperity to Providence, Pawtucket, Woonsocket, and the surrounding mill villages, as the mills secured contracts for war materials, and other local businesses supplied hard goods ranging from horseshoes to cannons.

By 1871, growth in the northern district of the state that had been known as Cumberland—the old Ballou Neighborhood—was extensive enough to warrant the incorporation of several new cities. Smithfield gave up some of its land to Woonsocket, which also absorbed all of the manufacturing villages, where Sullivan and Sarah had lived, into its town. Smithfield and North Smithfield remained, and the name Lincoln was chosen for the southeastern town, "in commemoration of the late martyred president of the United States."

As happened in New England, some of the profits were turned back into infrastructure and the towns were gradually modernized. Elevators began appearing in multiple-story office buildings, and iron rails were laid over every major thoroughfare during the war years, beginning with the Providence Pawtucket line in 1863, bringing the horse-powered street car, which made it easier for Sarah to visit the Bogle home. It also facilitated the growth of such suburbs as Elmwood.[1] Woonsocket's streets were paved in 1883, and sewer lines eventually followed.

Despite such profitable advancements, after the war many companies had to change their product line to stay in business; for example, the Burnside Rifle Company switched to manufacturing railroad locomotives. But the overall dynamics of the Reconstruction Era were not kind to Rhode Island, and it might be said that the South won an economic victory over Little Rhody. With

Reconstruction, money became available to build textile factories in the South, close to where the cotton was grown. Improvements in automation meant that less-skilled workers would monitor rather than operate the machinery. In contrast, the cotton mill industry in the North had not kept up-to-date technologically; by the end of the war, enough modern steam-powered plants had been built elsewhere that the New England mills of the Ballous became quaint historical oddities.[2]

Farms that by 1865 had averaged fifty to ninety-nine acres and tried to gain an economic edge with tobacco, scarce in the North during the war, were by 1875 abandoned, their land reverting to forest, their owners killed in the war, and "the best brains and the boldest spirits [gone] to the city."[3]

William's and Edgar's future was just as uncertain as their father's had been twenty years earlier. The fortunes of Woonsocket affected Sarah, because her income as a piano teacher relied on sufficient families with disposable income to educate their daughters in this graceful but inessential skill; lessons rarely came before food on the table.

Sarah's scrimping and saving had another purpose as well, an obligation to Sullivan she still had to fulfill. Sullivan's second grave was not intended to be permanent, either by his family or the church, and one of Sarah's priorities with her limited funds was to inter him permanently; she just had to decide where. Assuming Sullivan had never been taken out of the receiving tomb at Grace Church cemetery, something there was never any rush to do given the state of his scant remains, there was no marker, no memorial, nothing there to show who and what he had been. It was impersonal and hardly befitting a man renowned for dying so noble a death.*

* The plot records for this cemetery, though incompletely preserved, do not show a burial in the ground.

When Providence was a one-street town, families had buried their dead on their own lots and farms. As the population grew, plain and practical burial grounds were established, usually on land that was, at that point, on the outskirts of town. By 1722, King's Chapel started the practice of offering a graveyard adjacent to a church, and soon, other churches followed suit.[4] When the Episcopalians sited Grace Church as their cathedral in an already developed neighborhood of downtown, buying out the land of a theater, they had to establish its cemetery some miles south in the Elmwood district, in 1834, and enlarged it in 1845 to a total of eight acres. Not only was this relatively small cemetery rapidly filling up, it was now inconveniently far for Sarah to travel to from her residence in Woonsocket.

Happily for Providence, its need for larger burial grounds coincided with a new movement for large urban open spaces, and in the 1840s, a businessman suggested building a large cemetery in the new style, which would have "beauty of situation, amplitude of space, and capacity for improvement." Located near the Seekonk River, where wild swans were often—and still are—found, it was named Swan Point Cemetery. Local engineers laid out winding paths, effectively subdividing the tract into a hundred plots, each containing many burial lots; Swan Point featured specimen trees, water features, architecturally elegant structures, and meandering paths—a place of beauty to provide solace to grieving survivors. A great many churches and other cemeteries bought sections within, and hundreds of reburials took place during the 1850s. A great many military monuments honored the dead from previous wars. Swan Point became the most prestigious last resting place in the region, and this is where Sarah wanted Sullivan and herself to be buried, if she could afford it.

In 1858, half of its land already sold, Swan Point was rechartered as a nonprofit corporation, and Seth Padelford, the man on whose ticket Sullivan Ballou had run and lost for the office of attorney general, was on the board of directors. At that time, land in Swan Point sold for 25 cents a foot, minimum.[5] For those wanting to assemble a family plot for multiple graves around a central monument, the cost approached $250. A single grave and burial cost eight dollars.[6]

The cemetery bought adjacent land whenever possible, and the last purchase, in 1865, extended the cemetery north to the boundary with Pawtucket, and out to the river on land sold by Seth Padelford. It was on this land that Sullivan Ballou was buried the third and final time. Because the land was not used for burials prior to this date, Sullivan could not have been reinterred there before that date.*

There is an unverifiable legend that the land on which Sullivan is buried was donated to the family. Inasmuch as the location of his large family-size plot is in an exceptionally beautiful, prime spot, close enough to see the river when the leaves are off the trees in the winter but not so close as to be subject to its excesses, it is unlikely Sarah could have raised the purchase price by herself. While it is possible that Sullivan's extended family contributed, Seth Padelford was well placed to assist in its donation. Given that the raw ground had to be sculpted into the balance of the cemetery, and that the transfer would not have taken place in winter, 1867 is a reasonable date to assume Sullivan's placement in permanent ground.

Several towns, North and South, vie for the honor of having started Memorial Day as a designated day to decorate the graves of the honored dead. Wherever it started, the war had occasioned so many graves in need of cleaning and decoration after a winter had passed, that the custom was quite widespread before the end of the

* Despite the helpfulness and candor of the cemetery staff, and the excellent database linking names to location, business records of burials from the nineteenth century are unavailable. Solving the date of Sullivan's burial was one of the hardest analyses done for this book.

In the decades of peace following the upheaval and emotional devastation of the Civil War, the people of America vowed to remember and honor their dead. This fin de siècle drawing uses words from the song "The Blue and the Gray" (1867) to commemorate that memorial day, when the women of Columbia, Michigan, decorated the graves of soldiers of both the North and South. *From author's collection.*

decade by way of keeping alive the memories of the late conflict, of its causes, its costly sacrifices and of the devoted patriotism that brought it to a success.[7] The *Providence Evening Bulletin* news story on its observance as a citywide event in May 1868 mentions Sullivan Ballou's grave in Swan Point, so this date brackets the other into, at most, a three-year range.

Organized by the major Union veterans association, the Grand Army of the Republic (GAR), surviving soldiers mobilized in front of their armories and paraded to the downtown, where flags flew at half mast, and the buildings were decorated with both patriotic and mourning bunting. The populace had brought wreathes and flowers to designated places, from which these were loaded into carriages for delivery.

> Exchange Place, in the heart of downtown, was the site of a long ceremony. The entire High School student body attended, and every other school sent at least one hundred young scholars. Each child carried a handful of flowers, "earth's fairest adornments, joyous, voiceless harmonies " offered in tribute by fair and gentle and loving hands.

The teenagers sang "America," a special prayer was offered, the inevitable oration followed, and the ceremony wrapped up in a light rain with the singing of the doxology and a benediction. But that was just the beginning. General Burnside, the mayor, other civic dignitaries, the GAR units, the Mowry-Goff private school cadet corps, led by the American Brass Band, without whose presence no occasion in Providence was complete, then set off to visit the major cemeteries. The closest and first visited was that of Grace Church, where platoons of men fanned out bearing crosses, wreathes, and bouquets, and "literally enveloped the sacred mounds with the choicest floral offerings."

The moving mass of flowers passed through town to the North Burial Ground, the Catholic Cemetery, and Swan Point Cemetery.

So novel and touching was the sight that crowds gathered along the streets and roads to watch the carriages pass, despite a drenching downpour of rain. So many heroes were buried at each site that the GAR posts split up. Major General Burnside, his staff, and GAR Post No. 10, all mounted, rode in past the gates of Swan Point and down South Avenue, where they dismounted. Led by a guide, they marched around the grounds for the next seventy minutes, visiting the graves of thirty-five of their fallen comrades.

> The supply of flowers was abundant, and the graves were plentifully decorated, in some instances the mound being completely covered and bouquets placed upon the stone whenever its form would admit. . . . It was very effecting to witness the care and attention devoted by many veteran officers to leaving the amplest memorials upon the resting places of beloved commanders. The graves of Colonel Slocum, Major Ballou and Lieutenant Prescott bore especial marks of the love with which their memories are cherished. No stone yet marked the resting place of Colonel Slocum. . . . The grave of Major Ballou is also devoid of any monument.

Prescott already had a "handsome monument," but many graves were still marked with wooden staves while their families saved money for headstones or monuments. The unmarked graves eight years after their deaths reflect the high cost of monuments and the financial hardships of the postwar period, especially on families headed by widows. In the federal census taken in May 1870, Sarah, Catherine, Lucy and the two boys, apparently a compatible fivesome, were still sharing a house, now in Smithfield with a sixtyish couple, their living conditions somewhat improved. Sarah's personal property was valued at three thousand dollars, three times what she and Sullivan had in 1860. Even given wartime inflation, this was an accomplishment, but it did not mean it was all ready cash.[8] After the war, Sarah's brother John settled in Wilmington, Delaware, where, in 1871, he married twenty-three-year-old Catherine Leahy, born in Galway, Ireland; they had three children.

That year, Sarah and her family, in their role as relatives of a prominent figure who died in the war, had a very public duty to perform at one of the biggest galas ever to be staged in Rhode Island. On September 16, 1871 Rhode Island was dedicating the Soldiers' and Sailors' Monument in the heart of downtown Providence. Seats for 2,300 hundred family members were erected on three sides of the monument, and passes to them distributed. A group of civic marshals was invested to receive and assist the families. A choir of three hundred had a reserved place, as did every public official elected from Rhode Island. Seth Padelford was governor at last, and watched four thousand men and sixteen bands parade up to Exchange Place before he stood to remark,

Top detail of the Soldiers' and Sailors' Monument in Exchange Place, with the dome of city hall behind it. *Author's photo.*

> We meet to do honor to the brave men who have given up their life for their county, and whose names, on tablets of bronze, are immortalized on the beautiful monument about to be uncovered before you.

The crowd wept during the dirge but, when the monument was uncovered, rolling cheers swept through "the vast multitude which filled the square."[9] Reverend Augustus Woodbury gave a lengthy oration in which the sacrifices of all were equated as honorable. He spoke expected words about a citizen soldiery, faithful to democracy, full of patriotism for the republic, warmed by the memories of their loved ones back home, volunteering to go into battle and not flinching from the severest challenge. He spoke unexpectedly of soldiers who sang to ease their way down long roads, and who picked flowers as they passed, and tucked them into hat or buttonhole to brighten their uniform. He recalled how McDowell's words on the eve of the first battle, "I rely on the Rhode Island Brigade," had "been confirmed upon a hundred fields."

Through the efforts of the men now commemorated on this monument, Woodbury reminded the crowd, "The Union stands, and it stands for Liberty!" As a good orator, he challenged the crowd to action:

> Could a voice come down from those serene heights where souls of heroes dwell, it would have no doubtful tone, it would speak no hesitant word. "We are content," it would say, "to have died for liberty, . . . this has been our privilege. We have given you a country which you will ever be proud to call your own. We have established in the western world an empire where a true freedom may abide in undisturbed possession, and peace may reign for the lasting welfare of mankind. We are content. It is for you to maintain inviolate the liberties we have won—to preserve the nation we have saved."[10]

After hours of such ceremony, the families of the honored dead went home to lives that were irretrievably changed by the war. Some women had remarried; others like Sarah, who had very meaningful relationships in their first marriage, chose to remain faithful to that bond despite financial hardships.

The raising of monuments was a unique dynamic of the Civil War. Colonel Bartow's men had placed an impressive stone marker on Henry Hill before 1861 was over. Everywhere, units and states were raising funds to mark their positions on battlefields. Hometowns of fallen soldiers were erecting monuments in their town or courthouse squares.

For those who had played a particularly key role in the war, and in whose townfolk the fire of remembrance burned particularly bright, large-scale military-themed monuments were erected over individuals' graves whenever they could be financed, sometimes a decade or two after interment, sometimes by the family, often by group donations. Fund-raising for these, however, competed with solicitations for town and regional monuments.

Sometimes in the North, the fund-raising was spearheaded by a post of the Grand Army of the Republic. All posts were named after a local veteran, and Sullivan's was GAR Post No. 3 Central Falls, the town where he has served as town moderator in the 1850s, for all practical purposes an extension of the Ballou Neighborhood of the Cumberland. The records of this chapter no longer exist, so drawing conclusions about any role it might have played in placing the monument over Sullivan's grave is problematical. Even the date of the unveiling is uncertain, though presumably it was after the gale of September 8,1869, during which "many trees were prostrated and broken down."[11]

The GAR chapter named for Colonel John Slocum launched a major fund-raising campaign, complete with a brochure and prospectus, in 1886. One event announced by posters:

> Slocum Post, No. 10, Department of Rhode Island, Grand Army of the Republic, respectfully announces a grand fair and bivouac, : to be held in the Infantry Building, Providence, commencing Easter Monday, April 26, 1886, and continuing four days.[12]

Twenty-five years after Slocum's death, the GAR raised monies sufficient to emplace a block of stone carved on each of its sides with the names of the battles in which he fought since the Mexican War. Its top is bedecked with superbly carved soldier's accoutrements, his hat, sword, and jacket, appearing so realistic as to be ready to be picked up in a moment's notice before departing for battle. Elegant and moving, it is one of the finest pieces of sculpture in a cemetery that has much good sculpture. It was dedicated on November 30, 1886, with an enormous procession and memorial service reported on a full page of the *Providence Journal.*

Much of Victorian-era cemetery decoration was allegorical: the broken Greco-Roman pillar indicating a life cut short, sturdy angelic sentinels, Masonic or religious symbols. Neoclassical themes made a comeback, and "very typical of the 1870s" were "obelisks

Colonel John Slocum's magnificently carved monument, a fine piece of Civil War sculpture. *Author's photo.*

atop a base, or urns on a base.[13] Sometimes these were enhanced with carved wreathes or draperies. Evidently Sarah preferred a monument that testified more to the whole man, not just a military career that had been so brief, and when the time came to erect one for Sullivan, she chose a simple, elegant design.

Sullivan's monument is a large, undecorated obelisk about nine feet tall, on a double base. Carved from white granite, it may have come from a quarry in Westerly. The lowest base contains no writing; the higher one has BALLOU carved in raised lettering. On the pediment of the obelisk is incised part of the closing phrase from his letter to Sarah:

Sullivan Ballou
Major 2nd R E G T
R. I. Vols.
Died July 28, 1861
Aged 32 years

"I wait for you there,
Come to me and lead
thither my children."

While biblical quotes were frequently employed, it was a rare thing for monuments or stones to contain quotes from the deceased. The obelisk sits in the center of a generously sized family plot, and he is buried adjacent to it under a small flat headstone within its bounds. It is unknown if a memorial event similar to Slocum's was held for Sullivan.

The letter quoted on his monument first went public about six to eight years after his death. The first printed versions of this letter began to appear in biographies of special war heroes and Brown University Alumni who had died in combat between 1865 and

The obelisk stands over the family plot of the Sullivan Ballou family in Swan Point Cemetery. *Author's photo.*

A close-up of the obelisk's inscription. *Author's photo.*

1868. The local newspaper printed it, for interest, excerpted from the minutes of the local GAR chapter, in the 1870s, and a copyrighted decorative version appears to date from 1890. There is no evidence his letter to Sarah was used as part of a contemporary formal fund-raising drive, but that cannot be entirely ruled out. Considering how many prospectuses were printed for Slocum's monument, and how few survived, it is possible that if they ever existed, all were lost. More probably, the letter was quoted to create an emotional climate in which donations might be offered.

Life for Sarah was not all about the dead, however. Edgar and William were then attending Mowry-Goff, the most elite private school in Providence, formed by the merger of two privately run male academies. It was the hometown equivalent of the preparatory academies to which Sullivan had been sent in his teenaged years, and gave his sons excellent preparation for future life. Uncle Henry's son, Henry Jr., was going there at the same time, and perhaps Henry assisted with the Ballou boys' tuition, which had to be much higher than the approximately $14 per pupil for public school. In 1873, Sarah got a small financial boost from the federal government when she belatedly applied for new pension benefits approved for her sons after the laws were revised in 1866 and 1868. She received a modest windfall of $146 per son in retroactive payments, and William was still eligible for his $2 per month for another couple of years. Her own rate remained the same until her death. (It was also the same monthly pension amount for which Sullivan would have been eligible to receive for the loss of one foot, had he survived.[14])

Twelve years into her widowhood, Sarah became fast friends with the wife of the new minister at St. James Episcopal Church in Woonsocket, Mrs. James Francis Powers. Mrs. Powers was in poor health, went out infrequently, received many callers and kept a diary of her friends' visits as well as tidbits about their lives and the activities in the parish. Her 1873 diary survived, in the care of the

Rhode Island Historical Society. Usually listed as Mrs. Sullivan Ballou, Sarah appears in her diary at least twice a week, in the company of Uncle Henry, her mother, sons, and Mary Brownell, her close friend. All these women paid calls on each other multiple times a month, and the diary provided a glimpse into the dynamics of Sarah's busy everyday life, and its intertwining with that of friends and family, as well as evidence of news affecting them, that cannot come from census records.

On April 2, Mrs. Powers recorded that the parish was busy with preparations for Easter services. Sarah Ballou's musical talents had been pressed into service—she was in charge of the children's choir, which was going to sing at the festival. On the Monday following Easter, Sarah brought the little singers to the minister's house for Mrs. Powers to critique. Two days later, she was back, and Mrs. Powers "helped Mrs. Ballou a little on her dress," after working on props. On Thursday, Mrs. Powers went over to the Church Hall to assist with rehearsals.

All turned out well on the appointed date. The children sang their three songs well, doing credit to Sarah's patient coaching. The rest of the evening was a series of tableaux on a mixture of humorous and religious topics.* Mrs. Powers found the evening's offerings to be rather provincial, but the families declared them "good and highly entertaining." As for Sarah, it was proof she had created a busy social life for herself within the circle of her church, as she had in her community.

On the afternoon of May 7, on her way to visit Mary Brownell, Sarah was thrown from the wagon and injured. She was brought to Mary's to be nursed. By May 8, the minister visited a "quite

* Tableaux had been staged for at least four centuries and were a popular form of amateur theatrics. They consisted of costumed men and women who struck and held poses while poetry or a narration was read. The "actors" might move in choreographed motions, or just pose like a painting.

disabled" Sarah at Mary's house. Apparently, Sarah healed up well enough from her accident for, ten days later, she and Mary were back in Woonsocket and called at the minister's house, in the company of Henry Ballou.

On May 24, Mrs. Powers had undergone an operation at home to remove a tumor from her cervix, and her friends took turns visiting that evening to cheer her. The following day, Edgar brought her a bouquet of flowers. The two Sarah Ballous took turns calling to keep tabs on her condition and to cheer up the patient, who had little in the way of painkilling medicine.

On Thursday, June 19, "the sultriest day of the year," Reverend Frank Powers went to town "to attend the graduation ceremonies of Edgar and Harry Ballou at Mowry and Goff's. On Friday, June 20:

> Mrs. Sullivan Ballou came in with Henry and Edgar and the boys spoke to me the essays they prepared for their graduation and which I thought did them much credit. . . . Edgar's was "Education, the chief defence of Nations," and called for more originality of thought than Harry's. I was very well smitten indeed. Edgar's voice is very rich and smooth. Two fine boys.

When the Powers left for a parish near Kennett Square in Pennsylvania in September, Sarah and Mary Brownell were among the last to bid them farewell.

In 1874, perhaps through the recommendations of friends, an exciting opportunity came Sarah's way. The school committee, part of the structure of Providence city government, was looking to hire a new secretary. The school system had been steadily growing and now had a high school and thirty-seven primary schools with up to fourteen classrooms each, plus several grammar schools, all spread over seven districts. It was overseen by a sixty-member school committee under the ultimate jurisdiction of the mayor. Beginning in

February of that year, the bylaws committee began meeting to identify duties that would be shifted from the school superintendent to the newly enhanced position of the secretary of the committee. The school committee was all male, and the secretary had always been a male, but somewhere along the way, it was suggested that Mrs. Sullivan Ballou could perform the job quite capably.

The new duties involved keeping the employment records of teachers and substitutes: dates of hire and resignation, transfers, promotions, and rates of compensation. The secretary was to certify all school payrolls to the city. In addition, accounting ledgers for the purchase of school books and supplies were to be maintained, all bills presented for payment verified, and approval given to the city to pay the vendors. As before, the secretary took the minutes of the regular evening-held board meetings, and also served as secretary to the finance committee.

The bylaws stated that, during the school year, the secretary was expected to be in the office "at least five hours of every weekday, and at such other times as the School Committee shall prescribe."[15] Whether this can be interpreted to mean the previous employee slacked off is unclear. The job paid $1,000 a year, a tidy sum for an era, although the assistant commissioner of the patent office received $2,500 for supervising three hundred fifty clerks, and the assistant secretary of the interior made $3,500.

In this decade, almost no women in America held civil service positions. The few exceptions were the "treasury girls" in Washington, D.C., whose pay was set below that of their male counterparts; and some postmistresses that Lincoln had appointed in rural communities, often widows taking over their husband's appointment. For a group of men to have even proposed a woman for a job as high paying as this one was novel. However, Sarah's supporters were sufficiently impressed by her abilities and talents to refuse to back off, and committee members lobbied one another behind the scenes for their preferred candidate, Mr. Shaw, Mr.

Green, or Mrs. Ballou. Presumably all prospective secretaries had been interviewed at some point previously.

The dry records of the December 11, 1874, school committee meeting do not fully do justice to the drama behind the scenes that culminated that evening when they met to elect their new secretary. The rare appearance of the mayor at a school committee meeting was only so he could throw his weight behind the candidate he supported. The meeting began at 7:30 P.M. with the prompt adoption of the new bylaw that held the superintendent "hereby released from any duties that are by this article imposed upon the secretary." As for who would fill the post, the gentlemen began with an informal ballot, likely all that had ever been necessary in the past. When that proved inconclusive, a motion "to take a formal ballot" passed. Thirteen ballots later, at midnight, Sarah Ballou was declared elected with the minimum number of votes—twenty-four—required from the forty-four members present. Mr. Shaw had nineteen and Mr. Green, one.[16]

In many respects, Sarah's new job was similar to the one Sullivan had done while clerk for the House of Representatives in the General Assembly. Now she kept the records in the same kind of large, heavy, bound ledger books, her neat left-handed script covering the pages in book after book. Important actions, she underlined in red

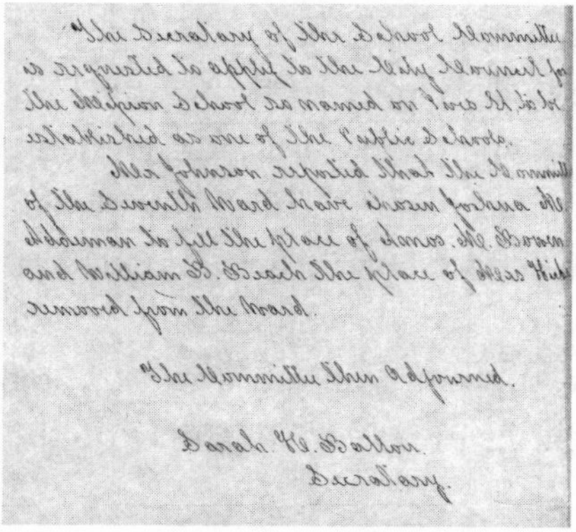

An excerpt of Sarah Ballou's handwriting from the school committee ledgers. *Courtesy of the Providence City Archives.*

using a ruler, and annotated in the margins, the latter something he had done in the state ledgers. There may have been a handful of other women across America working at this level, but Sarah was a true pioneer. The secretary was reappointed every year, so this was no sinecure; if she underperformed, there were men waiting to take her job. Sarah, however, won over the men on the school committee. At her next election, the vote was unanimous, as it was to be for the next fifteen years.[17] Sarah had triumphed. She now had the security of a regular paycheck forty times greater than her pension, and it transformed her life.

As Sarah began her term of office, a new City Hall was under construction from 1873 to 1878 at Dorrance and Washington on Exchange Place, replacing a performance hall that had also been called City Hall and stood on that same lot. The new building opened in 1878, and Sarah put in her five hours a day, in the marble splendor of the new building.[18] As she came in and out of the building, other employees greeted her respectfully, and, over the span of years, friendships formed. Sarah now belonged in her own right, not just as Sullivan's widow.

In 1875, the year Latimer Ballou started three terms as congressman, the state census showed the transformation of Sarah's life from a decade before. She had moved into an upper-class area of Providence and was living at 19 Barnes Street with her mother and the boys. Barnes Street was two blocks from Bowen Street, where Dr. Jabez Bowen's apothecary shop had sold chocolate "by the Pound, Box or Hundred-weight" in the 1700s.[19] It was a neighborhood of large wooden townhouses and gardens. Most homes were three stories tall and had full basements. Close to the campuses of Mowry-Goff School and Brown University, the neighborhood was also close to downtown. Its only drawback was the steep hill Sarah had to climb up and down on her daily walk to work. Sarah's dwelling unit was shared with the

Bradford family, but the family was obviously much more prosperous than before.*[20]

For the first time in fifteen years, Sarah again had a servant. Sarah Mallett was Black, one of the many Cape Verde Islanders migrating to Providence at that time. Forty-seven, widowed, unable to read or write, Mallett was born on St. Helena, the island of Napoleon's exile.

Edgar continued in school and graduated from Brown in 1877; whether he attended on his mother's resources or some sort of scholarship that might have been arranged for the sons of veteran alumni is unknown. It is unclear if Edgar had already started Brown University the fall of 1873, or commenced once his mother got her good job. On her own, Sarah had been able to replicate Sullivan's education for her eldest son, a considerable accomplishment that must have given her great satisfaction. After graduating at Mowry-Goff, William worked as a clerk in downtown Providence for several years.

In 1880, the family still lived at the pleasant house on Barnes Street, and Edgar now working as a "counselor," along with Charles F. Ballou, apparently in a law firm in downtown Providence. Charles Ballou remained a counselor for many years; the word may be a euphemism for a graduate of law school who never passed the bar. The term "lawyer" is otherwise used in the city directories of the period.

The first time he cast a vote for president, Edgar was able to vote for a Ballou cousin. In 1880, James Garfield, Sullivan's cousin, was elected president of the United States. He was another son of a widowed Ballou mother who encouraged his education, Eliza Ballou, daughter of James "the Astrologer" Ballou, part of the family that moved to Richmond, New Hampshire, in search of

* This dwelling unit no longer stands; the one presently at this address was constructed around the turn of the century.

farmland around the turn of the century. Rutherford Hayes said of him,

> There is a great deal of strength in Garfield's life and struggles as a self-made man. . . . From poverty and obscurity, by labor at all avocations, he became a great scholar, a statesman, a major general, a Senator, a presidential candidate. . . . The truth is, no man ever started so low that accomplished so much, in all our history. Not Franklin or Lincoln even.

While serving as General Rosecrans' chief of staff, Garfield had supported arming fugitive slaves to fight the Confederates instead of returning them to their plantations. As the so-called Jim Crow laws of the 1870s eroded suffrage and the rights of the newly freed, Republican Garfield developed a reputation as their champion. He won the election by the narrowest margin in history up to that point, 9,500 votes. (He won sufficient electoral votes, but a third party candidacy diverted 308,000 popular votes.)

Eliza Ballou Garfield was the first mother ever to attend her

As the Republican candidate, and president, James Garfield was known as a champion of the rights of emancipated slaves, and opposed Jim Crow laws that eroded their hard-won freedoms. *Author's collection.*

son's inauguration. Unfortunately, Garfield was gunned down at a railway station as he waited to board a train only two hundred days into his presidency. His assassin, a disgruntled man passed over for a diplomatic post to France, was hanged after trial; Garfield lingered for eighty days, succumbing eventually to infection caused by the nonsterile probing of his wound by several physicians.

Edgar was apparently not admitted to the bar, or did not like the work, and as early as 1882 availed himself of a new opportunity.

The transcontinental railroad, proselytized by President Buchanan, deferred during the war years, was finally organized and built by Civil War veterans managing teams of immigrant laborers. When it linked both coasts in 1869, it shifted the center of the United States from the coastal colonies to the geographic center of the continent. Boston and New York were no longer the preeminent markets for manufactured goods. New England lost her position in the textile world, along with investments, jobs, and development. The development of railroads, gold and silver mining, the exploitation of coal fields, created a boom economy in the midwest. Farms and orchards followed in the wake of irrigation canals. There were many opportunities for a sharp young man, and bright young men of the East Coast started to head west, among them the sons of the Ballous and Bogles.[21] Family tradition holds that Edgar lived in Denver during the 1880s, possibly as early as 1882.[22] His Brown alumni data says only that he was involved in "railroading" there.[23] The transcontinental railroad had opted for better ground and bypassed Denver, which then went on a railroad building boom to connect itself to the rest of the state and the main continental line. Around the time Edgar arrived, Denver had a population of 35,000 and was as lively as the New England mill towns had been in the 1820s.

Edgar's departure from Rhode Island began a decade of great change for Sarah, too, even though she continued to work for the school committee. Latimer Ballou's wife, Sarah, died, as did their friend Christopher Robinson. Josiah Richardson, only age 58, died in 1881 and was buried quietly in Swan Point; Governor Burnside's funeral that same year was another enormous, military-style event. The acrimonious divorce of the Spragues, which filled the newspapers with scandal for years, occurred in 1882. The former governor had continued his love affair with Nelson Viall's sister, Mary Eliza, even after they both married, and her tell-all book was avidly read. Uncle Henry, perhaps the single most stalwart male figure in Sullivan's and Sarah's lives, died in 1882. Sullivan's sister, Hannah Francis, and his mother, Emeline, had both died in 1876.

Happiest by far of all the changes in her life was the marriages of her sons. In 1884, both of Sarah and Sullivan's sons married for the first time. Family connections explain how the two Ballou brothers from Rhode Island eventually married two sisters from Chicago, half a continent away. They also provide a likely provenance for the Chicago Historical Society's handwritten copy of the famous letter Sullivan Ballou wrote to Sarah on July 14, 1861. One of the brothers, during courtship or marriage, might well have given a copy to their bride, in whose family it remained until donated to the society.

The first to take a bride was twenty-seven-year-old Edgar, who married Mabel Beatrice Hurlbert. No details of the wedding have been traced, although she likely came from the Connecticut branch of the Hurlbert/Hurlbut clan, which traditionally named at least one women per generation Mabel since the 1740s.* Where they met and where they married are unclear, but Denver was their home; a Mrs. Mabel Ballou was found listed in the 1890 directory for that city, listed as a dressmaker. (If Edgar's location of employment was outside the city boundaries, he would not have been listed.) Relatively little is known of their married life, except that if

* When all else fails, the onomastic or family naming patterns provide important clues to the researcher.

there were children before her death in the early 1890s, they did not survive.[24]

Later that same year, on his parent's wedding anniversary date, October 15, twenty-five-year-old William married twenty-two-year-old Laura Courtelyou Hutchins in Evanston, Illinois. Although Laura's father, Carleton, was a Massachusetts man, the family had been settled in Illinois since before the Civil War. How had the young people met?

Perhaps Laura had come east on a visit to paternal relatives. Or perhaps William had gone west. William's first cousin, Fred Mason Bogle, just two months older than William, had followed in his father's footsteps and gone to work for the Gorham Silver Company, but as a salesman. By all reports, he was quite effective and the company gave him Chicago as his territory.[25] It was conceivable that William, took a break from working as a clerk in Providence, and traveled to the Midwest either in the company of Fred, or to visit him. He could then have met Laura in the Chicago area.

Laura's middle name, Courtelyou, reflects her family's Dutch heritage passed down through her mother's ancestors, who were among the earliest founders of New Amsterdam (New York City.)* Laura's mother, Sarah Stanley, was widowed in her first year of marriage and, at age twenty-four, married Carleton Samuel Hutchins. Three of the five children born to them in Chicago survived early childhood. The eldest daughter married out of the circle of this book. The two youngest daughters, May or (Mary) Celeste Hutchins, born in 1859, and her sister, Laura Courtelyou Hutchins, born in

* The primogenitor, Jaques (spelled Courteljau) was born in Utrecht, Holland about 1625 and emigrated to New Amsterdam (New York City) in 1652. He married Neeltje Van Duyn, another émigré, had six surviving children, moved to Long Island and embarked upon a career of public service to his colony. He was a contemporary of Pierre Billieu, possibly a younger scion of the Ballou clan of New England. See Appendix 1.

1862, were well schooled. May attended Dearborn Seminary and Rockford College, "acquiring an intimate knowledge of the best in literature and music." Presumably Laura had a similar education.[26]

The father of the two girls, Carleton Hutchins, was rich, the Ballou family was venerable and so passed muster, and William joined the Hutchins family. The *Evanston Index* reported that, on October 15,

> Wednesday afternoon at 4 o'clock one of the most notable and brilliant society events of the season occurred at the residence of Mr. and Mrs. Carleton S. Hutchins, on Hinman avenue, the occasion being the marriage of their daughter, Miss Laura Hutchins, to Mr. William B. Ballou, of Providence, Rhode Island. Bishop Charles Edward Cheney, of Chicago, and Dr. George C. Noyes, of the First Presbyterian Church, were the officiating clergymen. . . . Every appointment was rich and elegant, and the affair was one of the finest of its kind. A large number of relatives of both bride and groom, and many friends were present. Among those in attendance were the following: Mrs. Sarah Ballou of Providence . . . Mr. and Mrs. Ballou left on an evening train for their future home in Providence, R I.[27]

The Evanston newspaper is silent on the attendance of the groom's brother, so perhaps Edgar did not attend. But if not at his brother's wedding in 1884, then at some subsequent family gathering, Edgar met the bride's sister, May.

The same month that Colonel Slocum's monument was dedicated, November 1886, the postmaster of Springfield, Massachusetts, John Rice, decided to go public with the story of how Amos and Margaret Benson of Sudley saved his life after the First Battle of Manassas. The month before, after attending a veterans' reunion at Gettysburg, Rice had gone south to see them, and had a most cordial reunion. When he asked if there was anything he could do to repay their kindness in tending him under the fencepost, they demurred but noted that the community struggled to pay off the $200 debt for the rebuilding of their church destroyed during the war. Rice's published account raised $235 in three days, from veterans and complete strangers, and the sum was sent promptly by money order to Manassas. The congregation replied with thanks, Mr. Benson noting, "It has converted Mrs. Benson, for while she always rendered service as far as she could to your suffering soldiers, she has never been reconstructed until now."[28]

In 1886–87, still working as secretary to the school board, Sarah was living at 50 Barnes Street, just a block away and across the street from her previous house. Built in 1860, and still standing, this one is a fine two-story wooden house with basement, large side porches, and rear garden. In 1886, Peter Bogle now passed away, and joined his wife, Hannah Francis, in the Mineral Spring Cemetary, under their large headstone. William and his wife were now living in Fall River, Massachusetts, where he was a partner in a hardware store, Ballou and Aldrich, at 125 Main Street, not far from the mills, an investment possibly funded by cash Laura brought into the marriage.[29]

Fall River is not so terribly far away, on the far side of Bristol, but Sarah may have found herself very lonely when Catherine Shumway herself finally died, March 5, 1889, of a pulmonary embolism. Catherine may have had pneumonia and was noted as debilitated. Her death occurred at 29 Lloyd Street, just two blocks from Barnes Street.[30] She was buried one space away from Sullivan in the plot in Swan Point. On November 1 of that year, Sarah turned in her resignation to the school committee, where it was eventually accepted with great regret. The woman they had not originally wanted to hire for a man's job they now praised, for her graciousness, courtesy, her intelligence and her even handedness, displayed these past seventeen years. To replace her, they hired a man, however.[31]

The 1890 Providence City Directory listed Sarah as having

moved to Fall River, presumably with William and Laura, who were expecting a child, perhaps their first. Yet their son, Stanley Bowen, was born March 8, 1891, in Chicago, Illinois.[32] Laura had chosen to go home to her own mother and family for her lying-in and birth. Things were not going well in their lives; Stanley died in infancy, and either Laura did not want to come back to Massachusetts, or William's vocation did not lie in a hardware store. By 1891, he is listed as removed to Chicago, presumably having sold his share of the business. In 1893, the firm of Aldrich and Wells appears to have expanded, and began advertising, something not done prior to William's departure.[33]

Their second child, a daughter Kathryn, was born in 1893. A posting about him in the Ballou Bulletin Board, a modern-day family association newsletter, notes that William worked

> in the food brokerage business for nearly sixty years. 1889 was a founder of firm of Ferrin and Ballou, Chicago; 1897 came to New York to open branch, but three years later entered business alone.[34]

William's future now centered on New York City, and if Laura preferred big-city living, she should have been happy, for he choose a prosperous area of New Jersey, East Orange, in which to make their home while he commuted into Lower Manhattan via railroad to work at a brokerage house that supplied grain and fruit internationally. William's office at 100 Hudson Street was a short six blocks from the Astor House and City Hall, three blocks from Broadway, and four blocks south of Canal—the location and route of his father's lying-in-state and funeral procession.

Meanwhile, Edgar must have remained in touch with his sister-in-law, May Hutchins Woodward: After their respective spouses died a few years apart, the two wed in January 1897.[35] Now the two brothers were married to two sisters. By all accounts, Edgar and May had a long and happy marriage. They had no children together but Edgar was an affectionate father to the three Woodward girls. A whole new chapter in his life opened up. His move back to the upper Midwest may date from this marriage.

Sarah had no reason to stay in Fall River on her own, so at an unknown date she returned to Rhode Island. She was now fifty-five years old and totally alone in the world, practically speaking. It was common for women to join together in setting up households where they could share the chores and more importantly, companionship. Sarah moved over twenty times in her life, and the only ones on record are those that can be documented either by a city directory or a census, which were compiled every five or ten years. During the 1890s, she may have moved more times than can be estimated, or she may have found a congenial arrangement and stayed put.

By the time of the 1900 federal census, Sarah was living with her friend, Mary Brownell, in Smithfield, and may have been there for some time, perhaps even during the great blizzard and hurricane of

An exceptionally fine image of Mary Brownell taken about forty years before Sarah went to live with her. *From author's collection.*

1897. Mary had for many years made a home for her elderly aunt, and once she passed away, there was room in Mary's spacious homestead estate for her good friend to join her. Over a hundred years old, its inventory revealed a home used to entertaining, with far more chairs and sofas, wineglasses and goblets, tables and light stands than the average house. Amid its many carpets, featherbeds, and counterpanes, the wealthy Brownell heiress lived in comfort, and kept her own carriage. A maid named Julia Shugrell from Ireland was employed, and twenty-five-year-old attorney, Everett Walling, boarded with them.

Sarah had a good friend and interesting companion in Mary, who

> was a woman of queenly presence and great grace of manner, of marked intellectuality, deeply interested in local history and possessed of a large amount of useful information. She loved life. She extended a generous and charming hospitality.

She was "very tall and a remarkably well proportioned woman with noble features," what was later called "statuesque." Judge Wilbur once noted the "finest looking couple he ever saw was in Louisville Kentucky when General Sherman walked across the hall with Miss Brownell on his arm." In later life, her beautiful wavy hair was a crown of white."

"Her very large circle of appreciative friends was young and old, rich and poor." No surprise for a woman described as a "large hearted and whole souled friend who loved to dispense good things." One year, she sent out seventy Christmas presents. "She was a true neighbor, helping in the joys of life and comforting in sickness; she lent herself to the lives of those about her." Before becoming an invalid in 1902, Mary had been very involved in club work, and she still received friends at home when feeling up to it. She was the "last of that distinguished coterie of women . . . women of rare intelligence and character."[36]

Census data normally follows strict protocols, but every once in a while, a census taker can be charmed into a candid notation. Sarah was not the respondent for this interview for the 1900 census, because her state of birth is incorrect, so perhaps it was Mary who was behind it, but under "occupation," the notation for Sarah Ballou was "lady of leisure." How nice for Sarah to at last be in that situation!

Her brother, John Shumway, had lived with his family in New Jersey for many years, but by 1892 they had moved to Philadelphia, where he worked as a laborer on the railroad, a harsh job for a man in his mid-fifties. John had the least professional situation of anyone in his generation within the Shumway or Ballou families. His application for a government pension indicated he had back trouble, and a significant loss of hearing, which he dated to his second attack of typhoid fever in the army. By the later part of the century, as the veterans aged, the U.S. government was besieged by pension requests from surviving Union veterans and their widows, and had established medical examining boards to review all cases. John was examined every two years, trying to increase his pension above fifteen dollars a month due to his hearing loss; he was deaf in both ears and could not hear anything unless it was yelled at him from under two feet away.[37] John's pension file has to be one of the largest at the National Archives, several hundred pages long, and contains results of medical exams which give even his pulse and blood pressure.

He had joined both army and navy veterans organizations, as well as a fraternal organization, the Order of Red Men, which dated from the Revolutionary War. All of these marched him to his grave in North Cedar Hill Cemetery on February 12, 1908, after one of the more unusual—but not unique to the Shumway family—deaths.* While walking to work on February 8, John's deafness caused him to fail to hear an approaching train of the

* John had a great-uncle who died the same way.

Philadelphia and Reading Railroad, which struck him. He died shortly afterward in a local hospital.[38]

His widow, Catherine, immediately applied to receive his pension to cover burial fees or her own expenses, as "my husband has left me very poor."[39] She spent the remaining twenty years of her life petitioning to receive the pension that stopped with his death, but the bureaucracy strangled her at every step, complaining she sometimes wrote her name with an *a* instead of an *e*, asserting she had not filed timely and no arrears were due her, or that his death was not related to his war injuries. Notaries, lawyers, the GAR Post pension committee, congressmen, and the Society for Organizing Charity wrote letters on her behalf. She herself even wrote to President Woodrow Wilson, noting that she was "starving" and had a "tubercular stomach," telling him her spirit guides had told her he would listen and help her get her fair due.[40] Her widowed life was especially dour; she was evicted one year on Easter, thrown out into the street. Working as a laundress to support herself, she lost a hand to a device aptly named a mangle, which wrung water out of clothes.[41]

She collapsed on the street of heart disease, and died in the hospital four weeks later. Although desperately poor when she died in 1928, Catherine Leahy Ballou had left the impression in her neighborhood, and with her landlord, that the government owed her a substantial sum of money. Accordingly, a decently middle-class funeral was held, and she was interred next to John. The government was duly petitioned, and the usual "no" came back, though the government sought to know how the undertaker was appointed.[42] Her landlord, the undertaker, and the lawyer that represented them both, got neither the back rent, $127 in funeral costs, nor the attorney's fees. It was, in all ways, a sad ending to the life story of a man who had served his country well but, like many veterans, never broke out of the cycle of poverty.

Mary Brownell died in 1907, and Aunt Sarah Ballou in 1908. By the time of the 1910 census, Sarah had joined William, his wife, and her granddaughter Kathryn at their home at 18 Winthrop Terrace, East Orange, New Jersey. Twenty-one-year-old Kathryn worked as a teacher.[43] At age seventy-five, Sarah was likely not as spry as she once was, but may have been able to enjoy a trip to nearby New York City, where the age of electricity had arrived—twenty blocks of Broadway were now lit with electrical advertising and already known as the Great White Way. But we may surmise that, in East Orange, Sarah lived out her days quietly, watching the world go by at a greater distance than before.

World War I had come and almost gone when Sarah succumbed to a major stroke on April 19, 1917. Her physician, Arthur Thompson, who had attended her since 1913, noted she suffered generally from arteriosclerosis, and his notes on her death certificate may mean that she had suffered prior strokes.[44] She also suffered the plight of old people who go to a strange town to retire with their children, and are away from the seat of their community involvement for some years before they die: Sarah had no obituary in any newspaper. A simple announcement in Providence, under "deaths," stated that she had passed away in New Jersey, that her funeral would be April 28 at Swan Point, upon the arrival of the "3 P.M. train from New York. Carriages will be at the station."[45] On that day, her mortal remains were laid next to those of her husband, though her spirit had already joined him nine days earlier in the reunion promised for fifty-six years.

Sarah H. Ballou
wife of
Major Sullivan Ballou
Died
April 19, 1917
Her 82nd Year

William promptly notified the Pension Office of her death, and pension number 25 was cancelled with a rubber stamp marked "dead," which took little note of the struggles of the woman who had received it for more than five decades.[46]

Although there was time to make the journey, it was unclear if Edgar was able to attend his mother's funeral. From 1904 through 1908, he and his family lived in Appleton, Wisconsin, where he was employed as a bookkeeper for the Hackworthy Construction company.[47] About 1911, Edgar moved his family to Sierra Madre, a community in the foothills of the Los Angeles basin in Southern California. He and May were affluent enough to spend part of their summers at the shore, in Long Beach. They built a charming and capacious two-story house on Ramona Street in this pleasant suburb of Pasadena in Los Angeles County where,

> after retiring from active business life, he acquired a lemon ranch in which he took keen interest. He also became closely identified with community affairs, serving as secretary of the Chamber of Commerce and as city clerk. His friends knew him as a man of ability and many fine qualities of character.

There were many echoes of the Civil War in southern California, and it became a destination for many former Yankee and Rebel soldiers. It is likely that, as a civic leader, Edgar Ballou knew and socialized with some of these veterans, now famous people, some of whom were intimately involved in the Civil War in the same months and places as his father.

This rural area also attracted many great men of the new century: Henry Ford, Luther Burbank, and Thomas Edison, among others. D. W. Griffith began the movie industry in Sierra Madre. Edgar, who was called Ned by his wife, and May had only to stroll from their house to watch the early movies being filmed.

Following Sarah's death, William continued his career as a

businessman. In 1917, his name could be found on the letterhead of Thompson, Conklin & Co., "Foreign and Domestic Brokers and Commission Merchants," with offices in New York and Liverpool, selling "Dried Fruits, Beans, Canned Goods, etc." Their office was at 100 Hudson Street.[48] In October 1921, after thirty-seven years of marriage, Laura Courtelyou Ballou died.[49] William decided to move, perhaps no longer needing the larger premises that had once housed his extended family.

About this time, something went very wrong in the relationship with William and his daughter, Kathryn, possibly related to his courtship of a someone who may have been a neighbor in Essex County, widowed around the same time he was, a woman named Doretta Ganley.[50] An American born of German parents, she had seven children, her youngest born the year Sarah died. In 1923, William moved into New York City; since this information was taken from his death certificate, there is no way to know if Kathryn went with him, but she dropped out of the Orange Directory for a while.

The family history book on the Ballou clan, *The Elaborate History of the Ballous,* listed Sullivan Ballou "junior," Uncle Henry's son, as working as a broker in New York City, without any details as to whether he was a fruit broker with William's firm, or a stockbroker. Sullivan Junior died in 1925.

The family bulletin said that William, in "1930 joined Steve Reggio Co., food brokers, 105 Hudson Street New York City, as office and sales manager."[51] By that year, he was living in multicultural Brooklyn, married to Doretta, whom he appeared to have wed no later than 1925. Four of her seven children, Frank, Edgar, Walter, and Marion, respectively twenty, eighteen, sixteen, and thirteen years old, lived with them in an upscale neighborhood near Prospect Park. Frank worked as an insurance clerk, Edgar as a grocery boy, and Walter as an insurance agent; Marion was still in school. In 1929, the United States entered the Great Depression,

William's last office was in this stylish Art Deco–style building. *Author's photo.*

William Ballou's last residence in Brooklyn on Avenue J. *Author's photo.*

when many persons could find no work, so it was quite an accomplishment to have so many family members working.[52] They paid eighty-five-dollars rent on their apartment in a forty-eight-unit apartment house at 11 Midwood Avenue near Prospect Park, a 526 acre oasis of green. Their neighbors were mostly native New Yorkers, some of Russian and German extraction who were working as insurance salesmen, a civil engineer, nurses, and business owners. William was then living just a few miles from the location where his great grandfather, Dr. Joseph Bowen, saved lives aboard the prison ship *Jersey* in the Revolutionary War.

In 1925, Kathryn, Sarah's granddaughter, lived at 260 Scotland Road, South Orange.* Her very pleasant upper-middle-class neighborhood was built out in large, two-story, single-family houses with gardens, in which she presumably boarded. Kathryn was then working as an accountant in New York City and could take the Orange Railroad into the city from the conveniently close Highland Avenue Station. Perhaps still objecting to Doretta, she had apparently opted not to join—or remain in—the boisterous household of her father, new stepmother, and teenaged stepsiblings. She remained in South Orange through 1930, still working at the same job. This is the last known listing for her there.[53] She next turns up eighteen years later, married to a man by the last name of Strachan, living in San Jose, California. There are Strachans in Essex County New Jersey, and perhaps she married one of them before moving west. She was at least forty at the time of her marriage, and there is no record she ever bore any children.

In 1931, the William Ballou family moved to 1818 J Street, on the other side of Prospect Park. A two-story, two-family house on a corner lot with a garage, this home was in a neighborhood of mostly single family homes. The Ballous are not listed as having

* Her house no longer stands; the area has been converted to retail and service businesses.

had a telephone throughout the thirties. William was able to commute to his job on Hudson Street by riding the BMT elevated subway line between Avenue J and Chambers Street.

In 1924, Edgar Ballou died suddenly and unexpectedly at the age of sixty-eight, possibly from appendicitis. Edgar has lived to twice the age of his father, although not the full life span of most of his family. A goodly, kind, religious man, he became, late in life, a civic-minded Ballou like his progenitors, and his passing was noted and mourned by many. His obituary in the local newspaper read,

> The sudden passing of Edgar F. Ballou . . . on Sunday came as a shock to the entire community. The end followed an operation for acute intestinal trouble performed Saturday night at the Pasadena hospital.
>
> Only a few days previously Mr. Ballou had been about town apparently in his usual health, and Mrs. Ballou and her daughters, the Misses Woodward, had gone to Long Beach for their summer stay. Consequently his many friends found it difficult to believe that he had really passed beyond.
>
> A beautiful twilight funeral service was held Wednesday afternoon at the home in the presence of a large circle of friends. The many floral offerings placed under the direction of Mr. Frank Monroe Smith testified to the high esteem in which Mr. Ballou was held.

Edgar was buried in an oasis of calm and green, the cemetery adjoining the grounds of the Episcopal Church of Our Savior, which has many Civil War burials, some with beautiful soldier-style sculptures.

Only one of Edgar's stepdaughters, Rena, married, to C. Lester Giddings of Los Angeles. Jean and Hazel lived on in the family home, nursing their mother until her death in 1929.

Jean focused her life around community work as an active member of St. Catherine's Guild at the Church of the Ascension Episcopal Church, but, of greater significance to this family, she was also on the board of directors of the Sierra Madre Red Cross. During both world wars, she was director of production for the local chapter and was subsequently honored with a fifty-year pin for continuous service.

By the time of the First World War, when Jean Woodward began her work with it in California, the Red Cross had 562 chapters and had provided assistance in the San Francisco earthquake, the Galveston Hurricane and the Cherry Mine disaster. Jean died October 29, 1960, at age seventy-two.

Hazel remained in touch with Ballou family members on the East Coast. It was her bits of information that allowed the trail of Edgar's later years to be followed. She did not die until August 12, 1974 at the age of eighty-nine, after a long illness. All of these family members rest together in the large family plot under the Ballou-Woodward headstone.

William continued to work at his job until his eighty-eighth birthday, when he retired. He continued to see the doctor who was his neighbor in his old neighborhood, Dr. Peter Shammon, who noted a decline in William's health. From not eating well, his weight dropped to 135 pounds, slim for a man who was 5' 11". Just after his eighty-ninth birthday, on January 20, 1948, William's doctor paid him one last visit at 10:00 A.M., and later that day, at 6:25 in the evening, William died from natural causes.[54]

Both of Sullivan's sons had lived to "honorable manhood." Even though Sullivan had never mentioned William as having blue eyes, the way he had exclaimed over Edgar's, the undertaker's records note that William, too, inherited his father's blue eyes. Now the last of them "went thither" to heaven to a reunion with their parents. Doretta Ballou signed paperwork with his undertaker to send William north; on January 24, he was buried in the family plot adjacent to Sarah and Sullivan's. Evidently, she lacked money for a headstone, for William's grave remains unmarked to the present day.[55]

William had made his last will in 1946, revoking previous wills, listing two survivors, his wife and daughter, and specifically excluding Doretta's children, whom he had not legally adopted. His attorney was appointed executor, and after paying his debts and final expenses, everything was left to Doretta. William had no real estate, owned a 1942 Packard Clipper Sedan, and had about $11,000 in bank accounts jointly held with Doretta. He also had an inheritance of $7,600 from his cousin, Jennie Mason Ballou of Woonsocket, who had predeceased him by two years. He held stocks of no value, and two gold watches, perhaps one of them Sullivan's.

A life insurance policy for $2,000 dollars was split evenly between his wife and daughter, and this provided the revelation of the degree of estrangement between William and Kathryn. When the executor attempted to notify Kathryn, the only address they had was the business office of her husband, in Burlingame, California. When the process server arrived, he declined to inform them where Kathryn was, indicated she would evade service, and provided them only with the name and address of her attorneys in New Jersey, who accepted the documents. Kathryn had walled herself off from her father. Another month went by before she signed documents to receive her $1,037, in San Mateo County, California.* Subsequently, she became widowed, and nothing more is known of her life or lifestyle, until she suffered a cerebral thrombosis that resulted in her being placed in the Grant Convalescent Home in Los Gatos, at an unknown date. About January 24, 1972, she had a second stroke; death followed on February 6.[56] The

* Because Kathryn's death certificate was filled out by people who did not know her history, it provides less information than usual. In 2010, when the 1940 census is released, it will be possible to learn more about her marriage.

public administrator handled her last arrangements, and she was cremated as an indigent on February 24. Her remains are still held in the receiving vault at Oak Hill Memorial Park, waiting for burial longer than her grandfather ever did.[57] Her death ended this branch of the Ballou clan, although more distantly related Ballous were now dispersed across America, like the Shumways. (Both clans keep in touch digitally through Web sites and e-mail, trying to reconstruct their genealogies.)

Given how many times Sarah moved, and her frail health in her last years, her possessions at the time of her death were most likely minimal. Whether she still kept with her a locket of dark hair and a packet of treasured letters—no one knows. The outlook for the survival of any of her personal papers is not good. William's own effects were likely dispersed, if not by Doretta, then by her son, Francis Ganley, when he cleared out her things.* If Kathryn Ballou had any of her grandmother's possessions, they were lost to the family with her transfer to the nursing home and subsequent death.

Sullivan's battlefield letters, all but the most famous, written in his hand, found their way into the possession of the Rhode Island Historical Society, which has no provenance for them. But especially because they are loving and effusive, Sarah may have kept these with her, and William might even have donated them when he returned her body to Swan Point. Enough other people sufficiently treasured the most famous of his love letters to her to have

* When Doretta died in Brooklyn in 1955, a bond of $2,000 covered her estate. All her daughters had married; her sons lived nearby. Francis died in 1989; Walter married Florence Bokowski, a Brooklynite of Czech-Polish descent, and they had two children. Edgar died in Brooklyn in 1983, apparently released from Mattawan State Hospital in Beacon, New York, a facility for the insane, where he was confined in 1955.

hand-copied them at least eight times over in the nineteenth century, and it is in this format they survived to delight modern audiences. A new copy turned up in an attic in Massachusetts while this book was being written.

Whether Sarah took the original to her grave with her is almost irrelevant. Her fifty-six-year wait was over, and those who believe in reunions on the other side may assuredly believe in this one. From their gravesite, in the cooler months when the leaves are off the trees, the waters of the river can be seen in the background, and sometimes the lucky visitor will see a pair of swans swimming together in the Seekonk. Swans also mate for life.

Notes

Abbreviations Used

ACR: *The Alabama Confederate Reader*

CCW: *Report of the Joint Committee on the Conduct of the War, in Three Parts,* (Washington, 1863)

CWDB: Civil War database at civilwardata.com

LDS: Family History Library, Church of the Latter Day Saints, Salt Lake City, Utah.

MNBP: Manassas National Battlefield Park

NARA: National Archives and Records Administration, Washington D.C.

NPS: National Park Service

OR: United States War Department. *War of the Rebellion, A Compilation of the Official Records of the Union and Confederate Armies.* 128 Volumes. Washington 1881–1902)

RIHS: Rhode Island Historical Society

VHS: Virginia Historical Society

All notes are reference only, with the exception of Chapter 1, note 7; Chapter 3 note 25; Chapter 8, note 83; Chapter 15, note 75; Chapter 18: 15; Chapter 21, notes 21 and 29; Chapter 25, note 19.

Introduction Tell My Wife Not to Grieve

1. Shakespeare, William, *Julius Caesar*, Act 2, scene 2.
2. Shakespeare, William, *Henry VI*, Part I, Act 1, Scene 1.
3. Sullivan Ballou, first letter to wife, July 14, 1861, manuscripts, RIHS.
4. Sullivan Ballou, second letter to wife, July 14, 1861, manuscripts, RIHS.

Chapter 1 Where the River Runs Like Silver

1. A Naval History of the American Revolution, tabulation of American resources, acceseds 30 December 2004 at www.americanrevolution.org/navapll.html.
2. "The Narrative of Captain [Master's Mate] Dring," from his *Recollections of Jersey Prison Ship.* (Morrisania, 1865), accessed 31 December 2004 at Http://www.accessgenealogy.com/scripts/data/database.cgi?file=Data&report=SingleArticle&ArticleID=0012010.
3. Ibid; "The Jersey" at http://www.longislandgenealogy.com/prison.html.
4. "A Wonderful Deliverance," extracted from Reverend Thomas Andros, "The Old Jersey Captive, or a Narrative of the Captivity of Thomas Andros." (Boston: 1833), accessed 30 December, 2004 at http://www.accessgenealogy.com/scripts/data/database.cgi?file=Data&report=Single Article&ArticleID=02021.
5. Dring.
6. *New Jersey Gazette* July 24, 1782.
7. Adin Ballou, *An Elaborate History and Genealogy of the Ballous in America*, (Providence, RI. By authors, 1888,) 2–4. At the time of his death, Mathurin left more than 81 acres to his family, in addition to his homestead of 25 acres. Equivalent land came to the family from Hannah's parents, the Pikes, and the most from an aunt who left them a large tract along the Massachusetts border.
8. Ibid. 9, 80.
9. Antoinette Forrester Downing, *Early Homes of Rhode Island*, (Richmond, VA.: Garret and Massie, 1937), 58.
10. Marian Klamkin, *The Return of Lafayette*, 1824–1825, (New York: Charles Scribner=s Sons, 1975), 25.

11. Ibid. 30.
12. Ibid. 30.
13. Adin Ballou, *History,* 505.
14. Ibid., 508.
15. Thomas M. Daniel, *Captain of Death: The Story of Tuberculosis,* (Rochester, N.Y.: University of Rochester Press, 1997), 93.
16. Ibid., 111, 120, 164.
17. Probate records for will of Hiram Ballou
18. Joseph Bowen, Will, Rhode Island Genealogical Register, Volume 9, Number 2, October 1968, 124.
19. Harriet Beecher Stowe, *Oldtown Folks,* (Boston 1869), 28, quoted by: Jane C. Nylander, *Our Own Snug Fireside, Images of the New England Home,* 1760–1860. (New Haven, CT: Yale University Press, 1994), page 41.
20. Ibid.
21. Adin Ballou, *History,* 508.
22. Sullivan Ballou, to wife, second letter of July 14, 1861, manuscript collection of the Rhode Island Historical Society, Providence Rhode Island.
23. Hiram Ballou, Will
24. Probate Court Record in association with Hiram Ballou will.
25. Ibid. 26. Catherine Clinton, *The Other Civil War, American Women in the Nineteenth Century,* (New York: Hill and Wang, 1984), 46-48, 90-91, 104.
27. Lydia Maria Child, *The Mother's Book,* (Boston: Carter and Hendee,1831), reprint edition (Bedford, MA.: Applewood Books, 1992.), 81.
28. Horatio Rogers Jr. "Sullivan Ballou," in *Brown University in the Civil War,* (Providence 1868), 94.
29. Ibid., 93.
30. Benjamin Greenleaf, A.M., *Introduction to the National Arithmetic, . . . Designed for Common Schools and Academies,* (Boston: Robert S. Davis & Co., 1876, fourth edition), 231.
31. "Public Speaking in An Outspoken Age, Oratory in 19th Century America," accessed 27 February, 2005 at www.assumption.edu/ahc/rhetoric/oratory.html.
32. Child, Mother's, passim.

Chapter 2 Whose Sons Are Foremost in Duty

1. Jabez Bowen biographies in: *Biographical Sketches of the Graduates of Yale College,* 1757, (New York: Henry Holt, 1907), 452-454;
2. Richard M. Bayles, *History of Providence County, Rhode Island, Volume 1,* (New York: W. W. Preston & Co., 1891), 266, accessed 14 September, 2004, at http://www.rootsweb.com/~rigenweb/article293.html. Hiram Ballou donation from Erastus Richardson, *History of Woonsocket* (Woonsocket: S. S. Foss, 1876), accessed 25 January 2005 at www.rootsweb.com/~rigenweb/article89.html.
3. Adin Ballou, *History,* 209; History of Cumberland in *History of the State of Rhode Island with Illustrations,* (Boston: Albert J. Wright, 1878), passim, accessed 25 April 2004 at http://www.rootsweb.com/~rigenweb/article251.html.
4. Tambora, accessed 1 January 2004 at http://volcano.und.edu/vwdocs/volc_images/southeast_asia/indonesia/tambora.html
5. Ibid.
6. Ibid.
7. John Williams Haley, "Great Gales," 179-181, *Stone Bank History of Rhode Island, Volume III,* (Providence, R.I.: Providence Institution for Savings, 1939), passim; Florence Simister, "The Hurricane of 1818," Streets of the City, WEAN broadcast. Script pages 261-262, undated. Typescript at RIHS.
8. Anthony Tully, "The Year Without a Summer (Tambora Volcano Part II)," accessed 3 January 2005 at www.indodigest.com/indonesia-special-article-20.html.
9. Adin Ballou, *History,* 22, 357, 498, 1050; Richardson, Woonsocket, 134-136.
10. Richardson, *Woonsocket,* passim.
11. Aimee Falardeau, Blackstone Valley Virtual Museum, "The Blackstone River: From Sewer to National Park," quoting Army Corps of Engineers, New England Division, Blackstone River Watershed Reconnaissance Study Volume 2 August 1997, accessed 6 May 2003 at www.bvlearnet.org.exhibits/home/river; Richardson, Woonsocket; Betty Buckley and Scott Nixon, University of Rhode Island, "A Historical Assessment of Anadromous Fish in the Blackstone River," accessed 6 June, 2004 at http://www.nbep.org/pubs/blackfish-hist.pdf.

12. Johnson, Elizabeth J and Wheaton, James Lucas, IV, *History of Pawtucket Reminiscences and New Series of Reverend David Benedict,* (Pawtucket, RI:, Spaulding House Publications, 1986), 13.
13. John Williams Haley, "Cotton and Rhode Island," 172-175, *Stone Bank History of Rhode Island, Volume III,* passim; "The Cotton Gin's Impact on the Cotton Industry," accessed 17 January 2005 at inventors.about.com/cs/inventorsalphabet/a/cotton_gin_2.htm,.
14. "The Cotton Gin's Impact on the Cotton Industry," accessed 17 January at 200inventors.about.com/cs/inventorsalphabet/a/cotton_gin_2.htm, 5.
15. Records of the Probate Court of Cumberland, Rhode Island November 4, 1839, 425, 442,448-9 microfilm at LDS Library, Salt Lake City.
16. Rogers Jr., 94.
17. Whitney R. Cross, *The Burned-Over District; the Social and Intellectual History of Enthusiastic Religion in Western New York,* 1800-1850 (Ithaca, NY: Cornell University Press, 1950), passim.
18. Alexander Campbell, *Delusions: An Analysis of the Book of Mormon,* (Boston: 1832), 13 and passim.
19. C. Clark Julius, "Biography of Joseph Smith," accessed 18 December 2004 at http://www.lds-mormon.com/jsmith.shtml.
20. Rogers Jr., 94.
21. Noah J. Arnold, "The History Of Suffrage In Rhode Island," *The Narragansett Historical Register,* Volume VIII. July 1890. No. 2, 305–331, accessed 29 December 2003 at http://www.rootsweb.com/~rigenweb/article229.html; Jane Lancaster, "The Battle at Chepachet: An Eyewitness Account," *Rhode Island History,* RIHS Volume 62 Number 1, Winter Spring 2004, 19.
22. Christopher Robinson, letters to Thomas Dorr, March 6, 1834 and August 29, 1835, in the Manuscripts collection of the Brown University Library.
23. Noah J. Arnold, "Suffrage."
24. Adin Ballou, *History,* 545.
25. Noah J. Arnold, "Suffrage."
26. Richardson, 115; Woonsocket Guards, Resolution on the Death of Sullivan Ballou, manuscripts at RIHS.
27. Edward Field quoted in John Williams Haley, "The Call to Arms," 119-121, *Stone Bank History of Rhode Island, Volume III,* (Providence, R.I.: Providence Institution for Savings, 1939), 120.
28. *Records of the Colony of Rhode Island and Providence Plantations in New England, printed 1862, Volume 7, June 1775.*
29. Rounders/Townball accessed on May 5, 2002, at www.chaosmedia.com/Rounder/Rounders-Docs.html and "The Doubleday Myth" at www.hickoksports.com/history/doubleday.shtml.
30. "Catalogue of the Officers and Students of Nichols Academy, Worcester, MA 1847", archives collection of the Henry J. Howland Conant Library, Nichols College, Dudley MA.
31. Wilson's Arte of Rhetorique 1560. Ed. G. H. Mair. Oxford: Clarendon Press, 1909
32. Ibid.
33. "American Eloquence" published in the *United States Democratic Review,* July 1854, accessed 25 April 2005 at http://cdl.library.cornell.edu/cgi-bin/moa/moa-cgi?notisid=AGD1642-0034-7.
34. Walt Whitman, Prose Works, 1892, V. November Boughs, "Father Taylor and Oratory" Accessed 24 April at http://www.bartleby.com/229/5003.html.
35. Nichols Academy Catalogue 1845-1846, (Worcester, MA: T. Whittemore Butterfield, 1846), Conant Library, Nichols Academy, Dudley, MA.
36. Rogers Jr., 94.
37. Nichols Academy Catalog.
38. Ibid.
39. St. Paul's Episcopal Church Web site accessed 2 January 2003at www.stpaulspawtucket.org/history.html.
40. Robert Grieve, *An Illustrated History of Pawtucket, Central Falls and Vicinity,* (Pawtucket, R.I. Pawtucket Gazette and Chronicle 1897), 181.
41. Ibid.
42. Harvey Strum, "Not Forgotten in Their Affliction:" Irish Famine Relief from Rhode Island, 1847 *Rhode Island History* RIHS Volume 60 Number 1 Winter 2002 27-31.
43. American Eloquence.

Chapter 3 Whose Daughters Are Peerless and Bright

1. Biographical records of Amherst students accessed 13 June 2001 at www.amherst.edu/~riyanco/genealogy/acbiorecord/menu.html; Amherst College catalog and student lists accessed same date at http:/clio.fivecolleges.educ/Amherst/catalogs/; John Shook,

Union College at "American Professors of Philosophy and Theology," accessed 7 February 2005 at www.pragmatism.org/amreican/American_professors.htm.

2. Graduates of Auburn Theological Seminary, 36. Fax from Auburn Alumni office.
3. "About Auburn," and "Historical Highlights," accessed 8 February 2005 at www.auburnsem.org/about/history.asp.
4. The Root of American Religious Liberty Roger Williams accessed on 12 December 2004 at www.churchandstate.us/church-state/wm-cot1a.htm; Elisha Potter, Memoir concerning the French Settlements of the Colony of Rhode Island (Providence: S. S. Rider 1879.) reprint (Baltimore: Genealogical Publishing Company, 1968), 5.
5. Alistair, Horne, *Seven Ages of Paris,* (New York: Alfred Knopf, 2002),79.
6. Franklin Bowditch Dexter,"John Hart Fowler," in *Biographical Sketches of the Graduates of Yale College, Vol. IV, July 1778–June 1792,*) (New York: Henry Holt, 1907), 666.
7. Biography of Daniel Waldo, Chaplain, Centenarian, accessed 7 February 2005, at www.geocities.com/Heartland/Fields/4791/danielwaldo.html.
8. Marriage Record in Vital Records of Saybrooke, CT accessed at Genealogy.com; "Sidney," accessed 7 February, 2005 at www.sidneychamber.org/history.htm.
9. Graduates of Auburn fax from Alumni Office at Auburn.
10. Arthur Goodenough, *The Clergy of Litchfield County,* (NC: Litchfield County University Club, 1988), 236. "Washington," in: *Nathan and Varney's Massachusetts Gazetteer,* 1890, accessed 21 March 2005 at www.capecodhistory.us/Conn1890/Washington1890.htm; "About Washington," accessed 8 February 2005 at www.washingtoct.org.about.html.
11. Child, *Mother's,* 10.
12. Carolyn J. Lawes, *Women and Reform in a New England Community, 1815–1860,* (Lexington: University of Kentucky Press 2000), 13.
13. Ithamar B. Sawtelle, *History of Townsend,* (Published by author 1878), 151.
14. Lawrence Academy pamphlet on benefactor Eliel Shumway, Lawrence Academy, (Groton MA 1913) collection of the American Antiquarian Society, Worcester, MA.
15. Sawtelle; Townsend Vital Records, 1836-37.
16. Sawtelle, 151.
17. Lawes 23, 13
18. Sawtelle.
19. Email from Rev. Susan Horgan, Petersham Orthodox Congregational Church, Received 22 March 2005. "Petersham," in: *Nathan and Varney's Massachusetts Gazetteer,* 1890, accessed 21 March 2005 at www.capecodhistory.us/Mass1890/Petersham1890.htm; www.firstparishpetersham.com/history/html accessed 21 March 2005.
20. Lawes, 4.
21. Lawes 95.
22. Notes on household Life Displays at the Merchant House Museum in New York City.
23. Dan Huntington biography in the Porter-Phelps-Huntington family papers at Amherst College Archives and Special Collections accessed on 7 February 2005 at www.amherst.edu/libary/arhcives/findingadis/pph/descript2.html.
24. Ledger Book of Worcester, MA, death records for 1845, manuscripts, American Antiquarian Society, Worcester, MA.
25. Probate records state he died intestate.
26. Probate Court Proceedings in re Columbus Shumway, Massachusetts Trial Court Record Center Case 53327 Reference ID number 73724 Location EB 101 017-002-0006-0006.
27. Lawes, 98.
28. Robert Doherty, *Society and Power, Five New England Towns, 1800–1860* (Amherst: University of Massachusetts Press, 1977) 31. Quoted in Lawes, 30.
29. Christine Stansall, *City of Women: Sex and Class in New York, 1789–1960* (Urban, IL.: University of Illinois Press, 1982), Appendix A Table 9. Quoted in Lawes, 133.
30. Lawes, 5.
31. Reverend Thomas Wentworth Higginson, "Women and the Alphabet: A Series of Essays," (Boston and New York: Houghton Mifflin Company, 1881), accessed 27 March 2005 at www.wwhp.org/Resources/righsworceseter.html.
32. "Why Worcester?" an excerpt from Worcester Women's Heritage Trail, (Worcester Women's History Project: 2005), accessed 22 July 2004 at www.wwhp.org/resources/whyworcester.html.
33. Lawes, 73–75.
34. *Worcester City Directory, 1845–1851,* (Worcester: Henry J. Howland, annually).

35. Child, *Mother's,* 58–59.
36. Ibid., 21.
37. Ibid., 19.
38. Ibid., 42.
39. Lawes, 48-49.
40. Lawes, 11.
41. Lawes, 55.
42. Lawes, 75.
43. Lawes, 54.
44. Lawes, 51.
45. Child, Mother's, 20.

Chapter 4 Joy Was in His Mild Blue Eyes

1. Biographical note on John Walcott Fowler on Ancestry.com.
2. *Ballston Journal,* 20 August, 1850.
3. *Poughkeepsie Press* 1852.
4. "Centennial History of Ballston Spa" p 93 and French, J. H. Gazetteer of the State of New York (Syracuse, N.Y.: R. Pearsall Smith, 1860), 274-5.
5. *Poughkeepsie Press* 1852.
6. Rev. H. Ludlow letter to Sarah Shumway Ballou, 1856. Sarah Ballou pension file.
7. Diploma from Cherry Valley Academy, Cherry Valley Library.
8. Cherry Valley Academy catalog passim.
9. Lawes, 99.
10. Reverend Theodore Parker Sermon On the Ideal Public Function of Women, accessed 5 March 2005 at http://www.vcu.edu/engweb/transcendentalism/authors/parker/parkeronwomen.html
11. Lawes 169.
12. Ibid. 166.
13. Report of the Worcester Female Employment Society, Presented by the Executive Board at the Second Annual Meeting, October 12, 1857 (Worcester, Mass.: Henry J. Howland, 1857), 4, 5, 8, 11, 7, quoted in Lawes, 178.
14. Child, Mother's 62.
15. Ibid. 62, 95, 88.
16. Andover Catalogue and Web site accessed 27 January 2005 at www.andovoer.educ/ about_andover/ notable_alums.htm.
17. Andover Catalog 7, 8, 13, 24,
18. "A Barrel on a Pitchfork," recollections of graduate Horace Eaton, accessed 10 March 2005 at www.andover.edu/about_andover
19. Ibid.
20. Rogers Jr., 94.
21. Brown University, Library Records, archives.
22. Rogers Jr,. 95.
23. National Law School Catalogue, collection of the Free Library of Philadelphia.
24. Whitman, Father Taylor.
25. American Eloquence.
26. Ibid.
27. Ibid.
28. Ibid. and Rogers Jr. on Sullivan Ballou, 95.
29. Rogers Jr., 95-96.
30. Woonsocket's Original Mill Villages accessed 11 Janaury 2003 at www.woonsocket.org/ village.htm and/owners.htm.
31. National Law School Catalogue
32. Rogers Jr., 95–96.
33. Thornwell, 149.
34. *Star* November 25.
35. Antebellum North Carolina: A Social History, Electronic Edition Guion Griffis Johnson, http://docsouth.unc.educ/nc/johnson/chapter7.html.
36. Parker Sermon.
37. Thornwell, 132,.
38. Lawes, 41.

39. Johnson, Antebellum
40. Thornwell, 145
41. Ibid.
42. Parker Sermon
43. *Official Gazetteer of Rhode Island,* listing for Woonsocket, email from RIGENWEB list.
44. *Catalog of the Carrington Library* (Woonsocket, R.I. Samuel Foss, 1854), manuscripts at RIHS.
45. Interview with Tom Shanahan, Valley Falls librarian; extracted from analysis of the state record books at RI State Archives.

Chapter 5 Our Lovings Prospered Well

1. Sullivan Ballou letter to wife, 1858, manuscripts, RIHS.
2. Richardson, *Woonsocket.*
3. Barbara Lesko, "Rhode Island & Its Role In American Egyptology," KMT: *A Modern Journal Of Ancient Egypt,* Volume 9 Number 3 Fall 1998.
4. Thornwell, Emily, *The Lady's Guide to Perfect Gentility, in Manners, Dress, and Conversation, in the Family, in Company, at the Piano Forte, The Table, in the Street, and in Gentlemen's Society. Also a Useful Instructor in Letter Writing, Toilet Preparations, Fancy Needlework, Millinery, Dressmaking, Care of Wardrobe, the Hair, Teeth, Hands, Lips, Complexion, etc.* (New York: Derby and Jackson, 1856.). 118, accessed 27 March 2005 at www.wwhp.org/Resources/Thornwell_lady_s_guide.html.
5. Sullivan Ballou to wife, June 26, 1861, manuscripts, RIHS.
6. Federal Census, 1860, Woonsocket, Rhode Island.
7. Sullivan Ballou, letter to wife, June 26, 1861, manuscripts, RIHS.
8. Sullivan Ballou, letter to wife, July 10, 1861, manuscripts, RIHS.
9. Sullivan Ballou, letter to wife, July 10, 1861, manuscripts, RIHS.
10. Sullivan Ballou, letter to wife, June 20, 1861, manuscripts, RIHS.
11. Charles A. Mills, *Love, Sex And Marriage In The Civil War* (Alexandria, VA.: Apple Cheeks Press, 1995), 13.
12. Carol K. Bleser, and Lesley J. Gordon, *Intimate Strategies of the Civil War, Military Commanders and Their Wives,* letters of Thomas J. Jackson to Mary Anna Jackson, (Oxford: Oxford University Press, 2001), 56-59.
13. Sullivan Ballou, letter to wife, July 14, 1861, manuscripts, RIHS.
14. Horatio Rogers, "Sullivan Ballou", a biography in *Brown University in the Civil War, a Memorial* (Providence, 1868), 97.
15. Ibid., and Bayles, *History of Providence County,* Chapter III, The Bench and Bar.
16. Sullivan Ballou, various letters to wife, manuscripts at RIHS.
17. George Opdyke, *Treatise on Political Economy,* 1851. accessed 17 November 2003 at http://cdl.library.cornell.edu/cgi-bin/moa/moa-cgi?notisid=AGD1642-0028-200.
18. Frederick Law Olmsted, *The Cotton Kingdom,* (New York: Mason Brothers, 1861), first published as a series of letters to the *New York Times,* 1853, 422-436; (Web site 4, 6.) Accessed 3 December 2003 at http://history.sandiego.edu/gen/civilwar/02/olmsted.html.
19. Ibid.
20. Senator James Henry Hammond, "On the Admission of Kansas Under the Lecompton Constitution," speech before the United States Senate, 4 March, 1858, accessed 10 May 2004 at www.sewanee.edu/faculty/Willis/Civil_War/documents/Hammond/Cotton.html.
21. American Eloquence, 46.
22. Hammond speech.
23. Sullivan Ballou, Letter to Latimer Ballou, June 11, 1861, manuscripts at RIHS.
24. Sullivan Ballou, Letter to Sarah Ballou, 1858, manuscripts at RIHS.
25. Catherine Martin Larkin, (What was Pawtucket Like 100 Years Ago? (1928, 5 Accessed 3 February 2004 at www.rootsweb.com/~rigenweb/Pawtucket100years.html.
26. Senator Charles Sumner, "Crimes Against Kansas," speech to the Senate, May 19-20, 1856, 2. Accessed on 26 February 2003 at History 367, American Civil War, University of Puget Sound Web site. http://www.anselm.edu./academic/history/hudbrulle/CivWar/text/documents/doc13/htm.
27. Donald, David, *Charles Sumner and the Coming of the Civil War* (New York: Alfred A. Knopf, 1967)
28. Ibid.
29. Ibid., 298.

30. "The Caning of Charles Sumner," Secession Era Editorials Project, accessed 15 January 2003 at http://history.furman.edu/~benson/docs/sumenu.htm
31. Ibid.1. Donald, p 289
32. Sumner, "Crimes Against Kansas,"
33. Donald, Chapter 7 passim
34. Ibid.
35. Abraham Lincoln, quoted in Shelby Foote, *The Civil War, A Narrative, Vol. 1 Secession to Fort Henry* (Alexandria, VA,: Time Life Books, 1998), 47.

Chapter 6 We Live in Hard and Stirring Times

1. Elbert B. Smith, *The Presidency of James Buchanan* (Lawrence, Kansas: The University Press of Kansas, 1975), 23.
2. Sullivan Ballou, letter to wife, letter of July 3, 1861, manuscripts at RIHS.
3. Sullivan Ballou, letter to wife, letter of July 19, 1861, manuscripts at RIHS.
4. Abraham Lincoln, "House Divided Speech," Springfield, Illinois, June 16, 1857.
5. Sullivan Ballou, to wife, second letter of July 14, 1861, manuscripts at RIHS
6. Sullivan Ballou, letter to wife, 1858.
7. Ibid.
8. Email to author from Bill Kibby-Johnson, expert on nineteenth-century pianos, (uk-piano.org) January 15, 2003; Survey of various contemporary ads for pianos by author.
9. Bayles, Chapter III, Bench and Bar, passim.
10. Michael Simoncelli, "Battling the Enemies of Liberty: The Rise and Fall of the Rhode Island Know-Nothing Party," *Rhode Island History,* Volume 54, Number 1, February, 1996 RIHS, 5.
11. Bureau of the Census, 1860 Federal Census for Rhode Island, Cranston, microform edition, entry for the Sullivan Ballou family, 261.
12. State of Rhode Island General Assembly. House of Representatives, May 1857, Ledger Version, *Meets and Resolves,* Rhode Island State Archives, Providence, Rhode Island.
13. History of the Rhode Island General Assembly, passim, accessed 17 April 17, 2000 at www.rilin.state.ri/studteaguide/genhist.html.
14. State of Rhode Island, General Assembly, House of Representatives, "Rules and Regulations to be Observed in the House of Representatives of the State of Rhode Island and Providence Plantations," accessed 8 March, 2003 at memory.loc.gov/cgi-in/ampage?collID=rbpe& fileName=rbpe17/rbpe171/17101600/rbpe1710600.db.
15. Rogers Jr., 97.
16. State of Rhode Island, General Assembly, House of Representatives, "Rules and Regulations to be Observed in the House of Representatives of the State of Rhode Island and Providence Plantations."
17. State of Rhode Island General Assembly. House of Representatives, May 1857, Ledger Version, *Meets and Resolves,* Rhode Island State Archives, Providence.
18. Ibid.
19. Rogers Jr., 97.
20. State of Rhode Island General Assembly. House of Representatives, May 1857, Ledger Version, *Meets and Resolves,* Rhode Island State Archives, Providence.
21. Ramona, E. Pekarek, America on the Brink of Civil War, Kenneth Stampp's *America in 1857,* Summary of Chapter 12, accessed 14 January 2003 at httpl://carbon.cudenver.educ/~rpekarek/Stampp12.html.
22. David M. Potter, *The Impending Crisis,* 1848–1861 (New York: Harper & Row, 1976), 466.
23. Ibid. 467.
24. From an anecdote formerly located on the Exeter Web site at http://library.exeter.edu/dept/Archives/chron.html. When the first Black student was admitted in 1858, several Southern students withdrew from the college.
25. "Panic of 1857," accessed 10 January 10, 2003 at www.harwich.edu/depts/history/pp/ahh13/tsld040.htm;.
26. Ibid.
27 "S. S. Central America," accessed January 14, 2003, available from www.shipofgoldinfo.com/journey.html and shipofgoldinfo.com/disaster.html.
28. Catherine Martin Larkin, "What was Pawtucket Like 100 Years Ago?" 1928, 5, accessed 15 February 2003 at www.rootsweb.com/~rigenweb/Pawtucket100years.html.
29. Thomas H. O'Connor, *Lords of the Loom, The Cotton Whigs and the Coming of the Civil War,* (New York: Charles Scribner's Sons, 1968), 126.

30. Potter, 43.
31. Ibid.
32. Ibid.
33. State of Rhode Island, General Assembly. House of Representatives, May 1857, Ledger Version, *Meets and Resolves,* Rhode Island State Archives, Providence.
34. Death Ledger, Pawtucket, 1858.
35. Death Notices, Pawtucket *Gazette and Chronicle,* April 30, 1858, 3.
36. John Russell Bartlett, *Memoirs of Rhode Island Officers* (Providence: Sidney S. Rider & Brother, 1867), 250.
37. Rogers, 97.
38. James Fenimore Cooper, *The Last of the Mohicans.* Internet; accessed 2003
39. Tom Standage, *Victorian Internet* (New York: Berkeley Books, 1999), 74–91.
40. Sullivan Ballou letter to wife, 1858, manuscripts at RIHS.
41. Bayles, *History of Providence County Volumes I and II* (New York: W. W. Preston and Co. 1891), 31-34.
42. Sullivan Ballou letter to wife, 1858, manuscripts at RIHS.
43. Sharon Ann Murphy, "Life Insurance in the United States through World War I," 1–8, accessed 14 January 2003 at www.eh.net.encyclopedia/murphy.life.insurance.us.php.
44. Sullivan Ballou letter to wife, 1858.
45. Standage, 74–91.
46. Johnston, Elizabeth J and Wheaton, James Lucas, IV *History of Pawtucket Reminiscences and New Series of Reverend David Benedict,* Pawtucket, RI,: (Spaulding House Publications, 1986), 243; Providence Journal, November 5, 1858.
47. Mary Chesnut, *A Diary from Dixie,* (New York: Portland House, 1977), 130, 142-143.
48. "Law Professor Shines Light on Mrs. Dred Scott," accessed 3 May 2003 at http://www.uiowa.edu/~fyi/oldfyi/issues97-98/022798web/law_022798.html.
49. The role of the Chace and Buffum families is discussed at The Phillips History of Fall River, accessed 4 February 2003 at http://www.sailsinc.org/durfee/phillips3-15.pdf.
50. Chuck Arnig, National Park Service Ranger and Underground Railroad expert, quoted in the *Providence Journal,* accessed 11 March 2003 at www.projo.com/cgi-bin/include.pl/seasonal/blackhistory/underground/prails.htm.

Chapter 7 Our Cause Is Just and Holy

1. Kris Van den Bosche, *Please Excuse All Bad Writing, A Documentary History of Rhode Island During the Civil War Era.* Letter of Eliza Lanphear Colvin to Sarah Lanphear, May 3, 1857; pamphlet, (Peace Dale, R.I.: Rhode Island Historical Document Transcription Project. 1993), 19.
2. Rogers Jr., 97.
3. The State Houses of Rhode Island, (Providence, R.I.: Rhode Island Historical Society, 1988), 35- 41.
4. Sullivan Ballou, "Report of the Joint Special Committee on the Title of the State to Lands in the Woonasquatucket Valley," (Providence, Rhode Island: Public Park Association; Providence Press Company, 1884), 3.
5. Ibid.
6. Bartlett, *Rhode Island Officers,* 250.
7. Horatio Rogers, "Sullivan Ballou," a biography in Brown University in the Civil War, a Memorial (Providence, 1858), 97.
8. Legal Fees in the 1850's from the "Descendants of Caleb Baron," accessed 19 April 2003 at www.freepages.genealogy.rootsweb.com~jcbarron/BarronCalbe.htm; www.Lydsander Spooner.org/BIOch7.htm, same date; Shelby Foote, *The Civil War, A Narrative, Vol. 1 Secession to Fort Henry,* (Alexandria, VA, Time Life Books, 1998).
9. Rogers Jr., 97.
10. National Park Service, "Thomas Jefferson at Harper's Ferry," Harper's Ferry National Historical Park Web site, accessed 8 March 2003 at www.nps.gov/hafe/jeffrock.htm.
11. Stephen Vincent Benet, John Brown's Body, available from www.smithsonianmag.si.edu/smithsonian/issues97/aug97/object_aug97.html.
12. John Brown's Raid accessed 3 Febraury 2004 at http://www.civilwarhome.com/johnbrown.htm.
13. "Secession Era Editorials Project," 1-6, accessed 15 January 2003 at http://history.furman.edu/~benson/docs/jbmenu.htm.
14. *Providence Journal,* October 20, 1859.

15. John Michael Ray, "Rhode Island Reactions to John Brown's Raid," *Rhode Island History,* October 1961, Vol. 20 No. 4, 101–103.
16. Ibid., 103.
17. Thomas J. Jackson, wartime letter to Mary Anna Jackson, accessed on 3 February 2005 at www.civilwarhome.com/johnbrown.htm,
18. Rogers Jr., 97.
19. Potter, 386–389.
20. Elbert Smith, *Buchanan,* 57–58
21. Sullivan Ballou, "Report of the Joint Special Committee on the Title of the State to Lands in the Woonasquatucket Valley," (Providence, Rhode Island: Public Park Association; Providence Press Company, 1884), 9.
22. Ibid, 11,30,27.
23. Ibid. 32-36.
24. William E. Baringer, and Earl Schenck Miers, Ed. In Chief. *Lincoln Day by Day A Chronology 1809-1865. Vol. II 1861.* (Washington: Lincoln Sesquicentennial Commission, 1960), 265, 273.
25. Ibid., 274–275.
26. Kelsey Ballou Sweatt, "Abraham Lincoln in New England," Address in Woonsocket, 1928, printed document in manuscripts, John Hay Library, Brown University, Providence, R.I.
27. Ibid.
28. Baringer and Miers, 274–275; *Providence Journal* March 8, 1860.
29. Sweatt.
30. Ibid.
31. Florence Parker Simister, *Streets of the City,* "Abraham Lincoln and Providence," Book 1, 204, and Volume Two, June 1, 1953-May 28, 204-5, scripts of radio broadcasts on WEAN radio station, Providence, library of RIHS; Baringer and Miers, 274-275.
32. Ibid.; Sweatt.
33. Latimer Ballou, Introductory Remarks Welcoming Abraham Lincoln and Audience, quoted in Sweatt; also notation about 1500 in audience and "packed to suffocation;" Simmister, Streets of the City, "Lincoln and Providence," 204-5. .
34. Abraham Lincoln, "Address at the Cooper Institute," New York City, February, 27 1859, 5/paragraph 56, available from wysiwyg://48/http://douglassarchives.org.linc_a89.htm; Internet; accessed January 15, 2003.
35. Ibid., paragraph 13.
36. Ibid., paragraph 69.
37. Ibid., paragraph 49.
38. Ibid., paragraphs 62–65.
39. Ibid., paragraph 69.
40. Sweatt, and *Providence Sunday Journal Magazine* clipping, "Lincoln in Rhode Island," no date, in the card file/Rhode Island History collection at the Providence Public Library, main branch, Providence, Rhode Island; Simister, "Abraham Lincoln and Providence,"
41. Baringer and Miers, II, 276.
42. Richardson, *Woonsocket,* 94.
43. Bayles, *History of Providence County,* 48.
44. Providence Neighborhood Profiles, 2, accessed January 7, 2003 at.www.providenceri.com Neighborhoods/elmwood.html.
45. Rhode Island Historical Preservation Commission, "Statewide Historical Preservation Report, Elmwood, Providence, P-P-3" (Providence: June, 1979), 13.
45. Rhode Island Historical Preservation Commission, "Statewide Historical Preservation Report, Elmwood, Providence, P-P-3" (Providence: June, 1979), 13.
46. Cranston, Rhode Island, Town Records, Deed Book No. 40, 379 and Book 3, 479. Microfilm, Library of the Church of the Latter Day Saints, Salt Lake City, Utah; Sullivan Ballou letters to wife, June 30 and July 3, 1861.
47. Bureau of the Census, 1860 Federal Census, Rhode Island.
48. Cranston, Rhode Island, Town Records, Council Meeting April 2, 1861, Microfilm, Library of the Church of the Latter Day Saints, Salt Lake City, Utah.
49. Letter from Seth Padelford containing donation for Free Kansas cause accessed 29 September 2004 at http://www.territorialkansasonline.org/cgiwrap/imlskto/index.php?SCREEN=show_document&document_id=102434&SCREEN_FROM=keyword&selected_keyword=Finance&startsearchat=0&PHPSESSID=0973cefe6ba670859153b9b0cd351be0

50. State of Rhode Island, Election Returns, Report of Special Committee Approved to Count the Votes for General Officers 1861, C#00171, Rhode Island State Archives, also email from Ken Carlson at the State Archives.
51. Patrick T Conley, and Paul Campbell, *Providence, A Pictoral History.* (Norfolk, VA: The Donning Company, 1986), Chapter 6.
52. Potter, 440.
53. Ibid., 405-414.
54. Ibid.
55. Ibid.
56. Potter, 407; Yanek Mieczkowski, *The Routledge Historical Atlas of Presidential Elections.* (New York: Routledge, 2001), 52-54.
57. Potter, 428; Mieczkowski, 52-54.
58. Potter, 427.
59. "Address of the Republican State Central Committee to the Electors of Rhode Island," accessed 2003 at www.memory.loc.gov.
60. "The Republican Platform of 1860," accessed 15 January 2003 at wysisyg://30/http://douglassarchives.orgrepu_b19.htm; 1–4.
61. Potter, 424.
62. Murat Halstead quoted in Donald E. Reynolds, *Editors Make War: Southern Newspapers in the Secession Crisis,* (Nashville, TN, Vanderbilt University Press, 1966), 59.
63. Atlas of U. S. Elections, accessed 23 February 2004 at www.uselectionatlas.org/USPRESIDENT/GENERAL/pe1860data.html.
64. PBS program Web site, *The West* accessed 3 February 2005 at http://www.pbs.org/weta/thewest/program/episodes/two/westwardfree.htm.
65. *Spartanburg Carolina Spartan* quoted in Reynolds, 78.
66. Abraham Lincoln to Samuel Galloway, June 19, 1860 in Basler, ed, *Works of Lincoln IV,* 80. quoted in Potter, 434.
67. Bayles, *Providence County,* 28–30.
68. Rogers Jr., 46.
69. Mieczkowski, 53.
70. Phillip Van Doren Stern, ed., *The Life and Writings of Abraham Lincoln,* (New York: The Modern Library, 1940), 599.
71. Reynolds, 125.
72. Reynolds, 58, 94.
73. Reynolds, 94, 127.
74. Reynolds, 58, 127.
75. James Heintze, "Fourth of July Dinners Prior to the Civil War," 2, accessed 26 March 2003 at www.american.edu/heintze/dinner.htm;.
76. Shelby Foote Interview on CSpan, 2002.
77. Brayton Harris, *Blue and Grey and Black and White: Newspapers in the Civil War.* (Washington D.C., Brassey's, 2000.), 23.
78. Potter, 442–443.
79. Reynolds, 40.
80. Edith Ellen Ware, *Political Opinion in Massachusetts During the Civil War and Reconstruction.* (New York: AMS Press, 1968,) 40.
81. Klein, *Days of Defiance, Sumter, Secession and the Coming of the Civil War* (New York: Vintage Civil War Library, 1999) 164.
82. "The Union Saved," *Harrisburg, PA, Telegraph,* November 7, 1860, accessed on 14 May 2003 The Valley of the Shadow Project Web site at www.iath.virginia.edu/vshadow2/articles/hburg.nd60.html.
83. Reynolds, 149.
84. Ibid. 141.
85. Potter, 445.
86. Shelby Foote, *The Civil War, A Narrative,* Vol. 1 Secession to Fort Henry. (Alexandria, VA, Time Life Books, 1998.)
87. Nylander, 271–273.
88. Nylander, 262-264 quoting various contemporary newspapers.
89. James Buchanan, "State of the Union Address", U.S. Congress, December 3, 1860, 1-3; 90. Buchanan, State of the Union Address, U.S. Congress, December 3, 1860, 19, 20, 22;1.

91. Reynolds, 141.
92. Reynolds, 150.
93. *Richmond Enquirer,* December 25, 1860, accessed on 14 May 200 at www.iath.virginia.edu/vshadow2/articles/rich.nd60.html.
94. Klein, 164.

Chapter 8 The President Called on the Land for an Army

1. James Chester, Inside Sumter in '61, in *Battles and Leaders of the Civil War Volume I,* (reprint: Edison, N.J.: Castle, no date. Original, 1897), 55-56.
2. Baringer and Miers, 3.
3. Ware, 65.
4. Baringer and Miers, 3, quoting CW IV 170-1.
5. Potter, 559.
6. Potter, 390.
7. Baringer and Miers, 3.
8. Potter, 497-504.
9. Ware, 65.
10. Potter, 478, 490.
11. Christopher Memminger letter to John Rutherford, November 27, 1860; Howell to "My Judge" November 11, quoted in Shanning, *Crisis of Fear,* 283–248, quoted in Potter, 501.
12. Potter, 493.
13. Ibid., 479.
14. In Louisiana, the counties dominated by the large sugar planters favored secession; these outpolled the areas of small farmers. See "The Secession of the Southern States" at http://www.civilwarhome.com/southernseccession.htm, accessed 3 February 2004.
15. Henry Adams, *The Education of Henry Adams,* (Boston: 1918), accessed 23 August 2003 at www.bartleby.com/159/3.html.
16. *Harrisburg Telegraph,* December 22, 1860, accessed 25 April 2004 at the Valley of the Shadow Web site at www.iath.virginia.edu/vshadow2/articles/; Leech, 29.
18. Leech, 5.
19. Ibid.
20. Potter, 389.
21. Ibid.
22. Leech, 36.
23. Malcolm C. McMillan, *The Alabama Confederate Reader* (Tuscaloosa: University of Alabama Press, 1963), 42–45, quoting speakers in Virginia; Mrs. Clay, *A Belle of the Fifties* (1905) 147-148; *Congressional Globe* 2 Session 36, Congress XXX (1861), 486-7.
24. Ibid.
25. Reynolds, 178.
26. Potter, 563.
27. Ibid., 528.
28. Ibid., 556.
29. Ibid., 515, 517.
30. Simister, Volume V, 104.
31. Potter, 560.
32. Baringer and Miers, III, 11–21.
33. Leech, 13.
34. Ibid.
35. Adams, 3, 3.
36. William C. Davis and editors, *First Blood, Fort Sumter to Bull Run,* (Alexandria, VA: Time Life Books, 1983), 27.
37. Leech, 3.
38. Ibid., 2.
39. Ibid., 1.
40. Ibid., 33.
41. Ibid., 5.
42. Charles P. Stone, "Washington on the Eve of the War," 7–24, *Battles and Leaders,* 14–15.
43. Leech, 37.
44. Ibid., 41.

45. Ashahel Adams Shumway, *Genealogy of the Shumway Family,* (Atlantic City, N.J.: 1909) reprint in facsimile, (York, PA: George Shumway, 1971), 240; "Night Train to Baltimore," Baltimore City Paper Online accessed 9 August 2003 at www.citypaper.com/2002-02-20/pf/charmed_pf.html
46. Ward Lamon quoted in Miers, III, 20–21.
47. Baringer and Miers III, 21.
48. Shumway Family, 249.
49. Leech, 62.
50. Baringer and Miers, III, 23; Pratt, 5.
51. Stone in *Battles and Leaders*, 25.
52. Ibid.
53. William A. Croffut, *American Procession, 1855-1914,* (Boston: Little, Brown and Company, 1931), 41-43.
54. Stone in *Battles and Leaders*, 25.
55. Ibid.
56. Benjamin P. Thomas, quoted in Baringer and Miers, III, 24.
57. Croffut, 41-43.
58. Abraham Lincoln, "First Inaugural Address," March 4, 1861, 7, accessed 20 November, 2001 at www.americancivilwar.com/documents/lincoln_inaugural_1.html.
59. *Wilmington Daily Herald,* March 5, 1861, Harris, 26.
60. Baringer and Miers, III, 26.
61. *New York Times,* March 7, 1861 quoted in Baringer and Miers, III, 27.
62. Bartlett, *Rhode Island Officers,* 250.
63. Sullivan Ballou second letter to wife, July 14, 1861.
64. Unpublished Diaries of George Manchester, Manchester Family.
65. *Providence City Directory 1860,* (Providence: H. H. Brown 1860), 201, 203.
66. Web site of the Rhode Island Attorney General www.riag.state.ri.us/history/default.htm
67. Barenger and Miers, III, 26 quoting Barton II 8, Jacob Schuckers, *Life and Service of Salmon P. Chase,* 207.
68. Baringer and Miers, III, 28-9
69. Baringer and Miers, III 33, *National Intelligencer* April 2, and *New York Herald* April 3, 1861.
70. Bartlett, *Rhode Island Officers,* 250.
71. Rogers Jr., 97.
72. Potter, 577.
73. Woodbury, First, 2.
74. Potter, 579.
75. *Baltimore Sun,* April 15, 1861 in Baringer and Miers, III, 34.
76. *Providence Journal,* April 13, 1861.
77. Ibid.
78. Report of Major Robert Anderson, retreat from Fort Sumter accessed 5 May 2002 at http://www.civilwarhome.com/anderson.htm.
79. *Richmond Enquirer,* April 16, 1861 accessed 1 May, 2004 at www.vcdh.virginia.edu/vahistory/reconfiguring/enquirer041661b.html.
80. Stone in *Battles and Leaders*, 7.
81. Woodbury, *First,* 3.
82. Ware, 67.
83. There was some friendly competition over which state responded most promptly to Lincoln's call for volunteers to defend Washington. Regardless of in state muster dates, Pennsylvania and Massachusetts regiments departed the most promptly, and arrived first, followed within a day by New York and Rhode Island. See "Pratt Street: First Blood in Baltimore," at http://www.us-civilwar.com/aldie/baltimore.html.
84. Ware, 69.
85. *Providence Journal,* April 13, 1861.
86. *Worchester Spy,* April 27, 1861 in Ware, 68.

Chapter 9 I'm Off to the War with the Good Men and True . . .

1. Woodbury, *Second,* 14.
2. Acts and Resolves, Special Session of the Rhode Island Legislature, April 1861, 212–222.
3. Woodbury, *Second,* 14.

4. Acts and Resolves, Special Session, 212–222.
5. Brayton Harris, *Blue and Grey and Black and White: Newspapers in the Civil War.* (Washington D.C.: Brassey's, 2000), 44.
6. Ware, 68.
7. Simister, "The Parade of Volunteers for the Civil War," *Streets of the City,* Undated broadcast (except for notation "Read Feb 11" pages 217–218. Undated typescript at RIHS.
8. Albert E. Sholes, "Personal Reminiscences of Bull Run; Read at the Thirtieth Annual Reunion of the First Rhode island Regiment and the First Battery Association at Lakewood, Rhode Island, July 21, 1910 by Albert E Sholes of Flushing, New York." No publisher.
9. Analysis of data, civil war database and regimental records. More correctly, Woodbury.
10. Woodbury, *First,* extrapolated from Appendix D.
11. Woodbury, *First,* 9–10.
12. Lt. McPherson, commander of Alcatraz Island, quoted in E. Porter Alexander, *Military Memoirs of a Confederate,* (New York: Charles Scribners Sons, 1907) reprint (New York: Da Capo Press, 1993, 5-6.
13. Sullivan Ballou letter to wife, first letter of July 14,1861; Payscale, Battles and Leaders, second footnote, 150.
14. John Usher in Rufus Rockwell Wilson, *Intimate Memories of Lincoln,* 382–83, quoted in Mrlincolnswhitehouse.org accessed 6 October 2003.
15. *Republican Vindicator,* (Staunton, VA) April 26, 1861, page 1 column 1, footnote from Mark M. Boatner III. *The Civil War Dictionary,* (New York: Vintage Books, Random House, 1991), 376, 699.
16. Upton Sinclair, *Manassas A Novel of the War,* (New York: The MacMillan Company, 1904). (Grosse Point, Michigan: Scholarly Press, 1968), 351.
17. Baringer and Miers, III, 36; Oates, CB, 4-5; report of Mayor of Baltimore, footnote, *Battles and Leaders,* 150–151.
18. Stephen B. Oates, *Clara Barton, A Woman of Valor,* (New York: The Free Press, 1994), 5.
19. Geoffrey Perret, *Lincoln's War,* (New York: Random House, 2004,) 39.
20. Harris, 48.
21. Leech, 66
22. David Hunter, *Report of the Military Services of Gen. David Hunter, U.S.A.: During the War of the Rebellion, made to the U.S. War Department, 1873.* (New York : D. Van Nostrand, 1873) 7.
23. Baringer and Miers, III, 36. Abraham Lincoln A History, Volume Four, 1.
24. Leech, 59.
25. Baringer and Miers, III, 36. Denny 6,
26. Leech, 80; Stone, *Battles and Leaders,* 7.
27. Leech, 80; John G. Nicolay, and John Hay, *Abraham Lincoln, a History,* (New York: the Century Co., 1890), 96.
28. Harris, 48.
29. U.S. Naval Academy Web site, 1860's, accessed 24 November, 2004 at www.usna.edu/Virtual Tour/150years/1860.html.
30. Woodbury, *First.* 24.
31. Oates, 11.
32. Sholes.

Chapter 10 Then to the South We Bore Away

1. Ware, 70
2. Leech, 70
3. Baringer and Miers, entries for last week of April, 1861.
4. *Staunton Spectator,* April 30, 1861, accessed 2 January 2005 at http://jefferson.village.virginia.edu:8090/xslt/servlet/ramanujan.XSLTservlet?xml+/vcdh/xml_docs/valley.
5. Johnston H. Skelly to his mother, in Alan Sessarego, *Letters Home II, Camp Life and Battles.* (Gettysburg, PA: Americana Souvenirs and Gifts, 2001), 4.
6. Civil War Database on Sumner Henry Needham; Colonel Jones report for April 19, 1861 accessed 12 December 2004 at http://www.civilwarhome.com/jones.htm.
7. Leech, 88
8. Woodbury, *First,* oath
9. Woodbury, *First,* 28–29; Alice Hunt Sokoloff, *Kate Chase for the Defense, a Biography,* (New York: Dodd, Mead and Company, 1971), 56.

10. Private Harrison H. Comings, Eleventh New York, *Voices,* 23.
11. Jefferson Davis, "Address to the Confederate Constitutional Congress, April 29, 1861," accessed 12 February 2005, at Civil War Battlefield Guide, Charleston Harbor, Fort Sumter (James McPherson)http://college.hmco.com/history/readerscomp/civwar/html/cw_000201_fortsumteris.htm.
12. Woodbury, *First,* 32.
13. Leech, 87.
14. Ibid.
15. *New York Herald,* May 14, 1861 accessed 2 January, 2005 at www.vcdh.virginia.edu/vahistory/reconfiguring/herald051461.html
16. James B. Fry, Adjutant to McDowell, in Battles and Leaders, 171.
17. "Joseph Mansfield," in Boatner, 508.
18. Woodbury, *First,*
19. Acts and Resolves May 1861.
20. Edwin W. Stone, *Rhode Island in the Rebellion,* (Providence, R.I.: George H. Whitney, 1864), xxi.
21. *Providence Post,* June 3, 1861 quoted in William Greene Roelker, "Civil War Letters of William Ames," *Rhode Island Historical Society Collections, Vol. XXXIII (23),* October, 1940, 73–92, 77.
22. Robert Hunt Rhodes: Elisha Hunt Rhodes, *All for the Union,* (Lincoln, R.I.: Alan Mowbray Inc.: 1985), 12.
23. Jacob D. Cox, "War Preparations in the North," *Battles and Leaders,* 88.
24. Orrin Robbins, "Headed Into a Hurricane Part I," *Civil War Times,* February 2001, 22.
25. Rhodes, 13-14.
26. Rhodes, 14.
27. Bayles, Chapter VII, "Providence City During the Rebellion," 208.
28. Acts and Resolves, May 1861, 52.
29. Acts and Resolves, Report of General Burnside on the First Rhode Island Regiment, 89,
30. Acts and Resolves, June 1862, 146-151
31. Acts and Resolves, May 1861, 52.
32. August V. Kautz, *Customs of Service for Non-Commissioned Officers and Soldiers.* Second Edition, (Philadelphia: Lippencott, 1865). Reprint, (Mechanicsburg, PA: Stackpole Books, 2001), 15.
33. Acts and Resolves, May 1861, 17.
34. Lecture by John Perry, author of *The Lady of Arlington, the life of Mrs. Robert E. Lee,* at the Women in the Civil War Annual Conference, 2004, Richmond, VA.
35. McDowell, CCW, 37.
36. Rhodes,15.
37. *Providence Journal,* June 14, 1861.
38. Kautz, 223-225, 21–26.
39. Aldrich, 5.
40. Rogers Jr., 98.
41. Edward S. Farrow, *Farrow's Military Encyclopedia,* Vol II. (New York: Published by the Author, 1885).
42. Articles of War, US Army Regulations of 1861 accessed 3 February, 2005 at www.usrgulars.com/Regulations%20Home.html.
43. Rogers Jr., 98–99.
44. Woodbury, "Sermon," April 21, 1861, 7.
45. Sullivan Ballou letter to Latimer W. Ballou, June 11, 1861, manuscripts of the RIHS.
46. Will of Sullivan Ballou, Cranston City Hall; Rogers Jr., 99.
47. Stone, *Rhode Island in the Rebellion,* 289.
48. Descriptive notes on reverse of photographs in graphics collection, RIHS.
49. *Providence Journal,* June 13, 1861.
50. Analysis of list of medals of honor awarded during the Civil War by author.
51. *Providence Post,* June 15, 1861.
52. Rhodes, 18-19.
53. Woodbury, Sermon, April 21, 1861, 8.
54. Rhodes, 19.
55. Roelker, October, 78.
56. Stone, *Rhode Island in the Rebellion,* 289; Bayles, History of Providence County, 42.
57. Rhodes, 19.
58. Woodbury, *Second,* 23.

59. Mary Rebecca Clark Sturdevant, *Thomas March Clark, fifth Bishop of Rhode Island: a Memoir by his Daughter,* (Milwaukee, Wis. Morehouse [c 1927]), 89.
60. Ibid.
61. Rhodes, 19.
62. Bishop Clark, letter in Sturdevant, 89.
63. Ibid.
64. Fort Schuyler Web site accessed 24 October 2004, at www.maritimeindustrymuseum.org/schuyler.htm; Thomas M. Aldrich, *The History of Battery A, First Regiment Rhode Island Light Artillery in the War to Preserve the Union, 1861–1865.* (Providence, Snow & Farnham, printers, 1904), 6.
65. Rhodes, 19.
66. Bishop Clark, letter in Sturdevant, 89.
67. Ibid.
68. The journey was fatiguing for everyone; the exact cite for the condition of the railroad cars did not come to hand.
69. Bishop Clark, letter in Sturdevant, 89.
70. Aldrich, 6.
71. Rhodes, 20.
72. Aldrich, 7.
73. Bishop Clark, letter in Sturdevant, 89-90.
74. Adams, *Education* Chapter 8, 44.
75. Roelker, 79.
76. Aldrich, 7.
77. Elisha Hunt Rhodes, Speech to Rhode Island Soldiers and Sailors Historical Society 1878-79 printed in the Military Order of the Loyal Legion of the U.S., Rhode Island, Volume I Personal Narratives of the Rebellion, (Wilmington, S.C.: Broadfoot Publishing, 1933), 8.
78. Chaplain Jamison under his pen name of "Tockwotton," letter to *Providence Press,* June 27, 1861 quoted in Roelker, October, 1941, 79, footnote 31.
79. Rhodes, Speech, 8.
80. Sullivan Ballou letter to his wife, June 25, 1861, manuscripts of the RIHS.
81. Rhodes, Speech, 8-9.
82. Bishop Clark, letter in Sturdevant, 89.
83. Ibid.
84. Rhodes, 20.
85. Henry Dewitt, engineer, letter to *Providence Journal* June 26, 1861, quoted in Roelker, October, 80, footnote 33.
86. Bishop Clark, letter in Sturdevant, 90.
87. Aldrich.
88. Bishop Clark, letter in Sturdevant, 91.
89. Woodbury, *First,* 30.
90. Aldrich, 7.
91. Sullivan Ballou letter to wife, June 23, 1861, manuscripts of the RIHS.

Chapter 11 From Hill to Hill, from Peak to Peak . . .

1. George Cary Eggleston, *A Rebel's Recollection,* (Cambridge: H. O. Houghton and Company,1874), 21. Accessed 29 December 2003 at http://docsouth.unc.edu/eggleston/eggleston.html
2. All Potomac information from Potomac Adventure on the WETA Web site, www.weta.org/potomac Regions and ecology accessed 12/21/01 and 1/7 /02. Site no longer up.
3. Pierre Gustave Toutant Beauregard, "First Bull Run, First Manassas," *The Century Magazine,* Vol. XXIX, November 1884, 1.
4. Alexander, 4.
5. Gerald Patterson, "Gustave," *Civil War Times Illustrated,* July/August 1992, 30.
6. Eggleston, 3.
7. Eggleston, 20.
8. (Staunton, VA) [Republican] *Vindicator,* April 26, 1861.
9. Narration from Historical Tour of Richmond.
10. Thomas Cutrer, ed., *Longstreet's Aide: The Civil War Letters of Major Thomas J. Goree,* (Charlottesville: University Press of Virginia, 1995), Goree, letter to mother, June 23, 1861, 18.
11. Ibid.

12. Eggleston, 21.
13. Goree, letter to mother, October 18, 1861, in Cutrer, 49–50.
14. Eggleston, 36-37.
15. Eggleston, 37.
16. Robert T. Coles, *From Huntsville to Appomattox: R. T. Coles's History of 4th Regiment, Alabama Volunteer Infantry, C.S.A., Army of Northern Virginia,* edited by Jeffrey D. Stocker. (Knoxville: University of Tennessee Press, 1996.) A monograph treating both the regiments in which Figures served is J. Gary Laine and Morris M. Penny, *Law's Alabama Brigade in the War between the Union and the Confederacy,* Shippensburg PA, 1996), 5.
17. Ibid.
18. Eggleston, 31-32.
19. James Cooper Nisbet, *Four Years on the Firing Line.* (Chattanooga, TN: The Imperial Press, c. 1914), x; Allen, 7; Thomas, 343; Ed Jackson and Charly Pou, This Day in Georgia History accessed 1 Febraury 2005 at http://www.cviog.uga.edu/Projects/gainfo/tdgh-sep/sep06.htm.
20. Nisbet, x, 10.
21. Randall Allen and Keith S. Bohannon, editors, *Campaigning with "Old Stonewall" Confederate Captain Ujanirtus Allen's Letters to His Wife,* (New Orleans: Louisiana State University Press, 1998), 11.
22. Nisbet, 10-12 passim.
23. Ibid.
24. West Point Alumni Organization email.
25. Allen, 12.
26. Nisbet, 17.
27. Scarborough, 433 and 483.
28. Davis, 31.
29. Ibid. 61.
30. (Netherton et al. 1978: 251-59).
31. Goree, letter to mother, July 6, 1861, in Cutrer, 21.
32. Goree, letter to mother, June 23, 1861, in Cutrer, 19.
33. Goree, letter to mother, July 6, 1861, in Cutrer, 20-21.
34. Eggleston, 115.
35. Alexander, 13.
36. Ibid., 16.
37. Beauregard, *Century,* 3.
38. Goree, letter to mother, June 23, 1861, in Cutrer, 18.
39. William C. Davis, *Battle of Bull Run,* (Garden City, New York: Doubleday and Company, 1977), 61.
40. Beauregard, letter to Jefferson Davis.
41. Goree, letter to mother, July 6, 1861, in Cutrer, 21.
42. Cox in *Battles and Leaders* I, 96.

Chapter 12 In the Watch Fires of a Hundred Circling Camps

1. Sullivan Ballou letters to wife, June 26 and first of July 14, 1861.
2. Albert Greene letter of June 25, 1861. manuscripts at South County Museum, Narragansett, Rhode Island.
3. Reverend Augustus Woodbury, "Sermon to Have Been Preached April 21, 1861," (Providence: Cook and Danielson, 1861), 8.
4. Sullivan Ballou letter to wife, July 3, 1861.
5. John Harmon McElray, *The Sacrificial Years, A Chronicle of Walt Whitman's experience in the Civil War,* (Boston: David R. Godine, 1999), 4.
6. Bishop Clark, letter in Sturdevant, 91.
7. Woodbury, *Second,* 24.
8. Museum of the Confederacy exhibits.
9. Private Warren Lee Goss, "Recollections of a Private", *Century Magazine,* 107–113, 1884, 108, accessed 15 October 2004 at Cornell University Making of America Web site at http://cdl.library.cornell.edu.
10. Aldrich, 10.
11. Sullivan Ballou letter to Charles Brownell, June 25, 1861.
12. Ames, letter to mother, June 25, 1861, in Roelker, 80.
13. Rhodes, 20.

14. Sullivan Ballou letter to Charles Brownell, June 25, 1861.
15. Greene letter of June 25, 1861.
16. Henry T. Blanchard, Second Rhode Island, letter to parents, June 25, 1861, manuscripts, Historical Society of Washington, D.C.
17. Davis, 76; Sullivan Ballou letter to Brownell, June 25, 1861.
18. Blanchard letter June 25, 1861.
19. Lt. William Ames to mother, June 26, 1861, in William Greene Roelker, "Civil War Letters of William Ames," *Rhode Island Historical Society Collections,* 82.
20. This quote is likely from Denny, but the page number proved elusive.
21. Baringer and Miers, quoting Meigs diary, 5.
22. Baringer and Miers, citing Thomas and Randall.
23. Sullivan Ballou letter to wife, June 26, 1861.
24. Ibid.
25. Ibid.
26. Sullivan Ballou letter to wife, July 10, 1861.
27. Sullivan Ballou letter to wife, June 30, 1861.
28. Woodbury, *First,* 33.
29. Sullivan Ballou letter to wife, June 30, 1861.
30. Goss, 108.
31. Aldrich, 9.
32. Kautz 22.
33. CCW McDowell 37.
34. Ibid.
35. Lieutenant George Bell USA, OR, II 338.
36. Davis, 12.
37. Meigs, CCW, 247, 242.
38. Goss 108.
39. Ibid.
40. Robert Goldthwaite Carter, *Four Brothers in Blue* 1913 reprint edition (Oklahoma City: University of Oklahoma Press, 1999), 8.
41. Ames letter in Roelker, 14.
42. Davis, 77.
43. James M. Perry, Touched by Fire, (New York: Public Affairs Books, 2003). 3; respective listings of each name in Boatner.
44. Boatner, 69.
45. U. S. Mexican War Web site, Corpus Christi, TX Library accessed 24 September 2004 at www.library.ci.corpus-christi.tx.us/MexicanWar/milesds.htm; Hispanics in the Indian Wars Web site, accessed same date at ww.nps.gov/foda/Fort_Davis_WEB_PAGE/About_the_Fort/In_the_Wake_of_Columbus.htm.
46. Brigadier-General Theodore Runyon, U.S.V., *Officers of the Volunteer Army and Navy who served in the Civil War,* (L.R. Hamersly & Co., 1893), accessed 6 June 2005 at http://www.all-biographies.com/soldiers/theodore_runyon.htm.
47. Eggleston, 16–17.

Chapter 13 Rally Round the Flag Boys

1. William Tecumsah Sherman, letter to wife, Brooks D. Simpson, and, Jean V. Berlin, eds, *Sherman's Civil War, Selected Correspondence Of William T. Sherman, 1860–1865,* (Chapel Hill, NC: The University of North Carolina Press, 1999), 125.
2. Abraham Lincoln, "Address to Congress," July 4, 1861.
3. Bishop Clark, letter in Sturdevant, 93.
4. Davis, 77.
5. Leech, 109.
6. Rev. Byron Sunderland D. D., Senate Chaplain, Pilgrims of Faith: Congressional Prayers for the Fourth of July, Prayer for July 4, 1861, accessed 30 November 2004 at gurukul.edu/heintze/Prayers.htm.
7. Lincoln, "Address to Congress," July 4, 1861.
8. Galusha A. Grow, This Hour of National Disaster" speech to the House of Representatives, July 4, 1861, accessed 3 November, 2004 at gurukul.edu/heintze/grow.htm.
9. William Russell quoted in Leech, 110.

10. Steven R. Weisman, *The Great Tax Wars: Lincoln to Wilson–The Fierce Battles over Money and Power That Transformed the Nation,* (New York: Simon and Schuster, 2002), 1, 9-11accessed 9 August 2003 at www.wnyc.org/books/4867.; and U. S. Senate Web site 1851–1877, July 4, 1861 www.senat.gov/artandhistory/history/minutes/Dramatic_Session.htm 11/3/04
11. "39th New York State Volunteers, Garibaldi Guard, Uniform Notes," accessed 23 January 2004 at www.ecs.gannon.edu/~frezza/39nysv.;
12. Leech, 109.
13. Beauregard *Century* 3.
14. *Providence Journal* July 3, July 4, 1861.
15. *Willimantic* (Conn) *Journal,* June 6 [or 7], 1861.
16. Rhodes, 21; Sullivan Ballou, letter to wife, July 5, 1861.
17. Woodbury, *First,* 79.
18. Rhodes, 21.
19. Sholes.
20. Sullivan Ballou, letter to wife, July 5, 1861.
21. Ibid.
22. Davis, 65.
23. Sullivan Ballou, letter to wife, July 10, 1861.
24. Enlistment ledger of New Bedford Naval Rendezvous, John Fowler Shumway Pension Record File, NARA.
25. Sullivan Ballou, letter to wife, July 5, 1861.
26. Rogers Jr., 100–101.
27. McDowell, CCW, 38.
28. Rhodes, 23.
29. Record of Civil and Military Service of Frank Wheaton, manuscripts at RIHS.
30. Army Form, Records of the Second Rhode Island Regiment, manuscripts at RIHS.
31. Sullivan Ballou, first letter to wife, July 14, 1861.
32. For example, see Willcox on the death of his mother, in Robert Garth Scott, *Forgotten Valor: The Memoirs, Journals and Civil War Letters of Orlando B. Willcox.* (Kent, Ohio: Kent State University Press, 1999), 179.
33. Augustus Woodbury, "Sermon," April 21, 1861, 6.
34. American Eloquence.
35. Rhodes, 23.
36. Aldrich.
37. Davis, 92.
38. Rhodes, 23.
39. Ibid.
40. Ibid.
41. Harriet Patience Dame accessed 4 August 2004 at: www.famousamericans.net/harrietpatiencedame; www.webster.state.nh/nhdhr/warheroes/dameh.html.
42. Ethel Hurn at "Springing to the Call a Documentary View of Women in the American Civil War," edited by C. Kay Larson, accessed 11 November 2004 at http://libraryautomation.com/nymas/civilwarwomen.html
43 Davis, 68.
44. Sinclair, 379.

Chapter 14 The Most Glorious Scene

1. Rhodes, 24.
2. Henry Blake, "Bull Run" from *Three Years in the Army of the Potomac,* excerpted in Don Congdon, ed., *Combat: The Civil War.* (New York: Mallard Press, 1967), 19.
3. Richardson, CCW, 19.
4. Ibid. 22.
5. Rhodes, 24.
6. Davis, 92.
7. Sullivan Ballou, letter to wife, July 19, 1861.
8. English letter in Rhodes, 32.
9. Blake in Congdon, 19.
10. Reverend George W Bicknell, *History of the Fifth Maine Regiment.* (Portland, ME.: Hall L. Davis, 1871), 22.

11. Heintzelman, CCW, 28.
12. Blake in Congdon, 20.
13. Leech, 120.
14. Ibid.; William Russell, My Diary, North and South, (London, 1863) II, 147.
15. Davis, 92.
16. Ibid., 93.
17. Bicknell, 33.
18. Blake in Congdon, 19.
19. Miles, OR.
20. Tyler, CCW, 205.
21. Rhodes, 24.
22. Thomas F. Meagher, "The Last Days of the 69th in Virginia," (NY: "Irish American," 1861)
23. Ibid.
24. Rhodes, Speech, 11.
25. McDowell, CCW, 39.
26. Sara Emma E. Edmonds, *Nurse and Spy in the Union Army The Adventures and Experiences of a Woman in Hospitals, Camps and Battle Fields.* (Hartford, CT: W. S. Williams and Co. 1865), 35-36.
27. Woodbury, *First,* 79.
28. Sullivan Ballou, letter to wife, July 19, 1861.
29. English letter in Rhodes, 32.
30. Sullivan Ballou, letter to wife, July 19, 1861.
31. George Putnam, "Before and After the Battle: A Day in Dixie," Knickerbocker Magazine, September, 1861, 5.
32. Woodbury, *Second,* 20, and First, 81.
33. Rhodes, 25.
34. English letter in Rhodes, 32.
35. Ibid.
36. Carter, Brothers in Blue, 8-9.
37. *Providence Evening Press,* July 22, 1861.
38. Rhodes, 24.
39. George Wilkes, "The Great Battle, Notes Taken on the Spot," (New York: Brown and Ryan, ND), 7.
40. Rhodes, 25.
41. Woodbury, *Second,* 29. verify
42. Sullivan Ballou, letter to wife, July 18, 1861; Rhodes, speech, 12.
43. Sullivan Ballou, letter to wife, July 19, 1861.
44. Blake in Congdon, 20.
45. McDowell, CCW. 37.
46. Willcox in Scott, 287.
47. Alexander, 17.
48. Willcox to Heintzelman, dispatch/note, OR, 310.
49. Leech 122.
50. Davis, 148.
51. Footnote, *Battles and Leaders,* 182.
52. Ibid.
53. McDowell, CCW, 46.
54. Meagher, 8.
55. Ibid.
56. Ibid.
57. Edmonds quoted in Robert E. Denny, *Civil War Medicine Care and Comfort of the Wounded.* (New York: Sterling Publishing, 1994), 32.
58. Davis, 102.
59. Meagher, 8.
60. While testifying with great propriety and deference to the chain of command at the committee on the conduct of the war, Tyler always maintained he—and the Union—lost a great opportunity that day. The source of this specific quote could not be resurrected in time for the publication deadline.
61. McDowell, OR, 308.
62. Tyler, CCW, 199; Various members of Twelfth New York, quoted in Davis, 119.
63. Barnard, CCW, 162.
64. Ibid.

65. Alexander, 23.
66. Fry, *Battles and Leaders,* 179.
67. Richardson, CCW, 21.
68. Whitman in McElray, 9.
69. Heintzelman, CCW, 29.
70. Ibid.
71. Bicknell, 25.
72. Meagher, 8.
73. Woodbury, *First,* 87.
74. Meagher, *Voices,* 86.
75. Franklin, CCW, 34-35.
76. Alexander, 27.
77. Ibid.
78. Ibid.; Beauregard, *Century,* 8.
79. Beauregard, quoted in Davis, 111.
80. Jubal Early, *Autobiographical Sketch and Narrative of the War Between the States.* (Philadelphia: 1912), 11.
81. Sullivan Ballou, letter to wife, July 19, 1861.
82. Sherman, letter to wife, end of June, 1861 in Simpson and Berlin, 118.
83. Berien McPherson Zettler, "War Stories and School-Day Incidents for Children," accessed 30 December 2001, at http://docsouth.unc.edu/zettler/aettler/html.
84. Whitman in McElray, 9.
85. Fry, *Battles and Leaders,* 183.
86. Davis, 153.
87. Richardson, CCW, 23.
88. General Joseph E. Johnston, "Report of The Battle of First Manassas", OR Series I Volume 2 [S#2] Chapter IX, 8, 23 November 2004 at www.swcivilwar.com/Johnston1stManassas.html.
89. Diary of Private George Anderson, Company I Fourth Alabama. Entry for July 21, 1861, made before he died. Diary taken by a member of the 71st New York from the corpse's pocket, published in the Northern press. Quoted in *R. T. Coles's History of 4th Regiment, Alabama Volunteer Infantry, C. S. A., Army of Northern Virginia,* Knoxville, 1996. A monograph treating both the regiments in which Figures served; J. Gary Laine and Morris M. Penny, *Law's Alabama Brigade in the War between the Union and the Confederacy,* (Shippensburg, PA: 1996), 26.
90. Jake Brouwer, "Observations from Above," accessed 19 April 2005 at www.aaaim.com/echo/v3n2/v3n2ObservationsfromAbove
91. Woodbury, *First,* 224.
92. McDowell, OR 308
93. Barnard, CCW, 161.
94. Sherman to wife, July 19/20, 1861, in Simpson and Berlin, 119.
95. *Providence Journal, July 22, 1861.*
96. Ibid.
97. McDowell, Dispatch to Scott, OR 308.
98. Edmonds, 33.
99. Davis, 154.
100. General Order 22, OR, 326-327; McDowell, CCW, 39.
101. Augustus Woodbury, "The Memory of the First Battle A Discourse Preached At Westminster Church on the 28th Anniversary of the Battle of Bull Run." (Providence, RI: E. L. Freeman & Son, 1889), 18.
102. Fry in *Battles and Leaders,* 183.
103. Keyes, CCW, 151.
104. McDowell, OR, 308.
105. McDowell, CCW, 131.
106. Keyes, CCW, 151.
107. Richardson, CCW, 22.
108. McDowell, CCW, 40.
109. Richardson, CCW, 24.
110. Barry, CCW, 148.
111. General Order 22, OR, 326-327.
112. Alexander, passim.

113. Blake in Congdon, 32.
114. Henry J. Raymond, editor, story written July 20, 1861 to file with *New York Times* quoted in Alan Hankinson, *First Bull Run, 1861,* (London: Osprey, 1990), 49.

Chapter 15 How Many Miles to the Junction?

1. Homer, *The Iliad.*
2. Woodbury, "Sermon," April 21, 1861, 6.
3. Smith, Dennis, *Report from Ground Zero,* (New York: Viking, 2002), 214.
4. Woodbury, "Discourse," 1889, 20.
5. Edmonds, 36.
6. Goree, letter to mother 7/20/61 in Cutrer, 23 – 24.
7. Zettler Chapter VI, 60.
8. Elihu Washburne, *Voices,* 95.
9. 1860 Federal Census for Virginia, Prince William and Fairfax Counties.
10. Barry, CCW, 145.
11. Alexander, 39.
12. McDonald, 42.
13. Davies, CCW, 114-115.
14. William Howard Russell, from either *My Diary North and South,* or *Celebrated Letter.*
15. Jon Krakauer, *Into Thin Air,* (*New York:* Anchor Books/Random House. 1999), 178.
16. McDowell, CCW, 41.
17. Blake, in Congdon, 22.
18. Wilkes, *The Great Battle,* 6–7, 28–9; and Colonel Dangerfield Parker, USA, "Personal Reminiscences," War Papers, 36, Washington, D.C. Division of MOLLUS, November 7, 1900.
19. *New York Tribune* July 27, 1861 "Report of the 79th Infantry at Bull Run," accessed 4 August 2004, www.jimlyons.com/civilwarts1861.html 2.
20. Woodbury, First, 87.
21. McDowell, CCW, 44.
22. Rhodes, letter to sister, July28, 1861, in Rhodes, 40.
23. Edmonds, 38.
24. McDowell, CCW, 41.
25. Barnard, CCW, 160.
26. Tyler, CCW, 201.
27. George M. Finch, "Boys of '61,"G.A.R. Papers, Vol. 1.,(Cincinnati: Fred C. Jones Post, 18910, 255, quoted in McDonald 40.
28. McDowell, CCW, 42.
29. Porter, CCW, 212.
30. John Hennessy, *The First Battle of Manassas, An End to Innocence July 18–21, 1861,* (Lynchburg: Virginia Civil War and Leadership Series, H. E. Howard, 1989), 37.
31. Tyler, CCW, 202.
32. Woodbury, *First,* 89.
33. McDonald, 42.
34. McHenry Howard, in Congdon, 33.
35. Woodbury, First, 90.
36. Ibid.
37. Blake in Congdon, 22.
38. Rhodes, 26.
39. Sholes, 6.
40. Barnard, CCW, 160.
41. Rhodes, speech 11-12.
42. *Providence Evening Press* quoted in Hennessy, 39.
43. Sholes, 6.
44. Ibid.
45. Blake in Congdon, 22.
46. All participants agreed the march was dusty and hot, especially when the overhead shade was lost. The exact personage who noted the forest shut out the breezes cannot be found at the publication deadline.
47. McDonald, 47.
48. Stedman, 23.

49. First Manassas, Report of General Joseph E. Johnston, October 14, 1861 accessed 30 May, 2005 at http://etext.lib.virginia.edu.
50. Heintzelman CCW 32.
51. Heintzelman CCW 30.
52. Blake in Congdon, 22.
53. Museum of the Confederacy Display.
54. Davis, 164.
55. Number 86. Report of Brigadier General M. L. Bonham, C. S. Army, commanding First Brigade, First Corps. OR 518.
56. Johnson, Battle Report
57. Ibid.
58. Alexander, 30.
59. Ibid.
60. Ibid. 31.
61. Ibid. 30–31.
62. Woodbury, Discourse.
63. Hennessy, 46.
64. Monroe, 6–7.
65. Blake in Congdon, 24.
66. Various sources give different times for the halt, which may reflect the time various companies spent resting. Wheaton may be considered authoritative for the whole.
67. Ames letter, July 22, 1861, in Roelker, 1941, 11.
68. Meagher, 12.
69. Porter, CCW, 212
70. Ibid.
71. Ibid.
72. Lt. Col (Former) Frank Wheaton, August 23, 1876 letter to Frances W. Goddard, discussing Goddard's Company of Carabineers (1st RI) Goddard Family Papers–RIHS (MSS 442).
73. Wheaton letter.
74. Wheaton letter
75. Contradicting claims exist regarding exactly which company or platoon composed the skirmishers. Lt. Shaw, Company F, says his company was the advance guard and had skirmisher "on each side of the road." *Providence Journal,* July 22, 1861; Monroe says the Second's skirmishers were on the flanks, not out in front, 12; all in Roelker, footnote 94 on page 17. Wheaton in his letter notes their positioning and dilemma, but not their composition.
76. Woodbury, Discourse 15.
77. Davis, photo caption between 178-179.
78. Esther Dogan Terrill, quoted in Johnson, *Horseshoe Curve,* 73.
79. D. S. Magruder, quoted in Denny, 34.
80. Rhodes, 26.
81. Esther Dogan Terrill, quoted in Johnson, *Horseshoe Curve,* 73.
83. Irwin McDowell, Report on First Manassas, August 4, 1861.
83. Ibid.
84. Zettler, 61,
85. Alexander, 32.
86. Richardson, CCW, 24.

Chapter 16 A Cannonball Don't Pay No Mind

1. *Biographical Cyclopedia* 191, ancestry.com.
2. Woodbury, First, 142-143.
3. *Biographical Cyclopedia,* 191.
4. Wheaton letter.
5. Papers of William Sprague, in Rhodes, 36. .
6. Greene letter July 25, 1861.
7. Wheaton letter.
8. Ibid.
9. Aldrich, 11–13.
10. Rhodes, 26.
11. English letter, in Rhodes, 33.

12. Greene, undated letter.
13. Wheaton letter.
14. Ibid. Also attested by Aldrich, Wheaton, Woodbury, and all others from the Second Rhode Island.
15. Wheaton letter.
16. Sprague papers in Rhodes, 36. .
17. Rhodes, 26.
18. Hennessy, 50.
19. Ames, letter to father, July 27, 1861, in Roelker, 1941, 13.
20. English letter in Rhodes, 33.
21. Letter in *Pawtucket Gazette*
22. Wheaton, letter.
23. Woodbury, Second, 32.
24. Wheaton letter.
25. Rhodes, letter to sister, 40.
26. Beauregard, *Century,* 13.
27. Woodbury, Second, 32.
28. McDowell, OR, 319.
29. Major William F. Barry, Battle Report, First Manassas in Official Reports (OR) Series 1, Volume 2, Chapter IX, 346 accessed 8 January, 2004 at Cornell University, Making of America at http://library5.cornell.edu.
30. Woodbury, *First,* 93.
31. Hunter, 8.
32. Woodbury, *Second,* 33.
33. Private James P. Smith, Rockbridge Artillery, Jackson's Brigade, Voices, 120.
34. Aldrich, 11–13.
35. Hennessy, 51.
36. Sprague papers in Rhodes, 36.
37. Aldrich, 11–13.
38. Lt. J. Albert Munroe, Reynold's Battery, in Voices, 100.
39. Captain John Imboden, Staunton Artillery, VA, "Incidents at Bull Run," *Battles and Leaders of the Civil War Volume I,* (reprint: Edison, N.J.: Castle, no date. Original, 1897) 232.
40. English letter, in Rhodes, 11–13.
41. Imboden, in *Battles and Leaders,* 234.
42. English letter, in Rhodes, 11–13.
43. J. Albert Monroe, *The Rhode Island Artillery at the Battle of First Bull Run,* excerpted from. *Reminiscences of the War of the Rebellion 1861–1865,* (Providence RI: N. Bangs Williams, 1881), accessed 14 July, 2005 at www.geocities.com/generalgreene1770/RIMOLLUS/Monroe.
44. English letter, in Rhodes, 11–13.
45. The bitter tone of this remark indicates a Northern battery, likely J. Albert Munroe,but the attribution is unavailable as the presses roll.
46. Coles
47. Hennessy, 48.
48. Robert T. Coles, *From Huntsville to Appomattox: R. T. Coles's History of 4th Regiment, Alabama Volunteer Infantry, C.S.A., Army of Northern Virginia,* edited by Jeffrey D. Stocker, Knoxville: University of Tennessee Press, 1996, 20.
49. Zettler, 61–62.
50. Alexander, 29.
51. Alexander, 33.
52. Lt. Vaughan, C Company, quoted in Coles, 27.
53. Woodbury, Second 32
54. Zettler, 65; Melvin Dwinell letter July 23, 1861, printed in Rome(GA) Tri-Weekly Courier, August 1, 1861.
55. Zettler, 65–66.
56. Wheaton letter.
57. Porter, CCW 213, 214
58. Fry, quoted in *Battles and Leaders*, 182.
59. Tyler, CCW, 200.
60. Wheaton letter.
61. Sinclair, 403.

62. Wheaton letter.
63. Wheaton letter.
64. Ames in Roelker, 19; *Providence Press,* July 29, 1861.
65. *Providence Journal,* Friday August 2, 1861.
66. *Providence Daily Journal,* July 26, 1861.
67. Wheaton, OR, 400.
68. *Providence Journal,* Friday August 2, 1861.
69. Private E. D. Patterson, Georgia, in Wiley, Reb, 265.
70. Address by Captain W. C. Ward, a private of Company G, Fourth Alabama Regiment, Law's Brigade, on Saturday May 3, 1900 to Camp Hardee, in Birmingham, Alabama, in Coles, 209.
71. *Providence Journal,* Friday August 2, 1861.
72. Ibid.
73. *Providence Press,* July 26, quoting unknown officer, quoted in Roelker, 19, footnote 101.
74. Woodbury, *Second,* 34.
75. Sergeant A. W. Chappell, letter of July 25 letter, archives, RIHS (I4/725)
76. Melvin Dwinell (Co. A) July 23, 1861 letter *Rome Tri-Weekly Courier,* GA. August 1, 1861.
77. Virgil Stewart (Co. A), quoted in George M Battey, Jr., *A History of Rome and Floyd County* [GA] 142-44, accessed at home.earthlink.net/~larsrbl/stewartva.htm on 30 December 2001.
78. Dwinnell letter.
79. Zettler, 66.
80. Dwinnell letter.
81. Zettler 66–67.
82. Dwinell letter.
83. The First Manassas, no author cited, Southern Historical Society Papers, Volume XXX, 1902, 272.
84. *Providence Daily Journal,* July 26, 1861 "CO C."
85. Sprague papers in Rhodes, 36.
86. Hazlett, First Lt of Artillery Griffin's Battery, CCW, 219.
87. Greene, letters July 25 and undated.
88. Hennessy, 53.
89. "DeW," letter of July 23, 1861 in the *Providence Evening Journal,* July 25, 1861.
90. Ames, letter to father, July 27, 1861 in Roelker, 17.
91. "Correspondant," in *Providence Daily Journal,* July 25, 1861.
92. *Providence Daily Journal,* July 26, 1861, "CO C"
93. Sprague Papers in Rhodes, 37-8.
94. English letter in Rhodes, 32.
95. *Providence Daily Journal,* July 26, 1861, "CO C"
96. Sergeant A. W. Chappell letter of July 25, 1861, manuscripts at RIHS.
97. "DeW" letter.
98. Woodbury, *First,* 99.
99. Hennessy, 57.
100. Coles, 21.
101. Penny 6.
102. Captain Thomas Goldsby, quoted in Davis, 181.
103. "DeW" letter.
104. *Providence Daily Journal,* July 26,1861, "CO C"
105. Major William F. Barry, Battle Report, First Manassas in Official Reports (OR) Series 1, Volume 2, Chapter IX, 346 accessed 8 January, 2004 at Cornell University, Making of America at http://library5.cornell.edu.
106. Woodbury, *First,* 96.
107. Hennessy, 57; John Reid, Eighth Georgia, Voices, 107.
108. Blake in Congdon, 24; Rhodes 26; Civil War Database.
109. Edmonds, 43.
110. Hennessy, 60.
111. Coles, 22
112. Private Eben Gordon, Second Rhode Island, Voices, 103.
113. *Woonsocket Patriot* July 26, 1861 noon edition.
114. Captain Edward D. Tracy, letter in *Huntsville Democrat* August 7, 1861, quoted in Coles, 200–201.
115. Line 1: Civil War Database; Line Two: OR.

116. Sholes, 6-7.
117. Rhodes letter to sister, Rhodes, 40.
118. W. S. King, Surgeon, U.S.A. quoted in Denny, 33.
119. Ames, letter to parents, July 22, 1861 in Roelker, 1941, 11.
120. Tyler, CCW, 201; Woodbury *First* 100.
121. Alexander, chapter 1, passim.
122. Ames, letter to father July 27, 1861 in Roelker, 1941, 13.
123. Sholes, 7.
124. Ames, letter to father, July 27, 1861 in Roelker, 1941, 13.
125. Comment mentioned in his diary, not cited Coles, 239.

Chapter 17 The Murdering Cannons Roar

1. *New York Tribune* July 27, 1861 "A Narrow Escape "accessed 4 August 2004, at www.jimlyons.com/civilwarts1861.html
2. Henry Ritter, NY 71st Company F, letter in the collection of the NPS at MNBP. accessed 17 April, 2000 at www.nps.gov/mana/letters/ritter.htm (no longer up).
3. Chappell letter.
4. Willcox quoted in Scott, 288.
5. Ritter, letter.
6. Doherty's report on his experiences as a POW at Sudley Methodist Church Field Hospital in the New York Post July 29, 1861 was subsequently printed in many northern newspapers.
7. Letter to the *Pawtucket Gazette.*
8. Sergeant Abner Small, Third Maine, *Voices*, 103.
9. Assistant Surgeon U. S. A., D. S. Magruder, quoted in Denny, 34.
10. Extrapolation from dates they passed through the lines to return home, Civil War Database.
11. Data analysis from Civil War Database.
12. Croffut, 51.
13. Ibid.
14. Edwin S. Barrett, "What I saw at Bull Run, An Address," (Boston: Beacon Press, 1886), 26.
15. Assistant Surgeon Melcher of the Fifth Missouri quoted in Denny, 40.
16. Henry Rivers, M. D. *Accidents: Popular Directions for Their Immediate Treatment,* (Providence, R.I. B. Cranston & Co., 1845) passim.
17. *Providence Journal,* July 29, 1861
18. William H. Pierce letter to father, July 24, 1861, manuscripts at RIHS.
19. C. Keith Wilbur M.D., *Civil War Medicine 1861–1865,* (Guilford, CT: Globe Pequot Press, 1998), 43–44.
20. Wilbur, 44.
21. *Providence Journal,* Friday August 2, 1861.
22. Woodbury, First, 119–120.
23. Alexander, 37.
24. Ricketts, CCW, 242.
25. Porter, CCW, 211.
26. Blake, in Congdon, 22.
27. Bicknell, 28.
28. Ibid, introduction.
29. Willcox in Scott, 289.
30. Blake, in Congdon, 22.
31. Bicknell, 39.
32. Josiah Nott, letter to a friend, July 23, 1861, published in the *Mobile Advertiser and Register* July 30, 1861, quoted in *The Alabama Confederate Reader*, 117–120.
33. Nott letter, ACR 118.
34. Nott letter, ACR 120.
35. Blake in Congdon, 26.
36. Private George Barnsley, Eighth Georgia. Voices, 118.
37. Beauregard, *Century,* 18.
38. Hollis, quoting an eyewitness, himself quoted in Penny, 8.
39. Ibid.
40. Sergeant Major Robert Coles, 4th Alabama, *Voices,* 121.
41. Penny, 8.

42. Davis, 198.
43. McHenry Howard, *Recollections of a Maryland Confederate Soldier,* quoted in Congdon, 33.
44. Davis 200–1.
45. Alexander, 37.
46. Fry, in *Battles and Leaders,* 182.
47. Averell quoted in Hennessy, 72 .
48. Blake in Congdon, 25.
49. Averell, CCW, 214.
50. Barnard, CCW, 161.
51. United States Census, Prince William County, 1860.
52. Beauregard, *Century,* 14.
53. Alexander, 35.
54. Davis, 204.
55. Ricketts, CCW, 243.
56. Eleana Henry, *Some Events Connected with the Life of Judith Carter Henry,* VHS, quoted in Davis, 205.
57. Records on Compton family, MNBP archives.
58. Alexander, 39.
59. Averill, CCW, 214.
60. Willcox quoted in Scott, 292.
61. Ibid. 291.
62. Meagher.
63. Willcox quoted in Scott, 293.
64. *Harpers* 153 note
65. Heintzelman, CCW, 31.
66. Averill
67. David Homer Bates, *Lincoln in the Telegraph Office,* (New York: The Century Co., 1907), 91.
68. Ibid.
69. Assistant U. S. Surgeon D. S. Magruder quoted in Denny, 34.
70. Dr. Mathew B. Reeves, History of Sudley Post Office accessed 28 April 2003 at http://nps-vipnet./history/SudleyPo/; Sudley Post Office Study Chapters 2 and 4, accessed 28 April 2003 at www/heritage/umd/edu/CHRSWeb/NPS/SudleyPostOffice.
71. Nicolay and Hay, 349.
72. Lt. Wm Blackford, 1st Virginia Cavalry, Voices, 129.
73. Hennessy, 97.
74. MacDonald, 113–117.
75. Nott, quoted in ACR, 118.
76. Stewart.
77. Uncited Heintzelman letter quoted in Coles.
78. Hennessy, 102.
79. Nathaniel Rollins, letter of July 25, 1861, in E. B. Quiner, "Correspondence of Wisconsin Volunteers," Vol.1, 115, Wisconsin Historical Society, quoted in Hennessy, 103.
80. William Todd, The Seventy-ninth Highlanders, (Albany, 1886), quoted in Davis, 218.
81. Again, a general conclusion of most officers; specific attribution unavailable.
82. Alfred Guernsey, and Henry Alden, *Harper's Pictoral History of the Civil War,* (New York: The Fairfax Press, 1866), 153, 157.
83. Howard quoted in Congdon, 34–35.
84. Nott, ACR,119.
85. Thomas Cooper DeLeon, *Four Years in Rebel Capitals,* (Mobile, AL: Gossip Print Company, 1893), reprint: (Time Life Books, 1983), 122–126.
86. Beauregard, *Century,* 16.
87. Barry, CCW, 147. or Major William F. Barry, Battle Report, First Manassas in Official Reports (OR) Series 1, Volume 2, Chapter IX, 346 accessed 8 January, 2004 at Cornell University, Making of America at http://library5.cornell.edu.
88. Heintzelman, CCW 28.
89. Fry, *Battles and Leaders,* 191.

Chapter 18 Yankee Doodle Wheeled About

1. Colonel Dangerfield Parker, "Personal Reminiscences", USA, War Papers, 36 Washington, D.C. Division of MOLLUS, November 7, 1900, 10.
2. Ibid., 6.
3. Ritter letter.
4. Horace Cunningham, *Field Medical Services at the Battle of Manassas (Bull Run)* (Athens: GA: University of Georgia, 1968), 18,
5. Putnam, 19.
6. Johnson, *Horseshoe Curve,* 95.
7. Louis. B. Duncan, The Medical Department of the United States Army in the Civil War.1985, *The Medical Department of the United States Army in the Civil War.* (Carlisle Barracks, PA: Medical Field Service School, 1931), Reprinted, various, including Gaithersburg, MD: Olde Soldier Books, Inc., 1997, 31.
8. *Providence Journal,* Friday August 2, 1861
9. Doherty
10. Charles J. Murphy, *Reminiscences of the War of the Rebellion and the Mexican War, Letter to the Editor of the Providence Journal, 60–63,*(New York: F. J. Ficker, 1882.)
11. Croffut, 50.
12. Edmonds, 41–2.
13. Munroe, 7.
14. Alexander, 41
15. Ricketts believed his own captured guns may have been trained on the fleeing Rhode Islanders. Southern sources are silent on this, although other guns were available to carry out this same objective, and some did move into position within range of Cub Run.
16. "Tockwotton" in *Providence Press,* July 26, 1861; testimonials from Ames in Roelker, 14; Dr. Rivers in *Woonsocket Patriot,* August 2, 1861.
17. Johnson, *Horseshoe Curve,* 80.
18. Davis, 210.
19. J. E. B. Stuart, "Report of Colonel J. E. B. Stuart, First Virginia Cavalry," July 26, 1861. Battle Report, First Manassas in Official Reports (OR) Series 1, Volume 2, Chapter IX, accessed 26 January, 2004 at www.swcivilwar.com/StuartReport1stMan.html.
20. Sprague papers in Rhodes, 39.
21. Bicknell, 31
22. Munroe, in *Voices,* 152.
23. English letter, Rhodes, 34
24. Ibid.
25. Rhodes, 30.
26. Munroe, in *Voices,* 152.
27. Stuart, OR.
28. Ibid.
29. Doherty.
30. Woodbury, *First,* 107.
31. Report of Col. J. E. B. Stuart, First Virginia Cavalry For The Battle of 1st Bull Run To General Joseph E. Johnston, July 26, 1861.
32. William Howard Russell The Battle of Bull Run: (Russell's Celebrated Letter New York: Rudd and Carleton 1861), 25.
33. Ibid.
34. Ibid., 12
35. Putnam, 5.
36. Putnam, 7.
37. Ibid.
38. Ibid., 7–8
39. Russell, 14–15.
40. Stedman, 36.
41. Putnam, 8.
42. Coles, 24.
43. Russell, 25–6.
44. Putnam, 9.

45. Putnam 13–14.
46. Richardson, OR, 25.
47. Blake in Congdon, 28.
48. Putnam, 10.
49. Putnam, 11, 13, 18-19.
50. Alexander, 45.
51. J. W. Reid, *History of the Fourth Regiment of South Carolina Volunteers,* (Dayton: np, 1975), 25, quoted in Hennessy, 129.
52. Leech, 125; Nicolay and Hay 352.
53. Hay 353.
54. Ibid.; Perret, 67.
55. McDowell telegram to Scott, 5:45 P.M. July 21, 1861 OR, Volume III, Chapter IX. 316.
56. Ibid.
57. Doherty
58. Ibid.
59. Bicknell, 33.
60. Sprague Papers, Rhodes 39
61. Rhodes, 30.
62. Woodbury, Discourse, 16.
63. Russell, 24.
64. Rhodes, 30.
65. Nicolay and Hay, 353.
66. Leech, 125.
67. General Scott telegram to Runyon, 8 P.M. July 21, 1861, OR Volume III, Chapter IX.
68. Nicolay and Hay, 355.
69. McDowell, OR, 316.
70 Nicolay and Hay, 354.
71. Keyes, CCW, 152.
72. Volley of telegrams between the War Department Headquarters, General Scott, Colonel McCunn, and McDowell, between 8 P.M. and midnight, July 21, 1861. OR Volume III, Chapter IX.
73. Thomas J. Scott, Pennsylvania Railroad, telegrams to Governor Curtin of Pennsylvania, the night of July 21–22, 1861,
74. Alexander, 50.
75. DeLeon, 122-26.
76. McDonald 129.
77. Colonel Kerrigan telegram to secretary of war, predawn, July 22, 1861, OR Volume III, Chapter IX.
78. General Scott.
79. Sherman telegram to Vice President Andrew Johnson at 10:11 A.M. July 22, 1861, telegram to Andrew Johnson. OR Volume III, Chapter IX.
80. Russell, 12.
81. Bates, 88.
82. Nicolay and Hay,343-346.
83. Nicolay and Hay, quoted in Baringer and Miers, 56.
84. Edwin S. Barrett, "What I saw at Bull Run, An Address," (Boston: Beacon Press, 1886), 30.
85. Rhodes, 30.
86. Putnam, 14.
87. Ibid., 15–16.
88. Stedman, 25.
89. Monroe 30.
90. Leech, 127.
91. Mary Henry, Diary, Archives of the Smithsonian Institution, Washington D. C., 2.
92. English, in Rhodes, 34-35.
93. Munroe, 7–8.
94. Whitman in McElray.
95. Henry, 3.
96. Blake in Congdon, 27–32.
97. Henry Wadsworth Longfellow, "Killed at the Ford," accessed 1 August 2004 at http://www.eagleacademy.org/killford.htm.

Chapter 19 Weeping Sad and Lonely

1. *Providence Journal,* July 21, 1861.
2. *Providence Journal,* July 22, 1861.
3. Extracted from *Providence Journal* stories between July 22–28, 1861.
4. Extract from a letter from an Officer in Company C [First?]. *Providence Daily Journal* July 26, 1861.
5. Sholes.
6. Aldrich, 20.
7. Blake, in Congdon, 29.
8. Meagher.
9. Blake in Congdon, 29.
10. Fry in *Battles and Leaders,* 176.
11. Henry, 2.
12. Putnam, 17.
13. Duncan, 34.
14. Eggleston, 44.
15. Putnam, 16.
16. Henry, 3.
17. McElray, *Whitman's,* 6.
18. Stedman, 39.
19. McElray, 6.
20. *Providence Daily Journal,* July 22, 1861
21. Ibid.
22. C. C. Gray, assistant surgeon U. S. A., quoted in Denny, 33.
23. Ibid. 35.
24. Ibid. 35.
25. Ibid., 36, and preceding quote from Murphy.
26. Murphy.
27. Murphy.
28. Doherty.
29. Murphy.
30. Murphy.
31. Beauregard, Century, 12.
32. Doherty.
33. "Parole," Boatner, 620.
34. Doherty.
35. Murphy.
36. Murphy.
37. Johnson, *Horseshoe Curve,* 96.

Chapter 20 Life's Tide is Ebbing Out So Fast

1. Henry, 2–3.
2. *Providence Journal,* July 2[5?], 1861 (date not especially legible)
3. Report of Lieutenant Colonel Frank Wheaton, Second Rhode Island Infantry. July 23, 1861 OR Chapter Ix 400 No. 41.
4. Woodbury, *Second,* 43.
5. Pierce letter.
6. Henry, 3.
7. *Providence Journal* July 28, 1861.
8. Frank Moore, *Women of the Civil War, their Heroism and Self Sacrifice,* "Mrs. Fanny Ricketts," (Hartford, CT: S. S. Scranton & Co.1866), 17–30.
9. Edmonds, 55.
10. Sholes
11. Aldrich, 15.
12. *Providence Journal,* July 29, 1861.
13. DeLeon 122-126.
14. *Providence Journal,* July 24,1861.
15. *Woonsocket Patriot,* July, 1861.

16. *New York Tribune* July 27, 1861 *Pawtucket Chronicle* Bull Run accessed 4 August 2004, at www.jimlyons.com/civilwarts1861.html
17. Greeley, CCW. 459.
18. Sullivan Ballou, to wife, second letter of July 14, 1861
19. Reverend Andrews, letter from Manassas.
20. Richmond Enquirer.
21. Moore, 25.
22. Bell Irvin Wiley, *The Life of Johnny Reb The Common Soldier of the Confederacy.* (New York: Bobbs Merrill Company, 1943), 90.
23. Appendix to Battle Report of Beauregard.
24. Doherty.
25. Doherty.
26. *Providence Journal,* July 30, 1861. *New York Times* August 6, 1861.
27. Gray in Denny, 37.
28. Reverend John Mines, letter to L.P. Walker, Secretary of War, Confederate State, in OR, Series II, Volume 2, Chapter IX, 1509-1510, and Confederate Government correspondence relating to his case, 1508-1512.
29. Ledger, deaths for 1861, Providence City Hall Archives
30. Josiah Richardson, statement attached to pension application of Sarah Ballou, Union Army Pension Records, Case 27, National Archives and Records Administration, Washington, D. C.

Chapter 21 And Our Hopes in Ruins Lie

1. Richardson statement, pension application of Sarah Ballou.
2. Sprague, CCW, 475.
3. Dr. James B. Greeley, CCW, 459.
4. The First Manassas, no author cited, *Southern Historical Society Papers,* Volume XXX, 1902, 272.
5. Laura Thornberry Fisher, Sudley "Post Office" from "Recollections" typescript in archives at MNBP.
6. Federal Census of 1860, microfilm edition, Prince William County VA mortality schedule.
7. Cunningham, Horace H., *Field Medical Service at the Battles of Manassas,* (Athens, GA: University of Georgia Press) 1968. Typescript draft at MNBP is divided into Confederate and Union parts, each with their own footnotes, Confederate footnote 16, quoting De Kay letter to *Louisville Courier,* August 27, 1861, quoted in the National Intellegencer, September 7, 1861.
8. *Providence Journal,* July 29, 1861.
9. Willcox in Scott, 303.
10. Penny, 8-9.
11. Wiley, 260.
12. Cunningham quoting the *New York Times,* August 6, 1861 in Confederate footnote 65.
13. *Richmond Daily Dispatch,* July 25, 1861.
14. Cunningham quoting Dr. E. F. Bouchelie, letter to editors, *Richmond Daily Dispatch* August 15, 1861. Confederate footnote 48.
15. The source on this quote just oozed away.
16. *Surgeon General of the United States Army, Medical and Surgical History of the war of the Rebellion,* 6 volumes, (Washington: 1870–1888) Part I Volume I, 1 Appendix.
17. *New York Times,* August 6, 1861.
18. Reverend Joseph A. Higginbotham, Diary, entries for end of July, 1861. Manuscripts at University of Virginia Library.
19. *New York Tribune,* August 17, 1861.
20. Edmonds, 298-299.
21. Fisher typescript: Written down seventy-six years afterwards, her testimony is a blend of what she saw for herself, and what adults told her. While she bears authentic witness to the devastation of her home, and the life long bitterness she bore, her sequences of events and dates of events are incorrect; she runs together the events of two years and battles. It is hard to date the episode of the dumping of the family possessions into the well behind the house. It is highly unlikely that any looting took place as the Second Division troops were waiting to attack on the morning of July 21. While the medics preparing the house for use on the afternoon of the battle might well have dumped household goods in the yard, it makes no sense for them to destroy the well, whose water they would need for the wounded. The badly wounded could not have vandalized, and it seems more to human

nature that the lightly wounded would have used the cups and dishes for their own use, rather than throwing them down the well. Only two other time frames remain for the battle of First Manassas. One would be during the retreat, but it seems unlikely that soldiers fleeing from enemy cavalry would take time to throw the flat iron down the well. The other is when the hospital was evacuated around July 26. Then too, the prisoner/nurses were too carefully supervised by Confederate soldiers to have the freedom of movement to do that. Also, by that time, relationships with the local people around Sudley were cordial since they had been feeding and nursing the sick. More likely, this event coincided with Second Manassas or the Confederate pull back in March, 1862, as do other parts of her testimony not included here as relevant.

22. Marianne Compton, Diary, archives of MNBP.
23. *Woonsocket Patriot,* July 24, 1861.
24. *Providence Journal,* Friday August 2, 1861.
25. Copy of resolution of the Woonsocket Guards, archives at RIHS.
26. Ibid.
27. *Providence Journal,* August 19, 1861.
28. Ibid.
29. Chen Song, "Applying for the Union Army Pension: A Summary for Historical Evidence," Center for Population Economics, February 26, 2000, accessed 12 May 2005 at www.cpe.uchicago.edu/publication/lib/pension_sum.pdf. While this quote is from the 1862 Pension Act, the provisions were the same when she first applied, and much of her subsequent dealings with the federal government were covered by this act.
30. Sarah Ballou Pension File, NARA.
31. Sullivan Ballou, will, Cranston City Hall.
32. Sullivan Ballou, will; Ledger Book of Providence County Probate Court, 1861, month of August, last section, page number illegible, microfilm edition, at the LDS Library, Utah.
33. *Philadelphia Ledger* quoted in the *Richmond Enquirer.*
34. Ames letters of August 4 to father and July 31, 1861 [to parents?] in Roelker, January, 1941, 24 and 21.
35. Handwritten Inventory, Second Rhode Island Regimental Band July 25, 1861, manuscript collection of the RIHS
36. Henry, 4.

Chapter 22 Though We Live in Winter Quarters

1. George Wise, *Campaigns and Battles of the Army of Northern Virginia.* (New York: Neale Publishing Company, 1916), 33.
2. Woodbury, *First,* 253.
3. *Richmond Dispatch,* July 24,1861.
4. Allen, 11, 21.
5. Allen, 31.
6. Coles 240, Notes to Page 30; Pvt. Otis D. Smith, 6th Alabama tourist, to "Mrs. Allen," August 18, 1861, typescript at MNBP.
7. Philip Thomas Tucker, *Burnsides's Bridge, the Climactic Struggle of the 2nd and 20th Georgia at Antietam Creek,* (Mechanicsburg, PA.: Stackpole, 2000.), 11.
8. Phoebe Yates Pember. *A Southern Woman's Story, Life in Confederate Richmond 1862–1865.* reprint (Marietta, GA.: Mockingbird Books, 1974) 123.
9. Cunningham printed 25. From Report of General Joseph E Johnston, August 17, 1861 OR, 7.
10. Wiley, *Reb,* 244.
11. Analysis by author from Civil War Database, of Twenty-First Georgia, all companies except E.
12. Captain E. B. Stiles, Company "E" Sixteenth Georgia, Wiley, Reb, 262.
13. William H. Phillips, Confederate Soldier, Wiley, Reb, 262.
14. Hankinson, 21.
15. Napier Bartlett, *A Soldier's Story,* 1875, reprinted in *Military Record of Louisiana,* (New Orleans: Louisiana State University Press, 1996).
16. Wise, 44.
17. *Historic Alexandria Quarterly,* Fall 1997 Volume 2 No 3 "John La Mountain and the Alexandria Balloon Ascensions." Passim.
18. Wise, 44.
19. Wiley, 59.
20. Governor William Sprague letter to Sarah Ballou, October, 1861, in manuscripts at RIHS.

21. Pension application of Sarah Ballou; Kautz, 1865, 274-283.
22. Adin Ballou, *History,* 1062; Olney Arnold Scrapbooks, collection of the Daughters of the American Revolution, Pawtucket, Rhode Island.
23. Nisbit 24.
24. Wiley, Reb, 60; Sarah "Sallie" Summers Clark of Level Green Farm, typescript at MNBP.
25. Wiley, Reb, 60.
26. G. L. Robertson, Texas, quoted in Wiley, *Reb,* 61.
27. Nisbit, 26.
28. Wiley, *Reb,* 64.
29. Allen. He also says "for love or money," on page 32.
30. DeLeon, 141.
31. Wise, 47.
32. Nisbet, 30.
33. Wise, 49
34. Wiley, *Reb,* 41.
35. Nisbit, 26
36. Wise, 51.
37. Nisbet, 25.
38. *Johnson's Common School Arithmetic* (Raleigh, NC: 1864), 38.
39. Wiley, *Reb,* 308.
40. Frederick Scholes, CCW, 454.
41. Wiley, *Reb,* Note 46 on 48.
42. Wiley, *Reb,* 63.
43. Greeley, CCW, 459.

Chapter 23 With Tender Care

1. Rev. Frederic Denison, *Sabres and Spurs, the First Regiment Rhode Island Cavalry in the Civil War, 1861–1865,* (no city: The First Rhode Island Cavalry Veterans Association Publisher, 1876), 45.
2. Testimony of Hon. Simon Cameron, before the Committee on the Conduct of the War, April 23, 1862 478.
3. Testimony of John Kane, before the Committee on the Conduct of the War, April 24, 1862 478-9.
4. http://www.nws.noaa.gov/ At this site, you can type in city and date and get historical weather records.
5. Rhodes, 56.
6. *Richmond Daily Dispatch,* November 13, 1861.
7. Rhodes, 53.
8. Ibid.
9. Robert Knox Snedon, *Images from the Storm,* (New York: The Free Press/Simon and Schuster. 2001), 15.
10. John Fowler Shumway pension file.
11. Private Joseph C. Martin, 102nd PA. *Diary,* 3, entry for February 11, 1862. accessed 19 December 2004 at http://cwdpa102ndregimentvolinf.com/jbmjan.htm.
12. Boatner, 108.
13. Rhodes, 56.
14. Snedon, 24.
15. Edmonds, 64–65.
16. Denison, 45.
17. Ibid.
18. Ibid., 41-44.
19. Ibid., 45.
20. CWDB and Denison, 45-46.
21. Denison, 46.
22. Ibid., 45.
23. Ibid., 46.
24. Ibid.
25. Ibid.
26. Ibid. 47.
27. Ibid.

28. Ibid. 48.
29. Ibid. 48-49.
30. Ibid. 49.
31. Ibid.
32. Greeley, CCW, 458.
33. By carefully cross referencing all accounts, the activities of undertaker Coleman have been discerned.
34. Greeley, 458
35. It is the author's opinion, as stated just above, that the most likely person to have provided this set of details to the *New York Times* was undertaker Coleman.
36. Testimony of Governor William Sprague, CCW 475.
37. Greeley, CCW, 458.
38. Denison, *Sabers,* 50–51,
39. Coleman, presumed, from press reports.
40. Sprague, CCW, 475.
41. Denison, CCW, 461
42. Greeley, CCW, 458.
43. Ibid.
44. Sprague. CCW, 475.
45. Ibid.
46. Coleman.
47. Greeley, CCW, 458
48. Ibid.
49. Ibid.
50. Coleman.
51. Coleman.
52. Greeley, CCW, 459.
53. Coleman
54. L. Vanloan Naisawald, "The Little Church at Sudley," *Virginia Cavalcade* Vol VIII Number 3 Winter 1958, 10.
55. Denison
56. Greeley, CCW, 461.
57. Douglas S. Freeman, *Lee's Lieutenants, A Study in Command,* One Volume Abridgement by Stephen W. Sears. (New York: Simon and Schuster, 1998), 319.
58. DeLeon, 139.
59. Snedon, 16.
60. Denison, 51.
61. Greeley, 459.
62. Denison, 52.
63. Ibid. 52-53.
64. Ibid.
65. Ibid.
66. Ibid.
67. Ibid., 53.

Chapter 24 Wreaths of Glory

1. Rhodes, 60.
2. *Philadelphia Public Ledger,* March 26 and 27, 1862.
3. *New York Times,* March 28, 1862.
4. *New York Times,* March 29, 1862.
5. *New York Times,* March 28, 1862.
6. *New York Times,* March 29, 1862.
7. *New York Express,* reprinted in the Providence Journal, April 1, 1862.
8. *New York Times* March 29, 1862.
9. Oxford Dictionary of Music, Online edition 2002.
10. *Providence Journal,* April 1, 1862.
11. *New York Express* reprinted in the Providence Journal, April 1, 1862.
12. Ibid.
13. *New York Times,* March 29, 1862
14. Ibid.

15. Ibid.
16. *New York Times,* March 31, 1862.
17. *Rochester's History, Glossary of Victorian Cemetery Symbolism:* Plants 11., accessed 27 September, 2002.at www.vintageviews.org/vvtl/pages/Cem_Symbolism.htm
18. *Providence Journal,* April 1, 1862.
19. Rhodes, 84. Actually, Rhodes' precise words were, "It is not like death at home."
20. *Providence Journal,* April 1, 1862.
21. Ibid.
22. Ibid.
23. Ibid.

Chapter 25 The Eagle of Freedom Shrieks

1. Motion by Senator Sumner, CCW, 449.
2. CCW, 449–483.
3. Robert J. Trout, *With Pen and Saber,* (Mechanicsburg, PA.: Stackpole Books, 1995), 19 & 21.
4. Testimony of Frederick Scholes CCW, 466-67.
5. Testimony of Daniel Bixby, Jr. before the Committee on the Conduct of the War, CCW, 476.
6. Scholes, CCW, 467.
7. *Richmond Dispatch,* April 8, 1862.
8. Ricketts, CCW, 463.
9. *Richmond Dispatch* April 9, 1862.
10. Report of the select Committee on the Conduct of the War, 456.
11. Ibid.
12. Drew Gilpin Faust, "Altars of Sacrifice: Confederate Women and Narratives of War," *Journal of American History* 76, March, 1990,178; Woodbury, speech, July 2, 1862, manuscripts collection, RIHS.
13. The U.S.S. *Preble,* Sloop of War, accessed 7 June 2002 at http://hub.dataline.net.au/~tfoean/prble.htm.
14. Acts and Resolves of the Rhode Island General Assembly, May 1862, 30.
15. Table in Song report, Filing for the Union Army Pension; Sarah Ballou pension file.
16. *The Providence Directory,* (Providence, RI: Adams, Samson & Co. June 1, 1863), 29.
17. Ledger, Deaths of 1863, Providence City Hall Archives.
18. *Providence Journal,* May 4, 1863.
19. Ibid.
20. CWDB, extracts from military records.
21. The Guano War of 1865–1866, accessed 15 January 2005 at www.zum.de/whkmla/military/19cen/guanowar.html and www.zum.de/whkmla/region/samerica/peru18210.html same date; and Department of State Listing of Ambassadors to Peru, 2, accessed 2 December, 2003, at www.state.gov/r/pa/ho/com/11144.htm
22. CWDB
23. John Fowler Shumway pension file.
24. Colonel Alanson M Randol, "The Second New York Cavalry at Appomatox Station and Appomatox Court House April 8 and 9, 1865," accessed 5 May 2004 at http://www.rootsweb.com/~nyononda/MANLIUS/2NDNYCAV.HTM/
25. Florence Simister, Streets of the City, Volume XII 1963–1964, 99–100. Typescript in the RIHS library.
26. Simister, "Abraham Lincoln and Providence."
27. "Sermon Suggested by the Assassination of Abraham Lincoln" (Providence, R.I. Anthony Knowles and Co., 1865) 21, 26, 22.
28. Leech, 510.

Chapter 26 We Shall Win the Day

1. Conley and Campbell, 86, 89.
2. Walter A. Nebiker, *The History of North Smithfield,* (Somersworth, NH: North Smithfield Bicentennial Commission, 1976),121.
3. Nebiker, quoting Bidwell, 1921, 115.
4. John Hutchins Cady, "Swan Point Cemetery: A Centennial History 1847–1947," (Providence R. I:. no publisher, 1947), 8.
5. Ibid., 17

6. Ibid., 19
7. The *Providence Evening Bulletin* June 1, 1868.
8. 1870 Federal Census, Rhode Island, Providence County, District 1, microfilm edition, 1-4 District Smithfield 1477; 644.
9. "Proceedings, Dedication of the Soldiers' and Sailors' Monument 1871." No publication data.
10. Augustus Woodbury, "An Oration Delivered at the Dedication of the Soldiers' and Sailors' Monument Erected by the State of Rhode Island," in Providence, September 16, 1871. (1871: A. Crawford Greene, Providence), passim, 16, 24–26.
11. Cady, 21.
12. Broadside, in Broadside files of the manuscripts division of the John Hay Library, Brown University; Dedication of Slocum Monument, Providence Journal November 30, 1886.
13. Cady, 20.
14. Table in Song report, Filing for the Union Army Pension; and Sarah Ballou pension files.
15. Records of the School Committee of the City of Providence, December 11, 1874, archives of the city; Diary of Mrs. Reverend Frank Powers, manuscripts, RIHS, passim.
16. Ibid.
17. Records of the School Committee of the City of Providence, December 11, 1874 through 1889, archives of the city.
18. Simister, "The City Hall and The City Hall," *Streets of the City,* Volume V, January 30, 1956 to January 27, 1957, 48–49.
19. Gertrude Selwyn Kimball, *Providence in Colonial Times,* (Boston: Houghton Mifflin 1912.) 344-345.
20. 1875 Rhode Island State Census, State Archives, Providence, Rhode Island.
21. James Garfield quote by Rutherford Hayes from Dead Presidents on Dead Presidents, Garfield, accessed 12 April 2005 at http://www.diplom.org/manus/Presidents/ratings/prez.html; Nebiker, passim.
22. Adin Ballou, *History,* 431–433, 1057.
23. Email to author from Brown University manuscripts, dating attendance/degree.
24. *City Directory of Denver 1890,* accessed at Ancestry.com, and Adin Ballou, History, 1057. Directory
25. Roster of Craftsmen at the Gorham Silver Company, accessed 5 September 2004 at The Owl at the Bridge Web site at www.owlbridge.com/roster02.shtml. This includes job titles, payroll and sometimes family records.
26. Courtelyou Genealogy, Ancestry.com; *The Ancestors of Two Sisters,* (Lincoln, NE: Brown Printing Service, 1954).
27. *Evanston Index,* October 16, 1884.
28. Amos Benson quoted in Johnson, *Horseshoe Curve,* 95–102.
29. *1886 Fall River Directory* (Boston: Sampson, Murdock & Co., 1886).
30. Death records, 1889 Death Ledger Card Catalog, State Archives, Providence, R. I.
31. Records of the School Committee of the City of Providence, November 1889.
32. File of Miscellaneous papers relating to the Ballou Family, LDS Library.
33. *1891 Fall River Directory* and Ad, (Boston: Sampson, Murdock & Co., 1891), 780; *Fall River Directory 1893 No XXIV* (Boston: Sampson, Murdock & Co., 1893)
34. January 1952, Ballou Bulletin Board newsletter, 2 pages collection of the American Antiquarian Society, Worcester, MA.
35. Adin Ballou, History, 1057.
36. *Woonsocket Evening Call,* September (after the 7th) 1907, and a tribute by the Fortnightly Club, November 15, 1907, both on Mary Brownell and quoted in Representative Men and Old Families of Rhode Island Volume 1 Part 2, 546–1088, (Chicago: J. H. Beers and Co. Chicago, 1908), 735–736.
37. Medical records in John Fowler Shumway pension file.
38. 1890 Federal Census, Rhode Island, North Smithfield; *Philadelphia Inquirer,* also death record in John Fowler Shumway pension file.
39. Letter of Catherine Shumway to Pension commissioner, May 13, 1908 in JFS pension file.
40. Catherine Shumway Letter to Woodrow Wilson, March 7, 1914 in John Fowler Shumway pension file.
41. Documents in John Fowler Shumway pension file.
42. Letter from Pension Commissioner to Undertaker, 1928 in John Fowler Shumway pension file.
43. 1910 Federal Census, New Jersey, Essex County, the Oranges.
44. Death certificate of Sarah Ballou, 1917; State of New Jersey.
45. *Providence Journal,* April 19, 1917.

46. William Ballou, letter to Pension Office, April 25, 1917, in Sarah Ballou pension file.
47. *City Directory Appleton WI, 1904–1908,* accessed in the microfilm edition: City directories of the United States. Appleton, WI [microform]. (Woodbridge, CT: Research Publications, 1990) 7 microfilm reels; 35, Segment 1. 1884–1901—Segment 2. 1904–1910, from the Appleton Public Library; Obituaries: Edgar Fowler Ballou *Sierra Madre News* August 22, 1924; Obituary, Mary Hutchins Ballou, *Sierra Madre News,* January 25, 1929, Jean Woodward, *Sierra Madre News,* November, 1968, Hazel Woodward, *Sierra Madre News,* August, 1974.
48. William Ballou letter to U.S. Pension Office, Sarah Ballou pension file.
49. *The Oranges Directory,* 1925.
50. 1930 Federal Census, New York: New York City, Kings County, Brooklyn; family bulletin.
51. January 1952, Ballou Bulletin Board newsletter.
52. 1930 Federal Census, New York: Brooklyn, microfilm, Los Angeles Public Library.
53. *The Oranges Directory,* 1930, (Lee, N.J.: Price and Lee, 1939).
54. Death certificate of William Ballou, King's County, Brooklyn, New York
55. Cemetery and undertaker records for William Ballou. Will and probate records of William Fowler Ballou, King's County Surrogate's Court docket number 2613–48.
56. Death Certificate of Kathryn Strachan, San Jose County, CA.
57. Records of Oak Hill Memorial Cemetery, San Jose, CA. Telephone interview.

Bibliography

Adams, Henry. *The Education of Henry Adams.* Accessed at Bartleby.com.

Aldrich, Thomas M. *The History of Battery A, First Regiment Rhode Island Light Artillery in the War to Preserve the Union, 1861–1865.* Providence, RI: Snow & Farnham, printers, 1904.

Allen, Randall and Bohannon, Keith S., eds. *Campaigning with "Old Stonewall" Confederate Captain Ujanirtus Allen's Letters to His Wife.* New Orleans: Louisiana State University Press, 1998.

Anonymous. "The Sentiments of an American Woman." Broadside in the collection of the American Antiquarian Association, Worcester, MA. Accessed on the Internet on August 15 2002 at www.americanantiquarian.org...rk/Domestic/Americanwomanlarge.jpg.

Anderson, Mary Eliza Viall. *The Merchant's Wife.* Boston: 1876.

Andros, Reverend Thomas. "A Wonderful Deliverance," extracted from *The Old Jersey Captive, or a Narrative of the Captivity of Thomas Andros.* Boston: 1833.

Arnold, Noah J. "The History Of Suffrage in Rhode Island," *The Narragansett Historical Register,* Volume VIII. July 1890. No. 2, 305–331.

Bacon, Edward F., Ph.B. *Otsego County New York Geographical and Historical.* Oneonta, NY: The *Oneonta Herald,* 1902.

Ballou, Adin. *An Elaborate History and Genealogy of the Ballous in America.* Providence, RI: 1888.

Ballou, Sullivan. Letters. Manucript collection of the Rhode Island Historical Society.

Ballou, Sullivan. "Report of the Joint Special Committee on the Title of the State to Lands in the Woonasquatucket Valley." Providence, RI: Public Park Association; Providence Press Company, 1884.

Battles and Leaders of the Civil War. Volume One. Edison, NJ: Castle, 1887.

Baringer, William E. and Miers, Earl Schenck, eds. in chief. *Lincoln Day by Day A Chronology 1809–1865. Vol. II 1849–1860.* Washington: Lincoln Sesquicentennial Commission, 1960.

Bartlett, John Russell. *Memoirs of Rhode Island Officers.* Providence, RI: Sidney S. Rider & Brother, 1867.

Bates, David Homer. *Lincoln in the Telegraph Office.* New York: The Century Co., 1907.

Bayles, Richard M. *History of Providence County* Volumes I and II. New York: W. W. Preston and Co., 1891.

Beauregard, Pierre Gustave Toutant, "First Bull Run, First Manassas," *The Century Magazine,* Vol. XXIX, November 1884.

Bicknell, Reverend George W. *History of the Fifth Maine Regiment.* Portland, ME: Hall L. Davis, 1871.

Blanchard, Henry T., Second Rhode Island, letter to parents, June 25, 1861. Manuscripts, Historical Society of Washington, D.C.

Blesser, Carol K. and Gordon, Lesley J, eds. *Intimate Strategies of the Civil War, Military Commanders and Their Wives.* Oxford: Oxford University Press, 2001.

Boatner, Mark M. III. *The Civil War Dictionary.* New York: Vintage Books, 1991.

Bowman, John S., ed. *The Civil War Almanac.* New York: World Almanac Publications, 1985.

Brayton, Gladys W. *Other Ways and Other Days.* East Providence, RI: Globe Printing Company, 1975.

Buchanan, James. "State of the Union Address," U.S. Congress, December 3, 1860.

Carter, Robert Goldthwaite. *Four Brothers in Blue.* 1913 reprint edition. Oklahoma City: University of Oklahoma Press, 1999.

Chappell, A. W. (Sergeant, Second Rhode Island). Letter of July 25, 1861. Manuscript at RIHS.

Chesnut, Mary. *A Diary from Dixie.* New York: Portland House, 1977.

Childs, Lydia Maria. *The Mother's Book.* Boston: Carter and Hendee, 1831. Reprint Bedford, MA: Applewood Books, 1992.

Clinton, Catherine. *The Other Civil War, American Women in the Nineteenth Century.* New York: Hill and Wang, 1984.

Coles, Robert T. *From Huntsville to Appomattox: R. T. Coles's History of 4th Regiment, Alabama Volunteer Infantry, C.S.A. Army of Northern Virginia.* Edited by Jeffrey D. Stocker. Knoxville, TN: University of Tennessee Press, 1996.

Congdon, Don, ed. *Combat: The Civil War.* New York: Mallard Press, 1967.

Conley, Patrick T. and Campbell, Paul. *Providence, A Pictoral History.* Norfolk, VA: The Donning Company, 1986.

Croffut, William A. *American Procession, 1855–1914.* Boston: Little, Brown and Company, 1931.

Cross, Whitney R. *The Burned-Over District; the Social and Intellectual History of Enthusiastic Religion in Western New York, 1800–1850.* Ithaca, NY and London: 1950.

Cunningham, Horace H. *Field Medical Service at the Battles of Manassas.* Athens, GA: University of Georgia Press, 1968. Also, a pre-publication typescript with notes, at MNBP. Cited separately in text.

Cutrer, Thomas W., ed. *Longstreet's Aide: The Civil War Letters of Major Thomas J. Gore.* Charlottesville, VA: University Press of Virginia, 1995.

Daniel, Thomas, M. *Of Death: The Story of Tuberculosis.* Rochester, NY: University of Rochester Press, 1997.

Davis, William C. *Battle of Bull Run.* Garden City, New York: Doubleday and Company, 1977.

Davis, William C. *The First Battle of Manassas.* Fort Washington, PA: Eastern National, 1995.

De Leon, Thomas Cooper. *Four Years in Rebel Capitals.* Mobile, AL: *Gossip Print Company,* 1893.

Denny, Robert E. *Civil War Medicine Care and Comfort of the Wounded.* New York: Sterling Publishing Company, 1994.

Donald, David. *Charles Sumner and the Coming of the Civil War.* New York: Alfred A. Knopf, 1967.

Dring, Thomas. "The Narrative of Captain [Master's Mate] Dring," from his *Recollections of Jersey Prison Ship.* Morrisania, 1865.

Duncan, Capt. Louis C. *The Medical Department of the United States Army in the Civil War.* Carlisle Barracks, PA: Medical Field Service School, 1931.

Dwinell, Melvin. Letter of July 23, 1861. Printed in the Rome, GA, *Tri–Weekly Courier,* August 1, 1861.

Early, Jubal. *Autobiographical Sketch and Narrative of the War Between the States.* Philadelphia: 1912.

The Early Records of the Town of Providence Volume III: being part of the third book of the town of Providence otherwise called the book with brass clasps, Section 13. Providence RI: Snow & Farnum City Printers, 1893.

Edmonds, Sara Emma E. *Nurse and Spy in the Union Army: The Adventures and Experiences of a Woman in Hospitals, Camps and Battle Fields.* Hartford, CT: W. S. Williams and Co. 1865.

Eggleston, George Carey. *A Rebel's Recollections.* New Orleans: Louisiana State University Press; reprint edition, 1996.

Farrow, Edward S. *Farrow's Military Encyclopedia,* Vol II. New York: Self-published, 1885.

Fisher, Laura Thornberry. *Reminiscences,* 1932 typescript in the Manassas National Battlefield Park files.

Foote, Shelby. *The Civil War, A Narrative, Vol. 1 Secession to Fort Henry.* Alexandria, VA: Time Life Books, 1998.

Freeman, Douglas S. *Lee's Lieutenants, A Study in Command.* One volume abridgement by Stephen W. Sears. New York: Simon and Schuster, 1998.

General Biographical Catalogue of Auburn Theological Seminary 1818–1918. Auburn, NY: Auburn Theological Seminary Press, 1918.

Gleeson, Alice Collins. *Pawtucket, R.I.* The Automobile Journal Publishing Company, undated.

Green, Albert. Civil War letters at the South County Museum, Narragansett, Rhode Island.

Greenleaf, Benjamin A.M. *Introduction to the National Arithmetic, 1842.* Boston: Robert S. Davis & Co., 1876; reprint.

Grieve, Robert. *An Illustrated History of Pawtucket, Central Falls and Vicinity.* Pawtucket, RI: Pawtucket Gazette and Chronicle, 1897.

Guernsey, Alfred and Alden, Henry. *Harper's Pictoral History of the Civil War.* New York: The Fairfax Press, 1866.

Hankinson, Alan. *First Bull Run 1861.* London: Osprey Publishing, 1990.

Harper's Weekly Journal of Civilization. September 26, 1857, Vol I No. 39.

Harris, Brayton. *Blue and Grey and Black and White: Newspapers in the Civil War.* Washington, D.C.: Brassey's, 2000.

Hennessy, John. *The First Battle of Manassas,* Lynchburg, VA: H. E. Howard, 1989.

Henry, Mary. *Diary.* Smithsonian Institution, Washington D.C.

Hess, Earl J. *Liberty, Virtue and Progress, Northerners and Their War for the Union.* New York: Fordham University Press, 1997.

Horne, Alastair. *Seven Ages of Paris,* New York: Alfred Knopf, 2002.

Hunter, David. *Report of the military services of Gen. David Hunter, U.S.A: during the War of the Rebellion, made to the U.S. War Department, 1873.* New York: D. Van Nostrand, 1873.

Johnson, Elizabeth Harrover, Conner, E.R. III, and Ferguson, Mary Harrover. *History in a Horseshoe Curve, the Story of Sudley Methodist Church and its Community.* Self-published, 1995.

Johnston, Elizabeth J and Wheaton, James Lucas, IV. *History of Pawtucket Reminiscences and New Series of Reverend David Benedict.* Pawtucket, R.I.: Spaulding House Publications 1986.

Johnson, Robert Underwood and Buel, Clarence Clough, eds. *Battles and Leaders of the Civil War,* Volume I. New York: The Century, 1887.

Joint Committee on the Conduct of the War, Report, in Three Parts. Washington: Government Printing Office, 1863. Millwood, NY: Kraus Reprint Co., 1977.

Kautz, August V. *Customs of Service for Non-Commissioned Officers and Soldiers.* Second edition. Philadelphia: Lippincott, 1865.

Klamkin, Marian. *The Return of Lafayette, 1824–1825.* New York: Charles Scribner's Sons, 1975.

Klein, Maury. *Days of Defiance, Sumter, Secession and the Coming of the Civil War.* New York: Vintage Civil War Library, 1999.

Larkin, Catherine Martin. *What was Pawtucket Like 100 Years Ago?* 1928.

Lawes, Carolyn J. *Women and Reform in a New England Community, 1815–1860.* Lexington, KY: University of Kentucky Press, 2000.

Leech, Margaret. *Reveille in Washington 1860–1865.* Alexandria, VA: Time Life Books, 1941.

Lincoln, Abraham. First Inaugural Address, March 4, 1861.

McCusker, John J. *How Much is That in Real Money? A Historical Commodity Price Index.* Worcester, MA: American Antiquarian Society, 2001.

McMillan, Malcolm C. *The Alabama Confederate Reader.* Tuscaloosa, AL: University of Alabama Press, 1963.

McDonald, JoAnna M. *We Shall Meet Again, The First Battle of Manassas.* Oxford: Oxford University Press, 1999.

Martin, Private Joseph C. 102nd PA. Diary entry for February 11, 1862.

Meagher, Thomas F. "The Last Days of the 69th in Virginia." *Irish American,* 1861.

Mieczkowski, Yanek. *The Routledge Historical Atlas of Presidential Elections.* New York: Routledge, 2001.

Monroe, J. Albert. *Reminiscences of the War of the Rebellion 1861–1865.* Providence, RI: N. Bangs Williams & Company, 1881.

Moore, Frank. *Women of the Civil War, their Heroism and Self Sacrifice,* "Mrs. Fanny Ricketts." Hartford, CT: S. S. Scranton & Co., 1866.

Mullins, Lisa, ed. *Early Architecture of Rhode Island: The Archaeological Treasures of Early America.* Harrisburg, PA: National Historical Society, 1987.

Murphy, Charles J. *Reminiscences of the War of the Rebellion and the Mexican War.* New York: F. J. Ficker, 1882.

Murphy, Sharon Ann. "Life Insurance in the United States through World War II." Accessed January 14, 2003 at www.eh.net.encyclopedia/murphy.life.insurance.us.php.

Nebiker, Walter A. *The History of North Smithfield.* North Smithfield Bicentennial Commission, 1976.

Nicolay, John G. and Hay, John. *Abraham Lincoln, a History.* New York: The Century Co., 1890.

Nisbet, James Cooper. *Four Years on the Firing Line.* Chattanooga, TN: The Imperial Press, c. 1914.

Nylander, Jane C. *Our Own Snug Fireside: Images of the New England Home, 1760–1860.* New Haven, CT: Yale University Press, 1994.

O'Connor, Thomas H. *Of the Loom: The Cotton Whigs and the Coming of the Civil War.* New York: Charles Scribner's Sons, 1968.

Oates, Stephen B. *Clara Barton, A Woman of Valor.* New York: The Free Press, 1994.

Olmstead, Frederick Law. *The Cotton Kingdom.* New York: Knopf, 1853.

Opdyke, George. *Treatise on Political Economy 1851.*

Patsias, Maria. *Ghost and Vampire Legends of Rhode Island.* 3rd Story Productions, 2002.

Payne, Andrew. *Reminiscences of the Rhode Island Bar.* Providence, RI: Tibbets and Preston, 1885.

Pember, Phoebe Yates. *A Southern Woman's Story, Life in Confederate Richmond 1862–1865.* Marietta, GA: Mockingbird Books, 1974.

Perret, Geoffrey. *Lincoln's War,* New York: Random House, 2004.

Perry, James M. *Touched with Fire.* New York: Public Affairs Books, 2003.

Pierce, William. Letter of July 24, 1861. Rhode Island Historical Society Collection.

Philadelphia Public Ledger.

Potter, David M. *The Impending Crisis, 1848–1861.* New York: Harper & Row 1976.

Powers, Mrs. John. Diary, 1873. Unpublished manuscript in the collection of the Rhode Island Historical Society.

Putnam, George. "Before and After the Battle: A Day in Dixie," *Knickerbocker Magazine,* September 1861.

Ray, John Michael. "Rhode Island Reactions to John Brown's Raid," *Rhode Island History,* October 1961, Vol 20 No. 4.

Reeves, Dr. Mathew B. *Views of a Changing Landscape: An Archaeological and Historical Investigation of Sudley Post Office 44PW294, Manassas National Battlefield Park, Manassas, Virginia.* 1998. Report in the files of Manassas National Battlefield Park.

Reynolds, Douglas M. and Myers, Marjory, eds. *Working in the Blackstone River Valley: Exploring the Heritage of Industrialization.* Woonsocket, RI: Sheahan Printing, 1990.

Rhode Island Historical Preservation Commission, "Statewide Historical Preservation Report, Elmwood, Providence, P–P–3." Providence: June, 1979.

Rhodes, Robert Hunt. *All for the Union A History of the 2nd Rhode Island Volunteer Infantry in the War of the Great Rebellion.* Lincoln, Rhode Island: Andrew Mowbray Incorporated, 1985.

Richardson, Erastus. *History of Woonsocket.* Woonsocket, RI: S. S. Foss, 1876.

Rivers, Henry, M. D. *Accidents: Popular Directions for Their Immediate Treatment.* Providence, RI: B. Cranston & Co., 1845.

Rogers, Horatio, Jr. "Sullivan Ballou," chapter in *Brown University in the Civil War,* pp. 93–108. Providence, 1868.

Robinson, Christopher. Letters to Thomas Dorr, March 6, 1834, and August 29, 1835, in the manuscripts collection of the Brown University Library.

Roelker, William Greene. "Civil War Letters of William Ames," *Rhode Island Historical Society Collections,* Vol. 23, October, 1940, 73–92 and Vol 24, January 1941, 5–24.

Sawtelle, Ithamar B. *History of Townsend.* Self-published, 1878.

Scott, Robert Garth. *Forgotten Valor: The Memoirs, Journals, and Civil War Letters of Orlando B. Willcox.* Kent, OH: Kent State University Press, 1999.

Sessarego, Alan. *Letters Home II, Camp Life and Battle.* Gettysburg, PA: Americana Souvenirs and Gifts, 2001.

Shumway, Ashahel Adams. *Genealogy of the Shumway Family.* Atlantic City, NJ: 1909; reprint in facsimile, York, PA: George Shumway, 1971.

Sinclair, Upton. *Manassas: A Novel of the War.* New York: The MacMillan Company, 1904.

Silber, Irwin. *Songs of the Civil War.* New York: Columbia University Press. 1960.

Simister, Florence Parker. *Streets of the City.* A series of radio broadcast scripts covering fifteen years of local history reports. Typescripts at the Rhode Island Historical Society.

Simoncelli, Michael. *Battling the Enemies of Liberty: The Rise and Fall of the Rhode Island Know-Nothing Party. Rhode Island History,* Volume 54, Number 1, February, 1996. Rhode Island Historical Society.

Simpson, Brooks D. and Berlin, Jean V. eds. *Sherman's Civil War, Selected Correspondence Of William T. Sherman, 1860–1865.* Chapel Hill, NC: The University of North Carolina Press, 1999.

Smith, Dennis. *Report from Ground Zero.* New York: Viking, 2002.

Smith, Elbert B. *The Presidency of James Buchanan.* Lawrence, KS: The University Press of Kansas, 1975.

Snedon, Robert Knox. *Images from the Storm.* New York: The Free Press/Simon and Schuster. 2001.

Song, Chen. "Applying for the Union Army Pension: A Summary for Historical Evidence." Center for Population Economics, February 26, 2000.

Standage, Tom. *The Victorian Internet.* New York: Berkeley Books, 1999.

State of Rhode Island. Acts and Resolves of the State Legislature. 1853–1862. Rhode Island State Archives, Providence.

State of Rhode Island. Election Returns, Report of Special Committee Approved to Count the Votes for General Officers 1861, C#00171. Rhode Island State Archives, Providence.

State of Rhode Island. Office of the Attorney General at www.riag.state.ri.us/history/default.htm.

Stern, Phillip Van Doren. ed. *The Life and Writings of Abraham Lincoln.* New York: The Modern Library, 1940.

Stone, Edwin W. *Rhode Island in the Rebellion.* Providence, RI: George H. Whitney, 1864.

Sturdevant, Mary Rebecca Clark. *Thomas March Clark, Fifth Bishop of Rhode Island: A Memoir by his Daughter.* Milwaukee, WI: Morehouse, c 1927.

Sweatt, Kelsey Ballou. "Abraham Lincoln in New England." Address in Woonsocket, 1928. Printed document in manuscripts, John Hay Library, Brown University, Providence, RI.

Thornwell, Emily. *The Lady's Guide to Perfect Gentility, in Manners, Dress, and Conversation, in the Family, in Company, at the Piano Forte, The Table, in the Street, and in Gentlemen's Society. Also a Useful Instructor in Letter Writing, Toilet Preparations, Fancy Needlework, Millinery, Dressmaking, Care of Wardrobe, the Hair, Teeth, Hands, Lips, Complexion, etc.* New York: Derby and Jackson, 1856. Accessed March 27, 2005 at www.wwhp.org/Resources/Thornwell_lady_s_guide.html.

Trout, Robert J. *With Pen and Saber.* Mechanicsburg, PA: Stackpole Books, 1995.

United States Census Records 1790–1930. Microfilm edition, as specifically cited.

United States Congress. Report of the Joint Committee on the Conduct of the War, in Three Parts, Washington, 1863.

Van Den Bossche, Kris, ed. *Pleas Excuse All Bad Writing, a Documentary History of Rhode Island During the Civil War Era, 1854–1865.* Letter of Eliza Lanphear Covin to Sarah Lanphear, May 3, 1857, Providence, RI: The Rhode Island Historical Document Transcription Project 1993.

Walker, Anthony. *So Few the Brave: The Rhode Island Continentals 1775–1783.* Newport, RI: Seafield Press, 1981.

Ware, Edith Ellen. *Political Opinion in Massachusetts During the Civil War and Reconstruction.* New York: AMS Press, 1968.

Wilbur, C. Keith, M.D. *Civil War Medicine 1861–1865.* Guilford, CT: Globe Pequot Press, 1998.

Wiley, Bell Irvin. *The Life of Johnny Reb: The Common Soldier of the Confederacy.* New York: Bobbs Merrill Company, 1943.

Wiley, Bell Irvin. *Confederate Women.* Westport, CT: Greenwood Press, 1975.

Wilkes, George "The Great Battle, Notes Taken on the Spot." New York: Brown and Ryan.

Winchester, Simon. *Krakatoa: The Day the World Exploded.* New York: HarperCollins 2003.

Wise, George. *Campaigns and Battles of the Army of Northern Virginia.* New York: Neale Publishing Company, 1916.

Woodbury, Augustus. *The Campaign of the First Rhode Island Regiment.* Providence, RI: Sidney S. Rider, 1862.

Woodbury, Augustus. *The Second Rhode Island Regiment: A Narrative of Military Operations.* Providence, RI: Valpry, Anobell and Company, 1875.

Zettler, Berien McPherson. *War Stories and School–Day Incidents for the Children.* New York: Neale, 1912. Accessed December 30, 2001 at http://docsouth.unc.edu/zettler/zettler/html.

Index

Abbot Female Academy, 66
abolitionist movement, 31, 55, 58, 92–94, 131–134, 155
Aborn, Daniel, 2
Aborn, William, 471, 676–677
Accidents: Popular Directions for Their Immediate Treatment (Henry), 518
Ackridge, J. B., 284
Adirondack Mountains, 272
Aeronautics Corps, 414
African Americans
  and armed forces, 248
  Reconstruction era, 762–763
  in Rhode Island, 134
  in slavery, 260–261, 277
  voting rights, 33
Alabama
  as Confederate capital, 182
  and national debt, 336
  secession, 180, 181
  Alabama regiments, 231, 281, 413, 500, 501
  casualties, 527
  at Manassas, 478–479, 481, 497, 498
alcohol, drinking, 285, 569, 671–672, 688
Alexander, Edward Porter, 276, 292, 334, 444, 445, 575
Alexandria, Virginia, 234, 237–238, 273, 275
  occupied, by Union Army, 244–246
ambulance transport, field, 509–510
American Eloquence, 36–37
Amherst College, 42
amputation, 514–516, 519–520, 573, 601, 641
  surgical instruments, 515, 516
Anacostia River, 274
Anderson, Eliza Clinch, 169, 172
Anderson, Robert, 168–169, 175–176, 177–178, 180, 196, 204
Andersonville prison, 735
Anne S. K. Brown Military Collection, Brown University, 346, 468
Antietam Creek, 273
Appalachian Mountains, 272
Appomatox Court House, 735–736
Aqueduct Bridge, 274
Arkansas, secession, 234
Arlington House (Robert E. Lee's home), 244–245, 273, 303
armed forces. *see also* Confederate army; militias; regiments, by state; Union army
  Aeronautics Corps, 414
  after first battle of Manassas, 655–656
  camps, encampments. *see* camps, encampments
  death, from illness, 661–662
  deployment begins, 206–207
  deployment, prior to Civil War, 206
  discharges, for disability, 662
  discipline, 279–280, 280–281, 281–282
  equipment and supplies, 284–285, 327–328, 349, 369–370, 386–387
  federal, 206, 220, 221, 431
  inexperienced, 521–522
  intelligence, gathering, 427–428. *see also* spying, spies
  leadership. *see also* Scott, Winfield
  light artillery, 323
  medical practices, medicine. *see* medical practices, medicine
  military courts, 241
  naming conventions, for armies, 248
  officers, 330–331
  organization of, 305–306
  pay, 366
  prepared for battle, 423–426
  regulars, 532–533
  support staff, 280–281
  terms of enlistment, 230, 360, 416–417
  training, 299–301, 328–331, 338
  troop transport, 256–265, 284–285, 325–327
  weaponry, 306, 319–325
  winter quarters, 664, 667–671
  women, as soldiers, 372–375, 386–387
"Army of the Free" (song), 655
Army of the Potomac, final review, 739–740
Army of the West, final review, 740–741
artillery
  photo, of crew, 476
  role, in battle, 477
Astor House, New York City, 710
attorney general, duties, 198–199
Atwater, Dorrance, 735
Averell, William Woods, 532, 533–535, 537–538

baby waker, 435, 441–442
Balch, Joseph, 235
Ballou, Catherine Leahy, 772
Ballou, Charles F., 761
Ballou, Dexter, 70
Ballou, Edgar Fowler (Sullivan's son), 102, 743, 755, 757, 761, 763, 764–765, 768–769, 774, 778–779
Ballou, Eliza, 761–762, 762–763
Ballou family
  ancestors, 4–5, 6–7, 9, 23–24, xxxvi
  branches, 22–23, 26
  militia service, 34–35
  mills, 26–28
Ballou, Frances (Sullivan's sister), 121, 127
Ballou, George Coburn, 22, 25, 64
Ballou, Henry, 96, 757
Ballou, Henry (Sullivan's uncle), 77, 96, 127, 186, 650
Ballou, Hiram (Sullivan's father), 2, 22
  career, 7, 8–9
  illness and death, 10–12
  will and probate, 14–15
Ballou, James "The Astrologer", 761–762
Ballou, Janette (Sullivan's sister), 13
Ballou, Jonathan, 7
Ballou, Kathryn (Sullivan's grandaughter), 773, 775, 777, 780–781
Ballou, Latimer, 96, 251–252, 763
Ballou, Mathurin, 4–5
Ballou, Molly (Sullivan's grandmother), 23
Ballou, Oliver, 27
Ballou, Olney (Sullivan's cousin), 21–22, 32
Ballou, Sarah (Fales), 96, 127, 186, 773
Ballou, Sarah (formerly Shumway)
  after Sullivan's death, 649–650
  birth, 45–46
  childhood, 50, 52, 53–54, 54, 58, 64
  courtship of, 77, 80–81
  death, 773–774, 782
  education, 61, 62, 365. *see also* women's roles, education for
  finances, after Sullivan's death, 646–647
  finances, in Sullivan's absence, 350, 357–358, 365–366, 408, 741–742, 748–749, 755–756, 760–761
  injured in fall, 756–757
  later life, 769–770, 771
  letters, to Sullivan, 354, 367
  life without Sullivan, 729, 731–732, 733–734, 755–761, 763–764, 767–768
  marriage, 83–84, 87–89, 90, 91–92, 111, 140
  meets Sullivan, 77
  mourning, 622
  mourns, 616–617
  notified of Sullivan's death, 588, 590
  receives letter of condolence, 665–666
  receives pension, 666, 731–732
  as school secretary, 758–760
  told of Sullivan's desecration, 703–704
  waits for news, 570, 586–587
  wedding, 80–81
Ballou, Sullivan
  accepts military post, 249–250, 251–253
  arrives in Washington, 267–268
  birth, 9
  burial, 633–634, 637, 743, 745
  in business, 109–110
  childhood, 1, 2, 10, 11, 13–14, 16, 17–18, 22, 23, 35–36, xxvii
  concern, for sons, 360
  courtship of Sarah, 77, 80–81
  death, 631
  death, reported, 585, 612–613
  duties, in camp, 355–357, 363
  early career, xxvii–xxviii, 29–30, 78, 79–80, 89–90, 99–100
  education, 17–19, 23, 28–29, 37–38, 64–68, 70, 71–72, 365
  eulogy, 637–638
  honored, by Woonsocket Guards, 617–618
  law career, 122–123, 139–140, 144–145, 241
  leaves for war, 256–257
  letter, famous, xxxi–xxxii, xxxiii, xxxiv–xxxv, 764
  letters
    additional, 123–126, 251–252, 266, 268–270, 301–302, 306–319, 359–360
    preservation of, 781–782

to Sarah, xxviii–xxxii,
xxxi–xxxii, xxxiii,
xxxiv–xxxv, 268–270,
306–319, 345–351,
354–358, 364–368,
392, 407,
624–627
at Manassas, 462, 466, 469, 473,
482, 483, 485–486, 487
march, to Manassas, 379, 381–382
marches through Baltimore,
262–263
marriage, 83–84, 87–89, 90, 111,
140
meets Sarah, 77
militia service, 33–34, 35
monument, cemetery, 753–754
as officer, 330–331
parades, with regiment, 304
pay, military, 366
personal effects, 349–350, 357
photo, xxxviii
in politics, 99–100, 112–116,
119–120, 121, 136–138,
138–139, 144–145,
196–198, 200–202
poverty, 72–73
prescience, of death, 367–368
as public speaker, 128–130, 163
remains
desecrated, 690–697
journey home, 701–722
returned to Rhode Island,
717–722
reported dead, 610
source, of given name, 9–10
speech, at bridge inauguration,
128–130
teaching career, 71–72
tribute, New York City, 707–717
trunk arrives home, 624–625
undergoes amputation, 519–521
wedding, 80–81
will, 253–254, 650
wounded, 487–490, 496, 503,
506, 509–510, 517–519,
542, 554, 555–556, 601,
606, 627–628, 630
Ballou, William (Sullivan's son), 743, 755,
761, 765, 766, 768, 773, 774–775,
775–777, 777–778, 779–780
Ballou, Ziba (Sullivan's grandfather), 9,
23
Ballou's Illustrated, 61
Ball's Bluff, 663, 678
Baltimore, 219–221
railroad route, secured, 236
reception of Second Rhode Island,
261–263
sacked, 217–219
bands, military, 247–248, 264–265,
468, 510
Barry, William Farquar, 428
Bartlett, John Russell, 137, 155
Barton, Clara, 219
Bartow, Francis, 283, 300, 444,
657–658
photo, 657
Bartow's Brigade, 231, 283, 285, 343,
479
Bates, Edward, 185
battery, role, in battle, 474, 475,
476–477
"Battle Cry of Freedom" (song), 335
"Battle Hymn of the Republic" (song),
297
Beasley, Sarah, 374–375
Beauregard, P. T., 202–203, 287–288,
293, 294–295, 334, 341–342, 351,
353, 360, 384, 443–444, 604
attack plan fails, 480–481
closes in, at Manassas, 449–452
leadership, 526
at Manassas, 525–526, 528–529,
530–531
Bee, Barnard
dies, 528, 579
at Manassas, 481–482, 527–528
Bee's Brigade, 444
at Manassas, 456, 478–479, 481
Belisarius (British ship), 2
Bell, John, 166
Benson, Amos and Margaret, 607–608,
694–695, 766–767
Benton, Thomas Hart, 60
Berrian, Will, 591
Bicknell, George, 560–561
Black, Edward R., 192–193
Black Horse Cavalry, 291–292
Black River Association, 44–45
Blackburn's ford, 399–402
Blackstone Canal, 49, 134
Blackstone River, 1, 20, 27
Blair, Montgomery, 185
Blake, Henry, 569, 591–593
Blenker, Louis, 333, 352, 685
Block, Mary, 153, 590
Blue Ridge Mountains, 272, 273,
288–289
boardinghouses, 53–54
Bogle, Fred Mason, 765
Bogle, William, 121
Bolles brothers, 253
bone, shattered, on display, 515
Bonham, Milledge, 334, 351, 443
Bonham's Brigade, 290–291
Booth, John Wilkes, 738
Borders, S. A., 283
boredom, of camp life, 662–663, 673
Bowen, Clovis Hidlovus (Sullivan's
uncle), 29, 70
Bowen, Emeline Frances (Sullivan's
mother), 2, 6, 8–9, 17, 23, 28, 622
Bowen, Hannah Frances, 9
Bowen Jabez, 3, 21–22
portrait, 22
Bowen, Joseph, 2, 3, 4, 8–9, 11, 605, 777
Boykin, J. T., 284
Brady, Matthew, 148, 287
Breadbasket of the Confederacy, 272
Breckinridge, John, 157, 166
breechloading rifles, 462, 492
brigades, 248
Brooks, Preston, 97–99
"Brother Green" (song), xxv
Brown family, 26–27
Brown, John, 140–143
Brown, Joseph, 282–283
Brown, Moses, 134
Brown University, 6, 66–67, 186, 761
Anne S. K. Brown Military Collection, 346, 468
Brownell, Charles F., 139–140, 241
dies, 732–733
letter from Sullivan, 301–302
Brownell, Kady, 373
Brownell, Mary, 769–771, 773
Brownell, Richmond, 67
Bub, Frederick, 248, 476
Buchanan, James, 103, 105–106,
106–107, 108, 116, 119, 154,
169, 170–171, 172, 173–174,
179–180, 181–182
Bull Run, 447
Bull Run, Battle of. *see* Manassas, first
battle of
Bullock, Russell J., 155
Burgess, Walter S., 155
burials, 622–623, 633–635, 637–638,
641. *see also* dead, disposal of
Burns, Ken, xxxii, xxxiv
Burnside, Ambrose, 334, 418, 428,
462–464, 748
at Manassas, 474, 484
in North Carolina, 679–680
Burnside's Brigade, 305
at Manassas, 462, 464, 466,
494–495, 499, 501, 523–524
receives reinforcements, 499, 501
Bush, George H. W., xxxiii–xxxiv
Butler, Benjamin, 231, 234, 236
Butler, Nathan, 437

California, 184
California, early 1900s, 774
calling cards, 86, 87
Camden Station, Baltimore, 218–219
Camden Yards, 218
Cameron. Simon, 185, 595, 675–676
campaign practices, 161, 163–164
camps, encampments
Confederate army. *see* Confederate
army
equipment and supplies, 242, 246,
268–269, 349, 350, 357,
669–670
food, 268–269, 327–328, 328,
409–410
Keating house, 234–235
life, 301, 347, 355–356, 359,
662–663
Lincoln visits, 358
prepared for battle, 369–371
Rhode Island regiments, 265–269,
359
Richmond, Virginia, 279
spying, 305
Washington, D.C, 265–269, 303
winter quarters. *see* winter quarters
cannon, 323–324, 323–325
Parrot rifle, 435, 441–442
smooth-bore, 487
cantinières, 373–375
Capitol Building, 304, 338, 676
as barracks, 225
Carnegie, Andrew, 225, 540, 656
cartes de visite, 86, 87
casualties. *see also* hospitals, field
Confederate army, 490–491, 492,
493, 500, 527, 621
left on the battlefield, 557
mortal, 601, 610–611, 621
Union army, 325, 494, 499–500,
502–503, 678
casualty lists, 610–611
Catharpin Run, 447, 452
cavalry, 291–292, 681–683, 735–736
condition, of horses, 448
role of, 292
cemeteries
Rhode Island, 744–745
Victorian era, 752–753
Chace, Elizabeth Buffum, 134
Chain Bridge, 274
Chamberlain, Joshua Lawrence, 329
Chance (ship), 2
Chappell, Albert W., 490, 510
Chase, Salmon P., 185, 199, 337, 346
Cherry Valley Female Academy, 61–62
Cherry Valley, New York, 61–62,
121–122
Chesapeake Bay, 272, 274
Chesnut, James, 288
Chesnut, Mary Boykin, 131, 288
Chicago Historical Society, 764
Chickahominy River, 274
Child, Lydia, 54, 55–56, 63–64
Mother's Book, 16
childbirth, 101–102
Chimborazo Hospital Medical Museum,
516
Christian Commission, 630
Christmas, 1860, 173–174
Civil War
begins, 202–205
ends, 736–737
financing, 731-732, 336–338
imminent, 167–168, 171–172
issues and precipitants, 97–101,
107–108, 108–110,
109–110, 118–120, 140–144
Northern conceptions of, 214–215,
229–230, 335–336
popular conceptions of, 295–297,
340, 348

preparedness, 230, 234, 277
prescience, of death, 367–368
Southern bill of war, 234
women, as soldiers, 372–375, 386–387
Civil War (PBS documentary), xxviii–xxx
civilians
at the battlefield, 437–438, 453, 536–537
care, of Confederate army, 409–410
encounters with Union soldiers, 446–447, 453, 557–558
homes commandeered, 644–645
at Manassas, 452–453, 511–512
in military camps, 410–411, 415–416
tending the wounded, 607–608
Clark, Thomas, 260, 263, 264, 337, 588, 637–639, 702
Clay Battalion, Kentucky, 221
Clay, Cassius M., 221
Clay, Henry, 60
Clay, Virginia Tunstall, 183–184
Clinton, Sir Henry, 3
clothing
children's, 57, 343
for mourning, 588, 589
patriotic cocades, 211–212
Revolutionary War-era, 7
turning, 705
uniforms. *see* uniforms, military
women's, 75, 85–86, 86–87
Cobb, Howard, 180–181
Cocke, Philip St. George, 286–287, 334, 353
coffins, scarcity, 634–635
Collins, James, 513
Colonial America, 4–5, 6–7, 34
militias, 35
religion, 42–43
Colorado, 183
Comet of 1861, xxvi, 298–299
communication. *see also* postal service; telegraph
from the battlefield, 486–487, 540–541, 571–572, 576–577
confusing, 480
lack of, 395, 450, 457, 532
to Manassas, from Washington, 577–578
mounted courier, 394–395, 540
telegrams, 484
Confederate army. *see also* armed forces
after Battle of Manassas, 620–621
after first battle of Manassas, 657–658
camps, encampments, 277, 279, 280–281, 285–286. *see* Confederate army
care, of civilians, 409–410
cavalry, 291–293
closes in, at Manassas, 449–450
cohesion, of regiments, 443–444
divisions, 353
equipment and supplies, 284–285
leadership, 230–231, 244, 285, 286–288, 334, 353
at Manassas, 465
organization of, 276–277, 278–280, 282–285
as privateers, 678
recruitment, 278–279, 282–283
and slaves, 277, 280–281, 294
spies, 351
strategy, 286–287, 294–295
surrenders, 736–737
telegraph, 351
training, 338
Confederate states. *see also* individual states
capital. *see* Richmond, Virginia
collection of tariffs, 336–337
government, 182
hatred, of Yankees, 659–660, 672–673, 673–674
and national debt, 336
ports blocaded, 217, 677–678
ports destroyed, 216
President, 187
regiments, 231
seize forts, 179–180
"Confederate Yankee Doodle" (song), 553
Connecticut, 44–45
regiments, 215, 235, 522
Constitution (frigate), 226, 730
Constitution, guarantees of, suspended, 232
Constitutional Union Party, 90, 159
consumption, 10
Cooper, James Fennimore, 121–122
Cooper Union speech, 146, 148–152
Copley, John Singleton, 22
corps, military, 248
cotton gin, invented, 27–28
Cotton Kingdom (Olmstead), 94
cotton mills. *see* mills, cotton
Cotton Whigs, 90, 146, 154
Courtelyou family, 765–766
courtship, 73–76
of Sullivan and Sarah, 77, 80–81
Cox, Jacob Dolson, 296
Cranston, Rhode Island, 152–154
Croffut, William, 515–516, 557
Crosby brothers, 604–605
Cumberland Rangers, 35
Cumberland, Rhode Island, 5, 742
Curtis, Benjamin, 108
Cushing, Crawford, 447
Cushing, Eleanor, 447
Custer, George, 735–736, 740

Dahlgren, Ulrich, 735
Dakota territory, 183
Dame, Harriet Patience, 373
Daughters of the American Revolution (DAR), xxxviii
Davies, Thomas, 333, 352
Davis, Jefferson, 187, 234, 237, 276, 620, 621
at Manassas, 559
dead, the
decomposition of, 697
disposal of, 601, 636–637, 642–644. *see also* burials
recovery of, 683–700
remains as souvenirs, 659–660, 673, 690, 726–727
death, from illness, 661
Dedham, Massachusetts, 35
DeJournette, R., 493
Delaware, 207
regiments, 231
Democratic Party, 90
1860 convention, 156–157
Denison , Frederic, 682, 683, 690–691, 700, 724
Dexter Training Ground, 246, 253
divisions, military, 248
divorce, of Spragues, 764
Dix, Dorothea, 75
Dogan, Molly Benson, 453
Doherty, Edward, 511, 563–564, 565, 572, 604–605, 606, 607, 643
escapes, 628–629
Dorr Rebellion, 33
Dorr, Sullivan, 9–10
Dorr, Thomas, 32, 33, 142
Doubleday, Abner, 169, 176
Douglas, Stephen, 156–157, 160–161, 166, 249
Douglass, Frederick, 55, 143
Dred Scott case, 107–108, 132
Dring, Thomas, 3
drunkenness, 285, 569, 671–672, 688
dry goods stores, 29–30
Duffy, John M., 486
Duvall, Bette, 351
Dwinnell, Melvin, 492
Dyer, Cyrus, 243, 247
dysentery, 106

Early, Jubal, 334, 353
economy
and Civil War, 108–110, 336–338
New England, 118, 130–131, 154–155
Northern, 118. *see also* New England economy
Panic of 1857, 117–118, 154, 336
Reconstruction. *see* Reconstruction
and trade routes, 154
Edmonds, Sarah Emma, 372, 386–387, 416–417, 432, 618, 681
education, 36–37
for girls, 55–56, 62
Victorian era, 17–19, 68–70
Elaborate History of the Ballous (family history), 775
Elderkin, William, 593
Eldridge, Joseph, 513, 564
Eleventh New York Regiment. *see* Zouaves
Ellis, Julius, 554
Ellsworth, Elmer, 238
Elmwood neighborhood, Providence, 152–154
Emigrant Aid Society, 155
English, Samuel, 387, 466–467
Evans, Nathan, 432, 442–443, 445
at Manassas, 454–456, 465, 467, 479–480, 480–481
Ewell, Richard, 245, 285, 334, 353
Executive Mansion, 187–188. *see* White House (Executive Mansion)

Fairfax, Virginia, 290, 293–294, 294–295
Union army occupies, 387–393
famine, 1815-1816, 23–25
fashions. *see* clothing
1800s, 7–8
fence, split-rail, 449
Fire Zouaves. *see* Zouaves
Fish, Faith G., 638
flags, 254–255, 740
in battle, 486, 497–498, 527
Confederate, 468
flank march, 329
"Flight of the Doodles" (song), 650
Florida
and national debt, 336
secedes, 180
Floyd, John B., 179–180, 206
Foote, Commodore, 679
Ford's Theater, 737–738
Fort Adams, 226
Fort Beauregard, 679
Fort Clark, 678
Fort Donaldson, 679
Fort Hatteras, 678
Fort Moultrie, 168–169, 172, 175–176
seized by state, 179–180
Fort Pulaski, Georgia, 180
Fort Schuyler, 258
Fort Slocum, 656
Fort Sumpter, 174–175, 177–178, 180, 196, 200
attacked, 202–205
falls, 205–206
Fort Walker, 679
Foster, Abby, 63
Foster, Augusta, 375
Foster, Stephen, "Hard Times Come Again No More", 660
Fourth South Carolina, 432, 454–455
Fowler, Catherine Francis (later Shumway), 44, 52–53, 57–58, 61
Fowler, John, 59–61, 498
Fowler, Jonathan Amos, 61
Francis, Martha, 374–375
Franklin, William, 333, 431
Free Soil Party, 90

"Freedom's New Banner" (song), 21, 41
Freeman, Douglas, 697
Frontier Guards, 221–222
Fugitive Slave Law, 132
Fuller, Clifford, 488–489

games, 35
Ganley, Doretta, 775, 777, 781
Gardner, William, 490
Garfield, James, 239, 761–763
Garibaldi Guards, 341, 375
Garrison, William Lloyd, 55
Geneva Conventions, 629–630
Geological Survey, U.S. Department of the Interior, xvii–xix
Georgetown, Virginia, 273
Georgia, 657–659
- Andersonville prison, 735
- secession, 181
- seizes fort, 180

Georgia regiments, 282–285, 285, 658–659, 660–661, 672–674, 695–696, 735, 736
- casualties, 527
- as grave desecrators, 690–697, 698–699
- at Manassas, 479, 482, 490–491, 492, 497, 500, 544
- return home, 672
- winter quarters, 667–671

"Getting Dressed" (woodcut), 12
Gettysburg, xxxiv
"The Girl I Left Behind Me" (song), 229
Glenwood estate, as military camp, 235
Glory (film), 321
Glover, Thomas C., 283
Goddard, Emerson, 86
Goddard, Francis W., 491
Godey's Lady's Book, 81
Goree, Thomas Jewett, 425
Grace Church, Providence, 744
Grand Army of the Republic (GAR), 747, 751–752, 772
Grant, Ulysses S., 679
Gray, Charles, 556, 598–600, 630
Greeley, Horace, 164, 335
Greeley, James Bonaparte, 683, 690, 692–693, 693, 694, 724
Greene, Caroline, 27
Greene, Charles W., 243
Greenhow, Rose, 375
Griffin, Charles, 191, 431, 448, 481
Griffiths, Lucy, 532–533, 537
Grow, Galusha, 340
gunpowder, 320
guns, firing, 320–322
Gurley, Fanny, 593

Haines, Peter, 429
Hamilton, Algernon S., 283
Hammond, James, 94–95
Hampton's Legion, 343, 444
- at Manassas, 522

hard tack, 448
"Hard Times Come Again No More" (Foster), 660
Hardee's Rifle and Light Infantry Tactics, 299–300, 328–329
Harper's Ferry, 140–143, 216, 217, 273
Harper's Weekly, 61–62, 160
Harris, Edward, 78–79, 151
Harris, John (surgeon), 513, 555, 564, 630, 734
Hart, John R., 284
havelocks, 255, 357, 412
Hay, John, 185, 186, 221, 577
Hayes, Rutherford B., 762
Heintzelman, Samuel, 352, 395, 412, 431–432, 450, 506–507
- regiments, 523–524, 524–525

Henry Hill, 455, 474, 529, 533–534, 533–535, 538–539, 538–540, 543–546
Henry House, 532–533, 536–537
Henry, Mary, 375–376, 593, 596, 613–614, 654
Higginbotham, Joseph, 643
historical records, xxxii–xxxiii. *see also* acknowledgments
Historical Slang (Partridge), 559
Holloway, Robert, 248
Holmes, Theophilus, 353
hospitals, civilian, 219
hospitals, field, 503, 505–506, 509–510, 512–518, 516, 541–543, 606–607
- doctors removed from, 602–604, 605
- evacuation, 554–555
- as prison camps, 572–573, 598–601, 607–608, 615–616, 627–629
- supplies, 600–601
- surrender, 564–565, 597
- used for civilians, 661

hospitals, United States Marine Hospital, 518
hot air balloon, 414, 663
housekeeping, 56–57, 92–93
Houston, Sam, 60
Howard, McHenry, 530
Howard, Oliver, 333, 352, 431–432
Hunter, David, 221, 221–222, 352, 375
- at Manassas, 467, 472–473
- wounded, 472–473

Hurlbert, Mabel Beatrice, 764
hurricane, of 1815, 24
Hutchins family, 765–766
Hutchins, Laura Courtelyou, 765

Illiad (Homer), 423
illness and death, 661
illness and treatment. *see also* hospitals; medical practices, medicine
- amputation, 514–516
- appendicitis, 51–52
- bone injuries, 514–515
- childhood, 318, 319
- dysentery, 106
- hospitals. *see* hospitals
- infection, 100
- labor and delivery, 101–102
- measles, 478, 661
- tuberculosis, 10
- typhoid, 660–661
- wounds, 99, 513, 763

Imboden, John, 474, 474–476, 559–560
immigrants, 92
- Irish potato famine, 54
- as soldiers, 341

income tax, instituted, 731–732
Independence Day, 1861, 340–346
Industrial Revolution, 26–28
Inman, Hannah, 69
insurance, life, 127
intelligence, gathering, 427–428, 448–449, 457
- by telescope, 444–445
- intelligence, military. *see also* spying, spies
- Interior Department, U.S. Geological Survey, xxi–xxiii
- Irish immigrants, 54
- Irish potato famine, 38–39
- immigrants, to New England, 54

"Irish Volunteer" (song), 723

Jackson, Thomas J. "Stonewall", 353, 659
- acquires nickname, 527–528
- at Manassas, 465, 466, 527–528

Jackson's Brigade, 456
James rifle artillery, 591
James River, 274, 279
Jersey (prison ship), 3, 605
Jim Crow laws, 762
Johnson, Andrew, 739
Johnston, Joseph E., 273, 334, 353, 360, 395–396, 412–413, 443–444, 664, 680–681
- at Manassas, 479–480, 525–526, 529, 529–530

Jones, David, 353
Jones, Egbert, 181, 231, 281, 413, 478, 498, 565
- dies, 640–641
- photo, 500
- undergoes surgery, 521
- wounded, 500, 507, 556

Kanawha Rifles Militia Company, 205
Kansas, statehood, 97, 120–121, 128, 148–152, 183
Keating house, as military camp, 234–235
Keen, W. W., 556
Kentucky, 679
- regiments, 206, 221

Keyes, Erasmus D., 190, 231, 332–333, 352, 431, 434–435
- at Manassas, 522–523, 523

Kill Van Kull, 259
Kilpatrick, Judson, 735
King, William S., 505
King's Chapel, Providence, 744
Kinman, Wesley, 284
Knight, Jabez, 241
Knights of the Golden Circle, 116–117
Know-Nothings, 90, 92, 112

Ladies' Guide to Perfect Gentility in Manners (Thornwell), 74, 86
Lafayette, Marquis de, 5–6, 6–7
Last of the Mohicans (film), 122
laundry day, 588
Law, Evander McIver, 527
Lawes, Carolyn, 46
Lecompton state constitution, 120–121, 121, 128
Lee, Robert E., 141–142, 244, 286–287, 287, 487, 735–736
legions, 248
Libby, Luther, 602
Libby Prison, 602, 606
Library of Congress, 148, 326, 668
life insurance, 127, 302–303
light artillery, 323
Lincoln, Abraham, 103, 110
- after first battle of Manassas, 596–597
- assassinated, 738
- awaits inauguration, 184–186, 192
- cabinet, 185, 199–200
- campaign, 161, 162–164, 166–167
- Cooper Union speech, 146, 148–152
- death, 738–739
- elected President, 165–167
- fatalism, 222, 223
- and first battle of Manassas, 540–541, 571, 576, 577
- gives levee, 383
- inaugurated, 183–196
- inauguration threatened, 178–180, 191–192
- journey, to Washington, 186–187, 192–193
- kindness, 677
- life threatened, 222
- military service, 169
- nominated, 157–159
- prescience, of death, 737–738
- proclamation, 675
- replaces Winfield Scott, 664
- seeks financing, 337–338
- visits Camp Clark (Second Rhode Island regiment), 358–359
- visits New England, 146–152

Lincoln, Mary Todd, 193
Lincoln, Robert Todd, 64, 146, 738
Long Bridge, 274

Longstreet, James, 290–291, 294, 334
looting, by soldiers, 390–392
"Lorena" (song), 83, 609
Louisiana regiments, 353, 442, 450, 454–455, 671, 727
  at Manassas, 466–467, 468, 477–478, 496, 496–497
Louisiana, secession, 181
Lovell, Lucy Buffum, 134
Lowe, Thaddeus, 414
Lynch, Mike, 284

maggots, 517, 608, 641
Magruder, D. S., 505, 541
mail service, xxiii
Maine regiments, 329, 352, 371, 375, 382, 385
  at Manassas, 512, 522, 524, 560–561
  soldiers wounded, 513
  tour Washington, D.C., 677
Mallett, Sarah, 761
Manassas
  as attraction, for visitors, 658–660
  battlefield, 465
  borders, sealed, 613–615
  civilian residents, 452–453
  map, 458–459
  Matthews Hill, 454, 455, 457–458
  Stone Bridge, 580, 688
  strategic locations, 454–455
  trees, felled, 667–668, 685–686
Manassas, first battle of, 469
  armed forces, after, 655–656
  casualties, 471
  commentary, after, 650–652
  Confederate command post, 529–530
  Confederate reinforcements, 530–531
  Confederate strategy, 529, 533–536
  Confederates close in, 449–452
  dusty uniforms, 538
  Henry Hill, 455, 474, 529, 533–534, 538–540, 543–546, 557
  march to, 379–396, 385
  news of, in Washington, 540–541, 571, 576–577
  newspaper coverage, 565–570
  roadblocks, 385
  Stone Bridge, 292, 404, 417, 441, 442, 525–526
  strategy, 360, 363, 383–384, 393–394, 395–399, 419, 424, 426–427, 433, 485–486
  and Union army leadership, 485
  Union army retreats, 550–554, 558–564, 572, 573–574, 591–593
Manassas Gap Railroad, 275, 287–288
Manassas Junction, 278, 286–287
  Union strategy, 360, 363
Manassas (Sinclair), 376
Mansfield, Joseph, 236, 237, 245
maps
  Blackstone River, 20
  camps, encampments, 267
  Manassas battlefield, 458–459
  New England, 1800s, 20
  Northern Virginia, 361
  Rhode Island, xxii, xxiii
  United States, 1863, xxi
marching, 329–330
marriage, 88–89. *see also* Women's roles, as wives
marrige, courtship, 73–76
Maryland, 207, 219–220, 232, 260–261
  Annapolis Naval Academy, 226
  Baltimore, sacked, 217–219
  regiments, 231, 435–436
  secessionists, 435
"Maryland, My Maryland" (state anthem), 271

Mason, C. R., 277
Mason-Dixon line, 116
Mason, Stephen N., 155
Massachusetts, 42
  Dedham, 35
  laws, 53
  Townsend, 46
  Worcester, 48–49, 54–55, 58
  Massachusetts regiments, 206, 215, 223, 224–225, 231
  at Manassas, 524–525, 543
  soldiers wounded, 513
Matthews Hill, 454, 455, 457–458, 500
McClellan, George, 348, 664, 679, 680
  address, to army of the Potomac, 681
McCullough, David, xxix
McCunn, John, 578
McDowell, Irvin, 221, 236–237, 244, 245, 305–306, 325–326, 328, 332, 417–418
  brigade, incohesive, 427–429
  as commander, 426, 433, 578
  gluttony, 418
  interviewed, on eve of battle, 383
  at Manassas, 473–474, 484–485, 521–522, 531–532, 535–536, 537, 543–544
  overburdened, 578
  photo, 428
McLean, John, 108
Meagher, Thomas Francis, 385
measles, 478, 661
media. *see* newspaper coverage, of war
medical practices, medicine, 51. *see also* hospitals; illness and treatment
  ambulance transport, field, 509–510
  anesthesia, 519
  armed forces, 370, 373, 416–417, 489, 641–642
  battlefield, 503, 505–506, 509–510, 555–556, 573
  surgery, 51, 514–516, 519–520
  thumb-screw tourniquet, 489
  vaccinations, 253
  walking wounded, 510–511
Meigs family, 327
Meigs Montgomery, 327
Memorial Day, 745–748
Mercer, John, 285, 671–672
Metropolis (steamer), 257
Michigan, regiments, 352, 373, 543
Miles, Dixon S., 333–334, 352, 428
  at Manassas, 568–569
military courts, 241
militias. *see also* under individual states
  activated, in Civil War, 205–207, 209–211
  history of, 34–35, 169
  organization of, 210, 213–214
  payment, 211
  volunteers, 212–214
mills, cotton, 28, 78, 154–155. *see also* Panic of 1857
  Reconstruction era, 742–743
Mines, John, 556
minister, role of, 42, 43–44, 46, 47, 49
Minnesota regiments, 513, 543
Mississippi regiments, 353, 479
Mississippi, secedes, 180
Missouri, 207, 679
Mitchell, Mathias C., 427–428, 431, 436, 438
Montgomery, Alabama, 182
monuments, Civil War, 749–752
Mormon church, 31
Morrison, James J., 282, 283
Morse, Samuel, 122, 128
Mother's Book (Child), 16, 19
Mott, Lucretia, 55
Mount Tambora, 23–24
Mount Vernon, 273

mourning, 12–13, 590, 622–623
  clothing for, 588, 589
Mowry-Goff school, 755
Munroe (lieutenant), 557–558, 562
Murphy, Charles J., 555–556, 600, 601, 602–603, 606, 630

naming traditions, 9, 136, 764
Narragansett shout, 469
national debt, 336
National Hotel, Washington, D.C., 105, 106
National Museum of Health and Medicine, 515
National Park Service, xxx, 20
Naval Academy, Annapolis, 226
Needham, Henry Sumner, 232
Nesbit, John Cooper, 477
Nevada, 183
New England, 136. *see also* Connecticut; Maine; Massachusetts; New Hampshire; Rhode Island; Vermont
  Colonial, 4–5, 6–7, 33–34
  economy, 23–27, 78, 109–110, 118, 130–131
  famine, 23–25
  religion in. *see* minister, role of; religion
New Hampshire regiments, 305, 352, 373, 385, 438
  at Manassas, 472
New Jersey, 259–260
  regiments, 235
New Rochelle, New York, 258
New York City
  founding families of, 765
  tribute to war heroes, 707–708
New York Irish Relief Committee, 39
New York Public Library, 12, 16, 162
New York regiments, 206, 225, 226, 235, 352. *see also* Zouaves
  after battle of Manassas, 591
  at Manassas, 471–472, 484, 498–499, 511, 525, 543, 544–545
  soldiers wounded, 513
New York State
  Cherry Valley, 121–122
  Fort Schuyler, 258
  New Rochelle, 258
  Poughkeepsie, 60
  Rochester, 30–31
New York Times, 89, 94, 211, 421–422, 585
New York Tribune, 89, 151–152, 164, 335, 430
Newman, Burkett, 695–696, 699
Newport, Rhode Island, 138, 226
newspaper coverage, of Sullivan's fate, 704
newspaper coverage, of war, 421–422, 429–430, 443, 585–588
  battlefield, 565–570
  deaths reported, 585–586, 597, 610
  inaccuracy of, 415–416, 461, 587, 597
Nichols Academy, 37–38
Nicolay, John, 185, 186
"Nine Miles to the Junction" (song), 423
Nisbet, James Cooper, 284, 284–285
Nisbit, John Cooper, 668–669, 671–672
Norfolk, Virginia, navy yard, 217
North Carolina, 678, 679–680
  regiments, 353, 544
  secession, 234
Northern economy, 118, 154–155. *see also* New England economy
Nott, Josiah, 525, 526, 640
nurses, 219, 373–375, 386–387, 432, 557, 730

Oglethorpe Rifles, 658
Ohio Life Insurance and Trust Company, 117–118

Ohio, regiments, 215, 348, 352, 434
Ohio River, 272
Ohio (ship), 355
Oldtown Folks (Beecher Stowe), 12, 13
Olmstead, Frederick Law, *The Cotton Kingdom*, 94
Olney, Stephen, 6
Opdyke, George, 713–714
Order of Red Men, 771
Oregon, 184

"Paddy and the Know-Nothings" (song), 177
Padelford, Seth, 154–155, 155, 744–745, 749–750
Panic of 1857, 117–118, 154, 336
Parker, Samuel A., 155
Parker, Thomas, 390
Parkhurst, Charles, 96, 734
parole d'honneur, 605
Parrot rifle, 435, 441–442
Patterson, Robert, 231, 273, 328, 395, 396, 417
Patton, George S, Jr., ix
Patton, George Smith, 205
Patton, John Mercer, 205
Pawtucket, Rhode Island, 96–97
pay, military, 619, 646–647
Pember, Phoebe Yates, 660
Pennsylvania Railroad, 225, 578, 656
Pennsylvania regiments, 231, 232, 706
pension, widow's, 666, 731–732, 755
pensions, soldiers', 771, 772
People magazine, xxx
Peugnet, Eugene, 556, 573, 605–606, 606–607
Philadelphia, 706
Philadelphia Medical School, 117
Phillips Academy, 64, 65–66
Phillips Exeter Academy, 65, 117, 146
photography, 86
Pierce, William H., 612–613
Pike, Hannah, 5
Pike, Robert, 5
Pinkerton's detectives, 192
pioneers, 437
Poe, Edgar Allen, 102
political activism, 1800s, 30–31, 54–55
  sewing circles, 57–58
political parties, 90–91, 155–159
Porter, Andrew, 333, 352, 428, 448–449, 449–450
  bridgade, 532–533
  at Manassas, 472, 483–484
Portici (Manassas home), 529–530
ports blocaded, 217, 677–678
postal service, 77, 171, 364, 408, 409, xxvi–xxvii
Potomac River, 272–273, 274
Potter, Hazard A., 683
Poughkeepsie Lyceum, 60
Powers, Mrs. James Francis, 755–756
premonitions, of death, 367–368, 426
Prescott, Henry, 235, 362
presidential election, 1860, 157–166
  ballots, 159
  election results, 165–166
prison ships, 3–4
prisoners, 478, 557, 563–565, 663
  at field hospital, 572–573, 598–601, 607–608, 613–615
  released, 676–677
  sent to Richmond, 601–602
  surgeons, 602–604, 605–606, 630
privateers, 2
  Confederate, 678
Providence Journal, 461, 585, 586
Providence Marine Corps of Artillery, 233
Providence Press, 461
Providence, Rhode Island, 84–85, 138, 240–241
  cemeteries, 744–745
  churches, 344, 744
  First Baptist Church, 344
  Reconstruction era, 742–743
  school system, 757-758
  Soldiers' and Sailors' Monument, 749–750
  State House, 136
Providence Troop of Horse, 35
Putnam, George, 566, 567–568, 570, 595
Putnam, Israel, 566

Quakers, 132, 290

railroad routes, 224–225, 259, 393
  Georgia, 284–285
  and military strategy, 275–276, 286–288
  Richmond, Virginia, 237
  secured, 236
  security, 232, 234
  transcontinental, 763
  Virginia, 275
Reconstruction era
  African Americans in, 762–763
  Rhode Island, 742–743
records, historical, xxxvi–xxxvii
recruitment, Confederate army, 276–277
Red Cross, 735
Reeder (servant), 476
religion. *see also* minister, role of
  Colonial era, 42–43
  religious persecution, 49–50
  Revivalism, 46–47
  Second Great Awakening, 47
  and slavery, 117, 132
Republican Party, 90, 92, 102–103, 109, 111–112
  1860 convention, 157–158
Revivalism, 46
Revolutionary War, 2–4, 6–7, 34, 217
Revolutionary War America. *see also* New England, Colonial
  clothing, 7
  militias, 34
Reynolds, William, 323, 473, 474, 475
Rhode Island
  African Americans in, 134
  celebrates war's end, 737
  Colonial, 4–5, 6–7, 42–43
  Cranston, 152–154
  Cumberland, 742
  dead, recovery of, 675–676
  Dexter Training Ground, 246, 253
  first Memorial Day, 747–748
  General Assembly, 99–100, 119–120, 139, 243–244
  Independence Day, 1861, 342–345
  Industrial Revolution, 26–28
  legislature, 111–112, 113–114
  at Manassas, 475–477
  map, xviii
  militia, 33–34, 35, 207
  Newport, 138, 226
  Pawtucket, 96–97
  political factions, 1861, 197–198, 200–202, 207–208
  Providence, 84–85, 138, 342–345, 742–743, 744, 749–750, 757–758
  reaction, to battle of Manassas, 597–598
  Reconstruction era, 742–743
  recruitment, 238–241
  regiments. *see* First Rhode Island Regiment; Second Rhode Island Regiment
  slavery in, 31
  social values, 464
  state constitition, 138
  support for war, 621–622
  voting rights, 31–33
  Woonsocket, 8, 77–78, 84, 86, 742
  year without a summer, 24
  Rhode Island Historical Society, 356, 468, 756, 781
  Rhode Island regimental band, manifest, 653
  Rhode Island regiments, 213–214, 217, 222, 226–227, 232–233, 234–235, 238, 238–239, 246–247, 248–249, 416, 431
  arrives in Washington, 264–266
  camps, encampments, 267
  Carabineers, 491, 492
  casualties, 502–503, 561–562. *see also* Ballou, Sullivan
  cavalry, 683–684, 685, 686
  color guard, 486, 497–498
  crosses Sudley Springs Ford, 447–448
  departs Rhode Island, 254, 255–256
  encampment, Washington, D.C., 265–266, 301, 305
  flag, 254–255, 468
  goes into battle, 457–458
  journey, to Washington, 256–265
  at Manassas, 462, 466, 466–467, 469, 469–475, 477–478, 482–483, 485–487, 487–495, 487–496, 506–507
  marches through Baltimore, 261–263
  moves on Virginia, 369, 371–372
  in North Carolina, 679–680
  officers, 362
  parades to White House, 303–305
  photo, 468
  receive remains, 700, 702–703
  reorganized, 611–612
  reputation of, 574–575, 651–652
  return to Rhode Island, 619–620
  return to Washington, 590–591
  route to Manassas, changed, 436–437, 438–439
  soldiers wounded, 513
  taken prisoner, 557
  training, 299–300, 300
Rhodes, Elisha Hunt, 239, 246, 256–257, 258–260, 261–262, 264, 303–304, 358, 369, 370, 431, 454, 469, 504–505, 575, 702–703, xvii
  photo, 362
Rice, John, 607–608, 766–767
Richardson, Israel "Fighting Dick", 333, 352, 411, 412, 428, 431
Richardson, Josiah, 513, 565, 631, 633, 634
  returns to Manassas, 684, 689
  returns to Rhode Island, 647–648
"Richmond is a Hard Road to Travel" (song), 650
Richmond, Virginia, 237, 275, 278, 279
  after victory at Manassas, 579
  population, 279
Ricketts, Fanny, 614–616
Ricketts, James B., 499, 536, 537, 614–616
Rivers, Henry (surgeon), 513, 518, 519, 520–521, 555–556
  returns to Rhode Island, 624
  Robbins, 242
  Robinson, Christopher, 32, 78, 137, 138
  Robinson, James, 533
  Rochester, New York, 30–31
  Rockafellow, Harry, 573
  Roebling, Paul, xxxiii
  Rogers, Horatio, 17, 29, 67, 70, 139, 196–197, 201, 251, 253–254
Runyon, Theodore, 334, 352, 576
Russell, William Howard, 340, 383, 429, 565, 567

sabotage, 224–225, 393
Sanitary Commission, 630
Schenck, Robert, 352, 431, 433–434

Schenk, Robert, 332
Scott, Charles V., 591
Scott, Thomas J., 225, 578, 656
Scott, Winfield, 169, 189–191, 193, 216, 221, 230–231, 375, 433, 484
and first battle of Manassas, 571, 572, 576, 577, 577–578
resigns, 664
threatened, 192
secession, 167–168, 180–181
of Alabama, 180, 181
of Arkansas, 234
Confederate government, 182
and federal government, 182–183
of Florida, 180
of Georgia, 181
initial reactions, 167–168, 172
of Louisiana, 181
and military men, 189, 220
of Mississippi, 180
of North Carolina, 234
of South Carolina, 167–168, 172, 173–176
of Tennessee, 234
of Texas, 184
of Virginia, 209–210, 237
secessionists, 271–295, 658
Second Connecticut Regiment, 235, 352
Second New Hampshire regiment, 305, 431
Second Pennsylvania Regiment, 232
Second Wisconsin Infantry, 352
Seekonk River, Rhode Island, 744
Senate, United States
assault, in Senate chamber, 97–99
inestigates grave desecrations, 723–727
meets, during war, 338–340
Southern senators exit, 183–184
weapons in, 183
Sepoys, India, 729
September 11, 2001, xxxv
Seventh Georgia Regiment, 300
Seventh New York Regiment, 225, 235
Seventy-First New York Regiment, 226
Seward, William, 179, 184, 185, 199, 576
sewing circles, 57–58, 254, 730
Shakespeare, William, xxvi
shebangs, 413
shellfish, delivered to soldiers, 328
Shenandoah Mountains, 272
Sherman, William Tecumseh, 334, 335, 352, 431, 442–443, 740
at Manassas, 506, 522
Sholes, Albert, 212–213, 502–503, 590–591, 618–619
Shumway, Catherine Francis (formerly Fowler), 52–53, 57–58
dies, 767
Shumway, Christopher Columbus, 41–42, 43, 44–45, 46–48
death, 51–52
household, 50–51
Shumway family, 41–44, xxxii
ancestors, 49–50
Shumway, Henry C., 225
Shumway, John Fowler, 47, 355, 678, 730–731, 735, 736, 749, 771–772
Shumway, Pierre (Peter), 49–50
Sickles, Dan, 515
sideburns, 463
Sinclair, Upton, *Manassas*, 376
Sixth Massachusetts Regiment, 218–219, 223, 232, 236
Sixty-Ninth New York regiment, 416
skedaddling, 559
Skelly, Johnston Hastings, 232
Slater Mill, 96
slave rebellions, 172–173
slavery, 260–261
abolitionist movement, 31, 55, 131–134
defense of, 94–95
Dred Scott case, 107–108
and the economy, 117–118, 130, 154–155
first battles over, 97–98
Northern Virginia, 289–290
and polarization of the country, 97–101, 107–108, 108–109, 116–117
Rhode Island, 31
slaves
and the Confederate army, 277, 280, 294
population, 279
reaction to Union Army, 260–261
Slocum, John, 235, 240, 247, 424–425
burial, 622–623
death, reported, 585, 606, 610
dies, 505
at Manassas, 482–483, 493
monument, 752
photo, 362
remains' journey home, 701–722
remains, recovered, 693
tribute, New York City, 707–717
wounded, 493, 503–504, 542–543
Small, Abner, 512
smallpox, 253
Smith, Caleb, 185
Smith, James Young, 198
Smith, Joseph, 31
Smith, Kirby, 334
Smith, Samuel James, 243, 247, 362, 561
Smithsonian Institute, 188
Society for Organizing Charity, 772
Soldiers' and Sailors' Monument, Providence, 749–750
"Somebody's Darling" (song), 634–635
"Sorrowing Family" (woodcut), 12
South Carolina, 167, 175–176
Fort Moultrie, 168–169, 172, 175–176
Fort Sumpter, 173–176, 177–178, 196, 200, 202–205
regiments, 353, 432, 442
secession, 167–168, 172, 173–176
seizes forts, 179–180
Southern economy, connection with North, 130–131
"Southern Soldier Boy" (song), 741
"The Southern Wagon" (song), 135
Southern way of life, 94–95, 281–282
Sprague, William, 155, 198, 207, 209–211, 249–250, 277, 356–357, 428
divorce, 764
letter of condolence, 665–666
spying, spies, 305, 342, 375–376
Bette Duvall, 351
Star of the West (merchant ship), 180
State and National Law School, 60, 71–72
State of Maine (steamer), 257
Stedman, Edmund, 443, 597
Steere, William, 243, 706–707
Sternberg, G., 601, 604
Stone, Charles, 190, 191
Stowe, Harriet Beecher, *Oldtown Folks*, 12, 13
strategy, military, 286–287, 294–295. *see also* spying, spies
Confederate army, 412–413
and financing, 338
first Manassas, 360, 363, 383–384, 393–394, 398, 419–420, 421
and popular opinion, 340
and railroad routes, 275–276
Stuart, J. E. B., 141–142, 291–292, 334, 563–564
at Manassas, 539
takes prisoners, 573
Sudley Ford, 447
Sudley Mansion, 447
Sudley Methodist Church, 453, 513–514, 516–518, 541, 559, 564–565, 661, 688–689
photos, 688–689, xiv
Sudley Springs Ford, 447
Sullivan Ballou Chapter of the Grand Army of the Republic, xxvii
Sullivan, John, 6, 10
portrait, 18
Sumner, Charles, 55, 97–99, 100–101, 167, 206, 723–724, 738
Supreme Court, United States, 107–108
Swan Point Cemetery, 744–745

tableaux, 756
Taft, George, 38–39
tailoring profession, 7–8
Taney, Roger, 108, 196
telegrams, 484
telegraph
Confederate lines, 351
invented, 122, 128
lines, repaired, 225
use of, 250, 394, 395, 540
temperance movement, 92, 162
Tennessee, 679
regiments, 353
secession, 234
Texas Rangers, 291
Texas, secession, 184
Texas Troubles, 172
textile mills, 155
Thanksgiving, 1860, 170–171
Thermopylae, 230
Third Connecticut Regiment, 352
Third Maine regiment, 371
Thornberry, John, 541–542
Thornberry, Laura, 644–645
Thornwell, Emily, *The Ladies' Guide to Perfect Gentility*, 73–74, 86
Tidewater Virginia, 274
Tigers, Louisiana, 353, 455, 468, 477, 478, 496, 497, 507, 668, 671, 727
Tompkins, Charles H., 233, 362
topography. *see also* maps
of Virginia, 271–276
of Washington, D.C., 187–189
tourniquets, 519
thumb-screw, 489
Tower, Levi, 237, 243, 247, 362
burial, 623
dies, 505, 511
remains' journey home, 701–722
remains recovered, 693, 699
tribute, New York City, 707–717
wounded, 493–494
townball, 35
Townsend, Massachusetts, 46
trade routes, 154
train routes. *see* railroad routes
transportation. *see also* railroad routes
camp supplies, 371, 393
Lincoln, to Washington, 186–187, 192–193
troops, 250, 256–265, 284–285, 325–327
weaponry, 371
tuberculosis, 10
Turner, Charles W., 243
Twain, Mark, 188–189
Twelfth New York Infantry, 352
Twentieth Ohio Regiment, 215
Twenty-First Maine regiment, 329
"Two Brothers" (song), 461
Tyler, Daniel, 333, 352, 420–421, 433, 441–442
at Manassas, 480, 523
typhoid, 660–661

Underground Railroad, 31, 58, 132
Ungar, Jay, xxxiv
uniforms, military, 246, 284
dusty, 538
Eleventh New York regiment, 544–545
Garibaldi Guards, 341
havelocks, 255, 357, 412
Louisiana batallions, 450, 455

for women, 374
Zouave, 343, 455, 468
Union army, 338. *see also* armed forces; under individual states, regiments arrive in Washington, D.C., 225–227
at Ball's Bluff, 678
building, 230–231
casualties. *see* casualties
cavalry, 681–683
divisions, 352
equipment and supplies, 242, 246, 250, 277, 278, 410
hierarchy of, 246–248
inexperienced, 429, 506
leadership, 230–231, 231, 236–237, 242–243, 245, 332–334, 352, 427–428, 485, 506
marches on Virginia, 369–373
moves on Manassas, 369, 371–372, 376–394, 417–421
occupies Fairfax, 387–393
organization of, 210, 213, 214
preparedness, 350
recruitment, 238–241
regulars, 500, 501, 507
returns to Washington, 590–595
route to Manassas, changed, 436–437
strategy, 679, 680–681
support staff, 248, 268
sworn in, 233
uniforms, 246
United States Cavalry, 431
United States Congress, Committee on the Conduct of the War, 678–679
United States, in financial crisis, 336–338
United States Marine Hospital, 518
United States Marines, 431, 543
University of Virginia, 192

"The Vacant Chair" (song), 59, 633, 701
Van Buren, Martin, 21
Vassall, Sally, 219
Vermont, regiments, 206–207
Viall, Mary Eliza, 764
Viall, Nelson, 243, 362, 486, 610
Virginia, 207
Alexandria, 234, 237–238, 273, 275
early role, in war, 277–278, 339
economy, 275
Fairfax, 290, 293–294, 294–295, 387–393
Georgetown, 273
Manassas Junction, 286–287
map, xxiii
militias, 278
Newport News, 216
Norfolk Navy Yard, 217
northern, 288–294
Northern, 361
railroad routes, 275
Richmond, 237, 275, 278, 279, 579
secession, 209, 237
Tidewater, 274
topography, 271–276, 288–290, 293, 438–440
Union Army in, 244–246, 327–328
Virginia Female Institute, 277
Virginia regiments, 216, 217, 353, 663
at Manassas, 474–476, 478–479, 544
vivandières, 373–375
Volcano Explosive Index, 24
voting rights, 31–33
for Blacks, 33

Waddail, J. S., 283
Wade, Benjamin, 678
Wade, Jenny, 232
"Wait for the Wagon" (song), 1
Wallabout Bay, 3
War of 1812, 34
Ward, J. H. Hobart, 352
Washburne, Elihu, 193, 426
Washington, D.C
after first battle of Manassas, 590–596, 609–611, 618, 656
bordered by Confederate states, 187, 209, 216, 217–221, 234
bridges, 274
buildings and geography, 187–189, 221, 273–274, 304
Capitol Building, 225, 304, 338
celebrates war's end, 737
conditions, 106, 304–305, 338
first regiments arrive, 225–227
hospital, 219
in lockdown, 652–653
National Hotel, 105, 106
Patent Office, 227
railroad routes, 224, 232, 236
security, 190–192, 219–224, 227, 231–232, 656
Washington, Martha Custis, 244
Washington Monument, 188–189
water, lack of, 386
weaponry, 306
ammunition, 506–507
breechloading rifles, 462, 492
cannon, 323–325, 435, 487
evacuation, 561
experience, of being wounded, 488, 489–490
handguns, firing, 320–322
James rifle artillery, 591
rifled guns, 536
training in, 319, 320–325, 323–324
transportation, 371
weddings, 80–81
"Weeping Sad and Lonely" (song), 585
Welles, Gideon, 185
West Point Military Academy, 231
Southern graduates, 276
West Virginia, 272
western theater, 679
"What's The Matter?" (song), 105
Wheat, Chatham Roberdeau, 443, 496
Wheaton, Francis L. (surgeon), 241, 243, 364, 505
Wheaton, Frank (captain), 363–364, 498–499, 610–611
at Manassas, 482–483, 484–485
Wheat's Battalion. *see* Tigers, Louisiana
Wheat's Tigers. *see* Tigers, Louisiana
White House (Executive Mansion), security, 221–222, 231–232
Whitman, Walt, 410, 596–597, 597
Whitney, Eli, 27
"The Why and the Wherefore" (song), 209
Wide Awakes, 161
Willcox, Orlando, 431
Willard's Hotel, 193, 194
fire, 233–234
Williams, Roger, 4, 42–43
Williams, Thomas H., 642
winter, of 1861-62, 676
winter quarters, 673
Wisconsin, regiments, 352
Wisconsin regiments, 484, 543
women's roles, 15–16
childbirth, 101–102
education for, 55–56, 62, 66
employment, 63–64, 758–759
housekeeping, 56–57, 92–93, 588
as nurses, 219, 373–375, 386–387
political activism, 57–58
political activism, 1800s, 164
rights, 53, 62–63
in wartime, 251, 254, 277, 372–375, 386–387, 432, 557, 729, 730
as wives, 43–44, 66, 73–75
Woodbury, Augustus, 265–266, 424–425, 435, 472–473, 738–739, 750
Woodward, Jean, 779
Woodward, May Hutchins, 768–769
Wool, Brigadier General, 230
Woonsocket Guards, 33–34, 35, 207
honor Sullivan, 617–618
Woonsocket Harris Public Library, 78–79
Historical Collection, 13, 65
Woonsocket Light Infantry, 33
Woonsocket, Rhode Island, 8, 77–78, 84, 86
Reconstruction era, 742
Worcester, Massachusetts, 48–49, 54–55, 58
World Trade Center attacks, xxxi
wounded. *see also* hospitals, field
care of, 630, 641–642
recuperation of, 640
transported to Libby Prison, 629–630, 631
Wright, John, 243

York River, 274

Zettler, Berien McPherson, 409, 492
Zouave uniforms, 343, 455, 468
Zouaves, 233–234, 341, 343, 352, 377, 534, 537, 538, 539, 545, 549, 594, 721